APPLIED ECONOMICS: RESOURCE
ALLOCATION IN RURAL AMERICA

APPLIED
RESOURCE ALLOCATION

RUEBEN C. BUSE

ECONOMICS
IN RURAL AMERICA

DANIEL W. BROMLEY

IOWA STATE
UNIVERSITY
PRESS
AMES / 1975

RUEBEN C. BUSE
is Professor, Department of Agricultural Economics, University of Wisconsin, Madison. He holds the bachelor of science degree and master's degree from the University of Minnesota and received the Ph.D. degree from The Pennsylvania State University in 1959. His general research interests are in consumer behavior, research methods, and computer-assisted instruction.

DANIEL W. BROMLEY
is Associate Professor, Department of Agricultural Economics, and Director, Center for Resource Policy Studies and Programs, University of Wisconsin, Madison. He received the Ph.D. degree in natural resource economics from Oregon State University in 1969. Professor Bromley has published numerous papers on public decision making in the natural resource area and in the general area of rural development. He is coeditor of *Land Economics*. During the 1973–74 academic year he was on leave in Washington, D.C., spending six months in the office of Economic Analysis, a staff position for the Secretary of the Interior, and six months in the Economics and Sector Planning Division of the Agency for International Development.

© 1975 The Iowa State University Press
Ames, Iowa 50010. All rights reserved
Composed and printed by
The Iowa State University Press

First edition, 1975

Library of Congress Cataloging in Publication Data

Buse, Rueben C
    Applied economics.

    Includes bibliographies.
    1. Agriculture—Economic aspects. 2. Agriculture—Economic aspects—United States. I. Bromley, Daniel W., 1940– joint author. II. Title.
HD1411.B98   338.1′0973   74–19097
ISBN 0–8138–0115–X

CONTENTS

v

PREFACE

This is an introductory text covering the application of economic principles to problems of resource allocation. Few introductory texts concentrate on the theory of resource allocation with a rural emphasis and hence a void exists in the theoretical development of the production of food and fiber, the agribusiness sector, rural poverty, the rural community, and natural resource use and development. It is our belief that economic concepts are more quickly grasped—and more fully appreciated—when their development is integrated with a discussion of economic problems and issues.

The book is divided into three parts: Part I: A Perspective; Part II: Theoretical Aspects; and Part III: Economic Issues. In Part I, we present an overview of economic systems and a discussion of economic analysis in general. In Chapter 3, we provide a preview of the economic issues to be covered in Part III.

Part II consists of seven chapters dealing with regional specialization and trade, production economics, cost curves, supply curves, consumer demand, market equilibrium, and market structure and resource allocation. The material presented here provides an introduction to that body of economic thought normally referred to as microeconomics.

Part III contains five chapters devoted to more detailed treatments of the economic issues of the production of food and fiber, the agribusiness sector, human resources and rural poverty, the rural community, and natural resource use. Here, we introduce the student to the problems of public policy in these areas and employ concepts developed in Part II to aid in the understanding of the central economic issues and the choices in problem resolution.

While the book is intended primarily for the beginning student of economics, most topics are developed in sufficient depth that the student with previous exposure to economics will gain additional insights and a different perspective. The material has been used in mimeograph form for several years—along with study guides—for the first course in the Department of Agricultural Economics at Wisconsin. Most of the students had previously taken an economic "survey" (not principles) course, but the book is written with the assumption that the student has had no prior *analytical* economics.

We have included a bibliography of suggested readings at the end of each chapter, and the interested reader is encouraged to pursue these readings for an alternative explanation of concepts, for a more extensive coverage of certain policy issues, or because the readings may represent the "classical" work on the topic.

In addition to former students and teaching assistants who have aided us in this endeavor, we are much indebted to the helpful comments of Professor Bruce R. Beattie of Texas A & M University; and our colleagues Professors William Dobson, Peter Helmberger, A. C. Johnson, Jr., Willard F. Mueller, and William Saupe. We are indebted to Kathy Haygood and Susan Jewell for statistical assistance, and to Barbara Iles for the drawings. Marie Jacobsen, Madeline Kalscheur, Madeleine Macho, Cathy Pille, and Mary Simon have all typed portions of the manuscript and their contribution is greatly appreciated.

RUEBEN C. BUSE
DANIEL W. BROMLEY

PART 1: A PERSPECTIVE

The first part of this book provides an overview of different economic systems, of economic analysis, and of some issues of resource allocation. In Chapter 1 we discuss the central economic questions facing any society and explore some alternatives for achieving certain economic objectives. To some, economic systems have become rather like religious doctrine, with supporters and detractors arguing relative merits. However, unlike religious doctrine, economic systems provide feedback on performance while there is still time to take corrective action; there are many "judgment days," none being irreversible. Hence, there is no "correct" economic system and it is hoped that the discussion will convince the reader that an economic system is a means to an end and not an end in and of itself.

In Chapter 2 we present a cursory view of the scope and method of economics. Here we explain the role of economic models and the differences among assumptions, hypotheses, theories, and laws. Additionally, the concepts of policy, of social goals, of economic goals, and of means to achieve those goals are briefly discussed. Finally, in the social sciences, the personal beliefs (called value judgments) of the scientist play an influential role in the problems selected for study, in dictating the analytical approach to be pursued, in interpreting the results of the analysis, and in offering policy prescriptions. It is important that the reader recognize the different ways that value judgments can enter economic analysis.

In the final chapter of Part I, we present a brief overview of some economic issues to be covered in more detail in

Part III of the book. This chapter is intended to introduce the student to a few of the interesting economic problems to be discussed later, in the expectation that it will make the ensuing theoretical material more interesting. In this day of demands for relevancy, it is our belief that the introduction of some economic issues in Chapter 3 will illustrate how a knowledge of economic theory is necessary to understand the cause and effect of the issues, and—more importantly—how to design institutions to help solve the problematic situation.

Chapter 3 is divided into five sections, each corresponding to a chapter in Part III of the book. The sections are (1) the farm sector; (2) the agribusiness sector; (3) human resources: the rural poor; (4) the rural community; and (5) natural resource economics.

CHAPTER 1: A PERSPECTIVE ON ECONOMIC SYSTEMS

In any society, a basic problem is to allocate the endowment of fixed and variable resources to satisfy individual and collective wants. Where those resources are abundant, the allocation problem is trivial; where the resources are scarce, the allocation takes on overwhelming importance. Indeed, both the French Revolution (1789–1799) and the Russian Revolution (1917) were spawned from a basic disagreement over the allocation of economic returns from fixed and variable productive factors. In the process of allocating scarce factors to meet human wants, four basic questions require consideration: (1) What is to be produced? (2) What factors are to be used in producing those items selected in (1)? (3) How much is to be produced? (4) How is the return from that productive process (income) to be allocated? These questions are independent of the particular economic system that is chosen; they arise in planned economies as well as in market economies.

The central purpose of this chapter is to describe in general terms the alternative ways in which a society is organized in an economic sense. This will achieve several purposes. First, it will help the reader gain a better understanding of the precepts and institutions of economic systems upon which the rest of this book is based. Second, it will permit the reader to gain a broader perspective with which to view our economic system. By this we mean that economic systems are the results of man's imagination and his view of the "good life." There is nothing sacred about any of them. The decentralized capitalism of the United States is but one type of economic organization; centralized socialism is another. The degree of centralized control of the decision-making process directly affects the organization of the economic system. For example, in the United States or Western Germany, where decisions concerning resources and their use are primarily in the hands of individuals, one finds decentralized capitalism; in Germany under Hitler, where the decisions were made by the state, one finds totalitarian capitalism (fascism); in England, where some resources are owned by the state and others by individuals, one finds liberal socialism; and in the Soviet Union, where most resources are owned by the state (and also most production decisions rest there), one finds centralized socialism.

The next section consists of an overview of economic systems. Following that, we will turn to the ways in which different systems deal with the four fundamental choices listed above.

OVERVIEW

At one time, economic systems were largely classified in a series of "isms" such as capitalism, socialism, communism, and fascism.

These terms describe both the institutions that coordinated economic decisions and the ownership pattern of the resources used to produce them. Today it is difficult to neatly categorize an economy as being of one type or another. We will therefore use a different scheme to classify and describe the basic characteristics of economic systems.

Economic systems can be classified according to two basic characteristics of their institutions: (1) the methods used to coordinate economic decisions of the individual units in society and (2) the nature of ownership of its productive resources. The first, the coordination of economic decisions, can occur either through a market system where prices of factors and products provide signals to decision makers or through a central planning agency where factor and product prices are for accounting purposes only. As for the second categorization, when the productive resources are owned by individuals, the economy might be characterized as capitalistic; if the state owns all productive factors, it would be referred to as socialistic.

Theoretically, it might be possible to have private ownership of the factors of production, yet rather than have free market decisions, power would be vested in a central planning authority. Likewise, it might also seem possible to have the state own and control the factors of production and still permit some free market operation where prices play a guiding role. The Soviet Union permits a certain degree of this to go on and has experimented with even a greater role for the market system to play. However, the underlying philosophical inconsistencies almost preclude such combinations as public ownership of the productive factors with free market behavior or the private ownership of productive factors and a central planning authority. Nevertheless, as will be seen, many countries have systems that combine elements of several or all of these four characteristics.

In Figure 1.1 we have depicted six countries in a matrix describing factor ownership and decision making; factor ownership lies increasingly with the state as one moves to the right, while decision making becomes increasingly centralized as one moves down.

The United States economy is an example of decentralized decision making and private ownership of productive factors, while the Soviet Union is the archetypical centrally planned economy, with state ownership of productive factors. Sweden, Japan, the United Kingdom,

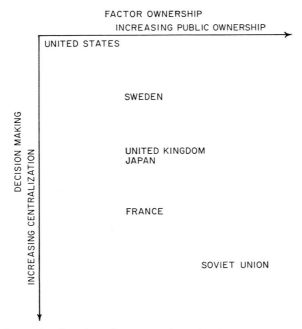

FIG. 1.1. A matrix of options for economic systems.

and France are listed as classic examples of the mixed economy. In these countries, the vast majority of productive factors are privately owned. However, central planning plays an increasing role as one moves down the list. Specifically, planning in Sweden is virtually limited to 5-year forecasts that are useful to businesses. At the other extreme of the mixed economies lies France. Here, planning is termed *indicative*—which means that it is less coercive than Soviet planning but more forceful than the planning of Sweden, Japan, and the United Kingdom. The purpose of French planning is to provide a set of guidelines to help direct the private and public sectors of the economy. Additionally, some government intervention takes the form of indirect control over credit and taxation.[1]

CHOICE PROBLEM

Before addressing the four main economic questions listed above, it would be well to outline the resource ownership aspects of the two extremes—capitalism and socialism.

1. For a more complete treatment of comparative systems, see the Suggested Readings at the end of the chapter.

In a capitalistic system, ownership of the productive resources is vested in individuals. This, however, does not preclude government ownership and operation of certain public services such as post offices, communication facilities, or natural monopolies such as public power systems.[2] The institution of private property is one that must be accompanied by elaborate guidelines for control, use, and transfer of the property, as well as rules for the allocation of rewards to the factor's owner. The use of such factors is clearly in the domain of their owner, subject to the condition that he does not impinge upon the rights of others.

The other principal form of factor ownership is that of socialism. Here, factors are owned and controlled by the state. Collective and state farms in the Soviet Union are classic examples. To illustrate the fact that different decision rules can prevail under one form of property ownership, consider the difference between the collective and state farms in the Soviet Union. On collective farms elected bodies of decision makers, while they must meet certain conditions of the region's plans, are free to exercise considerable control over certain decisions. This is not to imply that market prices guide these decisions, but it is to say that workers on the collective farms have some say in what will be produced and how it will be produced, and they have the opportunity to share in the profits of the enterprise after the harvest is in and the requirements of the plan have been met. Additionally, each family has a small private plot from which produce can be kept for home consumption or sold in the farmers' markets in larger towns. On the state farm this is not the case; each worker resembles a factory employee, with little participation in the decision process and little if any sharing of the economic surplus of the enterprise.

Of course the form of ownership of the productive factors is not independent of the way in which decisions are made, since one of the primary reasons for the Socialist Revolution in Russia was that the owners of one significant factor (land) were making decisions that had an undesirable effect on the landless peasants. The easiest way out to the revolutionaries appeared to be an alteration in the ownership of resources to preclude such behavior rather than an attempt to alter private decisions within the institutional context of private property.

Hence capitalism and socialism are the two extremes as regards the ownership of factors of production. We just saw that even in a socialist country individuals have access to small plots which they treat as private property. It would seem appropriate also to mention that in a capitalistic country the state does own certain productive enterprises.

2. The adjective "natural" has come to be attached to "monopoly" to denote those situations where a single seller of a good or service is deemed preferable to the normal situation of many independent producers. This will become clearer in later chapters, especially Chapter 10.

Amtrak, the nationalized railroad passenger service instituted in 1971, is a good example of this. Postal service is another.

We now turn to a discussion of the ways in which the two polar examples arrive at answers regarding (1) what to produce, (2) how to produce it, (3) how much to produce, and (4) how to allocate the national income.

WHAT TO PRODUCE

When discussing the choice of what to produce, it helps to classify economic units as either households or businesses; the household is a consumer and a resource owner, while the business firm is a producer and a resource user (see Figure 1.2). In a decentralized system, the ultimate decision about what is to be produced is said to lie with these households. The resources are sold in the marketplace by the households to firms, usually in exchange for money. These payments constitute the income of the household. The firms, once they have acquired the resources, use them to produce goods and services. These goods and services in turn are sold on the market by firms to

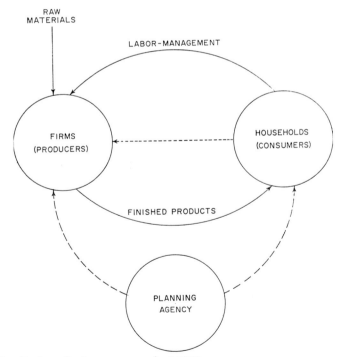

FIG. 1.2. Basic units in an economic system.

households in exchange once again for money. The entire process thus consists of two kinds of flows between households and firms. First, there are the flows of money. Money moves from households, via markets for goods and services, to firms. Then it flows back again from firms, via markets for resources, to households. Second, there are also nonmoney flows; labor and management skills flow from the household, via resource markets, to the firms; goods and services then flow from the firms, via product markets, to households.

The question of *what* to produce is in general decided by the consumers. The market provides a virtually automatic reading on consumers' desires. The phrase that describes this is *consumers' sovereignty,* and implies that the final choice lies with the consumer—that is, the firm responds to price signals received from consumers (dotted line in Figure 1.2); if too little is produced, prices will rise indicating the shortage, if too much is produced, prices will fall reflecting the surplus.

The freedom of consumers' choice also extends to the choice between present and future consumption. Members of a decentralized system are free to save part of their income and this savings then is used to produce capital goods which contribute to the capital growth of the economy. The adjustments of savings to investment desires are accomplished through the use of interest rates, that is, a price for money.

In contrast to the decentralized economy, decisions in the centrally planned economy are coordinated at the highest levels of government, generally through economic plans developed by a planning agency (see Figure 1.2). The primary purpose of such planning is to assure that resources are channeled into certain activities. Here, planning about what is to be produced starts from a basic decision about the allocation between present and future consumption, that is, between consumer items and capital investment. Then the composition of these two categories must be decided. The objective is to coordinate or harmonize the objectives of different sectors of the economy in order to optimize some objectives such as overall economic growth or growth in certain sectors.

In centrally planned economies, what is to be produced and how much is to be produced are worked out in detail according to the aims of the plan, the available resources, and the need for balance in the various sectors of the economy. Consumers usually must abide by the dictates of the plan regarding the quantity and quality of consumers' goods—thus the term *command economies.* Labor must carry out its task wherever needed, and managers are required to meet the production quota. If one industry does not fulfill its quotas, other industries will not have the necessary materials or machines, and the plan will fail to achieve its objectives. The coordination of the myriad of decisions that have to be made is aided by computers—and in actual practice, by considerable trial and error. Prices in such a system are set by edict and have no real guiding function as they do in a market system. In Figure 1.2 these informational flows are shown as dashed lines emanating from the planning agency.

The above-described planned economy does away with most of the consumer choice that characterizes the market economy of a private enterprise system. At most, consumers would be permitted to choose among the items that the government has decided to produce. Generally, labor is allocated by command and thus the question of why people work is partially answered. Since, however, administrative command is a rather poor way of motivating human beings, the planned system often compromises and tries to induce greater effort through wage differentials to guide labor supply into the right industries.

By way of perspective it should be pointed out that both extremes (centralized and decentralized) do not always work perfectly as described here. Specifically, there are those who maintain that the United States economy has little consumers' sovereignty that is not modified or influenced by incessant advertising campaigns to create wants and desires. Thus, instead of consumers sending signals (expenditures) to firms about what products are desired, one view is that firms send signals (advertising) to consumers which convince them to purchase certain products. Examples might be flashy superpowered automobiles and all sorts of quasi-useful medication for insomnia, headaches, anxiety, iron deficiency, and flatulence. The prime spokesman for this view is Harvard economist John Kenneth Galbraith.[3] As for the centrally planned economy, it too works imperfectly. Stories abound about Soviet stores stocked with items that consumers refuse to buy, and about lengthy queues to buy those items that the planners thought unpopular or unnecessary.

HOW TO PRODUCE IT

The second question concerns the appropriate combination of productive factors to achieve a certain level of production at the least possible cost. In a decentralized economy, factor prices play an important role in this process by indicating which factors are the scarcest, and hence which factors must be *economized*. While this will become clear in Chapter 5, intuition tells us that our choice of alternative means to accomplish some objective is greatly influenced by the relative price (cost) of the alternatives; relative prices dictate the choice of transportation modes for vacation-bound college students; relative prices play a

---

3. John Kenneth Galbraith, *American Capitalism: The Concept of Countervailing Power* (Boston: Houghton Mifflin, 1956), Chapter 8; *The Affluent Society* (Boston: Houghton Mifflin, 1958), Chapter 11; *The New Industrial State* (Boston: Houghton Mifflin, 1967), Chapter 18.

decisive role when the objective is to alleviate hunger; and relative prices are significant when a manager is considering alternative ways to produce a commodity. For example, if energy is very expensive relative to hand labor, one would find manufacturing processes that rely on manpower rather than on electricity or other energy forms. Hence, a decentralized economy relies on the market to emit signals about relative scarcity, which are then instrumental in the choice of how certain goods can best be produced.

In a centrally planned economy, relative scarcity is also vital in production decisions, although prices merely plan an accounting role. For instance, throughout the period 1920–1960, Soviet agriculture was plagued by a shortage of motorized equipment. This was the result of a conscious choice by the planners who thought that heavy equipment for construction of manufacturing facilities was of more importance than a mechanized agriculture. Put somewhat differently, it was judged less inefficient for animals and human beings to plant and harvest crops than to have them dig canals and haul steel and concrete for dams and for factories without the aid of heavy equipment.

Hence, while prices in a decentralized economy play the crucial role of indicating relative scarcity—and thus provide a basis for economizing on such scarce factors—prices in a centralized system are for accounting purposes only. The former system is maintained by its proponents to be more efficient in that the desire for profits will lead entrepreneurs to utilize the most effective (least cost) possible means. The proponents of planning argue that a decentralized system results in some individuals having several cars, two homes, four television sets, and extravagant wardrobes while other citizens walk, live in hovels, are illiterate, and are in rags—to say nothing of being continually hungry. This is not the place for an extended discussion on the relative merits of each system, but the reader should recognize that each system does certain things very well and does others quite badly.

HOW MUCH TO PRODUCE

In a decentralized economy, prices also play the important role of indicating to firms the ideal level of production. Just as discussed above, the choice of what to produce is closely related to the choice of how much; that is, rising prices indicate that certain goods are in short supply and would induce certain firms to begin production. But the entrepreneur must then decide the appropriate level of output. As will be seen later, the decentralized market is assumed to consist of many producers who respond to price changes by adjusting output. The assumption is made that each is too small a fraction of total industry production to influence price, and so acts as a "price taker." As a price taker, the entrepreneur takes the prevailing price as given, and, on the basis of production costs, decides the level of production that will maximize profit for the firm. If the industry (the aggregate of all like firms) is not producing sufficient quantities, the price will rise and two things will happen: (1) existing firms will produce more (the "how much" question), and (2) new firms will enter the industry in hopes of making some of the profit (the "what" question, and the "how much" question). On the other hand, if there is an excess supply, prices will tend to fall, signaling that individual firms ought to reduce output (the "how much" question). Additionally, falling prices will indicate to the marginal firms[4] that they ought to reduce output, as well as consider leaving the industry. This latter situation is again the "how much" question, as well as the "what" question.

In a centrally planned economy, prices play no such role and the basic question of how much of certain goods ought to be produced is decided as part of the overall plan. In the Soviet Union, where planning is generally imperative in nature, such guidelines take on considerable importance. In agriculture, production quotas are set for districts, regions, and republics based on previous production levels. Seeds and fertilizer are allocated to localities based on their need to meet the quotas, and mechanical equipment is allocated on the basis of greatest need. During the early 1970s, the Soviets seemed intent on improving agricultural production in the Asian part of the country and hence were sending much more equipment to the East than to the steppes of the Southwest. In industry, factory production quotas are set, and labor and material are allocated such that these targets might be achieved. Once production is complete, the output is allocated to outlets in districts, regions, and republics according to the plan. Since all stores are state owned, no entrepreneur is faced with economic hardship in the case of a shortage; this is not to say that consumers are indifferent to such events, however.

ALLOCATION OF INCOME

The final question that must be decided by a society is the allocation of income. Most are familiar with the communist dictum: from each according to his ability, to each according to his need. This is an ideal that the Soviets admit is still a long time off. At the moment, the Soviet system is characterized by: from each according to his ability, to each according to his work. This sounds vaguely like our own system, but vital differences do exist. In the centralized socialism of the

4. Marginal firms are considered the most vulnerable in an industry, and are usually the last to enter under a price rise and the first to leave under a price decline. More will be said on this later.

Soviet Union, everyone is guaranteed a certain level of income; granted it is not much, but its existence is in sharp contrast to our own system. Next, in that system, all individuals *can* find work. Critics would say *must* is a better word than *can;* still, the availability of jobs for all (between finishing the highest level of schooling attained and until retirement at approximately age 60) provides the system with an opportunity to use labor as a very significant form of participation in society, and hence to inculcate labor as both a duty and an honor.

Since there is no property income in the socialist system, all income is in the form of wages, salaries, or perquisites such as automobiles, better houses, longer vacations, and the like. Wages and salaries are set in a manner remarkably similar to those in capitalist countries; that is, "socially useful" jobs pay more, as do the same jobs in certain regions of the country. As indicated earlier, there is a desire to improve the development of agriculture in the East and hence the same work there pays better than in the western part of the country. All wages and salaries are set as a part of the various economic plans, with the sole purpose of inducing the right form of response from the populace so that the economic plans may be realized.

In contrast, income in a decentralized capitalistic system arises from the use by others of resources owned by the individual. Such resources may be his labor, his equipment, his money, his house, or his management skills.

Whereas the above descriptions approach the ideal of each system, there are wide divergences. In spite of the Soviet pronouncements to the contrary, they do indeed have a class society. It may not be classes on the basis of ownership of land and factories as before the Revolution, but it is a class society based on bureaucratic position. Managers, academicians, top-level scientists, and political functionaries are a social elite with high salaries, fancy housing, access to vacation villas, and opportunities to travel outside the Soviet Union. Hence, while class based on birthright has largely been abolished, class based on ascension within the system is still prevalent. In our own system, where income is supposedly allocated on the basis of an individual's contribution to production based on his ownership of productive factors, powerful unions—spawned to counteract the economic and political power of wealthy capitalists—have had a profound impact on changing that. Other influences on (retained) income are income taxes, inheritance taxes, and certain provisions for the holding of wealth. Furthermore, some critics would argue that things are out of balance when plumbers make more money than grade-school teachers. On the other hand, plumbers' unions have effectively limited the supply of plumbers, while teachers' unions have been notoriously ineffective. The point is that while the market—the supply of and demand for specific skill categories—works to a certain extent in the United States economy, certain factors have intervened to alter the results. More will be said on this in subsequent chapters.

SUMMARY

The foregoing discussion is intended to provide a perspective on economic systems and to set the stage for later theoretical and practical treatments of economic issues. The reader should realize that no economic system can be judged as right or correct; this is a position that can be formed only in the context of broader social preferences. Hence, it must be remembered that an economic system is not an end in and of itself, but rather a means to some other end. The centralized socialism of the Soviet Union derives from a long history of exploitation of the laboring class by superwealthy landed aristocracy. After the Bolshevik Revolution, the overriding objective was to eliminate class distinction that resulted in oppression for the less fortunate. Supposedly, the Soviet system has accomplished this. As for the United States, our system was spawned not from any great history of human suffering—though this is not to obviate the horror of European factories— but to escape religious intolerance and more generally unfavorable economic conditions (the potato famine, etc.).

Because of economic reprisals on the part of certain European countries (primarily Great Britain), it was imperative to build a productive capability that would permit the new colony to become self-sufficient and free from the imperialistic grip of the Old World. Hence, the motivating force was production.

The mixed economies are attempting to combine the best attributes of both extremes. The profit motive and private ownership of productive factors are retained to permit the greatest possible incentive for individual initiative. In addition, state ownership is encouraged in some enterprises to permit the more efficient provision of some goods and services that the private sector might tend to undersupply (medical care, education, some utilities, and the like). Additionally, some degree of planning is instituted in most mixed systems to avoid some of the pitfalls of an unbridled decentralized capitalistic system. We hope the reader keeps this perspective in mind as the theory in the following chapters is presented.

DISCUSSION QUESTIONS AND PROBLEMS

1. How might prices be used to encourage certain behavior in a centrally planned economy?
2. In a free market economy, does central planning for certain activities necessarily impinge on human freedom? Explain.
3. List several reasons why a centrally planned economy restricts the range of consumer's choice.
4. List several reasons why a free market economy results in certain very undesirable results for some members of the economy.
5. Does advertising play a useful role in a market economy or is it basically want-creation? Is want-creation an important aspect of a market economy? Why?

6. Explain the phrase: "Consumers vote with dollars." Relate your answer to question 4 above.

SUGGESTED READINGS

Bornstein, Morris; and Fusfeld, Daniel R., eds. *The Soviet Economy,* 3rd ed. Homewood, Ill.: Richard D. Irwin. 1970.

> An anthology of how the Soviet economy functions.

Commons, John R. *Legal Foundation of Capitalism.* Madison: Univ. Wis. Press, 1968.

> The basic work of the institutionalist school of economic thought, this book integrates economics and law as few have.

Halm, George N. *Economic Systems, a Comparative Analysis.* New York: Holt, Rinehart and Winston, 1951.

> A comparative theoretical and descriptive analysis of the economic systems of various countries.

Heilbroner, Robert L. *The Worldly Philosophers,* 9th rev. ed. New York: Simon and Schuster, 1965.

> Well-written treatment of some famous political economists.

———. *Between Capitalism and Socialism.* New York: Vintage Books, Random House, 1970.

> An excellent book comparing the two systems—their strengths and weaknesses.

Mandel, Ernest. *Marxist Economic Theory,* trans. Brian Pearce, vol. 1, 2nd ed. New York: Monthly Review Press, 1970.

> One of the more well-written books on Marxian economics.

Myrdal, Gunnar. *Asian Drama: An Inquiry into the Poverty of Nations.* New York: Vintage Books, Random House, 1972.

> A treatise on poverty in much of the less-developed world by one of *the* authorities on economic development.

———. *The Challenge of World Poverty: A World Anti-Poverty Program in Outline.* New York: Vintage Books, Random House, 1970.

> A continuation of *Asian Drama,* this book contains a set of actions for a world poverty program. Good perspective of economic systems.

Oser, Jacob. *The Evolution of Economic Thought.* New York: Harcourt, Brace & World, 1963.

> An excellent treatise on the development of contemporary economic thinking.

Robinson, Joan. *Economic Philosophy.* New York: Doubleday, 1964.

> A concise history of the development of economic concepts. It describes the development of the logic and ideologies since Adam Smith and elucidates the moral assumptions underlying current economic thought.

Schnitzer, Martin C.; and Nordyke, James W. *Comparative Economic Systems.* Cincinnati: Southwestern Publ. Co., 1971.

> A good treatment of comparative systems.

Soule, George. *Ideas of the Great Economists.* New York: New American Library of World Literature, 1952.

> A brief look at some of the premier economists.

CHAPTER 2: A PERSPECTIVE ON ECONOMIC ANALYSIS

Any society faces four fundamental economic questions. What is to be produced? How much of it is to be produced? How is it to be produced? How is the national income to be allocated?

We have seen that different societies choose to make these decisions in different ways. For instance, while the decentralized capitalistic economy relies on the marketplace for the first three questions, the centralized socialist economy relies on planning. While the market economy allocates income on the basis of property ownership, contribution to production, rent, dividends, and fortuitous foresight in risk taking, the centralized socialist system relies solely on the contribution of a worker's output to the goals of the society.

Economists have an important role to play in both systems, though that role differs considerably. However, one area of common concern is the efficient production of a given bundle of goods and services. More specifically, almost any society is interested in obtaining a given bundle of goods and services at the least possible commitment of productive factors. Put yet another way, the interest lies with obtaining as much as possible by way of goods and services from the society's endowment of productive factors—labor, land, capital equipment, and managerial talent. Whereas the United States economy relies largely on market prices to solve this problem, the Soviet economy relies on planning. Still, efficiency of production is important to both.

Consider the Soviet system. In each 5-year plan, Soviet planners must decide production levels for, among other things, clothes, automobiles, housing, space ships, farm equipment, airplanes, railroad equipment, movie theaters, and children's toys; more of some means fewer of others. Administered prices are used to allocate the goods and services that result from the current overall economic plan. While the consumer may indicate preferences by choosing to purchase certain goods and not to purchase others, prices generally do not fluctuate as reflections of shortages or gluts; that is, prices serve the primary role of accounting conveniences.

Consider the economy of the United States. Here, rather than relying on indicative or imperative planning, the marketplace is the usual guiding factor. However, the trade-offs that must be made in either system are at the heart of economics and derive from the scarcity of productive factors in the face of human wants and needs. Hence, the question of how to produce a given bundle of goods and services takes on similar flavor whether one is viewing a nonmarket (planned) economy or a market economy. The difference is that in the latter system prices play an allocating role. In either case, the sacrifice required to produce more of any one good is less if production is efficiently organized.

Advocates of the market approach argue that it saves all the manpower necessary to direct production and that it maximizes individual freedom to get ahead in one's own way. Yet the United States system is a series of paradoxes. Our technological advances have allowed us to send men to the moon, to equip our modern homes with the finest plumbing and bathroom fixtures, to produce more per acre of land with the new fertilizers, to have luxuriant wardrobes, and to have available what some claim to be the best medical care anywhere in the world. Yet industry pollutes the atmosphere. The effluents from our municipal sewage treatment plants pollute the waters. Fertilizers on farmlands drain off into the rivers and lakes and stimulate algae growth, thus destroying recreational and sporting sites. Detergents end up polluting lakes, rivers, and streams. The demand for sporting experiences is debilitating wildlife and threatening certain natural areas with ecological disaster. And, the "finest" medical care has become so costly that fewer and fewer individuals can afford it.

Whether concerned with pollution, medical care, or food production, the economist starts from the basic premise that productive resources are scarce, and develops a framework for analyzing and assisting in the solution of important economic and social problems. There are, of course, other views of what the economist does—or should do. It is our purpose in this book to present the rudiments of economic reasoning to aid the reader in viewing choice problems (trade-offs) and to aid in understanding the reasons why certain phenomena exist—whether such phenomena be pollution, high food prices, unemployment, poverty, depressed regions of the country, economic concentration, or the preservation of wilderness areas against the relentless march of "progress." Thus this book is focused on a selected set of issues and problems of economic significance and it introduces economic theory to help develop an understanding of those issues.

Because of the pervasiveness of the resource allocation problem, it is necessary to limit one's scope. Accordingly, we have chosen to focus on the rural sector for many of the economic issues discussed. The economic problems to be covered thus encompass food and fiber production; the processing, distribution, and marketing of same; poverty in general and rural poverty in particular; depressed rural communities; and natural resource problems. Traditional introductory economics books ignore many of these issues, and yet the study of these problems constitutes a significant portion of the total scientific man-years of professional economists in the United States. Almost every state has a land-grant university, and most of these universities have departments of agricultural economics. Agricultural economists have studied these problems for many years and have developed highly sophisticated models of market concepts, product supply, product demand, interregional trade, production economics, rural economic viability, and natural resource use and development. These issues affect all citizens, regardless of their residence—urban or rural. Indeed, the concern in 1973 over food supply, food prices, energy, and natural resource availability in general lends a particular air of significance to the analysis that follows.

SCOPE AND METHOD OF ECONOMICS

The usual definition of economics is that it is the study of the allocation of scarce resources among an infinite number of wants. It actually is much more than that; it is an abstract description of how the economic system of a society operates to achieve certain social goals. Real life is too complex to be comprehended in its entirety, and thus the description is simplified to promote understanding. Furthermore, the complexities of any economic system are so great as to defy comprehension as one complete, integrated, functioning unit. Thus the economist studies the economic system in small pieces by holding one set of variables constant while attempting to understand or describe the relationships among another set. For example, just as the physicist abstracts from the confounding influence of air resistance to study the law of gravity, so too the economist abstracts from the confounding influences of income changes when studying the relationship of the retail price of beef to the quantity people will buy.

In developing a framework with which to study economic phenomena, it is necessary to recognize several ingredients. First, we make some *assumptions* regarding the issue under scrutiny. If the responsiveness of consumers of ground beef to changes in the price of ground beef were to be analyzed, then it might be reasonable to assume that (1) a sample of households in a Denver suburb is representative of beef consumers nationwide; (2) ground beef is a homogeneous product that in all retail stores contains the same percentage of fat; (3) the income level of the household is important in influencing the response to changes in the price of the commodity; and (4) consumers wish to maximize satisfaction—given their income level. These assumptions would comprise a set for our analytical framework. Notice that if some (or all) seem unreasonable the analyst must make his framework more complicated or more extensive.

Second, it is necessary to articulate some hypotheses about the economic behavior of the households; such hypotheses constitute the basic question(s) to be answered by the investigation. More importantly, the hypotheses are instrumental in deciding which questions will be asked and how the study will be conducted. Hypotheses are derived from theories and it is thus necessary to consider the distinction between theories and laws. In early stages of the development of physics, there were theories of gravity, theories of thermodynamics, and theories of resistance to electricity flowing through a wire. Now there is a law of gravity, law of thermodynamics, and a law regarding the resistance to the movement of electricity through a wire (Ohm's law). Similarly, today there are theories about how the earth was formed and theories about the universe in general. In economics, there are theories about consumer behavior in the face of price changes, there are theories about firm behavior in the pursuit of maximum profit, and there are theories about the most efficient way to eliminate poverty and pollution. There are few economic laws. Still, the distinction between a theory and a law is relevant here. Consider the moon. Prior to the development of sophisticated devices, there were many theories regarding the origin of our closest planet. To some, the moon was (and still is) of religious significance and origin. But as we learn more of the facts from exploration, we are able to confront those facts with our theories and reject those that are incongruous. This iterative process—from theory to fact and back to theory—is the essence of scientific inquiry.

This brings us back to the notion of hypotheses. If a theory holds that the moon was formed by breaking away from the earth, a reasonable hypothesis would be that the same form of rock could be found on both planets. Hence, a testable hypothesis is derived from a theory, and the scientist's role is to verify that theory with empirical observations (facts). If the same form of rock is found on both planets, that particular theory is enhanced at the expense of a rival theory. This is not to imply that the case is closed—only that one theory now seems more plausible than another.

To return to the earlier example, the response of beef consumers to price changes can be assumed to follow from a theory of consumer behavior which indicates that a utility-maximizing consumer will decrease consumption of a commodity as its price increases, and increase consumption when the price falls. This is a theory that is subject to empirical testing. We might hypothesize that a 10 percent increase in the price of ground beef would cause an 8 percent decrease in the purchase of ground beef. This hypothesis would then guide us in our formulation of the above study, and it is hoped we would be able to assert—once finished with the study—that consumers in Denver in the $10,000 to $15,000 family income bracket decreased their purchases of ground beef by 12 percent in the face of a 10 percent increase in the price of ground beef.

In summary then, the framework includes assumptions, theories, hypotheses, and observable facts. The collection of components would often be referred to as an economic model of consumer behavior regarding the price of ground beef. A model, just as the more popularized notion of a model, is an abstraction with very specific purposes in mind. An aircraft engineer tests models in a wind tunnel for aerodynamic purposes, with extraneous parts of the airplane missing. An economist excludes certain things from his model by holding them constant. In the above example, we would assume that all other prices did not change during the course of our experiment. Additionally, we would assume that the income of the sample units did not change, and that tastes and preferences for ground beef and other goods did not change. These factors which are held constant are characterized by the phrase *ceteris paribus*—Latin for "all other things being equal." It is a phrase that appears many times in economics books.

POLICY MEANS AND ENDS

Economics is a social science. It is concerned primarily with those problems of resource allocation whose solutions require the cooperation, interaction, or, at a minimum, the sufferance of other individuals. Even the action of one person has implications for, is dependent upon, or is constrained by the individuals he knows and the institutional setting in which he lives. It is this institutional setting which determines how the individual or all individuals collectively in a society solve their economic problems. As we define the field of economics, the problem of resource allocation is the same for a backward agrarian society; a highly developed capitalistic society; or a modern, industrialized, communistic society. The goals they have collectively set for themselves and the institutions they have developed to solve their economic problems differ, yet the problems of resource allocation remain.

Because the emphasis here is on the problems and issues of human and natural resource allocation, we quickly encounter the notion of policy and policy recommendations. Policy actions are those that result in changes in the institutions that define the basis for collective action in restraint and liberation of individual action, and usually result from a given problematic situation. Economics may or may not play a role in this process, but where it does, the economist is involved in the development of models and data that will assist in the reformulation of the rules of the game.

Before proceeding further in the discussion of policies and

goals, it is important to define "institutions." While one might crudely call institutions rules of the game, a more elegant definition states that institutions are the range of laws, administrative codes, customs, organizations, traditions, and their interplay defining or circumscribing how a society deals with the complex of problems it faces. Specifically, it is helpful to distinguish two kinds of institutions: (1) primary institutions and (2) ancillary institutions. Primary institutions include the entire configuration of property rights, titles, and other legal notions that imply decentralized capitalism as both political and economic concepts. It is within this institutional setting that American society essentially operates. Ancillary to the above configuration is a rather impressive array of institutional contraints which further define or modify the basic tenets of our system. Examples include antitrust legislation, the Small Business Administration and its programs, farm programs, labor unions, and even the government subsidization of the distribution of third-class mail.

Policy, then, is the spectrum from the study and analysis of, to the passing of judgment on, the adequacy of these institutions (means) designed to achieve a predetermined goal (end). For example, if collective ownership of all resources by a society is one of its goals, the means (institutions) it utilizes to allocate resources will be oriented toward this goal. Similarly for the individual, if his goal is maximizing annual income, his behavior (means) will be directed toward achieving that end. One of the major activities of the economist is developing the analytics for evaluating the means of achieving a specific goal. This requires being able to specify the goals. Unfortunately, neither a society nor an individual can usually detail exact goals for several reasons.

First, ends and the means of achieving them are not clearly distinguishable even though the recent literature on public policy and decision making often seems to imply that they are. For example, the recent interest in planning-programming-budgeting systems (PPBS) that were introduced into the Department of Defense by Robert MacNamara assumes a prior designation of goals or ends and the systematic evaluation of alternative means to meet these ends. This is in contrast to the "muddling through" school of thought espoused by Lindblom.[1] Lindblom's emphasis is on a dialectic process of discovering goals or ends while alternative means of achieving them are being explored. Thus the true picture of the means/ends puzzle is more accurately portrayed as that of a continuum than as distinct polar opposites.

The means/ends problem is further complicated by the fact that goals for a society are, of necessity, vague. Social goals are usually vague because they must be stated in very general and abstract terms to satisfy the many viewpoints and interests of our modern society. Con-

1. Robert A. Dahl and Charles E. Lindblom, *Politics, Economics, and Welfare* (New York: Harper and Row, 1953).

sider the following quote from the report of the National Advisory Commission on Food and Fiber: "The Commission recommends that one of our National goals should be to insure that the services, cultural advantages and economic opportunities available to rural people are as good as those of urban people."[2] Or consider the following from the recommendations of the same advisory commission: "A major effort must continue to be made to achieve equitable incomes in agriculture. The goal should be to make earnings received by efficient farmers for their labor, management and investment comparable with earnings on similar resources outside of agriculture."[3]

What should be obvious from both of the above statements is their generality and their suitability for being interpreted as "all things for all people." As a consequence of this necessary ambiguity, progress in policy analysis requires developing approximate goals. For example, some accept the gross national product (GNP) as a surrogate for indications of human welfare. At best, it is nothing more than an approximate goal for human welfare; one that is theoretically defensible up to a certain point and, more importantly, one that is empirically observable. The necessity of measurable goals is probably the most important consideration in many respects and dictates the nature of approximate goals. For example, the real goal of a fire department is most likely fire prevention, but many departments view the efficient suppression of existing fires as a satisfactory goal. Or, while the real goal of police departments is crime prevention, many probably operate with the notion that their goal is to apprehend as many criminals as possible. Or, while many would view good highways as a logical goal for a nation to pursue, it is more proper to think in terms of a good transportation system in its entirety, and hence to view highways as but one alternative means of providing good transportation.

Third, policy analysis is further complicated by the fact that present goals and policies are continually being reevaluated and revised. Thus the analytical framework must develop the principles rather than specific recommendations. The institutions that man devises to guide his daily activities are never perfect—even at the time of their inception. As they function and their imperfections become obvious, alterations are justified, assuming, of course, that the benefits from such alterations outweigh the costs. This topic is covered in more detail in Chapter 15. For example, in the United States our society's notion of the goal of a good life is constantly being revised. Until recently, gross national product was accepted as an accurate measure of the nation's well-being. This is no longer considered adequate. In 1966 President Johnson directed

2. National Advisory Commission on Food and Fiber, *Food and Fiber for the Future* (Washington, D.C.: USGPO, 1967), p. 28.
3. Ibid., p. 33.

the secretary of Health, Education and Welfare to "search for ways to improve the nation's ability to chart its social progress."[4] In 1969 the department issued its findings in a document entitled *Toward a Social Report.* In the introduction to the report we find:

> Curiosity about our social condition would by itself justify an attempt to assess the social health of the Nation. Many people want answers to questions like these: Are we getting healthier? Is pollution increasing? Do children learn more than they used to? Do people have more satisfying jobs than they used to? Is crime increasing? How many people are really alienated? Is the American Dream of rags to riches a reality? We are interested in the answers to such questions partly because they would tell us a good deal about our individual and social well-being. Just as we need to measure our incomes, so do we need "social indicators," or measures of other dimensions of our welfare, to get an idea of how well off we really are.[5]

Furthermore, until recently economic growth was viewed as a solution to most if not all our problems; now it appears that some view economic growth as the cause of our problems. The literature that was generated during Earth Week of April 1970 is testimony to this latter sentiment.

Finally, the individual in our society is much better informed than in the past. Consequently, he is more aware of the fact that past surrogates for vague goals are inadequate and that some of our most highly regarded and widely articulated goals may not be worth the costs they entail. If high growth rates for the whole economy imply costs for certain subsectors of the economy (such as the inner city, minority groups, or the aged), a lower overall growth rate may be preferable. Similarly, a high growth rate with its attendant congestion and pollution is now being reevaluated. As a result, people are now concerned with formulation of policy on where people should live, where factories should be allowed to locate, where people should be allowed to drive cars, what crops a farmer should be allowed to grow, how much income a family should have, and a lengthy list of other items which would surely shock our forebears. To them the very essence of our system was that of each individual doing what was best for him in the belief that in the long run what was best for society would also emerge as a logical corollary. This is the cornerstone of our private enterprise economy, and it was not until rather recently that the public at large began to recognize that unfettered competition among firms and households has led to pollution, urban congestion, rural poverty, powerful labor unions, and a whole array of matters that require conscientious study, analysis, and public action.

4. U.S. Department of Health, Education and Welfare, *Toward a Social Report* (Washington, D.C.: USGPO, 1969), p. iii.
   5. Ibid., p. xii.

POSITIVE AND NORMATIVE ECONOMICS

The above is intended to illustrate that policy issues are inextricably linked to the notion of ends and means which are constantly changing and purposely inexplicit. To make headway, the scientist must designate certain concepts as approximate goals, and indeed in analyzing alternative policies, one cannot avoid the conflict between what is and what ought to be. The former notion is referred to as *positive economics* while the latter is considered *normative economics*. In other words, positive economics is directed toward the identification and articulation of what is, or perhaps more correctly, what people believe is the case. In contrast, normative economics is directed toward the specification of what ought to be the case.

As illustrations of the concept of positive and normative economics, consider the following propositions that an economist might make regarding poverty:

1. The poor are relatively worse off now than they were 30 years ago.
2. The poor should be counted as a special group in analyzing economic policy.
3. The poor should be treated preferentially so that they become less poor.
4. The poor should be given guaranteed incomes.
5. The poor should be given guaranteed jobs.

Proposition (1) would classify as a hypothesis which must be confronted with empirical data to determine its truth; until that confrontation, it is nothing more than a hypothesis, or pure conjecture. The proposition is neither a positive statement nor normative. If the proposition were made following a comprehensive analysis of the relative poverty of groups in the United States, the proposition becomes a positive statement; it expresses what is apparent fact as revealed by the empirical investigation. The second proposition could be referred to as a normative statement since it asserts what should be done regarding the poor—it is the opinion of the author of the proposition. Proposition (3) is also a normative statement since it asserts that the author is of the opinion that the poor should be given more income. Proposition (4) is a normative statement since it expresses an opinion, and likewise for proposition (5). Hence, propositions (2) through (5) are normative in nature, but they still differ significantly in character and it is important to explore those differences. First, proposition (2) is a normative statement of very narrow and limited scope; it merely asserts professional opinion of an economist regarding how economic policy analysis should be conducted. As such, it would qualify as a legitimate normative statement on the part of the economist. Propositions (3), (4), and (5) are more troublesome. If an economist made proposition (3), it would be classified as a normative statement that is in general considered outside the professional domain of an economist; that is, such a statement falls in the general category of social goals and is a political matter for social discourse and decision. An economist has no more authority in this domain than do poets, housewives, or business-men. This is not to say that economists should not speak out on such matters as private citizens. But the difficulty comes when—speaking as an economist, and hence with more than casual understanding of the con-cept of poverty—policy goals are outlined which are based on private views rather than on purely analytical foundations. This does not mean that the economist should not outline the economic implications of the existence of poverty. For instance, if research shows that poor diets result in unproductive workers, an economist is making a positive statement when he asserts if there is a desire to increase productivity of certain laborers, diets should be improved.

This brings us to propositions (4) and (5). If there has been a conscious public goal of eliminating poverty, these propositions become means to that end. While they are normative statements when they stand alone, they become positive statements when coupled with the prior con-dition that social policy is directed to the elimination of poverty, and with the empirical evidence that one or the other is the best way to eliminate poverty. With the social goal of eliminating poverty, but in the absence of any empirical evidence regarding the best way to achieve that goal, they both fall in the category of proposition (2)—that of pro-fessional opinion or conjecture.

While the above may strike the reader as unnecessarily detailed for an introductory text, it is imperative that the normative nature of the social sciences (of which economics is one) be understood. Most of what economists do by way of policy recommendations has implications for the relative wealth position of individuals and groups of individuals. In the discussion of the following chapters, we will avoid blatant pro-nouncements concerning what ought to be (normative economics) and will present an analytical framework for understanding what is. Addi-tionally, we will address the analytics of what might be, also a positive position. Thus this book is essentially positive economics. This is not to deny that our values have entered, for even in the selection of subject matter to be treated, value judgments play a part. Nonetheless, our concern is with the positive conceptual framework within which it is possible to understand economic matters in the world around us and to offer judgments on the economic consequences of one or several courses of action.

SUMMARY

It is our view that the economist is concerned with (1) analyzing and describing how individuals, groups, or societies solve their economic problems; (2) using this knowledge to improve the means of achieving prestated goals; and (3) further developing the analytics to help in (1) and (2). The important point is that the economist can study both means and ends; the relative efficiency of certain means is relevant, as is the analysis of which ends are incompatible in an economic sense. However, it is important that personal values be clearly identified when the economist enters the policy arena.

DISCUSSION QUESTIONS AND PROBLEMS

1. Criticize the definition of economics we have employed in this chapter.
2. What is a model?
3. Discuss the role of assumptions in developing a theoretical model.
4. Why are national goals so difficult to specify in advance?
5. Why is progress toward those goals which a nation does specify so difficult to measure?
6. List the kinds of institutional constraints that influence your behavior in daily life.
7. What is policy analysis?
8. When can it be dangerous for an economist to assert: "Property taxes should be lowered"?
9. Categorize the following statements as positive or normative:
   a. The unemployment rate is too high.
   b. If you wish to maximize profit you should use fewer laborers and more machinery.
   c. Based on our analysis, wages should increase next year at a rate slightly less than they did last year.
   d. Wages should be increased next year.

SUGGESTED READINGS

Bator, Francis M. *The Question of Government Spending: Public Needs and Private Wants.* New York: Collier Books, Crowell-Collier, 1962.
   Discusses the current role of the public sector in meeting private wants and public needs.
Blalock, Hubert M., Jr. *Causal Inferences in Nonexperimental Research.* New York: Norton, 1964.
   A highly recommended book covering the philosophy of research in the social sciences.
Boulding, Kenneth E. *Economics as a Science.* New York: McGraw-Hill, 1970.
   A collection of seven essays by one of the best known contemporary economists in the United States. Gives the reader a broad perspective of the scope and content of economics as a social, ecological, behavioral, political, mathematical, and moral science.
Buchanan, James M. Ceteris paribus: Some notes on methodology. *South. Econ. J.* 25 (1958):259–70.
   Author argues that the *ceteris paribus* assumption is a necessary and reasonable methodological procedure for studying market or firm equilibrium (microeconomics), but it is a hindrance and confounding influence in studying the economics of general equilibrium (macroeconomics).
Cohen, Kalman J.; and Cyert, Richard M. *Theory of the Firm: Resource*

Allocation in a Market Economy. Englewood Cliffs, N.J.: Prentice-Hall, 1965, pp. 17–27.

An elementary discussion of the methodology of model building in economics. It includes the nature of models, their construction, their testing, and their role in scientific explanation, prediction, and policy development.

Haveman, Robert H. *The Economics of the Public Sector.* New York: John Wiley, 1970.

An introduction to economic analysis of the public sector's activities.

Heller, Walter W. *New Dimensions of Political Economy.* New York: Norton, 1967.

An interesting book by a former chairman of the Council of Economic Advisors on economics and public policy.

Leontief, Wassily. *Essays in Economics: Theories and Theorizing.* New York: Oxford Univ. Press, 1966.

A good series of essays on theories in economics—their structure, their use, and their misuse.

Liebhafsky, H. H. *The Nature of Price Theory.* Homewood, Ill.: Dorsey Press, 1968, pp. 3–25.

Details the basic assumptions about human behavior that are required to study market behavior. Examines the question of why economic theory is such an important analytical tool for the economist. Briefly considers the importance and meaning of economic efficiency, economic welfare, and prediction from theory.

Lipsey, Richard G.; and Steiner, Peter O. *Economics,* 3rd ed. New York: Harper & Row, 1972, pp. 15–51.

A good discussion for the novice of what economics is and why it is termed a social science and of the methodology of the science of economics. Includes a broad description of the tools, techniques, and conventions of economics.

Mermelstein, David, ed. *Economics: Mainstream Readings and Radical Critiques.* New York: Random House, 1970.

A reader of traditional views on economic issues with companion articles by "radical economists" disputing the traditional view. Excellent for a wide spectrum of views.

Mishan, E. J. *Economics for Social Decisions: Elements of Cost-Benefit Analysis.* New York: Praeger, 1973.

Elements of benefit-cost analysis and its use in economic policy.

Mundell, Robert A. *Man and Economics.* New York: McGraw-Hill, 1968.

An easily comprehended discussion of the concepts of economics, its systems and methods, and their application to a wide range of every-day aspects of life.

Northrop, F. S. C. *The Logic of the Sciences and the Humanities,* 7th ed. Cleveland: World, 1967.

A good book on the research methodology of the social sciences.

Tweeten, Luther. *Foundation of Farm Policy.* Lincoln, Nebr.: Univ. Nebr. Press, 1970, pp. 1–57.

A discussion of the conflict of goals in a society. Author discusses the expectation of the rural sectors with respect to farm policies as viewed from their goals and values. He contrasts these policies with the expectations of the urban-industrial sectors as influenced by their goals and values.

CHAPTER 3: A PERSPECTIVE ON RESOURCE ALLOCATION IN RURAL AMERICA

The central purpose of this book is to help the student of economics to understand the complex issues facing the nation in the general area of resource allocation in rural America. Its focus is the issues and problems associated with such allocation, and its analytical framework is that of economics. It is not a book of economic theory alone; rather, it is a treatment of social problems from an economic point of view. The principles of economics pervade the roots of these problems, the issues surrounding them, and their impacts on society. Thus our central aim is not to teach theory for the sake of teaching theory but to teach economic theory in a way that the student gains an insight into its uses as an analytical framework for addressing important contemporary problems.

The primary purpose of this chapter is to provide an introduction to the economic issues that will be treated in considerable detail in Part III. Essentially, our aim is to highlight the basic economic aspect of the five areas covered in Part III to enhance the reader's interest and curiosity. Perhaps more importantly, it will also serve to provide a problem-oriented reference point from which to view the theoretical concepts to be developed in Part II. Because this is a book on economic concepts applied to problems of resource allocation, the brief treatment here of the problems is believed to be an effective way to create the proper perspective for the study of economic theory. The following five sections of this chapter will correspond to the five chapters of Part III of the book.

FARM SECTOR

While there are many possible ways to divide the issues pertaining to the production of food and fiber in the United States, they all directly or indirectly emerge from the rapid pace of technological advance in agriculture. We will concentrate on two major aspects: (1) the significant changes in the technology of the farming

27

TABLE 3.1. Man-hours per unit of production for selected crops and live-stock, United States, selected years 1925–1971

Item and Crop	1925-29	1945-49	1955-59	1965-69	1970-71[a]
Man-hours per 100 Bushels					
Corn	115	53	20	7	7
Wheat	74	34	17	11	9
Potatoes (per ton)	21	12	6	4	4
Cotton (per bale)	268	146	74	30	26
Soybeans	126	41	23	19	17
Man-hours per 100 Pounds					
Milk	3.3	2.6	1.7	0.9	0.7
Hogs	3.3	3.0	2.4	1.4	1.1
Eggs (per 100 eggs)	1.9	1.5	0.9	0.4	0.4
Broilers	...	5.1	1.3	0.5	0.4
Turkeys	28.5	13.1	4.4	1.3	1.0

Source: USDA, Agricultural Statistics, 1972, p. 541.

a. Preliminary.

sector and the impacts of these changes on agricultural output; and (2) the effect of such changes on incomes in agriculture, with specific reference to income distribution.

TECHNOLOGY AND OUTPUT

Production can be defined as the process by which a set of inputs can be transformed into outputs. As the level of outputs obtainable from a given set of inputs increases, the technology of production is said to have increased. Technology is a label used to refer to a wide variety of changes in production techniques and methods. New crop varieties such as hybrid corn, new and improved breeds of livestock, better equipment and machines, pesticides, and fertilizers and other chemicals are the more obvious examples. Technology also refers to the improved methods of combining the inputs. The improvement in managerial talent is an integral part of the technological revolution. Lacking the appropriate management decisions, the same machines, varieties, and materials might have been used in the wrong way or combination, leading to no increase in output.

Table 3.1 shows the man-hours needed to produce a selected

list of major farm commodities and is an excellent illustration of the on-going pace of technology in agriculture. For example, the hours required to produce 100 bushels of corn declined from 115 in 1925–1929 to 7 hours in 1970–1971; the man-hours to produce 100 bushels of wheat declined from 74 to 9 hours in the same period; and the man-hours to produce 100 bushels of soybeans declined from 126 to 17 hours. In livestock and livestock products, it took 3.3 hours to produce 100 pounds of milk in 1925–1929 and 0.7 hours in 1970–1971. The man-hours for 100 pounds of hogs declined from 3.3 to 1.1 hours in the same period, while that required for eggs decreased from 1.9 to 0.4 hours (per 100 eggs). For the production of turkeys, required man-hours fell from 28.5 to 1.0 hours per 100 pounds of meat.

Another interesting way to view the increased productivity of agricultural labor is to consider the number of persons supplied farm products by 1 United States farm worker. In Table 3.2 we have traced this trend for the period between 1910 and 1971. We can see from Table

TABLE 3.2. Total number of persons supplied farm products by one U.S. farm worker, selected years 1910–1971

Year	Persons Supplied[a]	Year	Persons Supplied[a]
1910	7.1	1963	30.7
1920	8.3	1964	33.2
1930	9.8	1965	37.0
1940	10.7	1966	39.6
1945	14.6	1967	42.1
1950	15.5	1968	43.4
1955	19.5	1969	45.1
1960	25.8	1970	47.1
1961	27.6	1971[b]	48.2
1962	28.6		

Source: USDA, Agricultural Statistics, 1971, p. 542.

Note: Includes persons in other countries supplied by U.S. agricultural exports.

a. Persons supplied per farm worker include the farm worker. For example, in 1910 the average farm worker supplied himself and 6.1 other persons.

b. Preliminary.

3.2 that the persons supported by each farm worker increased from 7 in 1910 to 48 in 1971; this means that 1 farm worker today supports himself and 47 other persons, while in 1910 he supported himself and 6 other persons. It also shows that the increase in productivity per farm worker is growing at an increasing rate. It took 35 years for the number supported by 1 farm worker to double from 7 to 14. It took 17 more years for the figure to double again to 28 (1945–1961), and in the 6 years from 1961 to 1967 it increased another 50 percent. As a result of the accelerating technological growth, a given level of output can be achieved today with one-seventh as many workers as in 1910.

The increases in output have been substantial as reflected by the number of man-hours required to produce a given level of output. The magnitude of these changes is more meaningful when compared to some reference point such as the other sectors of the United States economy. Therefore Figure 3.1 compares the increase in productivity per man-hour between farm industries and nonfarm industries. As can be seen, since 1947 labor productivity in agriculture has increased at a significantly faster rate than it has in nonagricultural industries.

In general, most of the new agricultural technologies have been labor saving. The new methods have permitted the farmer to substitute

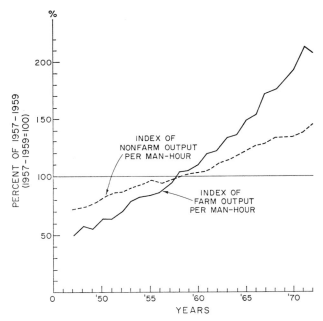

FIG. 3.1. Output per man-hour of farm and nonfarm workers, United States, 1947–1972. (From U.S. Council of Economic Advisors, **1973 Economic Report of the President,** Washington, D.C., Table C–34, pp. 230, 289.)

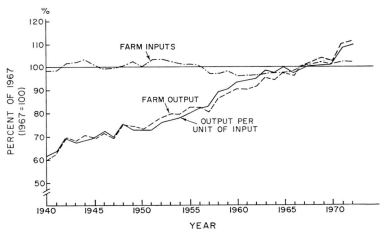

FIG. 3.2. Indices of farm output, farm inputs, and output per unit of input, United States, 1940–1972. (From USDA, ERS, **Changes in Farm Production and Efficiency,** Stat. Bull. 233, Washington, D.C.: USGPO, 1973; USDA, ERS, **Supplement V to Changes in Farm Production and Efficiency,** Washington, D.C.: USGPO, 1973.)

other inputs for labor. This means that over time there is less and less need for a given amount of labor to produce the required output. As we shall see later, another part of the reduced labor requirements grows out of the increasing specialization of farms. Many of the activities such as storage, transportation, processing, and selling have been taken over by business firms beyond the farm gate. The same also applies to farm inputs; the labor applied to the production of feed and the care of horses and mules has been replaced by firms that repair the trucks and tractors and sell fuel to farmers. Nevertheless, when the total range of inputs is included in the calculation, the same picture emerges. Output per unit of input has grown substantially over the past decades. The data for 1940 through 1972 are summarized in Figure 3.2. Here we see the relative change in farm output, inputs, and productivity during the period 1940–1972. Up through 1960 there was little change in the volume of farm inputs, and increases in total farm output reflected increases in productivity of the inputs. Since 1960 input productivity has leveled off slightly and the utilization of inputs has increased. Over the whole period, farm output has constantly increased. Thus there is a joint effect of inputs and productivity. Total input productivity (total farm output per unit of input) rose at an average annual rate of 0.5 percent per year from World War I to the beginning of World War II. In the last 30 years, the average yearly growth rate tripled to 1.6 percent per year. Thus we see that United States agriculture is enormously productive. Output has mounted steadily over the years, and productivity, however measured, has grown at a cumulative rate.

DISTRIBUTIONAL IMPACTS

The technological changes that permitted such significant increases in production have also promoted substantial transformation in the structure of agriculture. The new technologies have encouraged farms to become larger in size and fewer in number. Furthermore, the benefits of this tremendous increase in output have not been distributed equally among farm groups nor between farmers and nonfarmers. It can be seen from Table 3.3 that the number of United States farms increased until around 1935 (when it reached a peak of 6.8 million) and since then has declined steadily. Since World War II, the number of farms in the United States has decreased by 52 percent from 5.9 million in 1945 to 2.7 million in 1970. It is projected that by 1980 the United States will have only 2 million farms.

In spite of the rapid decline in farm numbers, the total amount

TABLE 3.3.   Number of farms, land in farms, and average farm size, United States, selected years 1910–1970

Year	Number of Farms	Land in Farms	Average Farm Size
	(thousand)	(million acres)	(acres)
1910	6,366	881	138
1920	6,453	957	148
1930	6,295	990	157
1935	6,812	1,054	155
1940	6,102	1,065	175
1945	5,859	1,142	195
1950	5,388	1,161	215
1954	4,783	1,160	243
1959	3,710	1,124	303
1964	3,158	1,110	349
1970	2,730	1,063	390

Source: U.S. Dept. of Commerce, Bureau of Census, 1964 United States Census of Agriculture, 1964, vol. 11, Ch. 8, Table 2; USDC, Bureau of Census, Census of Agriculture 1969 Preliminary Summary.

TABLE 3.4. Distribution of number of farms by size of farm, United States, 1950 and 1969

Size of Farm	Number of Farms 1950	1969	Percent of Total 1950	1969
(acres)	(thousand)			
Less than 100	3,016	1,096	56	40
100 to 499	2,068	1,268	38	47
Over 500	304	366	6	13
	5,388	2,730	100	100

Source: U.S. Dept. of Commerce, Bureau of Census, 1964 United States Census of Agriculture, vol. 11, Ch. 3, Table 7; USDC, Bureau of Census, Census of Agriculture 1969 Preliminary Summary.

of land in farms has changed very little in the past 35 years. The obvious consequence has been that the remaining farms are larger. This is clearly apparent in the last column of Table 3.3 where the average size of farms is shown to have increased from 150 acres per farm in the 1920s to almost 400 acres currently. It should be noted that this decrease in the number of farms and their increase in average size did not result from the already large farms getting larger. On the contrary, it was the result of several small, uneconomic-sized units being consolidated into one unit on which modern technologies became economically feasible. In fact, current statistical evidence indicates that in the past 20 years there has been a sharp drop in farms of less than 100 acres (Table 3.4).

While the farm sector fares well in terms of productivity and efficiency, there are some very important considerations on the income side. In spite of the willingness of the producer to provide the food and fiber a growing population requires, he has not received adequate compensation for this service. The available data point to a large number of very low-income farmers, along with a smaller number of medium-income ones and a few with relatively good incomes. There is also evidence that the latter group is receiving a smaller return on its capital, labor, and management ability than other sectors.

One indication of this discrepancy is the per capita income levels of farm versus nonfarm people. On the basis of the 1959 census, median farm income is estimated by the USDA to be only 56 percent of the United States median for comparable males employed in nonfarm jobs. Median rural nonfarm incomes on a comparable basis amounted to 89 percent of the United States median.[1] Table 3.5 further confirms the adverse position of farm income when expressed in terms of per

1. USDA, ERS, *Rural People in the American Economy*, Agr. Econ. Rept. 101 (Washington, D.C.: USGPO, 1966), p. 17.

TABLE 3.5.   Per capita disposable income of the farm and nonfarm population, selected years 1935–1972

Year	Income from All Sources of the			Per Capita Farm Income as Percent of Nonfarm Income
	Farm population	Nonfarm population	Total population	
	(dollars)			
1935	237	535	459	44.3
1940	245	671	573	36.5
1945	655	1,162	1,074	56.4
1950	841	1,458	1,364	57.7
1955	854	1,772	1,666	48.2
1960	1,100	2,017	1,937	54.5
1965	1,772	2,481	2,436	71.4
1970	2,610	3,414	3,376	76.4
1972	3,182	3,847	3,816	82.7

Source: USDA, ERS, Farm Income Situation, July 1973, Table 7H.

capita disposable income. The table reveals that on a per capita basis, farm incomes in the most favorable year of 1972 were 83 percent of nonfarm incomes. Although the disparity is less than in earlier years, it still exists. The problem is that most of this relative improvement has accrued either to owners of the largest farms or to those deriving income from nonfarm activities.

What is occurring is that a small proportion of all farmers is obtaining most of the income generated in agriculture. This is easily seen in reference to Table 3.6 where the distribution of farms by level of sales in 1972 is shown. As can also be seen in Table 3.6, less than 37 percent of all farms account for over 90 percent of the food and fiber marketed in the United States (farms selling $10,000 or more). These are the "commercial farms."

At the other extreme are the low-output farms, often referred to as "marginal farms." These are the farms where annual sales of output are less than $5,000. Some 1,457,000 farms, representing more than 50 percent of all farms, fall in this category. In total, owners of these farms market less than 5 percent of all the food and fiber produced in the United States. The weighted average net farm income of this group is $1,311 per farm operation. Many of the farms in this class are part-time, residential, and retirement farms. As a consequence, these farmers are not dependent upon agriculture as their sole source of income.

TABLE 3.6. Number of farms by value of sales class, United States, 1972

Sales Class	Number of Farms		Percent of Sales	Average Net Income per Farm[a]
	Total	Percent of total		
	(thousand)			
$20,000 and over	701	24.4	81.2	$20,138
$10,000-$19,999	353	12.3	9.2	6,736
$5,000-$9,999	359	12.5	4.8	3,533
$2,500-$4,999	420	14.6	2.7	1,929
Less than $2,500	1,037	36.2	2.1	1,061
TOTAL	2,870	100.0	100.0	

Source: USDA, ERS, Farm Income Situation, July 1973, Tables 1D, 3D.

a. Excludes nonfarm income but includes direct government payments.

Nevertheless, with an average income of $1,311 per farm, a sizable number of these farm families can be described as a poverty problem. We shall return to this problem in a later chapter.

The economic class of farms $5,000 to $9,999 contains the remaining farmers. This class of farms is comprised primarily of full-time farmers who are dependent upon agriculture for their livelihood. Over a third of a million farms fall in this class. They are actually not large enough to be considered truly commercial farms but are on the borderline, and are often referred to as "transitional."[2] Some farms in this group will be successful and move into the top two categories of Table 3.6; others will be unable to compete and will fall by the wayside. Although the farmers in this group depend upon the sale of agricultural products for a portion of their income, it was insufficient in 1972 to provide a reasonable living for themselves and their families. Consequently, many of these farm families also obtained a substantial amount of income from sources other than the farms.

It is of interest to review momentarily the size distribution of farms during the past 20 years to see the trends in farm size, number of farms, and their relative shares in total sales, marketings, and income. Earlier we asserted that the bulk of the reduction in farm numbers had occurred as a result of consolidation among the very small farms. In Table 3.7 several interesting facts are apparent. First, notice that the proportion of farms with sales less than $5,000 fell from 78.4 percent in 1949 to 63.3 percent in 1972. Second, notice that the proportion of farms

2. Willard W. Cochrane, *The City Man's Guide to the Farm Problem* (Minneapolis: Univ. Minn. Press, 1965), p. 20.

TABLE 3.7. Trends in sales and net income change by economic class of farm, United States, 1949, 1964, and 1972

	1949	1964	1972
Annual sales of $10,000 or more			
Farms	8.7%	26.0%	36.7%
Marketings	50.2	79.6	90.4
Net Farm Income	38.0	67.4	71.8
Government Payments	...	62.1	64.0
Annual sales of less than $5,000			
Farms	78.4%	74.0%	63.3%
Marketings	27.4	20.4	9.7
Net Income	37.2	32.6	16.1
Government Payments	...	37.9	20.9

Source: 1949 data from W. W. Cochrane, The City Man's Guide to the Farm Problem (New York: McGraw-Hill, 1966), p. 229; 1964 and 1970 data from USDA, ERS, Farm Income Situation, July 1972, Table 4D.

with sales in excess of $10,000 rose from 8.7 percent in 1949 to 36.7 percent in 1972. Consequently, whether size is measured in terms of acres or sales, the small farms are gradually giving way to larger and larger operating units.

As shown in the table, the large farms (those with $10,000 or more of annual sales) account not only for most of the marketings but also for almost three-fourths of all net income derived from the sale of agricultural products. Furthermore, their relative importance has been increasing steadily over the past 20 years at the expense of those farms with $5,000 or less of annual sales.

In 1949 farms with $10,000 of annual sales accounted for 8.7 percent of all farms, 50.2 percent of all the food and fiber marketed, and 38 percent of total net farm income. All three of these figures increased steadily through 1972 at which time this class of farms accounted for 37 percent of all farms, 90 percent of all marketings, and 72 percent of total net farm income. The important fact to be noted from these figures is that in 1970 approximately two-fifths of all farms accounted for more than three-fourths of all net farm income. This is the group of farms classified generally as commercial farms. They also received almost two-thirds of all direct government payments.

TABLE 3.8. Percent of U.S. farm operators working off the farm 100 days or more per year, 1934–1969

Year	Operators
1934	11%
1939	16
1949	23
1954	28
1959	30
1964	32
1969	40

Source: U.S. Dept. of Commerce, Bureau of Census, 1964 United States Census of Agriculture, vol. 11, Ch. 5, 1964, p. 518; USDC, Bureau of Census, Census of Agriculture 1969 Preliminary Summary.

In contrast, the small farms declined by one-third, while their share of marketing fell from 27 percent to 10 percent, and their share of net farm income declined by one-half (from 37.2 percent to 16.1 percent). Their share of government payments declined similarly. Thus many of the smaller farms, faced with a continually worsening agricultural income position, have supplemented their incomes from nonfarm sources. This is illustrated by the data in Table 3.8.

Table 3.8 indicates that an increasing percentage of farmers are working 100 days or more per year off the farm. Considering the fact that there are approximately 261 working days in a year, 100 days represent approximately 40 percent of the total annual working days available. In the 1934 census, 11.2 percent of all farm operators indicated that they worked off the farm 100 days or more. The number of farmers in such an employment status steadily increased through 1969 when it reached a level of 40 percent. A major proportion of this 40 percent of all farm operators is from the smaller farms. The importance of nonfarm income in total income increases consistently and substantially as the magnitude of average farm sales declines. In 1969, the latest census year for which data are available, the average net income of farmers selling more than $20,000 annually was $21,309 of which $3,936 or 18.5 percent was from nonfarm sources. For farms with $5,000 or less sales per year, nonfarm income comprises 84 percent of total income.

In summary, there are three distinct groups of farms in the United States. The first, loosely referred to as the commercial farm, encompasses approximately one-third of all the farms and is characterized as highly efficient, very productive, and capable of providing a sizable net farm income for the owner and operator. This group accounts for approximately 90 percent of the gross farm sales and for 72 percent of the net farm income in agriculture. The second group, often referred to as the marginal farm, contains approximately 50 percent of the farms and is the group that has been largely bypassed in the technological revolution in agriculture. As we will see in Chapter 11, farm programs tied to factors of production have failed to alleviate the income situation of these farms. Currently, this group accounts for less than 5 percent of total farm marketings (Table 3.6) and for approximately 11 percent of net farm incomes. The third group, referred to as the transitional farm, lies in between these two polar cases. The farms in this group are the smaller family farms that will not disappear, but neither will they become paragons of productive efficiency because of the substantial capital investments required to adopt the new technologies.

The reader may be pondering the following question at this point: Given the tremendous increase in agricultural output, why is there such a downward pressure on farm incomes? The reason is twofold. First, total net farm income has not kept pace with the growth in output. In fact, net farm income has been relatively stable since World War II at between $12 and $14 billion annually.

Figure 3.3 illustrates in greater detail the changes that have taken place since the beginning of World War II. Gross farm income increased more than 200 percent between the 1941–1945 period and 1972. Gross farm income includes the gross receipts from commercial market sales, government payments to farmers for programs such as the soil bank, agricultural conservation and wool programs, the value of farm produce consumed directly by the farmer and his family, and the value of housing provided by the farm dwelling. When this figure is netted of production expenses, the balance is net farm income. Notice from Figure 3.3 that net farm income has increased very little during a comparable period. Table 3.9 demonstrates that the widening gap between gross and net farm income is composed of production expenses. The new technologies usually require a bundle of inputs that must be obtained beyond the farm gate. Thus the technological revolution has linked the farmer evermore closely to the other sectors of the economy.

As will be seen later in this chapter, the rise in the proportion of inputs purchased by farmers not only strengthens the linkages of the farming sector with the rest of the economy but also subjects them to more price variability. When farmers produced most of their inputs (labor, fertilizer, forage for work animals), this linkage was weak. Now with the prevalence of synthetic fertilizers, and with the advent of the internal combustion engine for power, the degree of dependence upon

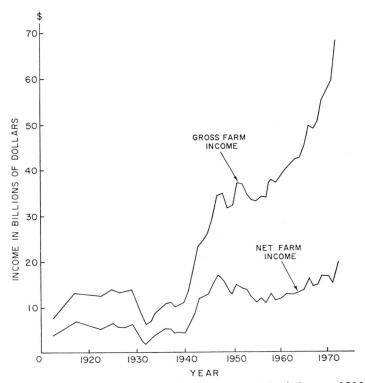

FIG. 3.3. Gross and net aggregate farm income, United States, 1910–1972. (From USDA, **Farm Income Situation,** Washington, D.C.: USGPO, July 1973, Table 1H.)

the rest of the economy is multiplied. As price changes occur elsewhere in the economy, farmers feel the effects in terms of higher prices for their factors of production that must be purchased and in the prices they receive.

Part of the problem arises from the fact that the market has not been ready to absorb the large increases in output. In contrast to supplies, the demand for agricultural products has expanded much more slowly. Even during the Great Depression, most Americans were reasonably well fed. As their incomes have increased, people have chosen to spend only a small portion of the increment on food and fiber and have allocated the greatest percentage to such items as houses, automobiles, television sets, and vacations. They have also spent more on convenience services that go along with food such as precooked dinners and frozen fruits and vegetables. As a consequence, the demand for the raw farm product has expanded little more than the growth in the population.

FARM PROBLEM AND FARM PROGRAMS

In summary, we have production (supply) increasing at a faster rate than consumption (demand). Ordinarily, in a market economy, rapid increases in supply would mean falling farm prices and incomes. The low prices and incomes working through the marketplace would ordinarily push people and resources out of agriculture and into other sectors where the opportunities were better. Because many farm people are ill-prepared to move out of agriculture, because there are often few opportunities for those desiring to move, and because of the large number of farmers, the government was persuaded to develop programs and policies to alleviate these problems. The USDA is charged with administering farm programs. Its philosophy has ranged from rigid mandatory programs to voluntary participation by farmers. The cost is substantial and there is constant pressure to reduce treasury outlay. The benefits of these expenditures do not, however, accrue solely to farmers. To understand the magnitude of government involvement, consider the data in Table 3.10.

The annual appropriations of the USDA can be shown to benefit directly or indirectly a rather broad segment of the United States population. As can be seen in the table, nonfarmers receive a larger share of the department's expenditures than do farmers; about

TABLE 3.9. Comparison of aggregate gross and net farm income for U.S. agriculture from 1941 to 1972

Period	Gross farm income[a]	Average Annual Value of Production expenses	Net farm income[a]
	(1)	(2)	(3)
		(billion dollars)	
1941-45	$21.2	$10.8	$10.4
1946-50	32.7	17.6	15.1
1951-55	36.1	22.0	14.1
1956-60	36.5	24.7	11.8
1961-65	42.2	29.2	13.0
1966-70	49.1	36.5	12.6
1972	64.9	48.8	16.1

Source: USDA, ERS, Farm Income Situation, July 1973, Table 1H.

a. Including government payments.

TABLE 3.10. United States Department of Agriculture's budget outlays for fiscal years 1961–1970 and estimated 1971–1972

Year	Programs Benefiting the General Public[a]	Programs Predominantly for Farm Income Stabilization[b]	Total Outlay
		(million dollars)	
1961	3,804	1,586	5,390
1962	4,182	2,121	6,303
1963	4,221	3,095	7,316
1964	4,387	3,068	7,455
1965	4,120	2,668	6,788
1966	3,881	1,624	5,505
1967	3,653	2,171	5,824
1968	3,853	3,451	7,304
1969	3,970	4,356	8,326
1970	4,302	4,005	8,307
1971[c]	5,315	3,387	8,702
1972[c]	5,825	3,677	9,502

Source: USDA, Food Costs--Food Prices, presented to the Committee on Agriculture, 92nd Cong., 1st Sess., July 1971.

a. Includes subsidized export of food commodities, domestic food distribution programs, and programs for the preservation and conservation of our agricultural and natural resources.

b. Includes all price and income support activities plus salaries and expenses of the programs.

c. Estimated.

60 percent of the USDA's budget for 1972 was devoted to services primarily for the benefit of the general public. About 40 percent went for price supports and other programs in which the farmer is the primary beneficiary.

One other aspect of Table 3.10 is that while the appropriations for the nonfarm sector have remained somewhat constant over the 10-year period, those for the farm sector have increased almost two and one-half times. Hence, while the number of farms has declined considerably in the past 10 years, the appropriations for price supports, supply management, and related programs have increased.

TABLE 3.11. Number of persons and percentage of total payments received by persons receiving $20,000 or more from cotton,
feed, and wheat programs in 1971

Program	Persons		Payments	
	Number	Percent of U.S. total	Dollars	Percent of U.S. total
			(million)	
Cotton	8,742	2.6	$308.1	37.7
Feed Grains	247	0.1	7.2	0.7
Wheat	1,112	0.9	32.0	3.6
	10,012	3.6	$347.3	42.0

Source: USDA, Farm Payment Limitations, a study presented to
the Committee on Agriculture and Forestry, 92nd Cong., 2nd Sess.,
March 1972.

While the magnitude of appropriations by the USDA is interesting, a more interesting question is who within the agricultural sector
receives the benefits of these programs. Table 3.11 is intended to cast
some light on this topic. The table was assembled as follows: all producers receiving payments of $20,000 or more in 1971 were separated
from the remaining producers. The proportion this group was of total
participants and total percentages of the payments they received are
shown in Table 3.11. The results reiterate the fact that a disproportionate amount of program benefits accrue to a small number of farmers.
Less than 3 percent of the cotton participants received almost 38 percent
of all government payments to producers. The other programs exhibit
the same phenomenon.

The table illustrates the major issues of the farm sector. The
marketplace provides unsatisfactory returns to farm producers. Yet
government programs to rectify the situation are also inequitable; farm
programs are tied primarily to factors of production—land and capital.
The larger farms have the greater endowment of these factors and hence
receive a larger share of program benefits. Those without many factors,
and hence those that might require price and income protection the most,
receive very few of the program benefits.

AGRIBUSINESS SECTOR

Modern agriculture is much broader than the commonly held
concept of farmers who produce the raw food and fiber. In
addition to the farmer, agriculture includes the input suppliers
who provide him with fertilizer, chemicals, gas and oil, machinery,

TABLE 3.12. Comparison of agribusiness volume by sectors, 1947 and 1967

	Year		Percent of Total		Percent Changed
	1947	1967	1947	1967	1947 to 1967
	(billion dollars)				
Farm Sector Input Purchases	$12.9	$30.7	17.6	24.3	+138
Farm Sector Value Added	16.4	12.3	22.5	9.8	- 25
Food and Fiber Processor Purchases from Farm Sector	$29.3	$43.0	40.1	34.1	+ 47
Marketing Sector Value Added	43.6	83.0	59.9	65.9	+ 90
Consumer Purchases of Food and Fiber	$72.9	$126.0	100.0	100.0	+ 73

Source: Adapted from materials in Henry B. Arthur and Ray A. Goldberg, The United States Food and Fiber Economy in a Changing World Environment, vol. 4 of technical papers published by the National Advisory Commission on Food and Fiber, Aug. 1967, section III, Table 1, exhibit III.

equipment, and the other supplies he needs; and the marketing firms that process, haul, and store the products. Each is important to the production of food and fiber, and together they make up what is frequently termed the *agribusiness* sector of our economy. Table 3.12 shows the relative magnitude of these three components of the agribusiness sector. The input and marketing sectors receive a much larger share of the consumer's expenditures than does the farm sector. In 1967 consumers spent $126 billion for food and fiber of which the input suppliers received one-fourth and the marketing firms two-thirds, leaving approximately 10 percent for the farm sector. Notice also in Table 3.12 that the relative position of the farm sector has declined over time. Consumers' purchases of agricultural commodities increased from $73 billion in 1947 to $126 billion in 1967, a 73 percent gain over the 20 years. At the same time, the value of the commodities contributed by the farm sector declined 25 percent (from $16.4 billion to $12.3 billion). In other words, in 1947, for each dollar spent by consumers for food and fiber, $0.22 went back to the farmer to pay him for the resources he used in producing the product. The remaining $0.775 went to either the farm input sector or the marketing sector. By 1967 the farmer's share had declined to $0.10 per consumer dollar.

The table illustrates three points. First, the range of tasks performed by the agribusiness sector is substantial. Second, the three sub-sectors—the agricultural supply industry, agricultural production, and the agricultural marketing sector—are all highly interdependent. And third, the farmer, seeing his relative importance in consumers' expenditures declining, feels he is being exploited by the other two sectors.

The third factor illustrated by Table 3.12 was described as a cost-price squeeze in the first section of this chapter. On the input side (cost side), farmers see rising prices for the supplies they purchase as well as rising dependence upon these inputs. We will examine the characteristics of these markets in more detail below. The price side of the squeeze refers to the falling prices farmers receive for what they sell. The problem is quite clear to farmers. They see the share going to the other two sectors of the agribusiness complex growing while their share is declining. They suspect that, because of their market structure, input suppliers and marketers are "price makers," while farmers are "price takers." Thus they blame elements of noncompetitive behavior in the two sectors for absorbing a part of the consumer's dollar that somehow is rightfully theirs.

MARKETING MARGIN

The difference between what the consumer pays for the food product and what the producer receives is generally referred to as the *marketing margin*. This margin includes all the costs of moving the product from the farm gate to the final consumer; it represents the costs of marketing the product. In other words, the farmer receives what the consumer pays after the costs of marketing have been subtracted.

The USDA regularly calculates the share of the consumer's food dollar that goes to the farmer. The share, as shown in Figure 3.4, varies from year to year, with the farmer getting more than 50 percent in some years and less than one-third in other years. In more recent years, the farm share has been between 38 percent and 40 percent. This means that the farmer receives approximately $0.38 to $0.40 out of each $1.00 the consumer spends for food. Many people wonder why it is that it costs more to get the product from the farmer to the consumer than to produce it; they suspect that it is because of either gross inefficiencies or large profits in the marketing system.

Obviously, the farmer is concerned not only with the share he receives but also the actual price per unit. The characteristics of the food marketing system are such that small changes in retail prices are magnified into large swings in farm prices. This instability makes planning difficult and frequently results in a poor allocation of resources. The extent of the problem is illustrated by the data in Table 3.13. The data indicate that while the marketing margin remains fairly stable over time, the farm value of commodities fluctuates considerably.

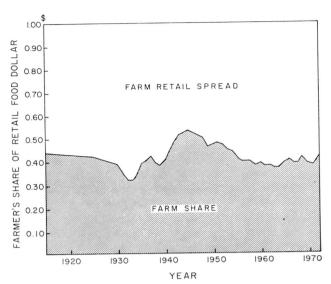

FIG. 3.4. Farmer's share of the consumer's retail food dollar, United States, 1915–1972. (From USDA, ERS, **Farm-Retail Price Spreads for Food Products**, Misc. Publ. 741, Jan. 1972; and selected issues of **Marketing and Transportation Situation.**)

TABLE 3.13. Yearly fluctuation in the retail cost, marketing margin, and farm value of the market basket of farm food products, 1914–1958

| Period | Average Percentage Change from Preceding Year | | | Farmer's Share of Consumer's Dollar |
	Retail cost	Marketing margin	Farm Value	
Entire Period, 1914-58	7.4	6.6	10.4	43
Periods of Rapidly Rising Prices[a]	9.5	6.9	16.5	45
Periods of Rapidly Falling Prices[b]	12.1	8.9	16.8	37
Periods of Relatively Stable Prices[c]	3.2	2.8	5.1	43

Source: Richard L. Kohls and David W. Downey, <u>Marketing of Agricultural Products</u> (New York: Macmillan, 1972), p. 106.

a. 1916-18, 1934-37, 1940-45.

b. 1921-22, 1930-32, 1938-39.

c. 1923-29, 1949-58.

When retail prices rise or fall, most of the change falls upon the farm price rather than being distributed proportionally between the marketing system and the farmer. For the period 1914–1958, marketing margins fluctuated slightly less than retail costs, and farm values fluctuated substantially more. This is because the marketing margin for a given market basket is constant in dollar terms. When a constant dollar margin is subtracted from a fluctuating retail price, the result is a larger percentage fluctuation in the farm price. For example, suppose that initially farmers received $0.50 out of each $1.00 the housewife spends for meat. If the retail price declines 25 percent (to $0.75) and the marketing margin remains constant at $0.50, the farm price falls from $0.50 to $0.25. In this example, a 25 percent reduction at the retail level is associated with a 50 percent reduction at the farm level. This is clearly reflected in Table 3.13 where price changes at the retail level are divided into periods of rapidly rising, rapidly falling, and stable prices. Clearly in periods of rapidly rising, falling, or stable retail prices the marketing margin changes much less than the farm value.

Farmers thus conclude that they are being exploited by middlemen who not only charge a large margin to market their products but insist upon the same margin in periods of high and low retail prices. In other words, the farmer feels he is a residual claimant on the consumer's food dollar and at the mercy of the middleman. We shall explore these problems in more detail in Chapter 12.

INPUT COSTS

As for the supply side of the market, we have stated that farmers are experiencing a cost squeeze arising from an increased dependence upon inputs acquired beyond the farm gate. Following World War II, the trend toward purchased inputs accelerated, and with it, an increased vulnerability to economic forces beyond the control of the farmer. In Figure 3.5 we have depicted the trend in the utilization of selected farm inputs; Table 3.14 verifies this trend. As the dependence on purchased inputs increased, a rise in their price resulted in net farm incomes that have not kept pace with increases in gross farm income (see Figure 3.3).

In summary, the farmer finds himself caught between fixed marketing margins and increasing input costs. The *parity ratio* is a concept devised to reflect the purchasing power of the farmer by computing an index of prices received by farmers to an index of prices paid by farmers. This ratio has been declining since 1950 (see Figure 3.6). Also shown is the index of prices paid by farmers (*parity index*). Notice that when the parity index is above the index of prices received, the parity ratio falls below 100. While we will later discuss objections with the concept of parity, it remains an important aspect in many people's notion about the relative well-being of farmers.

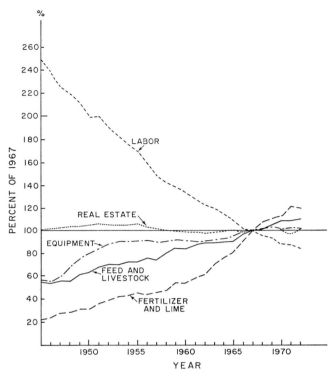

FIG. 3.5. Relative growth in utilization of selected farm inputs, United States, 1950–1972. (From USDA, ERS, **Changes in Farm Production and Efficiency**, Stat. Bull. 233, Washington, D.C.: USGPO, 1973; USDA, ERS, **Supplement V to Changes in Farm Production and Efficiency,** Washington, D.C.: USGPO, 1973, p. 13.

The period since approximately 1950 has seen a parity ratio below 100 and has led farmers, farm leaders, and politicians to charge that the marketing system is monopolized or at least organized to exploit the producer. This issue is a pervasive and frequently recurring one and has led to many investigations and research projects. It has also led to efforts on the part of Congress to improve the structure of the market via a long list of facilitative legislation.

FACILITATIVE SERVICES

In the free market economy, the buyer and the seller are each assumed to be small relative to the total market, to be many in number, and to have all the information to make the most advantageous purchases or sales. In our industrialized economy, the above conditions are never all satisfied. The separation of markets makes it difficult for buyers to inspect the merchandise and to accumulate all the information necessary to reach an agreement satisfactory to both sides. Buyers and

TABLE 3.14. Comparison of changes in the level of purchased and nonpurchased inputs in agricultural production, United States, selected periods 1940–1972

Year	All	Nonpurchased[a]	Purchased[b]
		1967 = 100	
1940-44	100	152	64
1950-54	103	141	74
1955-59	99	126	78
1960	97	112	84
1961	96	111	85
1962	96	108	87
1963	97	105	90
1964	98	104	92
1965	98	103	94
1966	98	101	97
1967	100	100	100
1968	101	100	102
1969	102	100	104
1970[c]	102	98	104
1971	102	97	104
1972	102	96	107

Source: USDA, ERS, Changes in Farm Production and Efficiency, Stat. Bull. 233, 1973, Table 29; USDA, ERS, Supplement V to Changes in Farm Production and Efficiency, 1972, Table 11.

a. Includes operator's and unpaid family labor, interest on operator-owned real estate, and other capital inputs.

b. Includes all inputs other than nonpurchased inputs.

c. Preliminary.

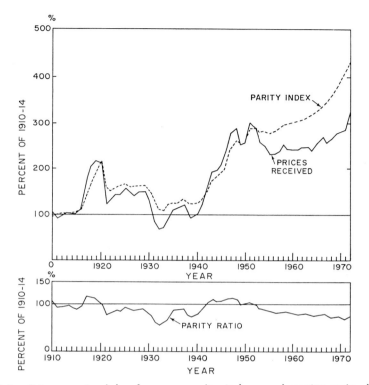

FIG. 3.6. Prices received by farmers, parity index, and parity ratio, United States, 1910–1972. (From USDA, ERS, **Agricultural Prices, Annual Summary,** Washington, D.C.: USGPO, June 1973, pp. 6, 8.)

sellers may be separated by thousands of miles (space) and by weeks or months (time); a farmer may want to sell his production in the fall but consumers may not want most of it until the following spring.

Our economy also fails to meet the requirement of many buyers and sellers. Markets are frequently characterized as many sellers facing few buyers, or many buyers facing few sellers. In either case, that side of the market in which there are few participants is subject to collusion to set price or other terms of trade. A market in which such distortions exist eventually results in inequities which society does not wish to tolerate.

As a consequence of these imperfections or departures from the ideal, the government makes an effort to correct or control the market in order to bring it closer to the ideal. In this regard, the government collects and disseminates information on market conditions such as prices, demand and supply conditions, and projections to all interested parties. It also establishes grades and standards to facilitate the description of the goods for buyers and sellers separated by time and space. Through the Department of Justice it attempts to protect farmers by policing monopolies and cartels that would distort the operation of the markets for agricultural products. In addition, laws and regulations are designed to prevent undesirable methods of competition by prohibiting large firms from using their market power to obtain an unfair price for the product.

As stated earlier, there is also a separation of agricultural markets in time. A large portion of farm output is harvested during a relatively short period. Even such nonseasonal products as livestock, dairy products, and eggs have high and low production periods during the year. Since the consumer desires these products throughout the year, provision must exist for storing commodities until there is a demand for them. In earlier years, private storage facilities often had such a competitive advantage that they could force the farmer to sell his products immediately after harvest when the price was the lowest. Governmental regulation of these facilities permits a farmer to obtain loans on that part of the crop he stores, thus enabling him to sell when he feels it is to his best advantage.

The time lag in agricultural production between planting and harvesting also creates a price risk. When the farmer plans his production, he has no clear idea as to what the price will be at harvest time. Drastic differences between the price he planned on and the price he actually receives could force him out of business. Ownership of commodities while they are in storage also involves a risk that prices could fluctuate so sharply as to bankrupt the business. As a consequence, farmers, who are basically specialists in production, and middlemen, who are engaged in the processing and storage or transportation of the commodities, are anxious to pass the risk of price change on to someone who specializes in this market function. The futures market is a service that shifts the risk of price change to those willing to assume it, in much the same way that a homeowner shifts the risk from fire loss to an insurance company.

In summary, there are many functions to be performed between the production phase and the consumption phase of agricultural commodities. Some of these functions are performed by the private sector, some are performed by the public sector, and some are performed by the private sector with considerable government participation. These services can generally be divided into two aspects: (1) services on the supply side of agriculture—the provision of inputs; and (2) services on the demand side of agriculture—the transportation, processing, and marketing of agricultural output. A detailed discussion of these is in Chapter 12.

HUMAN RESOURCES: THE RURAL POOR

In Chapter 13 we will spend a considerable amount of time developing the case of the rural poor, hence the discussion here will be very general in nature, as well as very brief. The process of economic development in a competitive economy can be a double-edged sword if the allocation of the fruits of that development is such that certain segments of the society do not share equally in the benefits of development. One of the fundamental premises of a market economy is that the allocation of rewards (income) is commensurate with the contribution of that particular productive factor to the value of the final product. This "trickle-down" hypothesis holds that if one sector of the economy is experiencing an increased level of economic activity all levels within that sector will get some part of the rewards.

While it may be true that the lowest laborer within a given sector shares in the "pie" according to the contribution that he makes, it is also evident that we now reject the idea that this share is automatically adequate for providing the laborer and his family with even the barest necessities; economic justice is not necessarily social justice. At a wage of $2.25 per hour, a worker fortunate to be employed 40 hours per week, 50 weeks per year, would gross only $4,500 annually. Reference to Table 3.15 reveals that in 1970 an urban family of 4 required a total annual income of almost $7,000 to maintain a *lower* budget existence; notice that an intermediate budget existence requires almost $11,000. While non-metropolitan residents are slightly better off, a metropolitan family is the hardest hit.

While some people consider poverty to be a relative concept, it is also an absolute concept; that is, if family income is below some minimum level needed for existence, that family lives in poverty. While some figures indicate that poverty in the United States is on the decline, there are still an estimated 30 million poor people—1 person out of every 8 persons.

In Table 3.16 we have depicted the size distribution of income for families in 3 selected years. The evidence indicates that in 1969 fewer families found themselves with incomes below $5,000 (in 1969 dollars) than in 1947. However, because more people now live in urban areas, and because costs vary depending upon the location of residence, the figures are not strictly comparable. Put somewhat differently, while the proportion of families having less than $5,000 income in 1969 is substantially less than it was in 1947, the problem has not diminished in proportion to the decline in the percentages in Table 3.16.

In December 1967 President Johnson released a report of his National Advisory Commission on Rural Poverty entitled *The People*

TABLE 3.15. Annual costs of urban budgets for a 4-person family and for a retired couple, 1967 and 1970

Item	Lower Budget			Intermediate Budget			Higher Budget		
	Urban U.S.	Metro areas[a]	Non-metro areas[b]	Urban U.S.	Metro areas[a]	Non-metro areas[b]	Urban U.S.	Metro areas[a]	Non-metro areas[b]
FOUR-PERSON FAMILY									
Total budget cost, 1967	5,915	5,994	5,564	9,076	9,243	8,332	13,050	13,367	11,640
Total budget cost, 1970	6,960	7,061	6,512	10,664	10,933	9,600	15,511	15,971	13,459
Cost of Consumption, Total	5,553	5,626	5,226	8,205	8,382	7,421	11,346	11,658	9,949
Food	1,905	1,933	1,780	2,452	2,491	2,281	3,092	3,162	2,785
Housing[c]	1,429	1,453	1,322	2,501	2,579	2,158	3,772	3,915	3,133
Transportation	505	481	610	912	916	894	1,183	1,204	1,091
Clothing and personal care	807	820	753	1,137	1,153	1,065	1,655	1,676	1,555
Medical care	562	580	480	564	582	483	588	606	505
Other family consumption	345	359	281	639	661	540	1,056	1,095	880

Source: U.S. Dept. of Commerce, Bureau of Census, Statistical Abstract of the United States: 1972, p. 350, Table 567.

Notes: These data are given in dollars and are based on spring prices. Four-person family refers to annual living costs at three levels for a family comprising a 38-year-old employed husband, wife not employed outside the home, 8-year-old girl, and 13-year-old boy. Retired couple refers to retired husband 65 years old or over and his wife.

a. Metropolitan areas as defined in May 1967.

b. Places with 2,500-50,000 population in 1960.

c. Includes the weighted average cost of renter and homeowner shelter, house furnishings, and household operations. Four-person families in the lower budget are assumed to be renters. A small allowance for lodging away from home city is included in the higher budget.

TABLE 3.15. Continued

Item	Lower Budget			Intermediate Budget			Higher Budget		
	Urban U.S.	Metro areas[a]	Non-metro[b] areas	Urban U.S.	Metro areas[a]	Non-metro[b] areas	Urban U.S.	Metro areas[a]	Non-metro[b] areas
Other Costs[d]	343	345	334	539	576	509	903	919	833
Social Security and Disability Insurance	345	352	316	387	389	377	387	389	377
Personal Income Taxes	719	738	636	1,533	1,586	1,293	2,875	3,005	2,300
RETIRED COUPLE									
Total budget cost, 1967	2,671	2,730	2,492	3,857	3,997	3,440	6,039	6,342	5,137
Total budget cost, 1970	3,109	3,188	2,872	4,489	4,679	3,917	7,114	7,503	5,949
Cost of Consumption, Total	2,975	3,051	2,748	4,210	4,384	3,681	6,187	6,485	5,301
Food	917	926	887	1,220	1,240	1,160	1,531	1,560	1,447
Housing[c]	1,077	1,141	884	1,554	1,674	1,194	2,429	2,638	1,805
Transportation	212	193	270	413	419	394	754	770	706
Clothing and personal care	254	257	247	408	412	394	618	616	623
Medical care	367	374	347	370	376	350	372	379	352
Other family consumption	148	159	113	245	263	189	483	522	368
Other Costs[e]	134	137	124	279	295	236	927	1,018	648

d. Includes gifts, contributions, life insurance, and occupational expenses.

e. Includes gifts and contributions and, at the intermediate and higher levels, an allowance for life insurance and personal income taxes.

TABLE 3.16. Percentage distribution of money income of families, United States, selected years, constant 1969 dollars

Annual Income Level	Years		
	1947	1960	1969
Less than $ 3,000	24.4%	16.8%	9.3%
$ 3,000 to 4,999	26.1	15.0	10.7
5,000 to 6,999	22.3	18.5	12.3
7,000 to 9,999	16.0	24.5	21.7
10,000 to 14,999	...	17.3	26.7
15,000 and over	11.3[a]	7.9	19.2
	100.0%	100.0%	100.0%
Median Family Income	$4,972	$6,962	$9,433

Source: U.S. Dept. of Commerce, Bureau of Census, Current Population Reports: Income in 1969 of Families and Persons in the United States, Series P-60, No. 75, 1970, p. 24.

a. Includes all those with incomes in excess of $10,000.

TABLE 3.17. Persons in poverty, by rural and urban residence, March 1965

Residence	All Persons		Poor Persons		Percent Distribution
	Number	Percent	Number	Percent	
	(million)		(million)		
United States	189.9	100.0	33.7	17.7	100.0
Total rural	55.3	29.1	13.8	25.0	40.9
Farm	13.3	7.0	3.9	29.3	11.6
Nonfarm	42.0	22.1	9.9	23.6	29.4
Total urban	134.6	70.9	19.9	14.8	59.1
Small cities	27.1	14.3	6.4	23.6	19.0
Metropolitan	107.5	56.6	13.5	12.6	40.1
Central cities	58.6	30.8	10.2	17.4	30.3
Suburbs	48.9	25.8	3.3	6.7	9.8

Source: National Advisory Commission on Rural Poverty, The People Left Behind, 1967, p. 3, Table 1.

Left Behind. It contained the commission's findings on the extent and seriousness of poverty in the United States. Table 3.17 (from the report) defines the extent of poverty in the United States in 1965. The definition of poverty used by the commission was based on the concept of a floating poverty line for families with different circumstances. They assumed that the average nonfarm family of 4 required approximately $3,200 to be above the poverty line and that a family of 7 required $5,205. The comparable levels for farm families were set at 85 percent of the nonfarm levels, or $2,720 for a family of 4.

Almost 34 million Americans were classified as poor in 1965. About 41 percent of the poor, 13.8 million people, lived in rural areas. In urban areas, 19.9 million people were poor. Almost half of these were residents of large metropolitan cities. Therefore, in terms of place of residence, the central cities and the rural nonfarm areas contained the largest number of poor persons.

Although most attention is given to poverty in the central cities, the incidence of poverty is highest in the rural areas; 25 percent of the rural population was defined as poor, in contrast to 14.8 percent of the urban population. Or, put differently, approximately 60 percent of all the nation's poor lived either in the open country or in small cities and villages. In the nation's central cities, only 17.4 percent of residents were classified as poor. This means that in rural areas, 1 out of every 4 persons was poor, in contrast to 1 of 8 in metropolitan areas, and 1 of 6 in the central cities. Thus the concept of poverty as strictly an urban problem is incorrect. The majority of the poor lived in rural areas or cities of less than 2,500 inhabitants. Furthermore, most of the rural poor did not live on the farm.

Some additional characteristics of poor families are shown in Table 3.18. This table was developed by the United States Department of Commerce in 1968 on the assumption that the poverty line for a nonfarm family of 4 was $3,743, and $3,195 for an identical farm family. The figure increases to $6,101 for a nonfarm family with 7 or more members.

An analysis of Table 3.18 indicates that poverty is most prevalent among fatherless families, especially among black families. In terms of the age of families, poverty is most prevalent among the very youngest and the very oldest families. Its incidence also increases as family size increases. The occupation of the family head also has a bearing on the problem. The greatest incidence of poverty is exhibited by farmers and farm laborers, and the least by the professional, managerial, and skilled craftsmen occupations. When several of these characteristics are combined in one family, the probability of poverty jumps sharply. For example, almost 90 percent of all families headed by a nonwhite female with 4 or more children are below the poverty line.

We have already shown that a major portion of United States

TABLE 3.18. Selected characteristics of families in relation to the incidence of poverty in 1969

Selected Characteristics	Families Below Poverty Line	
	Number	Percent of all families
	(thousand)	
1. Sex and Race of Head		
White male	2,490	6.0
White female	1,065	25.4
Negro male	609	17.8
Negro female	718	53.2
2. Residence		
Metropolitan areas	2,416	7.3
Nonfarm areas	2,123	13.4
Farm	408	18.3
3. Region		
Northeast	836	6.8
North Central	1,071	7.5
West	714	8.2
South	2,328	14.8
4. Age of Head		
Under 25 years	528	15.0
25-54 years	2,522	7.8
55-64 years	658	7.9
65 and over	1,243	17.6
5. Size of Family		
2 persons	1,896	10.7
3-4 persons	1,471	7.1
5-6 persons	901	9.1
7 persons or more	675	21.7
6. Work Experience of Head in 1969		
Worked at full-time job	1,995	4.9
Worked at part-time job	707	25.6
Didn't work	2,188	30.8
7. Occupation of Head Working in 1969		
Professional and managerial	310	2.7
Clerical and sales	215	3.6
Craftsmen and foremen	311	3.5
Operatives and kindred workers	499	6.0
Service and domestic workers	510	16.1
Nonfarm laborers	285	13.5
Farmers	349	21.6
Farm laborers and farmers	222	40.9
Armed forces	60	5.9
Head not working	2,188	30.8

Source: U.S. Dept. of Commerce, Bureau of Census, 24 Million Americans: Poverty in the United States, 1969, Current Population Reports, Series P-60, No. 76, 1970.

poverty is found in nonmetropolitan areas. Some other misconceptions must also be corrected. First, although a larger percentage of the non-white families are poor, the majority of our poor people are white. Second, although the rate of poverty increases with family size, nearly two-thirds of all poor families have no more than 2 children. Finally, more than 50 percent of all poor families were headed by a man or woman who had a job. This last fact should be emphasized: *most of our poverty families are not the result of any unwillingness to work.* Many family members worked all or part of the year but simply did not earn enough to be above the poverty level.

In summary, the poverty commission found that our national economic growth, and the technological change which permitted it, have affected our rural areas in perverse ways. The rapid adoption of new technologies in agriculture has increased labor productivity in rural areas at such a fast pace that employment opportunities there have declined at a very rapid rate. Furthermore, reduced manpower requirements have not been offset by industries moving into rural areas to absorb the surplus labor. In addition, developments in transportation and communications have expanded the ability of people to travel from one area to another to shop and to commute longer distances to jobs in the larger cities and towns. As a result, many rural communities are faced with declining employment opportunities, out-migration, and lowered tax bases and their consequent impact on local government revenues.

Many rural people have tried to get out of poverty by moving to urban areas. However, these migrants tend to have poor health, low education, and general lack of the types of training necessary to compete effectively with the urban labor force. Thus they end up trading rural poverty for urban poverty. Furthermore, the exodus has also meant that those left behind are frequently worse off than before. Since the most productive rural people are the ones most likely to be successful migrants, those who stay are either too young, too old, or too ill to work. Their chances of escaping from poverty or avoiding even deeper poverty have been reduced. Also, because the smaller remaining population is spread too sparsely across the countryside and cannot support or build the strong social and economic infrastructure the area needs, the quality of life in rural areas declines. Thus local government, schools, and churches are dying from lack of support. As the local infrastructure deteriorates, the chances for redevelopment diminish further.

RURAL COMMUNITY

While it makes more sense to talk of poor people than it does of poor areas, it is nonetheless convenient to view human income problems as separate from those issues that relate to groups of people living in certain areas. Because the focus of this book is on rural problems, we will devote Chapter 14 to a discussion of many of the problems facing the rural community and its residents. For now we will merely set the stage for our later discussion by highlighting some of the major problem areas.

Essentially, the rather elaborate network of rural communities throughout the nation was an accident of history rather than the result of any conscious design. As the frontier pushed west, there evolved a definite need for service centers to facilitate development of the young agricultural and forestry enterprises. Interesting work by sociologists traces the development of these communities, most of which were spaced so that the bulk of frontier families would be able to reach the town and return in a 1-day period. Since the fastest mode of transportation was horseback, it should be obvious why so many communities dot the countryside.

As transportation developed, the need for so many service centers declined, and only the better endowed ones survived. What we see today, then, is the culmination of approximately 60 to 70 years of "dying" on the part of most rural communities. With the advanced transportation network now available, most rural families think nothing of driving for several hours to reach a moderate-sized trade center. But, just as there are people left behind, there are communities left behind. Many rural towns refuse to give up, and they have launched extensive developmental efforts. Oftentimes such efforts merely exacerbate the frustration felt by rural residents since not every community can hope to attract industry or tourists. It is largely a matter of either moving the people to where the jobs are or moving the jobs to the people. In the absence of a national policy on population distribution, it seems likely that present trends will continue. The latest census (1970) seems to reveal one alteration in past behavior, although it is far too early to predict any trends. Specifically, there seems to be a slowing down in the agglomeration of economic activity in metropolitan areas, and there seem to be even a few indications that some firms prefer to locate in rural areas. How important this trend is and what impact it will have on the many rural communities are impossible to predict.

Let us then, very briefly, highlight some of the aspects of life in rural America. The welfare of the rural resident is closely tied to the socioeconomic climate of the rural community. It is the community which, through its schools, libraries, health facilities, churches, and government organizations, prepares its residents to participate in a modern society. Currently, the declining income of many rural areas, or the increasing size of farms in areas where per capita income is adequate, means that either there is a falling source of revenue available to local government or fewer and fewer people are demanding the services, or both. For example, in an economically depressed area, there is no income base upon which schools, roads, or health facilities can be built or supported. By way of contrast, in successful commercial farming areas, new technologies that tend to encourage large farms result in an adequate income base to support the desired services, but the declining population density makes it economically infeasible on a per capita basis to maintain the facilities. In either case, the ability of the community to provide the needed services declines. In the following discussion, we will mention aspects of education, health, and housing in rural areas.

EDUCATIONAL CONDITIONS

The commission on rural poverty found large rural-urban differences in educational quality and quantity.[3] In 1960 the average years of schooling for the urban population was 11.1 years. In contrast, the average for rural farm people was 8.8 years and for rural nonfarm adults 9.5 years. While today's rural youths are getting a better education than their parents, the level of educational achievement is still lower than their urban counterparts. Twenty-eight percent of the rural nonfarm youths and 23 percent of the rural farm youths aged 14 to 24 dropped out of school, compared to 21 percent of the urban youths of the same age. Furthermore, nearly twice as many urban youths attend college as do rural students. The rural students who do enroll in college have a more difficult time than the urban students.[4]

The quality of the educational system in rural areas is lower in terms of teachers, buildings, facilities, and curricula. The percentage of rural teachers not properly certified is almost twice as high as for urban teachers. There are still about 10,000 one-room schools in this country, mostly in rural areas; some still are without running water and indoor toilet facilities. A study by the Office of Education indicated many other discrepancies in physical facilities and programs in today's rural schools.[5] For example, fewer rural schools reported science and language laboratories than did urban schools.

As a consequence, in 1960, 700,000 adults in rural America had never enrolled in school and more than 19 million had not completed high school. Even among the young, those 18 to 24 years of age, more than 2.3 million rural youths had less than a high school education. This pool of adults experiences great difficulty in competing with its urban counterpart for employment.

3. National Advisory Commission on Rural Poverty, *The People Left Behind* (Washington, D.C.: USGPO, 1967), pp. 41–42.

4. John K. Folger, *Good Schools for Small Communities* (Raleigh, N.C.: Agricultural Policy Institute, N.C. State Univ., 1965).

5. James S. Coleman et al., *Equality of Educational Opportunity* (Washington, D.C.: USGPO, 1966).

HEALTH CONDITIONS AND FACILITIES

The commission was also profoundly disturbed by the health problems of low-income people in rural America[6] and claimed that there is a definite relationship between illness and income. Poverty and its associated conditions—inadequate nutrition and unsanitary living conditions—result in frequent and long illnesses, which limit an individual's ability to work.

In 1964 one-third of all maternal deaths in the United States were mothers in rural areas and small towns of less than 10,000. The lowest maternal death rate, 25 per 100,000 births, was found in the suburban areas surrounding the nation's largest cities; and the highest, 40.9 per 100,000, was found in the nonurbanized areas. Rural farm residents average fewer visits per person to a physician than rural nonfarm and urban residents. Moreover, children of low-income families living in rural areas are much less likely to have routine physical examinations than those of higher-income families or those living in metropolitan areas. This lack of medical care in the early years is particularly discouraging since the early detection and treatment of certain ailments can correct or prevent them. As a consequence, rural residents are much more likely to have disabling chronic health conditions than their urban counterparts.

The same relationship exists between dental care and income. One-fourth of the poor have never seen a dentist. In families with incomes of less than $3,000, only 1 out of 4 children under 15 years of age has ever received any dental care. In contrast, in those families with incomes of $7,000 or more, 3 out of 4 children had visited a dentist at least once during the year.

The specialized manpower required to provide the health facilities and services is also inadequate. The commssion states: "While about 30 percent of our population lives in rural areas, only 12 percent of our physicians, 18 percent of our nurses, 14 percent of our pharmacists, 8 percent of our pediatricians, and less than 4 percent of our psychiatrists are located in rural areas." A similar statement applies in the case of dental services.

The lower per capita incomes of rural people are a cause of the low level of rural health facilities as well as the main factor contributing to their maintenance at inadequate levels. Low-income people cannot afford to spend much on medical care. Concomitantly, the low-income areas do not have the resources to provide the facilities. Furthermore, the situation is expected to get worse. As rural population density declines further, it becomes economically impossible to operate a well-staffed hospital. The more affluent travel to distant cities to obtain their

6. National Advisory Commission on Rural Poverty, *People Left Behind,* pp. 59–68.

medical and hospital care; the poor remain, and services deteriorate further. In addition, as hospital and medical costs continue to climb, the overriding pressure is on further centralization of facilities to make operations more economical.

HOUSING CONDITIONS

Housing conditions in rural areas are not as good as in urban areas. The commission concludes, "Decent housing is an urgent need of the rural poor. They live in dilapidated, drafty, ramshackle houses that are cold and wet in winter, leaky and steaming hot in the summer. Running water, inside toilets, and screened windows are the exception rather than the rule."[7]

Based on the *1960 Census of Housing,* 27 percent of occupied rural housing was substandard, deteriorating, or dilapidated, compared with 14 percent for urban areas. The census found 9.2 million substandard housing units, 42.4 percent of which were located in rural areas. Less than 1 in 4 occupied rural farm dwellings had piped-in water. Thirty percent of all rural families still used an outdoor toilet. Fewer than half of all rural homes had central heating. These conditions also contributed directly and indirectly to the inability of the rural families to find and hold jobs providing an adequate standard of living.

The housing of special groups such as migratory farm workers, Spanish-Americans, and Indian-Americans is generally in dilapidated condition. Although twenty-eight states have enacted legislation establishing minimum standards for housing and sanitary conditions, most of it is still intolerable. "Of the 76,000 houses on Indian reservations and trust lands, at least three-fourths are below minimum standards of decency."[8] The houses are grossly overcrowded; more than half are too dilapidated to repair.

The local communities caught up and passed by in the surge of economic growth and technological change have been unable to cope with the problems they face. The recent changes have made the community ineffective. In the past, each rural community provided all the services required by the residents living around it. Today these units are too small to be practicable. Their tax base has eroded as the more able-bodied wage earners leave for jobs elsewhere. As a consequence, public services begin to deteriorate. As the communities decline, they offer fewer and fewer opportunities to earn a living and there is further out-migration of those already inadequately prepared, and a further deterioration in services. The vicious cycle must be interrupted. This will be the subject of Chapter 14. Some of the recommended policies

7. Ibid., p. 93.
8. Ibid., p. 98.

will permit people and communities to help themselves; others will attempt to alleviate poverty directly for those who cannot help themselves.

NATURAL RESOURCES

Our final area of concern is one that has grown in popularity over the past several years. The environmental movement has focused public attention on the problems of pollution and land use that raise interesting economic issues. Some relevant ones here include the question of what incentives exist for firms to pollute the air and the water? What incentives might be created to discourage such behavior? What form of incentive will achieve a most desired solution? Are property rights necessary to prevent pollution? Do property rights encourage socially undesirable behavior as regards the environment? Is conservation of natural resources analogous to nonuse? Is it proper to place economic values on natural amenities such as scenery? Is it possible? Is it meaningful in public policy context?

In Chapter 15 we develop the economic analysis that will provide answers to all of the above questions, as well as answers to other important questions.

By way of gaining a perspective on natural resources, it is helpful to recognize two aspects that differentiate them from ordinary goods and services that are the usual subject of economic analysis. The first differentiating trait is their general *irreproducibility,* and the second is the fact that *irreversibilities* often exist. These two aspects will be discussed in turn.

As for the irreproducible aspect, much of economics is concerned with the production, distribution, and consumption of goods and services that are deemed desirable by the consumer. Of central concern is the allocation of productive factors to attain those goods and services. However, in the case of a lake, a river, the Grand Canyon, a sunset, or a clear sky, we do not produce these "goods and services," though we most certainly allocate them among users, and over time. Much of natural resource economics is concerned with the allocation of these among users, and conservation is the term applied to a particular mode of intemporal allocation. It is true that some natural resources are enhanced by the expenditure of capital and labor to improve their utility to man, but in general we are dealing with a stock or a flow of scarce and valuable resources that cannot be recreated at will.

As for the irreversibility issue, certain natural resources are characterized by the presence of a use-level threshold which, if exceeded, results in extinction. Our actions can sometimes be irreversible; once the breeding stock of blue whales is so low as not to permit reproduction, we have irreversibly consumed the blue whale; once Lake Erie is devoid of living organisms, we may have irreversibly polluted its waters;[9] once an aquifer has been pumped beyond a certain level, we may reduce its porosity and hence have used it irreversibly.

These topics, as well as land use, water use, water pollution, and the federal government's role in natural resource development, will be discussed in more detail in Chapter 15.

One aspect of the land use controversy that is receiving considerable attention is that of conflicts on the rural-urban fringe. Several issues are pertinent here. First, as suburbanization pushes out from central cities, several things happen. It becomes more difficult to carry on agricultural pursuits among groups of houses, gas stations, root beer stands, and billboards. Second, as land moves into urban uses, its value rises considerably, and so its taxes. Since adjacent lands are now more valuable, farmers find their land taxed not on the basis of its agricultural value but on the basis of its value as homesites. The fact that they wish to keep farming is irrelevant; they are taxed on the higher basis.[10] A final form of difficulty is that urban residents are often offended by the smell of pigs, the dust from plows, and the noise from tractors at 6 A.M. The legislation would have states take steps to help avoid such conflicts in the future.

Another important consideration is that of water use in industry, homes, and agriculture, and the economic incentives to bring about a better use of that water. Many users pay little or nothing for the water they use, and as will be seen in Part II, a zero price on a factor of production results in rates of use that are most likely excessive. In Table 3.19 we have shown historical trends in water withdrawals for certain purposes in billions of gallons per day. Notice that while industry and agriculture have shown substantial increases, the use of water by steam electric utilities has grown the most, followed closely by public water utilities for domestic purposes.

Recent legislation dealing with water pollution states that it is now federal policy to move from a program of water quality standards for certain uses (such as domestic, recreation, and fishing) to one of using the best known technology for reducing pollution, and to an eventual goal by 1985 of no discharge into the nation's navigable waters. It is difficult to predict the necessary cost of an ultimate goal of no discharge, but a recent estimate of costs to achieve the 1983 goal of best technology indicates that it will be almost twice as expensive for treating industrial as well as municipal waste than complying with the water

9. A popular myth is that Lake Erie is indeed "dead"; this is far from the truth inasmuch as Lake Erie supports a bounteous fishery, though of less valuable species than formerly.

10. Several states have instituted differential or deferred taxing schemes that resolve part of this problem.

TABLE 3.19. Water withdrawals for selected years and purposes, United States including Puerto Rico (billion gallons per day)

Year	Total Water Withdrawals	Irrigation	Public water utilities	Rural domestic	Industrial and miscellaneous	Steam electric utilities
				Purpose of Withdrawals		
1900	40	20	3	2.0	10	5
1910	66	39	5	2.2	14	6
1920	92	56	6	2.4	18	9
1930	110	60	8	2.9	21	18
1940	136	71	10	3.1	29	23
1950	200	110	14	3.6	37	40
1960	270	110	21	3.6	38	100
1970	370	130	27	4.5	47	170

Source: National Water Commission, Water Policies for the Future, 1973, p. 7, Table 1-1.

quality standards set by the Water Quality Act of 1965. Those estimates are shown in Table 3.20.

Another relevant topic is that of the federal government's role in natural resource developments, that role in the past, and what it might become in the future. Figure 3.7 shows a 10-year trend in expenditures for various categories of water resource developments, and it is clear that water supply and waste disposal aspects have become dominant.

TABLE 3.20. Estimated additional costs for municipal and industrial waste-water management (billions of 1972 dollars)

Item	Capital Cost	Annual O&M in 1983	Cumulative O&M to 1983	Total Expenditures, to 1983
A. To Achieve Water Quality Standards Established under the 1965 Act				
Municipal wastes				
Collector systems	40	0.04	0.3	40.3
Treatment	15	1.5	9.0	24.0
Storm flows				
Combined sewers	32	0.40	2.0	34.0
Separate storm sewers	81	1.0	5.0	86.0
Industrial wastes	10	1.7[a]	11.9[a]	21.9
Thermal electric cooling	4	NA[b]	NA[b]	>4.0
Total	182	4.64	28.2	210.2
B. To Achieve a "Best Known Technology"				
Municipal wastes				
Collector systems	40	0.04	0.3	40.3
Treatment	40	3.3	23.1	63.1
Storm flows				
Combined sewers	54	0.65	3.2	57.2
Separate storm sewers	180	2.2	11.0	191.0
Industrial wastes	49	8.4[a]	59.0[a]	108.0
Thermal electric cooling	8	NA[b]	NA[b]	>8.0
Total	371	14.59	96.6	467.6

Source: National Water Commission, *Water Policies for the Future*, 1973, p. 513, Table 16-12.

a. Includes replacements costs.

b. Not analyzed.

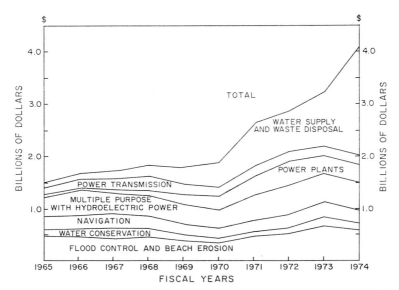

FIG. 3.7. Ten-year trend in expenditures for various water resource developments, 1965–1974. (From National Water Commission, **Water Policies for the Future**, Washington, D.C.: USGPO, 1973, Table 16–1, p. 504.)

With the legislation concerning "no discharge" discussed above, there is every reason to believe that this trend will continue. The federal government is now empowered to assist local government jurisdictions in financing waste treatment facilities, and that assistance can amount to as much as 75 percent in most instances.

SUMMARY

In this chapter we have presented a very cursory discussion of the farm problem and farm programs to deal with it, the agribusiness sector, rural poverty, the rural community, and natural resources. Our intent is to provide a brief overview of the economic aspects of these issues which will be treated in much more detail in Part III.

SUGGESTED READINGS

Cameron, Gordon C. *Regional Economic Development: The Federal Role.* Washington, D.C.: Resources for the Future, 1970.

An interesting book for the general reader, nontechnical but thorough.

Ciriacy-Wantrup, S. V. *Resource Conservation: Economics and Policies,* rev. ed. Berkeley: Univ. Calif. Press, 1963.

The first and best-known book on natural resource economics.
Cochrane, Willard W. *The City Man's Guide to the Farm Problem.* Minneapolis: Univ. Minn. Press, 1965.
A discussion of the farm problem in terms of the facts, the economics, and the politics surrounding the policy issues.
Freeman, A. Myrick; Haveman, Robert H.; and Kneese, Allen V. *The Economics of Environmental Policy.* New York: John Wiley, 1973.
A well-written book of interest to the beginning student.
Goodwin, Marshall R.; and Jones, L. L. The emerging food and fiber system: Implications for agriculture. *Am. J. Agr. Econ.* 53(1971):806–16.
Examines some recent forces of change and their implications for commercial agriculture in the United States.
Harrington, Michael. *The Other America.* Baltimore: Pelican Books, Penguin Books, 1969.
Perhaps the single most important book in pointing out the nature and extent of poverty in America.
Hathaway, Dale E. *Problems of Progress in the Agricultural Economy.* Glenview, Ill.: Scott, Foresman, 1964.
Contains some facts about the economic structure of agriculture, a description of government programs relating to agriculture, and an analysis of possible alternative economic policies.
Iowa State University Center for Agricultural and Economic Development. *Benefits and Burdens of Rural Development: Some Public Policy Viewpoints.* Ames: Iowa State Univ. Press, 1970.
A collection of papers from a symposium on the economic and sociologic aspects of rural development.
Marmor, Theodore R., ed. *Poverty Policy.* Chicago: Aldine-Atherton, 1971.
An excellent series of articles by experts in the field of poverty.
National Advisory Commission on Food and Fiber. *Food and Fiber for the Future.* Washington, D.C.: USGPO, 1967.
A report of a special commission appointed by President Johnson. Covers all aspects of policy for rural areas.
National Commission on Food Marketing. *Food from Farmer to Consumer.* Washington, D.C.: USGPO, 1966.
A report of a special commission appointed to examine the structure and performance of the U.S. food marketing system. Includes both a description of the current conditions of the sector plus public policy recommendations.
President's National Advisory Commission on Rural Poverty. *The People Left Behind.* Washington, D.C.: USGPO, 1967.
A condensed volume of the commission's recommendations.
Schultze, Charles L. *The Distribution of Farm Subsidies: Who Gets the Benefits.* Washington, D.C.: Brookings Institution, 1971.
Analyzes the distribution of benefits by size of farm and income group, and illustrates the impact of farm subsidies in farmland values.

PART 2: THEORETICAL ASPECTS

In this part of the book we develop the analytical framework that is ordinarily referred to as *microeconomics:* economics of the individual decision maker. However, our interest, and the analysis, are much broader in scope than the individual. While the analysis starts with the individual decision maker, whether producer or consumer, it is extended to the analysis of aggregate behavior in the marketplace. This then permits the development of an understanding of the economic phenomenon of greatest relevance in policy analysis—that of the aggregate effects.

Chapters 5, 6, and 7 are devoted to the firm and to its aggregate behavior as reflected in the market supply curve, while in Chapter 8 we develop the theory of consumer demand. In a decentralized economy, the consumer ostensibly dictates what will be produced and in what quantities. Chapter 9 then integrates the economic decisions of the individuals and firms making up demand and supply to explain the market-price phenomenon and how it is affected by various economic forces acting through the decisions of the individual firm or consumer.

Up to this point, the analysis has been predicated upon a series of simplifying assumptions. Finally, in the last chapter of the section, we explore the economic implications of relaxing some of the assumptions on the degree of competition within an industry. Market structure analysis refers to that branch of economics concerned with distortions in resource allocation which arise from an individual firm's power over aggregate production, and hence product price. In this chapter we provide a discussion of the theory of market structure and the implications of market power on the efficiency of resource allocation.

CHAPTER 4: SPECIALIZATION AND EXCHANGE

Specialization can take two forms: specialization of production and specialization of process. The specialization of production is defined as an economic entity such as an individual, a firm, or a region producing one particular commodity. Thus we can observe one region producing beef, another wool, and a third transistor radios. It is on this type of specialization that we will concentrate in this chapter, although the principles also apply to process specialization. In our modern society, specialization of processes within production is also very important. In this type of specialization, an individual, firm, region, or country confines itself to a single operation in the production of a particular product. Assembly lines are good examples, with each worker carrying out a particular task such as tightening a bolt or attaching a headlight. Process specialization generally leads to greater total output, since each activity is more efficiently performed by one individual in contrast to that individual performing several different tasks.[1]

The principles to be developed can be applied to both agricultural or nonagricultural production, and to process specialization within a given region. In this text we use the spatial distribution of agricultural production in the United States as the backdrop against which the analytic framework is developed and explained, although it could as easily be developed in the context of process specialization. Thus this chapter begins with the types of factors determining agricultural production and a description of its spatial distribution within the continental United States. This is followed by the notions of comparative advantage, the impact of transportation charges on regional specialization as developed by Von Thunen, and the concept of economic rent. Since the process of specialization creates a necessity for exchange, the final section will contain a discussion of some institutional factors that influence the development of specialization and exchange.

---

1. It is now also being realized that the repetitive nature of assembly-line jobs can decrease productive efficiency.

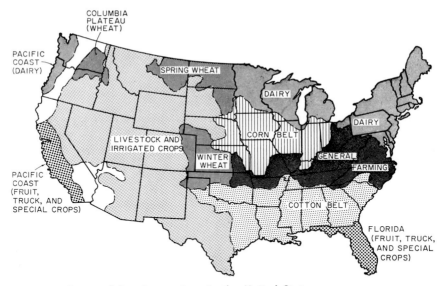

FIG. 4.1. Types of farming regions in the United States.

DETERMINANTS OF AGRICULTURAL PRODUCTION IN THE UNITED STATES

It is possible to classify agricultural enterprises into eight major categories and to demarcate the regions in which these farms or types of farms are the predominant agricultural activity. Figure 4.1 is a graphical representation of the eight major types of farming areas in the United States: (1) dairying in the Northeast states, the Lake states, and on the Pacific Coast; (2) feed grains and livestock in the Corn Belt; (3) cotton in the Southeast states, the Delta states, and part of the Southwest; (4) wheat in the Northern Plains, the Pacific Northwest, and the Central Plains; (5) general farming, including fruits and tobacco, in much of the Appalachian states; (6) livestock and irrigated crops on the range and mountain lands of the West; (7) specialty crops, including vegetables, in California and Florida; and (8) mixed farming areas scattered throughout the major regions but not shown in the figure. The latter classification is necessary since some areas have farms that are too heterogeneous for any other designation. These farms tend to predominate in the transition zones between the other seven more homogeneous regions. Before turning to a description of the eight types of farms and regions, it is necessary to briefly describe the primary determinants of specialization. These determinants are classified as (1) physical and (2) economic.

The major physical influences on locational aspects of farming activity can be grouped into one of four types: (1) climate, (2) topography, (3) soils, and (4) biological. Climate is a general term that describes levels of rainfall, temperature, and sunlight, and the variations in these variables. Obviously, the amount of rainfall is a crucial determinant as to the type of farming activity which can be conducted since some crops are extremely dependent upon moisture while others rely on artificial sources of water, such as irrigation. Even in areas where rainfall is adequate to grow certain crops, it may be that irrigation is used to augment production. Temperature is important because the length of the growing season restricts the plants that can survive in a given area. The frost-free period ranges from 2 to 3 months in the extreme northern sections of the United States to almost 12 months in the extreme southern and southwestern sections. Such differences will directly influence the type of farming that is possible. Another significant climatic consideration is the length of the daylight period. Different varieties of plants respond differently to short days and long days, while still others are insensitive to the length of day.

Topography is defined as the lay of the land or the general surface configuration of an area. With the advent of modern farm machinery, the lay of the land can play a most significant role in determining locational aspects of crop production. Certain species have been bred specifically for machine planting and harvesting. It is difficult to produce these items in areas where machines cannot maneuver, even if the soil, climate, and biological factors are favorable. The flat areas of the Great Plains produce less wheat per acre than do the rolling areas of Iowa, southern Minnesota, and Wisconsin, yet the terrain of the latter three states precludes the production of wheat on an extensive basis because it is difficult to maneuver large tractors and combines on hillsides.

One of the most significant physical features is soil. For example, many vegetables are grown on sandy soils. Anyone who has tried to grow garden vegetables such as beets and carrots is aware of the eventual effect of tight and heavy clay soils upon the development of a nice, well-shaped root. On the other hand, such items as cranberries are grown on very heavy clay soil because of its water-holding capacity. The same tobacco plant grown on different kinds of soil produces a different type of tobacco. On a light soil (such as sandy loam) it will produce a high-quality, light type of tobacco for cigarettes, while, if grown on heavy soil, it will yield a heavy leaf, useful only for cigars, snuff, and pipes.

The physical feature termed biological includes such things as insects, plant and animal diseases, and new varieties of plants and animals. For example, the boll weevil was an important reason why cotton production shifted from the states of Mississippi and Alabama to the states of Texas, New Mexico, and Arizona. The boll weevil thrives in the humid climate of the Southeast but not in the dry climate of the Southwest where cotton is grown under irrigation. As another example, consider the corn borer. Farms in the Corn Belt used to have more acres in corn production than they do now. It was discovered that continuous planting of corn facilitates the spread of blights such as the corn borer. Hence agriculture in the Corn Belt has diversified into soybeans and feed grains. The above are examples of biological influences which tend to reduce production and shift it out of a given area. Biological factors can also work in the opposite direction. Specifically, the development of new hybrid species has played a significant role in the locational pattern of agricultural production. A careful analysis of the acreage in corn indicates that the Corn Belt has been gradually edging northward into central and northern Wisconsin and Minnesota. Formerly the corn-producing areas were characterized by 100 to 120 frost-free days. Hybrid varieties of corn are now found where the number of frost-free days is only 80 to 90. The introduction of Brahma cattle from India into the United States is another example. Brahma cattle are much more resistant to the pests and insects of humid climates than are our own domestic breeds. By crossing these cattle with our Hereford and Angus breeds, cattlemen have been able to expand beef-producing enterprises into areas of the Southeast that were formerly unsuitable for livestock production.

These are the main types of physical considerations that play a crucial role in deciding what it is possible to produce in an area. Because this is a book on economics, our concern is less with that which is possible than with that which is feasible. It is the economic factors which determine from among the possible products those which are actually produced. The principle of comparative advantage and Von Thunen's principle describe the economic considerations determining regional specialization. But that requires a somewhat more rigorous approach, so before turning to those concepts, we will briefly describe the eight major types of farming regions in the United States as a backdrop for their development.

TYPES OF FARMING AREAS IN THE UNITED STATES

DAIRY FARMS

The dairy regions of the United States can be described as having a cool climate and ample and well-distributed rainfall; these factors favor excellent hay and pasture development. The soils and topography are usually not as favorable to field crops as are those in the Corn Belt. The region's proximity to major consuming centers is also an important consideration.

While dairy farms in the north central and northeastern areas of the country tend to be limited almost exclusively to dairy, those in the valleys of the West and in the South often include feed crops, hogs, poultry, and some beef cattle. This diversification is an outgrowth of the length of the growing season and the variety of soils.

FEED, GRAIN, AND LIVESTOCK FARMS

Although this region is frequently referred to as the Corn Belt, it is more correct to characterize it in more general terms. While corn is indeed the primary crop, other crops such as soybeans, hay, wheat, oats, and some pasture crops are also grown. Wilcox and Cochrane describe this region as containing at least three subregions.[2]

In the northern section, soils are not as productive as elsewhere in the region and, while corn and oats are grown, yields are not as great as on the more productive soils farther to the south. Hay and pasture make up the bulk of the feed supply for the dairy enterprises which dominate the area.

In the central portion of the Corn Belt, cash grain production predominates where the terrain is level. In this part, corn, oats, and soybeans are the principal crops. On those soils that are windblown and rolling along the Missouri and Mississippi rivers, cattle feeding and hog production are predominant. In the east central part of the Corn Belt, the soil is lighter and the farms in this region are somewhat smaller than for the balance of the Corn Belt and specialize in hogs and soft winter wheat.

The southern extremities of the Corn Belt are more rolling, with less productive soils. Instead of the cattle-fattening operations of the rest of the Corn Belt, here one finds considerable cattle grazing. In the southwestern part of the Corn Belt, wheat dominates, with corn and oats being less prevalent.

COTTON FARMS

We saw earlier how the length of the frost-free period can determine the northern border of a production area. Cotton is a good example. For successful cotton production, 200 frost-free days are considered necessary. The cotton region is limited on the east and south by rainfall patterns during the blossoming and picking seasons which reduce yields. Thus cotton farms are not found too close to the Atlantic Ocean and the Gulf of Mexico. The Mississippi Delta, with large areas of flat and level land, is intensively cropped. However, with the introduction of mechanization, irrigation, and long-staple

2. W. W. Wilcox and W. W. Cochrane, *Economics of American Agriculture* (Englewood Cliffs, N.J.: Prentice-Hall, 1960), p. 2.

(fiber) varieties of cotton, plus the boll weevil problem in the humid areas, Texas, New Mexico, Arizona, and parts of southern California have also become important cotton-producing regions.

On the fringes of the Cotton Belt, one finds farms that produce a variety of different crops. For example, along the eastern edge, peanuts, tobacco, and some truck crops are found, while on the western edge, grain sorghums compete with cotton.

TOBACCO AND FRUIT FARMS

Several types of tobacco are grown, depending upon the soils, rainfall, and other physical characteristics. In Virginia and North Carolina, flue-cured tobacco dominates, with some corn, cotton, and hay produced. Kentucky is where burley tobacco is raised in combination with pasture (bluegrass) for livestock. In southwestern Kentucky and northwestern Tennessee, one finds air-cured tobacco, with some feed crops. The southern Maryland tobacco area lies between Chesapeake Bay and the Potomac River

Fruit production is scattered along the border between Virginia and North Carolina and in northern Virginia, where the rolling topography permits the type of air "drainage" required for fruit crops.

WHEAT AND SMALL-GRAIN FARMS

The wheat-producing regions of the United States are characterized by level to slightly rolling topography, a level of rainfall too low for most other crops, and productive soils. Grazing is a logical complement to wheat production and these two enterprises are very commonly encountered throughout much of the region. In the Pacific Northwest, winter wheat (which is sown in the fall) is preferred, but if it is killed by frost or washed out by heavy rains, the land is replanted with spring wheat. The land is rolling and the rainfall varies between about 9 and 20 inches annually. Dry peas are often found in combination with wheat in this region, and summer fallowing is the common practice to conserve moisture. In the Great Plains, grain sorghums and cotton compete with winter wheat on the southern edge. In the northwestern part of the Great Plains, severe winters prohibit the winter wheats, and spring wheat is the principal crop alternating with summer fallowing.

LIVESTOCK AND IRRIGATED CROP FARMS

The eastern limit of this area—which is also referred to as the range livestock region—is a direct function of rainfall. Forage crops are also grown on relatively small, irrigated acreages to supplement the seasonal forage available from the native rangeland. In this region, rainfall can be as low as 3 inches annually and it is not uncommon to find rangeland that requires 100 acres to support one cow for a 3-month grazing season. The better rangeland receives 10 to 15 inches of rainfall annually, and thus a rancher requires only 50 acres to support one cow for a 3-month grazing season. The significant aspect of this region is the seasonal nature of the native forage. Cattle usually spend the winter months on the privately held lands of the rancher, while sheep may be grazed through the winter on the sagebrush and greasewood ranges of Nevada, Utah, western Colorado, southern Wyoming, and eastern Oregon. In the spring cattle and sheep will be moved to the foothill areas and will follow the melting snows up the mountains. Summer is usually spent on the mountains of this region where the forage is sufficient enough to require only 20 acres per cow for the 3-month grazing season. In the fall the foothill areas are once again grazed, and during winter, hay cut from irrigated pasture on the foothill ranches provides the necessary feed supply.

SPECIALIZED FARMS

Specialty crops are grown in a number of widely scattered areas well adapted to their production. The two largest regions in the United States are California and Florida. Soils, climate, and proximity to market are the dominant factors controlling their development. The Central Valley of California and the Willamette Valley of western Oregon grow a multitude of different food items ranging from avocados to yams. Most of these farms are irrigated. Other main activities include dairying, livestock raising, vegetable production, fruit production, tree farming, and grass seed production. Florida specializes in fruits and truck crops which can be produced in the winter months and hence command high prices in the North. It also produces sugarcane.

MIXED FARMS

The mixed farming areas in the East lie between the Corn Belt and the dairy region on the north and the Corn Belt on the south. The area is characterized by rolling land with rather low productivity. Hay and pasture must be rotated with other crops and, hence, livestock activities are carried on simultaneously with crop production. There are also general farming areas in the West. One example is the fruit and vegetable production that occurs along the western slope of the Wasatch Mountains in Utah. In this area fruit farms are found along the foothills where constant air movement prevents early freezing.

In summary, one can classify United States agriculture into eight general farming regions. Our classification is not unique and the reader may see elsewhere a description of nine farming regions, or ten farming regions, depending upon how finely one wishes to subdivide regions.[3] We believe that eight regions are sufficient to give a general feel for the locational characteristics of agricultural activity in the United States and to illustrate the influence of physical factors in delineating what it is *possible* to grow in a certain area.

ECONOMIC FACTORS DETERMINING SPECIALIZATION

It is not difficult to see how the physical factors limit the production possibilities of a region or area. Anyone with a knowledge of United States soils, topography, and climate will have no problem explaining why Maine produces little corn and North Dakota no cotton. But the physical factors can only carry our explanation to a certain point; they can eliminate those products that are infeasible but cannot discriminate among the remaining opportunity set. It is the economic considerations that determine the final product mix of a given area.

For example, assume you are a farmer and that you make a list of all possible products that you could produce on your farm. The list could include as many as 100 different crops and animal products. If you live in Ohio, you can cross off a large number of these products because of physical factors such as temperature and rainfall, or biological limitations such as insects and diseases. Conversely, a new species developed by the agricultural experiment station at the local university or the USDA will expand the list slightly. If your farm is in northern Maine or in California, the list would be considerably different than if your farm is in Ohio. Nevertheless, at this point your list still includes at least a dozen or more alternative products. All are within the physical constraints of your farm. The question then is, How do you choose among the remaining alternatives? It is the economic factors that finally determine, from among the list of viable alternatives, those products that are actually produced. The economic factors will be described as two principles—one called the principle of comparative advantage and the other, Von Thunen's principle.

The *principle of comparative advantage* states that you will produce those products where your production advantage is greatest, or your production disadvantage least. By use of this principle the student will be able to explain regional specialization in particular agricultural products. *Von Thunen's principle* further modifies the impact of the principle of comparative advantage by introducing transportation cost as an element affecting the producer's final decision. As an outgrowth

3. USDA, *Generalized Types of Farming in the U.S.*, Agr. Inform. Bull. 3, Feb. 1950.

of the study of these two principles, the concept of economic rent will be introduced as an explanation of the differentials in the values of equally productive land.

PRINCIPLE OF COMPARATIVE ADVANTAGE

In the preceding paragraphs it was stated that the physical factors determine the regional limits of production and the economic factors determine what is actually produced. How does the principle of comparative advantage work? Suppose that New York farmers can produce 30 bushels of wheat per acre worth $2.00 per bushel, and that Kansas farmers can produce 12 bushels of wheat per acre which, after subtracting transportation cost, is worth $1.85 per bushel to the farmer. The results are shown in Table 4.1. Obviously, the New York farmer has much higher yields and a much higher return per acre than the Kansas farmer. Why is it that New York farmers do not produce all the wheat? Another example: the South does not require dairy barns for cows and there is access to year-round pasture. However, the Dairy Belt is not located in the South but in the upper Midwest where farmers must make large investments in barns in order to protect the animals during the severe winters. Furthermore, if Wisconsin is a dairy state, why doesn't it produce all the fluid milk? A great proportion of the the total fluid milk in the United States is produced in the states of New York, Pennsylvania, and Vermont. Furthermore, if the East Coast has a comparative advantage in the production of milk, why is Wisconsin producing raw milk at all? Why not just butter or cheese? The answers to these questions can be found in the principle of comparative advantage.

The *principle of comparative advantage* states that a product will be produced where its ratio of advantage or disadvantage compared with alternative products is greatest in exchange for products from other areas. Several key words are in this definition. One of them is *ratio* and means the percent advantage or disadvantage of one area over another, and another key word is *exchange*. In its simplest terms, the principle states that farmers in each area will specialize in producing that product in which the area has the greatest edge over its competitors, and

TABLE 4.1. Per acre yields and farm prices for wheat in New York and Kansas

Area	Yield per Acre	Farm Price per Bushel
New York	30 bu	$2.00
Kansas	12 bu	1.85

will exchange the surplus commodities for those from other areas. Specialization without exchange does not make sense. If one needs bread, meat, and milk, specializing in bread production and not being able to obtain the milk and meat necessary for one's diet is foolish.

Exchange is thus an indirect way of producing something. An individual can either sew a suit of clothes for himself or he can, in effect, make that suit of clothes indirectly by specializing in some other product such as growing pumpkins and taking the income received from the sale of pumpkins and exchanging that for the suit of clothes produced by someone else. Furthermore, given the fact that resources are limited, it can be shown that there is a definite advantage to both individuals involved in the specialization of production and its exchange. In other words, even though one region may be completely inferior to the other in terms of all possible products that it can produce, the total output of both areas will be greater under specialization than without it.

A SIMPLE EXAMPLE

Let us take an example. Assume that two farmers need only wheat for bread and beef for steaks. A farmer in Ohio can produce between 10 and 20 bushels of wheat per acre or 350 to 450 pounds of beef per acre. In contrast, a Kansas farmer can produce 15 to 25 bushels of wheat per acre or 80 to 120 pounds of beef per acre. The comparison of production possibilities is shown in Table 4.2, assuming that the midpoints of each range are acceptable averages. Based on this assumption, the Kansas farmer's average yield of wheat is 20 bushels per acre and the Ohio farmer's yield is 15 bushels. In terms of beef, the Kansas farmer can produce 100 pounds of beef in an average year and the Corn Belt farmer 400 pounds on one acre of land.

An inspection of Table 4.2 indicates that the Kansas farmer can produce more wheat per acre than the Ohio farmer and the Ohio farmer can produce much more beef per acre than his counterpart in Kansas. The fact that the Ohio farmer is only 75 percent as efficient as the Kansas farmer in the production of wheat and four times as efficient in the production of beef makes the decision as to which product he

TABLE 4.2. Per acre yields of wheat and beef in Ohio and Kansas

Per Acre Production	Area		Ratio $(2) \div (1)$ (3)	Ratio $(1) \div (2)$ (4)
	Ohio (1)	Kansas (2)		
Wheat	15 bu	20 bu	1.33	0.75
Beef	400 lb	100 lb	0.25	4.0

TABLE 4.3. Comparison of total production per acre of beef and wheat with and without specialization

Product	Without Specialization[a]			With Specialization		
	Ohio	Kansas	Total	Ohio	Kansas	Total
Wheat (bu)	7.5	10	17.5	...	20	20
Beef (lb)	200	50	250	400	...	400

Note: Based on yields in Table 4.2.

a. Each farm using 0.5 acre for wheat and 0.5 acre for beef.

will produce an easy one (column 3, Table 4.2). Conversely, since the Kansas farmer is 33 percent more efficient than his Ohio counterpart in wheat production and only 25 percent as efficient in beef production, he will elect to produce wheat. Because the Kansas wheat farmer can produce more bushels of wheat per acre than the Ohio wheat farmer, he is said to have an absolute advantage in the production of wheat. Conversely, the Ohio farmer has an absolute advantage in the production of beef. The ratios in the last two columns of Table 4.2 yield the same information.

By specialization, the total output of beef and wheat is greater than if each had produced both products. This is demonstrated in Table 4.3, assuming each farmer has exactly one acre of land on which to produce the two products. Based on the yields in Table 4.2, the Kansas farmer would produce 20 bushels of wheat and the Ohio farmer 400 pounds of beef. If they had not specialized, total output would have been 17.5 bushels of wheat and 250 pounds of beef. Thus, in the example, specialization yields 2.5 extra bushels of wheat and 150 pounds of beef. Other allocations of each acre of land between wheat and beef production would yield similar results. In any case, both farmers have more commodities when they specialize and exchange with one another.

The above example is relatively simple but illustrates the rationale of the principle of comparative advantage in the case where each area has an absolute advantage in at least one commodity. Nonetheless, even though it is a relatively simple case, it was worthwhile for the two farmers to specialize and trade. Their joint output of the two farms will be larger than if each tried to produce and consume independently of the other. The net result in this case was more product for the two farmers to consume.

For a slightly more complicated case in which the Ohio farmer has an absolute advantage in the production of both wheat and beef, consider Table 4.4. He can produce more of either commodity on one acre than can the Kansas farmer. Since the Kansas farmer's yields per acre are less than the Ohio farmer's in both products, he is said to have

TABLE 4.4.   Per acre yields of wheat and beef in Ohio and Kansas

Per Acre Production	Area		Ratios	
	Ohio (1)	Kansas (2)	(1) ÷ (2) (3)	(2) ÷ (1) (4)
Wheat (bu)	20	15	1.33	0.75
Beef (lb)	400	100	4.00	0.25

an absolute disadvantage in both. Furthermore, assume that each farmer needs 10 bushels of wheat and 100 pounds of beef to survive through the year. Consequently, the two farmers must somehow produce 20 bushels of wheat and 200 pounds of beef. There are several possible alternatives by which these needs can be met: (1) one farmer produces the needs of both; (2) each farmer produces his own requirements; or (3) each specializes and then exchanges his surplus. If we assume they are rational, they will attempt to meet their needs with as few resources as possible and sell whatever surplus they can create. We consider each possibility in turn.

CASE 1:   *The Ohio Farmer Produces the Needs of Both Farmers*
      In this case the Ohio farmer would need 1.5 acres of land to produce the 20 bushels of wheat and 200 pounds of beef; however, the solution is not very interesting because there is no allocation problem and because it ignores the problem of how the Kansas farmer will buy wheat or beef from the Ohio farmer, since he produces nothing that he can use to exchange. If the Ohio farmer has only one acre on which he can produce wheat and beef, he is unable to meet the demands of both farmers. In this case, the resources of the Kansas farmer must also be utilized.

CASE 2:   *Each Farmer Produces His Own Requirements*
      If neither farmer specializes, the Ohio farmer will require 0.5 acres for wheat and 0.25 acres for beef, for a total land utilization of 0.75 acres to meet his needs. The Kansas farmer will require 0.66 acres to meet his wheat requirements and 1 acre to meet his beef requirements for a total of 1.66 acres of land. In this case, the total land requirement for both farmers jointly is 2.41 acres. The results are summarized in column 1 of Table 4.5.

CASE 3:   *Specialization of Production*
      The principle of comparative advantage states that each farmer will specialize in the production of that commodity in which he has the greatest advantage, or the least disadvantage. Examination of Table 4.4

TABLE 4.5.   Comparison of the amount of acres required to supply 20 bushels of wheat and 200 pounds of beef under alternative production pattern

| | Acres Required | | |
Area	W/o specialization	W specialization	Ohio only
Ohio	0.75	0.50 (Beef)	1.50
Kansas	1.66	1.30 (Wheat)	...
Total	2.41	1.80	1.50

Source: Based on yield data of Table 4.3.

indicates that the Ohio farmer can produce 1.33 times as much wheat as the Kansas farmer and four times as much beef. Therefore, the Ohio farmer has the greater advantage in the production of beef.

The data in column 4 of Table 4.4 show that the ratios for the Kansas farmer are all less than one. This means that the Kansas farmer has a disadvantage in the production of both wheat and beef. However, as the ratios indicate, his disadvantage is greater in one commodity than in the other. He can produce 75 percent as much wheat as the Ohio farmer but only 25 percent as much beef. Consequently, if he is going to produce, he will certainly produce that commodity where he can come the closer to competing with the Ohio farmer. In this case, he will produce wheat. Under these circumstances, the Ohio farmer will require 0.5 acres to produce the 200 pounds of beef, and the Kansas farmer will require 1.3 acres to produce 20 bushels of wheat that they jointly require. The Kansas farmer can trade one-half his wheat for one-half the Ohio farmer's beef; therefore, both their needs are satisfied.

The resources (land) required are summarized in Table 4.5. Note that with specialization their joint needs can be met with 1.8 acres in comparison to 2.41 acres without specialization. In this case, specialization and trading lead to minimizing the use of the amount of resources required to produce a given output. Had we chosen to ask the question in the alternative format, that is, What is the maximum amount of product that could have been produced with a given level of input? (for example, 1 acre of land per farmer), the results would have been the same. In other words, specialization would have resulted in a larger total output than each farmer producing his own requirements.

A MORE COMPLICATED EXAMPLE

In Table 4.6 we have extended the principle of comparative advantage to three commodities in three areas. Previous examples illustrated the principle as a partial explanation of regional specialization. It is equally valid as a partial explanation for intercountry differences. Hence,

TABLE 4.6. Output of selected commodities from a standard bundle of resources for three different areas and their ratios of advantage

Commodity	Units	Area A	Area B	Area C
		(output per resource bundle)		
Transistor Radios	Number	30	20	1
Motorcycles	Number	6	5	1
Cotton	Bales	1	2	10

	Ratios A/B	A/C	B/A	B/C	C/A	C/B
Transistor Radios	1.5	30.0	0.6	20.0	0.03	0.05
Motorcycles	1.2	6.0	0.8	5.0	0.20	0.20
Cotton	0.5	0.1	2.0	0.2	10.00	5.00

for this example we will use the commodities (1) transistor radios, (2) motorcycles, and (3) cotton. Furthermore, although the areas are labeled A, B, and C, they might be thought of as countries such as Japan, England, and Egypt.

The outputs in this example arise from the utilization of a standardized "bundle" of resources. This includes a fixed amount of land, labor, and capital. Thus, with this resource bundle, area A can produce 30 transistor radios, 6 motorcycles, or 1 bale of cotton. In contrast, area C can produce 1 radio, or 1 motorcycle, or 10 bales of cotton with the same standardized bundle of resources.

To use the principle of comparative advantage in this case, the output ratios comparing all the areas must be calculated. These ratios can be found in the lower half of Table 4.6. For example, the first column indicates that area A can produce 1.5 times as many transistor radios as area B, 1.2 times as many motorcycles, and 0.5 times as much cotton. It can produce 30 times as many transistor radios as area C and 6 times as many motorcycles but only 0.1 as much cotton. Comparing the ratios in the first 2 columns indicates that area A has a greatest absolute advantage over area B in transistor radios, and over area C in transistor radios. Consequently, area A will specialize in the production of radios. The 3rd and 4th columns compare the production of area B to that of areas A and C. The 3rd column indicates that area B is less efficient than A in the production of transistor radios and motorcycles, but it can produce twice as much cotton as can area A. The 4th column indicates that it is 20 times as efficient as C in transistor radios, 5 times as efficient in motorcycles, and only 20 percent as efficient in cotton. Area B has the least disadvantage over A in the production of motorcycles (0.8) and an absolute advantage over C in the production of the same commodity. Consequently, area B will be best equipped to produce motorcycles. Comparisons for area C are in the last two columns of the table. They indicate that area C has an absolute advantage over both areas A and B in the production of cotton. Consequently, it will specialize in producing that commodity.

The exercise of proving that the joint output of the 3 areas is maximized if A specializes in transistor radios, B in motorcycles, and C in cotton is left to the reader. It should be noted further that if the demand for motorcycles is greater than the ability for the resources of area B to supply it, area A could also produce motorcycles, since its second best advantage is in this commodity. Similarly, if area A has more resources than are needed to meet the demand for transistorized radios, it will produce motorcycles with its surplus resources.

TRANSPORTATION CHARGES

In this section we will consider the nature of the structure of prices in a region surrounding a market. This will lead to an understanding of how transportation costs influence the location of production relative to a particular market, and how this can result in two regions with the same natural endowment in resources producing different products, or different forms of the same products.

In its basic form, the principle of comparative advantage does not take into account transportation charges. Up to the present we have been assuming that producers can market all their output with no expense involved. Usually, however, the manufacturer must transport his product to market and transportation charges must be subtracted from the gross price. Since he must compete in the marketplace, the final decision as to which product is produced is dictated by the net comparative advantage which results from inclusion of transportation charges. The net effect is the same as though he used part of his resource bundle to transport the product, and part to manufacture it. As as result, transportation charges distort the pure "factory-gate" advantage of an area or of a producer.

For example, suppose that Table 4.6 depicts individual producers and that producer A lives a greater distance from the consumer market than producers B and C (see Figure 4.2). If producer A is to compete with producers B and C in the consuming center, the price of his product cannot exceed that of the other two producers. Therefore, producer A must use some of his resources to transport the commodity to the consumption center. The net effect is to leave fewer of his resources

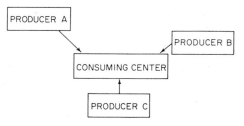

FIG. 4.2. Three producers at different distances from the consuming center.

to produce the transistor radios, motorcycles, or cotton. Consequently, the transportation charges reduce the yield per resource and hence change the comparative advantage among producers.

Returning to our example, suppose that producer A must use one-half his bundle of resources to transport the transistorized radio to the consuming center. Consequently, he can produce only 15 radios per standard bundle of resource. Because motorcycles are less fragile, they are not as expensive to transport. Consequently, he can produce 5 motorcycles. Furthermore, he is unable to produce cotton because transportation charges are greater than the resources he has available for producing it. The new yields and ratios are shown in Table 4.7.

TABLE 4.7. Relative output of selected commodities from a standard bundle of resources adjusted for transportation costs for three different producers and their ratios of advantage

Commodity	Unit	Producer		
		A	B	C
		(output per resource bundle)		
Transistor Radios	Number	15	20	1
Motorcycles	Number	5	5	1
Cotton	Bales	...	2	10

	Ratios					
	A/B	A/C	B/A	B/C	C/A	C/B
Transistor Radios	0.75	15.0	1.3	20.0	0.1	0.05
Motorcycles	1.00	5.0	1.0	5.0	0.2	0.20
Cotton	0	0	[a]	0.2	[a]	5.00

a. Since A produces no cotton, these ratios are technically infinite; but they are irrelevant for our purposes.

By comparing Tables 4.6 and 4.7, it is clear that the impact of the introduction of transportation charges has been to modify net comparative advantages. Since the areas from Table 4.6 can also be thought of as "producers," it can be seen that C will still produce cotton. But notice that B now has the comparative advantage over A in the production of transistor radios, and that A has the least disadvantage in producing motorcycles.

Although the physical factors gave producer A a natural comparative advantage in the production of transistor radios, and producer B an advantage in the production of motorcycles, economic factors such as transportation charges have modified this relationship. This concept, describing the way in which transportation charges influence the location of production in agriculture, is attributed to a German economist, Johann Heinrich Von Thunen. Von Thunen's principle is described in the next section and although it is usually applied to agricultural production, its underlying principle is also applicable to many other commodities and situations.

VON THUNEN'S PRINCIPLE

Von Thunen's principle states that the product with the higher transportation cost in relation to value will be produced near the consumption center. This means that perishable products will be produced nearer the areas of consumption than nonperishable products because of the higher cost of transportation. Fluid milk and fresh vegetables are good examples. The high cost of refrigerated transportation facilities, and the large potential loss due to spoilage, mean that almost every large city has in the surrounding countryside farmers producing farm produce and milk for the fresh market.

If perishable products are to be processed before consumption, or if the processing reduces their volume and weight substantially such as in the case of canned peas, other vegetables and fruits, and butter, the processing facilities will be located very near the producing area to minimize transportation costs. For example, the transformation of milk into butter in the area in which the milk is produced eliminates the need to pay freight charges on the water that is present in the milk but not in the butter. Cheese is a second example from which even a larger proportion of the water has been removed. Lumber is a third example. Lumber companies do not wish to pay for the costs of hauling bark (or slabs left over from converting trees into lumber) any farther than necessary. Sawmills are usually located very near where the timber is cut so that transportation costs per unit are as small as possible.

The Iowa corn producer with a large hog program is a further example of how the profit-maximizing entrepreneur, attempting to reduce transportation charges, markets his corn in the form of pork. Corn is a relatively large, bulky product and, consequently, the farmer cannot afford to transport it very far before the transportation charges have absorbed 100 percent of the value of the product. However, by converting 700 to 800 pounds of corn into 100 pounds of pork and shipping the corn to market in the form of pork, he reduces the marketing charges on the corn substantially. This explains the fact that only a very small percentage of all the corn produced in the Corn Belt actually appears on farm income statements as sales. Usually it appears in the form of sales of pork, beef, or milk.

Some other products lose little weight in conversion. These products are usually processed near where other factors are abundant. For example, wheat loses very little of its weight when it is converted into flour. Consequently, it is processed where other factors are important. Minneapolis was at one time noted as a flour-milling center of the world because the wheat was transported out of the West to Minneapolis where water was available to run the flour mills. This helps to explain, for example, why Pillsbury Mills and General Mills are located in this area. Minnesota iron ore is another example. It is produced on the Mesabi Range in northern Minnesota but it is not refined into steel there. Instead, it is loaded into large ore boats and hauled either to Pittsburgh, Pennsylvania, or to Gary, Indiana, and there refined into steel or other products. The reason is that these latter locations are closer to the sources of other materials necessary for processing, such as labor and coal. Gary, for example, is near a large metropolitan area where there is a large supply of labor. It is also near the Illinois-Indiana coal fields, and coal is an essential ingredient in the conversion of iron ore to steel. The proximity to coal also explains why Pittsburgh became the iron-ore–refining center of the United States. In terms of the final product, it is cheaper to transport the iron ore to the coal fields than to transport the coal to Minnesota and then the processed steel back to the East Coast where it is to be used.

The above examples outline the general results of the operation of Von Thunen's principle. Now let us see exactly how the principle works with a simple example. Suppose the data in Table 4.8 represent the production possibilities for an area that has the natural comparative advantage in production of dairy products. Table 4.8 is based on the assumption that a dairy farmer can sell his milk as milk, cream, or butter. Consequently, 100 pounds of fluid milk can be sold in the consumption center for $5.00, or converted into 12 pounds of cream, which is worth $4.00 in the consumption center, or converted into 4 pounds of butter for which consumers are willing to pay $3.60. The transportation charges are listed in column 3 of the table. A farmer living near the consumption center has the alternative of producing milk, cream, or butter. He must decide which of the three products will net him the greatest return. The data in Table 4.8 can be used to assist him in this

TABLE 4.8. Retail value and transportation charges per mile for alternative products obtained from 100 pounds of fluid milk

Product	Pounds "Q"[a]	Retail Value[b]	Transportation Costs[b]	Net Farm Price	
				10 miles[c]	1,000 miles[c]
Milk	100	$5.00	$0.002/mile	$4.980	$3.000
Cream	12	4.00	0.0002/mile	3.998	3.800
Butter	4	3.60	0.0001/mile	3.599	3.500

a. Per cwt of whole milk.

b. For "Q" pounds of product.

c. From consumption center.

decision. If a farmer decides to produce milk, 100 pounds of milk are worth $5.00 in the consumption center and it will cost him $0.002 per mile to transport this milk to market. In other words, if the farmer lives 10 miles from the market it will cost him $0.02 to transport 100 pounds of milk to the market. The 100 pounds of milk can also be converted into 12 pounds of cream worth $4.00 at the consumption center. Since cream is slightly easier to transport than milk, the charges per mile are less. Consequently, the farmer could transport the 12 pounds of cream to the consumption center for $0.0002 per mile. Similarly, for butter, the 100 pounds of milk marketed into the form of 4 pounds of butter have a value of $3.60 at the consumption center. Each mile that the 4 pounds of butter is transported will cost the farmer $0.0001. The example assumes that there are no charges of converting the milk from one product into another. In other words, if the farmer lives right next to the supermarket, he can get $5.00 for his milk, $4.00 if he sold it as cream, or $3.60 if he sold it as 4 pounds of butter. Obviously, if the farmer lives next to the supermarket, he would receive the greatest return from his resources by selling milk.

Suppose, however, the farmer lives 10 miles from the consumption center. Then, to determine his net returns, he must subtract the transportation charges of placing the dairy product on the market. In this case (as seen in column 4 of Table 4.8), he must subtract $0.02 for transporting the milk to the consumption center, leaving him with $4.98 for his milk. If he decides to convert it into cream, it would cost him $0.002 to ship the product the 10 miles to the consumption center, leaving him with a farm-gate price of $3.998 for the 12 pounds of cream. Similarly, subtracting the transportation charges for butter would leave him $3.599 for selling his 100 pounds of milk as butter. Obviously, the farmer living 10 miles from the consumption center still receives a larger price for milk than for either cream or butter. However, if a farmer lives

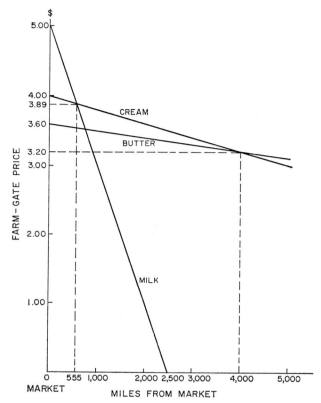

FIG. 4.3. Impact of transportation charges on the farm-gate price for selected
dairy products.

1,000 miles from the consumption center, the last column of the table
indicates that cream brings a higher net farm price than either milk or
butter. Therefore, as one moves out from the consumption center, transportation charges decrease the net farm price for the three products but
at differing rates. The effect of transportation charges on the farm-gate
price for the three products are depicted graphically in Figure 4.3.

It can be seen in Figure 4.3 that as one moves farther and farther
from the consumption center, the farm-gate (or net) price gets lower and
lower. For example, at 555 miles the net price of 100 pounds of fluid
milk is $3.89 and at approximately 2,500 miles the net price would be
zero. In other words, if a farmer lived more than 2,500 miles from the
market, he would have to be willing to produce milk for a zero price
because transportation would cost $5.00 or more per hundred pounds.
Similarly, one can draw a net price curve for cream and for butter. Notice
that although the zero-mile price is lower for cream than for milk, its

transportation charges are also lower. Consequently, the net price for cream declines more slowly than that for milk, and at 555 miles, the line tracing out the net price intersects the one for milk. This means that a farmer living 555 miles away would get $3.89 from selling either milk or cream. To the left of this intersection point (less than 555 miles), it would be more profitable for him to sell milk. To the right of this point, cream returns a larger net price per 100 pounds of milk produced.

Similarly, at 4,000 miles, transportation charges have reduced the farm-gate price for cream to the point where returns are larger for selling 100 pounds of milk in the form of butter rather than cream. Consequently, all farmers living more than 4,000 miles from the consumption center would be selling butter rather than cream or milk.

The results are probably more meaningful if one can visualize the producing areas surrounding a market center as a series of concentric circles. Each circle represents the boundary of a producing area. The boundaries are actually the intersection of net price lines for alternative products. This is obviously not a realistic depiction of all producing zones around a consumption center, but it does illustrate the point. As an example, the map of the producing regions resulting from Figure 4.3 is shown in Figure 4.4. It shows that transportation charges constrain the milk-producing area to within 555 miles of the city, the cream-producing area to the region lying between 555 miles and 4,000 miles from the center, and the butter-producing area to all farms more than 4,000 miles away.

It should now be clear as to how Von Thunen's principle can be used to explain some of the variations in the patterns of production that we see in the United States. For example, production of fluid milk in the northeastern part of the United States can be explained in terms of the large consumption centers located there, and the high cost of transporting fluid milk. Consequently, New York and Pennsylvania farmers find it profitable to produce fluid milk even though they do not

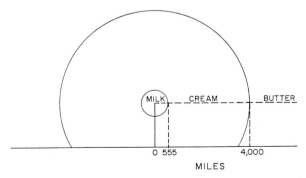

FIG. 4.4. The geographic location of production surrounding an isolated market.

have a natural comparative advantage when compared with states such as Wisconsin, Minnesota, or Michigan. Furthermore, the reasons for the location of dairy farms around each large metropolitan center should also be clear, as well as the reasons why most of the milk produced in northern Wisconsin and central and northern Minnesota finds its way into evaporated milk, butter, or cheese rather than remain as fluid milk.

The resulting net price differentials of farms at varying distances from a market can also be used to partially explain differences in the value of land. This is termed "economic rent."

LOCATION RENT

The issue of significant interest here is the impact of transportation costs on the rental values of land. Given that transportation charges influence the regional patterns of production through their impact on farm-gate prices, it can also be used to explain how areas with equal-quality land can command different prices or rental rates for their land. For example, assume that 1 acre can produce 1,000 pounds of milk and that all land is equally productive. Furthermore, assume that prices and transportation costs are as described in Figure 4.3 and Table 4.8 and that all costs of production are the same in the three areas. Under these assumptions, farm A located near the consumption center would realize a return of $50 per acre from producing milk; farm B producing cream 556 miles away, $38.90 per acre; and farm C more than 4,000 miles away from the consumption center producing butter, $32 per acre. Assume further that a farmer had the alternative of renting a farm in any one of the three regions. Clearly, farm A producing milk near the consumption center is the most desirable because it has the largest return per acre; however, if there is competition for the land, farmers will bid up the price of farm A until it just absorbs the difference in return per acre. In our example, since A has a return of $11.10 per acre more than farm B and farm B $6.90 more per acre than farm C, farm A will be able to command a rental premium of $11.10 over farm B. This premium would result because the renter, knowing the difference in returns, would be willing to pay up to $11.10 per acre more for farm A than for farm B. Similarly, in our example, farm B will command a $6.90 price premium per acre over farm C. These premiums are termed economic rent due to locational advantage. We will encounter this concept again later in the book.

The advantage of specialization is that through the trade or exchange of products all participants in the exchange economy are better off. This occurs because total aggregate output from a given level of resources is larger. Furthermore, the degree of specialization is directly dependent upon the ease with which exchange can be accomplished. If large numbers of people desire a product and the facilities exist to get it from producer to consumer, specialization will be encouraged. Good transportation and communication systems and a marketing system that facilitates the exchange of ownership of products all contribute to specialization. Furthermore, a large market that is the result of population concentrations or easy access to scattered consumers also facilitates specialization. One is more likely to find a cancer specialist, an orchid grower, or a gem cutter in New York City where there is sufficient demand for his specialty than in an area of remote villages not connected by roads. Also, one is more likely to find such a specialist at the hub of interconnecting roads, railroads, telephones, and telegraphs rather than in an area where communications between population centers are difficult or nonexistent.

Frequently, impediments to the free exchange of goods are erected. Such barriers as embargoes, tariff duties, legal restrictions, and other institutional barriers hinder exchange and thus reduce specialization and the economic benefits that accrue therefrom.

INSTITUTIONAL BARRIERS TO SPECIALIZATION AND EXCHANGE

Trade barriers such as tariffs, import duties, or quotas can distort the allocation of resources and the development of regional specialization and trade. The net result is an increase in the cost of production, reduced total welfare, and a transfer of income from one group of producers to another.

Trade barriers increase the cost of production and reduce total welfare by impeding the free flow of goods between countries or areas. As a result, each area cannot specialize but must produce to meet all its consumers' needs. For example, we have shown previously that if Wisconsin has a comparative advantage in milk production and Illinois in the production of corn, producers can maximize the amount they can produce with limited resources by specializing and trading. However, if a trade barrier exists between Wisconsin and Illinois, both areas must produce to meet all their needs. Consequently, Wisconsin must use some of its resources to produce a commodity in which it is less efficient, corn in this example; and Illinois must use some of its resources to produce milk, a product in which it is less efficient than Wisconsin. The net impact is a smaller amount of total output and increased production costs because the areas are using resources inefficiently. The consumers end up paying a higher price. Alternatively, it means that if each individual has a certain amount of income that can be used to purchase corn and milk, he must now use a larger proportion of this to purchase these basic commodities, leaving less of his income to purchase other commodities.

A second impact of trade barriers is that they reduce a country's willingness to adopt new technologies. Again, the consumer suffers through higher prices because of inefficient production techniques. For example, returning to our Wisconsin-Illinois example, if Wisconsin has a disadvantage in the production of corn, farmers will be stimulated to adopt new technologies in an attempt to lower their cost of production. There are examples in economic history where such attempts have changed a country from being at a net comparative disadvantage to having an absolute advantage in the production of a particular commodity. However, given there is a barrier that prevents outside competition from lower-cost producers, there may be no real incentive for farmers to attempt to lower costs.

Another major outgrowth of trade barriers is that they transfer income from one producing group to another. Health barriers in the production and transportation of fluid milk are an example. For illustrative purposes, assume that the city of Chicago will not accept any milk bottled for fluid consumption that has not been produced on a farm inspected by the city of Chicago milk inspectors. Given that Chicago inspectors will not travel more than 200 miles to inspect a farm, the net effect is a trade barrier to the transportation of fluid milk. The farm beyond 200 miles of Chicago cannot sell milk in the city of Chicago. Furthermore, given the demand for milk, farmers within this area now receive higher incomes because they can sell more milk than they otherwise would, and farmers outside the area can sell less milk. Consequently, there is a transfer of the income from a producing group beyond 200 miles to the producing group within 200 miles. There is also a transfer of income from consumers to producer, assuming that farmers within the 200-mile limit may have to increase prices to the consumer in order to expand production enough to meet total demand. As a consequence, consumers pay more for a given quantity of milk than they would have to without the trade barriers—resulting in a transfer of income from consumers to producers.

If our overall objective, then, is to maximize the total aggregate output and in some sense to maximize the well-being of the whole population, there can be no refutation of the argument for production in accordance with the principle of comparative advantage and specialization in trade. There are certain circumstances, however, such as the objective of national defense, or the protection of a domestic market, under which one can justify for certain periods of time interference with free trade among nations. For example, trade barriers can be used to protect a small "infant" industry until it grows large enough to compete effectively with the large competitors. The automobile industry may be an example. If the industry can produce 10 cars a day, it may only be able to produce them at a cost of $5,000 each. However, when the industry has developed to the point where it can produce 100 cars per day, the cost per car might be $2,000. Under such circumstances, one country may wish to protect its industry until it matures to the point where it can produce at the lowest possible cost. Under these conditions, consumers pay higher prices in the short run so that average prices may be lower in the long run. Another example is the development of the steel industry in Japan. Originally, Japanese steel mills were extremely inefficient and could not compete with United States methods of production. However, after a period of years the mills became so highly efficient that United States producers now find Japanese steel competing with their own in the United States markets. Unfortunately, the infant-industry argument is used all too frequently to protect an industry that will never become efficient. One can cite examples of many countries protecting an industry such as the steel or automobile industry with the argument that as the industry matures costs will decline and production become more efficient. Often, though, the establishment of trade barriers eliminates the incentives required for modernizations and improvements that can lower production costs. Furthermore, the political problems in removing the barriers are many times insurmountable. In summary, trade barriers tend to protect more inefficient industries than they do to promote the development of long-run efficient ones.

National defense is another argument often used in support of trade barriers. The country may want to assure itself of an uninterrupted supply of particular strategic commodities such as petroleum products, food and fiber, or rubber. During World War II, the United States placed an import duty on sugar to protect and encourage the development of the domestic sugarbeet industry. As a result, the United States currently produces sugar from sugarbeets at a higher price than it can be obtained from countries producing sugar from sugarcane. We also maintain import duties on petroleum products to assure ourselves of an adequate supply in times of national emergency.

Sometimes trade barriers such as embargoes are used to protect local industries from diseases which could have the impact of reducing total agricultural production. For example, Europe might place an embargo on Argentine beef because of the problems of hoof-and-mouth disease in the latter country. The embargo, by preventing the spread of the disease, may actually result in an increase in total aggregate output in the long run or, at a minimum, prevent a decrease in such output. In this case the embargo, although interfering with world trade and specialization, will have a net impact of lowering costs to consumers by impeding the spread of a cost-increasing disease.

Given specific conditions, the above are all valid economic arguments. One has to be careful, however, in using these arguments in favor of trade barriers. Frequently, the arguments are economically legitimate at the time the barriers are imposed; however, the time never seems to arrive for their removal. One must also keep in mind that trade is a two-way street and that the establishment of trade barriers interferes with the flow of commodities. Most countries export in order to earn dollars of foreign exchange with which to purchase items for import. Consequently, cutting off or reducing their ability to export in one way or another also reduces their ability to import.

Furthermore, when looking at or examining arguments in favor of trade barriers, one must always take into account who is making the argument and for what purpose. For example, senators from dairy states have often proposed import duties on dairy products from European countries in order to protect their local dairy industry. From the point of view of the dairy industry, this argument is acceptable. However, from the point of view of the consumers in the United States as a whole, this is an unreasonable argument in that it supports inefficiencies in one sector (dairying) at the expense of other sectors (consumers).

SUMMARY

We have thus seen how the physical and economic factors acting jointly determine the regional patterns of production. The physical factors determine what products can be produced in an area, and the economic factors as expressed in the principle of comparative advantage, and transportation charges as interpreted by Von Thunen's principle, determine what is actually produced. The net result is that locational advantages accrue to certain farms in certain areas and not to others, resulting in some farmland commanding a higher price than equivalent farms in other areas. Further, if the economic factors change, production patterns would also change. For example, if very large population centers developed in the western part of the United States, leaving the East Coast rural by comparison, the type of farming areas would also change, provided the physical factors permitted such changes. One might then expect large areas of fresh-vegetable production in Kansas, cattle grazing and wheat production in Ohio, and butter and cheese rather than fluid milk production in New York.

Finally, the advantages of specialization accrue to all who participate through exchange or trade. Without trade, specialization has no benefits. Institutional barriers such as trade restrictions can negate the effects of specialization by erecting barriers over which the products cannot pass. The arguments in favor of establishing institutional barriers are oftentimes overstated and the barriers generally are difficult to remove when they no longer are needed. Furthermore, the advantages accruing to the favored group must be weighed against the costs to other members of society.

DISCUSSION QUESTIONS AND PROBLEMS

1. Is the restriction on the importation of dairy products to the United States designed to aid the United States consumer or the United States dairyman? Are there any circumstances under which trade barriers might not be detrimental to United States consumer welfare?

2. What are the advantages and disadvantages of raising United States import duties on Japanese radios?
   a. To the Japanese producer and consumer?
   b. To the United States producer and consumer?

3. Suppose Illinois passed a law forbidding the movement of Wisconsin milk into Illinois, and Wisconsin has a comparative advantage in milk production.
   a. What would likely happen to the prices consumers pay for dairy products in Chicago?
   b. How would the erection of the trade barrier affect the distribution of income between consumers and producers of dairy products?

4. What factors can account for the loss of comparative advantage for a given product in a given area?

5. Evaluate the following statements:
   a. "Rich regions cannot afford to trade with poor regions because the standard of living in the rich region will be drawn down to the level of that in the poor region."
   b. "One area has no business producing a product that can be produced more efficiently in another area."

6. Does the saying "don't put all your eggs in one basket" have any merit in an economic world in which the principle of comparative advantage operates freely?

7. Contrast the role of economic specialization with that of diversification in maximizing the economic benefits of an individual. Of an economy.

8. Use the data in Table 4.Q.1, p. 98, to answer the questions:
   a. What factors could explain the differences in gross receipts/cow after allowance for differences in productivity?
   b. What factor(s) explain most of the difference in net income per cow between the Northeast and Western Wisconsin?
   c. Note that net income/cow is not sufficiently different in the two areas of Wisconsin to fully explain differences in land value per acre. What other economic factors could account for this difference?

9. What impact will a change in institutional barriers such as embargoes, import duties, etc., have on the value of inputs such as land within the protected area?

10. How would an urban renewal program that rebuilds a slum area with new, modern apartment buildings and houses affect the value of surrounding property? The extension of a bus line into a new area?

SUGGESTED READINGS

BASIC

Beckmann, Martin. *Location Theory*. New York: Random House, 1968.
   Good beginning text covering location of industry, location of an in-

dividual firm, allocation of land use, and locational aspects of economic growth.

Heady, Earl O. *Economics of Agricultural Production and Resource Use.* New York: Prentice-Hall, 1952.

Beginning material on regional specialization, transportation, and regional price variation, and a more advanced treatment of comparative advantage.

Snodgrass, Milton M.; and Wallace, Luther T. *Agriculture, Economics, and Growth.* New York: Appleton-Century-Crofts, 1970.

A discussion of agricultural trade policies and their impact upon specialization.

ADVANCED

Bressler, Raymond G., Jr.; and King, Richard A. *Markets, Prices, and Interregional Trade.* New York: John Wiley, 1970.

Excellent analysis of regional specialization and trade, and of the space, time, and form dimensions of commodities. Although mainly for the intermediate or advanced undergraduate student, certain parts would be of help to the beginning student.

Dunn, Edgar S., Jr. *The Location of Agricultural Production.* Gainesville: Univ. Fla. Press, 1954.

A theory of firm costs that explicitly includes distance as a variable.

TABLE 4.Q.1. Comparison of selected income and expense data on commercial dairy farms in three areas of the United States, 1966

		Area	
Item	Northeast[a]	Eastern Wisconsin[b]	Western Wisconsin[c]
1. Cows per farm	34	33	25
2. Cropland per farm	94 A	130 A	98 A
3. Land value per acre	$113	$254	$120
4. Milk production per cow (lb/year)	9,800	10,800	8,900
5. Gross receipts/cow	$561	$633	$517
6. Cash expenditures/cow	$368	$344	$251
7. Net income/cow	$193	$289	$266

Source: USDA, Farm Costs and Returns, Agr. Inform. Bull. 230, Oct. 1967.

a. New York and Pennsylvania.

b. Eastern Wisconsin Grade A milk area.

c. Western Wisconsin Grade B milk area.

Dunn developed the general theory of location of agricultural production as related to the geographical distribution of inputs and outputs and to the location of other economic activities. An appendix contains a complete review of, and comments on, the conclusions of earlier writers in this field.

Haberler, G. An assessment of the current relevance of the theory of comparative advantage to agricultural production and trade. *Proc. 12th Intern. Conf. Agr. Econ.* London: Oxford Univ. Press, 1966, pp. 17–55.

A good review of the current theory of comparative advantage, with a discussion by some of the leading economists in the field.

Sisler, Daniel G. International trade policies and agriculture. *Proc. 14th Intern. Conf. Agr. Econ.* Oxford: Oxford Inst. Agrarian Affairs, 1971, pp. 259–80.

A discussion of trade policies and trade barriers, their impact on agricultural trade between sections and on the growth of the agricultural sector within a country.

CHAPTER 5: PRINCIPLES OF PRODUCTION ECONOMICS

In this chapter we will begin to develop the analytical framework for decision making by the entrepreneur of a firm. The framework is generally labeled *production economics* since the emphasis is on the combining of inputs, often called factors of production, such that a product is created. The production process is also one of transformation since certain factors—labor, management, and raw materials—are transformed into a commodity.

When we think of an entrepreneur managing a business, we ordinarily envision an individual who, seemingly, intuitively knows how to perform this transformation process. Actually, it is an exceedingly complex task to run a successful enterprise and the analytics introduced in this chapter will both demonstrate that complexity and at the same time provide a systematic basis for making the necessary decisions. When discussing production decisions, it is helpful to distinguish among at least three distinct questions that the entrepreneur must ask. First, what product or products should be produced? Second, how much of any one product should be produced? Finally, which is the best possible means to accomplish that production? That is, how should inputs be combined in order to arrive at a product?

The first question, which products should be produced, can be viewed as logically prior to the other two; it is first necessary to determine a set of feasible products before turning to questions of "how much" and "how." The discussion in the previous chapter should underscore this notion. There it was seen that, at least in agriculture, there are distinct physical and biological determinants of what can be produced in a given region. Although there is some disagreement among economists on the matter, it is still convenient to view production as the result of combining four classes of factors of production—land, labor, capital, and management. The particular endowment of these, along with biological and physical factors, determine what it is *feasible* to produce. But more information is required before it is possible to ascertain what is *best* to produce from among the feasible alternatives.

The second question, how much to produce, assumes that the entrepreneur has narrowed down the choice of commodities to several and is faced with the problem of the ideal level of production for each.

Here, not only is it vital to have an understanding of the relationship between alternative levels and combinations of the factors of production but it is necessary to have information on the value (price) of the respective outputs, and to know the price (cost) of the various inputs to be employed. With the above data, it is also possible to simultaneously answer the final question, how the factors will be combined to produce the product.

Before turning to the analysis, it is necessary to state several important assumptions, a few of which will be repeated later. First, it is assumed that the entrepreneur wishes to remain in business over the long run. While a few might accomplish this feat in a market economy by operating at a financial loss year after year (say, by drawing on the larges of a rich relative), this would be the exception rather than the rule. Hence, in the following discussion it will be assumed that the entrepreneur desires to maximize profit from his business. Second, it will be assumed that the output of the firm is such an insignificant fraction of the total output of a particular product that there is no effect on market price when the production of the particular firm fluctuates. Third, it is assumed the entrepreneur knows with certainty the prices he must pay for productive factors, and the prices he can receive for his output. His purchase of factors is such an insignificant portion of their total supply that his transactions do not affect their price. Finally, we assume that production is instantaneous; we present production as output per unit of time—where time may be 1 year—but the analytics assume instant response from the utilization of variable factors.

The following analysis proceeds in four distinct steps. First, we introduce the concept of a production function. Second, we turn to a section on production decisions and optimality with three main subsections. The first deals with decisions regarding the ideal output level of a single product. Then we discuss the situation where the ideal mix of several variable factors must be determined. Finally, we analyze the situation where an ideal mix of two products is being sought. Through this analysis, it will be seen that we have developed the framework for deciding which products to produce, how much of each to produce, and how to produce them.

PRODUCTION FUNCTION CONCEPT

We begin by developing a production function for, say, corn that depicts the results of the application of various quantities of one variable input to a set of fixed inputs such as land, capital equipment, labor, and water. Equation 5.1 is an explicit formulation of a production function.

$$Y = f(X_f/X_l, \ X_c, \ X_h, \ X_w) \tag{5.1}$$

where

Y = output of corn in bushels
X_f = variable quantities of a specific fertilizer
X_l = a fixed quantity of land of a certain quality
X_c = a fixed quantity of capital equipment of a certain quality
X_h = a fixed quantity of human labor of a certain skill level
X_w = a fixed quantity of water of a certain quality

Notice that all inputs to the right of the vertical line in Equation 5.1 are *fixed factors;* the one to the left of the line—in this case fertilizer—is a *variable factor.* The formulation in Equation 5.1, though termed explicit, is still abstract in that it does not specify how increases in the level of X_f by 1, 10, or 100 units will affect the level of output of Y. Therefore, before a production function can be of any use to the decision maker, it must be quantified. In agriculture, production functions are determined experimentally by scientists at colleges and universities throughout the country, by the USDA, and by private concerns such as seed companies and fertilizer manufacturers. In addition, many farmers with long years of experience know how the output of a particular product will respond to varying levels of inputs.

As an example, Equation 5.2 can be used as a hypothetical simple production function relating the yield in bushels of corn per acre to the pounds of nitrogen applied per acre, with all other factors held constant.

$$Y = 25 + 0.5N \tag{5.2}$$

where

Y = bushels of corn per acre
N = pounds of nitrogen per acre

By substituting various levels of N in the equation, one can determine the bushels of corn per acre that will be forthcoming. For example, if a farmer applies 10 pounds of nitrogen to an acre of corn, the production function in Equation 5.2 reveals that he can expect to obtain a yield of 30 bushels of corn on that acre $(25 + 10 \times 0.5 = 30)$. By considering a series of values for N, it is possible to formulate a relationship such as that depicted in Table 5.1.

Table 5.1 is the tabular equivalent of the production function of Equation 5.2. Notice that the title in Table 5.1 is very specific; this

TABLE 5.1. Hypothetical production function illustrating the response of corn to nitrogen application (Webster Sandy Loam soil, Rock County, Wisconsin)

Pounds of Nitrogen per Acre	Bushels of Corn per Acre
0	25.0
10	30.0
25	37.5
50	50.0
80	65.0
100	75.0

is necessary because of the large number of factors which influence output—factors which are beyond the control of the entrepreneur. In agriculture, soil type and weather are two very important determinants of response to incremental applications of an input such as fertilizer, and it is therefore necessary to be very specific. In the production of steel, although it is easier to control the conditions under which production occurs, it is still necessary to be specific regarding the factors being held constant as one variable input is added or subtracted. The conclusion is that a production relationship such as that depicted in Table 5.1 would have little meaning for corn grown on a different soil type or in an area with a different climate.

By plotting corn yield on the vertical axis (ordinate), and the level of nitrogen on the horizontal axis (abscissa), a production function can also be expressed in graphic form. The data for Table 5.1 are illustrated in Figure 5.1. By plotting the production function, one can deduce a great deal of information about the relationship between the input and the output of the product in question. For example, Figure 5.1 indicates that under the assumed soil and weather conditions there is a yield of 25 bushels per acre when nitrogen application is zero. Figure 5.1 also indicates that the response of output to input is linear. This means that each additional pound of nitrogen adds exactly 0.5 bushels of corn to output. This is unusual and is rarely, if ever, found in agriculture. Generally, at some level of input, the production function will begin to decline. Thus Equation 5.2, Table 5.1, and Figure 5.1 are not consistent with the "real" world. In the next section we introduce some additional concepts which will permit us to develop a more reasonable

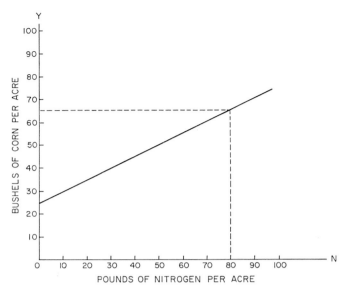

FIG. 5.1. Hypothetical production function for corn on Webster Sandy Loam soil, Rock County, Wisconsin.

production function; one that more closely approximates the true nature of the real production process.

TYPES OF PRODUCTION FUNCTIONS

When equal increments of a variable factor are applied to a complement of fixed factors, three possible responses can occur regarding output: (1) no change, (2) a decrease in output, and (3) an increase in output. While one might want to examine the reasons for all three types of responses, our current interest centers on the latter response where output increases as equal increments of an input are applied. It is conventional to classify production relations depending upon how output responds as the input level is increased. When output increases with the addition of equal increments of an input, it can either increase at a constant rate, increase at an increasing rate, or increase at a decreasing rate. This is referred to as exhibiting constant, increasing, or decreasing marginal returns to the variable factor. In essence, the classification is dependent upon the change in the slope of the production function. *Increasing marginal returns* implies a production function with a slope that is increasing; the production function is a type of curve that becomes steeper as more of the input is applied to the fixed factors. *Constant marginal returns* implies a production function with a slope that is the same for all levels of the variable input (Figure

TABLE 5.2.   Examples of production functions with increasing, constant, and decreasing returns to a variable factor of production

	Units of Input	Units of Output	Added Output (MPP)[a]
	X	Y	$\Delta Y/\Delta X$
	Increasing Marginal Returns		
	1	3	
			2
	2	5	
			3
Part A	3	8	
			4
	4	12	
			5
	5	17	
			6
	6	23	
	Constant Marginal Returns		
	1	2	
			2
	2	4	
			2
Part B	3	6	
			2
	4	8	
			2
	5	10	
			2
	6	12	
	Decreasing Marginal Returns		
	1	8	
			5
	2	13	
			4
Part C	3	17	
			3
	4	20	
			2
	5	22	
			1
	6	23	

a. MPP is the marginal physical product and is defined as the change in total output divided by the associated change in units of variable input required to produce it.

5.1). *Decreasing marginal returns* implies a production function with a slope that becomes less steep (decreases) as more of the variable input is applied. The numbers in Table 5.2 illustrate the three types of response.

Increasing marginal returns exist when each additional unit of input produces a larger increment to output than did the previous unit of input. For example, in part A of Table 5.2, the 3rd unit of input adds 3 units to output, while the 2nd adds only 2 units. The 4th unit of the variable input adds 4 units to output, compared to 3 for the 3rd unit. In other words, each additional unit of input adds more to output than the previous unit. The *added output* is defined as the marginal physical product of the variable factor (*MPP*). It is calculated by dividing the change in output by the associated change in the variable input required to produce it.

$$MPP = \Delta Y/\Delta X = (Y_2 - Y_1)/(X_2 - X_1) \qquad (5.3)$$

where

$$\Delta Y = \text{change in output}$$
$$\Delta X = \text{change in input}$$
$$Y_2 = \text{new output level}$$
$$Y_1 = \text{old output level}$$
$$X_2 = \text{new input level}$$
$$X_1 = \text{old input level}$$

It is assumed in Equation 5.3 that all other factors of production are kept constant. Hence, the *MPP* is the extra output that is forthcoming from the utilization of one extra unit of the variable input, while all other inputs are held constant.

Constant marginal returns exist when each additional unit of the variable inputs adds exactly the same amount to output as did the previous unit of the input. To put it differently, the marginal physical product of each unit of input is constant. For example, in part B of Table 5.2, the 2nd unit of input adds 2 units to output as do the 3rd, 4th, and 5th. In this case, the marginal physical product of each unit is 2. The production function for corn in Figure 5.1 also exhibits constant returns; the marginal physical product of nitrogen was 0.5.[1]

Decreasing marginal returns are said to exist when each additional unit of the variable input adds less to output than did the previous unit. In this case, *MPP* is decreasing with the addition of more inputs. In part C of Table 5.2, the 2nd unit of the input adds 5 units to output, the 3rd unit 4, and the 4th unit 3. Simply stated, less product is added to output by each subsequent unit of the input, and the marginal physical product declines from 5 for the 2nd unit of the variable input to 1 for the 6th unit of the variable input.

A graphic illustration of the three relationships as taken from Table 5.2 is shown in Figure 5.2. Notice that in all three cases the production function is increasing, but at different rates; it is this rate of increase that is of interest when talking of marginal returns to a variable factor. The rate of increase is the *slope* of the production function.

1. To test your understanding of the marginal physical product, calculate the *MPP* for nitrogen from Table 5.1.

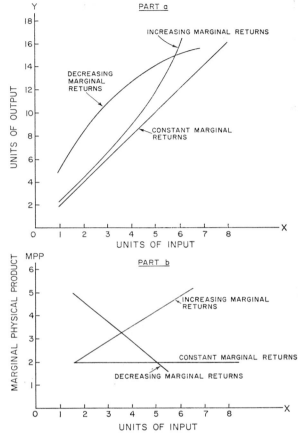

FIG. 5.2. Examples of production functions (part a) exhibiting constant, decreasing, and increasing returns to the variable factor, and of the marginal physical product functions (part b) associated with each production function.

The rate of increase is also the marginal physical product of the variable factor. Hence, the slope of the production function is the marginal physical product of the variable factor. In the lower portion of Figure 5.2, we have plotted the three marginal physical product functions. Notice which of the *MPP* functions corresponds to each production function.

CLASSICAL PRODUCTION FUNCTION

Although economists who specialize in production economics dislike the notion of a "typical" production function—and for good cause—there is a traditional concept of production relationships which the student who pursues economics to more advanced levels will encounter. Hence, to be consistent with conventional wisdom, we describe the concept of a "classical" production function. The student should be warned that such a relationship will rarely if ever be encountered in actual production function studies, yet the classical production function has certain pedagogical qualities that justify its discussion.

In the upper portion of Figure 5.3 is illustrated a combination of the three types of production relations depicted in Figure 5.2; this formulation depicts the classical production function. Here, the production function is labeled *total physical product* (*TPP*), a term that will

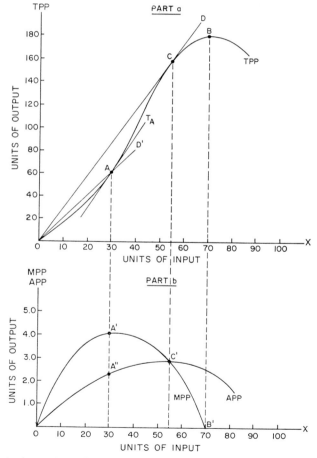

FIG. 5.3. A classical production function with its associated average and marginal physical product curves.

be used repeatedly throughout the remainder of the book. The classical function takes on the shape of a hill, and it is the different rates of change in output (slopes) that become of analytic interest. From zero to 30 units of the variable factor, output is increasing at an increasing rate. Between 30 and 70 units of the variable input, output continues to increase, but at a decreasing rate. Beyond point B (more than 70 units of the variable input), total physical product is actually less than if some smaller quantity of the input were utilized. As an example, up to a certain point the addition of workers on an assembly line will increase output. Beyond that point, as workers begin to get in each other's way, total production may be less than if fewer were involved in the process.

In addition to the notions of total physical product (TPP)—which is defined as the level of output—and marginal physical product, it is useful to understand the concept of average physical product (APP). *Average physical product* is defined as the total amount of output divided by the total level of the variable input used to produce that quantity of output. Algebraically, the average physical product is calculated as shown in Equation 5.4.

$$APP = Y/X = TPP/X \qquad (5.4)$$

where

$$
\begin{aligned}
Y &= \text{total output level} \\
X &= \text{total variable input level} \\
TPP &= \text{total physical product}
\end{aligned}
$$

For example, in Figure 5.3 an input level of 55 units yields 160 units of total physical output, so yield per unit of variable input is 2.91 units, calculated as shown in Equation 5.5.

$$APP = 160/55 = 2.91 \qquad (5.5)$$

In part b of Figure 5.3 we have plotted the average physical product and marginal physical product functions from the production function of part a. These two functions can be calculated quite simply from the TPP curve. Graphically, the average physical product for any level of a variable input is defined as the slope of a line from the origin (0) to the point on the TPP curve which is of interest. In Equation 5.5 we saw that the APP for 55 units of variable input was 2.91, which is the slope of the line OD. In geometry, the slope of a line is its "rise" divided by its "run." In this case, 160/55. Similarly, at point A, the APP is 2.0 since $TPP = 60$, and the level of variable input is 30 (line OD' has a slope of 2). Notice that in the segment of the production function from the origin to point C, any line drawn from the origin to a point on the production function will have a steeper slope as one selects higher points on the production function. Since the slope of these ray lines is the average physical product, it is seen that up until point C on the production function, higher levels of variable input will have a greater APP than previous levels of the input. Beyond point C, a ray line drawn to a point on the production function will have a lesser slope. Since the slope of the ray line is defined as the average physical product, this means that between the origin and point C the average physical product will be increasing, and beyond point C it will be decreasing. This is portrayed in the lower portion of Figure 5.3. At point C, the slope of all possible ray lines is as great as possible, and hence it is here that the average physical product (APP) will be a maximum.

As explained above, the slope of the production function (not the slope of a ray line to a point on the production function) is the marginal physical product of the variable factor. This can be determined geometrically by drawing a line tangent to the production function at the point of interest and computing its slope (as the rise over the run). It is clear that, at point A, the slope of a line tangent to the production function (T_A) is steeper than the slope of a ray line to point A (OD'). This means that the marginal physical product of the variable factor at point A is greater than the average physical product of the factor at point A as can be seen by comparing points A' and A'' in part b.

Notice the difference between the two functions in the lower portion of Figure 5.3. At point C, the slope of the production function is the same as the slope of the ray line, and the average physical product equals the marginal physical product (C' in part b). Beyond point C, the slope of the production function is less than the slope of the ray line, and the marginal physical product is less than average physical product. At point B the production function has a slope of zero. Hence, the marginal physical product is zero at that point (B' in part b) and the MPP function intersects the input axis at 70 units of input. Notice also that although the marginal physical product is negative beyond the point at which TPP is maximum, the average physical product will continue to be positive (though downward sloping) as long as there is a positive output from subsequent applications of the variable input.

From the classical production function, it is possible to discuss a common concept in economics—that of diminishing marginal returns. The earlier discussion on decreasing marginal returns relates to the same phenomenon—that as more of a variable input is added to a complement of fixed factors, the increment to total output from equal increments of the variable input will eventually decrease, and may ultimately approach zero. This is sometimes referred to as the principle of diminishing marginal returns.

Stages of the Classical Production Function. While the notion of stages of production is a venerable one in production economics, its value as a heuristic device has increasingly been questioned. Nonetheless, to provide a brief introduction to the concept of stages of a production function, we will not break with tradition here. The relationship between the marginal physical product function and the average physical product function is important in the notion of stages of the production function. Stage I of the classical production function is said to lie to the left of the point where the *MPP* and the *APP* functions are equal. In Figure 5.3 this would be the region from the origin out to point *C* on the production function. Stage II is said to lie to the right of the point of equality between *MPP* and *APP*, but to the left of the point where *MPP* equals zero (point *B* in Figure 5.3). Stage III is said to lie to the right of the point where *MPP* equals zero (point *B* in Figure 5.3).

TIME PERIOD CONSIDERATIONS

The production function we have developed and discussed has an implicit assumption regarding the time span of production. Production is not instantaneous. An increase in the level of application of an input will result in additional output only after sufficient time has elapsed to allow the input to be transformed. Thus the input and the output measured on the horizontal and vertical axes, respectively, must be specified with respect to a particular period of time, such as per hour, per day, per month, per year, or whatever period of time is required to permit the new level of the input to work its way through the production system and to be observed in the new level of output. The period of time will be different for different products. For example, the production process for Christmas trees is long. It takes, on the average, 8 years to grow a Scotch pine from a seedling to salable size. Thus, if Figure 5.3 were the production function showing the relationship between salable Christmas trees and labor hours applied, output (*Y*) would be salable Christmas trees per 8 years and the input (*X*) would be total labor hours per 8 years. Similarly, if Figure 5.3 represents the output of raspberries as a function of pounds of nitrogen fertilizer applied, the appropriate axis should be specified as pounds of raspberries per year and pounds of nitrogen per year. The fertilizer, which is usually applied in the spring, does not have any observable response until the harvest in late summer and fall. A shorter period would understate the true response of rapsberries to nitrogen. In fact, some of the nitrogen remains in the soil and is utilized by the plant in the second year. Thus there is a carry-over effect. In this case it might be appropriate to specify both inputs and outputs per 2 years rather than per year. As a third example, the output of a production line could be specified per 8-hour day or per hour as a function of the number of workers in the line that day or that hour.

In summary, the production process requires time. In the discussions that follow, the time unit is not specified but is implied in the labels. Consequently, for the sake of brevity, whenever we speak of input or output, we mean *input per unit of time* or *output per unit of time.* Whenever the time dimension is essential to the analysis it will be explicitly stated.

SHIFTS IN THE PRODUCTION FUNCTION

The concept of a production function is that it represents the maximum output available per unit of time from the complement of fixed factors and from the specified level of the variable input. It is possible to use a given quantity of the variable factor with the fixed factors and obtain less output than that indicated by the point on the production function corresponding to the level of variable factor being utilized, but never more output than that given by the production function. It will be recalled from Equation 5.1 that the fixed factors are always specified as representing not only a specific quantity but a specific quality as well. Hence, whenever either of these two aspects change for one or more of the fixed factors, the production function will shift upward or downward, depending on the nature of the change. It is important to understand why a change in the quantity of a variable factor is reflected in movements along the production function, while changes in the quality of the variable factor, or in either the quality or quantity of the fixed factors, are reflected in shifts in the production function.

For example, the hypothetical production functions in Figure 5.4 can be utilized to discuss this phenomenon. If TPP_0 is taken to represent the initial case, TPP_1 reflects the production function with improved quality of one or more productive factors (variable or fixed), or the greater quantity of one or more fixed factors. Conversely, TPP_2 would depict the situation with a lower quality of one or more productive factors (variable or fixed), or the decreased quantity of one or more fixed factors. New technology is generally said to shift a production function upward, reflecting a higher quality input.

PRODUCTION DECISIONS AND OPTIMALITY

The three types of production decisions discussed at the beginning of the chapter can be viewed in a slightly different manner. The three decisions can be classified as (1) factor-product decisions, (2) factor-factor decisions, and (3) product-product decisions. Used in combination, the three types of decisions help to provide the

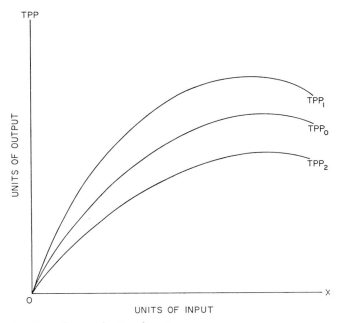

FIG. 5.4. Shifts in the production function.

entrepreneur with information for deciding what products to produce, how to produce them, and how much to produce of any particular product. Before proceeding to a detailed analysis of each type of decision, a short description and an example of each type are presented below.

The factor-product relationship was the general type of decision with which the concept of a production function was introduced earlier. Output is assumed to be dependent upon the amount of a single variable input that is combined with certain other fixed resources. For example, decisions as to how much labor to use in the production of Christmas trees, how much nitrogen fertilizer to use in the production of corn, or how much hired labor to use in the harvesting of potatoes are examples of this general type. The factor-product decision assumes that the entrepreneur may obtain any amount of the variable input that is needed. His basic problem, therefore, is to apply that amount which maximizes profit to the enterprise. In this type of decision, the entrepreneur must combine the physical factor-product information with input and output prices to determine the optimum level of the variable input.

The factor-factor relationship is relevant when several variable factors of production are used to produce one product. The entrepreneur must, therefore, decide which inputs he will use in the production of which product, and what amounts of each he will use, given their prices.

For example, a Wisconsin dairy farmer may vary the combination of grain and hay that he uses in feeding his dairy cows depending upon the prices of each and the amount of milk production he desires. Corn and protein supplement used in the production of pork, corn and silage used in the production of beef, plant population and fertilizer used in the production of corn, skilled and unskilled labor used on a production line, or public transportation and private automobiles used in transporting workers to their jobs are all examples of factor-factor decisions. The student should note that the last factor-factor example is in the area of public decision making in contrast to the first four which are intrafirm decisions. Much of the theoretical development that follows can also be applied to public decisions, and we will attempt to provide examples from this area.

The product-product relationship involves the determination of ideal levels of output between at least two technically independent[2] products capable of being produced by the firm. Here, output mix—rather than input mix—is the central concern. With limited resources for the purchase of variable factors, the expansion of one output implies a contraction of the other; it is important to use those limited resources in the wisest possible way. The decisions as to how to allocate farm labor among livestock or crop enterprises, cropland among alternative commodities, savings among alternative investment opportunities, or public funds between defense and welfare programs are all examples of a product-product decision.

Before proceeding to a detailed discussion of each type of decision, the several assumptions stated earlier should be kept in mind. The first assumption is that the entrepreneur buys his inputs or factors and sells his products without affecting their respective prices—he is operating in perfectly competitive markets. Consequently, prices are assumed to be determined by forces beyond the control of the individual manager and they are regarded by him as given. The second assumption is that prices and the production function are known with certainty. Consequently, once the optimum production decision has been made, the optimum production point changes only with changes in the production function. Finally, it is assumed that some inputs are fixed in quantity so that the decisions are in terms of short-run profit to which the principle of diminishing marginal returns applies.

FACTOR-PRODUCT RELATIONSHIPS

As indicated above, the problem here is to determine the most profitable point of operation for a single enterprise. This is

2. By technically independent we mean that the output of one of the products in no way depends upon the output of the other.

done by determining either the most profitable amount of input or the most profitable amount of output. Either decision results in the same utltimate answer, since inputs and outputs are connected in a specific fashion through the physical production function. Although production processes involving but a single variable input are not realistic in the study of most managerial decisions, the principles developed are general and can be applied to more complex production later. This section will focus on determining the optimum amount of one variable input.

Suppose that as an entrepreneur you were given the production function as illustrated by the schedule of quantities of inputs and outputs presented in columns 1 and 2 of Table 5.3. What would be the rule you would use to determine the level of output that will maximize profits? Several alternative methods could be used to attack the problem. The time-consuming method would be to calculate total cost, revenue, and profit for each level of variable input usage and then use that level for which calculated profit is a maximum. This method is both tedious and time-consuming; furthermore it assumes that all relevant points on the production surface are known and can be calculated. Unfortunately, this is not the usual case. We can, however, make use of some additional information about the production function that will help us to develop

TABLE 5.3. Determining the optimum level of a variable input for a hypothetical production function

Input X	Output Y	MPP $\Delta Y / \Delta X$	VMP (P_y = \$1)	VMP (P_y = \$2)
(1)	(2)	(3)	(4)	(5)
0	0			
		5	\$5	\$10
1	5			
		9	9	18
2	14			
		7	7	14
3	21			
		5	5	10
4	26			
		4	4	8
5	30			
		3	3	6
6	33			
		2	2	4
7	35			
		1	1	2
8	36			
		0	0	0
9	36			

a decision criterion. We know, for instance, that because of the principle of diminishing marginal returns, the variable input must sooner or later exhibit diminishing marginal physical product. Furthermore, we know that the entrepreneur is not interested in diminishing marginal physical product. Rather, there is interest in the money that the enterprise earns from the sale of products. Therefore, the entrepreneur's interests lie in how much can be added to revenues of the firm when the amount of the variable input used in the production process is progressively increased. This question is answered by comparing what the employment of each additional unit of the variable factor adds to revenues of the firm with what it costs to purchase the extra factor. Consequently, a *specific decision rule* is: use a variable input up to where the last unit employed creates just enough additional output to pay for its utilization in the production process. Another version of the same rule states that additional units of a variable input should be used so long as the addition of one more unit to the production process adds more to revenues than to costs. It can be proved that the point at which the increase in cost due to the utilization of one more unit of input is exactly offset by the addition to revenues for the output it creates is a level of inputs at which profits will be maximum.

The technical rule for the same principle states that the optimum use of a variable input occurs when the value of the marginal product (VMP) of the input is equal to the price of the input. The algebraic equivalent of this criterion is presented in Equation 5.6.

$$VMP_x = P_x \tag{5.6}$$

where

$$
\begin{aligned}
VMP_x &= \text{value of the marginal product of input } X \text{ in producing output } Y \\
P_x &= \text{price of the input } X
\end{aligned}
$$

The value of the marginal product is precisely what its label describes it to be: the value of the product produced by the last unit of the variable input, that is, it is the value of the marginal physical product. With the price of the final product given by P_y, we can write the value of the marginal product as[3]

$$VMP_x = (MPP_x) (P_y) \tag{5.7}$$

The marginal physical product of X in producing Y is shown in column 3 of Table 5.3. Note that the production function exhibits

---

3. When the assumption of a constant price (P_y) for the final product is relaxed, it is no longer sufficient to write the VMP of the variable factor X as

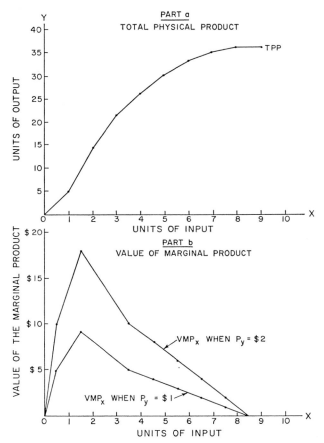

FIG. 5.5. Production function with two **VMP** functions.

diminishing marginal returns after the 2nd unit of variable input. If the price of output is $1 per unit, then based on Equation 5.7, the value of the product (VMP) produced by the 2nd unit of input is $9 = (9 \times \$1)$, by the 3rd unit $7, and by the 4th unit $5. Addition of the 7th unit of input produces 2 additional units of output $(MPP = 2)$, and the value of this additional output is $2. In the language of the economist, the VMP of the 7th unit is $2. Should the price of the output (P_y) change to $2, then the VMP at each level of input usage would be different. The value of the marginal product for outputs priced at $1 and $2, respectively, are presented in columns 4 and 5 of Table 5.3. The production func-

---

$(MPP_x)(P_y)$. In those instances where the price of the final product varies as a function of output (Y), the value of the marginal product is termed the marginal value product (MVP). We will use the former designation (VMP) almost exclusively.

tion of Table 5.3 is presented graphically in Figure 5.5, and the VMP functions for the two output prices are drawn in the lower portion (part b).

The ideal level of use for a variable input can be treated as two separate decisions. The necessary conditions are met when Equation 5.7 has been satisfied. Then the sufficient conditions are met when it is determined that the input level is the profit-maximizing level. For instance, it can be seen in the lower portion of Figure 5.5 and in Table 5.3 that for each VMP function (one for $P_y = \$1$; one for $P_y = \$2$) there are actually two levels of X which satisfy Equation 5.7. With $P_x = \$5$ and $P_y = \$1$, it is seen that $\frac{1}{2}$ unit of X has a VMP of $5, as does $3\frac{1}{2}$ units. If 1 unit were used, costs would be $5, and revenue would be $5 (5 units at $1 each) for a profit of zero. On the other hand, if 4 units of X were used, costs would be $20 (4 units at $5 each), and revenue would be $26 (26 units at $1 each) for a profit of $6. The same reasoning holds when the price of Y increases to $2 per unit.

With the discrete (lumpy) nature of the variable input X in the above example, the strict equality of Equation 5.7 can only be achieved with the fractions of units of the variable factor. In theory, the application of a variable input is viewed as a continuous phenomenon which permits the drawing of a smooth and continuous VMP function such as

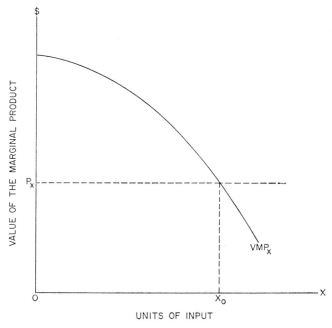

FIG. 5.6.   Idealized **VMP** function.

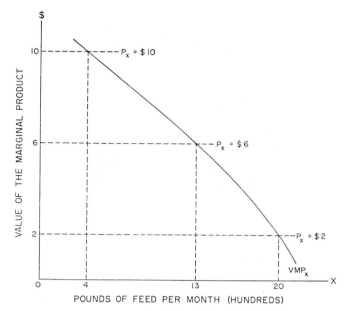

FIG. 5.7. The **VMP** curve of feed for broilers.

that in Figure 5.6. Then the exact amount of X to meet the conditions of Equation 5.7 can be determined.

DERIVED DEMAND FOR AN INPUT

Under certain assumptions regarding the period of analysis, it is possible to demonstrate that the value of the marginal product function can be considered as the demand curve for a variable factor. A *demand curve* is the relationship of alternative quantities of the factor that would be demanded by the entrepreneur at different prices for the factor. Assume that a farmer is a profit maximizing entrepreneur, that he knows the responses of his broilers to different levels of utilization of feed, and that he knows the price per pound of broilers. By utilizing that data he can construct a schedule of prices and quantities of feed he would be willing and able to buy per month at the local feed store. Such a schedule is shown in Figure 5.7. To be more specific, assume that the *VMP* curve in Figure 5.7 is for a broiler producer who buys feed in 100-pound lots (cwt) per month. The price of broilers is $30 per hundred pounds (cwt), and it is known from Equation 5.7 that the variable factor —feed—should be utilized up to the point where the value of the marginal product of last unit of feed (in this case cwt per month) is exactly equal to the cost of that unit of the factor.

The *VMP* curve is derived from the entrepreneur's knowledge of the response of the broilers to increments of feed per month (*MPP*) and the price of broilers (P_y). The curve is downward sloping since it is assumed that the producer would be in Stage II of the production function. If the price of feed were $10 per cwt, the farmer would maximize profit by utilizing 400 pounds per month. If the price were only $6 per cwt, profit would be maximized with 1,300 pounds per month of the feed.

The curve in Figure 5.7 is then the derived demand curve for feed, derived from the production function and from knowledge of the price of the final product, broilers. It should be pointed out that the *VMP* curve is the demand curve for a factor only in the single-variable factor case. The derivation of demand curves for a factor is complicated by the more realistic case of several variable factors and is reserved for more advanced courses.

Individual and Aggregate Demand. While the derived demand curve in Figure 5.7 is for an individual producer, there is also the notion of an aggregate demand curve for an input. While the individual producer uses his demand curve to decide upon the ideal level of feed to use in his broiler operation, the suppliers of broiler feed are extremely interested in the aggregate demand for their product. They want to know the total quantity of feed that would be purchased from them by all producers together at alternative prices. Recall that the derived demand curve for feed of the individual operator shows the quantity he should buy at alternative prices of feed. Each producer of broilers will have such a demand curve for feed, and the sum of these will represent the aggregate demand curve for broiler feed.

To derive the aggregate demand curve for feed, we need only recall that it depicts the total quantity which would be purchased at alternative prices. Knowing this, we can start by selecting a certain price, and summing the respective quantities which each producer would buy at that price. An example will clarify the concept. For the sake of simplicity, assume that there are only three broiler producers in the world and that their respective individual demand curves are illustrated by parts a, b, and c of Figure 5.8. The same relationship as in Figure 5.8 is also shown in Table 5.4. The table and the figure both illustrate the concept of how an aggregate demand curve for a factor of production is derived and the notion of a differential productivity of a factor across producers. To derive the aggregate demand curve, one merely adds the quantities that would be purchased at alternative prices by all producers (this is the definition of aggregate demand); this is the figure presented in the last column of Table 5.4 and is depicted graphically in part d of Figure 5.8. The perceptive student will note that we

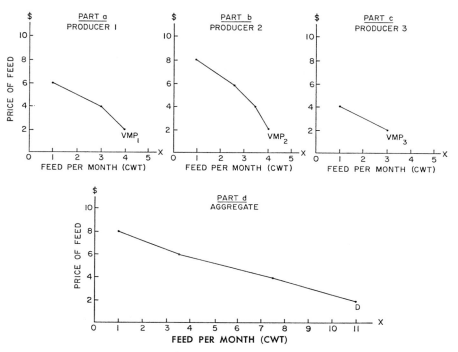

FIG. 5.8. Demand curves for broiler feed.

TABLE 5.4. Individual and aggregate demand schedules for broiler feed (cwt per month)

Price of Feed per Cwt	Feed for			Aggregate Demand
	Producer 1	Producer 2	Producer 3	
	(cwt/month)			
$2	4	4	3	11
4	3	3.5	1	7.5
6	1	2.5	0	3.5
8	0	1	0	1

could have derived the aggregate demand curve without Table 5.4 by simply adding horizontally across producers 1, 2, and 3 of Figure 5.8 for each price; that is, sum the quantities taken at $2 and make a point in part d at the height of $2 and at the quantity which corresponds to the sum. By repeating this for $4, $6, and $8, one would have four points in part d. Then, by merely connecting the points, the aggregate demand curve for all farms is obtained.

As we asserted earlier, it is the aggregate demand curve which is of interest to the seller of broiler feed, and once he knows the relationship depicted in Figure 5.8, he could determine the response of farmers to a slight increase or decrease in the price of feed. As will be seen in later chapters, this notion—referred to as the price elasticity of demand—is a most important one in economics.

The second concept illustrated in Figure 5.8 is that of a differential productivity among producers. This is reflected in the fact that each producer in Figure 5.8 has a different VMP curve. By remembering that the demand curve (VMP) is the marginal physical product of the input times price of the output, we can explain the fact that each producer has a different demand curve, even though the price of the output (broilers) is the same for all three. The derived demand curves (VMP) for producers 1 and 3 indicate that they are not as efficient in converting feed into broilers as is producer 2, and hence the derived demand curve for feed of producer 2 is above that of the other two. As a result of this efficiency on the part of producer 2, he is willing and is able to pay more for a given quantity of feed than producers 1 and 3. This result demonstrates the essence of the competitive system; the factors of production go to those producers who can bid the highest for their services. This is demonstrated in Table 5.4 where it is seen that producer 2 would continue to purchase feed even at the very high price of $8 per cwt, while neither of the others could afford to do so. Also notice that producer 1 is more efficient than producer 3 as evidenced by the fact that he would continue to purchase some feed at $6 per cwt, while producer 3 would not.

SUPPLY OF A PRODUCT

In the previous section we illustrated how the demand for a factor of production can be derived from the total physical product curve. It was assumed that the producer maximized profit and that he knew the price for which he could sell his output (broilers), and the price of the input (feed). By varying the price of feed while holding broiler prices constant, the input demand curve has been determined. Using the same basic assumptions and information, a set of quantities that show how much producers individually and in aggregate will produce at different output prices can also be derived. In this case, input prices are held constant and the output price is allowed to vary. If the results are presented in a tabular form, it is called an *individual supply schedule*. The sum of the individual supply schedules is the *aggregate supply schedule*. If the output price-quantity relationship is depicted graphically, it is called an individual or aggregate supply curve. We will utilize the same broiler production function to derive the supply curve for broilers.

The derivation of the supply curve is based upon the relationship between the VMP of the input and the price of the output. Recall that VMP is calculated by multiplying MPP by the price of the output (P_y).

$$VMP_x = (MPP_x) \ (P_y) \tag{5.8}$$

It is clear from the above equation that changes in the price of the variable input (X) do not affect the production function (TPP) or, therefore, the marginal physical product function (MPP_x). Hence, any changes in the VMP_x curve arise either from changes in the production function (and hence the MPP_x curve) or from changes in the price of the final product (P_y). An increase in P_y will shift VMP_x to the right (see lower portion of Figure 5.5), while a decrease in P_y will shift it to the left. As a more concrete example, consider the VMP curves for feed in producing broilers in Figure 5.9. VMP_1 assumes a fixed price for broilers of \$100/cwt throughout its length. If the price of broilers increases, it will be reflected in a shift in VMP_1 to the right. For example, if the VMP at 1,250 pounds of feed is \$5 when broilers are \$100/cwt (VMP_1), a change in broiler prices to \$200/cwt increases VMP to some larger value, say, \$7.50 (VMP_2), while a decrease would shift it to some lower value, say, \$3.00 (VMP_0). Consequently, as the price of broilers increases, the VMP of feed used in the production of broilers shifts right to VMP_2, VMP_3, and VMP_4. It is the relationship between these shifts in the VMP curve, as the price of the output changes, and associated changes in the profit-maximizing level of inputs that is used to determine the supply curve for a product. The profit-maximizing level of input use is determined by equating VMP with P_x, and then going from the appropriate VMP curve back to the TPP curve.

In Figure 5.9, each VMP curve represents the value of the marginal product of the input (feed) at different prices for broilers. As the price of broilers increases from \$100/cwt, VMP shifts to the right. As it shifts, the level of input which maximizes profit also increases. Thus it can be seen in Figure 5.9 (part b) that at \$100/cwt (VMP_1) the profit-maximizing level of input is 1,250 pounds of feed per month; at \$200/cwt (VMP_2) it is 1,650 pounds; at \$300/cwt (VMP_3) it is 2,100 pounds; and at \$400/cwt (VMP_4) it is 2,650 pounds of feed per month. Given the profit-maximizing levels of input, the TPP curve in part a is used to find the

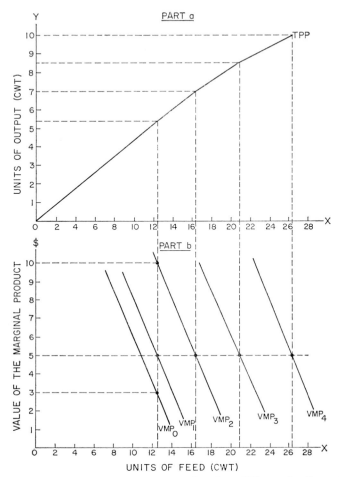

FIG. 5.9. Alternative levels of output as related to different broiler prices.

level of broiler output associated with that level of input. For example, 1,250 pounds of feed per month will yield 540 pounds of broilers; 1,650 pounds of feed, 700 pounds of broilers; 2,100 pounds of feed, 860 pounds of broilers; and 2,650 pounds of feed yields a profit-maximizing level of output of 1,000 pounds of broilers per month.

Thus for each broiler producer, we can write down the profit-maximizing levels of output associated with alternative broiler prices. This schedule of prices and quantities as developed from Figure 5.9 is shown in Table 5.5. This information is considered to be the supply schedule for broilers by a hypothetical producer. The quantities are those that he is willing and able to supply at each price of broilers, as-

TABLE 5.5. Schedule of prices for broilers and profit-maximizing quantities of broilers produced

VMP of Feed	Broiler Price per Cwt	Broiler Production per Month
	(dollars)	(pounds)
VMP_1	100	540
VMP_2	200	700
VMP_3	300	860
VMP_4	400	1000

Note: Derived from Figure 5.9, assuming constant feed price ($5 per cwt) and no change in other input prices.

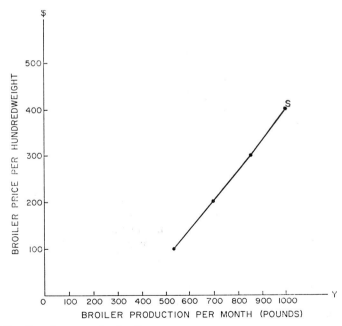

FIG. 5.10. Supply curve for broilers.

suming a certain price for inputs, a given total physical product curve, and that he wishes to maximize profit. The data from Table 5.5 are plotted as the supply curve in Figure 5.10. Given equivalent individual supply curves for other producers, the aggregate supply schedule for all producers could easily be obtained by summing the quantities that will be supplied at each price.

SUMMARY

The logic of the factor-product relationship is sufficient to develop the basic decision criteria needed to understand the principles used by entrepreneurs in maximizing profit. Given the physical production function relating inputs and outputs, when combined with price information on the inputs and outputs, a rule was developed to select the level of input usage which would maximize returns. Simply stated, this rule was that inputs should be added to the production process up to the point at which the value produced by the last unit of input is exactly equal to the cost of using that last unit ($VMP_x = P_x$). Furthermore, under certain assumptions, the VMP of the input is also the individual profit-maximizing entrepreneur's demand curve for that input. By aggregating the individual derived demand for the input over all users, the aggregate demand curve for the factor of production is obtained. Similarly, when the assumption of a constant output price is relaxed, the same basic factor-product relationship can be used to yield a supply curve for the product.

The above description of the production process involving one variable input is not very realistic. Nevertheless, the principles which have been developed in this section are general and will be applied to more complex production processes and decisions in the material that follows.

FACTOR-FACTOR RELATIONSHIPS

The production process discussed in the previous section dealt with only one input and one output; all other inputs were considered to be fixed in quantity. In the more usual case, a product will require the utilization of several inputs which are applied in varying proportion. Consider the case of a wheat farmer who combines labor hours and tractor power to grow wheat. Regardless of the level of labor hours and tractor power he is currently using, he could have produced the same output of wheat by utilizing less of one and more of the other.[4] Automobile assembly utilizing a combination of labor and capital (la-

---

4. Generally, this statement applies to certain ranges of each input. In the above example one could not produce wheat with tractor power and zero labor, although the reverse is possible. In the more usual case one input can substitute for another only within certain ranges of both inputs.

bor-saving devices) is another example. The factory could always use more labor and less capital, or more capital and less labor, to assemble the same number of automobiles per unit of time. Labor unions are very cognizant of the ability of other factors of production to substitute for labor, and as a consequence, attempt in their negotiations with management to forestall this type of substitution. Transporting people to a downtown metropolitan area is a third example; it can be accomplished with many different combinations of private automobiles and public buses.

It is possible to view the economic problem in the above examples as either one of selecting the least-cost combination of variable inputs to produce a given level of output or as one of selecting the combination of variable inputs that will yield the greatest possible net revenue. In the material that follows, the first situation will be of major interest. The concepts presented build upon those developed in the factor-product relationship of the previous section.

PRODUCTION SURFACE

Suppose that two variable inputs—labor and nitrogen fertilizer—are applied to a given piece of land to produce corn. In this case, it is not sufficient to show how quantities of labor will affect the output of corn when a fixed quantity of land is used, nor is it proper to talk only of the effect of fertilizer. A schedule that shows how the production of corn varies when both nitrogen and hours of labor are varied is needed. An example is presented in Table 5.6. The table contains 17

TABLE 5.6. The production of corn (bushels) per acre utilizing different combinations of labor and nitrogen fertilizer

Man-Hours of Labor per Acre per Year	Pounds of Nitrogen per Acre per Year									
	0	40	80	120	160	200	240	280	320	360
	Yield of Corn in Bushels per Acre per Year									
0	0	0	0	0	0	0	0	0	0	0
2	37	69	91	107	119	127	129	121	108	79
4	41	73	100	120	131	140	143	138	118	96
6	37	68	94	116	127	133	137	137	121	103
8	32	59	83	100	113	120	125	127	121	105
10	26	50	68	87	100	105	110	111	109	100
12	18	37	50	68	79	86	91	94	93	89
14	8	24	37	50	58	65	69	71	71	70

production functions of the type described in the previous factor-product example. The columns of the schedule show how much product (bushels of corn per acre per year) will be produced when various quantities of labor are applied on an acre of land with fixed quantities of nitrogen fertilizer. Thus, with zero pounds of nitrogen, 2 hours of labor can produce 37 bushels of corn; 4 hours, 41 bushels; 6 hours, 37 bushels; and so on. This corresponds to a production function with one variable input, namely, labor. Similarly, with 80 pounds of nitrogen per acre, 2 hours of labor can produce 91 bushels; 4 hours, 100 bushels; 6 hours, 94 bushels; 8 hours, 83 bushels; 10 hours, 68 bushels; and 12 hours, 53 bushels.

The rows of the table show how much product results from the application of various amounts of fertilizer to a fixed quantity of labor. For example, given 2 hours of labor, no nitrogen yields 37 bushels of corn; 40 pounds of nitrogen yield 69 bushels; 80 pounds, 91 bushels; and 120 pounds, 107 bushels. Similarly, the production response for corn to various applications of nitrogen when hours of labor per acre per year are fixed at 4, 6, 8, 10, 12, or 14 can also be determined. From the complete table, one can determine how many bushels of corn will be produced by any combination of fertilizer and labor. Futhermore, alternative combinations of labor and nitrogen that produce the same level of output can also be determined. For example, it can be seen that 37 bushels of corn can be produced by applying no nitrogen and 2 hours of labor per acre, or no nitrogen and 6 hours of labor, or 80 pounds of nitrogen and 14 hours of labor. Similarly, 120 bushels can be produced with either 120 pounds of nitrogen and 4 hours of labor or 200 pounds of nitrogen and 8 hours of labor. The manager who wishes to produce 120 bushels of corn must decide which of these combinations to use.

The 17 subproduction functions of Table 5.6 can also be illustrated graphically. However, in the case of two variable inputs and one output, it is not drawn as readily as for one input and one output. A three-dimensional diagram is required because we are dealing with three quantities—pounds of nitrogen, hours of labor, and bushels of corn. Consider each of the yield figures in Table 5.6. For instance, the number 8 in the lower left-hand corner shows that no nitrogen and 14 hours of labor per year will yield 8 bushels of corn. Assume that for each of these yields a block of a certain height is drawn to represent the yield; the higher the yield, the higher the block. The result would be a solid, three-dimensional figure similar to Figure 5.11. It would show all the relationships between the three quantities—pounds of nitrogen, hours of labor, and yield of corn—per unit of time.

If the units of nitrogen and labor were extremely small, the steps in Figure 5.11 would be smoothed out and would form a surface shaped like Figure 5.12. This is the physical production surface. Any point on the surface represent the yield of corn in bushels per acre resulting from a particular combination of nitrogen and labor.

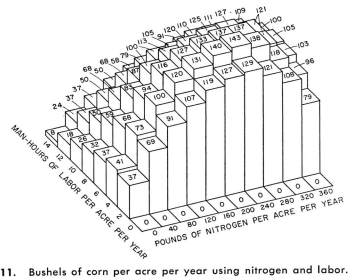

FIG. 5.11. Bushels of corn per acre per year using nitrogen and labor.

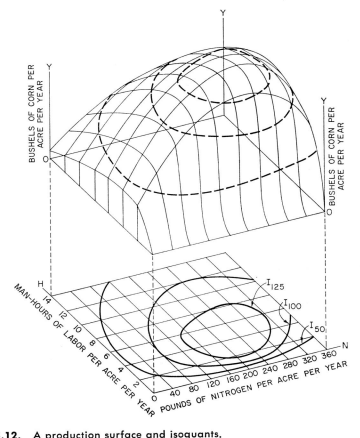

FIG. 5.12. A production surface and isoquants.

The surface clearly demonstrates the problem faced by the entrepreneur when more than one variable input is included in the production process. First, of all possible yields, what is the most profitable one? Second, what combination of nitrogen and labor should be used to produce that most profitable yield? The second question arises because a given corn yield can be produced using many different combinations of nitrogen and labor. To answer these questions we will need to develop the concept of an isoproduct curve.

ISOPRODUCT CURVE

The *isoproduct curve* is a curve showing all combinations of the two variable inputs that will produce a given level of output. It is more frequently called an isoquant ("iso" meaning equal, and "quant" meaning quantity). Thus the isoquant for 100 bushels of corn traces out all combinations of labor hours and pounds of nitrogen fertilizer which will produce 100 bushels of corn. Similarly, the isoquant for 125 bushels will trace out all combinations of the two inputs which will produce that yield.

The notion can be clarified by referring to the three-dimensional production surface in Figure 5.12. The isoquant labeled 100 in the lower part of the figure is a projection on the grid from the slice through the top portion of the figure. This slice traces out all those points on the production surface exactly 100 bushels above the base. If a perpendicular line is dropped from any point on the surface, it will trace out on the base grid those combinations of nitrogen and labor hours that will yield 100 bushels of corn. The reader can verify that these points are consistent with the data in Table 5.6. Furthermore, there are an infinite number of such isoquants in the production surface; we have drawn in only those for 50, 100, and 125 bushels of corn per acre per year. Just as isotherms connect all points on a map having the same temperature, and contour lines follow all points of the same elevation, so isoquants are lines connecting all points that yield the same product. Consequently, each production surface can be visualized as comprising a whole family of isoquants.

The isoquant is usually drawn in two dimensions, utilizing the idea of a contour line. If the production surface were viewed directly from above, and if isoquants were selected at certain production intervals and slices projected down on the base grid, we would obtain a flat, two-dimensional diagram as in Figure 5.13. The curve I_{100} represents all combinations of labor and nitrogen that can produce 100 bushels of corn, and I_{125} represents those combinations of inputs producing 125 bushels of corn. Because of the nature of the hypothetical data in Table 5.6, the isoquants are not exactly as we will draw them in future diagrams, but they are close.

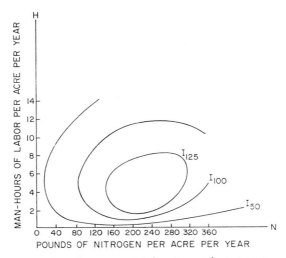

FIG. 5.13. Isoquants for nitrogen and labor in producing corn.

In Table 5.7, we have presented some hypothetical combinations of nitrogen and labor that could be taken from the production surface in Figure 5.12. Notice that through such a tedious process it would be possible to determine the least-cost combination of labor and nitrogen to produce corn. In this instance, it would be 4 hours of labor per acre per year, and either 80 or 140 pounds of nitrogen per acre per year, depending on whether one desired a yield of 100 bushels per acre or 125 bushels per acre. By assigning alternative prices to labor and nitrogen, we can determine the least-cost combination of inputs. In this example, a different set of prices for labor and nitrogen did not change the ideal input fix, but such is rarely the case.

LEAST-COST COMBINATION

There is a better way to search for the least-cost combination of inputs than the tedious calculations of Table 5.7. We can derive a formula or rule that will enable us to find the least-cost combination (*LCC*) of variable inputs more efficiently. It is the purpose of this section to develop such a decision rule.

To determine the quantities of two variable inputs that will produce a given output at minimum cost, the producer must know both the rate at which the variable inputs are substitutes in the marketplace (their relative prices) and how they substitute for one another in the production process (their technical substitutability). The rate at which they substitute for each other in production is termed the *marginal rate of substitution* (*MRS*), and the rate at which they substitute in the market-

TABLE 5.7. Alternative combinations of nitrogen and labor to produce 100 and 125 bushels of corn per acre per year, respectively

| Bushels of Corn per Acre per Year | | | | Variable Cost | | | |
| Y=100 | | Y=125 | | Y=100 | Y=125 | Y=100 | Y=125 |
X_1 (Nitrogen)	X_2 (Labor)	X_1 (Nitrogen)	X_2 (Labor)	P_{x_1}=$2 per pound P_{x_2}=$1 per hour	P_{x_1}=$2 per pound P_{x_2}=$1 per hour	P_{x_1}=$0.50 per pound P_{x_2}=$2 per hour	P_{x_1}=$0.50 per pound P_{x_2}=$2 per hour
100	2	190	2	$202	$382	$52	$ 97
80	4	140	4	164	284	44	74
90	6	150	6	186	306	51	81
120	8	240	8	248	488	68	128
160	10			330		90	

place is the *price ratio*. The least-cost combination of inputs X_1 and X_2 is achieved when the

$$MRS \text{ of } X_1 \text{ for } X_2 = P_{x_1}/P_{x_2} \tag{5.9}$$

We saw earlier that in producing a given level of output the utilization of an additional unit of input is profitable as long as its value of the marginal product (*VMP*) is greater than its cost (price). Since we are concerned with two inputs, X_1 and X_2, the best combinations should certainly require that each meet the above requirements. This condition is restated in Equations 5.10 and 5.11.

$$VMP_{x_1} = P_{x_1} \tag{5.10}$$

$$VMP_{x_2} = P_{x_2} \tag{5.11}$$

By dividing both 5.10 and 5.11 through by their respective input prices, each equation equals 1. Since $VMP_{x_1}/P_{x_1} = 1$ and $VMP_{x_2}/P_{x_2} = 1$, it follows that

$$VMP_{x_1}/P_{x_1} = VMP_{x_2}/P_{x_2} \tag{5.12}$$

Equation 5.12 implies that the criteria for cost minimization requires utilizing that level of X_1 and X_2 which equates the *VMP* of each input to its price. From previous discussions in the factor-product case, we know that the *VMP* of a factor is equal to its marginal physical product (*MPP*) times the price of the product; that is,

$$VMP_{x_1} = (MPP_{x_1}) \ (P_y)$$

$$VMP_{x_2} = (MPP_{x_2}) \ (P_y)$$

Substituting the above into Equation 5.12 yields

$$[(MPP_{x_1}) \ (P_y)]/P_{x_1} = [(MPP_{x_2}) \ (P_y)]/P_{x_2} \tag{5.13}$$

Dividing through by MPP_{x_2} and by P_y, and multiplying through by P_{x_1} yields

$$MPP_{x_1}/MPP_{x_2} = P_{x_1}/P_{x_2} \tag{5.14}$$

This equation states that the mixture of X_1 and X_2 should be such that the ratio of their *MPP*'s is equal to their relative prices. In other words, if the price of input X_1 is twice that of X_2, the utilization of X_1 should be such that its MPP is twice that of X_2. Notice also that the price of the output (P_y) drops out of Equation 5.13. This means that the price of the output has no influence on the least-cost combination of resources required to produce a given level of output. However, as we shall see later, the price of the output (P_y) does influence the profit-maximizing level of output. Equation 5.14 simply implies that, regardless of the level of output chosen, the variable cost of producing it will be minimized by applying the two inputs until the ratio of their physical productivities at the margin is equal to their price ratios.

Equation 5.14 can be further modified to make it even more meaningful and useful in the search for a simple decision rule for finding the LCC. By utilizing the definition of the MPP as the change in output divided by the change in input, further simplification is possible. By definition

$$MPP_{x_1} = \Delta Y/\Delta X_1$$
$$MPP_{x_2} = \Delta Y/\Delta X_2$$

Substituting the above into 5.14, and canceling the ΔY, we obtain

$$\Delta X_2/\Delta X_1 = P_{x_1}/P_{x_2} \tag{5.15}$$

where

$$\Delta X_2/\Delta X_1 = \text{marginal rate of substitution } (MRS) \text{ of } X_1 \text{ for } X_2$$

Equation 5.15 is identical to Equation 5.9. It states that the cost-minimizing combination of inputs is obtained where the MRS of X_1 for X_2 is exactly equal to the ratio of prices.

According to Equation 5.15, the determination of a least-cost combination depends in part on how the inputs are combined. This is described by the marginal rate of substitution (MRS). The rate of substitution indicates the amount by which X_1 must be changed to offset a change in the amount of X_2 to maintain production at a given level. It is usually defined as $\Delta X_2/\Delta X_1$, which is the slope of the isoquant at any given point.

The manner in which one input substitutes for another can be classified into three types of response depending on what happens to the MRS at different combinations of the inputs: (1) no substitution, (2) constant rate of substitution, and (3) changing rate of substitution. For the case in which no substitution is possible, the inputs can be combined in only one combination (a fixed proportion) for each level of output; no other way of combining inputs will yield the same amount of product.

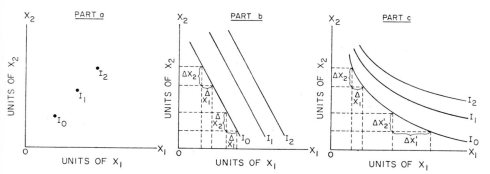

FIG. 5.14. Isoquants for different substitution possibilities between two inputs.

In this case the isoquant collapses into a point as illustrated in part a of Figure 5.14. An example would be the production of water from hydrogen and oxygen atoms. Each molecule of water is obtained by combining exactly two atoms of hydrogen with one atom of oxygen. Other examples would include tractors and drivers, automobile wheels and rubber tires, or fence wire and fence posts. As for the second case, one input substituting for another at a constant rate means that the amount of one input (X_2) replaced by the other input (X_1) does not change as the total amount of X_1 increases. In this case the MRS of X_1 for X_2 is constant, and the isoquant is a straight line. For example, if the MRS of two inputs in a particular production situation is equal to 2, two units of X_2 substitute for one unit of X_1 at all points on the isoquant. This case is illustrated in part b of Figure 5.14.

Examples of inputs that can be substituted at constant rates might include two grades of tractor fuel, two identical farm laborers, or corn and grain sorghum in the feeding of livestock. Generally when inputs can be substituted for one another at constant rates, this implies they are perfect substitutes and the LCC will result in the use of one or the other in the production process rather than some combination of the two. We shall see later that the one used will depend upon the relative prices of the two inputs.

The third case is where there is a changing rate at which one input substitutes for another; this is illustrated in part c of Figure 5.14. This means that the amount of X_1 required to permit a decrease in the utilization of X_2, while holding output constant, increases as the level of X_1 utilized increases. For example, in part c of Figure 5.14, $\Delta X_2/\Delta X_1$ is greater than $\Delta X'_2/\Delta X'_1$. Thus at low levels of X_1 (high levels of X_2), the marginal rate of substitution of X_1 for X_2 is greater than at high levels of X_1 and low levels of X_2. Decreasing rates of substitution arise because of the principle of diminishing marginal returns. Diminishing marginal returns implies that MPP decreases as more units of an input are utilized. Consequently, the MRS diminishes because MPP_{x_2} increases as less of X_2 is used, and MPP_{x_1} decreases as more of X_1 is used to replace the decreased X_2 (see Equation 5.14). There are many examples of decreasing MRS. Since the usual production function demonstrates diminishing marginal physical returns, the isoquants will typically be those shown in part c of Figure 5.14. Such isoquants are convex to the origin and are said to exhibit decreasing MRS as the level of X_1 increases.[5] Hay and grain in milk production, capital and labor in automobile assembly, and skilled and unskilled labor in building a house are all examples of inputs which can be substituted for one another over a certain range. As one uses a larger quantity of one of them, it is possible to economize on the other, but the ideal proportion changes with the absolute level of each.

The isoquants illustrate the left-hand side of Equation 5.15—the way in which one input substitutes for another in the production process. The right-hand side of Equation 5.15, the way one input can be substituted for another in the marketplace (price ratios), is illustrated graphically with an isocost (equal-cost) curve. When the prices of two inputs are known, all combinations of X_1 and X_2 which can be purchased for a given amount of money can be determined. For example, if P_{x_1} is \$0.60 per unit, and if P_{x_2} is \$1.00 per unit, then \$60 can purchase 100 units of X_1 or 60 units of X_2, or any combination of inputs X_1 and X_2 as shown by the \$60 isocost curve in Figure 5.15. Similarly, the \$30 isocost curve indicates that one can purchase 50 units of X_1 and 30 units of X_2, or 15 units of X_2 and 25 units of X_1. Because we have assumed that the cost of a unit of input is the same regardless of the amount purchased, the isocost curve has a constant slope equal to the (negative of the) ratio of the price of X_1 to the price of X_2. Because we saw how \$60 would purchase 100 units of X_1 if no X_2 were purchased, or 60 units of X_2 if no X_1 were purchased, we know that the intercept of the isocost curve will lie at 100 on the X_1 axis (abscissa), and at 60 on the X_2 axis (ordinate). The slope of the isocost curve can also be derived by recalling that the slope equals the "rise over the run." For our example, the rise is \$60$/P_{x_2}$ while the run is \$60$/P_{x_1}$. Forming the ratio of these two intercepts leaves P_{x_1}/P_{x_2} since the \$60 cancels out. This is illustrated in Figure 5.15.

---

5. The trait of "convexity to the origin" means that the slope of the isoquant increases from a large negative value to a smaller negative value as one moves to larger quantities of X_1. Conversely, as one moves to larger quantities of X_2, the slope of the isoquant becomes steeper. The negative slope throughout has nothing to do with the physical relationship between X_1 and X_2 but is simply a result of tipping the base grid of Figure 5.12 up to lay flat against the page as in Figure 5.13.

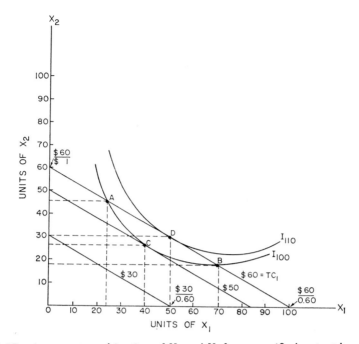

FIG. 5.15. Least-cost combination of **X₁** and **X₂** for a specified output level.

An alternative way to view the slope of the isocost curve follows. Let TC represent the total cost of using any volume of X_1 and X_2. Then

$$TC = (P_{x_1}) (X_1) + (P_{x_2}) (X_2) \tag{5.16}$$

To plot the isocost curve, modify Equation 5.16 by dividing through by P_{x_2} and rearranging terms to derive

$$X_2 = (TC/P_{x_2}) - (P_{x_1}/P_{x_2}) (X_1) \tag{5.17}$$

Now it is easy to see that when $X_1 = 0$, $X_2 = TC/P_{x_2}$; and when $X_2 = 0$, $X_1 = TC/P_{x_1}$. To make the isocost curve less general, we must specify the level of total cost to be considered—in the above example it was \$60. So, rewrite Equation 5.17 as

$$X_2 = (\$60/P_{x_2}) - (P_{x_1}/P_{x_2}) (X_1) \tag{5.18}$$

　　　　This is the equation of a straight line with an intercept on the vertical axis at $\$60/P_{x_2}$ and a slope of $-P_{x_1}/P_{x_2}$. This is the same isocost curve labeled TC_1 in Figure 5.15.

　　　　To return to the rule for the least-cost combination of two variable inputs (Equation 5.9 or 5.15), we can see that at point C in Figure 5.15 the rate at which the two inputs can be technically substituted for each other in the production process—the marginal rate of substitution of X_1 for X_2 (the slope of the isoquant at C)—is exactly equal to the rate at which the two inputs can be substituted for each other in the marketplace, that is, their price ratio (the slope of the isocost line).[6] At these levels of use for X_1 and X_2, 100 units of output can be obtained with the least possible variable cost. Similarly, for an output level of 110, point D depicts the least-cost combination of variable inputs.

　　　　Notice that because we have assumed that the prices of the inputs do not change in response to any action on the part of the firm, the isocost line has the same slope throughout; P_{x_1}/P_{x_2} is invariant with respect to combinations of X_1 and X_2. However, because of the physical aspects of production, we know that MPP_{x_1} and MPP_{x_2} change as the amounts of X_1 and X_2, respectively, are changed. Hence, as X_1 and X_2 are changed, the MRS of X_1 for X_2—which is, after all, a ratio of the two marginal physical productivities—varies. At point A, MRS is greater than is the price ratio—that is, MRS is a larger negative number; hence, the slope of the isoquant is steeper than the slope of the isocost curve. Recalling that the MRS is the ratio of the MPP of X_1 to the MPP of X_2, and that in Stage II of the production function the MPP of an input decreases as more of it is used, we can readily deduce that at point A, too much of X_2 is being used (its MPP is too low relative to X_1's MPP), and too little of X_1 (its MPP is too high relative to X_2's MPP). Thus X_1 should be substituted for X_2 in the production process. Conversely, at point B the opposite situation prevails with too much X_1 being used relative to X_2, and X_2 should be substituted for X_1. The adjustment process should continue until Equation 5.15 is satisfied; that will occur at point C.

　　　　Notice that the $\$60$ isocost line intersects the isoquant I_{100} at both points A and B. This means that either 46 units of X_2 and $23\frac{1}{3}$ units of X_1 or 18 units of X_2 and 70 units of X_1 could be used to produce 100 units of output. The cost of either combination would be $\$60$ (isocost curve $\$60$). However, since lower isocost curves represent lesser total cost, the same 100 units could be produced with the combination at C.

---

6. The MRS is defined as the negative of the slope of the isoquant (which itself is negative) and hence, even though the slope of the isocost line is a negative, it is convenient to write the decision rule as in Equations 5.9 or 5.15. Advanced texts show a great deal of variation in this regard—some equating MRS to $-P_{x_1}/P_{x_2}$, others using the approach taken here. At this stage, the student should be clear about the significance of the equality (instead of the sign).

At point C, 26 units of X_2 and 40 units of X_1 yield the same total output at a cost of $50.

In summary, point C is the least-cost combination of inputs that can be used to produce 100 units of output. In terms of the geometry of Figure 5.15, it is at the point where the lowest isocost line is just tangent to the isoquant I_{100}. Any higher isocost curve will intersect the given isoquant in more than one location, indicating that more than one combination of inputs can be used to produce the output at that given level of cost. Any lower isocost curve will not be tangent to the isoquant, thereby indicating that it is impossible to produce the given level of output with the lower cost.

FACTOR SUBSTITUTION WITH PRICE CHANGES

The economic logic of a minimum-cost combination is simple to apply. It states that given the ability to produce a given level of output with two different inputs, as long as the rate of substitution of one for the other is known, and as relative prices change, the substitution should be away from the more expensive input. For example, in a feeding situation, if the price of corn is twice that of barley, then at the current input mix, if one pound of corn substitutes for one pound of barley, it is obvious that too much corn is being utilized. Consequently, the feeding mixture should be adjusted to higher quantities of barley and lesser amounts of corn to achieve the least-cost feed combination. Furthermore, a change in the price ratio, resulting from an increase in barley prices, should cause the astute farmer to use less barley and more corn to the point where the ratio is again equal to the MRS.[7]

To illustrate this phenomenon, it is helpful to use Figure 5.16. Here TC_1 represents the isocost curve from Figure 5.15, where the price of X_1 was $0.60, and the price of X_2 was $1.00. Should the price of X_1 increase from $0.60 to $1.00, and should all $60.00 be spent on X_1, the entrepreneur would be able to buy only 60 units of X_1 instead of the 100 units he could formerly buy with the $60.00 (he could still buy 60 units of X_2 since its price is unchanged). From our earlier illustration, the slope of the isocost line is

$$(TC/P_{x_2})/(TC/P_{x_1}) = -P_{x_1}/P_{x_2} \tag{5.19}$$

Knowing that when the price of X_1 increases with the price of X_2 remaining unchanged the relative prices are different, we can deduce that the slope of the isocost line has changed, since it depicts relative prices.

7. Farm management specialists at state universities regularly publish conversion tables illustrating the relative values and substitution rates of one feed or grain for another. The human nutrition articles appearing in daily newspapers describe those foods that are the best nutritional buys and are another example of this economic principle.

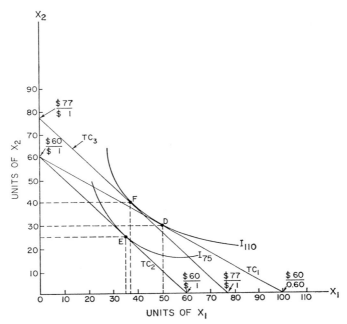

FIG. 5.16.   Least-cost combination of two inputs under two price ratios.

In this case, since P_{x_1} has increased, we know that $-P_{x_1}/P_{x_2}$ is now a larger negative number. Whereas before the ratio was $-0.6/1$, it is now $-1/1 = -1$. Instead of having a slope of -0.6, it now has a slope of -1.0. The new isocost curve is labeled TC_2 in Figure 5.16. Notice that the X_1 and X_2 intercepts of TC_2 are now both 60, indicating that with the new (higher) price for X_1, the entrepreneur could purchase 60 units of either by spending all $60.

From Figure 5.15 we saw that the entrepreneur could produce 100 units of output for $50, or, if he wished to spend $60, he could produce 110 units of output. To produce the 110 units, he would use 30 units of X_2 ($30) and 50 units of X_1 ($30) for a total outlay of $60. However, when the price of X_1 increases to $1 per unit, this same $60 will now buy fewer units of X_1, and hence result in less output. We see from Figure 5.16 that TC_2 is tangent to I_{75} (which represents 75 units of output) rather than to the initial isoquant (I_{110}). Now for $60 the entrepreneur could utilize only 25 units of X_2 ($25) and 35 units of X_1 ($35), which would yield 75 units of output. Thus, as the price of an input increases, the profit-maximizing entrepreneur uses less of it. Conversely, a decrease in its price will cause him to use more of it. Notice in Figure 5.16 that the reduction in use of X_1 is very substantial—from 50 to 35 (a decrease of almost one-third)—while the reduction in use of X_2, although its price did not change, is only 5 units.

Should the entrepreneur wish to achieve the original output level (I_{110}), it would require an outlay in excess of the former $60. This should be obvious since the price of one input (X_1) has increased from $0.60 to $1.00 per unit. Graphically this can be illustrated by a shift in the isocost line parallel to the new isocost line (TC_2), reflecting the new price ratio; this is TC_3. Notice that TC_3 is tangent to I_{110} at point F. Here 110 units of output could be attained utilizing 40 units of X_2 ($40) and 37 units of X_2 ($37) for a total outlay of $77 instead of the original $60.

EXPANSION PATH

Given that the entrepreneur can utilize two variable factors to produce a commodity, the first part of his management problem has been solved. The decision criteria for finding the combination of inputs to produce a given level of output at the lowest possible cost was shown to be at the point where the rate of substitution of one input for the other is exactly equal to their price ratio.

In earlier sections we described how an isoquant can be derived from the production surface for every possible level of output. Further, it has been demonstrated that for any given isoquant there is one input combination which has the lowest cost. Consequently, for every possible

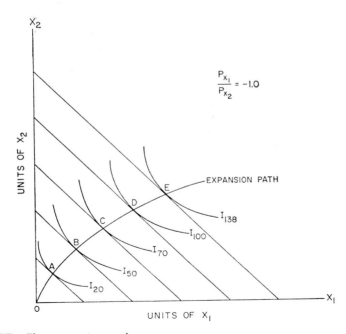

FIG. 5.17. The expansion path.

isoquant, a least-cost combination of inputs exists. This is illustrated in Figure 5.17.

The tangency points of the isoquants and the isocost curves depict the appropriate combination of inputs for each level of output and cost. The curve *ABCDE* connects all the points representing least-cost combinations and is called an *expansion path*. It is the path which a cost-minimizing entrepreneur would follow in expanding output. Our problem now is to determine which point on the expansion path *ABCDE* is the profit-maximizing one.

PROFIT-MAXIMIZING LEVEL OF OUTPUT

Conceptually, the problem of determining the profit-maximizing level of output is identical to that of the single-factor–product example of earlier sections. The best level is determined by proceeding out along the expansion path until the value of the additional product is exactly equal to the combined cost of the two inputs used to produce it. In other words, the entrepreneur moves from point *A* to point *B* to point *C* to *D,* until the marginal cost of the two inputs is exactly equal to the marginal value of the product they produce. There is no simple way of illustrating the most profitable input combination and output on an expansion path such as that shown in Figure 5.17. The best that can be said is that, as long as the additional cost of moving from one isoquant to the next is less than the additional revenue such a move generates, it is a profitable one. For example, if moving along the expansion path from *D* to *E* results in an increase in output worth \$38 and an increase in cost of \$35, the move from *D* to *E* is profitable. Furthermore, since the *VMP* was greater than the additional cost of the inputs, the entrepreneur should consider the possibility of expansion beyond point *E*. There is, however, a method of graphically finding the most profitable quantities of inputs and outputs. The inputs and outputs traced by the line *ABCDE* can be considered as a special subproduction function on the production surface. This concept is illustrated in Figure 5.18. The expansion path can be thought of as a special production function since it represents the least-cost combination of inputs associated with each level of output. Thus all points on the line *ABCDE* in Figure 5.17 are actually points on a least-cost production function *ABCDEFGH* which traces out the least-cost combination of inputs associated with each level of output on the production surface in Figure 5.18.

EQUIMARGINAL RETURNS

The general conclusions developed for two inputs also hold in the case of many inputs. The isoquants would be surfaces in (n) space as would the isocost relationships among n inputs. No matter how many inputs there are, the expansion path would still be a line, with each point

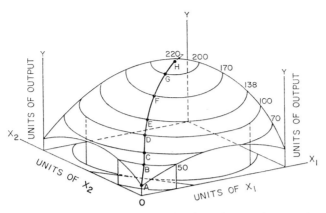

FIG. 5.18.   The production surface and the subproduction function.

on it representing the specific combination of inputs which minimizes the cost of that level of output. In this case a relative rise in the price of any one input will swing the expansion path away from the axis along which it is measured and thereby alter the proportion of inputs in favor of those whose prices did not change. As in the case with two inputs, profit would be maximized where the value of the marginal product of each input is equal to the price of that input:

$$VMP_{x_1} = P_{x_1}$$

$$VMP_{x_2} = P_{x_2}$$

$$VMP_{x_3} = P_{x_3}$$

$$\cdot$$
$$\cdot$$
$$\cdot$$

$$VMP_{x_n} = P_{x_n}$$

Each of the above equations must be satisfied simultaneously. Therefore, if one input costs twice as much as another input, it should be used at that level where its value at the margin is twice that of the other inputs. Furthermore, all inputs should be utilized up to the point where the contribution to revenue of the last unit of each is just equal to the cost of utilizing it. This is illustrated by Equation 5.20 and is a logical extension of Equation 5.12 to n inputs.

$$VMP_{x_1}/P_{x_1} = VMP_{x_2}/P_{x_2} = VMP_{x_3}/P_{x_3} \qquad (5.20)$$
$$= \ldots = VMP_{x_n}/P_{x_n}$$

The ratios are all equated to one on the assumption that the entrepreneur can obtain sufficient resources to increase output to the point that Equation 5.20 holds. It would always be profitable to do so, but if capital is limited, it may not be possible. For example, suppose a plant were utilizing three factors, X_1, X_2, and X_3, to produce a product (Y), and assume that $VMP_{x_1} = \$3$, $VMP_{x_2} = \$2$, and $VMP_{x_3} = \$4$. Further assume that $P_{x_1} = \$3$ per unit, $P_{x_2} = \$3$ per unit, and $P_{x_3} = \$2$ per unit. Then we would have

$$VMP_{x_1}/P_{x_1} = \$3/\$3 = 1;$$

$$VMP_{x_2}/P_{x_2} = \$2/\$3 = 0.67;$$

$$VMP_{x_3}/P_{x_3} = \$4/\$2 = 2$$

Clearly the three ratios do not satisfy the condition of Equation 5.20. It should be obvious that the plant is overutilizing input X_2, since the last unit, having cost \$3 to utilize, returns but \$2 of output. Therefore, by using less of X_2, MPP_{x_2} (and therefore its VMP) will increase eventually to \$3. After this adjustment, inputs X_1 and X_2 are being used at their optimum levels. Input X_3 is underutilized because the last unit costs \$2 but increases output by \$4. Clearly it would be profitable for the plant manager to obtain more of X_3 and use it to the point where its price and VMP are equal. Any further attempts to increase output by utilizing more of any one of the three inputs will result in a net reduction of profits because further applications of inputs will reduce their VMP's below input prices.

The situation is somewhat different when resources are limited. While Equation 5.20 still holds, the ratios would all equal some value larger than one. For example, suppose the plant described above was utilizing inputs X_1 and X_2 in such a manner that the following ratios were observed. The per-unit prices of the two factors are assumed equal as in the previous case.

$$VMP_{x_1}/P_{x_1} = \$30/\$3 = 10;$$
$$VMP_{x_2}/P_{x_2} = \$24/\$3 = 8$$

Assuming that resources are limited and it is impossible to increase the budget, it is still possible to increase profit. It is clear that by using one less unit of X_2 and applying that money to the purchase of an additional unit of X_1, the entrepreneur gains \$6 worth of output with no increase in input costs. This is because by utilizing one less unit of X_2 he gives up \$24 of output, but by spending the \$3 to buy one more unit of X_1 he gains \$30 of output, a net gain of \$6 (\$30 — \$24 = \$6). Because of the principle of diminishing marginal returns, shifting the expenditure for inputs from X_2 to X_1 will lower the MPP of X_1 and raise it for X_2. MPP_{x_1} decreases because utilizing larger quantities of X_1 means moving down the MPP_{x_1} curve. Consequently, VMP_{x_1} also decreases. MPP_{x_2} increases because employing lesser quantities of X_2 means moving up the MPP_{x_2} curve. Therefore, VMP_{x_2} will increase. Consequently, with a limited budget, it will always pay the profit-maximizing entrepreneur to shift utilization of resources from one input to another until the last dollar expended on each returns exactly the same amount. The concept is referred to as the *principle of equimarginal returns*. In our example, the manager would shift purchases from X_2 to X_1 up to the point where the ratios would be equal, say, at a VMP of \$27. He would then have the following situation:

$$VMP_{x_1}/P_{x_1} = \$27/\$3 = 9;$$
$$VMP_{x_2}/P_{x_2} = \$27/\$3 = 9$$

The profit-maximizing condition of Equation 5.20 holds. The last dollar expended for each input returns exactly the same amount. There is no method whereby the entrepreneur can increase profit. Given the limitation on the budget, he is at the optimum combination of inputs and output. If, however, he should suddenly find his budget for buying inputs expanded, then he would increase the utilization of both inputs up to the point where all ratios equal one.

SUMMARY

The factor-factor case is seen to be a mere extension of the factor-product case, with the added realism of more than one variable factor. We have expanded the notion of a production function to that of a production surface, and then introduced the concept of an isoquant. The least-cost combination of the two variable inputs was introduced, with the decision rule being that point in input space where the isoquant becomes tangent to an isocost line. This point is where the marginal rate of substitution of one input for another in the production process is exactly equal to their ratio of prices. The concept of an expansion path was developed, and its role in viewing not only alternative input combinations but alternative levels of output was discussed. Finally, the factor-factor case was generalized to more than two variable factors through the principle of equimarginal returns.

To conclude the treatment of production economics, we now turn to the consideration of production decisions between more than one commodity.

PRODUCT-PRODUCT RELATIONSHIPS

In the previous discussion, the production process was examined principally from the input side. Decisions associated with the amount of one input to use in the production of a product, and the ideal combination of inputs to use in the production of one product, were thoroughly described. Decisions as to how to allocate resources among the alternative possible products that can be produced are also important. This is a problem facing practically all entrepreneurs. For example, the farmer must make choices between the number of hogs or beef cattle to raise, the acres of corn or hay or soybeans to plant, or the amount of milk or grain to produce. Similarly, the processor of vegetables must decide on the amount of his product that he will sell in cans and the amount he will sell as frozen; or General Motors must decide on the number of deluxe, standard, or custom bodies of each type of automobile it will produce. In this section we will consider those factors required to choose a combination of products or enterprises that will yield maximum net revenue. The logic presented is the formalization of the procedure used in budgeting or planning a business enterprise. The analysis assumes that output of a production process is known in advance (with certainty), and that prices associated with outputs and inputs are also known. It further assumes the entrepreneur can sell whatever quantity of output he desires at the going market price. Finally, it is assumed that the two outputs being considered are technically independent—by which we mean that the cost of producing one of them (Y_1) is not a function of the output level of the other (Y_2).

PRODUCTION POSSIBILITIES CURVE

Assume that the manager of a production process can utilize the same resources to produce more than one output and is thus faced with the problem of deciding how much of each product he should produce to maximize firm profit. Given his resource base, he is faced with two different production surfaces:

$$Y_1 = f_1(X_1, X_2, X_3, \mid X_4, \ldots, X_n) \tag{5.21}$$

$$Y_2 = f_2(X_1, X_2, X_3, \mid X_4, \ldots, X_n) \tag{5.22}$$

How much of each product Y_1 and Y_2 will be produced is dependent upon the level of inputs utilized in each enterprise. The level of inputs utilized in turn is dependent upon how many inputs are available to the manager. The two possible situations are (1) the entrepreneur has unlimited resources at his disposal or (2) resources are limited.

When the inputs X_1, X_2, and X_3 are available in unlimited quantities, the problem reduces to one of considering each enterprise within the firm as a separate decision. The appropriate level of input usage—and hence output—is determined as described by Equation 5.20. The manager equates the value of the marginal product of each input to its price and uses the optimum amount of resources in each enterprise. Given that inputs are not limited, increasing the amount of X_1, X_2, and X_3 utilized in the production of Y_1 will have no impact upon the amount available for use in the production of Y_2. Although the production processes are located physically in the same firm and under the same manager, they are not related to each other as far as production decisions are concerned. The term *unlimited* does not mean that the inputs are free, but simply that the entrepreneur has sufficient capital or resources at his disposal to purchase or acquire all the variable inputs he will need to maximize profit (by utilizing each input up to the point where its *VMP* is equal to its cost).

As pointed out in the discussion of Equation 5.20, when the amount of inputs is limited for lack of adequate capital, the optimum amount of each may not be used in each enterprise. Consequently, the decision to increase the output of Y_2 by utilizing larger quantities of inputs reduces the output of Y_1 since variable inputs must be diverted from the production of Y_1 to the production of Y_2. The task of the entrepreneur is to determine the most profitable combination of enterprises (outputs), given the limited resources at his disposal.

A production possibility curve is a useful device for illustrating two production functions in one 2-dimensional diagram. In this section we will describe a production possibility curve and its derivation from least-cost production functions. Table 5.8 illustrates the physical data for the production functions Y_1 and Y_2 above (Equations 5.21 and 5.22).

TABLE 5.8. Production functions for Y_1 and Y_2 using the least-cost combination of X_1, X_2, and X_3 ($m) in each

Outlays for Inputs (m)	Alternative Y_1	Products Y_2
$ 0	0	0
4	1	2
8	5	8
12	8	11
16	10	14
24	12	18
32	13	22
40	14	23

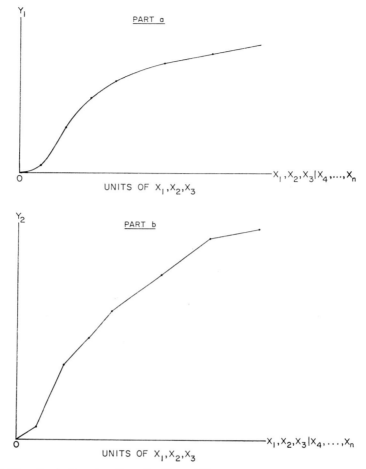

FIG. 5.19. Production functions for Y_1 and Y_2.

To simplify the graphics of the analysis, assume that the variable input is actually a composite of a least-cost combination of inputs X_1, X_2, and X_3 for each level of output of Y_1 and Y_2. Consequently, the *TPP* curves Y_1 and Y_2 are actually least-cost curves of total physical product; that is, the curves are taken along the expansion path in Figure 5.18. In this example the input bundle is first applied to the production of Y_1 only (column 2), and then to Y_2 only (column 3).

To further illustrate the concept in Table 5.8, consider parts a and b of Figure 5.19. There we have depicted two separate production functions—one for Y_1 and one for Y_2—with each reflecting the least-cost combinations of X_1, X_2, and X_3 applied to the complement of fixed factors $(X_4, \ldots, X_n)$. It is very important to note one crucial distinction at this point. As long as factor prices are assumed constant, it is possible to talk of physical quantities of X_1, X_2, and X_3 in their least-cost combination, or of total outlays for the three in their least-cost combination. This is the method used in column 1 of Table 5.8. For the sake of continuity between Table 5.8 and Figure 5.19, assume that the least-cost combination of X_1, X_2, and X_3 has a total per-unit cost of \$1. Then column 2 in Table 5.8 becomes Y_1 in part a of Figure 5.19, and column 3 becomes Y_2 in part b.

The decision process involves the application of X_1, X_2, and X_3—or similarly, the expenditure of \$m—for the production of either Y_1, Y_2, or some combination of the two. Suppose initially that financial conditions are such that \$24 represents the budget constraint for variable factors in some given unit of time. In this case, $m = \$24$ and the problem is to allocate \$24 such that Y_1 and Y_2 are produced in a combination that will maximize revenue to the firm. If all \$24 were spent in producing Y_1, there could be no Y_2, but it would be possible to obtain an output of 12 units of Y_1. Or, if all of it were spent to produce Y_2, there could be no Y_1, but the output of Y_2 would be 18 units. Additionally, if some of the \$24 were spent on producing Y_1, and the balance was spent on producing Y_2, it is possible to formulate a whole array of combinations of the two outputs. An example for $m = \$24$ and for $m = \$40$ is presented in Table 5.9.

The various possible combinations of output of both Y_1 and Y_2 that can be produced for $m = \$24$ are plotted in Figure 5.20 and connected by a smooth line drawn through the points. The resulting curve

TABLE 5.9. Production possibilities for two different levels of outlay for variable inputs in producing Y_1 and Y_2

| m = \$24 | | | | m = \$40 | | | |
| Expenditure (m) on Variable Inputs to Produce Y_1 and Y_2 | | Resulting Output of Y_1 and Y_2 | | Expenditure (m) on Variable Inputs to Produce Y_1 and Y_2 | | Resulting Output of Y_1 and Y_2 | |
Y_1	Y_2	Y_1	Y_2	Y_1	Y_2	Y_1	Y_2
\$ 0	\$24	0	18	\$ 0	\$40	0	23
8	16	5	14	8	32	5	22
12	12	8	11	16	24	10	18
16	8	10	8	24	16	12	14
24	0	12	0	32	8	13	8
				40	0	14	0

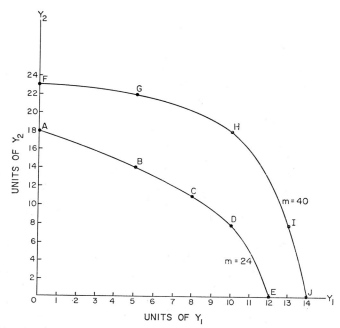

FIG. 5.20.   Production possibilities curves for two levels of total outlay.

$(ABCDE)$ is called the *production possibilities curve,* or the *transformation curve,* and it depicts the rate at which Y_1 can be transformed into Y_2; it shows what happens to the quantity of each product as the variable resources are transferred from producing Y_1 to Y_2. In other words, the production possibilities curve describes the maximum amount of one product (Y_2) which can be produced at particular levels of another product (Y_1) for a given level of expenditure for variable factors ($\$m$). In this sense some economists refer to the production possibilities curve as an *isocost curve,* since it does indeed relate various combinations of Y_1 and Y_2 that can be obtained with the same expenditure for variable factors.[8] While viewing the production possibilities curve as an isocost curve may aid the student in understanding the process, it is liable to cause confusion with the factor-factor case and hence that term will not be used again in the context of the product-product case.

In Figure 5.20 notice that the production possibilities curve for $m = \$40$ lies beyond that for $m = \$24$. This follows logically from the earlier discussion of a production function where a larger quantity of variable factors results in greater total physical product. In this case the

8. Lawrence A. Bradford and Glenn L. Johnson, *Farm Management Analysis* (New York: John Wiley, 1953), pp. 156–58.

output of each product separately—or in combination—is increased as the expenditure on variable factors increases.[9]

The Marginal Rate of Product Transformation. To discuss the decision-making process in the product-product case, it is first necessary to develop the concept of a marginal rate of product transformation. By definition, for a given point on the production possibilities curve, the marginal rate of product transformation describes the rate at which one output can be transformed into the other output.[10] Algebraically, it is

$$MRPT = \Delta Y_2 / \Delta Y_1 \tag{5.23}$$

The marginal rate of product transformation is actually the slope of the production possibilities curve. It can be illustrated graphically by drawing a tangent to the production possibilities curve midway between the two points in question. This is illustrated in Figure 5.21. At point A, a tangent line has been drawn to the production possibilities curve. The slope of this line is -1.33, and it is the exact $MRPT$ at that point.[11]

ISOREVENUE LINE AND OPTIMALITY

We have seen that the production possibilities curve depicts the rate at which two outputs can be substituted (exchanged) for each other in the production process. The concept of the rate at which two outputs can be exchanged in the market is the other item of data we need to determine the optimum combination of input.

From the earlier analysis of the factor-factor case, it should be clear that the rate at which products exchange for each other in the market is the ratio of their respective prices. Specifically, if we assume that a firm can produce both Y_1 and Y_2, the total revenue from the sale of those two products is written as

$$TR = (Y_1)(P_{y_1}) + (Y_2)(P_{y_2}) \tag{5.24}$$

9. At this point, it should become clear why the assumption of constant factor prices (for X_1, X_2, and X_3) is so crucial. If these prices increase, the entrepreneur could spend more for these factors yet still be on, say, the curve $ABCDE$. The difference would be that m would no longer equal $24 but some larger expense.

10. This is also defined as the marginal rate of product substitution. See John P. Doll, V. James Rhodes, and Jerry G. West, *Economics of Agricultural Production, Markets, and Policy* (Homewood, Ill.: Richard D. Irwin, 1968), pp. 135–41.

11. The student should be aware that computing the $MRPT$ as in Figure 5.21 will result in a slightly different value than computing it from the data in Table 5.9 (from which Figure 5.21 is derived). The reason is that in the figure we compute $MRPT$ at point A, while in the table we compute it between two points on the curve.

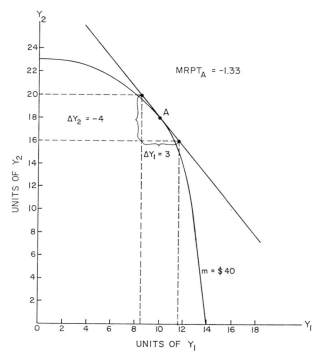

FIG. 5.21. The marginal rate of product transformation.

As with the total cost equation in the factor-factor case (Equation 5.16), rewrite the above as

$$Y_2 = (TR/P_{y_2}) - (P_{y_1}/P_{y_2}) \; (Y_1) \tag{5.25}$$

This is the equation of a straight line with a vertical intercept of TR/P_{y_2}, and a slope of $-P_{y_1}/P_{y_2}$. The effect upon the isorevenue line of changes in total revenue which it represents, assuming the relative prices remain unchanged, is to shift it away from the origin for higher levels of total revenue, parallel to its present slope. Lower levels of total revenue would be represented by parallel shifts toward the origin. As indicated, the analysis is identical to that for the isocost line in the factor-factor case. The steeper slope means that Y_1 is relatively more valuable than Y_2. An increase in the price of Y_1 will shift the Y_1 intercept closer to the origin. Conversely, a decrease in the price of Y_1 will shift the Y_1 intercept farther from the origin. Price changes for Y_2 would alter the Y_2 intercept. In both cases, the isorevenue line rotates around the intercept of the product whose price is unchanged. This will be explained in more detail in a subsequent section.

The criteria for determining the optimal combination of output such that revenue is maximized can now be developed. The rational producer will produce Y_1 and Y_2 in that combination which equates the rate at which the two are exchanged (transformed) in the production process ($MRPT$) with the rate at which they are exchanged in the market (relative prices). Specifically, this is given by

$$\Delta Y_2 / \Delta Y_1 = P_{y_1} / P_{y_2} \tag{5.26}$$

where $\Delta Y_2 / \Delta Y_1$ = marginal rate of product transformation.

This is depicted graphically in Figure 5.22.

The isorevenue line passes through all combinations of Y_1 and Y_2 that will yield a particular total revenue. For example, assume that Y_1 can be sold for \$2 per unit, and Y_2 for \$1 per unit; \$28 of revenue can be earned by selling 28 units of Y_2 and none of Y_1, or 14 units of Y_1 and zero units of Y_2. There are also other combinations of Y_1 and Y_2 that will earn \$28, such as 18 units of Y_2 and 5 units of Y_1, 8 units of Y_2 and 10

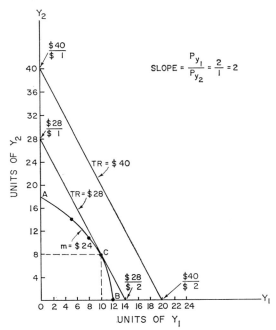

FIG. 5.22. The optimal combination of Y_1 and Y_2.

units of Y_1, or 4 units of Y_2 and 12 units of Y_1. When these and all other possible points that can earn $28 are plotted, they lie on a straight line called an *isorevenue line*. This isorevenue line, illustrated in Figure 5.22, passes through all combinations of Y_1 and Y_2 that can be sold for a total of $28. The line is straight because the prices of Y_1 and Y_2 do not change as the respective amounts of the two outputs change. The other iso-revenue line in Figure 5.22 represents a total revenue of $40. Notice that the expenditure of $24 on variable inputs ($m = \$24$) does not permit the realization of this higher total revenue. With $m = \$24$, a total revenue of $28 is all that is physically possible. As an exercise, the student should satisfy himself that no other combination of Y_1 and Y_2 will result in a higher revenue under the present set of output prices.

Another way of viewing the optimal mix of two products is to rewrite Equation 5.26 as

$$(\Delta Y_2) \ (P_{y_2}) = (\Delta Y_1) \ (P_{y_1}) \tag{5.27}$$

Now we see that if

$$(\Delta Y_2) \ (P_{y_2}) > (\Delta Y_1) \ (P_{y_1}) \tag{5.28}$$

the manager will know that an increase in the production of Y_2 will bring more revenue $(\Delta Y_2) \ (P_{y_2})$ than the resulting loss of revenue from reducing the production of Y_1: $(\Delta Y_1) \ (P_{y_1})$. Hence, in Figure 5.22 the firm is operating between points B and C on the production possibilities curve. Conversely, if

$$(\Delta Y_2) \ (P_{y_2}) < (\Delta Y_1) \ (P_{y_1}) \tag{5.29}$$

the entrepreneur would be better off to decrease production of Y_2 and increase the production of Y_1; that is, he is somewhere between point A and point C and should move toward C.

RELATIVE PRICES AND THE OPTIMUM COMBINATION OF OUTPUTS

Just as in the factor-factor case, we must concern ourselves with changes in the relative prices of the two outputs under consideration. In Figure 5.22 it was assumed that $P_{y_1} = \$2$, and $P_{y_2} = \$1$. We saw how this would lead to the production of 8 units of Y_2 and 10 units of Y_1, utilizing $24 for inputs and yielding $28 in total revenue. Assume that the price of Y_2 increases from $1 to $2. Since we know that the Y_2 intercept of an isorevenue line is given by TR/P_{y_2}, and we know that the isorevenue line will rotate around the intercept of the output whose price does not change, we can see that the new Y_2 intercept for the new isorevenue line (TR_2) representing \$28 will be \$28/\$2 = 14. The slope of the new isorevenue line is now (\$2/\$2) = −1. Notice that the Y_1 intercept has not changed since P_{y_1} did not change.

Following the price change, the entrepreneur can now realize \$28 of revenue (TR_2), but it is necessary to spend only \$12 on variable factors $(X_1, X_2, \text{ and } X_3)$ to realize that return $(m = \$12)$. Since the price of one of the outputs (Y_2) has doubled, it is intuitively obvious that the same level of total revenue can be obtained with a smaller expenditure on variable factors. In this case, 9 units of Y_2 (worth \$18) and 5 units of Y_1 (worth \$10) will bring \$28 of revenue. He will operate at point D in Figure 5.23.

However, assume that instead of being satisfied with only \$28 of total revenue the entrepreneur decides to spend as much as before on inputs. Hence, instead of continuing to spend \$12 on variable inputs, he once again spends \$24; that is, he again operates along the production possibilities curve $m = \$24$. But now, because of the optimization rule specified in Equation 5.26, he must be cognizant of the new price ratio between Y_1 and Y_2. This new ratio is given by the isorevenue line TR_2. *Shifting this line out parallel until it is tangent to the production possi-*

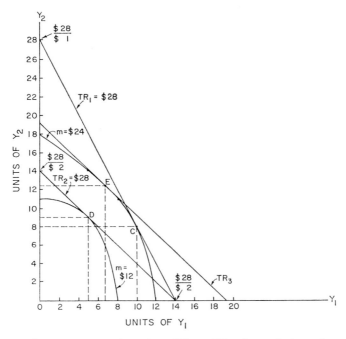

FIG. 5.23. The optimum combination of Y_1 and Y_2 when relative prices change.

bilities curve m = *$24 at only one point would result in tangency at point* E *in Figure 5.23.* At *E,* he would produce 6¾ units of Y_1 (worth $13.50) and 12½ units of Y_2 (worth $25) for a total revenue of $38.50, so for the outlay of $24 utilized initially, he now gets $10.50 more revenue. Hence, isorevenue line TR_3 represents $38.50 of total revenue. The student can determine the symmetry of the above analytics by determining the effects of other price increases and decreases in either Y_1 or Y_2.

GENERALIZATION TO MORE THAN TWO PRODUCTS

At the end of the discussion of the factor-factor case, we extended the analysis to the more general (realistic) situation where more than two variable inputs were utilized in production. In an analogous fashion, we will now extend the product-product case to include situations in which more than two outputs are produced by the same firm or decision-making unit. Recall that the optimality rule called for equating the marginal rate of product transformation with the ratio of prices. This was expressed formally as

$$\Delta Y_2 / \Delta Y_1 = P_{y_1} / P_{y_2} \tag{5.30}$$

If we assume that the firm produces goods Y_1, Y_2, and Y_3, we can write the optimality rule as

$$\Delta Y_2 / \Delta Y_1 = P_{y_1} / P_{y_2}; \tag{5.31}$$
$$\Delta Y_2 / \Delta Y_3 = P_{y_3} / P_{y_2};$$
$$\Delta Y_3 / \Delta Y_1 = P_{y_1} / P_{y_3}$$

That is, the entrepreneur would attempt to equate the marginal rate of product transformation for every pair of goods to the ratio of their respective prices. The expression $\Delta Y_2 / \Delta Y_1 = P_{y_1} / P_{y_2}$ can be rewritten as

$$(\Delta Y_2) \ (P_{y_2}) = (\Delta Y_1) \ (P_{y_1}) \tag{5.32}$$

But $\Delta Y_2 / \Delta Y_3 = P_{y_3} / P_{y_2}$ can also be rewritten as

$$(\Delta Y_2) \ (P_{y_2}) = (\Delta Y_3) \ (P_{y_3}) \tag{5.33}$$

Since the left-hand sides of both Equations 5.32 and 5.33 are equal, we know that the optimality rule calls for

$$(\Delta Y_1) \ (P_{y_1}) = (\Delta Y_3) \ (P_{y_3}) \tag{5.34}$$

This could have been derived as easily by rewriting the expression

$$\Delta Y_3/\Delta Y_1 = P_{y_1}/P_{y_3} \tag{5.35}$$

In general then, the optimality rule for n goods can be written as

$$(\Delta Y_1)\,(P_{y_1}) = (\Delta Y_2)\,(P_{y_2}) = (\Delta Y_3)\,(P_{y_3}) \tag{5.36}$$
$$= \ldots = (\Delta Y_n)\,(P_{y_n})$$

SUMMARY
  The product-product case is seen to be a more realistic extension of the factor-product case. First, it was necessary to develop the concept of a production possibilities curve. This was found to be—in the two-product case—a special case of allocating a fixed bundle of variable factors to either of two outputs exclusively, or to the two in some combination. The marginal rate of product transformation was developed as an indication of the rate at which one output could be transformed into (exchanged for) the other output in the production process. Revenue was seen to be maximized at that point where the marginal rate of product transformation is exactly equal to the price ratio for the two outputs. Next, the analysis was extended to show the effect of a change in relative prices on the optimal product mix. Finally, we extended the analysis to include the optimality rule for any number of goods.

SUMMARY
  In this chapter we have developed the analytical framework for understanding the role of economics in production decisions. The product-product case was seen to be concerned with the selection of several feasible products upon which the firm should concentrate its scarce productive factors. The exact mix of products was seen to be a function of their relative prices and the physical aspects of production which relate the relative effectivness of the firm in transforming variable factors into each of the several feasible products. As for the decision of how to produce a product at least cost, the factor-factor case was developed to illustrate that the firm is being most efficient when it combines its variable factors such that the ratio of their contribution to the value of output at the margin (their value of the marginal product) is equal to their ratio of prices.

DISCUSSION QUESTIONS AND PROBLEMS

1. In each of the following activities identify the inputs and outputs of the production surface.
   a. Producing corn
   b. Taking a math course
   c. Going to college
   d. Reduced air pollution
   e. Running a lakeside resort
   f. Running a high school
2. How would you measure the value of the marginal product of each of the above activities?
3. For each of the following pairs of inputs, draw the isoquant that to you describes the type of substitution that you think exists between them.
   a. Idaho and Maine potatoes to produce potato chips
   b. Regular and premium gasoline to power your automobile
   c. Coffee beans and water to produce coffee
   d. Labor hours and tractor horsepower to plow a field
   e. Your labor and a lawn mower to mow a lawn
4. For each of the following pairs of outputs draw the production possibilities curve that describes how the first output substitutes for the second, assuming a fixed level of the specified input.

INPUT	OUTPUT	OUTPUT
a. Hours of time	Your GPA	Going to the movies
b. Hours of time	Your GPA	Studying
c. Water	Hydrogen	Oxygen
d. Crude oil	Gasoline	Fuel oil
e. Potatoes	Chips	French fries
f. Advertising expenditures	Hamburger sales	Cheeseburger sales
g. Advertising expenditures	Hamburger sales	Malted milk sales

5. When we draw a production surface, we assume that the technology of production is given. What happens to each of the following, given an improvement in the technique of producing cornflakes?
   a. The total physical product curve
   b. The supply curve for cornflakes
   c. The demand curve for corn
   d. The demand curve for labor to manufacture cornflakes
6. In Japan, television sets are constructed with more hand labor and less mechanization than in the United States. Draw the isoquant and the isocost line that would explain the difference.
7. In Brazil most farms use labor-intensive production techniques and no mechanical power. Furthermore, most of the labor on the farm is family labor with no alternative sources of employment. Draw an isoquant and isocost line that would explain this combination of inputs.
8. Evaluate the following statements or recommendations:
   a. A good dairy farmer should be feeding one pound of feed for each three pounds of milk a cow produces.
   b. One should stop applying a resource at the point where the return from the last unit is the greatest.
   c. One should always attempt to maximize milk production/cow (or corn yields/acre).

    d. A farmer should continue applying fertilizer until he observes no further increases in the yields.

    e. Wisconsin corn producers should be applying an annual treatment of at least 200 pounds of 10-10-10 fertilizer per acre of corn each spring before or at planting time.

9. In Figure 5.16 the initial situation is assumed to be $P_{x_1} = \$1.00$; $P_{x_2} = \$1.00$; and $TC_2 = \$60.00$.

    a. What is the level of use of X_1 and X_2?

    b. What is the level of output?

    c. Assume P_{x_1} falls to \$0.60. What are the new levels of X_1, X_2, and of output?

    d. Assume the entrepreneur wished to produce only 75 units of output. What is the new level of total outlays for this production level?

    e. Assume P_{x_2} falls to \$0.60 per unit. What are the new levels of X_1 and X_2? Also, what output could now result from an outlay of \$60.00?

SUGGESTED READINGS

BASIC

Bishop, C. E.; and Toussaint, W. D. *Introduction to Agricultural Economic Analysis.* New York: John Wiley, 1958, Ch. 4–6, 9–12.
    (a) The Production Function: Chapters 4–6; (b) Factor-Factor Decisions: Chapters 9 and 10; (c) Product-Product Decisions: Chapters 11 and 12.

Castle, Emery N.; Becker, Manning H.; and Smith, Frederick J. *Farm Business Management: The Decision-Making Process.* New York: Macmillan, 1972.
    See especially Chapter 2.

Dillon, John L. *The Analysis of Response in Crop and Livestock Production.* New York: Pergamon Press, 1968.
    An excellent treatment of production economics.

Doll, John P.; Rhodes, James V.; and West, Jerry G. *Economics of Agricultural Production, Markets, and Policy.* Homewood, Ill.: Richard D. Irwin, 1958, Ch. 2–6.
    (a) Poduction Functions: Chapters 2–4; (b) Factor-Factor Decisions: Chapter 5; (c) Product-Product Decisions: Chapter 6.

Heady, Earl O. *Economics of Agricultural Production and Resource Use.* New York: Prentice-Hall, 1952, Ch. 2–9.
    (a) The Production Function: Chapters 2–4; (b) Factor-Factor Decisions: Chapters 5 and 6; (c) Product-Product Decisions: Chapters 7–9.

Lipsey, Richard G.; and Steiner, Peter O. *Economics,* 2nd ed. New York: Harper & Row, 1969, Ch. 14–16, 23.
    (a) The Theory of Production: Chapters 14–16; (b) Demand for Factors: Chapter 23.

Samuelson, Paul A. *Economics,* 8th ed. New York: McGraw-Hill, 1970, pp. 17–28, Ch. 27, 28.
    (a) Theory of Production: Chapter 27; (b) Pricing Factor Inputs: Chapter 28.

Snodgrass, Milton M.; and Wallace, Luther T. *Agriculture, Economics, and Growth.* New York: Appleton-Century-Crofts, 1970.
    See Chapter 12 for a treatment of production principles.

ADVANCED

Carlson, Sune. *A Study on the Pure Theory of Production.* New York: Kelley and Millman, 1965.

A classic book on production theory that is highly recommended to the serious student of production economics.

Doll, John P. The allocation of limited quantities of various resources among competing farm enterprises. *J. Farm Econ.* 40(Nov. 1959):781–89.

An example of the empirical application of the marginal conditions to determining the most profitable allocation of limited resources within a farm enterprise.

―――. A comparison of annual versus average optima for fertilizer experiments. *Am. J. Agr. Econ.* 24(May 1972):226–33.

A good example of how multiple input (nitrogen and plant population) production functions are developed and the results utilized to examine questions of profitability under different conditions.

Ferguson, C. E. *Microeconomic Theory,* 3rd ed. Homewood, Ill.: Richard D. Irwin, 1972, Ch. 5, 6, 13, 15.

(a) The Production Function: Chapter 5; (b) Factor-Factor Decisions: Chapter 6; (c) Marginal Productivity: Chapter 13; (d) General Economic Equilibrium: Chapter 15.

Heady, Earl O.; and Dillon, John L. *Agricultural Production Functions.* Ames: Iowa State Univ. Press, 1961.

For the advanced student wishing to pursue production functions in depth.

Henderson, James M.; and Quandt, Richard E. *Microeconomic Theory: A Mathematical Approach.* New York: McGraw-Hill, 1958.

The authors develop the microeconomic concepts with the help of mathematics. The level of mathematics required is not great. There is an appendix to help the reader review needed concepts.

CHAPTER 6: COST AND REVENUE FUNCTIONS

The primary purpose of this chapter is to extend the analysis and concepts developed in Chapter 5 to further the understanding of firm decision making. It will be recalled that in the previous chapter the focus was on variable factors—their cost and their effect on output. Now, we will turn to a different perspective for making decisions, one which is concerned with the cost to a firm of producing one more unit of output. In Chapter 5 the entrepreneur utilized information on product price(s), physical production relations, and input price(s) to arrive at an ideal level of input usage; output was determined by first deciding on the ideal level of input usage. Here the entrepreneur utilizes the same information to make decisions regarding the ideal level of output, with input usage then depending on this prior decision.

With profit maximization the objective of the firm, the results of viewing the decision process from these two different perspectives will be the same. The level of input usage, the level of output, and firm profit will be identical. There are two advantages of this different perspective: (1) by focusing on output directly, the entrepreneur can gear his decisions to the additional revenue that will be forthcoming from increments of output; (2) by comparing increments to revenue with increments to production costs, the entrepreneur can quickly reach a decision as to whether or not a different output level is to be preferred. This concept will become clearer as the material is presented.

This chapter contains three main sections: (1) the concept of a cost function will be developed, and its relation to a production function will be detailed; (2) the concept of a revenue function will be introduced; and (3) the decision process of the firm will be developed by integrating the two concepts—cost and revenue. Drawing on the material in Chapter 5, it will be seen that the profit-maximizing level of output occurs where the increment to revenue from an additional unit of output (marginal revenue) is just equal to the increment to cost of production (marginal cost).

COST FUNCTIONS

Prior to the development of the various cost functions, it is necessary to digress momentarily to a discussion of the concepts of *cost* and of *profit*. To economists, all costs are defined in terms of opportunity costs. By *opportunity costs* the economist means the value sacrificed when a factor is used in one endeavor rather than being used in its next best alternative endeavor. This will become clear by identifying several categories of opportunity cost. The first is concerned with factors of production that are purchased by the individual firm. Here we assume that if firm A wants to employ an additional unit of X in the production of commodity Y, it must be prepared to pay the present user of that factor an amount sufficient to bid it away from employment by that user (firm B). If factor X currently contributes \$4 worth of output to firm B's total revenue, we say that its opportunity cost of being sold by firm B to firm A is \$4.[1] If it has a value at the margin in excess of \$4 to firm A (its value of the marginal product), firm A can afford to bid the factor away from employment in firm B. The obvious example of this phenomenon is found in labor markets where one firm hires away from a competing firm an outstanding worker or a particularly good manager. In this case the value of the factor (labor or management) is greater in firm A than in firm B, and economic efficiency is served by having the reallocation occur.

The second category of opportunity costs is those that must be imputed by the firm. By imputed we mean that no explicit transaction occurs, yet the firm must consider the cost as a legitimate business expense. Two common examples of imputed opportunity costs are the expense of using the owner's capital in the enterprise, and the depreciation on plant and equipment. If the owner retains a stock of capital for use in the firm, it is necessary to charge as an expense the value foregone by not utilizing that money in its next best alternative. If that alternative is in a savings account at a nearby bank, the interest foregone by not putting it in the savings account is an opportunity cost to the firm of using the money in that way; it represents what the owner could have realized by employing the money in its next best use. The other imputed cost is that of depreciation on plant and equipment. If the entrepreneur fails to set aside money for the day that it becomes necessary to replace equipment, there is an incorrect accounting of the full cost of doing business. This depreciation is an opportunity cost that must be considered.

Other examples of opportunity cost more familiar to nonbusinessmen would be (1) the amount of money sacrificed to have a steak for dinner rather than a hamburger, (2) the income lost by storing money in a piggy bank rather than in a savings account, (3) the income sacrificed by an hourly worker for sleeping late, and (4) your reduced

1. This assumes that firm B represents the next best alternative use of factor X.

score on an examination as a result of spending the weekend at the beach instead of studying. These latter views of an opportunity cost, though only some of them pertain to actual money amounts, are also of importance.

In summary then, the concept of opportunity cost is central to all economics, and the student should begin to think in terms of all actions—and failures to act—as having their price. This price is the opportunity cost. In some instances this will be a price that exists in the marketplace; in other instances it is only imputed. But regardless of its degree of explicitness, it must be considered in any decision process. Before turning to the issue of cost functions, it is necessary to consider one more momentary digression—the concept of profit.

Several concepts of profit are employed in economics and it is necessary at this point to draw a distinction and to relate the concept of opportunity costs to that of profit. Traditionally, profit is defined as the difference between the total revenue of the firm in a given time period and the costs incurred by the firm for that same period of time. But which costs? Costs as an accountant might reckon them? Or as viewed by an economist? If profit is defined as the difference between total revenue and total opportunity costs, then if a firm is earning zero profit in a certain period of time, all is well. This implies resources are allocated in an optimal fashion. The term *normal profit* has come to mean the difference between total revenue and total actual costs, implying that if a return to capital and risk taking were imputed one would get to the economist's notion of opportunity cost. If some firms in an industry are more than covering all explicit and implicit opportunity costs, some would say they are earning "extra-normal" profit. Using the opportunity cost notion of costs, others would reply that they are merely making a positive profit. In the balance of this chapter—and in later chapters—we will view all costs from the opportunity-cost point of view. When we later talk of the implications of positive and negative profit in spurring a reallocation of resources, it should be understood that our cost curves are defined to include all opportunity costs of the firm.

TOTAL COST FUNCTION

Knowing how the prices of factors of production are determined, we can specify the total cost function and define it as the minimum possible cost of producing any given level of output.[2] Assume that Equation 6.1 is the production function for product Y, using inputs X_1 through X_n:

$$Y = f(X_1, X_2, \ldots, X_5 \mid X_6, X_7, \ldots, X_n) \qquad (6.1)$$

2. This is analogous to the situation with the production function which is defined as representing the maximum level of output attainable from any given combination of variable and fixed factors. Certainly a lower level of production is possible but the production function depicts the maximum.

In the preceding chapter we developed the concept of a least-cost production surface as the surface which, for each level of output, represents the least-cost combination of inputs required to produce that particular level of output. Since the production function in Equation 6.1 indicates that five variable factors are utilized in the production of Y, along with a number of fixed factors, we can express the total cost of producing Y as a function of the quantities of the various inputs multiplied by their respective prices. This formulation is depicted in Equation 6.2:

$$TC = (X_1)(P_{x_1}) + (X_2)(P_{x_2}) + \ldots + (X_n)(P_{x_n}) \qquad (6.2)$$

where

$$
\begin{aligned}
TC &= \text{total cost of production} \\
X_i &= \text{factors of production } (i = 1, \ldots, n) \\
P_{x_i} &= \text{prices (opportunity cost) of factors } (i = 1, \ldots, n)
\end{aligned}
$$

As an illustration of how costs of production might be classified, consider the hypothetical figures in Table 6.1. It is seen that, just as with the inputs, production costs are classified as variable costs and fixed costs.

Column 2 of Table 6.1 depicts the variable costs associated with production of Y. *Variable costs* are the costs associated with adding

TABLE 6.1. Hypothetical costs for the production of different quantities of output **Y**

Y	Total Variable Costs $(X_1, \ldots, X_5)$	Total Fixed Costs $(X_6, \ldots, n)$	Total Cost $(X_1, \ldots, X_n)$
(1)	(2)	(3)	(4)
0	$ 0	$10	$10
6	5	10	15
14	14	10	24
20	22	10	32
26	29	10	39
30	35	10	45
32	40	10	50
34	44	10	54
36	47	10	57
36	49	10	59

variable inputs to the production process. They will occur only if production is carried on. Generally accepted examples of variable costs would be labor, electricity, gasoline, and raw materials. Column 3 of Table 6.1 depicts the costs associated with the fixed factors. These costs will be incurred even if zero output is produced and are therefore commonly called *fixed costs*. Examples of fixed costs are real estate taxes, insurance, depreciation on equipment, interest on a loan, and amortization costs of land.

It should be noted that costs become fixed only after they have been incurred. Consequently, the point of view from which they are being considered may change their inclusion in fixed or variable costs from one situation to the next. For example, to the entrepreneur who is contemplating building a new plant, the interest he must pay on borrowed money is a variable cost until after the plant is built, from which time it is considered to be a fixed cost. Whether a particular item will be considered a fixed or variable cost also depends upon the length of time implicit in the production process. Generally, production can be considered in the short run or the long run. By *short run* is meant a period of time in which output can be altered but the basic size of the production facility cannot be changed. The *long run* is a period of time long enough to allow output to be changed by varying both the level of variable inputs as well as the size of the production facility. For instance, in the production function of Equation 6.1, the short-run planning period would be a period long enough to allow changes in inputs X_1 to X_5 but not inputs X_6 to X_n. The long run would be a period of sufficient length to allow the entrepreneur to alter all inputs if he so wished.

As an example, consider a bicycle assembly plant. The entrepreneur could adjust the amount of labor on a day-to-day basis by paying overtime, hiring part-time employees, or putting on two shifts. This factor can vary in the short run and its cost comprises the short-run variable cost. The depreciation on his plant, interest on any mortgage, and taxes would continue regardless of whether he produced zero or 200 bicycles a day. These would be considered as the fixed costs. However, if the reference period is considered to be sufficiently long, say 6 months to 1 year, the entrepreneur could also adjust the size of his plant in response to changes in demand for bicycles. If the enterprise is unprofitable, he could close down and sell the business, thereby eliminating fixed costs. If the demand for bicycles is growing, he could install automatic equipment or build a new and larger plant, as well as train and hire more laborers. Hence, it is conventional to characterize the situation by saying that in the long run there are no fixed costs.

It should be clear by now that what is short run to one entrepreneur may be long run to another; it depends upon the point of view from which one is planning a production process. For example, a dairy farmer would have the following types of costs: investment in buildings and in a dairy herd, land for pasture and crops, labor costs, and feed costs. If an individual entrepreneur is debating whether or not to go into the dairy business, all these costs would be considered as variable. He would have to include all of them in determining the appropriate (least-cost) combination of these inputs in milk production and whether or not to enter the business. During the planning phase, all the costs would be considered as variable because none of them has yet been incurred. However, once he has entered the business of producing milk, he would have incurred the costs of buildings, equipment, land, and a dairy herd. In this case these would be considered as fixed costs, and variable costs would probably be limited to feed and labor. If the length of time over which he is planning production is lengthened, he would be able to change the level of output by adjusting buildings, land, and cow numbers.

Thus, because the length of time required to change all inputs is dependent upon the commodity, the definition of short run and long run varies from one product to another. In the case of beef, the short run might be considered approximately 2 to 3 years because it could take that length of time to increase the basic breeding stock. For poultry, the short run is much less, while for a bicycle assembly it might be 6 months. In all three cases, the short run would be that length of time during which it is impossible to alter the size and nature of the basic production plant (which, in two of the three cases, includes animals).

Up to this point we have been discussing costs in rather abstract conceptual terms; we now turn to the more concrete (yet still conceptual) side. Specifically, there is a distinct relationship between the cost function of Equation 6.2 and the production function of Equation 6.1. A hypothetical relationship is illustrated in Figure 6.1.

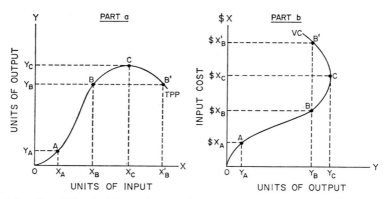

FIG. 6.1. The "classical" production function and its corresponding variable cost curve.

In part a of Figure 6.1 a hypothetical production function with only one variable input (X) is shown. This merely means that other factors which are also variable in the short run are—for the present analysis—being held constant.[3] In part b of Figure 6.1 we have plotted output (Y) on the horizontal axis instead of on the vertical axis as in part a. Of greater interest is the fact that the vertical axis in part b now depicts production costs—in this example consisting only of the expense of purchasing units of X. The units on the vertical axis of part b are $(P_x)(X)$ while the units on the horizontal axis of part a are merely X. Notice that the cost curve is a mirror image of the production function; the point at which diminishing marginal returns set in on the production function (the inflection point, A) also shows up on the cost curve as an inflection point (A). Likewise, there is direct correspondence for that point where average physical product is a maximum (B), and for the point where total physical product is a maximum (C).[4]

At this point we will expand the notion of production costs to include several categories, all of which are important to the individual firm. We start by disaggregating total costs of production into fixed costs and variable costs. Then we will introduce the concepts of average fixed cost, average variable cost, average total cost, and marginal cost.

FIXED COSTS AND VARIABLE COSTS

The total physical product curve depicts the effects on output of applying increments of the variable factor(s) to the complement of fixed factors. Hence, the cost curve derived from the production function reflects only variable costs. To incorporate fixed costs into Figure 6.1 (part b), it is necessary to recognize that fixed costs are those incurred by the firm but which are not a function of (do not vary with) output. Thus part b of Figure 6.1 can be modified to that of Figure 6.2.

Notice that in Figure 6.2 the variable cost curve of Figure 6.1 (part b) has been displaced upward by the amount of fixed costs (FC). Also notice that the shapes of the variable cost curve (VC) and the total cost curve (TC) are identical. Further note that the vertical difference between the two curves $(VC$ and $TC)$ is exactly equal to the magnitude of fixed cost $(FC = d)$.

To clarify the distinction between the three types of costs, hypo-

3. We will now abbreviate the designation of inputs on the input axis from the more extensive $(X_1|X_2, \ldots, X_n)$ to the more convenient X. It should be understood that this designation implies one variable input (X) applied to a complement of other factors $(X_2, \ldots, X_n)$. Some of the inputs in $X_2, \ldots, X_n$ may be varied in the short run, but are held constant in this analysis.

4. The student should note that input levels X_B and X'_B both result in an output level of Y_B (part a of Figure 6.1) and that the rational entrepreneur would never use X'_B. Similarly, in part b of Figure 6.1, output level Y_B could be obtained with a cost for X of either $\$X_B$ or $\$X'_B$. The entrepreneur, who spent $\$X'_B$ when $\$X_B$ would do, would obviously be irrational.

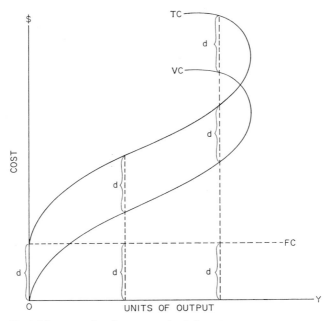

FIG. 6.2. Variable costs, fixed costs, and total costs.

TABLE 6.2. Cost schedules of a hypothetical firm producing antismog carburetors for mini-bikes

Output Y	Costs			Per-Unit Costs			Marginal (MC)
	Fixed (FC)	Variable (VC)	Total (TC)	Fixed (AFC)	Variable (AVC)	Total (ATC)	
(1)	(2)	(3)	(4)	(5)	(6)	(7)	(8)
0	$7,500	$ 0	$ 7,500	...	...	...	
							$3.00
1,000	7,500	3,000	10,500	$7.50	$3.00	$10.50	
							0.50
2,000	7,500	3,500	11,000	3.75	1.75	5.50	
							1.00
3,000	7,500	4,500	12,000	2.50	1.50	4.00	
							1.50
4,000	7,500	6,000	13,500	1.88	1.50	3.38	
							2.00
5,000	7,500	8,000	15,500	1.50	1.60	3.10	
							3.00
6,000	7,500	11,000	18,500	1.25	1.83	3.08	
							5.00
7,000	7,500	16,000	23,500	1.07	2.29	3.36	
							8.00
8,000	7,500	24,000	32,500	0.94	3.00	3.94	

thetical cost data for a manufacturing process are presented in Table 6.2. It is assumed that the firm has a fixed plant on which it must pay interest on the mortgage, property taxes, depreciation, and office salaries totaling $7,500 annually. Its variable costs include raw materials and supplies, selling expenses, power, and assembly line labor. The variable inputs are assumed to be in least-cost combination at every output level.

PER-UNIT COST CURVES

While to this point we have introduced three kinds of costs—variable costs, fixed costs, and total costs—four other kinds of costs are of interest to the economist as detailed in Table 6.2. Their importance derives from their critical role in the decision process. These four costs are (1) average fixed cost (AFC), (2) average variable cost (AVC), (3) average total cost (ATC), and (4) marginal cost (MC). Their computation and use in decision making are symmetrical to that of the average and marginal physical product curves. Each will be defined and described in the following sections.

AVERAGED FIXED COST

Average fixed cost is the fixed cost per unit of output; it is calculated by dividing fixed cost by the level of output (FC/Y). For example, in Table 6.2 the average fixed cost of producing 2,000 carburetors is $3.75 each—calculated by dividing $7,500 by 2,000 (see column 5).

One characteristic of the AFC is important to remember: average fixed cost falls continuously as more and more output is produced. This is true because, by definition, fixed costs are independent of output. Thus a fixed amount of cost is divided by increasingly larger output. For example, in Table 6.2 as output increases from 1,000 to 8,000 units, the fixed costs decline since the $7,500 is being spread over larger and larger amounts of output. This is illustrated in Figure 6.3, where column 5 of Table 6.2 is plotted as the curve AFC. The AFC curve continually declines, approaching closer and closer to the horizontal axis. Thus one effect of increasing total output is to lower fixed costs per unit.

AVERAGE VARIABLE COST

Average variable cost is computed by dividing variable cost by the quantity of output (VC/Y). In Table 6.2 it is obtained by dividing the total variable costs of production at each level of Y in column (3) by the corresponding output level. Because of the principle of diminishing marginal returns, average variable costs decrease, reach a minimum, and then begin to increase. In our example, variable costs per carburetor

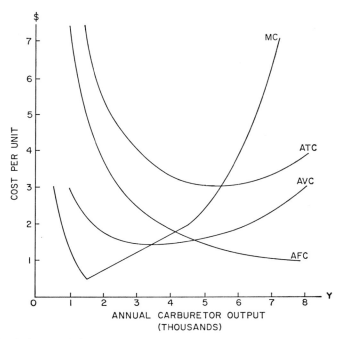

FIG. 6.3. Relation of the per-unit cost curves.

reach a minimum at 3,000 to 4,000 units annually. This is illustrated by curve *AVC* in Figure 6.3.

AVERAGE TOTAL COST

Average total cost is computed by dividing total cost by the quantity of output (TC/Y). It is the average of all costs per unit of output. In Table 6.2 the average total cost of production for 6,000 units is $3.08, computed by dividing their total production cost of $18,500 by 6,000. Since the total cost ($18,500) is the sum of variable cost ($11,000) and fixed cost ($7,500), it can be shown that *ATC* is the sum of *AVC* and *AFC*. The student can prove this by checking that column 7 is actually the sum of columns 5 and 6 in Table 6.2, and that the height of the *ATC* curve in Figure 6.3 is the *sum* of the heights of the *AVC* curve and the *AFC* curve at any given level of output.

Average total cost also reaches a low point but at a larger output than for the *AVC* curve (see Figure 6.3). This occurs because although *AVC* begins to increase, the fall in *AFC* offsets any increases in *AVC*. However, at some large level of output, the rate of decline in *AFC* will not offset rates of increase in AVC, and ATC begins to rise. The low point of the AVC curve is at 3,000 to 4,000 units of output, while average total costs are at a minimum around 5,300 units of output.

Notice that, as output levels increase, the vertical distance between average variable cost and average total cost becomes smaller and smaller. This is because the vertical distance between them represents average fixed cost which is continually declining.

MARGINAL COST

Marginal cost is defined as the additional cost necessary to produce one more unit of output. Ideally it is obtained by subtracting the total cost of producing Y units of output from the cost of producing $Y + 1$ units of output. Algebraically, it is generally expressed as

$$MC = \Delta TC/\Delta Y = (TC_2 - TC_1)/(Y_2 - Y_1) \qquad (6.3)$$

where

$$
\begin{aligned}
TC_2 &= \text{total cost of producing } Y_2 \\
TC_1 &= \text{total cost of producing } Y_1 \\
Y_2 &= \text{new output} \\
Y_1 &= \text{old output}
\end{aligned}
$$

Since the concern is with changes in per-unit cost, ΔY is generally taken to be 1.[5] This is illustrated in column 8 of Table 6.2 where the marginal cost reflects the change in total production cost per carburetor as the plant increases its output from, say, 3,000 to 4,000 carburetors per year. The marginal cost curve is depicted in Figure 6.3

The marginal cost of production is affected only by variable costs, since, by definition, it reflects the additional cost from additional output per unit of time. This change is reflected by changes in variable costs only.

RELATIONSHIPS AMONG COST CURVES

It is important that the student understand the relationship of the various cost curves to the production function and the relationship among the different cost curves.

5. It should be noted that marginal cost is always used as a per-unit concept. In this example we have depicted increments of output as being 1,000 but marginal cost is still the change in cost per unit for an increment of output. Additionally, when dealing with noncontinuous (discrete) increments, marginal cost is, in fact, an average over the interval of change.

To initiate this discussion of cost curves, we list the formulae for the different types of curves:

$$TC = FC + VC \tag{6.4}$$

$$AFC = \frac{FC}{Y} \tag{6.5}$$

$$AVC = \frac{VC}{Y} \tag{6.6}$$

$$ATC = \frac{TC}{Y} = \frac{FC}{Y} + \frac{VC}{Y} = AVC + AFC \tag{6.7}$$

$$MC = \frac{\Delta TC}{\Delta Y} = \frac{\Delta VC}{\Delta Y} \tag{6.8}$$

It is essential that the reader understand the relationship of MC to AVC and ATC. Part of the symmetry of the cost curves arises out of the fact that they are derived from the production function. Notice that AFC and MC have no relationship. This reflects the fact that total fixed costs are not affected by additional units of output. On the other hand, the relationship of the marginal cost curve to the average variable and average total cost curve is quite distinct. Knowledge of this relationship helps the economist solve everyday economic problems with a minimum of effort.

To facilitate the understanding of the relationship between MC and the average curves, consider the following example. Assume you have calculated your average grade in a course to be 80. If on your next exam you score less than 80, your overall average will fall because your marginal score is less than your average. If, on the other hand, your exam grade is above 80, your overall average will rise because your marginal grade is above your average grade. Furthermore, if your exam grade is exactly 80, your average will not change. This corresponds to the point where the marginal cost intersects (is equal to) average cost. The following diagram may also help.

Thus, when the marginal value is above the average, the average rises. When the marginal value is equal to the average, the average remains unchanged; and when the marginal value is below the average, the marginal value pulls the average down.

At this point it should be emphasized that the relationship of the marginal curve to the average curve is "one-way." By knowing what is happening to average costs, we can generalize about marginal costs but the reverse is not possible. Knowing whether marginal cost is rising

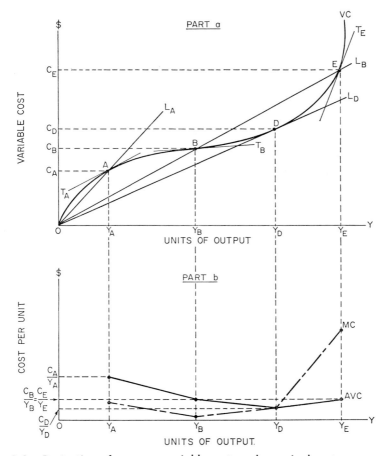

FIG. 6.4. Derivation of average variable cost, and marginal cost.

or falling will not allow us to state whether average cost is falling or rising. This is clearly illustrated in Figure 6.3 where the marginal cost falls and then starts to increase while the average cost curves continue to decline. As a final illustration of the relationship between the average and marginal curves, consider Figure 6.4.

In the upper portion (part a) of Figure 6.4, the curve labeled VC is the now-familiar variable cost curve. The straight lines (L_A, L_B, L_D, T_A, T_B, and T_E) require some explanation. From the definition of average variable cost (Equation 6.6), we know that it is the variable cost divided by output. Hence, at point A in Figure 6.4, average variable cost is given geometrically by C_A/Y_A; that is, the *slope* of the ray line L_A, which passes from the origin through point A, is C_A/Y_A and this is also average variable cost for Y_A units of output. Similarly, the slope of the ray line L_B is C_B/Y_B which is the average variable cost of producing Y_B units of output. Since the slope of L_B is constant and since it also intersects the variable cost curve at point E, we know that the average variable cost of producing Y_E is exactly the same as for Y_B. Since the slope of these rays lines is defined as average variable cost, it can be recorded as a magnitude (just as in Table 6.2) and it can also be plotted on a graph. In other words, since L_A is steeper than L_B (it has a greater slope), we know that the average variable cost of producing Y_A is higher than for producing Y_B (or Y_E for that matter). Now consider the ray line L_D. Point D is unique in that it represents that level of output (Y_D) at which average variable costs are as small as possible. Put differently, there is no other ray line from the origin with a slope less than that of L_D which can touch VC. Were we to plot the slopes of the ray lines as levels of average variable cost, our graph would be like AVC in part b of Figure 6.4. By connecting the four points we get a continuous curve. Notice that at output level Y_D, costs per unit of output (average variable cost) are a minimum. Similarly, since outputs Y_B and Y_E have the same ray line passing through VC, they must have the same AVC as shown in the lower portion of Figure 6.4.

Figure 6.4 can be used for a similar analysis regarding marginal costs. As those familiar with calculus will recognize, the slope of a curved line can be ascertained at any point as the slope of a tangent line at that point; that is, in part a of Figure 6.4, the slope of the curve VC at point A is given by the slope of the line T_A. Recalling that marginal cost is defined as the change in variable cost with respect to a change in output (Equation 6.8), it can be proved that this is the definition of the slope of the line T_A. Thus, by determining the magnitude of the slope of VC at various points along it, one can determine the marginal cost at those points. Since the slope of T_A is greater than the slope of T_B, the marginal cost at output level Y_A is greater than the marginal cost at output level Y_B. Notice that at point E the slope of T_E is much greater than the slope of either T_A or T_B. Also, notice that while the average variable cost is the same at both points B and E, the marginal cost is not the same. For point D, notice that the tangent line coincides with the ray line L_D. In other words, the slope of the tangent line is equal to the slope of the ray line. Thus, by the definition of the slopes, average variable cost equals marginal cost at point D (that is, at output level Y_D). Plotting the results in part b of Figure 6.4 results in the curve labeled MC.

If instead of using the variable cost curve in part a of Figure 6.4 we had employed the total physical product curve, part b of Figure 6.4 would have contained the marginal and average physical product curves. Since the variable cost curve is closely related to the total physical product curve, the corresponding average and marginal curves are also related. The relationship between the physical production function and the cost curves can easily be seen by referring to Figure 6.5. The marginal cost and average variable cost curves are mirror images of the marginal physical product and average physical product curves for the single variable factor case.[6] This relationship can be summarized in the following way:

PHYSICAL

(input–output)

1. When MPP is greater than APP,
   APP is *increasing*.
2. When MPP is equal to APP,
   APP is *maximum*.
3. When MPP is less than APP,
   APP is *falling*.

ECONOMIC

(output–cost)

1. When MC is below AVC,
   AVC is *falling*.
2. When MC is equal to AVC,
   AVC is a *minimum*.
3. When MC is greater than AVC,
   AVC is *rising*.

1. When MPP is greater than APP, MC is below AVC; when APP is increasing, AVC is decreasing.
2. When MPP equals APP, MC equals AVC; when APP is a maximum, AVC is a minimum.
3. When MPP is less than APP, MC is greater than AVC; when APP is decreasing, AVC is increasing.

In Figure 6.5, as in Figure 6.1, the close correspondence between the production function and the cost curves should be noted.[7] We have derived average physical product and marginal physical product curves from the production function and these are depicted in part c of the figure Additionally, the marginal cost and average variable cost curves have been derived from the total variable cost curve (part b) and are presented in part d. This concludes the treatment of cost curves and their relation to the production function. Decisions regarding ideal output require knowledge of these functions as well as information about the revenue side.

6. It is not possible to show symmetry (geometrically) for the multiple variable input case. The student can get an intuitive feel for the relationship in the two-factor case by referring to the previous chaper.

7. It will be noticed that since output beyond Y_c is not obtainable, the average variable cost and marginal cost curves (part d of Figure 6.5) do not exist beyond this point. At Y_c, MC goes to infinity since ΔY is zero. As for AVC, it actually begins to bend backwards, since more inputs are applied (which cost more money), yet output is actually less than at Y_c. To avoid undue confusion, this backward-bending portion of AVC is omitted from the figure.

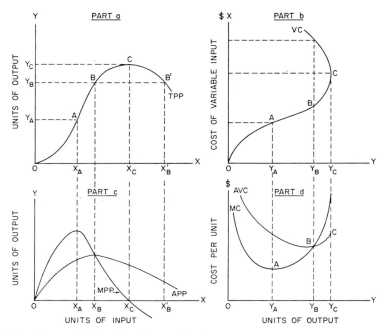

FIG. 6.5. The production function and cost curves.

REVENUE FUNCTIONS

In Chapter 5 we were concerned with the ideal mix of products, the ideal mix of inputs, and, to a certain extent, the ideal level of output for the individual firm. So far in this chapter we have introduced the notion of cost curves. We now introduce the concept of a revenue function—dealing first with total revenue, and then turning to average and marginal revenue.

TOTAL REVENUE

Total revenue is the total amount received by the seller; it is the value of production derived by multiplying total units of output by their price. Algebraically

$$TR = (Y) (P_y) \qquad (6.9)$$

where

$Y =$ quantity of output
$P_y =$ per-unit selling price of the output

Total revenue is also closely related to the production function since it shows the amount of money earned by a firm selling various levels of output. The production function relates physical outputs to inputs. Usually it is difficult, if not impossible, to compare directly physical units of outputs to inputs. Both must be in comparable units; monetary units provide this comparability. The total revenue curve translates the physical outputs into dollars and the total cost curve translates the inputs into dollars. The production function is, therefore, the intermediary through which revenues (through output) are related to costs (through the inputs).

    If the price of a commodity does not vary with the quantity of output a producer sells, total revenue will increase in direct proportion to increases in output. As an illustration, the levels of output for the production data of Table 6.1 and the accompanying total revenue schedule, assuming a constant output price, are shown in columns 1 and 2 of Table 6.3. The associated total revenue curve is plotted in part a of Figure 6.6. Notice that the slope is constant, implying total revenue is increasing at a constant rate. A higher price per unit will result in a steeper total revenue curve—a lower price, a lower curve. If the entrepreneur must lower his price in order to sell larger volumes of output, the total revenue curve will increase at a decreasing rate as shown in part b of Figure 6.6. As can be seen from columns 5 and 6 of Table 6.3,

TABLE 6.3. Hypothetical total revenue schedule under alternative output price schedules

Units of Output Y	Constant Price[a] Total revenue	AR	MR[b]	Declining Price Price	Total revenue	AR	MR[b]
(1)	(2)	(3)	(4)	(5)	(6)	(7)	(8)
0	$ 0	...		...	$ 0	...	
6	3.00	$0.50	...	$0.95	5.70	$0.95	0.95
14	7.00	0.50	0.50	0.84	11.76	0.84	0.76
20	10.00	0.50	0.50	0.75	15.00	0.75	0.54
26	13.00	0.50	0.50	0.66	17.16	0.66	0.36
30	15.00	0.50	0.50	0.60	18.00	0.60	0.21
32	16.00	0.50	0.50	0.57	18.24	0.57	0.12
34	17.00	0.50	0.50	0.54	18.36	0.54	0.06
36	18.00	0.50	0.50	0.51	18.36	0.51	0

Note: Based on output data from Table 6.1.

a. P_y = $0.50 per unit.

b. Actually <u>average</u> MR because of the discreet intervals.

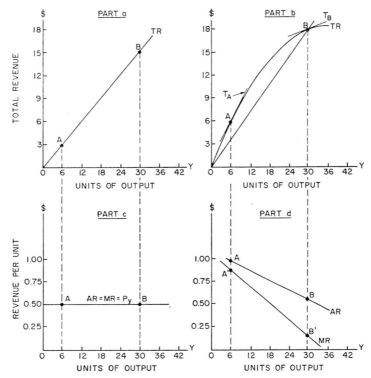

FIG. 6.6.   Revenue curves under two price assumptions.

the declining slope derives from the fact that price is decreasing; each additional unit of output adds less to total revenue than the previous unit.

In summary, when the entrepreneur can sell all his output at a constant price, the total revenue curve will be a straight line (that is, it has constant slope). If he must lower his selling price as his level of production increases, the slope of the total revenue curve will decrease. This difference in the behavior of the total revenue curve is most clearly described in terms of the marginal and average revenue curves.

AVERAGE REVENUE AND MARGINAL REVENUE

The average revenue and marginal revenue per unit of output are essential to decision making, with each playing a distinct role in the analytical process of determining the ideal output of a firm. Average revenue is defined as total revenue divided by the level of output:

$$AR = TR/Y \tag{6.10}$$

Average revenue is the value (price) received per unit of output. Marginal revenue is defined as the incremental revenue that could be earned from producing (and selling) another unit of output; it is the addition to total receipts (revenue) from selling one more unit of output. This is calculated as

$$MR = \Delta TR/\Delta Y = (TR_2 - TR_1)/(Y_2 - Y_1) \qquad (6.11)$$

where

TR_2 = total revenue from the new output level
TR_1 = total revenue from the old output level
Y_2 = new output level
Y_1 = old output level

The relationship among total revenue, average revenue, and marginal revenue is similar to the relationship among total physical product, average physical product, and marginal physical product, and the analysis of Chapter 5 will prove helpful in understanding parts c and d of Figure 6.6. The slope of a line from the origin to any point on the total revenue curve is the value of average revenue for that level of output. For example, in part a of Figure 6.6, the average revenue at 6 units of output would be the slope of the line OA. The slope is calculated by dividing the "rise by the run" as shown below.

$$AR_6 = \text{slope of } OA = \text{Rise/Run} = \$3.00/6 = \$0.50$$

This is plotted as point A in part c of Figure 6.6. Similarly, for 30 units of output (point B):

$$AR_{30} = \text{slope of } OB = \text{Rise/Run} = \$15.00/30 = \$0.50$$

This is plotted as point B in part c of Figure 6.6.

Notice that, since the slope of OA is identical to the slope of OB, average revenue is the same at all levels of output. This is simply another way of stating that the price of the output (P_y) is a constant—or the total revenue curve is a straight line. Part c of Figure 6.6 shows the average revenue (and marginal revenue) curve for a linear total revenue curve.

In the case of a declining price (part b), as output expands the slope of ray lines to the total revenue curve decline, average revenue declines as illustrated by part d of Figure 6.6.

$$AR_6 = \text{slope of } OA = \text{Rise/Run} = \$5.70/6 = \$0.95$$

This is plotted as point A in part d of Figure 6.6. For 30 units of output:

$$AR_{30} = \text{slope of } OB = \text{Rise}/\text{Run} = \$18.00/30 = \$0.60$$

This is plotted as point B in part d of Figure 6.6.

Marginal revenue for any output level was defined as the additional revenue to the firm from one more unit of output $(\Delta TR/\Delta Y)$ and can be depicted graphically as the slope of the total revenue curve at any given level of output. Without calculus the slope of a curve at a point is determined by the slope of a tangent line to that point. In part b of Figure 6.6, the slope of a tangent line (T_A) to TR at point A is approximately

$$MR = (\$7.50 - \$4.30)/(8 - 4) = \$3.20/4 = \$0.80$$

This magnitude is plotted as point A' in part d of Figure 6.6. The slope of the tangent line (T_B) at point B on the total revenue curve in part b is approximately

$$MR = (\$18.70 - \$17.40)/(34 - 26) = \$1.30/8 = \$0.16$$

This magnitude is plotted as point B' in part d of Figure 6.6.

The total revenue curve is linear when the price of output does not change as more of the firm's output is placed on the market (part a of Figure 6.6). Along such a linear function the ray line and a tangent line are everywhere coincidental to the function and hence average revenue equals marginal revenue at all levels of output. This is depicted in part c of Figure 6.6. Also notice that $AR = MR = P_y$. This can be verified by referring to columns 3 and 4 of Table 6.3.

In summary, a close examination of Figure 6.6 indicates a distinct relationship among the total, the average, and the corresponding marginal revenue curves. If average revenue is constant over the range of a firm's output, the firm can sell all it wishes at a constant price. In this case total revenue increases at a constant rate and average and marginal revenues are equal to each other and to the price of the product. If the firm must lower prices to sell larger and larger quantities of output, total revenue will increase at a decreasing rate. Average revenue will fall, and marginal revenue will be less than average revenue and will fall also. In fact, it can be proved that if AR is a declining straight line, MR will be declining twice as fast (it has twice the slope).[8]

8. For a further discussion of this, see C. E. Ferguson, *Microeconomic Theory* (Homewood, Ill.: Richard D. Irwin, 1972), pp. 93–96.

OPTIMUM LEVEL OF OUTPUT

It is now possible to combine the concepts of a cost function and a revenue function to discuss the optimum output level for the firm. First, recall that profit is defined as the difference between total revenue and total opportunity cost. Under the assumption that the entrepreneur desires to maximize profit, we will now develop the logic of how that objectve can be attained. Figure 6.7 presents an integration of the cost and revenue aspects of producing a commodity (Y); that is, the cost curves from Figure 6.2 have been combined with the revenue curve of Figure 6.6 (part a).

At an output level Y_A, it is clear that total cost (TC) exceeds total revenue (TR). The entrepreneur would be unwise to seriously consider this output level. As output is increased to Y_B, it is seen that total cost still exceeds total revenue. But notice that variable cost (VC) is just equal to total revenue. At Y_B the entrepreneur is able to cover the variable costs of production, though not fixed costs. Notice that, as output increases, total revenue is increasing faster—has a steeper slope—than total cost, and at an output level of Y_C, the two are equal. As output is increased toward Y_D, the difference between total revenue and total cost becomes an increasingly large positive amount. At Y_D, the two

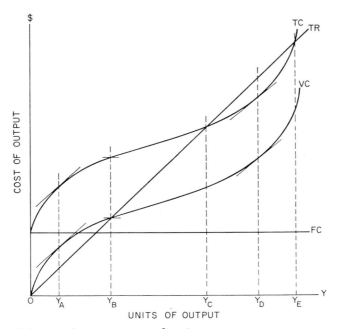

FIG. 6.7. Relation of cost to revenue functions.

curves (TR and TC) are as far apart as they will ever be, and as output is increased beyond Y_D, they begin to move together. At output Y_E, total revenue again equals total cost.

The following conclusions can now be drawn. At Y_A, total losses are maximized. At Y_B, variable cost, but not fixed cost, is covered by total revenue. At Y_C, all costs are covered. At Y_D, total revenue exceeds total cost by the greatest possible magnitude. At Y_E, again (as at Y_C) total revenue equals total cost.

With profit defined as $TR - TC$, it is clear that the entrepreneur would wish to maximize this difference. We have seen in Figure 6.7 that this difference is maximized at Y_D units of output. But there is a more direct way of determining optimum output levels than checking the difference between total revenue and total cost. That method is to employ the marginal revenue and marginal cost concepts from earlier sections. Recalling that marginal revenue is the slope of the total revenue curve, and that marginal cost is the slope of the total cost curve, it is possible to directly determine that output level where profit is a maximum. Notice in Figure 6.7 that at output level Y_A the tangent lines to both VC and TC are parallel to the total revenue curve. That means that marginal cost is equal to marginal revenue. However, it was seen earlier that Y_A was a loss-maximizing level of output.

Now consider output level Y_D. Here too, marginal cost (slope of TC and of VC) is equal to marginal revenue (slope of TR). But also notice that the difference between total revenue and total cost is positive. Hence, we can state that the necessary condition for profit maximization is that output be adjusted until that point is reached where the cost of one more unit of output (marginal cost) is exactly equal to the revenue derived from the sale of that incremental unit (marginal revenue).

But since there are two places in Figure 6.7 where this condition is met (Y_A and Y_D), it is not sufficient to insure that profit will be a maximum. Another consideration is required. To develop that concept, it will be helpful to derive the marginal revenue, marginal cost, average variable cost, and average total cost curves from the curves in Figure 6.7. These latter curves are depicted in Figure 6.8.

As can be seen from Figure 6.8, two levels of output (Y_A and Y_D) satisfy the necessary conditions of $MC = MR$. But at Y_A, where losses are maximized, MC is declining. On the other hand, where $MC = MR$ and profit is a maximum (Y_D), marginal cost is increasing. This leads us to the sufficient conditions for maximum profit: that $MC = MR$ and that MC be increasing. The area $P_Y DEP_D$ represents the total profit from the sale of Y_D units of Y. If the price of Y were only P_F, the firm would reduce output to Y_F and would have a zero profit level. That is the case since at Y_F per-unit revenue (P_F) is exactly equal to per-unit total cost (ATC). If the price should fall to P_B the entrepreneur would produce Y_B units of output, thereby covering variable costs of produc-

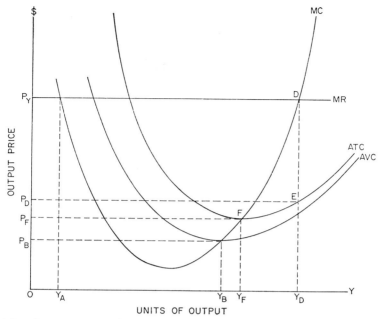

FIG 6.8.   Determination of optimum output level.

tion. At output prices less than P_B, losses would be minimized by not producing any output (see Figure 6.7). It should be recalled that a zero level of profit means that all factors of production, including management and capital, are earning their opportunity wage.

EFFECTS OF TECHNOLOGICAL CHANGE
ON THE IDEAL LEVEL OF OUTPUT

Considerable disagreement surrounds the proper way in which to view the phenomena of technological change and its impact —for the firm—on output levels, input levels, and profit. We have chosen to view technological change for the firm as something which causes a shift in the production function. An improvement in technology—represented by a better input (say, a more powerful fertilizer), a superior way to combine the same factors, or the introduction of a new factor of production into the firm—will shift the production upward as from TPP_0 to TPP_1 in part a of Figure 6.9.

First, notice the impact that such a shift in the production function has on the value of the marginal product (VMP) of X in the production of Y. With the old technology, a price of X at P_X would have implied the ideal level of use was X_0 units of the variable input, with a corresponding output of Y_0. With better technology, utilization of only X_0 units of the variable factor would result in the VMP of the

PART 2 : THEORETICAL ASPECTS

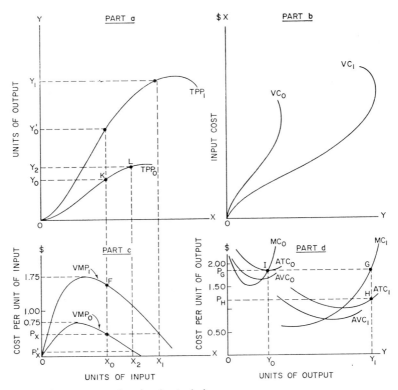

FIG. 6.9. The impacts of technological change.

factor X exceeding its price $(F > P_X)$, and the rational entrepreneur would increase use of X from X_0 to X_1. This would result in total output Y_1 instead of Y'_0 that would have resulted had the entrepreneur not increased use of X.

As regards the cost side, the technological improvement results in a shift in the variable cost curve from VC_0 to VC_1 (part b). The per-unit curves which are derived from VC_0 and VC_1 are presented in part d. To analyze the impact that this might have on profit, consider the curves MC_0, ATC_0, and AVC_0. At the old level of technology—and assuming that the price of output were P_G—marginal revenue (P_G) equals marginal cost at Y_0 units of output. Assume that product and factor prices are such that Y_0 represents the zero profit level for the firm (as shown in part d of Figure 6.9).

The improved technology results in a shift of the cost curves to MC_1, ATC_1, and AVC_1, respectively. Now, point G is where marginal revenue (P_G) is equal to the new marginal cost (MC_1), and Y_1 is the ideal level of output. Here, the area $P_G G H P_H$ represents profit earned

TABLE 6.4. Change in the value of capital investment per farm for selected types of commercial farms, 1957–1968 (current dollars)

Type of Farm	Capital Investment		Percent Change
	Average 1957-59	1968	
Wisconsin Dairy Farm			
TOTAL	$ 52,610	$ 89,520	70
Land and buildings	30,060	51,640	72
Livestock	9,260	14,980	62
Machinery and equipment	9,500	15,390	62
Corn Belt Hog-Beef Fattening			
TOTAL	92,920	166,640	80
Land and buildings	64,660	116,850	81
Livestock	11,900	21,610	82
Machinery and equipment	8,350	13,150	57
Corn Belt Cash Grain			
TOTAL	97,320	229,500	136
Land and buildings	88,230	208,320	136
Livestock	730	440	-40
Machinery and equipment	7,290	20,310	179
Irrigated Cotton Farm, Texas			
TOTAL	102,540	159,770	56
Land and buildings	86,560	138,750	60
Livestock	940	960	0
Machinery and equipment	14,520	19,560	35
Wheat-Pea Farm, Washington			
TOTAL	170,200	226,100	33
Land and buildings	149,300	195,920	31
Livestock	2,110	3,300	56
Machinery and equipment	17,020	25,670	51

Source: USDA, Farm Costs and Returns, Agr. Inform. Bull. 230, Sept. 1968.

by the firm as a result of the improved technology.[9]

If the improved technology occurs in some other industry than that being considered here, yet results in a fall in the price of factors used in producing Y, there would be no shift in the production func-

9. In later chapters it will be seen that the presence of profit in the short run entices others to enter the industry or for other firms currently in the industry to adopt the new technology. Both phenomena cause aggregate output to increase, eventually depressing price until profit is reduced—in the extreme case—to zero again for all firms.

tion for Y. Instead, assume, through technological improvement elsewhere, the price of X falls from P_X to P'_X. This would lead the entrepreneur to utilize X_2 units of X (where P'_X equals VMP_0) and to realize an output of Y_2. In this instance, we have moved along TPP_0 from point K (output Y_0) to point L (output Y_2). There would be a new set of per-unit cost curves (not shown) which would depict the level of profit corresponding to an output level of Y_2.

In general, economists conclude that technological change in agriculture has considerably increased the capital needs of the modern farm. Investment in a modern dairy farm includes milking parlors, milking machines, a bulk tank, etc., all of which require a substantial investment. Combines, tractors, and other special pieces of field equipment are other examples. As an illustration of the changes that have occurred in various types of agricultural activities, the data in Table 6.4 are instructive. Notice the change in capital investment over time within farm types, as well as the differential trends among farm types.

Because of the differences in acres of land required and types of equipment needed, the average capital investment per farm varies considerably from one type of farm to another. For example, a dairy farm in Wisconsin has a larger proportion of its total investment in livestock and equipment than any other type of farm. Similarly, a hog-beef farm in the Corn Belt has a larger percentage livestock and equipment investment than the cash-grain Corn Belt farm. Furthermore, wheat, cotton, and corn farms all have a major portion of their investment in land.

The substantial percentage changes in capital investment per farm in all types of farms dramatically illustrate the impact of technology on capital requirements; there has been a 50 to 150 percent increase in capital investments over the last 10 years. It is interesting to observe that the largest increases in capital requirements have come about in cropping enterprises, reflecting the greater technological advances in machinery and equipment that have taken place in these enterprises over the past decade.

Changes in technology not only require substantial investments but they also put a lower limit on enterprise size by increasing the level of fixed costs. Consequently, the farmer attempts to spread the fixed cost over more units of output by expanding the scale of his operations. This is reflected in Table 6.5, which shows the extent to which average farm size has increased over the same period of time. Technological innovation has also increased the price of land. Since land is the residual claimant on the profits of the enterprise, technological advance that increases profit increases the economic rent accruing to land. Even though the total amount of agricultural land in production in the United States has decreased slightly in recent years, the increase of eco-

TABLE 6.5. Change in the average size of farm for selected types of commercial farms, 1957–1968

Type of Farm	Size in Acres 1957-59	1968	Percent Change
Wisconsin Dairy Farm	157	192	22
Corn Belt Hog-Beef Fattening	247	285	15
Corn Belt Cash-Grain	232	320	38
Irrigated Cotton Farm, Texas	364	512	41
Wheat-Pea Farm, Washington	557	620	11

Source: USDA, _Farm Costs and Returns_, Agr. Inform. Bull. 230, Sept. 1968.

nomic rent accruing to land has been reflected in increases in the price of land. Coupled with the pressures put on land prices by urban expansion, this increase in the price of land has tended to encourage investments in land for its capital appreciation as well as for its productive potential. The net result has been cumulative and the cost of agricultural land has risen dramatically over the past decades.

In summary, technological progress is concerned with the new ways in which the basic factors of production are utilized. It involves new methods of production, new skills, and new inputs yielding lower costs and new products. Recent research has indicated that technological progress is a very important factor in the economic growth of a country. In a number of countries that have been studied it accounts for as large a proportion of the increase in output as do increased levels of inputs. One study concludes that increases in quantities of capital and labor account for about one-half the growth in total output in the United States, England, Canada, Germany, and Japan since World War II. The remainder is attributed to technological progress.[10]

LONG RUN VERSUS SHORT RUN

Up to the present, the cost curves have been derived from a production function that incorporates a given set of fixed and variable factors:

$$Y = f(X_1, X_2, \ldots, X_m | X_{m+1}, X_{m+2}, \ldots, X_n) \qquad (6.12)$$

10. E. Domar et al., "Economic Growth and Productivity in the United States, Canada, United Kingdom, Germany, and Japan in the Post-War Period," _Rev. Econ. Statist._ 46(1964):33–40.

where

$$Y = \text{level of output}$$
$$X_1, \ldots, X_m = \text{variable factors}$$
$$X_{m+1}, \ldots, X_n = \text{fixed factors}$$

This is a short-run description, assuming a cost commitment for a complement of fixed factors such as land, machinery, and buildings that does not change. However, in the long run, the entrepreneur can divest himself of these fixed factors by selling them or using them until they are worn out; or he may expand his fixed factors through investment. Thus, in this longer period of time, the manager can vary all inputs, including the size of plant, to obtain the most efficient size for the expected level of production. Consequently, the cost curves for different sizes of plants will be different. In the short run, it was seen that the average total cost curve rises because of the principle of diminishing marginal returns. As more and more of the variable factors (X_1 to X_m) are applied to the fixed factors (X_{m+1} to X_n) per-unit costs will initially decline and then rise. In a longer period, however, a new least-cost combination of all factors can be determined to most efficiently produce the new level of output. When all factors of production can be used in different proportions, the scale of operations is said to change,

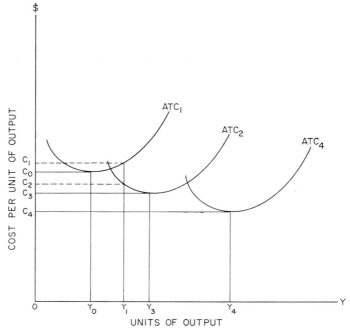

FIG. 6.10. Short-run average total cost under different scales of operation.

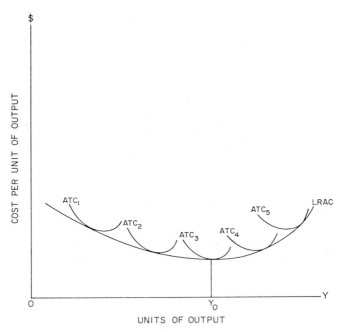

FIG. 6.11. The long-run average cost curve for a family of short-run average cost curves.

and the changes in cost that occur are said to be the result of *economies of scale.*

The quantity of fixed factors used determines the size or scale of the firm. The scale determines the limits on output per unit of time the firm can produce; within those limits the firm can vary its output by applying more or fewer variable factors to the fixed inputs.[11]

Each time the firm changes the level of fixed inputs X_{m+1} to X_n, the firm's scale of operation changes and the firm will be operating on a new set of short-run cost curves. For example, assume the firm in Figure 6.10 is operating on the short-run cost curve ATC_1, which has associated with it a particular combination of fixed factors. The least-cost level of output will be Y_0. If the entrepreneur wishes to increase output to Y_1, this can be accomplished in two ways: (1) by applying larger levels of the variable factors and hence expanding output along ATC_1, or (2) by changing the scale of plant to ATC_2 by utilizing a different mix of fixed and variable factors. The first method will increase

11. Economists also use a concept of *returns to scale*, which are defined as the increase in output arising from an increase in utilization of all factors in the same proportion. For our purposes, this is not a very interesting concept, since by now it is obvious to the reader that the input mix for a small firm to minimize costs is not a constant proportion of the optimal input mix for a very large firm.

per-unit total costs to C_1 because of diminishing marginal returns. In the short run this is the most feasible plan of action for the firm. In the longer run, however, the firm can build the new larger-scale plant with short-run costs ATC_2. The firm will be able to produce output Y_1 at a cost per unit of C_2 instead of C_1. The optimum level of output for this scale of plant is Y_3 units at a per-unit cost of C_3. Similarly, if expected output is Y_4 units, the optimum scale plant will have a short-run cost curve of ATC_4 and minimum per-unit costs of C_4.

In the long run then, it is possible to conceive of an infinite number of possible scales (or sizes) of firms. A series of average total cost curves would result from such an array and are depicted in Figure 6.11. The curve that is tangent to the family of ATC curves is called a long-run average cost curve. By definition, the long-run average cost curve ($LRAC$) depicts for any output level the locus of least-cost points for all possible scales of the firm.

Some economists refer to the long-run average cost curve as a "planning curve." The entrepreneur decides approximately what output level is desired and then uses that as a guide to build the optimum-size (least-cost) plant. Once the plant is constructed, output decisions imply movements along an average total cost curve (short run).

ECONOMIES AND DISECONOMIES OF SCALE

As the scale of firms becomes larger, certain economies of scale can be realized. This means that after adjusting all inputs optimally, the average cost of production decreases as plant size (scale) increases. In Figure 6.11 $LRAC$ decreases up to output Y_0 because of certain factors leading to lower costs at the large output levels. Economies of scale grow out of technical efficiencies in the production process; the two principal causes are (1) division and specialization of labor and (2) indivisibility of inputs.

Everyone is familiar with the economic advantages of specialization of labor. A small-scale plant does not have sufficient volume to permit its labor force to specialize on one phase of production at all times. On the other hand, a large plant can have one laborer learn a particular task because there is sufficient volume to keep him completely occupied at that one particular task. This process of specialization leads to shortcuts and increased speed, which in turn leads to lower cost per unit of output. It is well to point out that specialization can also lead to monotony which can counteract efficiency and lead to increasing costs.

The ability to lower costs by employing larger and better technological methods is also well understood. But this is primarily an advantage for the larger firms with more flexibility. New technologies, instead of being infinitely divisible, come in lumps. A new machine to automatically weld bicycle frames is not feasible for the small firms producing 4 or 5 bicycles per day. In contrast, as firms get larger they can buy automatic welders that have capacities of 25, 50, or 200 frames per day. The larger firm can install the welders in the combination that fits its daily output. Self-propelled combines, cotton pickers, corn pickers, milking parlors, automatic grain dryers, and sewage treatment plants can be efficiently utilized only on large production units. Another factor tending to lower costs is management. Up to Y_0 in Figure 6.11, better and more efficient management methods and practices reduce cost. Management is also frequently a "lumpy" input in that an entrepreneur must purchase either all or none of a new manager. Management, therefore, can be thought of as being incompletely divisible. Consequently, up to output level Y_0 the cost of management is spread over larger and larger levels of output, reducing average total cost. Beyond Y_0, the enterprise becomes so large that the coordination and communication in management systems must become so extensive that per-unit costs will eventually rise.

In summary, there are several forces that bring about economies of scale. First is the lumpiness of inputs. Second is the possibility for specialization of labor that comes with greater volume. But demand factors for the products of the firm, coupled with the nature of other producers in the industry, govern the limits of such expansion.

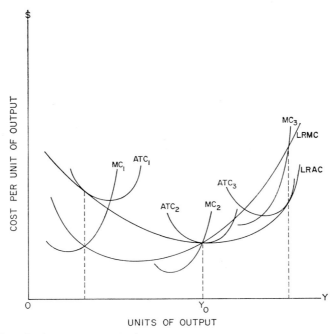

FIG. 6.12. The long-run marginal cost curve.

LONG-RUN MARGINAL COST

In addition to the long-run average cost curve, there is a long-run marginal cost curve that is defined as the change in total cost resulting from a one-unit change in the output of the firm when it has sufficient time to adjust its scale of plant. In Figure 6.12 notice that the long-run marginal cost curve intersects the various short-run marginal cost curves at that level of output corresponding with the point of tangency between short-run average total cost (ATC) and long-run average cost ($LRAC$). Also notice that, for output levels less than Y_0, the tangency of ATC and $LRAC$ is to the left of the minimum point of ATC, and for output levels greater than Y_0 the tangency point of ATC and $LRAC$ is to the right of the minimum point of ATC. It can also be seen that the optimum scale of plant in the long run is that where the short-run average cost curve is tangent to the long-run average cost curve at the minimum point of both. This occurs only for ATC_2 at Y_0.

Firms will not automatically construct the optimum scale of plant and operate at the least-cost per-unit level of output. As we shall see in later chapters, the actual scale of plant and level of output will vary with the level of demand for the product and upon the level of competition among firms in the industry (their number).

SUMMARY

This chapter is the logical corollary to the theory of production presented in Chapter 5. The cost function is derived from the production function, and provides the basis for decision making on the part of the entrepreneur. The revenue function also arises from the production function, and, together with the cost function, provides the basis for determining that output level that will maximize profit. The profit-maximizing level of output is that where the increment to cost (marginal cost, MC) is exactly equal to the increment to revenue (marginal revenue, MR), and where marginal cost is an increasing function of output. An important distinction between the short run and the long run must be recognized. While short-run output adjustments are possible, it is usually necessary to alter the scale of the firm (invest in a larger plant) to capture the significant scale economies which are potentially available from larger organizations. However, there is a point at which such cost savings begin to disappear. This occurs at the output level that corresponds to the minimum point on the long-run average total cost ($LRAC$) curve. The cost curves form a necessary link to the concept of commodity supply.

SUGGESTED READINGS

BASIC

Cochrane, Willard W. *Farm Prices: Myth and Reality.* Minneapolis: Univ. Minn. Press, 1958, pp. 85–106.
> Chapter 5 contains a good description of the process of technological change in agriculture; for the beginning student.

Doll, John P.; Rhodes, James V.; and West, Jerry G. *Economics of Agricultural Production, Markets, and Policy.* Homewood, Ill.: Richard D. Irwin, 1968, pp. 53–64, 154–81.
> A discussion of the costs of production and the production process through time.

Ferguson, C. E. *Microeconomic Theory.* Homewood, Ill.: Richard D. Irwin, 1968, pp. 207–42.
> An excellent discussion of the theory of cost. The mathematical footnotes contain excellent proofs of the economic propositions developed in this chapter.

Heady, Earl O. *Economics of Agricultural Production and Resource Use.* New York: Prentice-Hall, 1952, pp. 349–81.
> A theoretical discussion of returns to scale and its impact upon the size of the farm firm in the United States.

Lipsey, Richard G.; and Steiner, Peter O. *Economics,* 3rd ed. New York: Harper & Row, 1972, pp. 213–21, 227–69, 253–58.
> A good discussion of returns to scale and returns to size.

Samuelson, Paul A. *Economics.* New York: McGraw-Hill, 1970, pp. 441–58.
> Contains a good treatment of cost theory.

ADVANCED

Alchian, Armen A. Costs and Outputs. *Readings in Microeconomics.* Edited by William Breit and Harold M. Hochman. New York: Holt, Rinehart and Winston, 1968, pp. 160–72.
> Author proposes a different formulation of the firms' cost functions. By distinguishing between the rate of output and the volume of output, the author provides a theoretical explanation for quantity discounts.

Bachman, Kenneth L.; and Christenson, Raymond P. The Economics of Farm Size. *Agricultural Development and Economic Growth.* Edited by Herman Southworth and Bruce F. Johnston. New York: Cornell Univ. Press, 1967, pp. 234–57.
> The authors discuss the economics of farm size, scale, and resource productivity. They explore the problems of farm size in different regions of the world and then summarize our current state of knowledge with respect to the overall economic efficiency of different sizes of farms.

Berry, Russell L. Break-even analysis: A practical tool in farm management. *Am. J. Farm Econ.* 54(Feb. 1972):121–25.
> A good example of how the marginal principles developed in this chapter can be used by a firm manager in his decisions; describes the use of break-even charts in exploring alternative farm firm sizes. The break-even charts use linearized conventional cost and revenue concepts.

Brewster, J. M. The machine process in agriculture and industry. *J. Farm Econ.* 32(Feb. 1950):69–81.
> A discussion of the impact of technological advance on the organization of farm production at the firm level.

Herdt, Robert W.; and Cochrane, Willard W. Farm land prices and farm
    technological advance. *J. Farm Econ.* 48(May 1966):243–63.
        Illustrates the use of firm theory to explain the rising value of farm-
        land. The authors build a theoretical framework and use it to esti-
        mate the demand for and supply of farmland.
Krause, Kenneth R.; and Kyle, Leonard R. Economic factors underlying the
    incidence of large farming units: The current situation and probable
    trends. *Am. J. Agr. Econ.* 52(Dec. 1970):748–61.
        An analysis of the factors giving rise to economies of size and scale
        in farm firms in the United States.
Viner, Jacob. Cost Curves and Supply Curves. *Readings in Microeconomics.*
    Edited by David Kamerschen. Cleveland: World, 1967, pp. 197–228.
        The classical piece on cost curves.

DISCUSSION QUESTIONS AND PROBLEMS

1. By going to college you are foregoing an income; this is your opportunity
   cost. What is *your* opportunity cost and how did you calculate it?
2. Estimate your total cost of attending college this semester, being sure to include your opportunity cost. How do you decide if it is worth it?
3. If you are the proprietor of a firm producing lecture notes for a course,
   how would you (a) calculate marginal cost and (b) determine the optimum
   number of sets of notes to produce if you know the professor is selling
   his notes for $5 per set?

   Suppose that Xerox develops a duplicating machine that reduces your
   duplicating and paper costs by 60 percent. Explain the following by use
   of diagrams: (a) the impact of the new machine on costs and profits in the
   short run, (b) the impact on long-run profits, and (c) the impact on the professor if he does not use the new technology.
4. If General Motors can perfect a robot that can assemble automobiles as
   efficiently as a worker and cost the equivalent of 2 years' wages but last
   for 10 years, what will happen to the proportion of capital and labor used
   to produce automobiles?
5. What is likely to be the effect on employment in an area of minimum
   hourly wage legislation (a) if labor is in short supply, or (b) if there is a
   surplus of labor?
6. Suppose you are the president of a skilled-trade union. What should your
   policy be and what must you give up (a) if you want to maximize employment of your current union membership; or (b) if you want to maximize
   hourly earnings of your members?
7. What is likely to be the effect on employment of union members in an
   industry with rapid technological progress but where negotiated wage contracts call for wage increases that are greater than increases in labor
   productivity?
8. Suppose your friend's father told you he buys feeder pigs at 6 weeks of
   age, feeds them until they weigh 195 pounds, and then sells them. Suppose,
   in addition, he told you that when he buys the small pigs he anticipates a
   minimum selling price of $15/cwt but that he was willing to sell his hogs

as long as he received at least $12/cwt. At a price lower than $12/cwt, it is cheaper to shoot the pigs than to feed them to market weight.

a. Would you consider the man to be a poor businessman? Since $10/cwt is better than the return of 0 he would get when he shoots them, how would you justify his statement in economic terms?

b. What would you know about his average fixed cost per 100 pounds of pork?

CHAPTER 7: FIRM AND INDUSTRY SUPPLY

In Chapters 5 and 6, we discussed the concepts of production and of cost curves derived from production functions for individual firms. In this chapter, we will use these concepts to develop the notion of a short-run supply curve for the individual firm and, from that, the supply curve of all the firms producing the same product—an industry.[1]

In the first part of this chapter, we describe the relationship between the cost curves of individual firms and the industry supply curve. It is subdivided into two sections: (1) how a single firm's output changes in response to changes in its price and (2) how the industry supply curve is related to the supply curves of the individual firms within the industry. In the final section of this chapter, we will describe the responsiveness of market supply to changes in product price. In this section, the concept of supply elasticity and the factors influencing it are developed. Additionally, there is a discussion of factors which result in shifts in the supply curve of an individual firm and of an industry.

SUPPLY CURVE OF A FIRM

In economics, supply always means the series of prices and corresponding quantities that will be offered at those prices.

Specifically, the term *supply* is defined as the quantity of a specific commodity which a producer(s) would be willing and able to place on the market in a specified time period at alternative prices, *ceteris paribus*. *Ceteris paribus* is a Latin phrase meaning "all other things being held constant." The "other things" refer to prices of all inputs (both fixed and variable) and the technology defining the production surface. Should either of these items change, the net result is a new supply schedule for the firm; that is, the ability and willingness to supply a given quantity at a particular price will be different from what it was before. By defining factor prices and technology as constant, the economist is able to isolate the impact of product price on the

1. The long-run situation will be discussed in Chapter 9.

quantity of a commodity the firm will place on the market. Once the basic relationship is clear, the other variables can be introduced one at a time to see what impact they have on the supply of a commodity. If we did not use this technique, the simultaneous changes of more than one variable would make it impossible to isolate the impact on supply of any one of them. Notice that supply is a concept that implies a series of quantities, each with the associated price which is just adequate to induce a producer(s) to place that quantity on the market. It can thus be thought of as a supply schedule or a supply curve, tracing out the series of prices and the corresponding quantities that they will be ready and willing to sell at that price. It can be specified in terms of what the individual firm is willing and able to place upon the market *(individual or firm supply)* or in terms of the total quantity all firms or producers are willing and able to place on the market *(aggregate or industry supply)*. The industry supply is the accumulation of the activities of each firm in the industry. Hence, we begin by developing the firm's supply curve. The previous chapter developed in detail the conceptual differences between long-run and short-run decisions by the firm. The importance of the time frame is also reflected in the definition above ("in a specified time period"). The question then is, How is the firm's supply schedule related to the individual firm's cost curves in the short and long run?

Before embarking upon the actual derivation of supply curves, it is first necessary to distinguish between the economist's usage of the word "supply" and the more common, everyday usage. For example, market news reports frequently refer to supply as what should actually be called production. The market news reporter will state that the amount of cattle available on today's market is the supply of cattle available. The number of cattle on the the market is, in actuality, the production and represents but one point on the individual farmer's supply curve. Given the market price, it is the quantity he actually brings to the market on that day. In contrast, the farmer's supply curve indicates what he would do at all possible alternative prices, not just at the market price.

In Chapter 6 we saw that the profit-maximizing level of output for a firm is the level where the additional revenue from another unit of output is equal to the additional cost ($MR = MC$). It was demonstrated that the producer wishing to maximize profits would produce the quantity where one more unit of that commodity would bring him neither more nor less revenue than it costs to produce it. The profit-maximizing output level for alternative product prices is graphically illustrated in Figure 7.1.

For the firm in perfect competition, we know that it cannot influence the price at which its output is sold and hence $MR = P$. In Figure 7.1, if the product can be sold for P_0, the firm typified by this

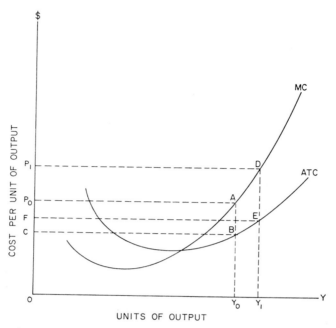

FIG. 7.1. The profit-maximizing level of output under alternative product prices.

diagram would be maximizing profit if it produced Y_0. At this combination of price and quantity, the firm would enjoy a profit equal to the area P_0ABC. Should the price of the product increase to P_1, the producer would be wise to increase his output to Y_1 in the short run and enjoy the larger profit by so doing (P_1DEF). If he expects this higher price to prevail, he may wish to expand the capacity of his plant and thereby reduce per-unit cost of production. We know from the previous chapter that this is a long-run adjustment. In the short-run situation depicted in Figure 7.1, the producer can respond to price changes only by adjustments along the marginal cost curve.[2] Given the fact that short-run adjustments in the profit-maximizing output level of the firm will be guided by the equality of price and marginal cost, it should be obvious that the marginal cost curve fits exactly our earlier definition of a supply curve. If it is assumed that producers are rational in their operation and strive to maximize profits, the marginal cost curve will describe the various quantities of output that a single producer will be willing and able to place on the market at alternative prices.

2. This assumes a given scale of plant. Recall that in the long run, when the scale of the firm is altered, the production function shifts, as do the cost curves derived therefrom. Hence, a new and larger facility would have a different marginal cost curve. If the firm enjoys economies of scale, the marginal cost curve will be shifted downward and the ideal output would be larger than in Figure 7.1.

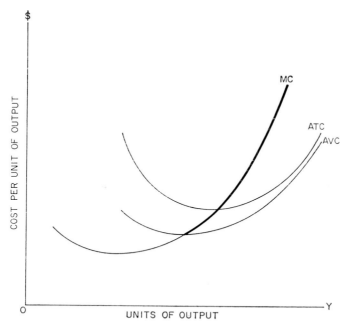

FIG. 7.2. The supply curve of the firm in the short run.

We showed earlier that a producer will continue to operate in the short run as long as the price of the product is greater than the average variable cost, even through the price is less than the average total cost.[3] Hence, our definition of the supply curve for the individual firm includes that portion of the marginal cost curve which lies above the average variable cost curve. The heavy portion of the marginal cost curve in Figure 7.2 would be the supply curve for the firm depicted in the diagram. In summary, the firm's short-run supply curve is its marginal cost curve above average variable cost.

A MODIFICATION

The previous discussion of the supply curve for a firm assumed that all factors were priced at their opportunity cost. When there is a disparity between the actual cost of a factor of production and its opportunity cost, it is necessary to modify the concept of a supply curve for the firm. The refinement begins with the recognition of two distinct values for a factor of production: (1) its acquisition cost (value) and (2) its salvage value. The acquisition cost of a factor is what an entrepreneur must pay for the factor—usually thought of as fixed assets such as machinery and buildings. The salvage value for that factor is

3. See Chapter 6.

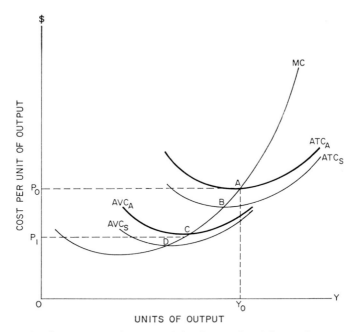

FIG. 7.3. The short-run supply curve of the firm under different factor prices.

the value that could be realized by the entrepreneur should he wish to dispose of the factor rather than use it in production.

This difference can be reflected in the per-unit cost curves and is depicted in Figure 7.3. The curve labeled ATC_A is the average total cost curve with factors valued at their acquisition cost, while AVC_A is the corresponding average variable cost curve. The curve labeled ATC_S is the average total cost curve with factors valued at their salvage value, while AVC_S is the corresponding average variable cost curve.

If the price of output is assumed to be P_0, we know that the profit-maximizing entrepreneur would produce Y_0 and make a zero profit, but be covering the opportunity cost of all factors. However, if their salvage value results in a disparity between what was paid for them and what could be obtained for them elsewhere, ATC_S becomes relevant. Furthermore, the earlier definition of a supply curve as representing that portion of the firm's marginal cost curve above average variable cost requires further modification. Specifically, there are two average variable cost curves, depending upon the assumption about factor values. In Figure 7.3, the supply curve for the firm must include the segment CD of the marginal cost curve. Hence, if the price of the product should fall to P_1, the entrepreneur might still continue to produce over a considerable period of time for the simple reason that return per unit, though less than adequate if factors are valued at their acquisition price, is sufficient in light of the worth of those factors in another use (their salvage value).[4]

In summary, certain types of production inputs are not completely used up in a particular production period. Fixed assets decline in value over their lifetime and hence there is a disparity between their acquisition value and their salvage value. This necessitates modifying the basic theory of the firm's supply to take account of this phenomenon. It is this modification that provides the rationale for the otherwise unexplainable observation that output continues at prior levels in spite of falling prices. It should be noted that this phenomenon is particularly relevant in United States agriculture as long as the returns on factors in agriculture are in excess of their salvage value. This will be treated again in Chapter 9.

INDUSTRY SUPPLY CURVE

While the concept of firm supply is important, it is a component of a more important concept—that of industry supply. The *supply curve of an industry* is defined as the schedule of quantities which all firms combined are willing to place upon the market at each possible price in a given period of time. The definition makes it clear that the total industry supply is obtained by summing the schedules of all the individual firms in the industry. Once again, the time period must be carefully specified because of its impact upon the scale and number of firms in the industry. In the short run, both the scale of firms in the industry and the number of firms are fixed. In a longer time period, existing firms can change their scale and firms can either exit or enter the industry. Long-run supply must reflect these possibilities. Since it is difficult to explore the ramifications of all possible changes simultaneously, we start with a simple example of short-run industry supply and then proceed to introduce the complexities described above.

The short run is defined as a period too short for new firms to begin producing. The number of firms in the industry is therefore fixed and the industry supply is the summation of the individual schedules of existing firms. If we know that there are only four firms in the country which produce a specific commodity, we can view the aggregate supply of that commodity at a given point in time as the amount which

4. This concept is referred to as the *fixed asset theory* in the literature and is discussed in Glenn L. Johnson and Lowell S. Hardin, *Economics of Forage Evaluation*, Sta. Bull. 623 (Lafayette: Purdue Univ. Agr. Exp. Sta., Apr. 1959); Clark Edwards, Resource fixity and farm organization, *J. Farm Econ.* 41 (Nov. 1959): 747–59; and Glenn L. Johnson, The state of agricultural supply analysis, *J. Farm Econ.* 42 (May 1960): 435–52. We present another brief discussion of the fixed-asset theory on pp. 294–95.

TABLE 7.1.   Derivation of an industry supply curve from the
supply curves of four hypothetical firms

Price	Firm A	Firm B	Output of Firm C	Firm D	The Industry
(1)	(2)	(3)	(4)	(5)	(6)
0	0	0	0	0	0
2	0	0	0	0 .	0
4	20	0	0	0	20
6	38	30	0	0	68
8	50	50	0	0	100
10	58	65	30	0	153
12	65	75	60	30	230
14	70	83	80	60	293
16	75	87	90	80	332
18	80	90	95	90	355
20	83	92	100	95	370

all four producers would be willing and able to place on the market at
specified prices. This could be thought of as the aggregate supply of the
commodity or as the industry supply. The industry is defined as the
collection of firms which produce a certain commodity. If the supply
curves of all actual and potential firms associated with the production
of a specific commodity are known, the *aggregate supply* curve for a
commodity is the horizontal summation of all the marginal cost curves
(above average variable cost) of those firms which are, or would be,
producing the commodity in the short run.[5] This is illustrated in
Table 7.1.

For each of the four firms illustrated in the table, the data
represent the individual firm's supply schedule above AVC as shown
in Figure 7.4. Notice that firm A is a low-cost firm. Its minimum AVC
is $4 per unit at 20 units of output. At any price less than $4 per unit
it will produce zero output and will begin producing when the price is
$4 or higher. When the price rises to $6 per unit, firm B will produce
30 units, and firm A will produce 38 units, for an industry output of 68
units. As the price of the product rises to $10 and $12, respectively,
firms C and D will begin to supply output. Consequently, the minimum

5. This is true only for "constant cost" industries to be discussed later in
this chapter. More advanced texts treat the more complicated situations.

price at which all four firms will be producing is $12 per unit. At this price, total industry output will be 230 units (Table 7.1).

Firm D is the highest cost firm in the industry. It is often referred to as the marginal firm since it is the last firm to enter the industry when prices rise, and the first to leave when they fall. At a price of $12, the marginal firm is just making enough to cover opportunity costs on its resources and will remain in the industry; the other three firms are all earning positive profit since their cost per unit is less than for firm D and less than the price received per unit.

Summing the marginal cost curves of the individual firms yields the supply curve of the industry as shown in the last column of Table 7.1 and in the lower section of Figure 7.4. When the price is less than $4, there will be no output by the industry. At a price of $4, firm A will enter production and 20 units will be produced. As the price rises to $6, firm A will expand output along its marginal cost curve. Consequently, from point *A* to point *B* (in Figure 7.4) the industry supply curve is simply the marginal cost curve of firm A. At $6, firm B enters the industry and its output is added to that of firm A. As the price rises from $6 to $10, the production of both firms increases as

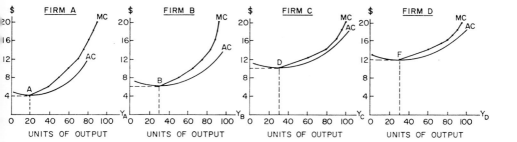

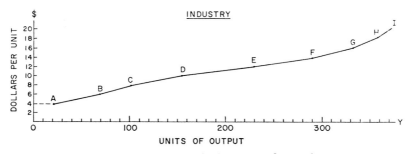

FIG. 7.4. Derivation of an aggregate supply for a four-firm industry.

they maximize their net revenue by expanding output along their respective marginal cost curves. Consequently, the segment *BC* of the industry supply curve is composed of the marginal cost curves of firms A and B. At point *C*, firm C enters the industry and at point *D*, firm D does likewise. At a price of $16, the industry supply curve indicates that 332 units of output will be supplied by the four firms: 75 by firm A, 87 by firm B, 90 by firm C, and 80 by firm D. Similarly, other points on the curve represent the combined contribution of firms A through D as determined by their separate and independent profit-maximizing decisions.

The supply curve of the industry is therefore *ABCDEFGHI*, comprising the sum of the marginal cost curves above average variable costs of all potential and actual firms in the industry. It should be clear that as the price of the output rises, the output of the industry increases for two reasons: (1) the output of each firm already in production increases as it expands output along its upward-sloping marginal cost curve and (2) other firms in the industry begin production.

SUPPLY RESPONSE

The economist is often concerned with understanding the cause and effect relationships between economic variables. In this chapter, for example, we are concerned with explaining how the quantity of a commodity placed on the market by firms is related to a price change. Also of interest are changes in input prices, the length or time period, and the number of firms. Additional variables such as expectations, risk, and weather are also frequently included in the analysis. To facilitate the analysis of supply response, economists have developed several concepts to describe certain market phenomena. Three of them are (1) supply elasticity, (2) changes in supply, and (3) shifts in supply.

ELASTICITY DEFINED

Up to the present we have been describing the relationship of the price of a commodity to the quantity producers are willing to sell per unit of time. Our supply theory indicates that as the price of the product goes up, the quantity supplied will go up. The economist is often interested in asking *how much* the quantity changes in response to a change in price, and in comparing the response of commodity A to a change in its price with the response of commodity B to a change in its price. Unfortunately, the particular dimensions in which commodities are quoted are arbitrary; sugar may be quoted at $0.10 per pound, at $0.01 per ounce, or 100 rupees per kilogram. The dimensions are also difficult to compare. For example, how does one compare a change in the supply of hours of labor to wage rates with a change in the supply of bushels of tomatoes to the price of tomatoes? Or the supply of pretzels in ounces with that for beer in gallons—with regard to a change in their respective prices?

The concept of elasticity has been devised precisely with these comparison problems in mind and helps to avoid arbitrariness in a considerable range of comparison problems. *Elasticity* is a measure of responsiveness and compares the percentage change in one variable to a percentage change in another. For example, given two variables Y and X, the definition of elasticity of Y with respect to X is defined as in Equation 7.1.

$$E = (\Delta Y/Y)/(\Delta X/X) = \% \text{ change in } Y/\% \text{ change in } X \qquad (7.1)$$

where

$$\Delta Y = \text{ change in } Y$$
$$\Delta X = \text{ change in } X$$

Note that this definition is completely general; X and Y could be any two variables. For example, Y could be the size of McDonald's hamburgers, and X could be the price of economics textbooks, in which case we would talk about the elasticity of McDonald's hamburgers with respect to textbook prices. In more meaningful terms, Y could be the quantity supplied of a particularly commodity such as steak, and X could be its price. In this case we would have the elasticity of quantity of steaks supplied in terms of its own price. This is referred to as *price elasticity of supply*. If Y is the quantity of steaks consumers would be willing to purchase and X the price of steaks, this E would be the *price elasticity of demand*. The formula can be visualized by reference to Figure 7.5. The line AA represents the relationship between a variable Y with respect to changes in X. The elasticity measures the responsiveness of a change in Y to a change in the level of X. The change in X is from X_1 to X_2 (ΔX). The corresponding change in Y is from Y_1 to Y_2 (ΔY).

Elasticity is a dimensionless number; it is purely abstract, which permits us to compare the supply elasticity of automobiles with the supply elasticity of candy bars, and to conclude—on the basis of empirical analysis—that one is more "supply elastic" than the other. Additionally, it is important to recognize that elasticity may be either positive or negative. In Figure 7.5, as X increases so does Y; the elasticity is positive. If the line AA sloped downward, as X increased, Y would decrease; the elasticity would be negative.

Although Equation 7.1 is useful as a general concept, it is in-

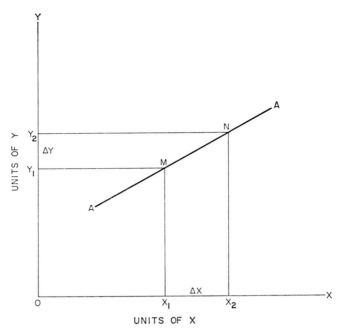

FIG. 7.5. Graphic illustration of the concept of elasticity.

sufficiently specific. For example, using Equation 7.1, the elasticity between points M and N in Figure 7.5 will differ depending upon whether
it is calculated as a change from M to N or from N to M. Furthermore,
the distance between points M and N will also affect the result. Consequently, Equation 7.2 will be used to compute elasticity.[6] The logic
used to develop Equation 7.2 from 7.1 is illustrated in the next section
on supply elasticities.

$$E = [(Y_2 - Y_1)/(Y_2 + Y_1)]/[(X_2 - X_1)/(X_2 + X_1)] \qquad (7.2)$$

where

Y_2 = new quantity of Y
Y_1 = old quantity of Y
X_2 = new quantity of X
X_1 = old quantity of X

The definitions of the Y's and X's depend upon the type of elasticity in
which we are interested.

6. This is ordinarily referred to as the formula for *arc elasticity*. For a
more detailed discussion of other methods of calculating elasticities, see Appendix A
to this chapter.

ELASTICITY OF SUPPLY

As indicated earlier, supply elasticity indicates the percentage change on the output of a commodity with respect to a percentage change in its price.[7] The percentage change in quantity is given by

$$(Y_2 - Y_1)/[(Y_2 + Y_1)/2] \qquad (7.3)$$

where

$$Y_2 = \text{new quantity of } Y$$
$$Y_1 = \text{old quantity of } Y$$

The new and old quantities are added together in the denominator (and then divided by 2) to obtain an average elasticity. Otherwise the elasticity will differ, depending upon whether the difference between Y_2 and Y_1 is computed as a percentage of the new quantity (Y_2) or of the old quantity (Y_1). By averaging the two we obtain one consistent elasticity.[8]

Similarly, the percentage change in price is given by

$$(P_2 - P_1)/[(P_2 + P_1)/2] \qquad (7.4)$$

Again, the subscripts refer to new and old prices, and the denominator is an average. Given the definition of supply elasticity, we can form the ratio of expressions 7.3 and 7.4 obtaining

$$E_s = \frac{(Y_2 - Y_1)/[(Y_2 + Y_1)/2]}{(P_2 - P_1)/[(P_2 + P_1)/2]} \qquad (7.5)$$

Since the 2's cancel, we can rewrite Equation 7.5 as

$$E_s = \frac{[(Y_2 - Y_1)/(Y_2 + Y_1)]}{[(P_2 - P_1)/(P_2 + P_1)]} \qquad (7.6)$$

For example, suppose that when the price of commodity A rises from \$3 to \$5, the quantity supplied changes from 10 to 20 units. The supply elasticity between these two points is calculated as follows:

$$E_s = \frac{[(20 - 10)/(20 + 10)]}{[(5 - 3)/(5 + 3)]} = \frac{(10/30)}{(2/8)} \qquad (7.7)$$

$$= (10/30) \times (8/2) = (1/3) \times (4) = 1.3$$

7. For those familiar with calculus, supply elasticity is given by
$$E = (dq/dp)(p/q)$$
where $q = $ quantity supplied
$p = $ price per unit
8. This is clarified in Appendix A to this chapter.

In this case, a 1 percent increase in price is associated with a 1.3 percent increase in quantity sold.

There are three general types of supply elasticities: elastic, inelastic, and unitary elasticity. An *elastic* response is one in which the change in quantity offered in response to a 1 percent change in price is greater than 1 percent ($E_S > 1$); an *inelastic* response occurs when the change in the amount offered relative to a 1 percent price change is less than 1 percent ($E_S < 1$); and a response of *unitary elasticity* is when the percentage change in quantity supplied is exactly equal to the percentage change in price ($E_S = 1$). Equation 7.7 is a specific example of an elastic response. A price increase of 67 percent is associated with a change in quantity of 100 percent. If the change in quantity had been less than 67 percent, the response would be classified as inelastic. If the 67 percent change in price had resulted in a 67 percent increase in the quantity offered, it would have reflected unitary elasticity.

For linear supply curves, one can infer their elasticity from the axes they intercept. A linear suppply curve that extends to the origin has unitary elasticity. Any linear supply curve that intersects the vertical axis has an elasticity greater than one and is said to be elastic. Any linear supply curve that intersects the horizontal axis has an elasticity of less than one and is said to be inelastic. It should be noted that in part b of Figure 7.6, supply curve S_2 is more elastic than S_1, though both are elastic. Similarly, in part c, supply curve S_1 is more inelastic than S_2, though both are inelastic.

The nonlinear supply curve exhibits all three types of supply elasticity as demonstrated in Figure 7.7. The line tangent to the supply curve S at point A intersects the vertical axis. Therefore, at A, S has an elasticity greater than one. By similar logic, at point B the elasticity of S is unitary, and at point C it is inelastic. Therefore, depending upon the curvature, a nonlinear supply function can contain an elastic as well as an inelastic portion.

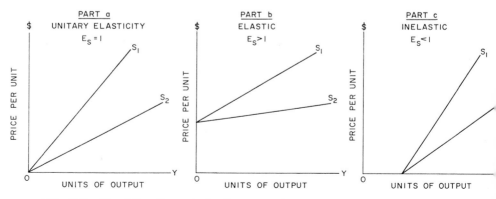

FIG. 7.6. Elasticity of supply for linear supply curves.

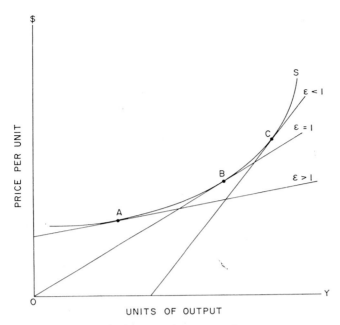

FIG. 7.7. Elasticity of supply for a nonlinear supply curve.

DETERMINANTS OF SUPPLY ELASTICITIES

We have seen that supply curves of products can exhibit different elasticities. Some products are highly elastic, with a small change in price bringing about a large change in the quantity supplied. For others, supply is highly inelastic, meaning that a price change will have relatively little effect on the quantity supplied. The question naturally arises as to what factors influence supply elasticity. These factors include the shape of the firm's marginal cost curve, differences in the firm's cost structure, the time allowed for adjustments to take place, and a number of other factors of lesser importance such as expectations of the entrepreneur, storability of the product, and alternative opportunities for inputs. Each of these factors is discussed in turn.

In general, if the firms comprising the industry can expand output with only small increases in marginal cost, the industry supply curve will be more elastic than in the case where MC rises rapidly as output is expanded. In other words, if the marginal cost function for all firms producing a product is relatively flat (as is that of firm D in Figure 7.4), the industry supply elasticity will be relatively large. If, on the other hand, the firms in the industry have MC curves similar to firm A in the same figure, the cost of producing an extra unit of output increases sharply and the industry supply curve composed of such firms will be rather unresponsive to price changes (relatively inelastic).

A second factor influencing elasticity is a difference in the per-unit cost curves of potential and existing firms in the industry. If potential firms have only slightly higher cost than existing firms, the industry supply curve will be more elastic than in the case where potential firms' cost curves are much higher than the existing firms. For example, if all potential firms have cost curves only slightly above the going price for the product and there are many potential producers, small increases in price will make it profitable for a large number of new firms to enter the industry. In this case, the individual firm's marginal cost curve could be relatively steep, but the difference between firms' costs are very small. The industry supply curve would, therefore, be highly elastic because of the tendency of new producers to enter the industry with very small changes in price. For example, the elasticity of supply for many farm commodities is relatively high because of the high number of potential producers of these commodities. A small change in price leads to a large expansion in the number of farmers producing a particular commodity. If, for example, the price of soybeans rises relative to the price of other crops such as corn or barley, farmers will take some acres out of other crops and plant more soybeans. Soybean output will therefore increase substantially in response to a relatively slight increase in price.

Time is another important factor influencing the elasticity for a particular commodity. Since supply is defined as the quantity producers are willing to place on the market per unit of time, the length of time implicit in the definition of a particular schedule or curve will have an impact on the degree of responsiveness of producers. As the time period lengthens, the supply curve tends to become more elastic. Economists usually differentiate three time periods: the very short run, the short run, and the long run.[9] Depending upon production peculiarities of the particular commodity under consideration, the definition of the length of time varies from one commodity to the next. Properties of each of the time periods are described below.

THE VERY SHORT RUN

The very short run is defined as the period of a single day or a very few days. It is a period so short that even changes in variable input usage are impossible. Hence, supply will be limited to what is available in inventories. As an example, a cooperative of fishermen located in a large ocean city supplies the population with seafood. Each morning this small fleet of fishing vessels goes out to catch fish which

9. The student should not be confused by the addition here of a third time horizon. We have merely added a period with little relevance in production theory but of great importance in supply and market analyses. Samuelson refers to the very short run as "momentary." See Paul A. Samuelson, *Economics* (New York: McGraw-Hill, 1964), pp. 378–80.

will be sold in a local fish market that day. Given a price change during the day, there would be very little increase in the quantity of fish offered for sale by the fishermen. There could be some response, since, if the price changes were favorable enough, the fishermen might decide to consume less of their own catch and sell it instead. In this case, the very short run is defined as one marketing day, since it is the period within which no changes in output are possible; the fishermen are unable to adjust their output to a change in price.

For another commodity, the short run would be different. In the case of pork, the short run might be a period as long as several weeks. A sudden change in price could result in a few farmers marketing their pigs a week or two ahead of schedule. However, since the number of marketable hogs available for sale is fixed, the change in price can only speed up or slow down the number arriving on the market within very narrow limits. Consequently, in this case, the very short run could be defined as the period encompassing several weeks. The basic concept of the very short run is a period of time insufficient for producers to change their level of output by changing scale of plant or by adjusting variable inputs; they can at best adjust their sales by selling from stocks. As a consequence, the supply curve is relatively inelastic.

THE SHORT RUN

As seen earlier, the short run is a period defined as being long enough for supplies of a commodity to be altered by increases or decreases in current output, but a period not long enough for scale of plant to be altered. Variable inputs can be adjusted, but fixed factors cannot.

In the case of the fishermen, the short run would be a period of several days. This would allow the fishermen to adjust their variable inputs used in catching fish. Variable inputs might include the number of hours fished per day, number of lines used in catching fish, and the number of fishermen per boat. For example, given an increase in price, the fishermen may attempt to catch more fish by encouraging a friend who is a carpenter to join the fishing fleet. In this case, changing the price on a given day would result in little response of the quantity of fish offered. However, if the new price is maintained for a period of several days, an increase in the quantity of fish marketed would be observable because fishermen would have an opportunity to increase their output by applying more variable inputs in the production process.

In the hog example, the short run would be one of 12 to 18 months. This would be sufficient time to allow farmers to change their breeding plans in response to the price change. It would also allow them sufficient time to feed their hogs to heavier weights.

THE LONG RUN

The long run is defined as a period of time long enough to allow the production unit to adjust the scale of the plant and equipment in response to changes in price. This is the time period associated with the long-run cost curves. As an example, it would allow the fishermen to (1) build new boats, (2) increase the size of the fishing fleet, (3) build bigger boats that can go farther out to sea, and (4) allow the fishermen to recruit and train new fishermen to man the larger fleet.

In the case of hogs, it is a period of several years which would allow more hog houses to be built and more equipment such as feed-mixing plants and hog feeders to be manufactured and installed. The supply curve in this period of time will be the most elastic of all.

In summary, the elasticity of supply is dependent upon the length of time. The length of time is in turn defined differently, depending upon the commodity under consideration. For any given commodity, it is least elastic in the short run, because production cannot be changed, and most elastic in the long run, because it is a period long enough to allow all inputs to be recombined in the most efficient manner.

OTHER FACTORS

Within any given period of time, the elasticity of supply for two commodities can be different, depending upon a number of other factors such as expectations, storability, and the ease with which the resources can be shifted from the production of one commodity to the production of another.

Expectations of producers play an important role in the response of quantity supplied to a change in price. If the fishermen had reason to expect that the price changes were strictly temporary in nature, they would be less inclined to change their output than if they felt the price changes were permanent in nature. Therefore, a small price change that producers expect to be maintained with a high degree of certainty will bring larger increases in output than a large increase in price that producers do not believe will be maintained in the future. The reason for this is that most production processes, particularly in agriculture, require a long period of time, and few resources can be changed once the process is initiated. Consequently, it is both the level and the stability of the farmer's expectation that is important.

A good example of the role of expectations in the response of farmers to price changes is that of the price-support program in a developing economy. Many developing countries attempt to encourage farmers to increase the output of particular agricultural commodities by guaranteeing to support the prices of these commodities at a predetermined level. Frequently, because of the lack of adequate administrative capabilities and funds to carry through on a support payment, the farmer observes that the promised price supports never materialize. Consequently, in the following production period, the announced high price for a particular commodity brings no response from farmers. In contrast, in other countries where the support program did operate efficiently and farmers had confidence in the program, they would respond. In summary, the more certain the expected price, the larger the response of output to a price change, and the more elastic the supply curve.

Another factor that influences the ability of the producer to respond to a price change within a given period of time is the storability of the product. An owner of a perishable product has little choice except to move the product at almost any price. Consequently, a commodity that is not storable will have a more inelastic supply than a commodity that can be stored for any given period of time. For example, fish are not storable; consequently, a sudden change in price within the marketing period will not induce fishermen to withdraw fish from the market and store them until the following day. Wheat, on the other hand, is easily stored. Owners or producers of wheat have more control over the time in which they sell it and, consequently, they respond more readily to price changes. In summary, storable commodities are more responsive to changes in price, and they will exhibit greater supply elasticity.

The ease with which resources or inputs used in producing a given commodity can be shifted to the production of another commodity is still another factor which influences the elasticity of supply. If it is difficult to alter the facilities to produce some other product, the supply will be relatively more inelastic than if such adjustments are easy and relatively inexpensive. In other words, the elasticity of supply is a function of the alternative uses for the inputs used in producing a commodity. If the inputs have no alternative uses (the VMP in the next best alternative is zero), supply will tend to be inelastic and producers will not be able to respond much to a change in price. Wheatland in Kansas is an example; there are relatively few alternative income-generating uses for such land. Consequently, the farmer uses this land to produce or it generates no income at all. In contrast, an acre of land near Detroit, Milwaukee, or Chicago that is producing commercial vegetables has many alternative uses. Consequently, given a small drop in the price of vegetables, it could be used in an urban development program, in an industrial park, or to produce other agricultural commodities. In this case, small changes in product price will shift the resources from one product to another.

As for some comparative elasticities of supply among vegeta-

TABLE 7.2. Some comparative supply elasticities for major and minor vegetable crops produced for fresh market, selected periods 1919–1955

Vegetables	Short-Run Price Elasticity	Long-Run Price Elasticity
Major		
Green lima beans	0.10	1.70
Cabbage	0.36	1.20
Carrots	0.14	1.00
Cucumbers	0.29	2.20
Lettuce	0.03	0.16
Onions	0.34	1.00
Green peas	0.31	4.40
Green peppers	0.07	0.26
Tomatoes	0.16	0.90
Watermelons	0.23	0.48
Minor		
Beets	0.13	1.00
Cantaloupes	0.02	0.04
Cauliflower	0.14	1.10
Celery	0.14	0.95
Egg plant	0.16	0.34
Spinach	0.20	4.70

Source: Marc Nerlove and W. Addison, Statistical estimation of long-run elasticities of supply and demand, J. Farm Econ. 40 (1958): 861-80.

bles, Table 7.2 is instructive. Notice the difference between long-run and short-run elasticities. Also notice that in the short run, the major vegetables tend to exhibit greater supply elasticity than the more specialized minor vegetables.

Supply elasticities may also vary depending upon whether prices are increasing or decreasing. Theoretically, as prices rise, new firms enter into production when price becomes equal to the minimum

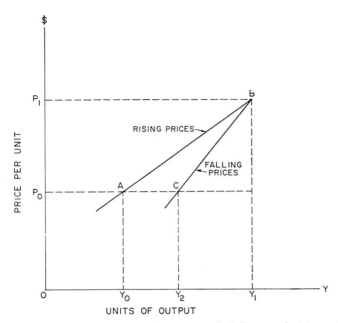

FIG. 7.8. Hypothetical industry supply curve with falling and rising prices.

point on their average total cost curve. However, when prices are declining, these same firms do not exit from the industry until prices drop below the average variable cost curve. As a consequence, the supply curve is more elastic for increases in price than for decreases in price. The difference between the two elasticities will be greatest in those industries with high fixed costs relative to total costs. This "ratchet effect" is illustrated in Figure 7.8. When the price changes from P_0 to P_1, output of the industry expands from Y_0 to Y_1. However, if prices then fell back to P_0, industry output would only decline to Y_2 because all the firms entering in the segment AB did not exit.

As will be seen in Part III of the book, supply elasticity is a crucial element in the development of economic policy. In agriculture, elasticity of supply plays a central role in the design of price-support programs. For example, if supply is relatively inelastic, efforts to raise prices by reducing aggregate production will probably be more successful than for commodities that are relatively supply elastic. At the present, generally reliable estimates of supply elasticities are not available. Economists estimating supply elasticities have had a great deal of difficulty because of the influence on supply of outside, noncontrollable factors such as weather, and the inability to quantify such factors as change in technology. Much work still remains to be done in this field before satisfactory supply elasticity estimates are obtained.[10]

SHIFTS IN SUPPLY VERSUS CHANGE IN QUANTITY SUPPLIED

The supply curve describes the relationship between the prices of a product and the quantities of that product producers will place on the market at that price, *ceteris paribus;* that is, if all other factors remain unchanged. For any given supply curve, the factors that are assumed to remain fixed are the prices of all inputs used to produce that product and the physical production process used to transform the inputs into outputs. Therefore, a movement along a given supply curve (a change in the quantity supplied) must be differentiated from conditions leading to a shift of the supply curve.

A shift in the supply curve means that more or less of the good will be offered on the market at the same price. A change in the quantity supplied means a movement along a given supply curve. For example, assume that S in Figure 7.9 is the original supply curve and that for some reason supply shifts to the right to S_2. This means that at every price producers are now willing to supply a larger quantity than formerly. Consequently, at price P_0 the change in quantity supplied from Y_0 to Y_2 is due to a shift in supply. Similarly, a decrease in the quantity offered from Y_0 to Y_1 at price P_0 would be the result of a shift in the supply curve to the left. In contrast, a movement from A to B on supply curve S in Figure 7.9 does not constitute a shift in supply; it is a change in the quantity offered growing out of a change in the price from P_0 to P_1, *ceteris paribus.* Thus a change in the quantity supplied from Y_0 to Y_2, due to a change in price from P_0 to P_1, is defined as a change in the quantity supplied. In contrast, a change in the quantity supplied from Y_0 to Y_2, with price remaining constant at P_0, is due to a shift in the supply curve from S to S_2 because one of the factors included in the *ceteris paribus* assumption has changed. These supply shifters are described in the next section.

SUPPLY SHIFTERS

A contraction or expansion of supply (supply shift from S to S_1 or to S_2) may be the result of a change in production cost, a change

10. An excellent discussion of the problem in estimating supply elasticities (and an extensive bibliography) can be found in Marc Nerlove and Kenneth L. Bachman, The analysis of changes in agricultural supply: Problems and approaches, *J. Farm Econ.* 42(1960): 531–54.

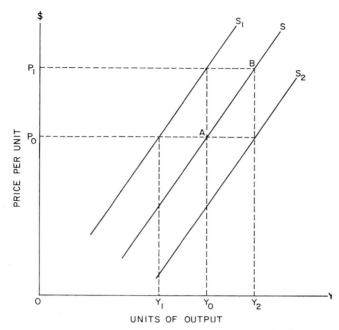

FIG. 7.9. Shift in supply versus a change in quantity supplied.

in technology, or a change in the number of producers. In the case of agriculture, a fourth supply shifter is also very important—a change in weather. Each of these factors and its impact upon the supply curve will be described briefly.

As we saw earlier, changes in the price of inputs used to produce a particular commodity have a direct impact on the supplier. If the price of an input increases, given no other changes, it will increase the per-unit cost of production. This will be reflected in the supply curve by the fact that producers will be willing to supply only a particular quantity at a higher price. The impact of the increase in input prices is a shift to the left of the supply curve from S to S_1 (Figure 7.9). Specifically, if producers were willing to supply Y_0 units of output at price P_0, after the increase in input prices they will be willing to supply only the same quantity at a higher price (P_1). Conversely, a decrease in input prices will shift the supply curve to the right, meaning that producers are now willing to supply a given quantity at a lower price.[11]

11. The reader should verify that a shift to the right in the supply curve is identical to a downward shift and that a shift to the left in the demand curve is identical to an upward shift.

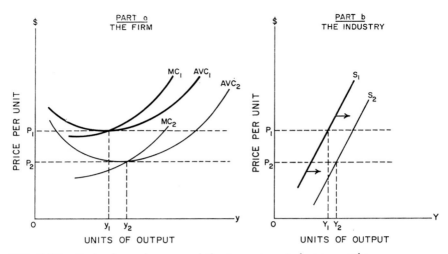

FIG. 7.10. Technology change and the impact on industry supply.

Changes in production technology will also be reflected in shifts of the supply curve of a commodity. As was shown earlier, the derivation of the aggregate supply curve for a particular commodity assumes a given production process. This process is assumed to transform inputs into products at a given rate (or cost). When a new technological innovation is used, the rate of transformation of inputs to outputs is changed. These changes shift downward the marginal cost curves of the individual adopting firm. The first firm to adopt the new technology lowers its cost and achieves positive profits. These profits induce other firms also to adopt the new technology. As the marginal cost curves of more and more firms shift downward, the industry supply curves shift to the right as illustrated in Figure 7.10. Under the old technology, the typical firm in the industry had cost represented by AVC_1 and MC_1 and the equilibrium industry price was P_1. However, as more and more firms adopt the new technology, cost curves MC_2 and AVC_2 become typical, and the industry supply curve begins to shift from S_1 to S_2. The firm that hesitates finds itself forced by the falling market price either to adopt new technology or to leave the industry. As a consequence, the net impact of the new technological innovation is a lowering of the per-unit cost curves and the industry price from P_1 to P_2, and increasing industry output from Y_1 to Y_2.

A third shifter of aggregate supply is the number of producers. Since aggregate supply is defined as the horizontal summation of the supply curves of individual producers (see Figure 7.4), an increase in the number of producers over all ranges of production costs will shift the supply curve to the right. Correspondingly, a decrease in the number will shift it to the left.

A final factor shifting the aggregate supply curve—and one that is peculiar to agricultural supply curves—is weather. One usually is not concerned with this factor when describing the supply for industrial products. However, in agriculture, this factor turns out to be a very important influence on supply. Unfortunately, it is also the one that is least predictable. Abnormally good years can result in a shift of the supply curve to the right, meaning that producers will now supply larger quantities at any given price than originally had been anticipated. Conversely, extremely unfavorable weather will shift the supply curve to the left. Thus, when describing a supply curve for an agricultural product, it is assumed that it is for a period of "normal weather."

SUMMARY

In this chapter we completed the discussion that began in Chapter 5 and was expanded in Chapter 6. Here, our concern has been the operational aspects of the firm's cost curves rather than their theoretical foundation as in Chapter 6. The notion of individual and aggregate supply was developed, and the very important concept of supply elasticity was introduced. The factors that are important in determination of elasticity were also detailed.

These concepts are essential to the analysis and discussion of resource allocation problems in Chapters 10 through 15.

APPENDIX A: ALTERNATIVE MEASURES OF ELASTICITY

As seen earlier, elasticity is defined as the percentage change in one variable associated with a 1 percent change in the quantity of another variable. One formal definition of elasticity was given as

$$E = (\Delta Y/Y)/(\Delta X/X) \qquad (7.A.1)$$

When elasticity is measured between two points on a line, we refer to it as *arc elasticity;* when measured at one point on a line, we refer to it as *point elasticity.* When using arc elasticity, the resulting elasticity will vary, depending upon which "end of the arc" is considered the starting point. This will become clear by reference to Figure 7.A.1.

If we determine the elasticity of the line in Figure 7.A.1 in

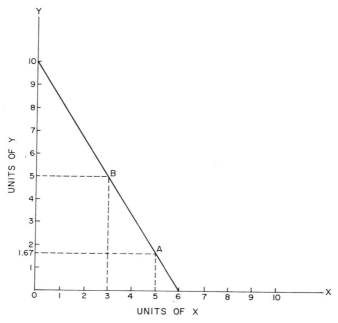

FIG 7.A.1. Arc elasticity of a straight line.

moving from *A* to point *B* we would obtain, according to Equation 7.A.1:

$$E = (\Delta Y/Y)/(\Delta X/X) = (3.33/1.67)/- (2/5) \qquad (7.A.2)$$
$$= - 1.99/0.40 = -4.98$$

On the other hand, if we determine elasticity in moving from point *B* to point *A*, we would obtain, according to Equation 7.A.1:

$$E = (\Delta Y/Y)/(\Delta X/X) = - (3.33/5)/(2/3) \qquad (7.A.3)$$
$$= - 0.67/0.67 = - 1.00$$

It should be clear why there is a need for a more precise formulation than that presented in Equation 7.A.1. Accordingly, arc elasticity is determined by the equation

$$(7.A.4)$$

$$E = \frac{(Y_2 - Y_1)/[(Y_2 + Y_1)/2]}{(X_2 - X_1)/[(X_2 + X_1)/2]} = \frac{(Y_2 - Y_1)/(Y_2 + Y_1)}{(X_2 - X_1)/(X_2 + X_1)}$$

where

$$Y_2 = \text{new level of } Y$$
$$Y_1 = \text{old level of } Y$$
$$X_2 = \text{new level of } X$$
$$X_1 = \text{old level of } X$$

Now, as should be verified by the student, the arc elasticity is — 2.00.

It is possible to talk of arc elasticity for curved functions, though with a great loss in precision. Consider Figure 7.A.2. To utilize the concept of arc elasticity for the movement between points C and D on curve GG would obviously be very misleading. Likewise, the use of arc elasticity for movements between points A and B would be of questionable validity, though less extreme than between C and D. For this reason, it is necessary to deal with the concept of point elasticity. Notice that as the difference between the two points of interest becomes less, the accuracy of our elasticity estimate increases. At point H, we can obtain a very precise measure of elasticity; here the arc is infinitely small. At point H, the elasticity of the curve GG will be identical to the elastic-

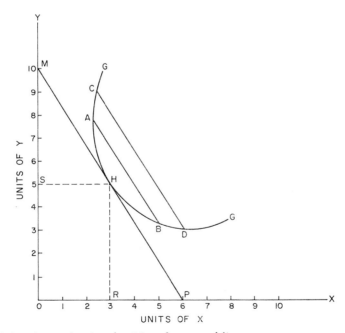

FIG. 7.A.2. Arc and point elasticity of a curved line.

ity of the straight line (*MP*) since the two are tangent at *H*. Recall the formula for the elasticity is sometimes written as

$$E = (\Delta Y/Y)/(\Delta X/X) = (\Delta Y/Y)\ (X/\Delta X) \qquad (7.A.5)$$

This can be rewritten as

$$(\Delta Y/\Delta X)\ (X/Y) \qquad (7.A.6)$$

Recall also that the slope of a straight line such as *MP* is given by $\Delta Y/\Delta X$ or

$$OM/OP = HR/RP = MS/SH = -5/3 \qquad (7.A.7)$$

If we utilize one part of Equation 7.A.7, we can write the slope of *MP* as

$$HR/RP \qquad (7.A.8)$$

Substituting this for $\Delta Y/\Delta X$ yields

$$E = (HR/RP)\ (X/Y) \qquad (7.A.9)$$

But, at point *H*, $X = OR$, and $Y = HR$. Hence Equation 7.A.9 becomes

$$E = (HR/RP)\ (OR/HR) = OR/RP \qquad (7.A.10)$$

Hence, to determine the point elasticity of a curved line such as *GG*, we can draw a tangent to the curve at the desired point and extend it so that it cuts the horizontal axis at point *P*. Drop a perpendicular from the tangency point to the horizontal axis and call the intersection *R* as in Figure 7.A.2. The elasticity at the point is then *OR/RP*. Notice that when *OR* is greater than *RP*, elasticity is less than — 1 (say — 1.5) and the curve is said to be elastic at that point. If *OR* is equal to *RP*, we have unitary elasticity. When the elasticity is between — 1 and zero, *OR* is less than *RP* and the curve at such a point is said to be in-elastic. Note that when calculating the price elasticity of a product, quantity is ordinarily plotted along the X axis as in Figure 7.A.2. In that case Equation 7.A.10 would become:

$$E = RP/OR \qquad (7.A.11)$$

SUGGESTED READINGS

BASIC

Bishop, E. C.; and Toussaint, W. D. *Introduction to Agricultural Economic Analysis.* New York: John Wiley, 1958, Ch. 13, 15.

Discusses time and producer uncertainty in production decisions. Chapter 16 describes factors causing year-to-year variation in the aggregate supply of agricultural output.

Capstick, Margaret. *The Economics of Agriculture.* New York: St. Martin's Press, 1970, Ch. 4.

Discusses the supply of agricultural products from the point of view of the economic structure of Western Europe and the United States.

Heady, Earl O. *Economics of Agricultural Production and Resource Use.* New York: Prentice-Hall, 1952, pp. 672–703.

Discusses individual and aggregate supply functions in agriculture. Devotes a great deal of attention to the time frame of reference because it is critical to an understanding of agricultural supply and supply adjustments.

Krishna, Raj. Agricultural Price Policy and Economic Development. *Agricultural Development and Economic Growth.* Edited by Herman M. Southworth and Bruce F. Johnston. New York: Cornell Univ. Press, 1967, pp. 497–540.

Contains a list of short-run and long-run price elasticities of acreage for 12 different crops in less developed countries and regions, for the United States and for the United Kingdom. Analyzes the effect of various price policies on farmers' response in developing countries.

Mellor, John W. *The Economics of Agricultural Development.* New York: Cornell Univ. Press, 1966, pp. 208–12.

Deals with factors affecting farmers' response to price changes in developing economies under policies to raise prices and output and with policies to stabilize prices.

ADVANCED

Falcon, W. F. Farmers' response to price in a subsistence economy: The case of West Pakistan. *Am. Econ. Rev.* 54(May 1964):580–92.

Describes the problems of obtaining quantified supply elasticities in developing areas of the world. Presents evidence showing that farmers do respond to price changes in a low-income economy.

Ferguson, C. E. *Micro-economic Theory,* 3rd rev. ed. Homewood, Ill.: Richard D. Irwin, 1972, Ch. 8.

An excellent geometrical development of the theory of short-run and long-run supply for firm and industry under many alternative conditions for the firm and in the industry.

Heady, Earl O.; et al., eds. *Agricultural Supply Function—Estimating Techniques and Interpretations.* Ames: Iowa State Univ. Press, 1961.

A compilation of papers on the problems, research methods, and results of investigations of supply functions in U.S. agriculture.

DISCUSSION QUESTIONS AND PROBLEMS

1. Comment on each of the following statements:
   a. Firm X showed a net loss the past 2 years. It is inefficient and should get out of the industry.

    b. Positive profit should be taxed at 100 percent, since the tax won't drive any firms out of business.

    c. A recession once in a while is good for industry because it forces the inefficient resources and firms out of business.

2. What is the impact of a sales tax paid by the retailer on the aggregate supply curve of the industry? What will happen to the supply curve if a sales tax must be paid each time the product changes hands, that is, by the producer, the jobber, the wholesaler, etc.?

3. Explain why a rise in the price of wheat will shift the supply curve for corn.

4. What would be the impact on the supply curve for Ford automobiles if there were a 20 percent increase in the price of steel?

5. Based on the fact that United States farmers produced one million bushels of corn annually between 1900 and 1905 at an average price of $0.54 per bushel, and two million bushels between 1940 and 1945 at an average price of $0.45 per bushel, an economist concluded that the United States supply curve for corn is downward sloping. What is your conclusion from the above "facts"?

6. If someone published (say, in the *New York Times*) the formula for Coca-Cola, what might happen to the supply curve for the industry?

7. Explain the process of adjustment if the only fried chicken stand in your community was making large positive profits.

8. How will an increase in the price of automobiles be reflected in the number of automobile workers employed by the industry?

9. What would be the impact on the employment of welders in the steel industry of a union-negotiated increase in welders' wages in the automobile industry? (Assume their wage contract in the automobile industry still has 2 years to run.)

10. Why is the supply of agricultural products very inelastic in the short run? Would the long-run supply curve be more or less elastic?

11. Explain why the supply curve for a firm is that portion of marginal cost above average variable cost rather than above average total cost.

12. What is the elasticity of supply of a perfectly vertical (linear) supply curve? Of a perfectly horizontal (linear) supply curve?

CHAPTER 8: CONSUMER DEMAND

Up to this point we have seen that a producer makes several important decisions, namely, what to produce, how to produce it, and how much of it to produce, and we have investigated the conceptual basis used by economists to describe how those decisions are made. However, all of what we have gone through is still incomplete. It is incomplete because it says nothing about the basis for all private production decisions—the notion of consumer demand. We saw in the early chapters that in a free enterprise economy it is largely the wishes of consumers which dictate the kind and quantity of commodities that will be produced;[1] that is, the competitive system is said to respond to the wishes and desires of consumers. This is usually referred to as "consumer sovereignty." In this chapter we develop the conceptual basis of consumer demand so that the student understands the way in which consumer behavior produces a set of signals which producers find useful in deciding how much to produce and what to produce. In the following chapters we will put together the two sides of the market (the supply side of Chapters 5, 6, and 7, and the demand side of this chapter) so that market equilibrium and the forces establishing a market price can be explored. The student will then have all the basic tools necessary for an analysis and discussion of policies, programs, and issues of resource allocation.

OVERVIEW

In economics, *demand* is defined as a schedule showing the amounts of goods or services which consumers are able and willing to purchase in a given market at a given array of prices in a given time period. The words "able" and "willing" are emphasized because they are keys to determining the demand for a particular commodity. The word "able" refers to the ability of a consumer to purchase a particular good and is a function of income and wealth. "Willing-

---

1. We say "largely" because several writers argue that consumers, rather than guiding production decisions, are instead manipulated to a certain extent by large firms employing persuasive advertising. For one view of this argument, see John Kenneth Galbraith, *The Affluent Society* (Boston: Houghton Mifflin, 1958); and *The New Industrial State* (Boston: Houghton Mifflin, 1967).

TABLE 8.1. Hypothetical demand schedule for apples, by a typical
individual, Oaksville Market, 1973

Price	Quantity/Week
(each)	(pounds)
$0.10	3.0
0.15	2.5
0.20	2.0
0.25	1.5
0.30	1.0
0.35	0.5
0.40	0.0

ness" refers to the consumer being prepared to purchase and is determined by individual preferences. The "given array of prices" means
that there are alternative prices which allow choice between quantities
of the good or service at these different prices. The "given time period"
emphasizes the fact that the time frame of reference is important to the
definition and must be clearly stated. Thus the demand schedule is
specific to a particular time and place. The place may be as specific as a
particular city or as general as the United States. Similarly, the particular
time may refer to the demand per day, per week, or per year.

It should be emphasized that the schedule or function of prices
and quantities is a list of alternative possible situations of which only
one can exist at any one time. Such a schedule is illustrated in Table 8.1.
The schedule relates the various quantities of apples a consumer would
purchase at possible alternative prices. The demand schedule shows, for
example, that if the price is $0.10 per apple, the individual will purchase
3 pounds of apples per week; at $0.20, 2 pounds; and at $0.30, 1 pound;
etc. As we shall see, the fact that the consumer is not consciously aware
of what he would purchase at prices other than the one he finds in the
marketplace does not alter the fact that there is a schedule. If the price
had been different, the quantity purchased would also have been different.

The demand schedule of Table 8.1 can be depicted also in
graphic form as shown in Figure 8.1. The line D is called the demand
curve. It represents the quantity of apples that the individual is able
and stands ready to buy at each possible price. The demand curve can
be a straight line or it can be curved, with its form determined by the
individual's preferences as will be seen below.

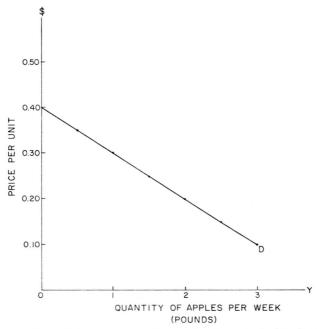

FIG. 8.1. Hypothetical demand curve for apples by a typical individual, Oaksville Market, 1973.

Note also that in Figure 8.1 the demand curve slopes downward and to the right. This is a characteristic feature of demand curves, and it is sometimes referred to as *the law of demand*. It is a shorthand way of saying that there is an inverse relationship between prices and quantities. In other words, the consumer will buy more of a commodity at a low price than at a high price. It should also be noted that the demand curve—like a production function—depicts a maximum concept. At any given quantity, a consumer would not be willing nor able to pay more than that corresponding price, though he surely would be willing to pay less to obtain that same quantity.

It is important to make a distinction between the demand of an individual and the demand of groups of individuals. Our earlier definition was not very specific in this regard, so let us begin by stating that the demand curve for an individual depicts the alternative quantities that the individual is willing and able to purchase at alternative prices, *ceteris paribus*. Before one can talk of demand by an individual consumer, it is necessary to control for such factors as (1) the income of the consumer, (2) tastes and preferences of the consumer, and (3) prices of substitute and complementary products. Should any one of these items change, the net result will be a new demand schedule for the individual.

TABLE 8.2. Aggregate demand schedule for apples of four consumers, Potsville, U.S.A., 1973

Price per Pound	Individual				Aggregate Demand
	A	B	C	D	
	(quantity/week in pounds)				
$0.10	3.0	4.0	1.0	2.0	10.0
0.15	2.5	3.2	0.5	1.0	7.2
0.20	2.0	2.9	0.3	0.2	5.4
0.25	1.5	2.6	0.1	0.0	4.2
0.30	1.0	2.4	0.0	0.0	3.4
0.35	0.5	2.2	0.0	0.0	2.7
0.40	0.0	2.1	0.0	0.0	2.1

In other words, his ableness and willingness to purchase a certain quantity at a given price will be different from what it was before. By defining income, tastes and preferences, and prices of other commodities as constant under *ceteris paribus,* we can isolate the impact of changes in the price of a commodity on the quantity of a commodity that a consumer will buy. Once the basic concept is clear, each of the other variables can be introduced one by one to see what impact they have on the demand for a commodity. If, for example, in considering the demand for Coca-Cola we allow the prices of coffee, of beer, of milk, and of other commodities to change continually, it would be difficult to assess the impact of the change in the price of Coca-Cola on the quantity of Coca-Cola taken off the market.

INDIVIDUAL AND AGGREGATE DEMAND

Aggregate demand is merely the sum of the demands of all individuals that are able and willing to purchase the commodity.[2]

It is calculated by adding, *at each price,* what each individual is willing to purchase. For example, if we have a demand schedule for four indviduals (A, B, C, and D), as illustrated in Table 8.2 and Figure 8.2, the aggregate demand at $0.10 is simply the sum of the quantities each of the individuals—A, B, C, and D—are willing and able to purchase at $0.10. If we knew the individual demand curves for all consumers,

2. The student will notice the analogy between individual and aggregate demand and individual and aggregate supply, as discussed in Chapter 7.

we could derive the aggregate demand curve as in Table 8.2 or as in Figure 8.2.

Notice in the table and in the figure that at a price of $0.25 per pound individual D has dropped out of the market. Also, notice that at $0.30 per pound individual C drops out. At these points, we would say that the demand by individuals C and D is ineffective demand. Similarly, most students have an ineffective demand for Rolls-Royce automobiles, yachts, and Caribbean cruises. This is not to say that they do not desire such items, merely that their demand—at current levels of income and price—is ineffective.

In summary, an individual's demand for a good or a service is but one component of the aggregate demand for that good or service. When all individuals' demand curves are added together, we have aggregate demand. That aggregation may be for a given region of the country (say a state, or several states), for a given socioeconomic class, or for a given age class. A recording studio likely has quite good demand information by age class, which would lead it to produce, for example, 5 Lawrence Welk albums per year and 500 albums of "acid rock" over that same period of time, with the production of Chopin, Bach, and Strauss

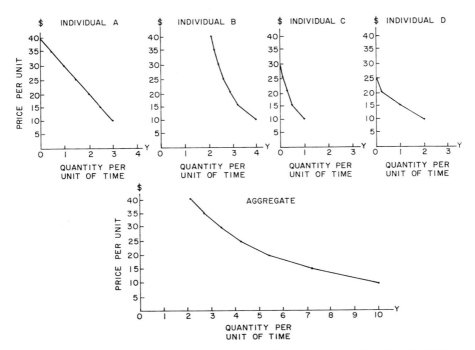

FIG. 8.2. Individual and aggregate demand for apples, Potsville, U.S.A., 1973.

likely falling somewhere in between those two extremes. Thus far, the demand concepts have been developed in an intuitive manner. We will now develop the theoretical basis on which the demand curve of the consumer for a particular commodity is derived. The discussion will be divided into three sections. The first section examines the consumer's willingness to consume as reflected by indifference curves. The second section examines the consumer's ability to purchase the commodity as constrained by his budget line. The final section illustrates how the indifference curve, as reflecting the consumer's willingness, and the budget line, as reflecting ability, combine to produce the individual demand curve for a particular commodity.

For the sake of perspective, it is necessary to point out at this stage that the approach to be developed below is the result of a long evolution of economic thought that dates back to the turn of the century. The initial view of consumer demand, developed primarily by William Jevons, Karl Menger, and Leon Walras, argued that the downward slope of the individual consumer's demand curve emanates from the diminishing utility the consumer obtains from each additional unit he consumes (diminishing marginal utility), and hence he is only willing to pay a lesser price for additional units. It assumes the consumer maximizes total satisfaction by allocating income among goods in such a manner that the marginal utility derived from the last dollar spent on one good is exactly equal to the marginal utility derived from the last dollar spent on all other commodities.[3] The neoclassical approach to be discussed below eliminates the need to assume that utility of the consumer is measurable. As such, it is intellectually more appealing than having to assume that the utility derived from eating subsequent apples can somehow be measured. Both approaches result in the same thing though—the understanding and explanation of consumer behavior.[4]

THEORY OF CONSUMER DEMAND

In this section we divide the theory of consumer demand into two major components. First, we theoretically describe the willingness of the consumer to purchase different combinations of goods. Second, we develop a theoretical description of the consumer's ability to purchase different combinations of goods as constrained by his

3. For excellent discussions of the evolution of economic thought, see Robert L. Heilbroner, *The Worldly Philosophers* (New York: Simon and Schuster, 1965); Jacob Oser, *The Evolution of Economic Thought* (New York: Harcourt, Brace & World, 1963); and George Soule, *Ideas of the Great Economists* (New York: Viking Press, 1952).

4. For an elementary discussion of the marginal utility approach to consumer demand, along with the indifference curve analysis, see Richard H. Leftwich, *The Price System and Resource Allocation*, 4th ed. (Hinsdale, Ill.: Dryden Press, 1970).

budget. Finally, we integrate these two components to derive one particular point on the consumer's demand schedule or curve.

INDIFFERENCE CURVE

The neoclassical, or indifference curve, approach to consumer demand was originally developed by an English economist, Francis V. Edgeworth, and by the famous Italian sociologist-economist, Vilfredo Pareto. Although their work occurred around the turn of the century, it fell to two famous English economists, J. R. Hicks and R. G. D. Allen, to popularize the approach in the 1930s.

Assume that we have a consumer who has only two commodities, steaks and pork chops, upon which he can spend his monthly income. Consequently, we could represent all possible combinations of pork chops and steaks our consumer could consume in one month on a graph such as in Figure 8.3. Ignoring for the moment any limitations that the consumer's income might impose on what he can buy, any point in Figure 8.3 represents a possible combination of steaks and pork chops that can be consumed per month. Consider any combination—say point A. This point indicates that the consumer would consume P_1 pork chops

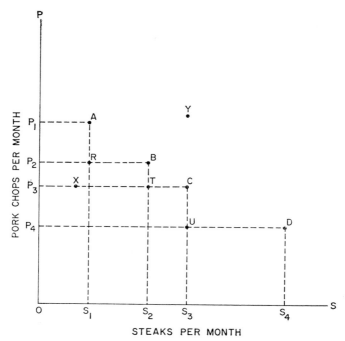

FIG. 8.3. Alternative combinations of pork chops and steaks consumed per month by a hypothetical consumer.

and S_1 steaks per month. Obviously the consumer would prefer some points to others and be neutral with respect to still other possible combinations. For example, consider the combination represented by point X. Clearly point A is preferable to point X because it represents a larger quantity of both steaks and pork chops. Similarly, the consumer would prefer point Y to points such as A, B, C, and X because it represents a larger quantity of one or both commodities.

Other combinations on Figure 8.3 are not as clearly preferable to A, X, or Y. In fact, one can theoretically find a series of points or combinations of the two commodities for which the consumer would have no preference. For example, suppose point B is one such point. If the consumer is indifferent between points A and B, the amount of steak and pork chops represented by points A and B are such that he does not care which combination he has. Theoretically one could find such a point by taking away $P_1 - P_2$ pork chops and asking the consumer the following question: What is the additional number of steaks that would compensate you for the loss of pork chops? After some thought, the consumer would answer: $S_2 - S_1$ additional steaks would exactly compensate me for the loss of $P_1 - P_2$ pork chops. The consumer is therefore saying that he is *indifferent* between combination A and combination B.

We can repeat the experiment by asking the consumer to forego the consumption of $P_2 - P_3$ pork chops. This time he tells us it would require an additional $S_3 - S_2$ steaks to compensate him. The loss of $P_3 - P_4$ pork chops requires compensating our consumer with an additional $S_4 - S_3$ steaks. We now have four points—A, B, C, and D—representing four combinations of steaks and pork chops to which our consumer is *indifferent*. In other words, he derives the same satisfaction or utility from consuming combination A of pork chops and steaks as from consuming combination D.

One can obtain as many points as necessary by making the units of pork chops and steaks as small as desired. By connecting all these points we obtain an indifference curve labeled U_1 in Figure 8.4. Thus the consumer is indifferent between all the combinations of steak and pork chops represented by line U_1 which passes through points A, B, C, and D. An *indifference curve* is defined as a set of points representing different combinations of goods, all of which give the consumer the same level of satisfaction.[5]

Several important assumptions underlying the derivation of the indifference curve should be noted. First, the consumer is rational; this means that he prefers a larger quantity of a commodity to a smaller

---

5. The student should notice the similarity between the isoquant of production theory and the indifference curve in demand theory. In the former, we have a locus of points defining the combinations of two inputs to produce a given level of production (or output), while in the latter we have a locus of points defining the combinations of two inputs to produce a given level of satisfaction or utility.

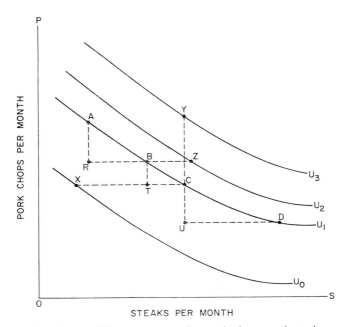

FIG. 8.4. A family of indifference curves for pork chops and steaks.

quantity; he prefers point Z to point B in Figure 8.4. It is not necessary that we be able to measure the amount by which he prefers Z, just that it is preferred. Second, since all points on U_2 are equivalent to Z, it means that indifference curve U_2 represents higher levels of satisfaction (or utility) than U_1, and U_3 higher levels than U_2. Third, indifference curves can never intersect. The intersection of U_2 and U_1, for example, would mean that a lesser quantity of the goods (point C) could be preferred to a larger quantity of both (point Z). This would imply some combinations on U_2 would represent a lower level of satisfaction than combinations on U_1. This is logically inconsistent with the previous two assumptions. Fourth, the consumer need not state how much he prefers U_3 to U_2, or U_2 to U_1. He can merely rank them in order of increasing preference; the consumer is assumed to have ordinal utility. For example, the consumer may not be able to say that steak gives him 5 units more utility than pork chops, or that gum gives him 3 units more utility than a candy bar, but merely that he prefers a given quantity of steaks to a given quantity of pork chops, and 1 package of gum to 1 candy bar. In other words, he can rank commodities in order of preference. Finally, the indifference curve slopes downward from left to right, meaning that there is a diminishing rate at which one good substitutes for another to maintain a certain level of utility. In other words, the greater the quantity of pork chops the consumer has, the smaller the amount of steak that will be required to replace 1 pork chop to maintain total satisfaction. For example, in moving from point A to B in Figure 8.4, the consumer is willing to substitute RB steaks for AR pork chops. However, at point C, to induce the consumer to accept CU fewer pork chops (equal to AR), it is necessary to compensate him with UD steaks (and UD is greater than RB). This phenomenon is termed the *principle of diminishing marginal rates of substitution*. The marginal rate of substitution is a measure of the slope of the indifference curve. It is defined as the number of units of one commodity necessary to replace one unit of the other commodity to maintain the same total satisfaction.

In addition, we must make two more assumptions, one with respect to the consumer's behavior, and the other with respect to a restriction on his behavior. Our analysis assumes that the consumer is interested in maximizing utility; that the consumer seeks to pick a combination of pork chops and steaks on the highest possible indifference curve. The final assumption is that the consumer has limited income. This assumption simply means that the consumer faces the problem of allocating income among alternative possible goods and services. If income were not limited, it would always be possible to move out to higher and higher indifference curves; there would be no problem of choice. It is the existence of an income constraint which limits the degree to which he can move out from indifference curve U_1 to indifference curve U_2, or to $U_3, \ldots, U_n$. We will examine this concept more closely under the next section related to the consumer's budget constraint. But first it is necessary to elaborate on the concept of an indifference curve.

In earlier discussions we talked in terms of physical quantities of pork chops and steaks and we now will discuss these goods in terms of dollars and in terms of physical quantities. This reformulation of the analysis is accomplished by replacing "pork chops per month" on the ordinate with "money spent on pork chops per month."

Figure 8.5 depicts various amounts of money allocated to the purchase of pork chops (at \$1 per pork chop) and the number of steaks purchased during the month. For instance, our consumer can spend \$40 for pork chops and also buy 10 steaks to attain a certain level of utility (point A on U_1). Alternatively, it would be possible to attain that same level of utility by spending only \$30 on pork chops but purchasing 15 steaks (point B). Or, there are several other combinations depicted in Figure 8.5 and in Table 8.3.

A central concept in economic theory is that of diminishing marginal utility—a concept that can be illustrated using Figure 8.5 (or Table 8.3). For the consumer to be indifferent as between points A and B, he gives up \$10 in pork chops in exchange for 5 more steaks. We would be correct therefore to assume that each steak is worth approximately \$2 (column 4, Table 8.3) in that particular range of quantities

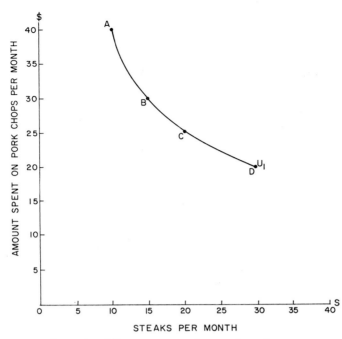

FIG. 8.5. Hypothetical indifference curve for steak and money spent on pork chops.

TABLE 8.3. Combination of steaks and money spent on pork chops yielding equal utility per period of time

Point in Figure 8.5	Dollars for Pork Chops	Number of Steaks	Marginal Rate of Substitution[a] between Pork Chops and Steaks
(1)	(2)	(3)	(4)
A	$40	10	
			$2.00/steak
B	30	15	
			1.00/steak
C	25	20	
			0.50/steak
D	20	30	

a. Stated in terms of dollars per steak.

of the two goods. As the consumer moves from *B* to *C*, $5 less is spent
on pork chops, and 5 more steaks are purchased. Remaining on the
same indifference curve implies our consumer is willing to trade $5
worth of pork chops for 5 additional steaks. It is safe to conclude that
each steak is worth approximately $1 to our consumer (column 4, Table
8.3). Finally, in moving from *C* to *D*, the consumer evinces indifference
between $5 less for pork chops and 10 more steaks (from 20 steaks to 30
steaks). Now, each steak would appear to be worth $0.50.

What this exercise demonstrates is that as the consumer acquires more steaks per unit of time, his evaluation of them—their worth
to him—falls. An alternative way of viewing the concept is that at *D*
the consumer would sacrifice 10 steaks per week (*CD*) for only $5 worth
of pork chops. However, in moving from *C* to *B*, the additional $5 worth
of pork chops results in a sacrifice of only 5 steaks.

It will be recalled that the shape and position of the indifference curves are a reflection of the consumer's tastes and preferences, and
that we would expect great individual differences. For example, if a
consumer considers two commodities as perfect substitutes, there would
be a willingness to exchange them in constant proportions. In part a of
Figure 8.6, commodities *X* and *Y* are considered perfect substitutes over
the relevant range depicted, and hence the indifference curves are linear,
reflecting a constant marginal rate of substitution. An example of perfect substitutes would be Idaho potatoes and Maine potatoes; our facilities for discrimination are sufficiently weak that the two commodities
are termed perfect substitutes. If, however, growers of Idaho potatoes
have succeeded—through incessant advertising—in convincing consumers
that their product is indeed superior, then the indifference curves would

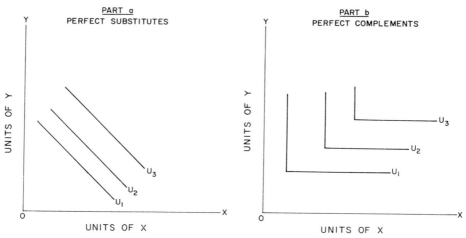

FIG. 8.6.   Two families of indifference curves reflecting different assumptions
about characteristics of commodities **X** and **Y**.

be curved as in earlier figures. This will have an effect upon the demand curve which is derived from the indifference curves.

At the other extreme is the situation where two commodities are considered perfect complements. This arises when the two must always be used in some fixed proportion. A fairly common example would be left and right shoes. Indifference curves for perfect complements are depicted in part b of Figure 8.6.

By way of summary, the concept of indifference curves provides one-half the foundation upon which demand theory rests. The indifference curve is a reflection of the willingness of a consumer to purchase certain bundles of commodities and is based on his tastes and preferences. The other aspect—ability to purchase—derives from the budget constraint of the consumer.

BUDGET CONSTRAINT

In any given period of time, a consumer faces a budget constraint which describes—given the prevailing set of prices—the various combinations of goods that can be purchased. For example, assume that a consumer has $50 per month to allocate between pork chops and steaks. The various ways of allocating this $50 between steak and pork chops is illustrated in Table 8.4.

In the table, alternative A indicates that the consumer would spend all $50 for pork chops, and would buy zero steaks. Alternative E is at the opposite extreme where nothing would be spent on pork chops and all would go for the purchase of steaks. The intermediate points are some combination of steak and pork chops.

Where steaks are $2 each, the data in Table 8.4 indicate that the maximum number which could be purchased per month is 25. This is plotted as point E in Figure 8.7. Notice that this would leave nothing to be spent on pork chops. At the opposite extreme (alternative A), we saw above how all $50 would be spent on pork chops, with nothing

TABLE 8.4. Alternative allocation of $50 per month between steaks and pork chops

Alternative	Number of Pork Chops at $1 each	Number of Steaks at $2 each	Number of Steaks at $1 each
A	50	0	0
B	30	10	20
C	20	15	30
D	10	20	40
E	0	25	50

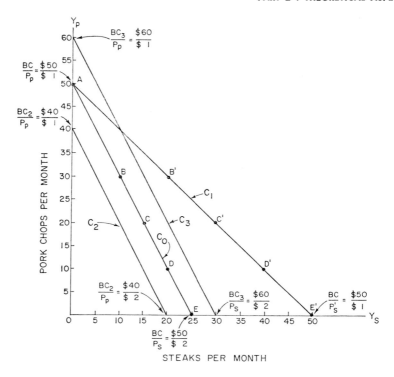

FIG. 8.7. Budget constraints under two different assumptions regarding the price of steak, and three alternative budgets.

spent on steak. This is plotted as point *A* in Figure 8.7. Notice that the various combinations between these two extremes are plotted on the line between points *A* and *E*. This locus of points for different combinations of steak and pork chops constitutes the budget constraint.[6] Line C_0 in Figure 8.7 is the graphic representation of the budget constraint. Line C_1 in Figure 8.7 constitutes the budget constraint when the price of steak is $1 each. Notice the relation between the amount allocated to pork chops and the number of $1 steaks depicted by the last column in Table 8.4. It should be obvious that if steaks cost only $1 each, the consumer could—by allocating all $50 to the purchase of steak—obtain 50 per month (point *E'*), rather than the 25 under the higher price.

To develop the concept of a budget constraint, we can employ the approach used in Chapter 5 when dealing with input usage of the firm. Let *BC* represent the amount budgeted each month to be spent on steak and on pork chops. Then,

6. Other texts refer to this as the budget line, or the isocost line.

$$BC = (P_S) \, (Y_S) + (P_p) \, (Y_p) \tag{8.1}$$

where

$P_S =$ price per steak
$Y_S =$ number of steaks
$P_p =$ price of pork chops
$Y_p =$ quantity of pork chops

We know from the analysis of Chapter 5 that the equation for the budget line is

$$Y_p = (BC/P_p) - (P_S/P_p) \, (Y_S) \tag{8.2}$$

This is the equation of a straight line with a vertical (ordinate) intercept of BC/P_p and a horizontal (abscissa) intercept of BC/P_S. In the above examples, $BC = \$50$, $P_S = \$2$, and $P_p = \$1$. It is clear that Equation 8.2, with these numbers inserted, yields line C_0 in Figure 8.7. If $P_S = \$1$, the equation would give us line C_1; that is,

$$C_0 = 50 - 2Y_S \tag{8.3}$$

$$C_1 = 50 - Y_S \tag{8.4}$$

are the equations for the budget constraint lines C_0 and C_1 in Figure 8.7.

At this time it is important to make a distinction between shifts in the budget constraint and changes in its slope. As for the latter, Equations 8.3 and 8.4 depict two budget constraints with the same vertical intercept (50) but with different slopes. One (C_0) has a slope of -2, the other (C_1) has a slope of -1. The slope of the lines is given by the ratio of the two prices P_S/P_p. This can be computed alternatively by recalling that the vertical intercept is BC/P_p, and that the horizontal intercept is BC/P_S. Since we know that the slope of a line is its rise over its run, we can form

$$(BC/P_p)/(BC/P_S) \tag{8.5}$$

which reduces to

$$P_S/P_p \tag{8.6}$$

It should be clear that the size of the budget determines its position in Figure 8.7. Hence, a shift arises out of a change in the budget available. Budget constraints C_0 and C_1 are for a monthly budget of $50. Budget constraint C_2 is for a monthly budget of $40, while C_3 is for a monthly budget of $60. Both of the latter two constraints have a slope which depicts the price of steak at $2 each.

Different budget levels—holding relative prices constant—result in parallel shifts of the budget constraint, while changes in relative prices result in movements of the intercept along the axis of the good whose price has changed. If the price of steaks changes, the intercept on the horizontal axis (abscissa) will change. If the price of pork chops changes, that intercept will change. As for the direction of that move to a new intercept, recall that the intercept is given by

$$BC/P_i$$

where

$$P_i = \text{the price of any good depicted on an axis}$$

Hence, if P_i increases, BS/P_i is a smaller quantity and would move the intercept closer to the origin. On the other hand, a decrease in P_i causes BC/P_i to be a larger quantity and moves the intercept away from the origin. This concept is central to the derivation of a demand curve and should be thoroughly understood before proceeding.[7]

CONSUMER EQUILIBRIUM UNDER A BUDGET CONSTRAINT

We are now in a position to combine the consumer's willingness to purchase commodities—represented by his indifference map—with his ability to make such purchases—represented by his budget constraint—given his income and relative prices. From this, a combination of pork chops and steaks that the consumer is both willing and able to purchase can be derived. Recall that the assumed objective of the consumer is to attain the highest level of utility that his income will permit. Put in the context of our earlier discussion, the consumer wishes to attain the highest indifference curve subject to the budget constraint.

In Figure 8.8, assume that the consumer is currently at point N. Here a monthly budget of $50 is being allocated between pork chops ($40) and 5 steaks at $2 each. The consumer is on the $50 budget constraint but is not on the highest possible indifference curve; that is, for the same expenditure of $50, it is possible to achieve a higher level of utility. By moving from point N to point A, the consumer can attain a higher level of utility (U_2) and still spend only $50 per month. Whereas

7. The student should satisfy himself that a doubling of both prices in this analysis leaves the slope of the budget constraint unchanged, although it will shift the constraint toward the origin.

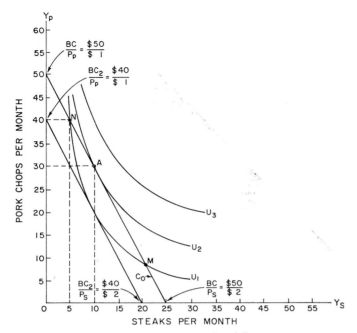

FIG. 8.8. Integration of budget constraint and indifference curves.

at N there were 5 steaks purchased, leaving $40 to spend on pork chops, the superior position results in 10 steaks being purchased, leaving $30 to spend on pork chops. It is at point A that the budget constraint is just tangent to the highest possible indifference curve. Notice that the $50 budget line intersects lower indifference curves (for example, M on indifference curve U_1) but combination A is preferable because U_2 represents a higher level of utility to the consumer. Given his budget (C_0), point A is the most desirable combination. At any point either to the left or to the right of point A on budget line C_0, the consumer would be on lower indifference curves. Furthermore, it should be noted that points to the northeast of A (beyond A, say on U_3) are unattainable because of the budget constraint, and points to the southwest of A are attainable but undesirable because they lie on lower indifference curves.

We can summarize the foregoing by asserting that the utility-maximizing combination of any two commodities (in this case steak and pork chops) is found at that point where the marginal rate of substitution (MRS) between the two commodities is exactly equal to the ratio of their prices. Or, algebraically,

$$MRS = - P_s/P_p \tag{8.7}$$

We already know that the price ratio is given by the slope of the budget constraint, and we know that the marginal rate of substitution (*MRS*) is the slope of the indifference curves; the indifference curves depict the rate at which a consumer can substitute one commodity for another and still maintain the same level of utility.

At point *N* in Figure 8.8, the marginal rate of substitution between steaks and pork chops is far in excess of the relative prices of the two goods, and the individual is in equilibrium where the two are equal—at point *A*; that is, at *N*, the consumer would be better off (reach a higher indifference curve) with fewer pork chops and more steaks. At *M*, the opposite is true.

Given the concept of consumer equilibrium, we can now proceed to derive the individual's demand curve for a commodity based on tastes and preferences—the indifference map—as constrained by income—the budget line.

DERIVATION OF A CONSUMER DEMAND CURVE

To derive the demand curve for a commodity, it has been seen necessary to hold certain things constant—the *ceteris paribus* caveat. It is now time to formally introduce those conditions into the analysis. Several have already been discussed—tastes and preferences held constant and income held constant. The final important one is that the prices of all other goods are held constant. Recall that it would be impossible to understand consumers' reaction to changes in the price of steaks if the prices of other items also change, particularly if there were price changes for other food items. Hence, we must fix all other prices. Finally, since the consumer chooses between steak and many other goods, it is necessary to expand our analysis from one of pork chops and steaks to "all other goods" and steaks. Figure 8.9 depicts the quantity of all goods except steak on the ordinate, and quantity of steaks on the abscissa.

Now it is necessary to rationalize the presence of a budget constraint in a diagram such as Figure 8.9. Before, it was easy to talk of pork chops and the price of pork chops. But what is the price of "other goods"? Simply put, we know that the important issue in consumer demand is relative prices between steaks and the other goods. Hence, we can arbitrarily set the price of other goods equal to unity and proceed with our analysis. Budget constraints C_0, C_1, and C_2 in Figure 8.9 reflect a budget constraint of $50, a price of other goods equal to unity ($P_G =$ $1), and a price of steak of $2, $1, and $5, respectively. When the price of steak is $1, the budget line C_1 is tangent to indifference curve U_3 at point *D*. Here the consumer is on the highest possible indifference curve and is purchasing 25 steaks per month, leaving $25 to be spent on other goods. If the price of steaks were increased to $2 each, budget line C_0 is relevant and is tangent to the highest possible indifference

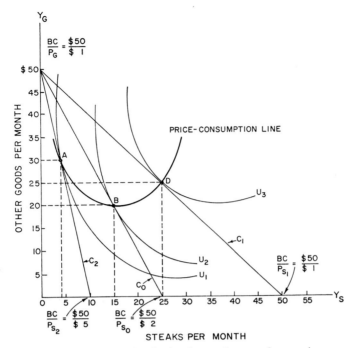

FIG. 8.9. Derivation of an individual's demand curve for steaks per month.

curve (U_2) at point B. Here 15 steaks per month are being purchased at $2 each, leaving $20 to be spent on other goods. Finally, if the price of steaks should rise to $5 each, budget constraint C_2 becomes relevant. Tangency with the highest possible indifference curve is at point A, where 4 steaks are purchased per month, leaving $30 to spend on other goods. The line joining points A, B, and D is called the *price-consump-tion line*.

The demand curve for steaks of the individual depicted in Figure 8.9 can now be expressed—as we have defined it earlier—as a schedule (or curve) relating different quantities of a commodity that would be purchased at different prices per unit of time. In Figure 8.9, point A indicates that 4 steaks per month would be purchased when their price is $5 each. This point is plotted as point A in Figure 8.10. When the price of steaks falls to $2 each, we see that 15 would be purchased per month. This point is plotted as point B in Figure 8.10. Finally, when the price of steaks falls to $1 each, we see that 25 would be purchased per month (point D, Figure 8.9). This point is plotted as point D in Figure 8.10.

One topic of importance in economics, but one which is left

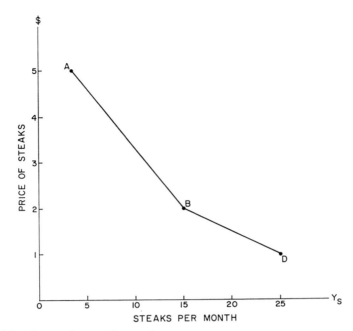

FIG. 8.10. Demand curve for steak.

for more advanced study, concerns the nature of the consumer's response to a price change. As the price of steak increased in Figure 8.9 from $1 to $5, the decrease in the quantity of steaks purchased consists of a *substitution effect,* and an *income effect.* The first reflects the consumer switching to lower-priced goods in the face of a higher price for steak. The latter reflects the fact that the consumer's real income has decreased. In the case of a price decrease, the substitution effect would be in the direction of more expensive goods, and the income effect would be in the form of an increase in real income.[8]

In summary, given an indifference map, a fixed income, and all prices but one held constant, one can describe what the consumer would do under all possible alternative prices for a product by obtaining the price-consumption line. The price-consumption line depicts the pairs of product prices and equilibrium quantities the consumer would purchase. The necessary price-quantity data to plot the individual consumer's demand curve are obtained from the price-consumption line. They can be either plotted to obtain the demand curve or listed to ob-

8. For more detail on this see C. E. Ferguson, *Microeconomic Theory* (Homewood, Ill.: Richard D. Irwin, 1972), pp. 58–60; and Richard G. Lipsey and Peter O. Steiner, *Economics* (New York: Harper & Row, 1972), pp. 146–47.

tain the demand schedule. In the next section we will examine the impact on the demand curve of relaxing the assumption that "all other variables are held constant."

SHIFTS IN CONSUMER DEMAND

The shape and position of the demand curve is dependent upon those factors which we have held constant in earlier analyses. As long as these other factors—the consumer's income, the prices of other goods, and the tastes and preferences of the consumer—do not change, the consumer's demand curve will not change. If that is the case, we can talk of *movements* along a demand curve. The causal factor here would be a change in the price of the good depicted in the demand curve (part a of Figure 8.11). In contrast, a *shift* in the demand curve is the result of a change in one of the *ceteris paribus* conditions (part b of Figure 8.11). This section will treat the impact on the individual's demand curve when these other factors change.

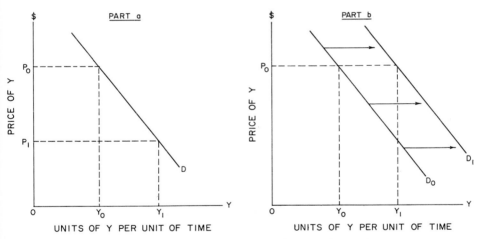

FIG. 8.11. Distinction between a movement along a demand curve versus a shift in the demand curve.

CONSUMER'S INCOME

Figure 8.12 depicts the effect of an increase in a consumer's income on the demand curve. The budget constraints C_0 and C_1 represent two alternative prices for steak at the initial income level, while C'_0 and C'_1 represent the same relative prices at a higher level of income. Demand curve D in part b of Figure 8.12 corresponds to budget constraints C_0 and C_1 (low income), while demand curve D' corresponds to

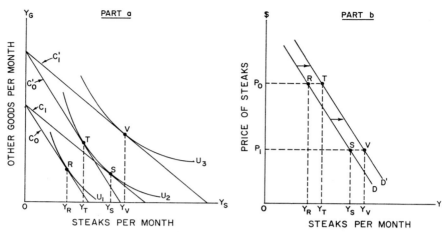

FIG. 8.12. Effect on the demand curve for steaks from an increase in the consumer's income.

budget constraints C'_0 and C'_1 (high income). With the low-income budget constraint lines, the tangency points are at R and S, indicating that the consumer would demand Y_R steaks at a price P_0, and Y_S steaks at the lower price (P_1). The high-income budget lines are tangent to the indifference curves at T and V. At this higher income, the consumer would demand Y_T steaks when the price is P_0, and Y_V steaks at price P_1. Notice the impact on the demand curve from this increase in income. We can conclude that as income changes, it shifts the individual's demand curve to the right or the left through a change in the budget lines.

Normally, an increase in the consumer's income will lead to a rightward shift in the demand curve for a commodity, and a decrease in income will lead to a leftward shift. In fact, economists classify goods as normal or inferior, according to how their demand curve shifts as income changes. A *normal* good is one for which the demand curve would shift to the right as income rises. An inferior good's demand curve would shift to the left as income rises. The classic example of an inferior good is potatoes, where higher incomes permit people to buy other kinds of food (perhaps steaks), and their reliance upon inexpensive foods to satisfy their hunger is reduced. Other examples might be low-priced cars, black and white television sets, and mail-order clothes. In summary, an increase in income shifts the demand curve to the left for inferior goods and to the right for normal goods. Conversely, a decrease in income shifts the demand curve to the right for inferior goods and to the left for normal goods.

The concept of normal and inferior commodities is very useful for anticipating the impact of changes in income on economic growth. For example, in cases where national income per capita is growing rapidly, industries that are engaged in producing normal goods can expect the aggregate demand for their commodity to grow as consumer demand shifts to the right over time. On the other hand, industries that are engaged in producing inferior goods can anticipate falling demand for their product as the aggregate demand curve for their products shifts to the left. The conclusion is that, for industries producing normal goods, future prospects in terms of sales and volume of output are bright, while for industries producing inferior commodities, future expectations are at best dim.

At this point it should be recognized that the direction of causality in the real world may not be as straightforward as the above discussion implies. For example, the preceding discussion may lead the reader to conclude that as incomes rise, consumption also increases, and therefore the major determinant of consumption is income. Generally, in a market economy, an individual's productivity is the major determinant of income. In underdeveloped areas of the world, the relationship may operate in both directions, creating a cycle whereby low income breeds low levels of consumption, which, in turn, limits the individual's ability to increase his income. In such countries, people at the lower income levels have very poor diets, resulting in low energy levels. Low energy levels in turn result in low productivity and thus low income. Consequently, the low income prohibits or restrains the individual from improving his diet and productivity. It is for this reason that development programs in many areas of the world attempt to break the cycle by improving the diets of low-income people. Once the cycle is broken and individuals obtain adequate diets and adequate levels of nutrition, the higher levels of energy and increases in productivity lead to increases in income. This is one reason why in less developed countries there is much emphasis on improving agricultural output. Our food aid programs to these countries also have this as their major objective, for example, upgrading diets as a method of improving productivity. Unfortunately, many of these programs have had political repercussions because free milk, wheat, or other foods undercut local producers.

One final word is in order regarding normal goods. Economists often classify normal goods as either luxuries or necessities, depending on the magnitude of the shift in the demand curve in response to an increase in income. Color television sets, motor boats, and electric knives are examples of luxuries, while food and functional clothing would be termed necessities. More will be said on this later in the chapter.

CONSUMER'S TASTES AND PREFERENCES

A change in tastes favorable to the commodity will lead to a shift to the right in the demand curve, and an unfavorable change in taste will lead to a shift to the left in the curve. This is brought

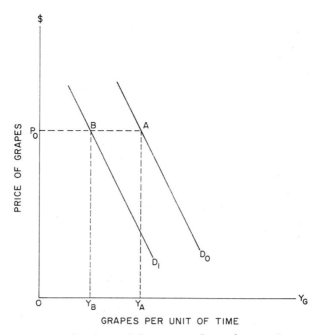

FIG. 8.13. Effects on the demand for grapes from changes in tastes and preferences.

about by shifts in the consumer's utility function (and corresponding adjustments in the indifference curves). As an illustration, consider point A on the hypothetical demand curve D_0 for California grapes in Figure 8.13. At this point the price is P_0, and the quantity the consumer would wish to buy is Y_A. Now assume that there is a release of a news story which states that all table grapes were accidentally sprayed with an insecticide which may contain certain cancer-producing agents. This would persuade the individual to want to consume fewer grapes at each price. Thus, at price P_0, he will want only Y_B grapes. This new amount is less than that previously purchased at the same price. Consequently, point B lies on a new demand curve for grapes located at D_1. The change in tastes and preferences has therefore shifted the demand curve for grapes to the left. Subsequently, a nationwide advertising campaign by the California grape growers citing evidence that frequent eating of table grapes increases one's longevity could shift the demand curve from D_1 back to D_0.

Advertising is often used to change the tastes and preferences of consumers. For example, a claim by an advertiser that brand X gasoline gives more gasoline mileage and longer engine life is an attempt to accomplish two objectives: (1) it shifts the demand curve for brand X gasoline to the right by enticing consumers away from other brands; and (2) it makes the demand less susceptible to inroads by other advertisers by convincing the consumer there is no substitute for brand X gasoline at any price. In other words, advertising attempts to shift the consumer's preference away from competitors and to prevent a shift in the demand curve for brand X gasoline to the left through counterclaims by competitors.

When dealing with aggregations of individual demand curves, it is also important to recognize that changes in tastes and preferences come about through a change in population characteristics. The preferences of an individual are a function of age, education, place of residence, marital status, family size, race, etc. The aggregate demand for a commodity reflects the preferences of the population over which that aggregation took place. If the characteristics of a population are changing, the aggregate demand will also be changing.

PRICES OF OTHER GOODS

We know that most goods are interrelated and that a change in the price of commodity A will affect the amount demanded of commodity B. This section is concerned with the problems of shifts in the demand for one commodity due to changes in the price of another. For example, we know that certain products are reasonable substitutes for one another. Margarine and butter, turkey and chicken, coffee and tea, and Coca-Cola and Pepsi-Cola are examples. Normally, when the price of one of these commodities falls, you tend to buy more of it and less of of the other. For example, when the price of turkey falls, consumers will shift more of their poultry purchases from chicken to turkey. Consequently, a fall in the price of the substitute (turkey) causes the demand for chicken to shift leftward. Conversely, had turkey prices risen, consumers would shift more of their poultry consumption to chicken, and the demand curve for chicken would shift to the right.

One can also find a list of commodities which are generally consumed jointly. They are called complements. Coffee and cream, tea and lemon, bread and margarine, bacon and eggs, and skis and ski boots are examples. In the case of complements, an increase in the price for one of the pair will result in consumers' reducing their consumption of both items. For example, if the price of coffee rises, consumers will buy less coffee. Since it is a rather common practice for consumers to use cream in their coffee, this will also cause decline in the consumption of cream as manifest in a leftward shift in the demand curve for cream.

In summary, if commodities A and B are substitutes, an increase in the price of one will shift the demand curve for the other to the right. Conversely, a fall in the price of one shifts the demand curve for the other to the left. If commodities A and B are complements, the opposite phenomenon will be observed; that is, an increase in the price of one commodity will shift the demand curve for the other to the left. Conversely, a fall in the price of one shifts the demand curve for the other to the right.

CHANGES IN POPULATION
Thus far we have talked almost exclusively of the individual's demand curve for a commodity, and have demonstrated how changes in income, tastes and preferences, and the prices of other goods would precipitate shifts in that curve. The aggregate demand curve for a specific commodity reflects the same shifts as the individual's demand curves discussed immediately above. For instance, if the tastes and preferences of many individuals change (such as with the grape example), the aggregate demand curve for grapes will shift. This is true also for income changes and changes in the prices of other goods. When discussing the *ceteris paribus* conditions for aggregate demand, the number of individuals included in the aggregation must also be held constant. Consequently, an increase in population causes shifts in aggregate demand by the mere fact that there are now more people willing and able to purchase a given commodity. An example of this phenomenon is the burgeoning sales of records which followed the baby boom of the early 1940s; a significant increase occurred in the quantity of records sold, even though each individual consumer may have purchased the same number of records as their teenage counterpart during a preceding period of time.

Finally, the student should be aware of the fact that the impact of the demand shifters is additive. For example, if the commodity is a normal good, and income and population are both increasing, aggregate demand for the commodity will shift to the right by the summation of both effects. If the commodity is an inferior good, the net effect of increasing population and income may be difficult to predict without rather accurate data on responsiveness to these two factors. In the following section we explore a more precise measure of demand responsiveness to changes in income, changes in the price of related goods, and changes in the price of the commodity under consideration.

ELASTICITY: MEASURE OF RESPONSIVENESS
Up to the present we have been describing the relationship of the price of a commodity to the quantity the consumers are willing to buy. The law of demand states that as price goes up the quantity demanded will go down. The economist is often interested in asking how much the quantity changes in response to a change

in price, and in comparing the response of commodity A to a change in its price and the response of commodity B to a change in its price. Unfortunately, as discussed earlier, the particular dimensions in which economic quantities are quoted are arbitrary. The concept of elasticity has been devised precisely with these comparison problems in mind. Elasticity helps to avoid arbitrariness in a considerable range of comparison problems. Elasticity is a measure of responsiveness. It compares the percentage change in one variable to a percentage change in another. A review of Chapter 7 (and the Appendix to Chapter 7) will reveal that elasticity is given by

$$E = (\Delta Y/Y)/(\Delta X/X) = \% \text{ change in } Y / \% \text{ change in } X \quad (8.8)$$

where

$$\Delta Y = \text{change in } Y$$
$$\Delta X = \text{change in } X$$

We also know that the equation for elasticity is given by

$$E = [(Y_2 - Y_1)/(Y_2 + Y_1)]/[(X_2 - X_1)/(X_2 + X_1)] \quad (8.9)$$

where

$$Y_2 = \text{new quantity of } Y$$
$$Y_1 = \text{old quantity of } Y$$
$$X_2 = \text{new quantity of } X$$
$$X_1 = \text{old quantity of } X$$

The remainder of this section will concentrate on three specific measures of responsiveness: (1) price elasticity of demand; (2) income elasticity of demand; and (3) cross elasticity of demand. As for the first, price elasticity of demand measures the responsiveness of a change in the quantity demanded of a commodity to its own price. In this case Y_2 and Y_1 would be the two quantities of the commodity, and X_2 and X_1 the corresponding prices of that commodity. The second elasticity, the income elasticity, measures the response of a change in the quantity demanded to a change in the consumer's income. In this case, the Y's might refer to a consumption of food, and the X's to consumer income. The result (E) is referred to as the income elasticity of demand for food. The final elasticity, the cross price elasticity, measures the responsiveness of the quantity demanded of one good to a change in the price of another good. For example, if the Y's refer to the quantity of beef demanded and the X's to the price of pork, the corresponding estimate (E) will be the cross elasticity of demand for beef with respect to pork price.

PRICE ELASTICITY OF DEMAND

The price elasticity of demand indicates the degree to which consumers are willing to change their consumption (percentage-wise) of a particular commodity in response to a percentage change in its price, as indicated in Equation 8.10.[9]

$$E_d = \% \, \Delta \text{ in quantity of a good}/\% \, \Delta \text{ in price of a good} \quad (8.10)$$
$$= [(Q_2 - Q_1)/(Q_2 + Q_1)]/[(P_2 - P_1)/(P_2 + P_1)]$$

The size of the coefficient E_d indicates the degree of responsiveness in terms of percentage changes. There are two important points to consider with respect to demand elasticities. First, since a change in either price or quantity has a sign attached, the value of E_d will also be signed. Because the demand curve is downward sloping, the change in quantity will always be opposite in sign from the change in price. Hence, the price elasticity, E_d, will always be negative, indicating that the percentage change in quantity is opposite in direction from the percentage change in price. For purposes of convenience and clarity of exposition, we will usually ignore the negative sign of E_d and refer to the numerical value, that is, its absolute value.

Second, the student must refrain from a simple association of the slope of a demand curve with a numerical value for its elasticity. Because the elasticity will change all along a straight line demand curve, it is important to recognize position on the curve as well as its slope when estimating its elasticity.[10]

Consider the location on a linear demand curve. From Equation 8.8 it is possible to rewrite elasticity as

$$E_d = (\Delta Q/Q) \, (P/\Delta P) = (\Delta Q/\Delta P) \, (P/Q) \quad (8.11)$$

There are thus two components to elasticity: the point on the demand curve at which elasticity is to be measured (P/Q), and the reciprocal of the slope of the demand curve $(\Delta Q/\Delta P)$.[11] For two parallel linear demand curves, the slope is obviously the same, but P/Q is not.

As for slope, consider Figure 8.14. Here, demand curve D_1 is less elastic than D_2. This can be verified by comparing the change in

9. The student will no doubt be perplexed by our sudden shift in notation from Y's to Q's for commodities. Our only defense (and a very weak one at that) is that production theory is usually the domain of X's and Y's, while demand theory is the domain of P's and Q's. We have resisted the transition thus far into the chapter but now succumb to conformity.

10. For a detailed analysis of elasticity, see Lipsey and Steiner, *Economics*, pp. 91–96.

11. We say "reciprocal" since the slope of a demand curve drawn traditionally, with price (P) on the vertical axis and quantity (Q) on the horizontal axis, is $\Delta P/\Delta Q$. Here, we have $\Delta Q/\Delta P$.

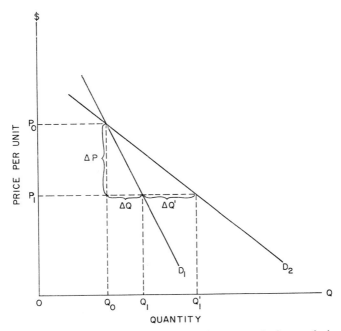

FIG. 8.14. Price elasticity of demand as a function of slope of the demand curve.

quantity from a drop in price of P_0 to P_1. The percentage change in quantity demanded for a given change in price is less for demand curve D_1 than for demand curve D_2; that is, $\Delta Q + \Delta Q'$ is larger than ΔQ, and hence E_d is less for demand curve D_1. The student should note that the comparison says nothing about the numerical value of E_d, simply that E_d for D_1 is less than for D_2.

Commodities are often classified according to the size of their price elasticity of demand. If the magnitude of E_d is greater than 1, we say the demand is *elastic*. For example, if the price elasticity of demand for beef is calculated as 1.5 (actually — 1.5), this means that the percentage change in quantity demanded is greater than the percentage change in its price. When the magnitude of elasticity is less than 1, we say the demand is *inelastic*. Again, using our beef example, if the elasticity of demand for beef is 0.8 (— 0.8), this means that the percentage change in quantity demanded is less than the percentage change in price. When the magnitude of the elasticity is equal to 1, we say that the demand is *unit elastic* or has *unitary elasticity*. This means that the percentage change in quantity demanded is equal to the percentage change in price. Figure 8.15 illustrates the relationship between the classes of demand elasticity. Part a of Figure 8.15 depicts a demand

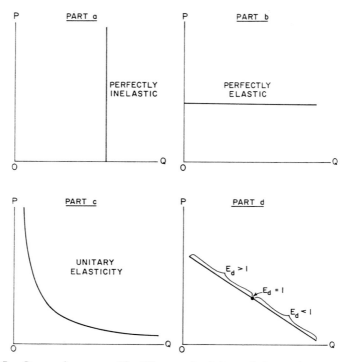

FIG. 8.15. Demand curves with different elasticities of demand.

curve that is perfectly inelastic, while part b depicts one that is perfectly elastic. The former illustrates that there is no change in quantity for a given percentage change in price, and the latter illustrates an infinite change in quantity for a given change in price. Part c illustrates a demand curve which has an elasticity of one at any point; that is, unitary elasticity. Part d shows that the numerical values of elasticity on a straight line demand curve continually change. It is for this reason that the student was cautioned earlier against assuming numerical values for E_d at any point on a specific curve.

This can be illustrated by reference to Table 8.5 where different price-quantity combinations for beef are presented. Note that the price elasticity of demand is different on different segments of the demand curve. At the higher prices, the elasticity is 3.0. This means that a 1 percent change in price results in a 3 percent change in the quantity demanded. At the lower price levels, the elasticity of demand is 0.2. This means that at the lower end of the demand schedule a 1 percent change in price will result in a 0.2 percent change in the quantity demanded.

TABLE 8.5.   Illustration of two price elasticities of demand for beef

Price per Pound	Quantity Demanded per Year	Elasticity
	(pounds)	
$5	2,000	
		-3.0 (elastic)
4	4,000	
3	7,000	
2	14,000	
		-0.2 (inelastic)
1	16,000	

$$E_d = \frac{[(4,000-2,000)/(4,000+2,000)]}{[(4.00-5.00)/(4.00+5.00)]} = 2/6 \times 9/-1 = -3.0 = elastic$$

$$E_d = \frac{[(16,000-14,000)/(16,000+14,000)]}{[(1-2)/(1+2)]} = 2/30 \times 3/-1 = -0.2 = inelastic$$

FACTORS AFFECTING ELASTICITIES

At this point it is logical to inquire as to why one commodity would have an elastic demand and another an inelastic demand. Although the question can be answered by use of indifference curves, the analysis is beyond the scope of this book. Consequently, we will answer this question in terms of three specific factors that influence the elasticity of demand. The first factor is the number of uses for the commodity. Those commodities that have many uses will tend to have more elastic demands. The more uses to which the commodity can be applied, the greater the variation in quantity demanded as price changes. A small decrease in price has the potential of bringing many new users to the marketplace to buy, and a rise in price will quickly drive them away from the good. On the other hand, if a commodity has few uses, it is those few users who will adjust and their potential impact is less. For example, suppose titanium was useful only for manufacturing aircraft frames. Since only the few aircraft manufacturers would adjust to changes in price, the impact would be smaller than in the case where it was used by a wide variety of industries. Soybeans, on the other hand, can be used to manufacture margarine, to supply proteins in feed, to make synthetic meats, and to make plastics. Hence its demand is more price elastic than if it could be used only for feed.

The second factor is the number of substitutes that exist for a commodity. Those commodities with many close substitutes will have more elastic demands than those for which no close substitutes exist.

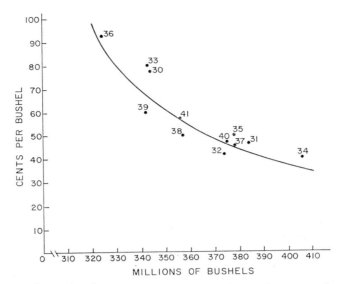

FIG. 8.16. Relationship between potato consumption and average farm prices, United States, 1930–1941. (From Warren C. Waite and Harry C. Trelogan, **Agricultural Market Prices,** New York: John Wiley, p. 44, Figure 6.)

While certain food products are relatively elastic among other food products, food products in general—for which few substitutes exist—are relatively inelastic.

The third factor affecting demand elasticity is the importance of the expenditure on the commodity relative to the consumer's income. The greater the relative expenditure, the greater the relative elasticity is likely to be. In simple terms this means that the larger the proportion of the consumer's income spent on the commodity, the more likely he is to be sensitive to changes in price for that commodity. This is the principal reason why the demand for a particular commodity is likely to be less elastic among high-income groups than among low-income groups. Generally speaking, demand is very inelastic for absolute necessities and for those luxuries of the rich that do not require very much of their income.[12]

Attempts have been made by various investigators to determine the elasticity of demand for important agricultural products. The usual method employed has been to compare the prices at which the various commodities have been sold on the market at different times and allow for changes in the values of the demand shifters. An illustration is given in Figure 8.16. Here the average seasonal price received by farmers in

12. Indeed it should be obvious that as one becomes quite rich the distinction between luxuries and necessities becomes blurred.

the United States for potatoes produced in that year is plotted as a function of the level of consumption in that year.[13] The period is from 1930 to 1941, with potato prices adjusted for changes in the general price level. The resulting points on the graph are what one would expect theoretically. The observations show larger crops bring lower prices than the smaller crops. A curve has been drawn through the observations to represent the average relationship between prices and quantities. This curve can be considered as representing an average demand curve for potatoes at farm prices during the period under consideration. It should be noted that the actual observations are scattered around the curve. This could be due to the demand shifters which have not been taken into account in this simple figure. For example, in the years 1930, 1933, and 1934, per capita income may have been below average, resulting in a shift in the demand curve to the right. By adjusting these three observations for the difference in per capita income, the points would be very close to the demand curve.

Examples of the price elasticities of demand for various products are listed in Table 8.6. Examination reveals that there is a wide range in the price elasticities of demand for agricultural commodities at the retail level. The values range from — 0.15 for cereals to — 2.35 for lamb. Notice also that the meats show quite elastic demands at the retail level, with beef at about unity, and pork the least elastic. The retail elasticity of demand for all meats (— 0.60) is less elastic than that for beef, pork, lamb, or chicken individually. This illustrates the principle stated earlier that there are fewer substitutes for meat than for an individual component such as beef, hence, the price elasticity for meat as a category is less than for any of the individual components. Greater substitutability exists within the class of meats than between all meats and other commodities. The greater the degree to which a consumer can substitute, the more elastic is the demand.

The same principle also helps explain the low price elasticity of demand for all foods collectively. There are no substitutes for food. It is this low price elasticity of demand for all foods that explains why a relatively small increase in the total quantity of food produced by farmers in a given year will tend to reduce farm prices substantially, and why small shortages will increase food prices rather dramatically.

Thus far our analysis has treated price elasticity for a given commodity as if it were rather uniform. In fact, as seen in Table 8.5, there is a difference in elasticity depending upon the point in the chain from producer to consumer at which elasticity is measured. Notice the difference in elasticities between the farm level and the retail level. This

13. The actual computation was between production levels and prices received—which is a supply concept. However, by assuming all production is consumed, it is possible to view the relationship as one of demand. See Warren C. Waite and Harry C. Trelogan, *Agricultural Market Prices* (New York: John Wiley, 1948), p. 44.

TABLE 8.6.   Price elasticities of demand for selected
agricultural commodities at the retail
and farm level

Commodity	Price Elasticity	
	Retail	Farm
Beef	-0.95	-0.64
Pork	-0.75	-0.45
Lamb	-2.35	-1.78
Chicken	-1.16	-0.74
All meats	-0.60	
Butter	-0.85	-0.66
Eggs	-0.30	-0.23
Fluid Milk	-0.29	-0.15
Fruit	-0.60	-0.20
Vegetables	-0.30	-0.10
Cereals	-0.15	-0.03
Potatoes	-0.20	-0.08
All foods	-0.34	-0.23
Nonfoods	-1.02	

Source: G. E. Brandow, Interrelations among
Demands for Farm Products and Implications for Control
of Market Supply, Pa. Agr. Exp. Sta. Bull. 680, Aug.
1961, Tables 1 and 10, pp. 17, 50.

can be explained by the fact that consumers do not buy a beef animal,
but rather roasts, liver, steaks, leather, etc. Each commodity at the retail level consists not only of the raw product but also some time, form,
and space utility discussed earlier. The steak has been processed, perhaps tenderized, and packaged. Hence, economists say that the demand
for beef at the farm level is a derived demand—derived from the demands of consumers for packaged steak, derived from the retailer's demand for a side of beef to cut up and package, and derived from the
processor's demand for carcasses to sell to the retailer. This is illustrated
in Figure 8.17 where D_F represents demand at the farm level and D_R
represents demand at the retail level.

The difference between the two demand curves depends upon
the amount of marketing cost necessary to convert a beef animal into

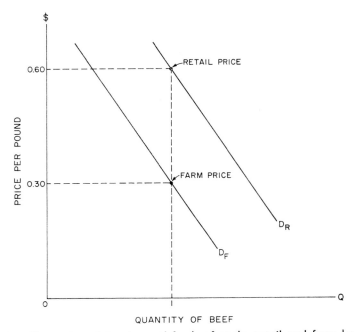

FIG. 8.17. Illustration of the demand for beef at the retail and farm levels.

the final products demanded by consumers. For example, D_R is the demand at retail for the meat products contained in the live steer. The curve D_F is the equivalent demand for this beef animal faced by the farmers. Curve D_F is derived from D_R by subtracting all the costs necessary to transform a live beef animal into edible beef and other products. In Figure 8.17 this marketing cost is \$0.30 per pound and includes the cost of slaughtering, processing, transporting, and packaging the products.

To repeat, the price elasticities at any level of output are always less at the farm level than at the retail level. The difference is dependent upon the size of the marketing charge.[14] For example, in Table 8.6 the price elasticity of eggs (for which the marketing margin is

14. This proposition can be proved as follows:
$$E_d = (\Delta Q/\Delta P)(P/Q)$$
Assuming that $\Delta Q/\Delta P$ is the same for both D_R and D_F, the elasticity at any given quantity (Q) is a function of only price (P). The lower the value of P, the lower the ratio P/Q, and, hence, the lower E_d. For example, in Figure 8.17 the elasticity at retail is
$$E_d{}^r = (\Delta Q/\Delta P)(0.60/1) = 0.6(\Delta Q/\Delta P)$$
The elasticity of derived demand at the farm is
$$E_d{}^f = (\Delta Q/\Delta P)(0.30/1) = 0.3(\Delta Q/\Delta P)$$
Obviously $E_d{}^r$ will always be greater than $E_d{}^f$. The larger the marketing charges, the larger the difference between the two prices, and hence between the two elasticities.

relatively low) only changes from 0.30 to 0.23 from the retail to the farm level. On the other hand, elasticities of fluid milk and cereals, more highly processed products with relatively high marketing margins, decrease by approximately 50 percent. This difference in elasticity between the retail and farm level is another reason why small changes in farm output can cause relatively large changes in farm prices.[15]

TOTAL REVENUE AND PRICE ELASTICITY

The amount of money spent by consumers on a commodity is of considerable interest to the seller since it represents the latter's gross receipts. The total value of the quantity sold is found by multiplying the quantity sold by the price per unit at which it was sold. To avoid confusion, we will use the term *total revenue* instead of the terms consumer outlays or seller receipts for the total value of quantity sold. Sellers are interested in knowing what will happen to their total revenue when the price of a commodity is changed. One may be inclined to conclude that when price falls, total revenue will also fall, and that when the price is raised, total revenue will increase. However, this is not necessarily the case. Because demand is downward sloping, a decrease in price will be accompanied by an increase in the quantity sold, but what happens to total revenue is dependent upon the amount by which quantity increases in relation to the price change.

This is easily determined if we know the price elasticity of demand. It is a direct expression of the relationship between the percentage change in quantity in response to a 1 percent change in price. Consequently, if we know the demand elasticity, we can immediately determine whether an increase in the quantity of the commodity sold in the market will cause total revenue to increase, decrease, or remain unchanged. Consider first the case of inelastic demand. In this case, E_d lies between 0 and 0.99.[16] An elasticity of less than 1 means that a 1 percent change in price results is less than a 1 percent change in quantity. In this case there will be an inverse relationship between total revenue and output. As price decreases, total quantity sold increases, but not sufficiently to offset the price decline and total revenue declines. When a commodity has an elasticity of demand of unity (1), decreases in price and corresponding increases in quantity exactly offset one another. In this case, regardless of the quantity of the commodity demanded, total revenue will remain unchanged. When demand is elastic, E_d is greater than 1, indicating that the percentage change in quantity is larger than

15. Economists define the reciprocal of the price elasticity of demand as *price flexibility*. A flexibility coefficient is interpreted as the percentage change in price due to a 1 percent change in the quantity marketed, *ceteris paribus*. Low price elasticities yield high price flexibilities and vice versa. We will return to this concept in discussing farm price variations in Chapter 12.

16. Remember that price elasticities of demand are actually negative quantities. For ease of discussion we use their absolute value.

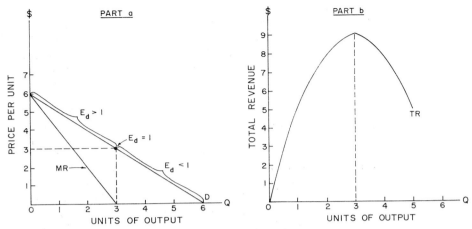

FIG. 8.18. Price elasticities of demand and total revenue.

the percentage change in price. Here, as price falls, total quantity sold will increase sufficiently to cause total revenue to increase.

The relationship is clearly exhibited in Figure 8.18. Curve D in part a is a demand curve. In part b the associated total revenue obtained by multiplying price by quantity for each possible quantity is illustrated. At relatively low levels of quantity demanded (high prices), price changes are in the elastic portion of the demand curve and increases in output will result in increased revenue. As the aggregate quantity sold increases, the point is reached ($Q = 3$) where total revenue is the maximum possible. This occurs where $E_d = 1$ in part a. As quantity sold is increased beyond this point, the inelastic portion of the demand curve is encountered, and total revenue decreases as further increases in quantity occur.

The data for Figure 8.18 is presented in Table 8.7. When

TABLE 8.7. Hypothetical demand schedule illustrating the impact of demand elasticity on total revenue

Price per Unit	Quantity Demanded	Total Revenue	Price Elasticity	Marginal Revenue
$6.00	0	$0.00		
			11.0	5
5.00	1	5.00		
			3.0	3
4.00	2	8.00		
			1.4	1
3.00	3	9.00		
			0.7	-1
2.00	4	8.00		
			0.3	-3
1.00	5	5.00		

price is decreased from $5 to $4 per unit, total revenue increases from
$5 to $8, an increase of $3. The significant increase in total revenue
associated with the decline in price can be explained by the fact that in
that range of the demand curve the price elasticity of demand is 3.0.
This means that a 1 percent decrease in price is more than offset by a 3
percent increase in quantity demanded, resulting in a net increase in total
expenditures by consumers. If prices fall another dollar (to $3 per unit),
there is a further increase in quantity sold that more than offsets the
decrease in price; total revenue increases $1 to a total of $9. However,
in the next segment of our example, the price elasticity of demand
changes to inelastic, meaning that the increase in quantity sold does
not offset the decrease in price. Consequently, the drop in price from
$3 to $2 per unit will result in total revenue falling $1 to a total of $8.
Similarly, if price is further reduced to $1 per unit, the inelastic demand
of that portion of the demand curve means total revenue falls $3.

Before leaving the discussion of the price elasticity of demand,
one additional fact should be noted. In the above we have been describing the change in total revenue resulting from a change in the quantity
sold. This is the standard definition of the concept of *marginal revenue*.
It was calculated in the last column of Table 8.7 by use of Equation 8.12.

$$\text{Marginal Revenue} = MR = \Delta TR/\Delta Q \qquad (8.12)$$
$$= (TR_2 - TR_1)/(Q_2 - Q_1)$$

where

$$TR_2 = (Q_2)\,(P_2)$$
$$TR_1 = (Q_1)\,(P_1)$$

In simple terms, marginal revenue describes what happens to
total revenue. If marginal revenue is positive, total revenue is increasing. When marginal revenue is zero, total revenue is not changing; and
if marginal revenue is negative, total revenue is decreasing. Thus we may
interpret part a of Figure 8.18 in another manner. As we move along
the demand curve (D) from the elastic portion to the unit elastic point,
and on into the inelastic portion, marginal revenue changes from positive to zero (at $E_d = 1$) to negative. This provides the economists (and
the decision maker) with concepts that are very helpful in analyzing a
problem. For example, if a businessman observes that as he increases
output—even though it brings a lower price—total revenue increases, he
can infer that marginal revenue is positive. He knows he is operating
in the elastic portion of his demand curve. Furthermore, he would
know that as long as marginal revenue is greater than zero, it would
pay to increase the quantity placed on the market, even though it results in a lower per-unit price.[17] In addition, when marginal revenue

17. This ignores the marginal cost of the added output. In reality, output
would be increased until marginal revenue *(MR)* equals marginal cost *(MC)*.

TABLE 8.8. Relationship between the price elasticity of demand and total revenue

| Change in | | Price Elasticity is[a] | | |
Quantity	Price	Elastic $(E_d > 1)$	Unitary $(E_d = 1)$	Inelastic $(E_d < 1)$
		TOTAL REVENUE WILL		
increase	decrease	increase	not change	decrease
decrease	increase	decrease	not change	increase

a. The student should recall that price elasticities are negative and hence $(E_d > 1)$ implies that elasticity is a larger negative number than -1.0 (say -1.8). Likewise $(E_d = 1)$ really means $E_d = -1.0$ and, for the inelastic column, $(E_d < 1)$ implies that the elasticity is less than -1.0 (a smaller negative number such as -0.5).

for an increase in output is equal to zero, he knows that is the quantity which maximizes total revenue in the market. Any further increases in output will show negative marginal revenues, indicating that total revenue is declining. Therefore, by knowing the relationship between marginal revenue and elasticity, it is possible to make rational economic decisions without calculating total revenue at each level of output; it is only necessary to calculate the direction and magnitude of change, not the absolute level.

This relationship is useful in understanding the various types of supply and acreage control programs in United States agriculture. It is known that the demand curve facing producers of agricultural commodities is inelastic. This means that quantities currently being offered by the producers fall in the inelastic portion of the demand curve for food. From the foregoing analysis, we know that in this situation an inverse relationship exists between total revenue and the quantity sold. In other words, if a procedure can be found to reduce the quantity sold, total revenue accruing to farmers would increase. This is the basic rationale behind the many policy proposals designed to curtail agricultural production. More will be said on this matter in a later chapter.

As can be seen, the elasticity of demand enters as one of the important factors determining the most desirable quantity to be sold. As long as the price elasticity of demand is less than 1, total revenue will be increased by raising the price and curtailing the quantity sold. If the elasticity of demand is greater than 1, either raising the price or curtailing the quantity sold will decrease total revenue. The relationship of price elasticity, changes in prices, changes in quantities sold, and changes in total revenue is summarized in Table 8.8.

INCOME ELASTICITY OF DEMAND

In an earlier section we described how an increase in consumer's income is reflected in the outward shift of the budget line. The new budget line will be tangent to the consumer's indifference curve at a different point. The result was observed in the marketplace (for normal goods) as a shift of the demand curve to the right. Conversely, it was also demonstrated that a decrease in income will shift the demand curve for normal goods to the left. The income elasticity of demand is merely a formalized way of measuring and describing how much the demand curve shifts and in what direction. The formula for income elasticity of demand is directly analogous to that of the price elasticity of demand; that is,

$$N_d = \% \ \Delta Q / \% \ \Delta Y \tag{8.13}$$
$$= [(Q_2 - Q_1)/(Q_2 + Q_1)]/[(Y_2 - Y_1)/(Y_2 + Y_1)]$$

where

Q_1 = quantity demanded in period 1
Q_2 = quantity demanded in period 2
Y_1 = consumer income in period 1
Y_2 = consumer income in period 2

As an example, suppose that consumers purchased 30 pounds of beef per capita in period 1 when their average per capita income was \$1,200. In period 2 their demand was 50 pounds per capita when their income was \$1,800. Given the change in income, this automatically means a shift in the demand curve. The degree of the shift is described by the magnitude of the income elasticity of demand. The calculations are shown below.

$$N_d = (50 - 30)/(50 + 30) \times (1,800 + 1,200)/(1,800 - 1,200)$$
$$= 20/80 \times 3,000/600 = 10/8$$
$$N_d = 1.25$$

The income elasticity of demand of 1.25 means that a 1 percent change in income has resulted in a 1.25 percent change in the quantity of beef consumed. It implies that the demand curve has shifted to the right, assuming all other things—including the price of beef—remain constant. If, in the above example, there had also been a change in the price of beef, we would have had great difficulty in calculating directly the impact of the change in income on consumption of beef. This is so because it would not be known how much of the change in quantity consumed was due to a change in the price of beef and how much was due to an actual change in income. This again illustrates the usefulness of the *ceteris paribus* assumption to clearly understand a relationship.

Consumption items can be classified into one of two classes depending upon the size of the income elasticity. These classes were defined as inferior goods and normal goods. *Inferior* goods are those for which the income elasticity of demand is less than zero (negative). This means that an increase in income will result in people consuming less of that commodity. Inferior goods might be items such as potatoes and lard. Another example is starchy food. As the individual consumer's income increases, he buys less of these items; consequently, the income elasticity is negative. A *normal* good is one which has an income elasticity that is positive, that is, greater than zero. Most commodities fall in this classification. It includes all agricultural commodities with the exception of the above items described as possibly inferior. Normal goods are further subclassified into two groups: necessities and luxuries. A *necessity* is an item for which the income elasticity of demand is between zero and 1.0. For a necessity, a 1 percent increase in income results in consumers increasing their expenditures for this commodity by less than 1 percent. A *luxury* is a commodity for which the income elasticity of demand is greater than 1. For such commodities a 1 percent increase in income results in consumers increasing their consumption of the commodity by more than 1 percent. Items such as fur coats, sports cars, and diamonds are probably included in this category. Beef, with an income elasticity of 0.47, and chicken, with an income elasticity of 0.37, are examples of normal goods defined as necessities. A porterhouse steak with an income elasticity of 1.40 is defined as a normal good that is a luxury. On the other hand, lard, with an income elasticity of —0.50, is an example of an inferior good.

These income elasticities are very useful in consideration of policy problems in agriculture. For example, one might expect from our previous discussion that as incomes increase people would tend to spend more, that is, consume more of particular commodities. However, the above information indicates that as incomes go up there is not a great increase in the consumption of agricultural commodities. The income elasticity of demand for all foods is approximately 0.26. This means that as consumers' incomes increase 1.0 percent, consumption of food will increase by only 0.26 percent.

The income elasticity of demand for food also varies by level of income and by country. As average levels of income increase in a country, the income elasticity for food will decline. The elasticity of 0.26 cited above is for the United States. Other countries of the world such as Brazil, Argentina, Pakistan, and India have much higher income elasticities. Given a 1 percent increase in income, consumers in one of those countries will spend most of it for food commodities. Consequently, the income elasticity for a less developed country might be as high as 0.7, 0.8, or 0.9 in comparison to 0.26 for the United States. One can expect that as incomes in these countries increase, their elasticities of demand will decline. Conceivably, one can visualize the day when everyone has adequate diets and that, consequently, all increases in income are spent for nonfood items. In this situation, the income elasticity of demand for food would be practically zero. If such a time does arrive, the ability of farmers to increase their marketings of foods and fibers as people's incomes increase will also decline to zero.

CROSS PRICE ELASTICITIES

The third and final variable included in the *ceteris paribus* assumption is the prices of other commodities. The *cross price elasticity* measures the degree and direction of the shift of the demand curve for commodity A as the price of commodity B increases or decreases. Equation 8.14 is the formula for calculating the cross price elasticity of demand.[18]

$$E_X = (\% \ \Delta Q^A)/(\% \ \Delta P^B) \tag{8.14}$$
$$= [(Q_2^A - Q_1^A)/(Q_2^A + Q_1^A)]/[(P_2^B - P_1^B)/(P_2^B + P_1^B)]$$

where

$Q_2^A =$ new quantity of Q^A
$Q_1^A =$ old quantity of Q^A
$P_2^B =$ new price of Q^B
$P_1^B =$ old price of Q^B

Each commodity can be influenced by the price of many other commodities. For example, the quantity of beef demanded will be influenced by the price of pork, chicken, fish, cheese, and possibly television sets as well as many other commodities. Therefore, the description of a cross price elasticity must include an indication of the commodity whose price is being considered. Thus the cross price elasticity is with respect to another commodity. A description of the cross price elasticity of demand for beef, given a change in the price of chicken, would be described as "cross price elasticity of beef with respect to chicken is —0.36." Or, if potatoes are the prices being used, "cross price elasticity of beef with respect to potatoes is +0.15." In the first case, the reader then knows that the price included in the denominator of the calculations is chicken, and in the second case it is potatoes.

An example of the calculation of the cross price elasticity of ham with respect to chicken and to potato salad is illustrated in Equations 8.15 and 8.16. Assume that the calculations are based on the observation of sales of ham in a local supermarket, given no change in the price of ham and the information presented in Table 8.9.

18. The value of E_x can vary from negative infinity to positive infinity, with the sign and magnitude used to classify commodities with respect to one another.

TABLE 8.9. Hypothetical data on food sales

	Week 1	Week 2	Week 3
Pounds of Ham Sold	315	435	365
Price of Chicken per Pound	$0.24	$0.36	$0.36
Price of Potato Salad per Gallon	$0.14	$0.14	$0.18
Price of Ham per Pound	$0.45	$0.45	$0.45

$$E_x^c = [(435 - 315)/(435 + 315)]/[(0.36 - 0.24)/ \qquad (8.15)$$
$$(0.36 + 0.24)] = 120/750 \times 0.60/0.12$$
$$= 60/75 = 0.8$$

$$E_x^p = [(365 - 435)/(365 + 435)]/[(0.18 - 0.14)/ \qquad (8.16)$$
$$(0.18 + 0.14)] = -70/800 \times 0.32/0.04$$
$$= -7/10 = -0.7$$

The cross price elasticity of ham with respect to chicken as calculated in Equation 8.15 is + 0.8, meaning that a 1 percent increase in the price of chicken results in an 0.8 percent increase in the quantity of ham sold in the supermarket. The cross price elasticity of ham with respect to potato salad as shown in Equation 8.16 indicates that a 1 percent increase in the price of potato salad results in a 0.7 percent decrease in the quantity of ham sold.

In calculating the cross price elasticity, the price of the commodity itself is assumed to be unchanged. Furthermore, the consumer's taste and preference, except for the one under consideration, must also remain unchanged. If they do not, the effect of the price of commodity B on consumption of commodity A will be confounded by the "other influences." In our example, if between week 1 and week 2 the price of potato salad has also changed, we would be unable to separate the impact on the quantity of ham sold to the change in the price of chicken from that of the change in the price of potato salad. Similarly, in examining the cross price elasticity of ham with respect to potato salad, had the price of chicken also changed, we again would be unable to separate out the impacts of the two price changes.

Note that the cross price elasticity indicates both the direction and magnitude of the shift in the demand curve. Given a decline in the other price, a negative sign indicates a shift to the left and a positive sign indicates a shift to the right. The converse would be true for a rise in the other price.

Frequently the economist is more interested in the sign of the cross elasticity than its precise magnitude because the sign is used to classify commodities as to their relationships to one another: *substitutes* for which the cross price elasticity is positive, and *complements*, for which the cross price elasticity is negative.

As the name suggests, substitute commodities will be substituted for one another in consumption. In our example, an increase in the price of chicken causes consumers to shift some of their purchases of meat to ham. The magnitude of the cross price elasticity also indicates the closeness of the relationship between the two commodities. If two products are easily substitutable for each other (beef and pork), the cross price elasticities will be much greater than for two products which are not good substitutes (beef and cigars). Brandow estimates, for example, that the cross price elasticity of demand for beef with respect to pork is 0.10, and with respect to ice cream, 0.003. He also estimates that the cross price elasticity of demand for all nonfoods with respect to food is − 0.20, meaning that a 1 percent increase in nonfood prices will decrease the consumption of both food and nonfood items.[19]

SUMMARY

In this chapter we have seen how the preference functions of the consumer can be used to deduce indifference curves which,

in turn, reveal willingness to purchase different combinations of commodities. When combined with a budget constraint (which limits ability to purchase) the utility-maximizing combination of two bundles of commodities could be found. By altering the price of one of these bundles we saw that a demand curve for that bundle could be derived for the individual consumer. By aggregating over all consumers we obtained the notion of aggregate demand.

Given a definition of a demand curve, we next became concerned with differentiating between movements along a specific demand curve and shifts in that demand curve. The former phenomenon was seen to be caused by a change in the price of the commodity itself, while the latter (shifts) were seen to be caused by changes in tastes and preferences, incomes of consumers, the prices of other goods, or—in terms of aggregate demand—by changes in population.

The concept of elasticity was introduced to provide a convenient index for describing the magnitude and direction of such changes. The elasticity permits the economist to directly compare the changes in vastly different commodities. The measure of elasticity also permits classifying commodities into normal goods, inferior goods, luxuries, necessities, substitutes, and complements.

19. George E. Brandow, *Interrelations among Demands for Farm Products and Implications for Control of Market Supply*, Bull. 680, Pa. Agr. Exp. Sta., Aug. 1961, Table 1, p. 17.

In the following two chapters, we will combine the concepts developed here, with those from previous chapters describing market supply, to explain the interactions between demand and supply and the implications for product prices. Thereafter, the concepts of market structure, price analysis, and resource allocation will be explored.

SUGGESTED READINGS

BASIC

Burk, Marguerite C. *Consumption Economics: A Multidisciplinary Approach.* New York: John Wiley, 1968, Ch. 5–7.

> An interdisciplinary approach to the subject of consumer demand. The author discusses the impact of psychological, anthropological, sociological, and economic factors upon consumer demand.

Due, John F. *Intermediate Economic Analysis,* 3rd ed. Homewood, Ill.: Richard D. Irwin, 1956, Ch. 6.

> Describes the characteristics of a demand curve and its associated marginal revenue curve from the point of view of an individual seller of the product (a firm). Includes the case of one of many sellers (a competitive industry), one of a few sellers (monopolistic competition and oligopoly), and a single seller (monopoly).

Ferguson, C. E. *Microeconomic Theory.* Homewood, Ill.: Richard D. Irwin, 1972, Ch. 3.

> A detailed geometric analysis of special topics in consumer demand, using indifference curves. Includes the income and substitution effects of a price change; definition of normal, superior, and inferior goods; substitution and complementarity among goods, and an analysis of leisure and income choices by a consumer.

Leftwich, Richard H. *The Price System and Resource Allocation,* 4th ed. Hinsdale, Ill.: Dryden Press, 1970.

> See especially Chapters 4 and 5 and Appendix to Chapter 5. Presents the theory of individual consumer demand from both the classical utility and the indifference curve approach. The appendix contains an easily understood discussion of the income and substitution effects of a change in the price of a commodity.

Linder, Steffan B. *The Harried Leisure Class.* New York: Columbia Univ. Press, 1970.

> An economic analysis of the demand for time. The author argues that as an economy develops and per capita incomes grow, time becomes an increasingly scarce good to the consumer and hence an important determinant of the demand for goods and services.

Lipsey, Richard G.; and Steiner, Peter O. *Economics,* 3rd ed. New York: Harper & Row, 1972, Ch. 8 Appendix, Ch. 9.

> The appendix presents a third theoretical approach to the theory of consumer demand called *revealed preference theory.* Chapter 9 provides a critique of demand theory and summarizes the wealth of empirical knowledge about demand that economists have accumulated.

Mellor, John W. *The Economics of Agricultural Development.* Ithaca, N.Y.: Cornell Univ. Press, 1966, Ch. 3, 4.

> Describes how the aggregate demand curve shifters—population and income—are used in planning economic development.

Stonier, Alfred W.; and Hague, Douglas C. *A Textbook of Economic Theory.* New York: John Wiley, 1961, Ch. 2–4.

    A strictly geometric development, analysis, and discussion of the theory of individual consumer demand, aggregate demand, the slope of the demand curve and factors affecting its position and slope, and several other special topics related to the analysis of consumer equilibrium of two or more goods.

Working, Elmer. What do statistical demand curves show? *Quart. J. Econ.* 41(1927):212–35.

    A well-known article in the literature of demand analysis. It analyzes the reasons why it is difficult for the economist to estimate a true demand curve from marketplace data.

ADVANCED

Alchian, Armen A. The meaning of utility measurement. *Am. Econ. Rev.* 18(Mar. 1953): 26–50.

    Discusses the objectives and meaning of measurement in general, and of utility measurement in particular, the methods of measuring utility, and some of the implications of utility measurement for demand theory.

Fellner, William. *Modern Economic Analysis.* New York: McGraw-Hill, 1960, Ch. 14–15.

    A detailed development of the theory of rational consumer choice from the perspective of marginal utility analysis (Chapter 14) and from the analysis of indifference curves (Chapter 15).

Goreux, L. M. Demand Analyses for Agricultural Products. FAO Planning Studies, No. 3, Rome, 1964, pp. 117–32.

    A practical example of how the concepts of demand shifters can be utilized by economic planners. Discusses methods that can be used to estimate the rate at which the aggregate demand for a commodity within a particular country is shifting due to changes in population and per capita income.

Henderson, James M.; and Quandt, Richard E. *Microeconomic Theory: A Mathematical Approach.* New York: McGraw-Hill, 1958, Ch. 2.

    The theory of consumer demand in mathematical terms. The mathematical concepts used in developing the demand concepts are reviewed in an appendix.

Hicks, J. R. *Value and Capital,* 2nd ed. Oxford: Clarendon Press, 1946, pp. 11–52, 305–14.

    A complete and detailed presentation of the indifference curve approach to consumer demand theory. An appendix (pp. 305–14) contains a mathematical presentation of the theory.

———. *A Revision of Demand Theory.* Oxford: Clarendon Press, 1956.

    Uses the concept of revealed preferences to develop the theory of consumer demand.

Leibenstein, Harvey. Bandwagon, snob, and Veblen effects in the theory of consumer demand. *Quart. J. Econ.* 64(May 1950): 183–207.

    The author expands the theory of individual consumer demand to include effects such as style or fashion, exclusiveness, and conspicuous consumption. He describes the impact of each of these effects on the elasticity of demand curves.

Schultz, Henry. *The Theory and Measurement of Demand.* Chicago: Univ. Chicago Press, 1938.

    The most widely known work on demand analysis. It combines a detailed review of demand theory up to that time with a large number of statistical studies.

DISCUSSION QUESTIONS AND PROBLEMS

1. What would the term *ceteris paribus* include in defining the demand curve for each of the following?
   a. Butter
   b. Sailboats
   c. Lincoln Continentals
   d. College degrees
2. What would you expect the demand curve for college degrees to look like? Why?
3. Would you expect the indifference curves of an individual consumer to be constant over a period as long as 5 years? 20 years?
4. Explain why the demand curve for salt is inelastic.
5. Would a sales tax on salt raise much revenue?
6. What can you conclude about the behavior of the demand curve for stainless steel razor blades, if Gillette sold 300,000 packs in 1967 at a price of $0.89 per pack and 600,000 packs in 1969 at a price of $1.09 per pack?
7. What does advertising of a specific brand name product attempt to accomplish with respect to an individual's indifference curve for a product versus all competing products? Explain with the use of indifference curves.
8. Natural gas and oil are substitutes in the heating of homes. What would you expect to happen to the demand for natural gas if the price of oil were to increase?
9. Give at least one example of a good that would fit in each of the following classifications:
   a. An inferior good
   b. A luxury
   c. A good that has a positive cross price elasticity of demand with respect to skis
   d. A good that has a negative cross price elasticity with respect to Ford automobiles
10. Suppose you were stocking a store in a very wealthy neighborhood and that economic forecasts were for continued prosperity.
    a. How would knowing the income elasticities of various products help you decide which items to stock?
    b. If the economic forecasts were for a downturn in the economy, would you be inclined to stock a different class of items? Why?
    c. How would your stocking policies differ in a predominantly poor neighborhood?
11. Suppose you were the president of Shell Oil Corporation. A market analyst has told you that the cross price elasticity of demand for Shell gasoline with respect to all other major brands is approximately +1.0 for each brand.
    a. How can you use this fact to explain to your board of directors why "gas wars" affect your sales and profits adversely?
    b. What are some of the strategies you might use to reduce the impact of price changes by your competitors on your sales volume?
    c. Why is it good strategy on your part to encourage the President to speak out against increases in automobiles prices? In steel prices?

CHAPTER 9: MARKET EQUILIBRIUM

In Chapters 7 and 8 we developed the dual concepts of firm supply and the aggregate supply of all firms, and of the individual's demand for a commodity and the aggregate demand of all individuals. To this point, the price that will exist in the marketplace—and how it is determined—has been treated little, if at all. In this chapter we will describe the forces of supply and demand as they operate simultaneously to determine the market price and hence the quantity of a good that will be exchanged. In the process we will show how a market economy simultaneously allocates resources among firms and industries so as to maximize the output of those goods and services desired by consumers. This is referred to as "market equilibrium analysis." In essence this chapter is the synthesis of most of what has been presented earlier in Chapters 4 through 8. The technical conditions of production and the operating costs of a business jointly establish the costs of producing a product and hence the supply conditions of the industry. These were discussed in Chapters 4 through 7. This is the *cost side* of the industry—or the *supply side*. The *revenue side* is determined by the demand conditions of the industry. Product demand determines the quantity of product a firm can sell at any one price, or the price it can get for any quantity it chooses to sell. The aggregate demand curve can also be an important factor in influencing the structure of an industry. By *structure* is meant the degree of competitiveness among firms. The notion of structure will be discussed in more detail in Chapter 10.

The analysis of the interaction of revenue and costs or supply and demand presented in this chapter will rest upon a series of basic assumptions. First, we assume a free market. This means that there are no outside controls of any type which influence or establish artificial market conditions to which a business firm must adjust. Governmental intervention—federal, state, or local such as price regulation, moral suasion, tariff barriers, or trade restriction and antitrust regulation—all establish artificial controls to which business firms in an industry will respond. The resulting allocation of resources will differ from what it would be within an economy free from all such restraints.

Second, we assume the market is competitive. Economists distinguish two types of competitive situations, *pure competition* and *perfect competition*. The latter is a refined condition of the former in that it requires the additional assumption of perfect knowledge. Our analysis in this chapter rests upon the assumption of pure competition. Hence, we will describe the attributes or conditions necessary for an industry to be considered purely competitive. This is the subject of the next section.

The third assumption of this chapter is that entrepreneurs maximize profits. Obviously not all firms try to maximize profits at all times, but it is certainly one of their goals. A business firm cannot long exist if it does not provide a reasonable return to all its factors of production.

These assumptions do not imply that a free, purely competitive market is an ideal. No economist would argue that the conditions of a free, purely competitive market composed of profit-maximizing firms describes the United States economy or any other economy for that matter. Yet these conditions are not without some degree of historical validity in this country as well as in many other countries in the Western Hemisphere. It is safe to conclude that many of the conditions described here do exist in our economic system. Yet, the real issue here is their use as theoretical constructs which when taken together offer a reasonable explanation of human behavior regarding matters of choice in the face of scarcity.

This set of conditions and assumptions and the analysis that flows from them is merely a convenient starting point. Our final objective is to be able to analyze the efficiency of resource allocation under different market conditions. Once these assumptions are employed to build a model of economic behavior, the economist can then proceed to investigate behavior implications of relaxing one or more of them. It is much easier to begin with an analysis of a purely competitive economy than a more realistic market structure. In economics, as in other social sciences, the more nearly one approaches reality the more difficult things become. Indeed, as the following chapter will show, much of economics is devoted to the study of the implications of relaxing some of the assumptions that are made in this chapter. For example, in physics you study the laws of motion assuming no friction. This is unrealistic since all motion in the real world always involves some friction. Once the basic laws of motion are clearly understood, they can be modified to take friction into account. The same philosophy is applied in this textbook and in the main of economics.

The assumptions we spell out in the beginning pages of this chapter have two other points in their favor. First, the theory developed serves as a convenient "norm" against which actual or theoretical performance of other market structures can be contrasted. Second, although not perfectly competitive nor totally profit oriented, conditions in a sufficient number of industries are close enough to these ideals that they do provide a great deal of insight into the actual operations of real markets. Thus in the final analysis the assumptions may not be as highly abstract as the casual observer might at first conclude.

In this chapter we develop the analytics of market equilibrium in several steps. First, we briefly define a market. Then we describe the attributes associated with a market that is purely competitive. Following that discussion we describe the equilibrium in one marketing period. This is the *static* case and it is represented by a "snapshot" of a market.

Second, we will move to the case of *comparative statics,* which may be characterized as a situation where snapshots exist for two or more different time periods.[1] Finally, we will present a general discussion of the allocation of resources in a competitive market economy.

PURELY COMPETITIVE MARKET

A *market* is composed of a group of buyers and sellers in close enough contact so that an exchange of goods and services is achieved among them. It is a geographical area or space within which buyers and sellers are aware of each other's transactions. Viewed in this way, the actual limits of a market are dependent upon the extent to which buyers and sellers communicate with each other and the characteristics of the product which permit it to move between buyers and sellers.

Under this definition, a market could be local, regional, national, or international, depending upon how widely the impact of one exchange affects other transactions. For some commodities where it is difficult to move the commodity long distances because of relatively high transportation costs, the number of potential buyers or sellers is limited to a small geographical area. Sod for landscaping, earth for landfill, or trash from the local community are examples of commodities in which there are many small local markets with little commingling of participants from one market in another. As a consequence, prices are dependent upon strictly local conditions. In contrast, automobiles, lumber, stocks, and bonds are bought and sold across the United States and their prices are determined according to countrywide costs and revenue conditions. Similarly, diamonds, gold, and wheat are bought and sold across the world. Their prices are affected by worldwide conditions of demand and cost.

In Chapter 5 we listed several assumptions as being necessary

---

1. By *equilibrium* we mean the arrival at a generally stable condition—a balancing—of two opposing forces such as supply and demand. *Static* refers to an instantaneous view of the balancing of such forces, while *comparative statics* refers to two or more instantaneous views. In the latter situation we compare two or more time periods and record the effect on the values of certain economic variables of interest. On the other hand, *dynamics* includes time as a variable and offers continuous monitoring of the economic variables as we move from one period to the next.

prerequisites to the development of the analytics of production economics. Foremost among those was the assumption that entrepreneurs desired to maximize profit. Second, we assumed that the purchase of inputs by each firm, and the total output level of each, was such an insignificant fraction of the total market that no firm could exert influence over input or output prices by its production decisions. Third, we assumed that each entrepreneur had perfect knowledge of all input and product prices. Finally, we assumed that the production response on the part of a firm was instantaneous.

In this chapter it is necessary to elaborate on the above list of assumptions, as well as to relax several of them. As for the elaboration, we begin with the concept of resource mobility. Up to the present, this has been an implicit assumption of our analysis. When economists talk of a purely competitive market, the requirement is that all necessary resources can enter and exit the industry unimpeded. This implies that land, labor, and capital will move into and out of the industry in pursuit of maximum return. For example, a skilled craftsman earning $3.20 in Gary, Indiana (his home), is assumed perfectly mobile and would quickly take a job in South Chicago at $3.50 per hour, provided his daily transportation costs are not greater than this potential income differential. This assumption means that all resources can move into and out of the market readily in response to price signals.

Under this assumption, the profit-maximizing businessman will move into those product lines that promise a higher rate of return and away from those that promise a lower return. In summary, the perfect mobility of resources includes the entry and exit of resources to firms, and of firms to industries. In reality we know that this assumption is rather unrealistic. Resources are often highly specialized and immobile. There is specialization of occupations, such as coal miners, aircraft engineers, blacksmiths, and neurosurgeons. Likewise, capital invested in equipment is not really very mobile. Patents, copyrights, and trademarks also limit free entry. Thus, in reality, the movement of resources will take place only over a long period of time. Nevertheless, in our competitive model we assume that this movement takes place very rapidly.

Another assumption that must now be mentioned explicitly is that of homogeneous products. This assumption is merely another way of saying that when we discuss equilibrium in the marketplace, we are dealing with producers of a very specific commodity which is homogeneous across all the producers in that market. For economists to discuss and analyze markets, it is necessary that the commodity be well defined. It makes no sense to talk of demand and supply unless one talks of the demand for a specific item at a specific point in time. It is not enough to describe the demand for bread alone, but some specificity must be given such as rye bread, whole wheat bread, sourdough bread, etc. This also means that there is no distinction between one firm's product and that of another; the product is interchangeable and no buyer will prefer the product of any particular seller over that of another seller. As indicated in the previous chapter, the primary goal of advertising is to reduce the degree to which consumers view two different brands of a commodity as being homogeneous.

One assumption that will be relaxed is that regarding perfect knowledge. Earlier we had assumed that both firms and consumers were in possession of all necessary information about prevailing prices, production patterns and methods, and attributes of competing products. By that we meant that producers in a particular market (that is, producing a specific commodity) have perfect knowledge of their production function and cost curves, as well as information about what all other producers in the same market are doing. Recall from above that they cannot exert any influence over other producers, but this does not preclude knowledge of others' actions. In addition to this, they know the nature of the demand for their particular commodity.

A second kind of knowledge relates to the owners of productive factors (land, labor, capital, entrepreneurship). This assumption requires that the owners are in possession of considerable information with respect to the alternative opportunities for the resources, their comparative advantage, and any other requisite information for maximizing returns to the resource.

The third kind of knowledge pertains to consumers of commodities. Specifically, the buyer is assumed to be aware of all products which are either substitutes or complements for the commodity in question, and he can make a rational comparison among them. This means that he knows all prevailing prices and the quality and nature of each product.

This assumption assures that a single price will prevail for any one product. If all consumers are fully informed, the producer cannot charge more than the going price without losing sales. If two prices existed, consumers would know it, and since we are assuming homogeneous commodities, two prices would not long prevail. The implication of the above assumptions regarding the extent of knowledge on the part of producers and consumers is most relevant in the area of market adjustment processes. If we were to assume thoroughgoing perfect knowledge on the part of all participants, the upshot would be that all adjustments would be instantaneous. In fact, the essence of this chapter is to explore the nature of that adjustment process; hence we relax the assumption of thoroughgoing perfect knowledge and assume that producers have knowledge of production functions and cost curves, but not necessarily of all product prices; that is, they are assumed to know the prices at which they can obtain productive factors but not to know the exact prices that will prevail for output.

MARKET EQUILIBRIUM IN A SINGLE PERIOD: THE STATIC CASE

Everyone can quote the familiar phrase "price is determined by supply and demand" but few can tell why this is so or can explain the process whereby this occurs. With the understanding of the supply and demand sides of the market, we can now turn to the exposition of that equilibrating process. Consider the demand and supply curves illustrated in Figure 9.1. Assume that the diagram represents the demand and supply situation for peaches sold in the central market of a large metropolitan area each day. The curve S_0 represents what peach producers are willing and able to offer at each price (supply), while the curve D_0 represents how many peaches buyers are willing and able to purchase at each price (demand). Since buyers demand more at lower prices than at higher prices, and producers offer more at higher prices than at lower prices, the demand and supply schedules for peaches in this market will intersect. Thus there is some price at which offers and bids are equal. At this market price, every willing buyer can find a willing seller, and every seller a buyer.

The intersection of the two curves in Figure 9.1 indicates an equilibrium price of $3 per bushel. At this price, 700 bushels of peaches

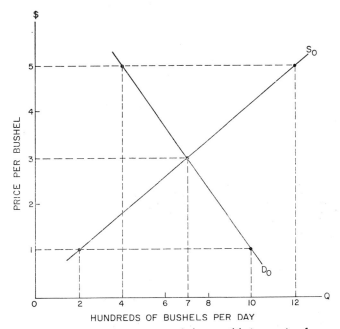

FIG. 9.1. Demand and supply curves and the equilibrium price for peaches.

will exchange hands each day; it is the intersection of demand and supply that determines the market clearing price and the quantity that will change hands. This still leaves the basic question unanswered: Why is the intersection significant? Why couldn't the price be something else?

The answer is that only at this particular price ($3) are there no sellers with unwanted peaches on their hands, and no buyers seeking to buy but unable to satisfy their wants; the forces of demand and supply in this market are in equilibrium. As an example, consider the price of $5 per bushel. At this price consumers would buy only 400 bushels, while producers would offer 1,200 bushels. Because more is offered for sale (1,200) than would be purchased (400) there is a surplus of 800 bushels. As long as there is a surplus at a particular price (sellers wanting to sell more than buyers are willing to buy), the price must fall. In our example, as long as the price is above $3, there woud be a surplus offered for sale and a consequent downward pressure on price as producers sought to sell their product.

The same argument applies when price is below $3, say $1 per bushel. At $1, producers would be willing to sell only 200 bushels, while buyers want to purchase 1,000 bushels, and there would be a deficit of 800 bushels. In this situation, buyers will bid up the price until it reaches $3, where the number of peaches offered for sale is just equal to the amount demanded.

At the intersection of the demand and supply curves, surplus or deficit problems do not exist. At this point, there are no sellers making price concessions to attract buyers, nor are there waiting lines of buyers trying to buy quantities that are not available. It is thus an equilibrium price. This price will prevail until some fundamental change occurs in the forces determining the demand or supply schedules. When such an event occurs, the demand or supply will shift, leading eventually to a new equilibrium price and quantity.

MARKET EQUILIBRIUM OVER SEVERAL PERIODS: COMPARATIVE STATICS

We have pointed out in previous chapters the necessity of the *ceteris paribus* assumption in developing the concepts of demand and supply. When one of the factors included in this assumption changes—such as technology or input costs on the supply side, or consumers' incomes, or tastes and preferences on the demand side— there is a shift of the demand and/or supply curves. The result is a disequilibrium in the forces of supply and demand and the market reacts by seeking out a new equilibrium price and quantity. In the real world, the conditions of demand and supply are continually changing, and if

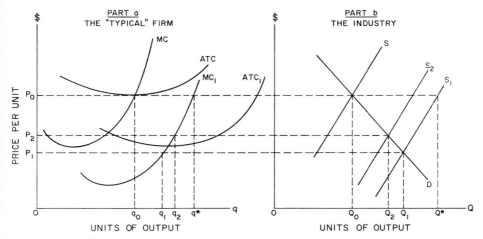

FIG. 9.2. Market adjustment to cost-decreasing changes on the supply side of a competitive industry.

one is to understand the phenomena observed in the marketplace, one must understand the effect of changes in the conditions of demand and supply, reflected in shifts in these curves, on the equilibrium market prices and quantities. In this section we will examine the impact of the various demand and supply shifters on the equilibrium price of a commodity.

SUPPLY SIDE

In earlier chapters we saw how changes in the production process led to alterations in the costs of production. Specifically, an improved technology makes it possible to produce the same quantity at a reduced cost. Similarly, production costs fall when input prices fall. The question then becomes: Given a change in the basic cost conditions of firms in the industry, what is the impact on industry price and output? We assume that there has been a change in the cost conditions (either a new technology or a fall in input prices) of the "typical" firm as depicted in part a of Figure 9.2. The firms buying inputs at the lower price experience a downward shift in their per-unit cost curves (to ATC_1 and MC_1). As more and more firms adopt the cost-reducing methods, there is a corresponding shift from S to S_1 in the industry supply curve as depicted in part b of the same figure.[2]

As can be seen in Figure 9.2, the changes that have occurred at the firm level result in the aggregate quantity of the commodity that

2. Recall that the industry supply curve is the horizontal summation of the marginal cost curves of the firms in the industry. When these curves shift, the industry supply curve shifts as well.

producers are willing and able to place on the market at a price of P_0 to increase from Q_0 to Q^*. This is because the prevailing price (P_0) would lead the typical firm to produce q^* which, when aggregated across all firms, produces a total industry supply of Q^*. Assuming no change in demand conditions, consumers would be willing only to clear the market of the smaller quantity Q_0. The surplus $(Q^* - Q_0)$ will tend to drive the price down to equilibrium price P_1 where the aggregate quantity purchased by consumers is Q_1. As this happens, the profit-maximizing firm, producing the level of output that equates marginal cost and marginal revenue, will move along its marginal cost curve until at price P_1 it produces output q_1. Thus the impact on the industry of a cost-reducing perturbation is a lower commodity price and greater output.

However, the new market equilibrium is short lived, since with P_1 the typical firm illustrated in part a is not covering all input costs. We must also consider the impact of this change on the number of firms in the industry and the level of resources utilized by the industry. Since there are resources earning less than their opportunity cost, as evidenced in part a, resources and firms will exit from the industry. The supply curve for the industry will shift to the left and the process continues until a new stable industry equilibrium is established at price P_2 and output Q_2. At this level the marginal firm is just covering costs, and the typical firm of part a is earning some positive profit.

Notice that the process causes the price to the consumer to fall. While this is desirable for the consumer, the impact on specific firms within the industry can be less agreeable. Specifically, if the new technology is initially adopted by only a few firms, their output, and the output of the industry, will increase but must be sold at a reduced price. To those firms that were barely covering all their production costs before the new technology was available (earlier defined as "marginal"), the adjustments hardly constitute desirable news. These marginal firms may lack the capital or the repayment capacity to invest in new technology and, hence, when competitive firms adopt such devices, the marginal firms are put at even more of a competitive disadvantage. As the number of firms in an industry adopting the new technology increases, the aggregate output increases, and prices might fall even more. As prices fall, the marginal firms will begin to drop out and resources exit. As they move out of the industry, the aggregate supply curve will shift back to the left (fewer marginal cost curves being summed) and an eventual equilibrium will be reestablished with fewer firms in the industry, the aggregate supply curve being S_2, the aggregate output being Q_2, and the equilibrium price being P_2.

In a competitive industry, firms are strictly quantity adjusters. The price is determined by the market through the aggregate behavior of all firms in the industry acting strictly as price takers. This has important resource allocation implications. It ensures that the economy is getting the maximum output per unit of resource. As new methods of producing more output per unit of resource appear on the horizon, the system ensures that they will be incorporated into industry production processes, yielding a greater total bundle of goods and services for members of that economy. Within the total economy, the result is to release resources for other industries and users and permit greater total output. Agriculture is a good example of an industry where this innovative incentive has had profound implications. In such crops as wheat and corn, the pressure to be the first to utilize a new high-yielding variety is strong. For those who get the larger yields early, the prevailing price will result in higher profits. Several years later when the new variety has come into more widespread usage, the price begins to drop, and this early advantage disappears. As we shall see later, the United States consumer has been a direct beneficiary of this process.

To enhance understanding of the market adjustment process we turn to the contrasting situation of a cost-increasing influence as illustrated in Figure 9.3. Initially, the industry is at equilibrium with an output of Q_0 (part b) and a price of P_0. The typical firm (part a) is producing q_0 and is earning zero profit. Recall that zero profit means that the firm is covering the opportunity cost of all factors.

Now assume that the cost of productive factors increases so that there is an upward shift of the ATC curve of the typical firm to ATC_1. Notice that this does not cause the minimum point of ATC to move to the left or to the right. This change would imply that some firms were unable to continue operating when per-unit cost is above price. As firms leave the industry, the aggregate supply curve shifts to the left, say, to S_1.

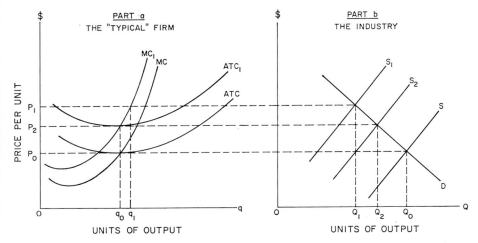

FIG. 9.3. Market adjustment to cost-increasing changes on the supply side of a competitive industry.

This results in a price increase which would lead the typical firm of part a to increase its output to q_1. As the news spreads that firms in this industry are earning positive profit, other firms would enter and the aggregate supply curve would shift back to the right. For ease of explanation, assume that it shifts back to S_2. Here the industry output would be Q_2, and the equilibrium price would be P_2. Notice that the typical firm ends up producing the same level of output as previously (q_0), but at a higher per-unit cost (ATC_1) and price (P_2). As for the industry, there are fewer firms than at the initial position (S), but more than at S_1. The new equilibrium is at a smaller industry output and at a higher equilibrium price.

DEMAND SIDE

Perhaps the commonest form of adjustment in the purely competitive market is that made in response to changes on the demand side of the market. The famous saying, "Build a better mousetrap and the world will beat a path to your door," is one way to state this phenomenon, namely, that the demand for the better mousetrap will reward those who produce it, and those who continue to produce the ordinary mousetrap will find their business declining. Such was the fate of former manufacturers of buggy whips, quill pens, kerosene lanterns, parchment, candles, wooden plows, and potbellied stoves. The point is that firms respond to changes in the demand for their product and the aggregate of firms responds to the new demand situation. Since an individual firm in a purely competitive industry is a price taker, we know that the demand curve for the individual firm in pure competition is nothing more than a price; there is no curve or schedule for the firm as depicted in part b of Figure 9.2—such a curve (or array of prices and quantities) exists only for the aggregate of firms which we call the industry.

Because of the differential nature of adjustment when demand is increasing as distinct from when it is decreasing, we will investigate the case of market adjustment in an industry where demand is shifting to the right and in one where demand is shifting to the left. Before embarking upon this discussion, we will restate the various *ceteris paribus* assumptions that will give rise to the demand adjustments.

A large number of factors can cause changes in consumer demand. The most important of these factors are a change in consumer income, a change in the price of other products which complement or substitute for the commodity, a change in tastes and preferences, and a change in the number of buyers in the market. The impact of each of these factors on the direction of shift in the aggregate demand for a commodity has been described earlier and will not be repeated here. Figure 9.4 summarizes the effect of various factors shifting demand on

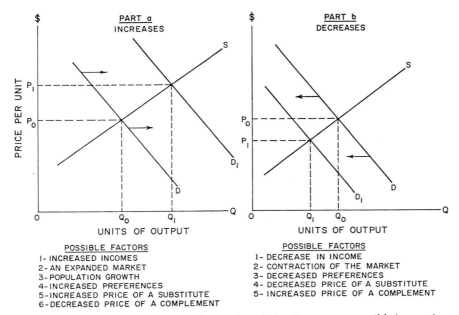

FIG. 9.4. Shifters of aggregate demand and the impact on equilibrium price and quantity.

the market-clearing price and quantity. It is assumed that the reader is familiar with the logic underlying each assumed shift from the individual consumer's point of view. Consequently, attention in this section will focus on effects on the market equilibrium price and quantity of demand shifts and the actions and reactions of firms to the shifts.

Part a of Figure 9.4 illustrates the impact upon market equilibrium of an increase in aggregate demand. Assume that D is the demand curve and S is the supply curve for a particular commodity. An increase in per capita consumer income will shift the demand curve to the right (to D_1), provided the commodity is a normal good. The net impact is an increase in the equilibrium price from P_0 to P_1, and an increase in the quantity that will be bought and sold from Q_0 to Q_1. It means that as consumer incomes expand, the demand for commodities which are normal goods will also expand. In contrast, commodities such as wheat, which have very small income elasticities, will not expand very rapidly. The other factors that will shift the demand curve to the right are listed below part a and include increases in the number of consumers either through population growth or through expanding the market served by the product. Encouraging marketing firms to expand their sales to overseas markets is an example of such market expansion. Other possible sources of the rightward shift in the aggregate demand are a change in tastes due to concentrated advertising campaigns, increases in the price of substitute commodities, or a decrease in the price of complementary commodities. All result in an increase in the equilibrium price and quantity.

Part b of Figure 9.4 illustrates a decrease in the demand for a commodity, resulting in a lower equilibrium price and quantity. Some of the factors that can decrease the demand for a commodity (shift it leftward) include a decrease in consumer incomes, an increase in the price of complements, or a contraction of the market either directly due to a tariff barrier or import quota, or indirectly through a decrease in the price of a substitute. For example, if D is the demand curve for beef, a decrease in the price of pork relative to beef will result in consumers shifting some of their meat purchases from beef to pork. Thus the market for beef has diminished, and the demand for beef will shift leftward from D to D_1. The net impact of a decrease in the demand for a product is a lowering of the equilibrium price and quantity. A final factor is a change in consumers' tastes away from a commodity. For example, federal Food and Drug Administration studies indicated that the artificial sweetener, cyclamate, induced cancer in test animals. Publication of this finding caused people to shift away from low-calorie products containing the sweetener. As a result, producers of diet drinks were able to sell a smaller quantity at a lower price.

We have seen that rightward shifts in demand will increase the equilibrium price and quantity, while leftward shifts in demand cause the opposite effects. We now turn to an analysis of the impact of these shifts on firms and resources within the industry.

AN EXPANDING INDUSTRY AND MARKET ADJUSTMENT

Assume an industry is in equilibrium as depicted in part b of Figure 9.5, with an aggregate output of Q_0 and an equilibrium price of P_0. The typical firm is depicted in part a. Now introduce a change into the market situation in the form of an increase in the demand for the product of this particular industry. This can be represented by a new demand curve D_1. Since, in the short run, firms can increase output only along their marginal cost curve, we can expect a price rise to P_2. At the higher price, it is obvious that firms will be willing to place larger quantities on the market and each will increase its output (to q_1 for the typical firm). Since the manner in which Figure 9.5 is drawn indicates that prior to the demand shift the typical firm was just covering all opportunity costs, the price rise permits the typical firm to earn positive profits.

Our theory indicates that positive profit in any sector of the economy is a strong inducement for resources to flow into that industry. Specifically, new firms will be started or existing ones will expand.

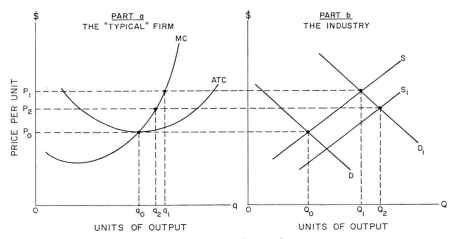

FIG. 9.5. Market adjustment in an expanding industry.

When this occurs, the supply curve of the industry will shift to the right (S_1). The new equilibrium price is P_1 in the diagram.[3] As the price becomes established at P_2, the typical firm will be led to reduce its output somewhat (from q_1 to q_2) and a new industry equilibrium would be established with aggregate output being Q_2, per-unit price being P_2, and the typical firm earning less profit than immediately following the increase in demand. The industry now consists of more firms than previously, the new firms having entered in response to the short-run positive profits earned by firms already in the industry.

Many examples of this phenomenon might be cited. An obvious one is that of computer software firms. These are businesses which provide computer programs and consultant services to business firms. As the computer has become cheaper to use, it has become feasible for most medium-sized businesses to take advantage of what a computer can offer. However, rather than hiring people to do the technical work, and instead of purchasing expensive computers which are too large for the needs of most businesses, specialty firms have developed to provide this service. The first few firms comprised an industry in the sense we are using that term, and these firms had substantial profits as businesses bid for their services. Employees of these software firms, realizing the potential for profits, then used their knowledge and experience in the software business to get loans from lending institutions, start their own businesses, and compete with their former employers. As more

---

3. The student should realize that there is nothing magical about the location of S_1 and that its position depends upon the extent of new entry into the industry, the technology of the new firms, and other factors. Here P_2 happens to be above P_0, but it is equally plausible for S to shift to the extent that P_2 is below P_0. We will have more to say about this later in this chapter.

and more firms became established, profits diminished as prices were forced downward. Eventually an equilibrium is reached where positive profits are essentially eliminated.

A DECLINING INDUSTRY AND MARKET ADJUSTMENT

To carry over our example into the area of a declining demand for a product, and to investigate the market adjustments which follow such a situation, we will use as a hypothetical example the desk calculator industry. In Figure 9.6, part b depicts the initial demand conditions for desk calculators (D), the initial supply conditions for the industry (S), the initial aggregate output (Q_0), and the initial equilibrium price (P_0). Part a depicts the typical firm in the industry producing q_0, receiving a price of P_0, and earning zero profit.

In this case we assume that the growth in the computer industry is reflected in fewer and fewer firms buying desk calculators. The low operating cost and convenience of the computer make it a better product. In this situation, we will observe a demand shift to the left and a short-run decline in aggregate output (to Q_1). With present suppliers willing and able to produce along the initial supply curve (S), but with demand decreased, the prevailing price will be P_1. From our earlier discussions we know that the typical firm depicted in part a would reduce its output to q_1. While at this price and output level the typical firm might still be covering variable costs per unit, it is not covering total per-unit costs. Should demand continue to be weak, firms will drop out of the industry in the long run. The resources can earn higher returns elsewhere. As more firms follow suit, the aggregate supply curve will shift to the left (to S_1).

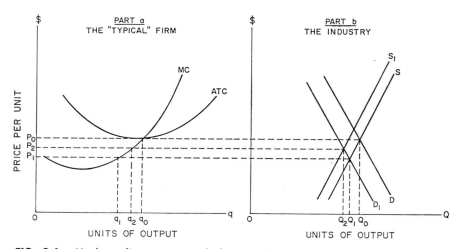

FIG. 9.6. Market adjustment in a declining industry.

Assume that the firm and resource adjustment is such that the new industry equilibrium is at the point where aggregate output is Q_2. The prevailing price is P_2, and the output of the remaining firms would increase slightly to q_2. As can be seen in part a of Figure 9.6, the typical firm depicted there would still be operating at a loss; that is, some factors will be earning less than their opportunity cost. If Q_2 and P_2 represent the new equilibrium position of the industry, the typical firm depicted in part a must decide how long it can continue to earn less than the opportunity cost on all its productive factors. If these factors must be hired, there is little chance to cut corners. Indeed, the usual result is that one of the factors which is not hired—the owner's labor and entrepreneurial input—is the principal bearer of this deficient return. Unless demand conditions change for the better, or unless the cost of factors falls, we know that the typical firm in the figure could not endure in the long run.

ELASTICITIES AND MARKET ADJUSTMENT

We have seen that prices tend to rise in response to a rightward demand shift with no shift in supply, or in response to a leftward supply shift with no shift in demand. Conversely, prices will tend to fall in response to a leftward demand shift with no shift in supply, or in response to a rightward supply shift with no shift in demand. In both cases, given a disturbance in the marketplace, equilibrium will eventually require an adjustment both in the output of the individual firm, in the number of firms in the industry, in the aggregate output, and in the equilibrium price. However, it cannot be assumed that a given change in demand or supply conditions always causes a proportional change in both equilibrium price and quantity. When a supply shift is the cause of a market readjustment, the percentage change in price and quantity from the old to the new equilibrium depends upon the price elasticity of demand. If the market disequilibrium is due to a demand shift, the relative change in price and quantity depends upon the supply elasticity.

If the supply curve is relatively elastic, a given rightward shift in demand will increase price less and sales more than if the supply curve is relatively inelastic. For example, in Figure 9.7, the supply curve S' is relatively more elastic than S. As a consequence, for a given change in demand from D to D_1, the price P_1 is above P'_1, indicting that price will rise less with a relatively elastic supply curve.[4] Similarly, the equilibrium quantity, Q'_1, is greater than Q_1, indicating that the more elastic the supply curve, the greater the impact on sales for a given change in demand. Therefore, with an inelastic supply curve, a given increase in demand raises price more than with an elastic supply, but equilibrium quantity increases less.

4. For a review of supply elasticities, see Chapter 7.

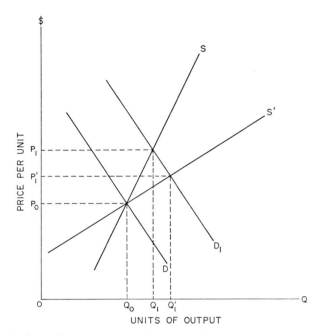

FIG. 9.7. Market adjustment to a rightward shift in demand under two assumptions of supply elasticity.

In a similar manner, one can illustrate the effect of different price elasticities of demand on the relative change in market-clearing prices and quantities for a given shift in the aggregate supply curve. For example, in Figure 9.8, D is relatively more elastic than D'. The shift in supply from S to S_1 decreases price from P_0 to P_1 in the case of the more elastic demand, and from P_0 to P'_1 for the more inelastic curve. The impact on sales of the shift in supply is larger for the more elastic demand curve, as illustrated by the fact that Q_1 is to the right of Q'_1. In summary, with a given rightward shift in supply, price will fall more with an inelastic demand curve than with an elastic one, and the equilibrium quantity will increase less.

It should be clear that elasticity is a very useful concept. When demand shifts occur—for whatever the reason—the elasticity of supply is the key element in determining the extent to which the price of the product will change in response to this demand shift. Similarly, when supply curves shift, the elasticity of demand is the key element in determining the extent to which the price of the product will change in response to this supply shift. Additionally, when the price elasticity of demand is greater than unity ($E_d > 1$), total revenue in that industry will increase as the price falls and will decrease as the price rises. When

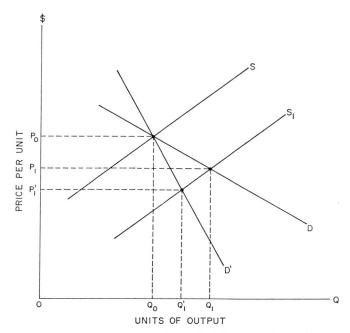

FIG. 9.8. Market adjustment to a rightward shift in supply under two assumptions of demand elasticity.

the price elasticity of demand is less than unity ($E_d < 1$), total revenue in that industry will decrease as the price falls and will increase as the price rises.

The above discussion on the comparative statics of market adjustment omits the intermediate steps whereby a market moves from one equilibrium to a new equilibrium position. Lack of perfect knowledge and the physical inability to make instantaneous responses mean that there may be a series of intermediate prices and quantities established in the market before a new equilibrium is attained. The cobweb theorem is utilized to trace the nature of this type of adjustment process.

COBWEB THEOREM
When prices are traced over a period of years, we observe a cyclical pattern; one year prices will be high, the next they will be low. These cycles develop because of the time lag between the decision to change production and the time when the results of this decision can be empirically ascertained in the marketplace. This is particularly true in agricultural commodities. As indicated earlier, on annual crops this lag is generally 1 year; for broilers the lag may be 3 to 4 months; for

cattle the lag may be 3 to 4 years; for tree crops (nuts, citrus, fruit) the lag may be as much as a decade.

To the extent that expectations about future prices are a function of past prices, and adjustments in the production process are made on the basis of these expectations, there will be a delay in the feedback to producers of the price information which serves as a basis for their future production decisions. This can also result in a cyclical behavior in prices. For example, in one year the quantity of corn supplied is small, and the price is high. This high price encourages producers to plan for an increase in production which, however, does not mature until the next year. When this increase in production comes on the market, prices are forced down, and consequently, many producers find that the prices upon which they planned their production were not realized. The optimistic or pessimistic price expectations and the accompanying changes in production they produce result in a cyclical pattern of prices that looks like a spider web when traced on a demand and supply diagram. This is the source of the name the "cobweb theorem." This is illustrated in Figure 9.9.

The demand and supply curves in the figure are defined somewhat differently from our earlier definitions. The demand curve D represents the price at which a given quantity of production can be sold in a

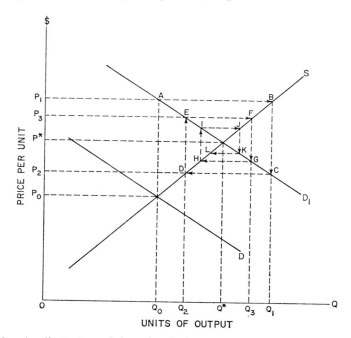

FIG. 9.9. An illustration of the cobweb theorem.

given time period, while the supply curve depicts the relationship between the price in one period and the quantity that will be produced in the following time period. The time period is taken to be the length of time between a decision to produce and the completion of production. The supply curve S is drawn on the assumption that there is a time lag of one period in the response of production to price. This means that one period is required between the time the decision to produce is made and the time when production is forthcoming. For example, if price P_1 prevails in time period 1, the assumptions of the figure are that the quantity Q_1 consistent with price P_1 will appear in the marketplace in time period 2.

Given the demand and supply as defined above, the market depicted in Figure 9.9 is in equilibrium, with the quantity forthcoming being Q_0 at a market price of P_0. Assume there is a shift in the aggregate demand curve to D_1. Since production is a time-consuming process, there will be no new quantity forthcoming until the following period. Consequently, the price rises to P_1, the price consumers would be willing to pay for quantity Q_0 under the new demand conditions. At this higher price, P_1, the quantity Q_0 is cleared from the marketplace. Producers will respond to the higher price P_1 after a time lag of one period and offer quantity Q_1 which can only be disposed of under current demand conditions at price P_2. At this price, (P_2), sellers will only be willing to offer quantity Q_2 in the next period, while consumers would be willing to pay P_3, which would lead to production of Q_3 in the following period. Thus price and quantity are seen to oscillate period by period, starting with point A and moving in succession to point L. We can see that the process will eventually lead to a new equilibrium at Q^* and P^*. Notice that the amplitude of the price oscillation decreases and, given no further shifts in demand or supply, we can expect that P^* and Q^* would be a stable equilibrium. It will remain at that equilibrium until a new market disturbance sets off another oscillatory pattern.

It should be observed at this point that while the geometrical argument depends on the slopes of the curves, the theoretical argument is actually dependent upon the relative elasticities of demand and supply. In Figure 9.9, the supply curve is steeper than the demand curve, and this condition leads to a contracting spiral, or dampening in price oscillations. Not all markets exhibit the type of oscillatory pattern that leads eventually to the stable equilibrium depicted in Figure 9.9. Figure 9.10 shows the effect upon the pattern of prices over time of different relative slopes or elasticities of demand and supply. In part a of the figure, the converging case described above is presented. In part b the supply curve has less slope (is more elastic) than the demand curve, and the cobweb diverges outward in an explosive pattern of production and prices. In part c, the supply and demand curves are such that we have perpetual oscillation.

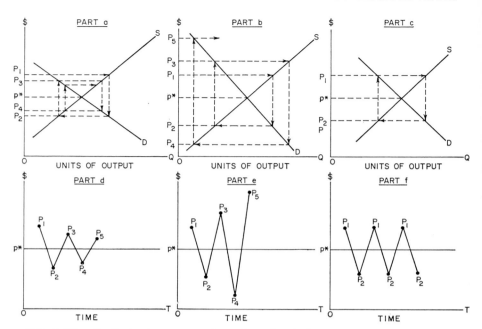

FIG. 9.10. Cyclical price patterns from the cobweb theorem under different elasticities of supply and demand.

Much more complex dynamic models are also described in the literature, with some defining the adjustment process as requiring 1, 2, or even 3 periods.[5] For example, the model may state that farmers make 60 percent of the required adjustment in the first period, 30 percent in the second period, and the remaining 10 percent in the third period. Frequently, they also include considerations of risk and expectations. Obviously, if participants in the marketplace are accustomed to market oscillation, they will include these elements in their production and consumption decisions. As shown in Figure 9.11, the introduction of such expectations will tend to dampen the oscillations. When price is above normal, buyers, knowing it will fall, are willing to pay less than if their expectations were not incorporated (point *b* rather than *a*). Similarly, sellers will discount above-normal prices and produce less than if price was assured (point *d* rather than *c*). The net result of this type of market behavior is that demands are kept down as prices rise above normal in expectation of lower future prices. At below-normal prices, consumers

5. Much of the pioneering work in this area is due to Marc Nerlove, *Dynamics of Supply* (Baltimore: Johns Hopkins Press, 1958); and *Distributed Lags and Demand Analysis for Agriculture and Other Commodities,* Agr. Handbook 141, USDA, Washington, D.C., 1958. The student with a knowledge of calculus is referred to the two works for more details.

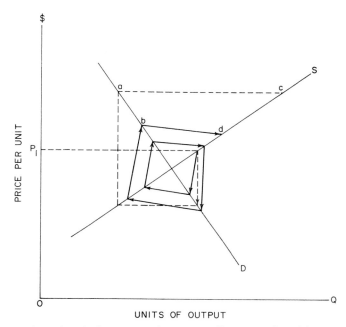

FIG. 9.11. The cobweb theorem with price oscillations reduced by expectations.

pay a higher price in anticipation of higher future prices. In this case, because of expectations, the possibility of a diverging or explosive price cycle is reduced.

Models have also been developed for the case of two or more interrelated markets. A well-known example is that of the corn-hog cycle. The corn-hog cycle explains changes in the production and prices of hogs in terms of the price of corn. Briefly, the demand for corn in any period is dependent upon the price of corn in the same period. The supply of corn is a function of the previous period price received by producers. The demand for hogs is expressed as a function of the price of hogs in the same period. Hog supply depends upon both the price of hogs and the price of corn in a previous period. In the complete model, the corn cycle is independent of the hog cycle but the converse is not true; the hog cycle is dependent upon the corn price in previous periods. In this case the stability in the hog market is highly dependent upon the corn market. More complex variations of this model have also been developed.

Thus the cobweb model is a useful analytical tool for explaining price fluctuations or cycles in a market. It demonstrates that the tools of supply and demand are not limited to analyzing static situations and that the existence of a potential equilibrium in a market does not guarantee it will ever be attained. It is most appropriate for explaining the cycle in nonstorable commodities, since with storable commodities it is possible to even out such cycles through storage and speculation. We will explore the role of such economic activities on market behavior and performance in Chapter 12.

FIXED-ASSET THEORY

In Chapter 7 we introduced the fixed-asset theory and discussed the implications for an industry supply curve. The concept is important in understanding the nature of the farm problem as it will be discussed in Chapter 11, and the human poverty issues discussed in Chapter 13. Recall that there is not always a single price for a factor of production, but that there is an acquisition price and a salvage value. The *acquisition price* reflects what an entrepreneur must pay for a productive factor, while the *salvage price* reflects its value in use elsewhere and is determined by what the owner could obtain for it upon disposition.

Consider Figure 9.12. The curve labeled VMP_1 reflects the

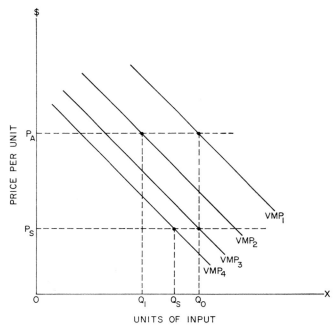

FIG. 9.12. Resource adjustments to alternative product prices under the fixed-asset theory.

value of the marginal product of a productive factor. If the per-unit price of the factor (X) is P_A, the rational entrepreneur will utilize Q_0 units of it to produce the product. Assume that shortly following purchase of the factor (assume it is a piece of equipment such as a tractor) the price of the final product declines. Since $VMP = (MPP)\ (P_Y)$, where P_Y represents the price of the final product, the VMP function will shift downward to VMP_2. From Chapter 5 we know that the rational entrepreneur would reduce his use of the productive factor to the point where $P_A = VMP_2$; that is, he would now reduce the number of tractors employed in the production of the good under consideration from Q_0 to Q_1. However, economists noticed that in agriculture, observed behavior failed to bear out this prediction. It was observed that as farm prices fall, most producers continue to produce at the same level (with the same complement of equipment) and in some instances have been known to increase output. This is exactly opposite of what we would expect from the theory developed in Chapter 5.[6]

The explanation can be found in the two-price concept discussed above; that is, a piece of equipment purchased to perform a specific task (such as a tractor) has little flexibility to be used outside the activity for which it was initially purchased. Given this fact, its value at the margin is somewhat less. Put differently, the amount that a farmer could receive for a tractor from a nonfarmer or another farmer is likely to be less than what he paid for the machine, even though it is still in the crate. In other words, because its salvage value (value in use outside the firm) is less than its acquisition price, it remains fixed in its present use. In Figure 9.12 let P_s represent the salvage value of tractors. With this assumption, we can see that the price of the final product would have to fall substantially before the number of tractors in agriculture would begin to drop, and hence before we would observe a decline in agricultural production. Only when the product price falls sufficiently to shift the value of the marginal product curve to, say, VMP_4 would there be a reduction in tractor usage (Q_s).

Since assets are synonymous with factors of production, it should also be recognized that such variable factors as labor also have an acquisition and a salvage value. Hence the entrepreneur who plans on a return of, say, $2.00 per hour would impute this return as part of per-unit production costs. However, as the price of the product falls, he is forced to realize that his labor outside agriculture may bring only $1.50 per hour. Given this, his salvage value for labor is less than what he figured on in the planning stage (his acquisition cost) and he remains "fixed" in agriculture. This will be discussed in Chapters 11 and 13.

6. This is a good example of a case where empirical observation leads to a refinement in theoretical concepts.

LONG-RUN ADJUSTMENTS

In Chapter 6, in our discussion of cost curves, we detailed the concepts of long-run average cost and long-run marginal cost.

That discussion concluded with a warning that any discussion of plant scale and long-run adjustments required the consideration of demand conditions. Now that the discussion of comparative statics is complete, it should be clear that demand conditions are important determinants of the ultimate scale of a firm and hence of the average total costs of the firm. Depending upon a firm's share of the total market, it may be impossible for it to expand to the scale which corresponds to the minimum point on its long-run average cost ($LRAC$) curve. Indeed, the incentive for bigness in business (by which is meant not only absolute size but share of the market) comes from the desire to capture all possible economies of scale. This issue will be discussed in more detail in Chapter 10.

For now, it is important to recognize that the comparative statics analysis of the previous section ignored a very important consideration and that is the *external* factors which dictate the cost conditions of all firms. By external we mean those things beyond the bounds and control of the individual firm and industry being analyzed. In contrast, the analytics of Chapter 6—specifically those of the long-run average and marginal cost curves—were concerned with factors *internal* to the firm such as technology and specialization of factors. The economies and diseconomies obtained were internal to the firm. However, as firms enter or leave an industry in response to demand shifts, the suppliers of inputs to those firms in that industry experience shifts in the demand curve for their product. Recall from Chapter 5 that we can derive the demand curve for productive inputs from the production function (and product price) of a firm; the aggregate of these derived demand curves for a particular factor constitutes the market demand curve which producers or suppliers of that factor face. This shift in demand for factors influences the input-supply industry just as the shift in consumer demand influences the industry of most direct interest. This adjustment process is the subject of this section.

The analysis which follows is classified in advanced books as *pecuniary external economies and diseconomies*—pecuniary referring to monetary;[7] that is, as the output of industry A expands, it permits the expansion of those industries which supply inputs to A. Depending upon the economies of scale within these supply industries (internal to them), the cost of inputs to industry A will be either higher or lower.

---

7. This should be kept distinct from *technological* external economies and diseconomies—a situation which denotes a physical interdependency between firms rather than a monetary interdependency. The classic example of technological economies and diseconomies is that of pollution, a subject to be treated in Chapter 15.

If the supply industries are operating at a scale less than that which is optimal (minimum average cost), the expansion will permit internal (to them, external to A) economies to be realized and will result in reduced input prices for A. On the other hand, if the supply industries are operating a scale greater than that which is optimal (minimum average cost), the expansion will result in internal (to them, external to A) diseconomies and will lead to increased input prices for A.[8] Examples of inputs in which this situation can occur are transportation costs, electrical energy, and intermediate products which are used by the industry to produce its final product.

There are three possibilities corresponding to the industry's experience with the changes in factor costs: (1) a constant-cost industry; (2) an increasing-cost industry; and (3) a decreasing-cost industry. A constant-cost industry is one which can expand its acquisition of productive factors to meet any increase in demand for its product without having to pay higher or lower prices for its inputs. Thus, as the output of the industry changes, there is no change in the location of the typical firm's per-unit cost curves. The analysis of a constant-cost industry was presented in Figure 9.5.

INCREASING-COST INDUSTRIES

In Figure 9.13 we start with the basic situation as depicted in Figure 9.5. D and S represent the initial demand and supply curves, respectively, and ATC and MC represent the average total cost and marginal cost curves of the typical firm. The initial output of the industry is Q_0, the initial price is P_0, and the typical firm is producing q_0. As demand shifts to D_1, new firms enter the industry in pursuit of the extranormal profit, and existing firms expand output along their marginal cost curve (to q_1). The added productive capacity requires more inputs. Such demand drives up the price of productive factors such that the per-unit cost curves of the typical firm are displaced upward. For example, as the computer software industry expands, the demand for computer programmers and computer language specialists will increase. This could be expected to have a positive effect on wages paid these people. In the aggregate, it can be argued that the individual firms already in the industry must meet these higher wages (or lose their good employees to the new firms) and hence, costs of production within the industry increase. This leads to an upward shift in ATC to ATC_1 and to MC_1. Whereas under the constant-cost assumption a new equilibrium was determined at the intersection of S_1 and D_1 (point C), the effect of

8. If the demand for A's product is contracting instead of expanding, the conclusion would be the converse to that detailed.

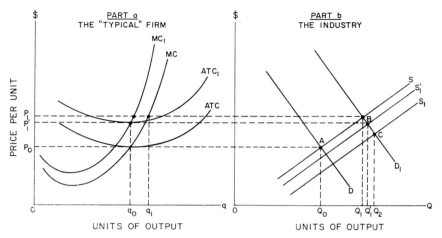

FIG. 9.13. Long-run adjustments in an increasing-cost industry.

higher factor prices is to actually shift S_1 to S'_1, with a new equilibrium output of Q'_1, an equilibrium price of P'_1, and an output for the typical firm (q_0). There is no way to predict what will happen to the equilibrium output per firm. It may remain constant as shown in Figure 9.13 or it may increase or decrease. Furthermore, there is nothing magical about the particular location of S'_1—the crucial determinants are the extent of price increase in the supply industry (or industries) and the number of new firms entering the industry. Indeed, S'_1 could be to the left of S. The central result is that in an increasing-cost industry, output is less—and price is higher—than in a constant-cost industry. The relevant comparison in part b of Figure 9.13 is between points B and C.

DECREASING-COST INDUSTRIES

The final type of industry is that which experiences lower prices for its productive factors as it expands to meet the increased demand for its product. Consider Figure 9.14. The initial conditions find equilibrium output to be Q_0 for the industry, q_0 for the typical firm, and an equilibrium price of P_0.

As a specific example, consider the computer software industry. Assume that when computer software firms first became popular they comprised a small part of the total market for the equipment of such computer manufacturers as IBM and Control Data Corporation. As a result, these latter firms face a limited demand for their machines. As the demand for computer services grows, we could observe a shift to D_1, a short-run price of P_1, and an industry output of Q_1 (the typical firm

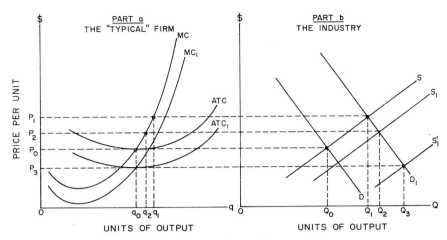

FIG. 9.14. Long-run adjustments in a decreasing-cost industry.

would produce q_1). However, we know that the higher price will attract other software firms into the industry and shift the supply curve to S_1, resulting in a lower price (P_2), a larger output by the industry (Q_2), but a lower level of output for the typical firm (q_2).

As the computer software industry flourishes, the manufacturers of computers can produce computers at lower per-unit costs (achieve internal scale economies). Hence, scale economies external to the computer software industry may make lower production costs possible as the industry expands (even with the higher wages being paid the software personnel). If such scale economies are large enough, the cost curves of the individual software firms might be shifted downward (to ATC_1 and MC_1 in Figure 9.14) and cause the industry supply curve to shift downward to S'_1. This implies a new equilibrium price in the market of P_3, a new industry output (Q_3), and a new output level (q_0) of the firm depicted in part a. For the typical firm, the new output level just happens to correspond to the old output level. This is purely a coincidence resulting from the location of S'_1. Also, the location of S'_1 implies that the typical firm earns zero profit.

As another example of external economies, consider the expansion of the transportation industry in a developing country. Initially, commodities are expensive to move, and firms experience considerable costs in merely getting their product to market. However, as the transportation network develops, per-unit costs fall. This cost saving is brought about by forces completely outside the industry and the firm and may not have been generated by demand shifts for the commodity under consideration. For example, the expansion of the railroads into the western frontier early in our history had nothing to do with the demand for beef on the East Coast, nevertheless it certainly bestowed certain cost advantages on those producers who could get their livestock to a shipping point. In this case, as the industry expanded and as more rail lines were established, the beef industry was characterized by decreasing costs.

In summary, in a purely competitive industry, adjustments to changing demand conditions are dependent upon the time period under consideration. In the short run, firms adjust output by moving along their marginal cost curve (short-run supply curve). In the long run, both firm scale and the number of firms may change. The exact nature of the adjustment process is dependent upon both internal economies and diseconomies, and external economies and diseconomies. In the former, the entrepreneur responds to changing market conditions by scale adjustments, assuming constant factor prices. He allocates resources according to signals he receives from within his firm and industry to obtain the optimum factor combination to minimize costs. In the case of external factors, the entrepreneur must take into account the external economies and diseconomies and the resultant factor price signals from outside the firm and industry.

This entire discussion can be best consolidated by the long-run average cost (*LRAC*) curves in Chapter 6 as illustrated by Figure 9.15. Here, the long-run average cost curves for some hypothetical situations illustrate the essence of constant-cost industries, increasing-cost industries, and decreasing-cost industries.

Part a of the figure indicates that regardless of the level of demand the long-run average cost curve for the firm is given by LRAC. In part b, the increasing-cost industry indicates that as the demand for that industry's product grows, and as individual firms attempt to expand—or, as new firms enter—the price of productive factors required by the industry increases. Consequently, the long-run average

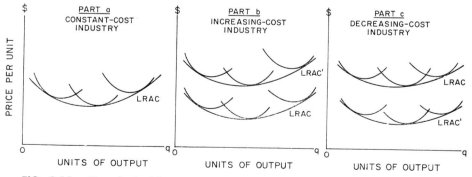

FIG. 9.15. Hypothetical long-run average cost curves for constant-, increasing-, and decreasing-cost industries.

cost curve increases from $LRAC$ to $LRAC'$ as consumer demand expands. For the decreasing-cost industry, the situation is symmetric, but reversed.

RESOURCE ALLOCATION IN A COMPETITIVE ECONOMY

In earlier chapters we described the allocation of productive factors within a firm to achieve a certain level of output at minimum cost or to achieve a maximum revenue for a certain cost of production. Now we will review very briefly the essence of resource allocation within the whole economy to show how, if it worked smoothly, the competitive economy operates at maximum efficiency when resources are free to move about in response to the signals emitted in each marketplace. The discussion should not be construed as an argument that the system really operates as smoothly as described. Instead, it should be viewed as an explanation of the logical conclusions of the premises of the purely competitive economy. If the premises are true, the conclusions stated here are also true. Since many (if not all) of the premises are only approximately true in the marketplace, the student should be aware of the tenuous nature of the following results.

To review, an economic system that is purely competitive is assumed to be characterized by the following conditions in each market:

1. There is such a large number of both buyers and sellers that no one can influence price through his actions.
2. Firms in pure competition in any market produce a standardized product. This means that any buyer of the product is indifferent as to the seller from whom he purchases it since the products are perfectly substitutable one for another.
3. The factors of production are completely mobile and free to move from one industry to another to secure greater returns. In other words, there is no barrier to the flow of capital, labor, or management out of one industry and into another.
4. Both buyers and sellers operate in an economically rational manner so as to maximize profits or utility.

In the preceding material, we developed a theoretical framework describing how prices for resources and consumer goods and services are determined in a competitive market and how these prices act as signals to producers and consumers in that market. In this we viewed a single competitive market in isolation. This type of analysis is termed *partial equilibrium* analysis. It is concerned with the equilibrium in a particular market in contrast to equilibrium in all markets in an economy.

It is clear from our observations of the world around us that there is interaction among markets. To really understand the resource allocation process one must take into account these market interrelationships. This type of analysis is termed *general equilibrium* analysis. General equilibrium analysis is an approach which permits us to study the determination of prices and quantities in all markets in the economy simultaneously. It ties together and summarizes the major principles we have covered, and it demonstrates how a perfectly competitive economy answers the major questions: What is to be produced? How shall it be produced? How will the resulting product be distributed? In the process of describing how an economy achieves general equilibrium, we will gain insight into how the system provides consumers with the maximum possible satisfaction from the given distribution of resources.

To clarify the explanation, we will use as an example a two-sector economy producing two products, fish and nuts. The two basic sectors are (1) a business sector composed of firms producing fish and nuts and buying resources, and (2) a consuming sector comprised of households which provide all the resources and consume the output. A simplified representation of our hypothetical economy is illustrated in Figure 9.16.[9] When this purely competitive economy is in equilibrium, the magnitude of money flowing from firms to households in payment for resources will be exactly equal to the money payments from households to firms for fish and nuts.[10]

Up to this point we have been concerned with parts of this general economy. Although we can learn a great deal about the price of fish by analyzing the product and factor markets for fish when the price of nuts is assumed fixed, our present analysis will permit us to learn a great deal more about the economy by allowing us to relax the assumption of constant prices for nuts. Similarly, when studying the price of resources used in the fisheries, we will no longer be required to assume the price of other resources to be constant. Thus in partial equilibrium analysis, we are concerned with some of the firms on the left and part of the households on the right of Figure 9.16. The general equilibrium analysis of this section considers all relationships among firms on the left side and all households on the right side as well as the relationships between firms and households.

Assume now that Figure 9.17 reflects the present equilibrium prices and quantities for each of the two commodities. As for the producers of fish and nuts, each individual firm will visualize the horizontal

9. While it should be noted that this is a simplistic view of any real economy, it is sufficient to illustrate many of the essential features of the interactions among various factors and product markets. It is beyond the scope of this text to discuss the more sophisticated general equilibrium models which include others sectors such as government, a foreign sector, savings, investments, and intermediate goods.

10. In fact, each stream represents a different way of measuring the size of the economy, the first by measuring income and the second by measuring product value.

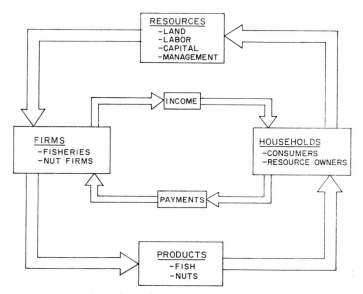

FIG. 9.16. Flows in a hypothetical two-sector economy.

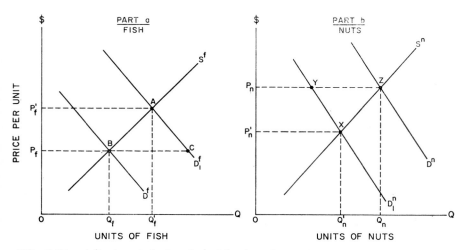

FIG. 9.17. Adjustments in two industries in a two-sector economy.

line P_f or P_n as its demand curve and sell that quantity of fish or nuts which maximizes its net profits. Furthermore, in equilibrium, each firm in the industry will be earning zero profit. Aggregate output of all firms in the fish industry will result in Q_f units of fish, and firms in the nut industry will produce Q_n units of nuts.

Each resource will be receiving its value marginal product. The ratio of the *VMP* of the resource to its price will be equal for all resources. On the demand side, the marginal utility the consumer receives from the last unit of nuts and fish consumed is exactly equal to their respective prices. Furthermore, the price of the product exactly reflects the cost of the last unit of each resource used to produce it. This insures that the utility the consumer receives from the last unit of fish and nuts is exactly equal to the cost of the resources sacrificed to produce it. If these conditions were not met, either costs could be reduced or consumers' satisfaction increased by shifting resources from fish to nuts or vice versa.

Assume it is discovered that the high oil content of nuts leads to coronary problems and, consequently, the inhabitants of our simple world reduce their consumption of nuts and replace this with a larger consumption of fish. From earlier sections we know that this is equivalent to a rightward shift in the demand curve for fish to $D_1{}^f$ and a leftward shift in the demand curve for nuts to $D_1{}^n$. In the *very* short run there will be an excess demand for fish $(C - B)$ and an excess supply of nuts $(Z - Y)$. The shortage of fish will result in consumers' starting to bid up the price of fish by offering individual firms a higher price (up to P'_f). As the time frame lengthens, the firms supplying fish, responding to the higher prices and extranormal profits, will attempt to expand production along their marginal cost curves. In order to expand, they must acquire additional quantities of the variable resources. Since it is assumed that there are no surplus resources or unused capacity in the economy, these resources must come from other industries; in our example, from the nut industry which is experiencing losses. The nut-producing firms will be willing to release inputs because of the excess supply. As a consequence, nut producers will begin contracting output along their marginal cost curves. In the short run they will use fewer variable inputs such as labor, power, and other supplies.

As there is expansion in the fish industry—and contraction in the nut industry—we can expect that point A might represent a new equilibrium in the former and point X might represent a new equilibrium in the latter. The long-run situation would be characterized by new boats, plants, and other equipment in the fish industry and a liquidation of trees and equipment in the nut industry. Employment in the fish industry would be higher, employment in the nut industry less; the share of total national income arising from nut production would be down.

While the short-run adjustment was primarily in terms of price, the longer-run adjustment process involves firm output, scale of firms, numbers of firms, aggregate output, employment, and income payments. The change in consumer preferences has precipitated a whole series of events that reverberate through the economic system. Theoretically, fac- tors are perfectly mobile so that following the perturbation the two industries reach a new equilibrium where firms have achieved the least-cost scale of operation, and consumers would consequently be receiving the respective quantities of fish and nuts at the minimum possible social cost.

This simple example illustrates how in theory a competitive economy operates in an efficient manner to allocate resources in response to the desires of consumers. The market mechanism always works to equate price with marginal cost. This means that the consumer pays no more than the marginal cost of producing the product. Since the consumer equates the price he must pay for the product to the marginal utility he derives from its consumption, the market mechanism insures that each resource is allocated to the production of that commodity which adds the most to the consumer's utility or satisfaction. Therefore, insofar as the available resources permit, it maximizes total satisfaction of all consumers.

There is, in effect, a voting system in which the consumer votes by buying, and the producer responds to this vote by shifting resources according to the purchases. Total utility is said to be maximized because the marginal utility to society from the last unit of product produced is just equal to its marginal cost in terms of the resources used to produce it.

In summary, if the competitive economy were characterized by the many assumptions made in this and earlier chapters, it could be said that the economy would produce those goods and services valued most by consumers and would produce those goods and services at the lowest possible cost, and owners of productive factors would be rewarded according to the contribution of their factors to the total value of the product. In fact, these assumptions are often unrealistic and the following chapter is devoted to a discussion of one of the major areas in which some of the assumptions are not met.

SUMMARY

In this chapter we combined the concepts of production—which form the foundation of the supply side of the market—with the concepts of demand theory. This leads to the concept of market equilibrium and of the ability to describe market adjustments over time. The precipitating factors for market adjustments were seen to be shifts in supply curves or shifts in demand curves. The concept of elasticity—

both demand and supply—were used to illustrate the relevance of these concepts in explaining market adjustments. The cobweb theorem and the fixed-asset theory were detailed as examples of refinements in the theory of markets. The process of long-run adjustment was developed to illustrate the impact of relaxing the assumption concerning the ability of all producers to buy inputs at the same price. Here we explored the concepts of constant-cost, increasing-cost, and decreasing-cost industries. Finally, a general discussion of resource allocation in a competitive economy was presented to illustrate the usefulness of the theory in explaining the process of economy-wide adjustments.

SUGGESTED READINGS

B A S I C

Bawden, D. Lee. An evaluation of alternative spatial models. *J. Farm Econ.* 56(Dec. 1964): 1372–79.

    An overview of how the basic concepts of demand, supply, and market equilibrium are modified in light of real-world observations. The author defines, classifies, and evaluates economic models according to how they utilize the concept of space (location) in explaining eonomic activity.

Cochrane, Willard W. *The World Food Problem: A Guardedly Optimistic View.* New York: Thomas Y. Crowell, 1969.

    An example of the application of the concepts of demand and supply curves in the analysis of a real-world problem. The author analyzes the shifts in the aggregate demand for food due to population growth throughout the world. He compares the rate of growth in aggregate demand to shifts in (growth in) aggregate food supply for various countries and regions of the world.

Dean, Edwin R. Social determinants of price in several African markets. *Econ. Develop. Cult. Change* 11(Apr. 1963): 239–56.

    An attempt to extend basic price theory. Describes an experiment in local markets in Africa where determination of the market price includes the impact of such noneconomic variables as the social relationship of buyer and seller and the age-sex group of buyer and seller.

Due, John F. *Intermediate Economic Analysis,* 3rd ed. Homewood, Ill.: Richard D. Irwin, 1956, Ch. 18–19.

    A discussion of the current theoretical thinking on the role of profits and economic rents in the theory of cost and prices.

Ezekiel, M. The cobweb theorem. *Quart. J. Econ.* 12(Feb. 1938): 255–80.

    The theoretical framework for this model was developed independently by three different economists. The name, cobweb theorem, was proposed in another early article by yet a fourth economist. The above article is the most frequently cited work on the cobweb. It contains a discussion of the adequacy of the theorem for explaining commodity price cycles as well as specific references to the four original articles on the subject.

Leftwich, Richard H. *The Price System and Resource Allocation,* 4th ed. Hinsdale, Ill.: Dryden Press, 1970, Ch. 13, 18.

    The author develops the principles underlying resource pricing and utilization in purely competitive products and resource markets. He describes how these markets allocate resources among different uses, areas, and products among participants. Chapter 18 describes how an economy composed of purely competitive markets operates to ensure the greatest possible level of consumer satisfaction from a given distribution of resources.

Low, Richard E. *Modern Economic Organization.* Homewood, Ill.: Richard D. Irwin, 1970, Ch. 6.
    Defines and describes the various types of scale economies that can exist within a firm and a plant and the problems of defining and of measuring optimum scale.

Rees, Albert. The effects of unions on resource allocation. *J. Law Econ.* 6(Oct. 1963): 69–78.
    (See annotation under Rottenberg.)

Robinson, Joan. What is perfect competition? *Quart. J. Econ.* 8(Nov. 1934): 104–20.
    A famous early article. The author very carefully defines and analyzes perfect competition. Includes a lengthy discussion of the role of normal profits.

Rottenberg, Simon. The baseball players labor market. *J. Polit. Econ.* 64(June 1956): 242–58.
    The two articles by Rees and Rottenberg utilize the tools of microeconomics to point out the impact on resource allocation of imperfections in two different markets: (1) baseball players and (2) labor unions and collective bargaining.

Samuelson, Paul A. *Economics,* 9th ed. New York: McGraw-Hill, 1973, Ch. 20, 21, 23, 24, 32.
    A clear elementary discussion of the elements of pricing in competitive markets. Chapter 32 contains a description of general equilibrium analysis and ideal welfare pricing.

ADVANCED

Bator, Frances. The simple analytics of welfare maximization. *Am. Econ. Rev.* 47(Mar. 1957): 22–59.
    The author brings together all aspects of microeconomics into one well-known review of welfare maximization in a perfectly competitive market economy. The treatment is completely nonmathematical.

Baumol, W. J. *Economic Dynamics.* New York: Macmillan, 1951, Ch. 7.
    A nonmathematical discussion of comparative statics, dynamics, and the cobweb theorem.

Bressler, Raymond G., Jr.; and King, Richard A. *Markets, Prices and Interregional Trade.* New York: John Wiley, 1970.
    Illustrates the adaptability and power of the theoretical tools of demand and supply in the analysis of markets and market equilibrium. The book reviews price theory and then extends the concepts to include the variables of time, form, and space in determining market price.

Johnson, Glenn L. Alternatives to the neoclassical theory of the firm (NTF). *Am. J. Agr. Econ.* 54(May 1972): 295–304.
    The author defines neoclassical theory of the firm and discusses recent important efforts in the literature to define alternatives. He deals with shortcomings of the theory as revealed by agricultural economists. He describes accomplishments to date and suggests further needed developments of the theory.

Leibenstein, Harvey. Allocative efficiency vs X-efficiency. *Am. Econ. Rev.* 56(June 1966): 392–415.
    The author estimates allocative inefficiencies of resources in the

United States as being small. He argues that microtheory pays too much attention to allocative efficiency at the expense of other types of economic efficiency which he call X-efficiencies.

Robinson, Joan. Euler's theorem and the problem of distribution. *Econ. J.,* (Sept. 1934): 398–414.

The author examines the famous "adding up" criteria of distribution theory. She provides an answer to the question contained in the criteria, "If each factor is paid its marginal product, how do we know that the total payments will just 'add up' to the value of the product which they produced?

Viner, Jacob. Cost curves and supply curves. *Z. Nationalokonomie* 3(1931): 22–46. Also reprinted in American Economic Association, *Readings in Price Theory*. Chicago: Richard D. Irwin, 1952, pp. 198–232.

The classic reference in clarifying the relationship of short-run and long-run cost schedules. A geometric development of the relationship between supply curves and the different possible types of cost situations in a purely competitive industry. It includes a discussion of internal and external economies of scale.

Worchester, Dean A. A reconsideration of the theory of rent. *Am. Econ. Rev.* 36(June 1946): 258–77.

A review of the various approaches to the theory of rent or surplus.

DISCUSSION QUESTIONS AND PROBLEMS

1. The Brazilian government regularly destroys a portion of its coffee harvest to increase its revenues from coffee sales abroad. Is this a rational economic policy?
2. Explain the following statement (use a supply and demand diagram): The demand for *each* farmer's wheat is perfectly elastic, while the demand for *all* wheat is very inelastic.
3. Why does the operation of demand and supply in a competitive economy assure the most efficient *economic* allocation of resources?
4. Discuss the proposition that the most efficient economic allocation of resources may not be the most desirable allocation of resources.
5. Explain why an industry such as computer manufacture might be an increasing-cost industry because of *internal* diseconomies. Because of *external* diseconomies.
6. Discuss what economists mean by "perfectly mobile factors of production."
7. Explain the relevance of time in the determination of supply elasticities.
8. Make a distinction between external and internal economies and diseconomies.
9. Of what relevance is the market-share concept in realizing scale economies?

CHAPTER 10: MARKET STRUCTURE AND RESOURCE ALLOCATION

The case of the decentralized private enterprise system has been developed in the previous chapters. It culminated in the assertion that firms, pursuing profits in their own self-interest, caused resources to flow from firm to firm and industry to industry as profits varied, thus assuring that each resource would produce the maximum output and that consumers would obtain the maximum utility. Up through the latter part of the nineteenth century, this theory was adhered to by economists and policymakers alike. It assumes that competition prevails and that each entrepreneur operating in his own self-interest is guided as if by an invisible hand toward obtaining the best solution for all.[1] In this view of the economic system, any interference by nonmarket forces such as government or other artificial restrictions would subvert the operation of the invisible hand of competition and cause the system to be less efficient.

A century or more ago, many small independent firms were indeed the rule. Productive activities were centered in agriculture, the extractive industries, handicrafts, small manufacturing firms, and traders. Enterprises were primarily organized as individual proprietorships or partnerships that often developed and then dissolved within one generation. This is now all changed. The individual proprietorships and partnerships have largely given way to modern corporations that exist indefinitely, grow to be large-scale organizations, accumulate large amounts of capital, and with it, economic power in the marketplace. With the growth of large business, economists observed that the decline in competition and the supposed automatic and spontaneous operation of the marketplace could not be counted on to maximize output from the available resources.

As economists observed the economic problems that existed in the form of concentrations of economic power, solutions were proposed that necessitated the establishment of government controls. Up through World War II, the United States and Canada were virtually alone in the world in regard to their official opposition to large concentrations

---

1. Adam Smith, *The Wealth of Nations* (New York: Modern Library, 1937), p. 432.

of market power in the hands of a few firms. It has been the stated policy of the United States government since 1890 to prevent monopoly and to maintain a competitive economy. The first important piece of legislation stating this policy was the Sherman Antitrust Act of 1890. The act stated: "Every contract, combination in the form of a trust . . . or conspiracy, in restraint of trade or commerce among the several states or with foreign nations, is hereby declared illegal." (Sec. 1). "Every person who shall monopolize, or attempt to monopolize, or combine or conspire . . . to monopolize any part of the trade or commerce among the several states, or with foreign nations, shall be deemed guilty of a misdemeanor. . . ." (Sec. 2). The Sherman Act has since been buttressed by many additional pieces of legislation whose intent is to strike down monopolies and activities which restrain competition in the marketplace.

This book is not the place to develop rigorous arguments on the full array of issues involved in the concentration or control and regulation of economic power. Our purpose in this chapter is to develop some analytical devices that will help the student to understand the economic effects of imperfect competition. The case of perfect competition was studied earlier because it sheds light on the efficiency with which the market mechanism allocates resources. It will be seen here that the success of the market system in solving resource allocation matters is closely related to the degree of market imperfections in the system.

Thus in this chapter we have four main tasks: (1) to explain alternative forms of market structure—from the extreme of pure competition to the opposite extreme of pure monopoly; (2) to explore in more detail the economic theory of pure monopoly; (3) to detail the economic effects of monopoly in terms of resource use, output, and product price and to discuss ways to regulate monopoly; and (4) to present a discussion of that branch of economics known as industrial organization theory.

ALTERNATIVE FORMS OF MARKET STRUCTURE

In earlier chapters we have discussed the assumptions of the purely competitive economy and the role that these assumptions play in the theoretical concepts. The assumption which will be dealt with here concerns that of the number of sellers in a given market.[2] Our traditional assumption regarding numbers is that there are many firms, none of them large enough to have an influence on product price because of their output policy. At the other extreme is the case of monopoly where there is but one producer or seller of a good or service. Our discussion in this chapter will focus primarily on the

2. Recall that we refer to a *market* as a group of buyers and sellers in close enough contact so that an exchange of goods or services takes place.

theory of monopoly but, to add perspective to the discussion on monopoly, consider the following listing of the different forms of market structure. The first three refer to the selling side of the market, while the latter three refer to the market for inputs.

1. Monopoly: Total supply controlled by one seller.
2. Oligopoly: The existence of more than one seller, but still few enough so that the actions of one or several can have a significant effect upon the market price to other sellers.
3. Monopolistic competition: The existence of many sellers in a given market yet the product of each is, in some way, different. Here it is assumed that there are sufficient producers so that the actions of one do not significantly influence the price or quantity sold of the others, yet each feels he can influence his demand by nonprice competition.
4. Monopsony: Only one buyer of a particular good or service, the direct antithesis of pure competition on the buying side.
5. Oligopsony: The existence of more than two buyers, but still few enough such that the actions of one or several can have a significant effect upon the market price of the other buyers.
6. Monopsonistic competition: The existence of many buyers in a given input market, yet the demand for inputs by each is somehow differentiated.

The above taxonomy of market structure is summarized in Table 10.1. As stated earlier, the four types of firm/product combinations are the clear and distinct cases that exist among the variety of types possible between A and D. Furthermore, when the selling and buying side are placed together as in Table 10.1, it is easily apparent that the market could consist of any of a large number of possible buyer-seller arrangements; for example, a firm might be one of several thousand purchasers of labor in a given town but be the only outlet of some good or service. Or it might be the only purchaser of uranium in the

TABLE 10.1. A classification of alternative types of market structure

Number of Firms/Product Type	Activity of the Firm	
	Selling	Buying
A. Many Firms/Homogeneous Product	Perfectly Competitive	Perfectly Competitive
B. Many Firms/Differentiated Product	Monopolistic Competition	Monopsonistic Competition
C. Few Firms/Homogeneous or Differentiated Product	Oligopoly	Oligopsony
D. One Firm/Unique Product	Monopolist	Monopsonist

country, yet produce many different types of products, all but one of which is also produced by many other firms. Economists, for each of the six relatively distinct market situations, have analyzed the degree of imperfection of resource allocation each entails. We now turn to a detailed examination of one of these, the monopolist.

MONOPOLY CASE

In monopoly there is but one seller of a particular product. Thus the firm constitutes the entire industry. Further, since there are no close substitutes, the firm does not have to worry about how its actions affect other firms' behavior nor does it have to face any competition from other firms producing the same or a similar product. As we shall show, the monopolist frequently enjoys in the long run large positive profits that a firm in a competitive industry could not hope to enjoy.

The reader may wonder why a monopoly would long exist since other firms or entrepreneurs, observing large profits, would try to enter the same market and share in some of those profits. Many factors can lead to the establishment and perpetuation of a monopoly. The control of a raw material supply is one. Bauxite, an essential ingredient in the production of aluminum, was at one time controlled by the Aluminum Company of America (Alcoa). As a result, Alcoa had a monopoly in aluminum. Exclusive rights to a particular production process such as a patent or a secret is a second source. E. I. du Pont de Nemours and Company had a patent on cellophane that gave it a monopoly in this product. Coca-Cola Company has managed to keep the recipe for Coca-Cola secret and as a result maintains tight control over the production of this popular beverage. For years, Minnesota Mining and Manufacturing (3M) had patent monopolies in Scotch tape and the Thermofax copier. A third source of monopoly is the economies of scale inherent in some types of production processes. These are the so-called natural monopolies. They arise when the minimum average cost of production occurs at the scale of plant that can supply the entire market demand. The natural monopolies are generally the public utilities such as electric power, telephone communications, transportation, and sewage disposal companies. The final source of monopoly is the market franchise and licensing. A market franchise is a contract whereby some governmental unit gives the entire right to market a particular good or service to a particular firm. In return, the firm agrees to permit the government to control certain aspects of its conduct such as the price it can charge or the return it can earn on its investment. Local cable television companies and public utilities are examples. Franchises are also issued by private firms, and by this procedure it is possible to limit the number of firms selling their product and the prices that they will charge. Local automobile agencies and specialized food chains are examples. Licenses are frequently required as a condition of entry into many fields. Doctors, dentists, and distributors of liquor are some examples. In each case, the license requirement can be used as a method of controlling entry and thereby restricting competition in a particular market.

DEMAND SIDE

The monopoly firm, being the only firm in the industry, faces the aggregate demand curve for the commodity; it is this curve that shows the alternative price-quantity combinations for the commodity. Whereas a firm in a competitive industry can sell its total output at the same price, a monopoly can increase sales only by reducing price. In Figure 10.1, the aggregate demand curve indicates that if the monopolist wishes to increase sales from Q_0 to Q_1, a price reduction from P_0 to P_1 would be necessary.

The significance for decision making should be obvious; in the competitive industry, each firm is small in relation to the total output of the industry. There, the manager of each firm knows that the level of its output will not materially affect prices of the product it sells, and hence

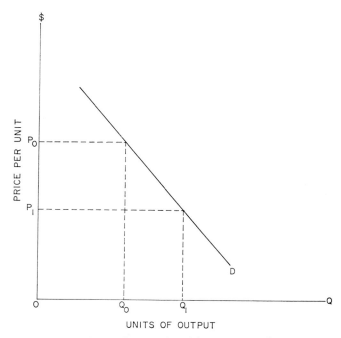

FIG. 10.1. Aggregate demand curve faced by a monopolist.

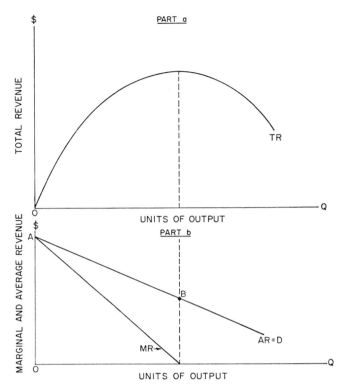

FIG. 10.2. Total revenue, average revenue, and marginal revenue of a monopolist.

it views that price as a parameter (a constant) when it decides how much of the product to produce and the best techniques to produce it. Put somewhat differently, we know that the decision rule for how much to produce is that production should be increased until marginal costs become equal to marginal revenue—until the increment to total costs just equals the increment to total revenue. For the competitive firm, the price at which each additional unit can be sold does not vary, and hence marginal revenue is a constant.

This is not the case for the monopolist. Since he is the industry and hence faces the aggregate demand curve for his product, he knows that the quantity he produces will affect price. The market demand curve becomes the monopolist's average revenue curve because it tells him the average price he can get for any quantity he sells. The marginal revenue will thus lie below and to the left of the demand curve. This relationship (originally developed in Chapter 8) is illustrated in Figure 10.2.

Recall that the elasticity of demand changes as one moves along the demand (average revenue) curve. Between points A and B the price elasticity of demand is greater than 1; at point B demand is unitary elastic; and to the right of point B the price elasticity of demand is less than 1.

Recall that marginal revenue is defined as the change in total revenue with respect to a change in total output, and hence it is the slope of the total revenue function. Marginal revenue and average revenue are related by Equation 10.1

$$MR = AR - AR/E_d \tag{10.1}$$

where

$$
\begin{aligned}
MR &= \text{marginal revenue} \\
AR &= \text{average revenue (price)} \\
E_d &= \text{price elasticity of demand}
\end{aligned}
$$

This formulation can be used to prove that at that output level where marginal revenue equals zero, the price elasticity of demand is unitary (point B in Figure 10.2). At output levels less than this point, that is, where marginal revenue is positive, total revenue can be increased by expanding output up to this point; at output levels greater than this point, total revenue can be increased by reducing output until this point is reached. Since marginal costs are never zero for productive endeavors, we can conclude that a monopolist would always produce at some output level to the left of point B. The exact level of output is determined (as will be recalled from earlier chapters) by the equality of marginal revenue and marginal cost ($MR = MC$). Before turning to that we must briefly review the cost aspects of a monopoly.

SUPPLY SIDE

Aside from the fact that a monopolist comprises the industry in a particular commodity or service market, there is no prior reason to assume that his costs of production will differ conceptually from those of a very large firm in a competitive industry; that is, we here assume that the monopolist will have cost curves that resemble those developed in Chapter 6. Specifically, we assume that he experiences average total costs which decline initially and then begin to rise as output is pushed to greater levels for a given scale of plant.

PROFIT-MAXIMIZING OUTPUT BY A MONOPOLIST

Recall that profit-maximizing behavior implies an output level that results in the greatest possible (positive) difference between total revenue and total cost; that is,

$$TP = TR - TC \tag{10.2}$$

where

$$
\begin{aligned}
TP &= \text{total profit} \\
TR &= \text{total revenue} \\
TC &= \text{total cost}
\end{aligned}
$$

As before, we know that this occurs where $MR = MC$. Another way to view this is to rewrite Equation 10.2 as

$$
\begin{aligned}
TP &= (AR)(Q) - (ATC)(Q) \tag{10.3} \\
TP &= (AR - ATC)(Q)
\end{aligned}
$$

where

$$
\begin{aligned}
AR &= \text{average revenue} \\
ATC &= \text{average total cost} \\
Q &= \text{quantity produced}
\end{aligned}
$$

In the case of a firm in a perfectly competitive industry, price equals average revenue, which equals marginal revenue ($P = AR = MR$). In the long run, marginal cost will equal average total cost. Hence the equality of marginal revenue and marginal cost implies—in the long run—$P = AR = MR = MC = ATC$. In contrast, the monopolist faces a downward-sloping demand curve and average revenue is above marginal revenue ($AR > MR$). Hence, in equating marginal revenue and marginal cost, price (average revenue) will be above average total cost. Consider Figure 10.3.

The monopolist seeking to maximize profit would produce output level Q_0, where $MR = MC$ (at point A). Notice that at this level of output the per-unit total cost of production (ATC) is P_c (at point E), yet the per-unit price (average revenue) is P_0. This difference ($P_0 - P_c$) represents profit per unit, and the area P_0BEP_c represents *monopoly profit*. Alternatively, note that total revenue is given by the area P_0BQ_00, and that total cost is given by the area P_cEQ_00. The difference (see Equation 10.2) is monopoly profit. With $MR = MC$, no other output level will yield greater profit.

Several other aspects of this situation merit discussion. First, Figure 10.3 illustrates both the short-run equilibrium of the firm and of the industry. Since the monopolist is the industry, its level of output is the level of output of the industry.

Second, in determining the monopolist's profit-maximizing behavior, nothing was said about the firm or the industry supply curve. Recall that a supply curve relates the quantity supplied to the price offered. In a competitive industry the firm's short-run supply curve is

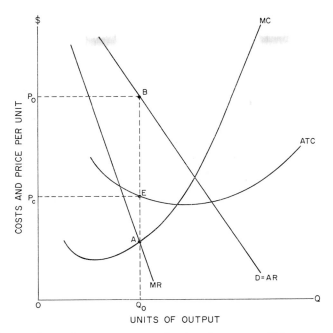

FIG. 10.3. Profit-maximizing output and price of a monopolist.

its marginal cost curve above average variable costs. The industry supply curve is the horizontal sum of the marginal cost curves of the firms in that industry. In a monopolized market, the quantity the monopolist will place upon the market depends upon marginal revenue, not upon market price (average revenue). Since the monopolist equates MR and MC, a much steeper demand curve might have a marginal revenue curve that passes through point A in Figure 10.3. In that case, output would not change, though market price (at output Q_0) would be higher than depicted in the figure. Since there is no *unique* relationship between market price and quantity produced, there is no supply curve.

Third, in the competitive situation, we made a distinction between long-run and short-run equilibrium based upon conditions in the industry before and after entry and exit. There is no such distinction in a monopolized market. There is, of course, a distinction between long-run and short-run equilibrium for a monopolist according to whether or not the firm can adjust its scale of plant. We will discuss this in more detail below.

Additionally, we saw in Chapter 9 that there is nothing particularly unique about producers making short-run profits. Positive profits occur in many industries in the short run and their existence constitutes a signal to other enterprising people to become involved in the same endeavors. The crucial element in the monopoly case is the ability to limit entry of other potential producers. We have already discussed several forms this effort might take. For example, one way to limit entry is to own the patent rights over the only known process by which a certain commodity can be manufactured. In the case of a rare input (for example, bauxite for aluminum), one company may control all the known supply. In any case, if there are positive profits in monopolized industries, they will persist. In this type of market the signal for additional resources is subverted.

One of the common misconceptions concerning monopoly is that a monopoly will make a profit; consider Figure 10.4. Here we see an example of a situation in which production costs are of such a magnitude relative to the demand for the commodity that the monopolist incurs a loss given by the area $P_0 P_c B E$. In this illustration, the monopolist's costs are so high and the market demand so low that at no output will price cover average total costs. He minimizes losses by producing output Q_0, provided that P_0 is greater than average variable costs (not shown).

Another common misconception regarding monopolies is that they produce where demand is inelastic. This can never be rational for, as can be seen, this would require producing where marginal revenue is negative. If the monopolist has any production costs at all (obviously

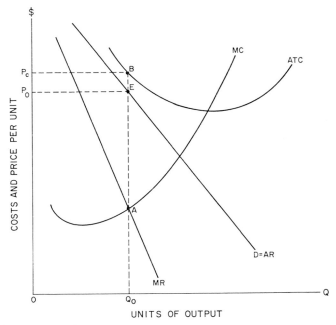

FIG. 10.4. A monopoly incurring losses.

the commonest situation), he will produce along the elastic portion of his demand curve; since marginal cost would be positive, the output level at which marginal cost equals marginal revenue must be where marginal revenue is positive also. This occurs only in the elastic portion of his demand curve. The roots of this misconception probably lie in the fact that any firm can profit by differentiating its product from those of its competitors. This is accomplished through advertising in the hope of developing brand loyalty. Examples where groups of firms attempt this are Idaho potatoes, Wisconsin cheese, and Florida citrus. By differentiating one's product, the demand curve becomes more inelastic, which means that it has some "tilt" as in the monopoly case. This means it is possible to maintain a long-run difference between average total cost and average revenue (positive profit). Once brand loyalty is established, the firm can raise its price somewhat and if the demand curve is at all inelastic (not horizontal), total revenue will increase over what it was at the lower price. But this is different than saying that a monopolist operates in the inelastic portion of his demand curve.

Before turning to the economic effects of monopoly, we briefly discuss the choice of scale of plant for a monopolist. In the purely competitive case, we have seen that a long-run adjustment process results

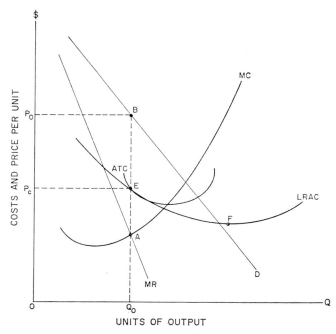

FIG. 10.5. The monopoly and long-run equilibrium.

in each individual producer ideally constructing that scale of plant which would equate the minimum point on the short-run average total cost curve (ATC) with the minimum point on the long-run average cost curve $(LRAC)$. In Figure 10.5 this would occur at point F. However, since the monopolist is constrained by market demand, the scale of plant will be as given by ATC in Figure 10.5. Notice that the equality of marginal revenue and marginal cost, though creating the greatest possible profit, means per-unit production costs are not necessarily as low as possible.

ECONOMIC EFFECTS OF MONOPOLY

Comparing the economic effects of a monopoly with those of a purely competitive market provides an understanding of why the monopolized market leads to inefficiencies in resource allocation. This comparison serves as the basis for developing guidelines as to the type of market performance that is desired and the type of market regulation that will cause monopolies to conduct themselves in a more desirable manner. The comparisons are with respect to prices and output and the impacts upon resource allocation and technological innovation.

PRICES AND OUTPUT

In Chapter 9 we concluded that if the industry were purely competitive, individual firms would—in the long run—operate the optimum scale of plant. Furthermore, long-run competitive equilibrium will lead to levels of output where price (the measure of product utility to the consumer) equals long-run marginal costs (the measure of the cost in resources to the economy of producing that product). In contrast we shall demonstrate that the monopoly will produce a smaller output for which it charges a higher price.

Figure 10.6 illustrates the comparative adjustments. The demand curve facing the industry is D. First assume that the industry is purely competitive and is comprised of 100 firms. S_0 is the sum of their marginal cost curves and is therefore the supply curve of the industry. The industry price will be P_1 and industry output, Q_1. At price P_1 each firm would observe a horizontal demand curve and a marginal revenue curve of P_1, and would elect to produce where $MC = MR = P_1$. Summed over all firms, the industry output would thus be Q_1. Notice that this is a short-run situation since per-unit profit is $C - D$, which would attract other firms to the industry.

Assume that one of the firms bought out the other 99 so that the industry now comprises one firm with 100 plants. Assume further

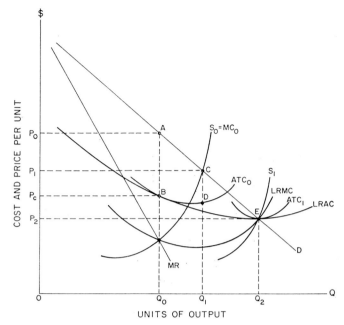

FIG. 10.6. Industry equilibrium output and price under competition versus monopoly.

that the newly monopolized industry has the same costs as that of the competitive firms. The former industry supply curve (S_0) is now the marginal cost curve of the monopolist.[3] The monopolist must now recognize the downward sloping nature of the demand curve he faces. This means that MR is less than price at every level of industry output. The monopolist, in choosing the profit-maximizing level of output (where $MC = MR$), elects to produce Q_0 units which can be sold at a price of P_0. In summary, in the short run, given identical cost structures, a monopolized market will sell a smaller total output at a higher price per unit than if the industry organized competitively.

In the long run, it is traditionally argued that firms would enter the competitive industry in pursuit of the short-run profits. Additionally, existing firms would expand output along their long-run average cost curve ($LRAC$ in Figure 10.6). Eventually the typical firm would be producing at the minimum point on its $LRAC$ curve, and we might envision an industry supply curve of S_1 which is the sum of all of the firm's marginal cost curves in the industry. Now aggregate industry output is Q_2 and equilibrium price is P_2. By way of contrast, the monop-

3. Notice that we did not say it was the *supply curve* of the monopolist since there is no such concept; S_0 is the *marginal cost curve* of the monopolist.

olist would continue to produce Q_0 and charge a price of P_0. Here, profits for the monopolist are P_cP_0AB.

Notice in Figure 10.6 that it is a mere coincidence that the demand curve (D) intersects $LRAC$ at the latter's minimum point; it could just as easily intersect $LRAC$ to the left of point E, or to the right of point E. The conclusions remain the same.

RESOURCE ALLOCATION

We have seen in earlier chapters that the price consumers are willing to pay represents the social value they place upon the product. Additionally, the long-run marginal cost curve represents the resource cost to the economy of producing that product. For the monopolist, product price exceeds both long-run and short-run marginal cost. Misallocation occurs in that too few resources are employed by a monopolist in his efforts to restrict output. Consider Equation 10.4.

$$(MPP_x)(P) = P_x \tag{10.4}$$

Recall from Chapter 5 that this is the rule for determining the ideal quantity of an input (X) to be used in the production of the commodity whose price is given by P, when the input is priced at P_x. Since we know that price (P) equals average revenue (AR) we can rewrite Equation 10.4 as

$$(MPP_x)(AR) = P_x \tag{10.5}$$

However, since the monopolist makes output decisions on the basis of marginal cost and marginal revenue (not marginal cost and price), we must write Equation 10.5 for the monopolist as

$$(MPP_x)(MR) = P_x \tag{10.6}$$

Here it is no longer correct to refer to this expression as the value of the marginal product; it is instead the marginal value product (MVP) and is written

$$MVP_x = (MPP_x)(MR) \tag{10.7}$$

We can now show the effects of monopoly upon the level of input use. Specifically, we know that, for any level of monopoly output, marginal revenue lies below average revenue ($MR<AR$). This leads us to assert that $MVP_x < VMP_x$; that is,

$$(MPP_x)(MR) < (MPP_x)(AR) \tag{10.8}$$

Since we have no reason to suspect that input price (P_x) is different as between the two market situations, we conclude that a monopolist would utilize less of factor X (or any other factor) in response to the decision rule

$$(MPP_x)(MR) = P_x \tag{10.9}$$

than if he employed the decision rule

$$(MPP_x)(AR) = P_x \tag{10.10}$$

TECHNOLOGICAL INNOVATION

One dynamic economic force is that of technological change. The continual development of new goods and services has significant impact upon the rate of growth and the level of output of an economy. Frequently it is argued that because he has no competitors the monopolist is less inclined to innovate than the purely competitive firm. Furthermore, the assertion is made that, when technological advances are made, the cost reduction merely results in extra profit for the monopolist.

On the other side of the coin, some would argue that, because a monopolist has complete claims on the profits to be realized from technological advance, innovation is more attractive. Second, it is argued that monopoly profits provide a source of research funds that permit technological innovation.

There is no clear conclusion as to the impact of monopoly on the rate of technological advancement of an industry. We could analyze the issue in more depth but to do so would take us beyond the scope of this book.

REGULATION OF MONOPOLY

There are at least two ways in which the behavior of a monopolist may be altered: through direct regulation of price and through taxing policies that reduce the monopolist's profits.

PRICE REGULATION

Certain goods and services lend themselves particularly well to production by a monopolist: railroad, telephone, electricity, and natural gas. Monopoly provision of these goods and services is economically desirable because of the economies of scale inherent in their production. These are the natural monopolies or public utilities where more than one producer would entail extensive and costly duplication of facilities. For example, if there were many companies that sold electric power in a given location, each would have to possess (and maintain) a complete network of wires and poles throughout the area. Given such redundancy of capital equipment, the per-unit cost of providing electric power would likely be prohibitive. By granting the rights of a monopolist to one firm, substantial cost savings result. But rather than permit the monopolist to behave as a monopolist, regulations are imposed to alter his behavior. Generally, the rates or prices that can be charged are regulated by a federal, state, or local commission.

In Figure 10.7 the unregulated monopoly would choose to produce Q_0, at a per-unit cost of P_B, and at a per-unit price of P_0. In this case, a monopoly profit of P_0ABP_B would be earned. Price regulation can take several forms. First, assume that the Public Utilities Commission insists that the monopoly produce electricity at that point where the marginal cost of production is equal to the marginal value to consumers from having the product (ideal price). Since the demand curve traces out the marginal value of a commodity or service at various quantities, this point of equality is found at point E in Figure 10.7. Hence, if a maximum price is established at P_1 (the ideal price), the marginal reve-

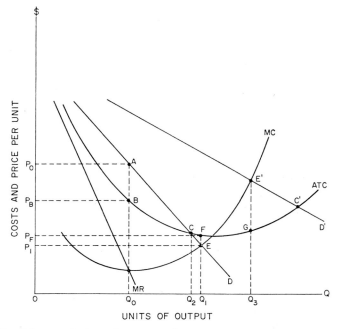

FIG. 10.7. Price regulation of a monopoly.

nue curve takes on a different nature; marginal revenue is now given by the line segmnts P_1EQ_1. With this new marginal revenue curve, it can be seen that an output level of Q_1 satisfies the condition that a monopolist equates marginal revenue with marginal cost. However, as illustrated in Figure 10.7, if the public utility has a cost structure such that the regulated price does not cover average total costs, it may be necessary to supplement total revenue (P_1EQ_10) with a lump-sum subsidy in the amount of the loss (P_FFEP_1).

A second price which insures covering all costs of production is a fair return price. This criterion sets a ceiling price at point C, the intersection of the average total cost curve and the demand curve. This price brings social costs closer into line with social benefits and provides a return to all factors of production, allowing the monopolist to break even. However, it does not completely correct the underutilization of resources in the industry, nor does it result in an output level beyond Q_2.

If the demand situation is such that the demand curve is D', the commission would regulate the price to that associated with point E' rather than the break-even point C'. In this latter case, the price per unit exceeds per-unit cost by the amount $E'G$, resulting in large profits for the monopolist. This profit can then be taxed away by requiring an annual license.

In summary, a price-regulated monopoly benefits the economy through a lower price per unit and a larger total volume of product than an unregulated one. Regulation prevents the monopolist from taking full advantage of his monopoly position. While some profit may continue to exist even with regulation, this may be taxed away by other devices.

LUMP-SUM TAX

Another method of regulating monopolies is through a lump-sum tax. Here the monopolist's excess profits are taxed away without affecting the price or the level of output. In Figure 10.8 it can be seen that the unfettered monopolist would produce Q_0 and sell the output for a price of P_0. By so doing, monopoly profit is given by the area P_0ABP_c. However, by the imposition of a lump-sum tax, the average total cost curve is shifted upward to ATC'. The lump-sum tax does not affect marginal cost since it is independent of the level of output (an example might be an operating license which must be purchased each year). With average total costs shifted up to ATC', the profit being earned by the monopolist is reduced to P_0AGP_G.

By raising the tax sufficiently, all the firm's excess profits can be captured by the regulatory agency. Since the tax is a fixed cost, it does not alter marginal costs. Further, there is nothing the monopolist can

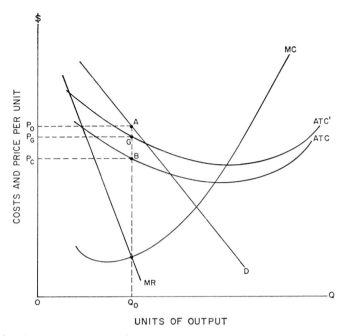

FIG. 10.8. Lump-sum tax regulation of a monopoly.

do to pass it on to consumers. If he raises his price, he would reduce his profits still further because he moves away from his profit-maximizing level of output.

In summary, the existence of a pure monopolist, like a firm in pure competition, is not as common as one might think. However, both theoretical extremes are useful in a heuristic sense. The difference between the theory of pricing in pure competition and pure monopoly is based on the demand and marginal revenue situations facing firms in the two types of industries and the conditions of entry. The differences have important implications for the efficiency of resource allocation and the maximization of consumer satisfaction.

We assumed that the cost curves of a monopoly were the same as those of firms in a competitively organized market and showed that under monopoly the consumer paid a higher price and received less product than under pure competition. Further, a purely competitive market uses a productive factor up to the point where the value of the marginal product of that factor is equal to its price. A monopolist only uses a factor up to the point where its marginal value product is equal to its price. This results in the monopoly using less of a factor than its counterpart in a competitive industry. The theory of monopoly pricing also reveals effective methods of regulation through fixed prices or a lump-sum tax to improve the allocative efficiency of the market.

ECONOMIC CONCENTRATION IN GENERAL

In the previous section we discussed and analyzed certain aspects of the polar opposites of pure competition and pure monopoly. Our aim in the present section is to discuss economic concentration in general terms, citing some specific examples and relating some of the recent theoretical and empirical work in the general area of market structure analysis.

The previous analysis of market types is based upon three basic characteristics of the industry: (1) the number of firms, (2) the degree of differentiation of the product by the industry's firms, and (3) the ease of entry or exit of the firms into and out of the industry. Based on these three characteristics, the theory provides us with a set of categories or models which can offer guidance and an understanding of the functioning of industries in our economy. For example, we saw how the concept of monopoly implies a single seller and barred entry and leads to certain conclusions about how a market system of monopolies would function and what one can do to improve the undesirable aspects of the behavior of such markets. Similarly, although not detailed in this text, the concepts of monopolistic competition or oligopoly lead to specific conclusions with respect to the functioning of such industries or markets. However, because of wide diversity in market or industry organization, these concepts have proved to be a rather imperfect guide. Part of the difficulty lies in the fact that few examples of industries epitomize any of the ideal types described in Table 10.1, but instead most lie somewhere between these two extremes. If one were to pictorially display the frequency distribution of all markets in the United States, the result would probably resemble Figure 10.9.

Another part of the difficulty lies in the fact that even within any of the intermediate types such as monopolistic competition or oli-

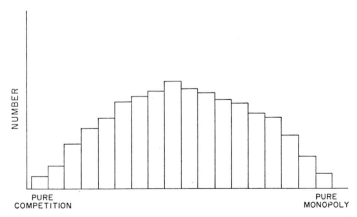

FIG. 10.9. Hypothetical frequency distribution of firm types as classified from pure competition to pure monopoly.

gopoly, there is wide latitude for differences in structure in a market. For example, oligopoly is the pattern of market structure that is characteristic of most of the manufacturing industries in the United States. An oligopolistic market structure is one in which firms have enough market power so that they are not simple price takers, yet there is enough competition among the firms so that they cannot view their market as their own. Hence, an oligopolist knows beforehand that any price change will affect his rival's demand. The latter's action, in turn, will be reflected back on his own demand curve. In this type of industry, a small number of firms generally dominate the industry and new firms find it difficult to enter. Still, an oligopoly of three sellers will likely behave differently from one of 20 sellers, or one of 50 sellers. Furthermore, two industries—A and B—might still differ even though in both industries 80 percent of the sales are accounted for by the three largest firms. In industry A, one firm may account for the remaining 20 percent, while in industry B a large number of firms may be sharing that 20 percent. Likewise, the largest firm in each of the oligopolistic industries (A and B) might have different degrees of influence on the industry. For example, the largest firm in industry A may account for 10 percent of sales, while in industry B the largest firm may account for 50 percent or more of sales; consequently, although both industries might be classified as oligopolistic, they could differ substantially in their effect on resource allocation. As economists studied such markets, they became increasingly aware of the many variations of the three basic forms on each side of the market, plus the variety possible within even one market type. It became apparent to some that a new way of viewing concentration of economic power was required; market structure analysis is the result of this development.[4]

Market structure analysis is a combination of the price theory described in preceding chapters as modified by the empirical studies of firm behavior in actual markets. There are three key concepts in market structure analysis: structure, conduct, and performance. It is assumed that the direction of causation runs from structure to conduct and finally reveals itself in performance (Figure 10.10). In other words, the structure of the market determines or strongly influences how the firms in that industry will behave—how they will set price, determine level of output, adopt new technologies, advertise, etc. How the firms behave (their conduct) in turn will determine the industry's performance, for example, how efficiently it allocates resources. And it is performance that is the crucial factor in evaluating whether or not an economy achieves certain predetermined goals. The understanding of what leads to bad or good performance helps one to modify that performance through adjustments to structure or conduct.

4. The material in this section is based mainly on the work of Joe S. Bain, *Industrial Organization,* 2nd ed. (New York: John Wiley, 1968).

FIG. 10.10. The line of causation from structure to conduct to performance.

If there are reliable relationships between the structure of an industry and its performance, then by knowing something of structure one can predict the performance of the industry in which he is interested. More importantly, if one can identify some features of market structure which cause poor industry performance, one has the key to designing policies (altering institutions) to change structure and thereby affect conduct and performance.

MARKET STRUCTURE

Market structure refers to the organizational characteristics of a given market. Bain's definition is

> . . . organizational characteristics . . . which determine the relations (a) of sellers in the market to each other, (b) of buyers in the market to each other, (c) of the sellers to the buyers, and (d) of sellers established in the market to potential new firms which might enter it. In other words, market structure for practical purposes means those characteristics of the organization of a market that seem to exercise a strategic influence on the nature of competition and pricing within the market.[5]

The characteristics most emphasized as the important variables of market structure are (1) market concentration, (2) product differentiation, (3) entry conditions, (4) growth rate of market demand, and (5) price elasticity of market demand. The first three are the most important elements.

MARKET CONCENTRATION

Market concentration is defined as the degree to which the supply of the product is controlled by the largest firms in the industry. The *concentration ratio* is a measure that takes account of both the number and size distribution of firms within an industry. A concentration ratio is computed by the following steps: (1) rank the firms in order (by total sales) from the largest down to the smallest, (2) start from the top and calculate the percent of total industry ouput for each firm in the industry.

The concentration ratio is an easily interpreted number. It tells one the percent of total sales concentrated in the hands of the top indus-

5. Ibid., p. 7.

try firms. The number represents one aspect of the power of the firms in the industry and is compiled by the Bureau of the Census. Every manufacturing plant in the United States is assigned to an industry on the basis of its primary product. Then concentration ratios are computed on the basis of the aggregate amount of shipments from plants controlled by the 4, 8, 20, and 50 largest firms in an industry. A list of concentration ratios for the top 4 and 8 firms in selected industries is presented in Table 10.2.

The 4-firm and 8-firm concentration ratios vary considerably

TABLE 10.2.   Concentration ratios in selected industries, United States, 1970

Industry	Concentration Ratio[a] in 1970	
	4 largest firms	8 largest firms
	(percent)	
Telephone Equipment	94	99
Motor Vehicles	91	97
Cigarettes	84	NA
Household Refrigerators	82	99
Greeting Card Publishers	75	85
Tires and Inner Tubes	72	89
Soaps and Detergents	70	79
Corn Milling	64	88
Aircraft	65	87
Aluminum Rolling	57	73
Computing	57	78
Blast Furnaces and Steel Mills	47	65
Farm Machinery	40	51
Petroleum Refining	33	57
Dehydrated Foods	33	52
Fences and Plywood	30	44
Meat Packing	23	37
Canned Fruits and Vegetables	21	33
Fluid Milk	20	NA
Newspapers	16	24

Source: U.S. Dept. of Commerce, Bureau of Census, Annual Survey of Manufactures: 1970, Value-of-Shipment Concentration Ratios M70(AS)-9, 1972, Table 4.

a. Concentration ratios show the percentage of total industry shipments controlled by the 4 or 8 largest firms.

NA = Not available.

from industry to industry. Notice that, in general, the agricultural commodities are processed by industries with the lower ratios. Also notice that the highly advertised products have some of the higher ratios. None of the industries would fit either the model of competition or of monopoly. Among the high-concentration industries such as telephone equipment, automobiles, cigarettes, and soaps, the top 4 firms have considerable market power. However, there is competition among them for the consumer's dollar and this is not described by the monopoly model. On the other extreme, the low concentration industries such as petroleum, meat-packing, fluid milk, and newspapers are not adequately described by either the oligopoly or pure competition models.

Most economists agree that the greater the concentration ratio in an industry or product class, the greater are the chances that the intensity, character, and efficiency of competition among sellers will be less than if the concentration ratios were lower. Obviously, as the number of firms in a particular market declines, the ability to control that market individually or collectively is increased. There are difficulties with such generalizations but the ratio is one indicator of the economic power that can exist in a given market.

PRODUCT DIFFERENTIATION

Product differentiation is defined as the existence of different preferences in the minds of consumers for individual brands of a product. A firm can introduce special features, designs, styles, brand names, conditions of sale, or other changes in order to differentiate its product from that of its competitors or rivals in the industry. The purpose is to make its output appear to be different from that of other firms. The degree of price elasticity of demand is partially determined by the availability of substitute products. Product differentiation is an attempt to reduce the number of substitutes.

Recall from an earlier discussion that the demand curve of a differentiated product is more inelastic than one for an undifferentiated product (see Figure 10.11). When its product is differentiated, a firm has more latitude to raise price since consumers have a certain attitude about the product (perhaps created by advertising) and view other very similar products as inferior (not perfect substitutes). Additionally, should any changes in market conditions affect the firm's demand curve, the firm may respond by changing the characteristics of the product and convincing consumers through advertising that its product is superior.[6] In general, the more highly differentiated the product, the larger the share of the industry's output controlled by the top 4 firms, and the more success they have had in increasing their share of the market. Data

6. This explains the incessant use of such adjectives as new, newer, improved, brighter, brightest, coldest, hottest, faster, fastest, etc., in advertising.

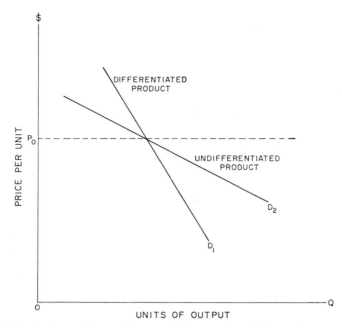

FIG. 10.11. Product differentiation and the associated demand curves.

TABLE 10.3. Average 4-firm concentration ratios by degree of product differentiation for 69 consumer goods industries, 1947–1970

Year	All firms	Average 4-Firm Concentration		
		Degree of Product Differentiation		
		Low	Medium	High
		(percent)		
1970	42	28	41	62
1967	41	26	40	62
1963	40	26	39	60
1958	37	24	37	56
1954	37	25	36	55
1947	36	28	35	50
Percentage Change 1947-70	6	0	6	12
Number of Industries	69	20	33	16

Source: Unpublished data supplied by Willard F. Mueller, Dept. Agr. Econ., Univ. Wis., Madison.

in Table 10.3 indicate that the top 4 firms in industries with a low degree of product differentiation (examples are creameries and meat processing) control 28 percent of total industry volume with little change
in their share over the 23-year period. In contrast, the highly differentiated industries (such as cigarettes) accounted for a much larger share
of the total market in 1947 (50 percent) and in addition were able
to increase their share to 62 percent by 1970.

Product differentiation thus appears to be an important element in how firms in an industry behave and in the success with which
they can gain a larger share of the market. In a later section on performance, this type of structural difference is reflected in the size of budget
devoted to advertising. Here advertising is designed to change consumer
wants and give the firm a tighter grasp on its customers. Other things
being equal, the firm with a differentiated product can behave somewhat
like a monopoly—produce a smaller output and obtain a higher price
per unit. The more clearly differentiated the product, the closer that
firm approaches monopoly.

ENTRY CONDITIONS

Entry conditions are defined as those market conditions that
affect the potential supply of rival firms ready to enter the industry, and
the ease of entry is another significant aspect of market structure affecting the competitiveness of the industry. In the same way that concentration ratios reflect the actual number of competing firms in an industry, the ease or difficulty of entry indicates the potential for competition.
In principle, entry barriers can be measured by the highest price above
cost the firm can charge without enticing new firms into the industry.
This is essentially a measure of the height of the entry barriers.

Barriers to entry can be illustrated by the following example.
Suppose in industry A there is only one firm—a monopolist producing a
particular product. This monopolist currently has no rival, but the
nature of the industry is such that should he raise his price even slightly
above the level which yields normal profits, a large number of new firms
would quickly enter the industry. In contrast, take a similar firm in
industry B. This firm owns a patented process which prohibits other
firms from producing the product. This firm can charge whatever price
will maximize profits and be unconcerned about new firms entering the
industry. Industry A has low barriers and industry B high barriers.

There are several other types of barriers to entry. One is scale
economies and the concept has been discussed earlier. Essentially, the
cost structure of the industry is such that the low point on the long-run
average total cost curve occurs at an output level that comprises a substantial portion of the aggregate industry demand for the product. Given
this, it is obvious that if several firms attempted to supply the total mar-

ket, each would be operating at a point on its long-run average total cost curve where per-unit production costs were substantially higher than if the total demand were supplied by only one firm. In this case there is a natural inclination for one firm to move into a dominant position in the industry.

Another type of barrier is due to absolute cost disadvantage. Because of long experience in developing technical know-how, established firms may have a significant advantage over potential entrants. Potential entrants may only be able to develop this expertise at a considerable cost. This raises their average costs above those of the going firms. The secret formula for Coca-Cola is an example. Any new firm would have to spend a great deal of money attempting to reinvent the formula. Developing access to particular inputs such as raw materials or credit may also raise the costs of potential entrants over those of established firms.

Product differentiation can also lead to barriers to entry into an industry. Consider, for example, the problem of a new firm attempting to produce a new line of automobiles. Not only must the firm underwrite substantial development and manufacturing costs but it must also attempt to convince the consumer that its product is at least as desirable as the more established brands. To accomplish this, considerable resources must be spent on advertising and promotion. This will raise the new entrant's average selling costs per unit above those of established industry firms, thus creating an effective barrier to entry. Put somewhat differently, the man who invents a new and better mousetrap and sits back and waits for the world to beat a path to his doorstep may find only the mailman delivering his bills.

The above aspects are frequently used to evaluate barriers to entry in a particular industry. The rapid turnover of firms in industries such as agriculture and retail trade and services is a sign of low entry barriers. They are characterized by undifferentiated products and relatively low capital requirements. In contrast, public utilities and transportation are industries with high entry barriers. Special governmental franchises plus tremendous scale economies are characteristic. In between lie the vast majority of United States industries producing most of the products we consume each day. Generally, product differentiation is the most important type of barrier, while capital requirements explain the lack of competition in only a few industries. However, what may be a high barrier for one industry may be low for the next; consequently, general statements on the extent of barriers as a dampening influence on competition are difficult to make.

GROWTH IN MARKET DEMAND

The rate of growth in market demand can play an important role in the degree of competition in particular industries. For example, in an oligopolistic industry in which demand is not growing, firms may base their behavior on the unchanging size of the market. Any effort to increase sales at the expense of one of the rivals will probably result in other firms fighting back. The net result is increased costs and reduced total industry profits. On the other hand, in an industry with a rapidly expanding demand, the aggressive firm can obtain a disproportionate share of this growth. Consequently, cutting price this year, even though it means less than normal profits, may result in a larger share of next year's market. Thus, in an industry with an expanding demand (a growth industry), firms are more likely to behave competitively than in one with a stable demand.

PRICE ELASTICITY OF DEMAND

The price elasticity of demand for the ouput of an industry can also affect the way in which firms in the industry behave. It may lead to the same differences in behavior as described above for firms in fast-growth versus slow-growth industries. For example, in an industry facing a highly inelastic demand, a cut in the price by one firm which is matched by all other firms will result in the total value of sales falling. An inelastic demand means that a decrease in price will result in a less than proportionate increase in the quantity sold and hence bring about a drop in total revenue. In contrast, the same price cut by a firm in an industry with an elastic demand will increase total sales and revenues. The larger volume can partly offset the lower per-unit profit resulting from the price cut. Certainly, the industry with the elastic demand is more likely to display price competition.

In summary, one can identify many elements of market structure, but seller concentration, product differentiation, entry barriers, growth in demand, and demand elasticity are the most important. Of these five, the latter two are of lesser importance than the first three. All these elements influence conduct, which in turn affects the allocation of resources (performance).

MARKET CONDUCT

The major elements of market structure which define the economic environment of an industry were described above. Structure is important because of the way in which it induces firms in an industry to behave, that is, how they set price, output, the characteristics of their product, and their marketing and research expenditures. Firm behavior patterns are termed conduct. *Conduct* is defined as the firms' policies toward their market and to their rivals in the market. Bain defines conduct as ". . . patterns of behavior that enterprises follow in adapting or adjusting to the markets in which they sell (or buy)."[7]

7. Bain, *Industrial Organization,* p. 9.

He lists the following significant dimensions of conduct:

1. Methods employed by the firm or groups of firms in determining price and output.
2. Product policy.
3. Sales promotion policy.
4. Means of coordination and cross-adaptation of price, product, and sales promotion policies among competing firms.
5. Presence or absence of an extent of predatory or exclusionary tactics directed against either established rivals or potential entrants.

To simplify the analysis, the discussion of market conduct will be divided into three major areas of behavior:

1. Firm behavior with respect to selling price.
2. Firm behavior with respect to the product.
3. Firm behavior aimed at coercing rivals.

Since pure competition permits no choice with respect to the above variables, and a monopoly has no rivals, the discussion is based on the assumption that the industry is oligopolistic.

PRICING POLICIES

The oligopolist sees his action as directly affecting that of his rivals and, consequently, he also knows that they will react to what he does as regards price policy. Hence, there is mutual interdependence among the firms and an aversion to policies that will tend to create major adjustments in pricing policy. Each firm has its own separate cost structure and calculates its own profit-maximizing price. However, mutual interdependence biases the firms toward acting jointly where possible by attempting to avoid price competition which might lead to unstable conditions in the industry—and the subsequent demise of some of the firms. The following are some of the methods by which firms achieve these objectives.

Agreements among firms. This is the most obvious form of establishing an industry-wide price. Such an agreement may simply cover the price at which all agree to sell the product or it may be expanded to include specifications for quantity, quality of product, selling practices, territories, and divisions of markets. The most recent such agreement came to light in the heavy electrical equipment industry. The executives of firms in this industry secretly met to set price on circuit breakers, transformers, and other heavy electrical equipment for sealed bids to governments and private agencies. The conspiracy allegedly grew out of decisions of the firms to maintain prices in the face of strong competition from their rivals.[8] The result was substantially higher prices on electrical equipment which were then passed on to the final consumer in the form of higher prices. This type of price coordination is illegal in the United States.

Price leadership. This is price coordination without any formal organization. Under the arrangement, prices are announced first by the leader who is usually one of the largest and best-established firms in the industry. The other firms quickly follow suit. This type of arrangement is most likely to exist in an industry where the product is difficult to differentiate. In this case, changes in price by one firm can lead to substantial shifts in market shares if the other firms do not quickly follow suit. This type of arrangement can lead to rigid prices which do not reflect the most recent changes in technology, particularly if the leader is an old established firm with conservative management. The "following" firms can adopt cost-reducing methods but may not pass these benefits on to the consumer.

Tacit Collusion. In this type of price policy, firms can take one another's responses into account without revealing any external signs that industry-wide prices in fact exist. As an example, consider an industry dominated by a few firms with a differentiated product. The differentiated product reduces the need for uniform industry-wide prices. Each firm uses approximately the same methods for calculating costs and prices and for changing these prices in response to changing demand in cost situations. Furthermore, all firms behave in a predictable manner with regard to models, quality, model changes, etc. Consequently, each firm can establish its price with the confidence that the other firms will also announce prices at about the same time and near the same level.

The automobile industry is an example. Models are introduced regularly at specified times, and prices of all manufacturers for a particular model are always very similar. Under this type of price-setting arrangement, the industry can keep prices at levels yielding some monopoly profits without resorting to illegal methods of collusion.

8. For a full description of this case see John G. Fuller, *The Gentlemen Conspirators: The Story of the Price Fixers in the Electrical Industry* (New York: Grove, 1962); John Herling, *The Great Price Conspiracy: The Story of the Antitrust Violations in the Electrical Industry* (Washington: Lewis, 1962); Richard A. Smith, The incredible electrical conspiracy, *Fortune,* April and May, 1961.

PRODUCT POLICIES

Product policies can assume many forms ranging from real or apparent product differentiation to the amount of advertising cost or the service guarantees on the product. Planned obsolescence (such as annual automobile model changes) is difficult to interpret as either enhancing or retarding performance and competition. It is difficult to determine whether annual model changes in the automobile industry reflect the independent competitive action of firms attempting to increase their share of the market, or whether such changes are an attempt to raise the aggregate demand for all automobiles relative to other goods by making people dissatisfied with last year's model. Regardless of the motives or the results, it is obvious that frequent model changes cause consumers to pay higher prices for automobiles. A study of the cost of such changes has revealed that during the years 1956 to 1960 the annual total cost for model changes amounted to approximately $700 per car. This does not include the additional costs due to greater gasoline consumption brought on by larger engines and transmissions and copious nonfunctional chrome and baubles. If these components are included, it is said that the total cost of model changes averaged about $5 billion per year over the period 1956 to 1960.[9]

Not only can product policies assume many different forms but the same policy may have a different impact on market performance under different conditions. For example, firms may be spending just that amount on advertising to inform consumers of the "true" merits of their products. However, suppose one oligopolist, in a campaign to capture a larger share of the market, decides to introduce a "new" product whose improvements are illusory rather than real. Other firms might respond by real improvements in their products' quality, in which case consumers benefit. Conversely, the same firms could decide to increase their advertising budgets to maintain their market shares. Alternatively, firms might respond by attempting to reach an agreement to produce a less durable and lower-cost product to protect their profit positions, or offer subsidies to retailers to promote their product. The net result is higher costs to consumers.

Product strategies are difficult to interpret and they can be combined in different ways, each of which embodies different implications for market performance. In short, given our current state of knowledge, it is difficult to predict from patterns of product policy the performance that will follow. The point is that firms generally do not act independently or without regard for the impact of their product policies on aggregate industry profits. Researchers have, however, observed that

9. Franklin M. Fisher, Z. Griliches, and Carl Kaysen, The Costs of Automobile Model Changes during a Decade, *Price Theory in Action,* ed. Donald S. Watson (Boston: Houghton Mifflin, 1965), pp. 217–20.

most industries are more independent with respect to product policies than with respect to their pricing policies.

COERCIVE CONDUCT

Pricing and product policies are the result of the structural characteristics of the market. The third type of market behavior, coercive conduct, attempts to change the structure. This type of behavior attempts either to drive its rivals out of the industry or to raise the barriers to entry of potential firms. Some of the more important types of coercive conduct are described below. The reader will notice some overlap with price and product behavior.

Price Cutting. This is the most obvious and notorious method of driving a rival out of the industry. Price cutting is a powerful tool in the hand of a financially strong firm that can force prices down below cost until the rival firm is eliminated. After the demise of the rival, the remaining firm is in a position to extract monopoly profits and otherwise distort the price structure. Alternatively, the purpose of price cutting may be to discipline a rival who initiated the price cutting. This can be done most effectively by driving the price down to unprofitable levels. When the victim has learned to cooperate rather than compete, prices return to higher levels.

Vertical Integration. This is a method of coercion whereby firms may raise the entry barriers to either potential or actual rivals. A manufacturing firm, by buying out all the retail outlets, can effectively hamper its competition by denying them access to marketing channels. The petroleum refining industry is a possible example. Since each retail outlet handles only one brand of gasoline, a potential competitor must either build competing outlets or attempt to entice retailers to drop the other brand. Similarly, a firm may integrate backwards, purchasing its raw material suppliers, thereby precluding competition from sources of supply.

In summary, it is easy to see that coercive conduct can change the structure of the market. It generally attempts to weaken rivals, eliminate rivals, or raise the barriers to entry of potential rivals. In any case, the outcome is a step toward market power, monopoly profits, and the inefficient allocation of resources. Of the three types of market conduct it is easiest to predict the consequences of coercion; pricing and product policies are much less clear. Two reasons for this are (1) our theory and methods of observations are still quite rudimentary in this field of inquiry and (2) it may be that structure is really more important than conduct in determining performance. Thus price cutting or planned obsolescence may be less important to policy decisions than the oligopolistic type of structure in which they exist.

MARKET PERFORMANCE

Market performance is an evaluation of the results of firm behavior and is based upon a comparison with some goal or norm, a few of which are listed here. We present a brief discussion of the implications of each in the final section of this chapter.

1. The economy should be efficient, employing its scarce resources so that they yield the greatest possible gross national product (total output).
2. The economy should fully employ its resources. Having resources idle reduces the real income of the economy more than using them inefficiently; consequently, although efficient utilization of resources is more desirable than inefficient utilization, inefficient utilization is preferable to no utilization.
3. The economy should be progressive. This means that it should be continually improving its production processes as well as the quality, quantity, and variety of goods and services produced. In other words, as new technologies are developed, these should be incorporated into the production process as rapidly as possible. Furthermore, there should be a continual search for new technologies to improve techniques and organize the factors of production.
4. The economy should be equitable. The economy should equitably distribute its output among its members on the basis of their efforts and resources, but provide some minimum to cover essential needs.

The performance of an industry, therefore, is evaluated in terms of how its performance as derived from individual firm behavior contributes to the 4 goals of the economy. More specifically, Bain lists the following principal variables of market performance:

1. The height of selling price relative to the long-run marginal cost of production and to the long-run average cost of production . . . , and the resultant profit margin.
2. The relative technical efficiency of production so far as this is influenced by the scale or size of plants and firms (relative to the most efficient), and by the extent, if any, of excess capacity.
3. The size of industry output relative to the largest attainable consistent with the equality of price and long-run marginal cost.
4. The size of sales-promotion costs relative to the costs of production.
5. The character of the product, or products, including design, level of quality, and variety.

6. The rate of progressiveness of the industry in developing both products and techniques of production, relative to rates which are attainable, and also economical in view of the cost of progress.[10]

If the price is considerably above long-run marginal or average cost of production, the presumption is that the firms are extracting extranormal profits and, consequently, the industry is weakly competitive. Similar arguments apply to excessive advertising costs and sluggishness in the adoption of new products and technologies. The conclusion is that, if the performance of the industry is less than that implied by the model of perfect competition, its structure is one that is other than competitive. The policy implications that flow from this are that performance must be modified by changing conduct, changing structure, or changing both.

SUMMARY

The market structure approach to the analysis of industries outlined above focuses on the problems of market performance as influenced by conduct and structure. Adequate performance is assumed to be based on the concepts of vigorous but fair pricing and product policies. Industries in which competition is weak exhibit excess profits, uneconomic size of plants, excess plant capacity, lack of progressiveness, and excessive advertising costs. Cutthroat competition involving sales at less than cost, price discrimination, and the exclusion of competitors may result in the elimination of competitors, and in the long run may destroy vigorous competition. The policy problem then is to develop policies leading to suitable structure and conduct.

The following statements probably best summarize conditions of structure and conduct which lead to adequate performance:

1. The more firms in the marketplace, the less the interdependence of price among them and the more difficult it is for sellers to communicate.
2. The more even the size distribution of firms in the market, the more difficult it is for any one firm to dominate the market to coerce rivals into following a particular price or to convince other firms to follow a product policy that maximizes its profits.
3. The greater the difference in design, quality, and customer acceptance among competing products, the more difficulty sellers will have in finding a mutually acceptable price for their differentiated products.
4. The easier it is for new firms to enter a market, the less likely it will be that firms in the market will be able to maximize their joint profits because this would attract new firms with whom they would have to share sales and profits.

10. Bain, *Industrial Organization,* p. 11.

SOME CONCLUDING COMMENTS

The performance goals discussed in the previous section are concerned with allocative efficiency, technical efficiency and progress, full employment, and equitable distribution of income. There are many ways in which a society may promote these goals and we will discuss only several as they pertain primarily to issues in rural America. Each will be taken up in more detail in the following chapters.

Allocative efficiency implies that resources are in the right place at the right time and perform the appropriate functions for the proper amount of return. An important element here is the possession of perfect knowledge on the part of owners of productive factors and producers of goods and services. A very important aspect of perfect knowledge then is market information. The agricultural sector is relatively well developed regarding the dissemination of market news. In fact, recent critics have charged that we know more about the value of a hog in different locations than we do the value of a person in different jobs. True or not, this does point up the extensiveness of marketing information services in agriculture. In industries characterized by very few firms, the demand for market information is less pronounced than is the case in agriculture. Indeed, one of the first tasks performed by economists in assisting a nation to achieve some greater degree of economic development is to establish information channels for factor and product data.

The goal of technical efficiency and progress within an industry is an important performance component and one of special relevance to agriculture. It was seen in Chapter 3 how the agricultural sector has increased productivity per man-hour faster than the industrial sector of the economy and much of this is due to conscious policy in the public sector. An interesting issue in market structure discussions concerns the role of research and development. Since the purely competitive firm is said to earn nothing more in the long run than enough to just cover opportunity costs, no funds are available to the firm to conduct significant research and development activities; experimentation must be confined to minor alterations in present practices. By way of contrast, a monopolist, with probable profits in the long run, can afford to allocate a portion of such retained earnings to research activities—either to develop new and better products or to investigate significant modifications in production technology. This concept, coupled with the feeling that agriculture is somehow different from other productive enterprises, led to the establishment of several forms of assistance to agriculture in the realm of technology enhancement.

One form this has taken is the network of agricultural experiment stations around the country where research on crops and livestock is conducted. Another aspect is the existence of a land-grant university in each of the states. Here the training of students is carried out in conjunction with the research activities of the faculty. The advancements made in food and fiber production technology by these institutions range from hybrid varieties of both crops and livestock to such items as artificial vitamin D for milk and rat poisons such as Warfarin. Hence, with the structure in agriculture approaching the competitive end of the spectrum, such activities have been aimed at improving the performance of the industry.

The full employment goal is less amenable to generalizations, so little will be said here. But two issues might be mentioned—both of them closely related. The inordinate degree of economic power held by certain sectors of the economy was a strong incentive to the creation of labor unions to counteract this power. It was felt that great economic power created the conditions which permitted the exploitation of labor and the arbitrary treatment of various segments of the labor force (often women and children). As the unions gained power—and hence became capable of influencing working conditions and wages—they tended to stifle the movement of certain resources (labor) among occupations. Hence, the notion of full employment, as that term has meaning in present-day circumstances, has taken on a rather different meaning. Specifically, an unemployment rate of 4 percent of the work force is viewed as acceptable—by all, no doubt, but those unfortunate ones who happen to be unemployed.

The second issue pertaining to full employment relates to the adoption of advanced technology in a modern society (also one of the goals). As will be seen in Chapter 13, labor-saving technology shifts the demand curve for labor to the left, resulting in fewer people being employed in certain sectors. As people are displaced from jobs—usually the jobs that can be assumed by machines are the more menial and repetitive—they require retraining. Hence, organized labor's concern for advancing technology is concentrated in certain sectors of the economy where economic power is the greatest—steel, automobiles, etc. One public program aimed at achieving the goals of full employment and efficient resource allocation is that of manpower training.

The final goal, the distribution of income in an equitable manner, will also receive more attention in Chapter 13. While the relevance of this issue in the context of a discussion on market structure may not be immediately apparent, recall that the concentration of economic power also carries with it the concentration of the claims to income which that power can bestow. One need only to look to the Morgans, the Rockefellers, the Vanderbilts, the Whitneys, and the Fords to see that economic concentration also results in the creation of enormous estates held by the fortunate few. While it is still probably true that our society presents a considerable opportunity for all to get ahead, let no one underestimate the advantage enjoyed by those born into families with the kind of wealth of those listed above.

If the reader is left with the impression that the articulation of such goals creates an insuperable policy task, he is indeed perceptive. As was stated in Chapter 2, social goals can provide only broad guides as to the general direction in which a nation would like to progress. To simultaneously talk of rapid technological change, full employment, and the equitable distribution of income may sound nice in theory, but they present considerable difficulties when it comes to policy implementation. In the chapters in the following section of the book, we will focus on particular policy issues which largely arise because of a dissatisfaction with the outcome of present market performance.

SUGGESTED READINGS

B A S I C

Caves, Richard. *American Industry: Structure, Conduct, and Performance,* 2nd ed. Englewood Cliffs, N.J.: Prentice-Hall, 1967.
> Applies the concepts of price theory and industrial organization to a discussion of the performance of U.S. industries. Deals with the way economic variables affect market structure, conduct, performance, and the nation's economic welfare.

Leftwich, Richard H. *The Price System and Resource Allocation.* Hinsdale, Ill.: Dryden Press, 1970, Ch. 6, 14, 15.
> Chapter 6 describes the market demand curve faced by firms under alternative market structure. Chapters 14 and 15 contain a detailed comparative analysis of the employment, utilization, and allocation of resources under monopoly and under monopsony.

Lipsey, Richard G.; and Steiner, Peter O. *Economics.* New York: Harper and Row, 1972, Ch. 16, 17.
> Price theory is used to describe actual market situations in which producers in competitive industries have tried to obtain monopolistic profits through collective action. Chapter 17 states the classical case for competition (and against monopoly) and predicts the likely impacts of monopoly power on economic performance.

McGuire, Joseph W. Are Businessmen Socially Responsible? and Milton Friedman, The Social Responsibility of Business Is to Increase Its Profits. Kenneth Elzinger, ed., *Economics: A Reader.* New York: Harper and Row, 1972, pp. 106–12.
> The two articles present contrasting points of view. The first offers evidence to show that the large firm is interested in goals other than profit maximization. In the second, Friedman argues that businessmen who encourage social responsibility in business would destroy the market mechanism.

Mueller, Willard F. *A Primer on Monopoly and Competition.* New York: Random House, 1970.
> A clear and concise development of the theory of monopoly and market power and alternative public policies available to promote competition.

Robinson, Joan. *The Economics of Imperfect Competition.* London: Macmillan, 1933.

A pioneer study of monopoly and monopsony; develops the basic concepts of the modern theory of monopoly markets.

ADVANCED

Clodius, Robert L.; and Mueller, Willard F. Market structure analysis as an orientation for research in agricultural economics. *J. Farm Econ.* 28(Aug. 1961): 515–53.

Discusses areas in which economists should expand their research efforts. Contains an excellent abstract of selected books and professional journal articles related to market structure analysis plus a summary of each of the more important empirical studies.

Garoian, Leon, ed. *Economics of Conglomerate Growth.* San Francisco: Recorder-Sunset Press, 1969.

Examines the issue of growing market power in the United States via conglomerate growth. Includes articles reviewing recent developments in conglomerate growth, a conceptual framework for its analysis, and its impact on agriculture.

Johnson, A. C.; and Helmberger, P. G. Price elasticity of demand as an element of market structure. *Am. Econ. Rev.* 57(Dec. 1967): 1218–21.

Develops a theoretical analysis demonstrating the importance of the price elasticity of the demand curve facing a firm on market conduct and performance.

Leibenstein, H. M. Allocative efficiency vs X-efficiency. *Am. Econ. Rev.* 56(June 1966): 392–415.

The author argues that the welfare loss in an economy due to allocative inefficiencies is trivial compared to the possible improvements due to nonallocative efficiency. He calls the nonallocative efficiencies X-efficiency and presents cross-country empirical evidence to demonstrate the importance of X-efficiencies in an economy.

Low, Richard E. *Modern Economic Organization.* Homewood, Ill.: Richard D. Irwin, 1970.

A detailed discussion of those variables of structure and conduct which affect market performance and of the policies to control market power and the enhancement of competition.

U.S. Cabinet Committee on Price Stability. *Industrial Structure and Competition Policy.* Washington, D.C.: USGPO, Jan. 1969.

Describes the methods by which firms with discretionary market power can exert inflationary pressures within an economy and the sources of this market power. It also presents a set of recommendations on ways to maintain competition without impairing economic efficiency.

Wilcox, Claire. *Public Policies toward Business,* 4th ed. Homewood, Ill.: Richard D. Irwin, 1971.

An excellent text devoted to the major types of public policies designed to improve market performance. It includes a discussion of the relative merits and shortcomings of each policy and its consequences for general welfare.

DISCUSSION QUESTIONS AND PROBLEMS

1. Discuss the relevance of demand elasticity for the monopolist.
2. Explain the significance of the short run and the long run in a competitive industry vis-à-vis a monopolistic one.
3. In what circumstances might a monopoly be desirable?
4. In what circumstances might a monopoly be undesirable?

5. What are the advantages of a lump-sum tax to regulate monopolies?
6. Justify the flow of causality from structure to conduct to performance.
7. Comment on the relevance of the performance goals for a centrally planned economy.
8. Prove that where price elasticity of demand equals unity the marginal revenue curve equals zero.
9. Make a list of firms in your town that are the sole seller of goods and services. What pricing and product policies might you suspect they employ? How might you empirically test your hypotheses?

PART 3: ECONOMIC ISSUES

In Part I (Chapters 1–3) we developed a perspective on economics, and in Part II (Chapters 5–10) we presented the theoretical concepts basic to an understanding of supply, demand, market equilibrium, and resource allocation. We now turn to more specific and detailed discussions of the areas of (1) the farm sector, (2) the agribusiness sector, (3) human resources and rural poverty, (4) rural communities, and (5) natural resources.

Earlier we discussed the main economic problems of any society and explored alternative ways of solving those problems. It was seen that the performance of economic systems may not always be what is hoped for, and most societies then set about to improve that performance. For instance, in a purely competitive system it might turn out the income distribution is a serious problem. For example, although the poor in our rural and urban areas may be receiving the value of their marginal product, their skill level is so low that annual earnings fall short of those needed to provide access to many goods and services. In this case, we have programs to provide them reasonable medical care, housing, aid to dependent children, etc. This is a way of transferring income from one group to another outside the market system. The important point is that there is a difference between the concept of social justice and the concept of economic justice in the marketplace. This is reasonable since one would expect the criteria for judging social justice to be much broader than those used to evaluate economic performance.

Any society allocates to its government the role of distributing the benefits of the economic system among its members spatially and temporally so as to provide social justice. It may choose one of several methods of accomplishing this objective. The government can take the direct approach by entering the market in such a way as to influence the demand for, or the supply of, a commodity, thus altering the equilibrium price. As seen in previous chapters, the effects ripple back through the factor markets and forward to the consumer. This is the primary emphasis of the government's role in Chapter 11.

Alternatively, the government may take the oblique approach and attempt to influence market performance by adjusting structure or conduct. This is the emphasis of government activities described in Chapter 12.

Finally, it may attempt to ameliorate performance by activities completely outside ordinary market channels such as transfer payments, regulation, or special institutions. This approach is utilized by the government for particular farm-support programs as detailed in Chapter 11. Also, this is discussed in Chapters 13 through 15 in the context of human resource problems, economic development in rural areas, and natural resource problems, respectively.

CHAPTER 11: THE FARM SECTOR

All governments have programs and policies for agriculture. This is noteworthy because they frequently do not have special policies toward other sectors. For example, workers in the service industries, such as barbers, television or automobile repairmen, lawyers, or economists, are very rarely considered for special attention because of the divergence between economic and social justice for these groups. Agriculture has much in common with these groups, yet in almost every country in the world it has received special attention for a number of reasons.

First, in the early stages of economic development, agriculture represents a major sector in the economy. In a young nation, it is not unusual for 70 to 80 percent of the labor force to be engaged in agricultural occupations and for 50 to 60 percent of the gross national product to be derived from agriculture. Governments have come to realize that for development to proceed there must be progress in this sector. This conditions them to look upon the problems of agriculture as special, even though in some countries this may no longer be necessary. In the United States there is an additional aspect to this lag. At one time most of the population was rural and, consequently, so were its representatives in the legislative bodies. These groups were naturally concerned with the problems of the people they represented. Since representation is much slower to change than the relative importance of agriculture in the economy, there is a tendency to continue to give special attention to agriculture because of its overrepresentation. In contrast, the service industries are the last to develop in an economy and hence they might be considered underrepresented.

Second, governments consider agriculture to be essential to their welfare. They view their supply of food and fiber as strategic and try to become as nearly self-sufficient as possible. In this way, should there be war, disruption of transportation, etc., the nation's welfare would not be jeopardized. Many of the production incentive programs of developing countries fit into this category.

Third, agriculture is viewed as a sector with special needs or characteristics. Farming is often looked upon as a way of life which instills in its citizens certain desirable characteristics such as being hard working, independent, frugal, etc. Additionally, as we shall see later, the adjustments in agriculture dictated by the marketplace are considered to be too harsh. Consequently, government policy is directed toward maintaining or increasing farmers' incomes either directly or indirectly.

United States agricultural policy contains some aspects of all three of the above. It has not developed suddenly nor under its own power. It has been a long and complicated evolutionary process. A better understanding of current programs is obtained by a short description of the evolution of the institutions and programs which we observe in agriculture today. This places the present in proper perspective.

A SHORT HISTORY OF GOVERNMENT IN AGRICULTURE

Until approximately 150 to 200 years ago the economic organization and development of agriculture and industry were very similar. Specifically, the differences between a firm in agriculture and a firm in industry were practically nonexistent. They were both small, independent operations, usually family owned, family operated, and highly dependent upon family labor. In agriculture the farm was small, generally because the number of people in the family limited the amount of land a farmer could handle. For example, one man with a hoe could handle approximately 2 to 3 acres. Consequently, if an individual had 10 children, he could probably farm 20 to 25 acres.

During this period, economic historians tell us that the capital-labor ratio was constant, reflecting the fact that there was little improvement in productivity. The technology was such that one man could handle but one hoe, one ax, or one plow. Increasing the capital by giving him an extra hoe or plow did not increase his ability to produce more since he still had but one set of hands. In addition, there was no product or service specialization in agriculture. The whole process from production to marketing took place on the farm. The individual farm firm raised the grain and the hay to produce milk. The family separated the milk, churned the butter, made the cheese, and hauled the milk to market where it was sold directly to the consumer. The farmer was the producer, the input supplier, and the distributor of the agricultural products. Because there was no specialization, there was no excess production. One man and his family farmed enough land to produce the products required to survive until the following harvest. If the year was good and the crop was excellent, there was excess produce to sell. If the year was bad, there was no excess produce. Trade was strictly in terms of surplus commodities, and was on an intermittent basis. Currently, this same situation still exists in many of the developing countries of the world. As long as there is no excess production, there is no stimulus for specialization because excess production leads to trade, and trade in turns acts as a stimulus for specialization.

About 200 years ago, with the advent of the industrial revolution, the development of towns and industry began to diverge from that of the rural and agricultural areas. Power in the form of steam gave a tremendous boost to the development of the nonagricultural industries. Labor productivity in industry began to increase since one individual could now operate more and larger machines; instead of one man weaving one piece of wool into one thread, he now had the power to weave dozens of pieces of wool into dozens of threads simultaneously. Consequently, we began to observe specialization of labor. When one individual operated several machines, there was increased production per individual. This increased specialization led to excess production and surpluses which, in turn, tended to stimulate trade. Trade then stimulated further specialization.

The increasing specialization in industry also stimulated agriculture. First, increases in labor productivity led to increases in wages which were reflected in increases in the demand for agricultural products. Second, the application of power to the processing of agricultural products lowered its per-unit costs which, in turn, were reflected in increasing sales of agricultural commodities in the United States and in Europe. Probably the best example of this was the invention of the cotton gin by Eli Whitney in 1793. This led to cotton's becoming the major crop of the South. The development of railroads was also a significant factor in the expansion of agricultural production frontiers by making it possible to economically transport agricultural commodities long distances.

Agriculture, on the other hand, did not change substantially during the "revolution." It was difficult to take direct advantage of the basis of the industrial revolution—the power source—because it was a stationary type of power. Industry could concentrate its production in a relatively small area; agriculture could not. During this period then, increases in agricultural output depended primarily upon expansion of the agricultural frontier.

The relative abundance of land and scarcity of labor stimulated the development of an agricultural technology that was oriented toward achieving gains in labor productivity rather than gains in land productivity.[1] As a consequence, farms tended to be scattered across the landscape rather than clustered together as in European countries. The communities which serviced them were likewise scattered and consequently

1. Vernon W. Ruttan, Economic Development, Political Power, and Agricultural Policy, *Agricultural Policy in an Affluent Society*, ed. V. W. Ruttan, A. D. Waldo, and James P. Houck (New York: W. W. Norton, 1969), pp. 1–22.

of low population, each being about one day's journey by horse from the next.[2]

In contrast, the industrial centers were concentrated not only in relation to space but also in terms of control. The increased productivity of labor led to a separation of the labor and ownership/management functions. It became apparent that with one individual concentrating on production, and another on management, the firm could produce greater quantities of output than when one individual attempted to handle all phases of production. Over time, the family-owned and family-controlled firm gave way to the corporation, leading to a further separation of ownership and management. As firms and factories required increasing amounts of capital to establish and maintain an economic unit, it became difficult for a single family to accumulate enough capital to build and maintain one of these organizations. Consequently, the corporate method of organization was developed. This allowed a wide range of individuals to become part owners in the factory and, by sharing in the ownership, share in the profits. The by-product was a separation of labor from management, and of management from ownership.[3]

A further feature of the corporation is that it has a perpetual life of its own. Its management need not be concerned with problems of dissolution or disruption of the organization upon the death of one of its owners. This means there is no natural opportunity for the redistribution of the large aggregations of economic power and wealth contained in many of these firms.

People who controlled the capital also controlled management; and the control of capital and the high concentrations of wealth led to abuses. The accumulation of capital in the hands of relatively few individuals gave them the wherewithal and the opportunity to consolidate the controlling interest of firms both within and across industries. Through such devices as trusts, common stockholdings (where one firm owns the controlling stock in others), interlocking directorates, and parent-subsidiary relationships, a small group of individuals at the financial apex could exert tremendous leverage on the decisions of whole industries. In this period we observe the growth of economic power as exemplified by individuals such as J. P. Morgan in banking, Rockefeller in oil, DuPont in chemicals, and James Hill in railroads. Thus during the nineteenth century this country's major industries such as petroleum, transportation, cottonseed oil, meat-packing, sugar, coal, and tobacco began to exhibit some form of market power.

In other cases specialization of function also provided the op-

2. Marion Clawson, *Policy Directions for U.S. Agriculture* (Baltimore: Johns Hopkins Press, 1968), p. 77.
3. See John Kenneth Galbraith, *The New Industrial State* (Boston: Houghton Mifflin, 1967).

portunity for a few large firms to exploit others. As the farmer moved more and more in the direction of specialization in production, he left to others the task of assembly, processing, storage, and the transporting of agricultural commodities after they left the farm. The nonfarm firms that developed to perform these functions were few in number and concentrated in particular geographic locations such as Chicago, Kansas City, and Minneapolis. This frequently meant that the farmer had to send his products to these central or terminal markets where he contracted with an agent to sell them for him. This practice led to many abuses, mainly at the expense of the farmer. His absence from the bargaining process resulted in his interests getting secondary consideration. This was particularly true in the meat-packing and milling industries where the firms were large enough to hold farm prices low on the farm side, while simultaneously extracting high prices from consumers.

On the consumption side of the market, the few large firms were also able to take advantage of consumers by mislabeling, deceptive packaging and advertising, adulteration, and other practices which raised real prices to consumers by lowering quality. On the input side, producers of agricultural inputs developed market power that permitted them often to overcharge the farmer for his inputs.

The above forces lead to considerable agitation by farmers for corrective legislation to promote the orderly marketing of agricultural products. With the decline of the agrarian geographic frontier, the common man could no longer find new opportunities or escape the system by migrating to new areas. He was forced to stay and attempt to modify its undesirable attributes. Farmers in the South and West developed strong political movements against monopoly. These farm organizations, supported by labor unions and independent businessmen, grew during the late 1800s until antitrust laws were enacted by state and federal governments. Since that period, the scope of public regulation has grown steadily.

Not all public regulation or control of business can be included under the concept of prohibited activities. Much of public policy is also directed to causing the activities of firms or individuals in the system to differ from those which they would voluntarily pursue. Thus it encompasses a wide variety of measures that differ in purpose and effect. Their common feature is modification of the economic consequences of the market by changing structure or conduct or directly softening the impact of performance.

Furthermore, public policy is not all regulatory in nature. It also creates the general environment within which economic activities are conducted. This includes such things as defining the legal status of a firm; the enforcement of contracts; maintenance of a monetary system; the provision of police and fire protection; the encouragement of certain private activities such as land settlement, soil conservation, and establishment of local schools; and the discouragement of other activities such as those which cause pollution, are hazardous to health, or are deceptive. In some cases these policies have grown out of common law and precedent. In others they are the result of specific legislative activity.

The next two sections will briefly sketch those pieces of legislation that influenced agriculture. The first describes those laws which facilitated the development of agriculture or those whose objective was the improvement of market structure or firm conduct. The second subsection describes the attempts by government to ameliorate market performance through direct intervention. These sections will then serve as background for an analysis of present governmental activities in agriculture.

FACILITATIVE LEGISLATION

Among a whole series of laws that have given special consideration to agriculture, probably the first in the United States was the Land Ordinance of 1785. This set up the rectangular system of land survey and registration. Its purpose was to get the land into the hands of private individuals through sales, and at the same time, to raise revenue. The law provided that land should be surveyed in 6-mile-square lots. The 36-square-mile sections of land were called townships. One section in each township was to be set aside and sold for educational purposes. This greatly facilitated the development of country schools all across the land.

While Congress expected that this act would put land into the hands of private individuals rapidly, it was not very successful. Interested land buyers did not have the $640 required to buy a section of land. Consequently, in 1885 Congress passed the Homestead Act. This was a further attempt to get land into the hands of private individuals rapidly by, in effect, giving it away. The basic provision of the act stated that an individual could settle on a one-fourth section of land (160 acres) and, if he lived on it for 5 years and improved the land, he gained free title to it.

A third act contributing substantially to the development of agriculture is the Morrill Act of 1862. This act established the land-grant college system across the United States. Under this act Congress granted blocks of land to individual states. These blocks were to be sold to raise funds for the establishment of a state-supported college devoted to the study and development of agricultural and mechanical arts. In the same year Congress also established the United States Department of Agriculture (USDA) as a separate organization. Formerly it had been a division of the patent office.

The Hatch Act of 1887 was another act of great importance to the development of agriculture. Under this act Congress made grants for research in agriculture to the colleges of agriculture by establishing agricultural experiment stations in each land-grant college. These experiment stations have provided the technological basis for most of the rapid developments in agriculture since 1920. By linking together the USDA and the expertise of the land grant colleges and the agricultural experiment stations, Congress created a very powerful mechanism for technological advance in the United States. Its primary purpose was to improve the welfare of farmers. The substantial increases in productivity provided the consumer with substantial benefits and reduced the number of farmers required to feed the country.

The Sherman Antitrust Act of 1890 is the cornerstone of our present-day efforts to encourage competition in product and factor markets. It was passed by Congress in direct response to the abuse of market power by certain large firms. It grew out of an investigation into charges of collusion among the large meat-packers. Essentially, it forbids any effort on the part of industry to collude to restrain free trade at competitive prices.

In 1914 the Clayton Act and the Federal Trade Commission Act were passed to correct certain weaknesses in the Sherman Act. The Clayton Act further defined types of activities considered to lessen competition or lead toward monopoly power, and it exempted labor unions. The Federal Trade Commission Act provided an administrative body to oversee and supervise the enforcement of the Sherman and Clayton acts.

The Sherman Act created problems for our export industries since small unorganized groups of firms were unable to compete for international markets with the strong cartels of many European countries. The Webb-Pomerance Act of 1918 permitted domestic firms to form export associations to effectively compete in foreign trade. It exempted such groups from prosecution under the Sherman Act. The Capper-Volstead Act provided a similar exemption for farm cooperatives.

After World War I, large chain stores and mass distribution outlets frequently tried to drive the smaller independent operator out of business by obtaining price concessions from their suppliers on the basis of their large volumes. They argued that the larger volumes lowered per-unit costs of the supplier. The independents felt that frequently the price concessions of the supplier were larger than could be justified economically and were really attempts to drive smaller firms out of the industry. The Robinson-Patman Act of 1936 was passed to circumscribe the methods a firm could use to descriminate pricewise against its customers. It prohibited discriminating among purchasers if it could not be justified as a cost difference or as an attempt to meet the price of a competitor.

The Capper-Volstead Act clarified the status of agricultural cooperatives under the Sherman and Clayton acts. In the early 1900s, the Supreme Court declared that agricultural cooperatives were actually a combination that restrained trade since they were groups of farmers joined together to obtain higher prices for their commodities. This was considered to be illegal under the provisions of the Sherman Act. Senators Capper and Volstead sponsored an act which provided that cooperatives were a legal form of organization exempt from prosecution under the Sherman Act. This formed the basis for a significant growth in the development of agricultural cooperatives in the United States.

Two other acts which proved to have direct and far-reaching consequences for agriculture were the Smith-Lever Act of 1914, and the Smith-Hughes Act of 1919. The first of these developed the agricultural extension service, and the second provided federal funds for vocational agricultural training in the universities and high schools of the nation. It was based upon the idea that the new techniques and methods of farming being developed by the land-grant colleges and agricultural experiment stations would be extended to farmers and to the industries associated with or servicing agriculture. As a result we now have the federal extension service whose function it is to extend new knowledge and techniques. The agricultural extension system is now being used throughout the world as a model to extend science not only to agriculture but to other industries and directly to consumers.

In the years since 1920, a considerable number of laws have been passed which were intended specifically to apply to the marketing of one or more commodities. The first such laws of substantial importance to agriculture were the Packers and Stockyards Act of 1921, the Grain Futures Act of 1922, and the Commodity Exchange Act of 1922. The Packers and Stockyards Act and the Grain Futures Act were attempts to protect the farmer from exploitation by other individuals in the marketing channel. They regulated the stockyards and the grain markets in the purchase and sale of farmers' produce.

The Commodity Exchange Act of 1922 regulates futures trading on the commodity exchanges in the United States. It specifically prohibits the manipulation of (or the attempt to manipulate) the price of commodities such as corn, oats, wheat, barley, rye, flaxseed, potatoes, wool, soybeans, and fats and oils. It thus protects both the farmer and the consumer from traders who would try to influence commodity prices for their own advantage. Other acts to facilitate trade in agricultural commodities included the U.S. Warehouse Act of 1916 providing for the licensing and supervision of warehouses and their operation; the Produce Agency Act of 1927 attacking certain practices of commission agents and brokers which defrauded the seller of produce; and the Perishable Agricultural Commodities Act of 1930 providing for licensing and auditing of commission merchants, brokers, and dealers handling fresh fruits and vegetables. Also, there are many laws affecting the handling of products by regulating their weights, measures, grades, standards, and container sizes: the Standard Container Act of 1928, the

U.S. Cotton Standards Act of 1916, the Tobacco Inspection Act of 1935, and the Wool Standards Act. The next chapter will have more to say on facilitating marketing by providing inspection services, grades, standards, and market news and information services.

The Agricultural Marketing Agreement Act of 1937 is also important to the producers of many agricultural commodities. It permits producers and handlers of agricultural commodities to join together to "promote the orderly marketing of their product" under supervision of the secretary of agriculture who can enter into marketing orders and agreements that permit controlling the supply and price of a commodity. It specifically exempts this type of collusive behavior in agriculture from the Sherman and Clayton acts.

A number of laws have also been aimed at protecting the consumer. Regulation in this area generally attempts either to assist the consumer in making informed decisions or to protect him from products that could be harmful. The Federal Food and Drug Act (Pure Food and Drug Act) of 1906 and expanded in 1938 regulates the contents and characteristics of products available to the general public. It requires that the contents be labeled and forbids misbranding or misrepresentation of contents. It also covers animal feeds and veterinarian supplies and thus protects the farmer as well as the consumer. The Meat Inspection Act of 1906 requires inspection of all meats and of all establishments processing meats and poultry. The Wheeler-Lea Act of 1935 made false and deceptive advertising an illegal and unfair method of competition. In addition to the above federal laws, many state and local standards and regulations apply to agricultural commodities.

All the above facilitate in one way or another the efficient allocation of resources. In earliest times, concern was with legislation to place those resources in the hands of citizens who could profitably employ them. Later acts were designed to improve economic efficiency by adjusting market structure or conduct to more closely approximate the purely competitive model. In some instances, particular groups faced a noncompetitive market situation, and the government, rather than attempt to enhance competition, permitted the groups to develop their own countervailing market power by suspending the antitrust laws. Agriculture received a number of such exemptions, for example, cooperatives and marketing agreements.

In other instances the competitive market situation was permitted or encouraged. However, the resulting performance was judged to be unjust for one reason or another. In this case policies were designed to moderate its impact. Again agriculture has been the beneficiary of a good deal of such legislation. However, it should be clearly noted that agriculture has not been the only heir of policies to restrict competition. Such policies as collective bargaining for labor and fair trade practices for the small independent retailer have also been approved.

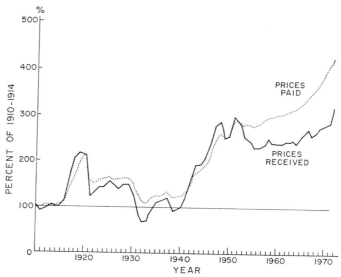

FIG. 11.1. A comparison of prices received and paid by United States farmers, 1910–1972. (From USDA, ERS, **1970 Handbook of Agricultural Charts,** Agr. Handbook 397, Washington, D.C.: USGPO, 1970, p. 7.)

AMELIORATIVE LEGISLATION

The 25 years before World War I have often been called the Golden Era of Rural America.[4] Total production increased by one-third but the demand for agricultural output was very strong. It was the most prosperous period in our history for farmers. Up until that time, increases in output were associated with equivalent increases in inputs. Yields changed very little and increase in crop acreage was the main input responsible for increases in output. Output per worker was constant until the late 1920s. Since then it has been increasing at an accelerating rate. During World War I, incomes and prices remained very favorable for farmers, and they were consequently stimulated to adopt some of the new technologies that were beginning to grow out of the Morrill Act, the Hatch Act, and the Smith-Lever Act.[5]

Immediately following World War I (1918), prices received by farmers fell substantially, as did the prices they paid for inputs. However, as indicated in Figure 11.1, prices received experienced the greater decline. As a consequence, net farm income fell substantially from its 1919 peak (see Figure 3.3). The resultant pressure from farm groups led to a number of bills in Congress that were designed to relieve the price-

4. M. M. Snodgrass and L. T. Wallace, *Agriculture, Economics, and Growth* (New York: Appleton-Century-Crofts, 1970), p. 40.
5. Recall these acts established the USDA, the agricultural experiment stations, and the extension service, respectively.

cost squeeze they were experiencing. Many of the proposals were attempts to make the marketing system for farm products more efficient.
The perceptive reader may have noted the large number of laws that
were described in the previous section adopted during the 1920s. The
hope was that by reducing the marketing margin the derived demand
for farm products would increase, thereby increasing farm prices and
incomes.

   Most of American agricultural policy since the late 1920s has
sought to maintain farmers' incomes by sustaining the prices of agricultural products at levels above the price that would result from the
unhindered interplay of demand and supply. Direct income supplements to farmers have never been politically feasible, hence the government has used other methods to raise farmers' incomes. The government has interjected itself into the market in many different ways and,
as will be seen in subsequent sections, has distorted the allocation of
resources as otherwise signaled by free market prices. Some of the principal pieces of legislation are described below.

   The McNary-Haugen plans, which never became law, were introduced in Congress and debated frequently during the 1920s. The
plans were based upon the price discrimination model for obtaining a
higher average price for all output, a process that requires separating
the market into a domestic and a foreign component. Domestic prices
were to be set at some fair level. All the production which could not
be sold domestically at that price was to be purchased by the government and sold abroad at whatever price it would bring. High tariffs
would prevent foreign imports from entering the higher-priced domestic
market. The government's loss on foreign sales was to be shared by
United States producers. Since the domestic price was higher and the
foreign price lower than the single price at which the product would sell
without the plan, farmers would receive a higher average net price. Because of its wide application in today's markets, the price discrimination
model is described below.

   Price discrimination occurs when a producer sells a commodity
to different buyers at different prices for reasons not associated with
cost differences. The success of a two-price plan is dependent upon the
markets having different elasticities of demand and the ability to keep
markets physically separated. The basic idea is to maximize total revenue by equating the marginal revenue of the last unit sold in each
market. The plan assumes that by restricting the amount sold on the
more inelastic (domestic) market, price and hence total revenue are increased. The excess is sold on the world market where demand is more
elastic. The resulting total revenue is larger than if all the production
were sold at one price.

   A graphic illustration of price discrimination is shown in Figure 11.2. In part a we have shown the (relatively inelastic) domestic

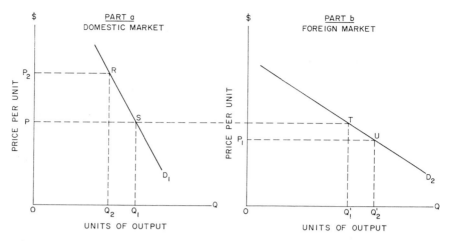

FIG. 11.2. The basic price discrimination model.

demand curve D_1, and in part b the (relatively elastic) foreign demand curve D_2. If the same price, P, were charged in both markets, a total quantity $Q_1 + Q'_1$ would be sold in both markets. Since the domestic demand is less elastic, by raising its price to P_2 and selling the smaller quantity (Q_2), the resulting total revenue OP_2RQ_2 is larger than the old revenue of $OP SQ_1$. The difference in quantity ($Q_1 - Q_2$) is added to the quantity (Q'_1) sold in the foreign market, resulting in a drop in the foreign price to P_1. The sum of the total revenue in the two markets at the different prices can be shown to be larger than if the same price were charged in each.[6]

$$(OP\ SQ_1 + OP\ TQ'_1) < (OP_2RQ_2 \times OP_1UQ'_2) \qquad (11.1)$$

The conditions under which a seller can successfully discriminate pricewise are, first, he must be able to control the supply available to particular buyers. Second, he must be able to prevent the resale of the commodity from a buyer in the low-priced market to a buyer in the higher-priced one. In the McNary-Haugen proposal, tariff barriers effectively segregated the two markets. In other cases, transportation costs, import duties, or geographic barriers can be utilized to effectively segregate the markets. As long as there is a difference in the elasticities of

6. To prove this, refer to Figure 11.2 and assume that $Q_1 - Q_2$ is one unit. The loss in revenue in the foreign market is $(P - P_1)Q'_1 - P_1$, while the gain in the domestic market is $(P_2 - P)Q_2 - P$. Obviously, the gain is larger than the loss, and hence total revenue is increased by transferring one unit from the domestic to the foreign market. The process is continued until the increase in total revenue in the domestic market is just offset by the loss in total revenue in the foreign market. This will occur where their respective marginal revenues are equal.

demand between two markets, total revenue can be increased by separating them and charging a higher price in the less elastic one. The price policy requires that marginal revenues in all markets be equalized to maximize total revenue.

The practice of selling excess production in the more elastic market is frequently termed *dumping.* The term is uually encountered in international trade in connection with the practice of selling at a lower price abroad than at home. There are also examples of the same principle being applied in domestic markets. The federal milk marketing orders in the Agricultural Marketing Agreement Act permit milk producers and handlers to sell milk to fluid users at a higher price than the milk used for manufacturing butter and cheese. The appliance manufacturer who sells the same machine at a higher price under his own brand name, and through a mail-order house at a lower price, is another example. Here, brand loyalty has made the demand curve for his own product relatively inelastic (Figure 11.2, part a). This is the tilt in the demand curve discussed in Chapter 10.

FARM INCOME PROBLEM

All during the 1920s and 1930s, the index of prices received by farmers remained at a level substantially below those which they paid for items they purchased (see Figure 11.1). Thus there was continuing pressure for federal legislation to remedy the income problem of agriculture. The first attempt to directly deal with this problem was the Agricultural Marketing Act of 1929. The law conceptualized the farm problem as growing out of disorderly marketing procedures. It viewed the farmer as having to sell his products immediately after harvest when prices were the lowest. If he could store his products and sell them in an orderly fashion throughout the year, he would obtain higher prices and incomes. The act established the Federal Farm Board and appropriated $500 million for its operation. The board was to buy commodities through cooperatives and store and sell them back to consumers throughout the year in an orderly manner, thus stabilizing farm prices. Unfortunately, 1929 brought on a drastic drop in farm prices growing out of the Great Depression (see Figure 11.1). By 1933 the board had spent all its funds and had acquired large quantities of farm commodities which it was storing, yet prices were still falling. The board was dissolved when Congress did not appropriate any further funds for its operation.

The period of the 1930s signaled a change in the basic approach to solving the farm-income problem. The two-price plan was designed to give farmers a protected domestic market, and the Federal Farm Board was to level out the peaks and troughs in farm prices; both involved withholding supplies from the market to raise domestic prices.

The farm board experience, plus falling demand during the early 1930s, emphasized the fact that prices could be adjusted only if production were kept in line with actual foreign and domestic demand. Beginning with the Agricultural Adjustment Act of 1933, the concept was modified to that of establishing fair prices for farmers, and in turn requiring them to limit production. Farm income was to be increased in two ways: (1) higher prices in the marketplace resulting from smaller market supplies and (2) direct government checks to cooperators for reducing output. The law provided funds for the program by imposing a special tax on the processors of agricultural products such as cotton ginners, wheat millers, and meat-packers. The act limited production by determining how many acres of a particular crop a farmer could plant. His acreage allotment was set as some proportion of his historical acreage for that crop. Farmers then signed contracts to reduce their acreage devoted to such products as corn, wheat, cotton, rice, tobacco, hogs, and milk in return for a certain cash payment.

The act also established the Commodity Credit Corporation (CCC) to support agricultural prices. The CCC used two programs to reach its objectives. For storable commodities it utilized nonrecourse loans. Under this system the farmer put his commodity in approved storage and obtained a loan on the stored quantity reflecting the fair price, that is, the support price. If the market price rose above the support price, the farmer could sell his stored commodities and repay the loan. If the market price stayed below the support price, farmers simply turned the stored commodities over to the government (the CCC) to repay his loan.

For nonstorable commodities—or those requiring special off-farm storage facilities—the CCC entered directly into the marketplace and stood ready to buy at a predetermined support price all the commodity offered. It disposed of these commodities through outlets which did not directly compete with commercial channels, such as school lunch programs, food donations through welfare programs, etc. In some cases it had to destroy the commodities as a last resort. This program has been used for products such as butter, eggs, turkeys, pork, and beef.

PARITY PRICES

The Agricultural Adjustment Act of 1933 also established the criteria of a fair price for agricultural commodities. A *fair price* was defined to be one that would give agricultural commodities the same purchasing power with respect to articles that farmers buy as that which existed in the base period 1910–1914.[7] This price was called the *parity*

---

7. Note that the period was part of the 25-year period described earlier as the "golden era of rural America." It was a period when prices and incomes of farmers were very favorable.

price. If a farmer sold a bushel of corn in 1910–1914 for $0.50 and bought a shovel with the proceeds, the parity concept required that when the current price of the shovel increased to $1.00 the current parity price of corn must increase to $1.00 per bushel. Thus, if prices farmers paid for goods and services changed, parity dictated that prices farmers received for the commodities they sold change by the same proportion. This relationship of prices received to prices paid was measured by the *parity ratio*.

$$\text{(11.2)}$$

$$\frac{\text{current index of prices received } \quad \text{(1910–14 base)}}{\text{current index of prices paid} \quad \text{(1910–14 base)}} \times 100 = \frac{\text{parity}}{\text{ratio}}$$

Using Equation 11.2, it is easy to see that when prices received by farmers increased less than the prices they paid, the ratio fell. Conversely, a rising ratio means that prices received are increasing more (or falling less) than prices paid. A ratio below 100 means that prices of farm commodities have a lower purchasing power than in the 1910–1914 base period. Thus a parity ratio of 80 in 1935 meant that prices farmers received for the products they sold had fallen relative to prices paid, and hence they possessed 80 percent as much purchasing power as in the base period.

The parity purchasing power of an individual farm commodity can also be calculated as follows:

$$\frac{\left(\begin{array}{c}\text{average price received} \\ \text{for a commodity} \\ \text{during 1910–14}\end{array}\right)\left(\begin{array}{c}\text{current index} \\ \text{of} \\ \text{prices paid}\end{array}\right)}{100} = \begin{array}{c}\text{current} \\ \text{parity} \\ \text{price}\end{array} \quad \text{(11.3)}$$

As an example, suppose wheat averaged $0.884 cents per bushel in 1910–1914, and in 1942 the index of prices paid by farmers was 150. In this case, wheat would have to sell for 1.5 times $0.884 or $1.326 to have the same purchasing power as in the base period. This would be the parity price for wheat in 1942.

This concept and the formulas illustrated by Equations 11.2 and 11.3 had a distorting effect on resource allocation. They operated to obstruct the adjustment of production to changes in demand, input costs, or changes in input efficiencies as reflected in changing relative prices. For example, over the period 1910 to 1950 the demand for cereal and grain products declined relative to the demand for meats, dairy products, fruits, and vegetables. Under such circumstances one would expect that the ratio of cereal to livestock prices should decline over the period. The parity ratio did not permit cereal and grain prices to fall relative to livestock products. This discouraged the transfer of resources from the production of one product to the other. Similarly, if the efficiency of resources has changed, a lower product price may still provide the producer with an adequate return. The parity price does not take this into account. It assumes that whatever input/output, marginal cost/marginal revenue, or factor price/value of the marginal product existed in the 1910–1914 period had to be maintained to provide farmers an equitable return.

The 1933 act was declared unconstitutional on the grounds that the processing tax was benefiting a particular group rather than the general welfare. However, the concept of parity price as being a fair price remained as an integral part of the way of thinking about farm price problems for many years.

SOIL CONSERVATION CONCEPT

The next attempt to alleviate the farm income problem was the Soil Conservation and Domestic Allotment Act of 1936. While it sought to accomplish the same objective as the 1933 act, the emphasis was on conservation rather than production controls. The act provided for payments to farmers for reducing their acreage of soil-depleting crops and increasing their acreages of soil-conserving crops such as legumes. Furthermore, the act made payments to farmers directly from federal funds rather than through the unconstitutional processor tax. The soil-depleting crops were defined to be almost identical to those included in the 1933 act. Although payments to farmers for certain soil-conserving practices are still a part of current farm programs, this act did not completely remedy the price and income problems and it was followed by a second act in 1938.

FLEXIBLE PRICE SUPPORTS

The Agricultural Adjustment Act of 1938 continued many of the provisions of the preceding acts, including the Commodity Credit Corporation and its price-support programs, as well as payments for soil-conserving practices. This act provides the basic framework for all major farm programs since the time of its enactment. In the 1938 law, support levels were specified as a percentage of the parity price as determined by Equation 11.3. For example, suppose that in 1939 the parity price for cotton was calculated to be $0.10 per pound. If the 1938 act stated that cotton was to be supported at a level of at least 80 percent of parity, the Commodity Credit Corporation would stand ready to buy all the cotton offered at 80 percent of $0.10, or $0.08 per pound.

Up until 1938, the level at which prices of commodities were supported was specified administratively. It could have been at any level the secretary of agriculture desired, including zero. The 1938 act established the precedent that prices for particular commodities be supported mandatorily at between 52 and 75 percent of parity. The secretary of agriculture could peg prices at the lower level in years of large anticipated supplies and at the higher level if supplies were expected to be smaller than deemed desirable. The objective of the law was to establish an ever-normal granary by maintaining a level of reserve stocks for future emergencies. The issue of the level of price supports has been debated in Congress nearly every session since 1938. Generally, supports at 75 to 90 percent of parity have been the rule.

With price supports at levels above those which would naturally balance supply and demand, surpluses are created. These must be neutralized (isolated from the market) or disposed of in some way to avoid further depressing farm prices. The losses associated with surplus disposal can be limited only if production is controlled. The problem with the controls was that they were attached to acreages rather than to physical units of output such as pounds or bushels. Land is but one of the inputs used in agricultural production. Given restrictions on its use, more labor and capital can be combined with less land to produce the same or a larger output. The farmer will naturally idle his poorer acres and use improved technologies on the remaining land. The reduced acreage produces more rather than less output. As a consequence, surpluses continued to accumulate as farm prices fell 20 percent between 1938 and 1940. Effective production controls required setting farmer quotas in terms of physical units of output rather than attempting to control one particular production input.

Programs to expand the demand for farm commodities first made their appearance in this act. It provided for the establishment of four regional scientific research laboratories to develop new uses and outlets for farm products. It also established direct distribution of surplus farm commodities to the indigent through a school lunch program, a low-cost milk program, and a food-stamp plan. We shall return to demand expansion programs in a later section of this chapter.

PRODUCTION INCENTIVES

In the early 1940s, conditions changed rapidly in favor of agriculture. The index of prices received by farmers increased from 100 in 1940 to 193 in 1943. Farm output also increased but not nearly so rapidly. Consequently, the objective of farm legislation became that of encouraging production. The same basic legislative mechanism was utilized by removing restrictions on production and by the addition of the Steagall Amendments to raise the support levels to 90 percent of parity. These levels were continued until 1948, at which time surpluses were beginning to build up again because of the price-support program. The large cost of this program was also beginning to alarm many legislators. On the other hand, farm leaders, remembering the disastrous period after World War I, were concerned that those conditions might be repeated. As a consequence, there was a struggle in Congress between those wanting to return to the more flexible provisions of the 1938 act and those wishing to retain the high rigid price supports of the war years.

The Agricultural Act of 1948 was a political compromise and also a move toward recognition of the impact of price signals on resource allocation. It provided for a return to the flexible price support instead of the fixed 90 percent level. The level of support was to vary inversely with the level of production. If, in a given year, farm output was below the average of recent years, the support price would be at a higher percentage of parity than if production was at a higher level. The flexible provision recognized the fact that prices do guide production and consumption decisions and thus that larger crops require lower prices to clear the market than do smaller crops.

The act also redesigned the parity formula to eliminate the distortions in prices and resource allocation that were becoming apparent under the old formula (developed in 1933). For example, shifts to mechanical power in farming altered the demand for horses which, in turn, decreased the demand for pasture, hay, and grains. The old parity formula was outdated principally because the 1910–1914 base did not allow for such changing relationships among agricultural commodities. The new parity formula did permit changes in price relationships to operate. The concept of fair purchasing power was still tied to the 1910–1914 base through the index of prices paid. To take account of changing relationships, the base period for the price of a commodity was based upon its relationship to all commodities in the most recent 10 years. The new formula was as follows:

$$\frac{\text{average price of a commodity last 10 years}}{\text{average index of all prices received last 10 years}} \times \frac{\text{current index of prices paid}}{(1910\text{–}14 = 100)} = \frac{\text{current parity price}} \qquad (11.4)$$

The formula adjusts relative parity prices for specific commodities for continuing market trends. Long-run persistent shifts in demand among commodities are reflected back to the farmer. The parity price for starches and cereals will fall as their demands decrease and those for meat and livestock products rise as demands for these products grow. This formula is still an impediment to the free response to market signals in that it ties prices to the index of prices paid in 1910–1914. It does not reflect changes in production technologies nor quantities bought or sold. A farmer's economic status is a function of both price per unit and quantity produced or purchased. Given the objective of establishing income quality, what was actually needed was an income-cost formula in which the gross income received per farm operator in the base period is multiplied by the current index of costs incurred.

In 1949 the secretary of agriculture, Charles Brannan, proposed a new type of farm program. The key feature of the Brannan Plan was a shift from a price standard to an income standard as a means of measuring and providing a fair return to farmers. Parity income was to be calculated on a moving base beginning with the period 1939–1948; each year the earliest year would be dropped and a new year added. A second feature was that all commodities would be sold at market-clearing prices. To keep farmers' incomes at the desired level, the difference would be made up by direct government payments (compensatory payments) to farmers. A third feature was that the income supports to any farmer would have an upper limit, thereby limiting the benefits to any individual. The program was strongly opposed by most farm groups and never passed. The concept of direct payments as opposed to market intervention as a means of providing equity did not receive further serious support until 1965. Further, efforts to limit the amount of payments one individual could receive were unsuccessful until the early 1970s.

SUPPLY CONTROL AND SURPLUS DISPOSAL

From 1950 to date there has been very little innovation in policies and programs to ameliorate the impact of market processes on farmers' incomes. The programs were generally modifications and combinations of policies found in one or more of the earlier acts. The decade of the 1950s saw a combination of continued price supports and movements toward voluntary participation in production control programs. The end result was large surplus stocks. The 1960s were opened by a major effort to introduce mandatory supply management along with income protection for farmers. The effort failed and the latter half of the decade saw public policy for agriculture move in the direction of voluntary programs and direct payments for those complying with programs to reduce production. Overlaying the total 20-year period was the continual struggle with overproduction and the high costs of managing the surplus. The Agricultural Acts of 1949 and of 1954 continued the main features of the federal program to support farm income through prices. The Korean War strengthened the demand for farm products and delayed the buildup of stocks. As a consequence, price supports were maintained at 90 percent of parity through 1954. After the Korean War, large stocks began to accumulate once again. This led to low crop and livestock prices and, consequently, pressure to once again lower support levels. In an effort to facilitate the movement of surpluses into international markets, and thereby remove the depressing effect of huge stocks and low farm prices, Congress passed another significant act.

The Agricultural Trade Development and Assistance Act of 1954 is more commonly known as Public Law 480 (PL 480). It had a number of subprograms which moved large quantities of our surplus commodities overseas under programs such as Food for Peace, sales in foreign currency rather than in dollars, and donations to the needy through voluntary agencies such as CARE, the United Nations Children's Fund, and Disaster Relief Funds. Although PL 480 did alleviate the situation somewhat, surpluses continued to grow. As farm leaders and legislators began to realize that total agricultural production in the United States was beyond the level which would yield fair prices for farmers in the marketplace, they once again sought methods of controlling production. The decision was to control production by removing cropland from production by banking it for the future.

The Soil Bank Act of 1956 was the first large-scale program since the 1930s to control output by limiting the land input. It was a two-part program in which farmers' participation was voluntary. Under the Acreage Reserve, farmers could receive payments for renting crop acres to the government, with participants being paid directly for each acre on the basis of their normal yield multiplied by the support price per bushel. The essential difference from earlier programs was that the land rented to the government could not be used for any other purposes. The second part of the program was the Conservation Reserve. Here the objective was to permit land to be taken out of production by renting it for periods up to 10 years. This land must be put into conserving uses such as grass. Payments averaged about $10 to $15 per acre.

The Conservation Reserve was a long-run program that retired whole farms as well as parts of farms. In fact, there was a bonus to a farmer who placed his whole farm in the Conservation Reserve. By 1960 about 6 percent (29 million acres) of the country's cropland had been retired by the program. When whole farms were completely removed from production, the other inputs associated with farming were also removed. The farm operator generally retired or took a nonfarm job. The reduction in the purchases of farm production inputs evoked opposition from local merchants and citizens who saw their livelihood threatened. This led to the political downfall of the program in 1960.

Despite the efforts to control production, the farm-income situation had not improved during the 1950s. Although estimates indicated that farm output was below the level which would have poured forth without the program, total output continued to climb. Crop yields increased on the remaining acreage until in 1960 total output reached a level 23 percent higher than in 1950, even though 29 million acres of cropland were in the soil bank. The index of prices received by farmers decreased from 259 to 239 on a 1910–1914 base. There was wide disagreement among farm leaders, economists, and legislators as to the appropriate policy to follow with respect to the agricultural price and income problem.

Failure of the Conservation Reserve to curtail total output, particularly with respect to feed grains, led the administration to seek authorization to impose mandatory acreage reductions in feed grains to control both feed grain and livestock output. Farmers objected to the mandatory features of the proposal and it was defeated. Instead, Congress passed the voluntary feed grain and wheat programs.

The Feed Grain Act of 1961 and the Agricultural Act of 1962 provided the basic enabling legislation during the 1960s. This was followed by the Food and Agricultural Act of 1965. Farmers did not have to participate in this program unless they thought it was profitable to do so. Furthermore, nonparticipating farmers could expand their acreage above previous levels if they wanted to. However, the government began moving toward lower price-support levels and farmers who did not participate received only the market price. These acts diverted acreages of specific crops to soil-conserving uses. The per-acre payments the farmer received for diverting his cropland were directly tied to the amount he diverted. Those farmers diverting a large percentage of their allotments received a higher per-acre payment than those diverting the minimum amount permissible. In addition to the cash payments farmers received for diverting acres, and the ability to obtain nonrecourse loans at the support price on the production of their remaining acres, participating farmers also received a direct payment for each bushel. The program was designed to separate income supports from the market mechanism and to provide incentives for keeping production within manageable limits.

Wheat was experiencing special difficulties in that farmers did not like the acreage restriction. Congress then passed the special Cotton and Wheat Act of 1964 which permitted a two-price plan for these commodities. This was a multiple-price plan that gave the farmer one price for his share of production which was consumed domestically and a lower price for that part which was exported. The purpose was to lower the farmers' marginal revenue on production in excess of that required to meet domestic requirements and, hence, to more closely approach actual market conditions in resource allocation. It is based upon the principles described earlier in this chapter in the price discrimination model.

The Feed Grain Act expired in 1964 and Congress then passed the Food and Agricultural Act of 1965 which carried forward through 1969 most of the provisions of earlier legislation. It also incorporated the dual system of price supports and direct payments to participating farmers. The 1965 act also established another long-term general land-retirement program called the cropland adjustment program. It permitted farmers to sign 5- to 10-year contracts with the USDA to retire cropland to conservation uses. In 1970 a new agricultural law extended for another 3 years the existing program of lower price supports, voluntary participation, and direct payments. Under a new "set-aside," farmers are required to set some acreage aside and keep it idle in order to qualify for program benefits. It also permitted farmers to use their remaining acreage for any crops which they wish to grow and sell without a subsidy. This provision gives farmers greater freedom in making their farm-operating decisions.

GOVERNMENT IN AGRICULTURE: AN OVERVIEW

The basic goal of the most recent legislation has been to give farmers more flexibility in their farm-operating decisions by not restricting acreage of particular crops on any individual farm. The acreage limitation and quotas serve only to determine the amount of land which must be set aside to qualify for loans and direct payments, and to determine the amount of product upon which the producer is eligible to receive income support. A second objective is the greater reliance upon the marketplace by using a support price nearer a market-clearing price, direct payments on that portion of the farmers' production required to meet current demand, and no support on any excess production above that level. Thus current programs protect farmers' incomes up to certain levels and simultaneously attempt to use the market mechanism to bring production in line with market demand.

This approach has been adopted after much trial and error. The economic costs of interference with the market mechanism are high. It creates false market signals leading to resource misallocation and excess production as producers always attempt to maximize returns. For each new attempt to control production, producers find new methods of partially circumventing its provisions. The current approach attempts to utilize the market as fully as possible to allocate resources and to impose overall production controls through cross-compliance requirements. This approach is directed toward permitting the marketplace to equate the cost of producing the last unit with the utility to consumers of consuming that last unit. Under this approach, producers can ignore price supports if they are efficient enough to produce at market prices. This improves technical efficiency. Before analyzing these features in more detail, an economic analysis of alternative methods of supporting prices is presented.

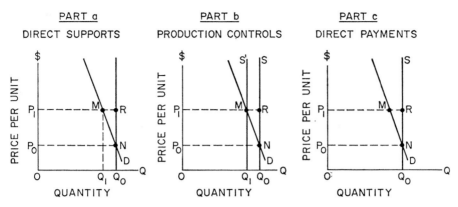

FIG. 11.3.   Economic implications of alternative price support programs.

ECONOMICS OF PRICE-SUPPORT PROGRAMS

Figure 11.3 illustrates the basic economic principles of alternative price-support mechanisms. Assume that D is the market demand and S the aggregate supply curve.[8] The market clearing price is P_0 and parity price is P_1. Assuming that government decides to support the price to farmers at P_1, it can employ one of three basic approaches: (1) directly support prices at P_1, (2) limit production to raise the market clearing price to P_1, or (3) pay farmers directly for the difference between P_0 and P_1. Depending upon the mechanism employed, the economic consequences will differ.

DIRECT PRICE SUPPORTS

In this approach, the government establishes a price floor at P_1 by standing ready to purchase in the marketplace all the commodity offered at that price. Since consumers will purchase only Q_1 units at P_1, the government acquires the quantity $Q_0 - Q_1$. It must remove this quantity from the market by storing it, selling it abroad, destroying it, or otherwise preventing it from influencing the market price. The net result is to drive the price to consumers up from P_0 to P_1. Farmers receive the total outlay $OP_1 RQ_0$ of which $OP_1 MQ_1$ is direct consumer outlay, and $Q_1 MRQ_0$ is indirect consumer outlay through treasury expenditures. There is also an additional cost not shown in part a. This is the expenditure to neutralize the price-depressing effect of the surplus; we shall have more to say on this later.

8. Market supply curves for agricultural commodities are generally highly inelastic since production tends to be an irreversible growth process. Except for the influence of weather, production that is forthcoming at harvest time was fixed a number of months earlier when the farmer planted his crops.

PRODUCTION CONTROL

In this approach, the government limits agricultural output by cutting supply from S to S' (part b). With the smaller supply, market price will rise to P_1, and since demand is inelastic, farmers obtain a larger total revenue ($OP_1 MQ_1$) than if they produced Q_0 units. The total payment to producers is direct consumer outlays. In comparison to direct price supports, farmers' total receipts are less by the amount $Q_1 MRQ_0$ because there is no surplus to be sold to the government. Since the farmer also saves expenses by producing the smaller quantity, the reduction in net income may be less than the reduction in total receipts ($Q_1 MRQ_0$).

Both procedures result in a misallocation of resources since consumers are forced to pay a higher price for agricultural products.

DIRECT PAYMENTS

In this case the government pays the producer directly for the difference between the market clearing price P_0 and the support price P_1 (part c). Each producer receives the amount $P_1 - P_0$ per unit of output in the form of a check from the treasury.

This method yields the same total receipts for the producer as direct price supports ($OP_1 RQ_0$). However, in this case a larger portion of it comes from the treasury ($P_0 P_1 RN$ versus $Q_1 MRQ_0$ in part a). This method is preferable to direct price supports in that total production clears the market at a price equal to consumers' marginal utility as reflected in P_0.

By way of summary, the direct-supports approach and the direct-payments approach encourage excess resources in agriculture by artificially inflating returns to productive factors. To partially compensate for this undesirable feature of price supports, direct payments can be limited to that level of production required to satisfy domestic needs. In part c, the producer would then receive the lower price (P_0) on any output in excess of Q_0. The lower price for the marginal units of output brings its price in line with its marginal utility to consumers. We turn now to a summary of current price-support methods.

CURRENT SUPPORT METHODS

Currently, farmers may produce as much as they wish at prevailing market prices. Each farmer is allocated his share (allotment) of the total output needed to meet anticipated demands. Those who produce more than their allotments are either ineligible for government loans and payments or they receive no support on the excess they must sell at the market-clearing price. Each farmer has a historical base acreage and production allotment (or quota). To qualify for price-support payments, the farmer is required to set aside a specified percent-age of cropland in his base acreage from crop production. His quota is calculated by multiplying his base acreage by an average yield. The amount of payment each producer receives is calculated as a percentage of his historical allotment.

The Commodity Credit Corporation (CCC) is the agency re-sponsible for agricultural price-support activities, and it supports prices in four different ways: (1) nonrecourse loans, (2) purchase in lieu of loans, (3) direct purchase in the marketplace, and (4) direct producer payments. Each method has the same objective: supporting producer incomes by guaranteeing a minimum price for his product. The overall mix of these methods has changed with time, shifting from an emphasis on direct price supports via loans and purchases to direct producer payments.

Price-support loans are made to eligible farmers through local offices of the Agricultural Stabilization and Conservation Service (ASCS), a division of the USDA. At harvest time the farmer obtains a loan equal to the support price times the units of product stored. If the market price should rise above the support level, the farmer sells the product and pays off the loan plus interest. If prices do not rise, the farmer permits the loan to mature. At maturity the CCC takes title to the commodity and the loan is paid off.

Purchases in lieu of loans are frequently used in areas where storage facilities are not available to the producer or the producer does not wish a loan. Under this method an eligible farmer offers his com-modities for sale to the CCC at the support level. The corporation is obligated to purchase all the eligible commodity offered to it. For a specified period of time the producer need not deliver the commodity immediately but can store it in his own facilities until he delivers it to the CCC.

Loans and purchases support the price at exactly the same level. The loan appeals to the producer who requires the money immediately and who has adequate storage available. The purchase route provides a convenient method of price support for the producer who does not need cash immediately, does not have storage, or does not want to go through the process of obtaining a loan.

Direct purchases are used for those commodities requiring processing or special storage or handling. In this case the government purchases the commodities from processors or handlers who have con-verted them into a more durable or transportable form. The CCC an-nounces the support price for such commodities and stands ready to purchase all that is offered. Merchants will sell commodities to the CCC whenever their price falls below support levels, thus placing a floor under the commodity.

Direct payments are made by the CCC to the producer at a

specified level per unit of product marketed. For example, under the feed grain program in 1970, the CCC supported the price of corn at $1.05 per bushel via loans and paid another $0.30 per bushel directly to eligible farmers. For wheat, the direct payments involved a much more complicated multiple-price system requiring marketing certificates. The net effect was that the farmer received the support price on all of his eligible output, an additional direct payment for that part consumed domestically, and another smaller direct payment per unit on that part that was exported. The methods of support used for various crops in recent years are

> Loans, purchases, and direct payments—corn and grain sorghum.
> Loans and purchases—barley, dry edible beans, flaxseed, honey, oats, peanuts, rice, rye, and soybeans.
> Loans and direct payments—upland cotton.
> Loans, purchases, and marketing certificates—wheat.
> Loans only—tobacco, crude pine gum (on rosin or its content in crude pine gum), extra-long staple cotton, and tung nuts.
> Purchases only—manufacturing milk, butterfat (butter, cheddar cheese, nonfat dry milk solids, and other dairy products when announced), and cottonseed.
> Direct payments only—wood, mohair, and sugar.

CROSS-COMPLIANCE AND SLIPPAGE

In attempts to lower total output, cropland diverted from production by price-support programs reached a peak of 65 million acres in 1962 and again in 1972 (Figure 11.4). Yet total agricultural output continued to expand for two reasons: the impact of land withdrawal on total output was much less than expected because of enterprise substitution, and farmers adjusted their remaining production inputs to compensate for the acres withdrawn.

In the early years, efforts to control production failed to recognize that when farmers decreased the acreage of one crop in compliance with the provisions of a particular support program, they frequently expanded the acres devoted to other crops. Participation in the benefits of one program was not contingent upon participation in others. It was possible for farmers to receive a payment under one production control program while not complying with another. The following illustrates the types of enterprise substitutions farmers were utilizing between 1952 and 1959 as reflected by the net change in acres devoted to particular crops.[9]

9. USDA, ARS, *Farm Production-Trends, Prospects and Programs*, Agr. Inform. Bull. 239 (Washington, D.C.: USGPO, May 1961), p. 32.

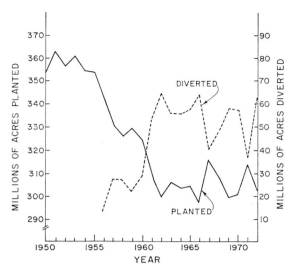

FIG. 11.4. Comparison of crop acres planted to crop acres diverted, United States, 1950–1972. (From USDA, Statistical Reporting Service, **Crop Production,** annual summaries, Washington, D.C.: USGPO, various years; USDA, **Agricultural Statistics,** annual issues, Washington, D.C.: USGPO, various years.)

	1,000 ACRES
Wheat	— 16,272
Cotton	— 11,661
Feed grains	+ 8,004
Soybeans	+ 8,533

As illustrated above, surpluses in wheat and cotton were being transferred to feed grains and soybeans. The efforts to restrict production were largely negated by the failure of the programs to require farmers to comply with all production controls if they wished to be eligible for price supports. Hence, the 1961 feed grain program and the 1962 wheat program and later legislation do require cross-compliance. Farmers have to demonstrate that they are reducing their acres devoted to all crops.

A second major problem with input controls is that farmers try to compensate. They offset acreage controls by divertting their inferior acres, increasing acreages in other areas, increasing the productivity of their remaining acres, or otherwise nullifying the control features of these programs. This is clearly illustrated in Figures 11.4 and 11.5. The reduction in acres in compliance with production-control programs did not reduce acres planted on a one-for-one basis, nor did it reduce total output. As can be seen in Figure 11.4, total cropland

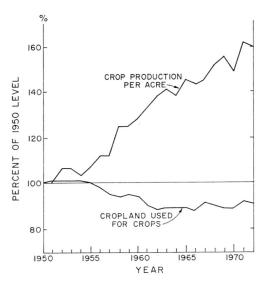

FIG. 11.5. Crop production per acre and cropland used for crops, United States, 1950–1972. (From USDA, **1972 Handbook of Agricultural Charts,** Washington, D.C.: USGPO, 1972, p. 14.)

planted in major crops has leveled out since 1961 at slightly more than 300 million acres, and diverted acreage at approximately 50 million acres. Notice further that there is a close inverse relationship between changes in crop acres planted and those diverted, but it is not perfect. For example, between 1960 and 1962 diverted acres increased by 36 million acres while crop acres planted only decreased 25 million acres over the same 2 years. Tweeten estimates that each acre diverted from production reduced total cropland by 0.8 acre.[10] When this is combined with the fact that the diverted acres are generally of lower productivity, total agricultural output has continued to increase year after year.

SURPLUS DISPOSAL

One of the direct results of government price-support activities via loan and direct purchases was the accumulation of surplus stocks. These stocks were costly to maintain and to service and consequently formed one of the pressure points in Congress for programs which would not create huge surpluses as a by-product of support activities.

Figure 11.6 illustrates the large buildup of surpluses of wheat and feed grains during the late 1950s and the early 1960s from programs

10. Luther Tweeten, *Foundations of Farm Policy* (Lincoln: Univ. Nebr. Press, 1970), p. 316.

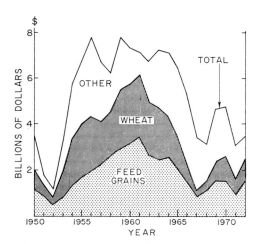

FIG. 11.6. Value of CCC inventories of wheat and feed grains, United States, 1950–1972. (From USDA, **Handbook of Agricultural Charts,** Washington, D.C.: USGPO, various years.)

characterized by high price supports via the marketplace and by ineffective production controls. The rising stockpile of surplus commodities in CCC inventories and loans reached a peak of $7.7 billion in 1956 and again in 1959. This is equivalent to about 60 percent of total income earned by all of agriculture in 1 year. Surpluses persisted at this level until 1963 when they began to decline to current levels of $3 to $5 billion. This decline is the result of two mutually reinforcing factors operating simultaneously: (1) a growing domestic and foreign demand for food and fiber arising out of increasing per capita incomes and (2) effective programs to reduce the rate of growth in surpluses, accompanied by efficient programs to dispose of surpluses.

The most popular method of surplus disposal has been "dumping abroad" (selling surplus at low prices on the world market). However, selling surplus commodities at subsidized prices abroad is resented by foreign producers and eventually brings retaliation by closing those markets to legitimate United States sales. As a consequence, Congress developed great resourcefulness in disposing of surpluses without antagonizing either domestic or foreign producers; that is, many of our surpluses were disposed of by donations to disaster victims or sold for foreign currencies under PL 480. The foreign currencies accumulated in this way are used to support local diplomatic missions or are loaned or granted back to the local government for economic development projects. Some are also bartered abroad for strategic materials that are stockpiled in the United States for emergencies. In this way much of the price-depressing effect of United States surpluses on domestic market prices can be tempered. Additionally, surpluses have been dumped at home. Again, however, considerable effort was devoted to minimizing the price-depressing impact on domestic markets and to avoid replacing commercial sales. Although the domestic food distribution programs can be justified on the basis of improved nutrition, their primary motivation has been the reduction of surpluses. Furthermore, there is more than a little doubt that the total consumption of food is actually increased. The money saved by the recipients of the foodstuffs is spent on products other than food.

The other factor responsible for declining surplus stock is the more effective production control programs. In effect, the government has managed to trade surplus commodities stock of the early 1960s for idle acres. Voluntary participation in the program was encouraged by the lower market support price and hence the market price available to the nonparticipant. This is clearly reflected in Figure 11.7. It can be seen that when the loan support price for wheat was dramatically reduced, the market price for nonparticipants followed suit, while the total return to participants remained high. The loss per bushel of wheat to farmers choosing not to participate was about $0.50 per bushel between 1964 and 1970.

PROGRAM COSTS

The smaller surplus, accompanied by increased farmer freedom, has not come without cost. The voluntary nature of the current

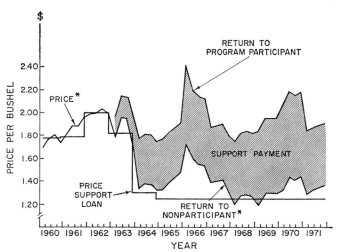

FIG. 11.7. A comparison of wheat prices and support rates to participants and nonparticipants in the wheat program, United States, 1960–1972. (From USDA, **1972 Handbook of Agricultural Charts**, Washington, D.C.: USGPO, 1972, p. 89.)

Table 11.1. Net U.S. government outlays for agricultural income support activities totals for 1934–1953 and annual 1953–1972

| Fiscal Year | Price Support Activities | | | | Surplus Disposal | | Total Cost |
	Market trans- actions	Direct payments	Acreage with- drawals[a]	Other[b]	Foreign programs[c]	Domestic programs[d]	
			(million dollars)				
1934-53	1,286	...	...	2,037	14	805	4,142
1954	474	...	...	154	26	170	824
1955	893	...	...	177	50	180	1,300
1956	1,111	...	243	232	70	249	1,905
1957	1,118	...	700	547	147	251	2,763
1958	1,153	...	815	394	101	200	2,663
1959	934	...	323	343	132	246	1,978
1960	1,014	...	370	560	311	317	2,572
1961	993	...	684	446	310	307	2,740
1962	1,279	...	1,201	370	282	448	3,580
1963	1,061	...	1,251	468	180	432	3,392
1964	1,258	462	1,113	472	212	458	3,975
1965	974	333	1,469	367	99	562	3,804
1966	756	488	1,319	332	240	391	3,526
1967	825	1,564	1,079	351	180	410	4,409
1968	798	1,279	955	297	70	596	3,995
1969	569	1,632	696	370	30	761	4,058
1970	569	1,931	1,128	601	98	1,127	5,454
1971	491	2,054	931	485	173	2,147	6,281
1972[e]	454	1,746	691	449	117	2,396	5,853
TOTAL	18,010	11,489	14,969	9,452	2,842	12,453	69,214

Source: USDA, Report of the Financial Condition and Operations of Commodity Credit Corporation, annual reports, various years; USDA, Agricultural Statistics, selected issues, various years.

a. Includes payments for all programs diverting acreage from crop production.

b. Includes administrative and research expenses of CCC and miscellaneous programs such as disease eradication, special subsidies, emergency feed grain, etc.

c. Includes the net cost of sale, barter, donation, and distribution of surplus commodities abroad under PL 480 and other programs.

d. Includes all programs distributing surplus commodities, such as school lunch and food stamp, and to institutions and needy persons. In some cases, cash subsidies are included.

e. Preliminary.

TABLE 11.2. U.S. Department of Agriculture budget outlays—fiscal year 1961, 1964–1970, and preliminary 1971, 1972

	1961	1964	1965	1966	1967	1968	1969	1970	1971 Estimates	1972 Estimates
					(million dollars)					
Programs that clearly provide benefits to consumers, businessmen, and the general public:										
Programs having foreign relations and defense aspects, including PL 480	2,138	2,255	1,946	1,817	1,473	1,243	997	962	1,046	994
Food distribution programs, including commodities distributed to the needy, school lunch, and special milk	514	792	693	596	700	900	1,208	1,567	2,777	3,292
REA and FHA repayable loans, and related salaries and expenses	229	300	359	298	192	372	540	338	-109	-28
Long-range programs for the improvement of agricultural and natural resources	923	1,042	1,122	1,170	1,288	1,338	1,229	1,435	1,601	1,567
Total	3,804	4,389	4,120	3,881	3,653	3,853	3,974	4,302	5,315	5,825

Source: Committee on Agriculture, _Food Costs--Food Prices_, U.S. House of Representatives, 91st Cong., 2nd Sess., July 1971.

TABLE 11.2. Continued

	1961	1964	1965	1966	1967	1968	1969	1970	1971 Estimates	1972 Estimates
	(million dollars)									
Programs which are predominantly for stabilization of farm income, but which also benefit others:										
CCC price-support, supply, and related programs	1,111	2,596	2,230	1,211	1,735	2,975	3,891	3,586	2,995	3,284
Cropland adjustment program, adjustment payments	...	...	...	...	44	79	76	75	75	68
Conservation reserve program	351	290	194	151	141	122	107	39	1	...
Federal crop insurance program (net)	-7	-1	1	11	-6	15	7	9	-3	...
Sugar Act program	70	87	92	88	82	84	87	93	88	85
Salaries and expenses for above programs	61	96	151	163	175	176	188	203	231	240
Total	1,586	3,068	2,668	1,624	2,171	3,451	4,356	4,005	3,387	3,677
Grand Total	5,390	7,457	6,788	5,505	5,824	7,304	8,326	8,307	8,702	9,502

programs has substantially increased program costs over earlier years (Table 11.1). The cost of the subsidies totaled more than $69 billion from 1934 to 1972. Of this total, price support and related operations accounted for $44 billion; PL 480 and related disposal programs, $15 billion; and other costs such as interest, wartime subsidies, and emergency programs, $9 billion. The table indicates that there has been a shift from market transactions (loans and purchases) to direct payments and input control (land). There has also been a shift in emphasis on the surplus disposal from using surplus commodities to subsidize foreign consumption to subsidizing domestic consumption.

These are the net costs of government income support activities in agriculture, and they are indirect in that they do not take account of higher food prices. The costs in Table 11.1 also ignore the impact upon other sectors of the economy as well as the secondary effects within agriculture.

A better indication of the magnitude of government programs to assist agriculture and the potential beneficiaries of the programs is illustrated in Table 11.2. This table breaks down the annual appropriations of the USDA into those programs benefiting farmers directly and those which also benefit other sectors of the economy. It indicates that USDA outlays do benefit a broad segment of the population. As can be seen from the table, the nonfarm segment receives a large share of departmental expenditures; however, over time, the share has declined. In 1961 about 70 percent of USDA program outlays were devoted to services and programs providing benefits to the general public, and 30 percent went for price support and other programs in which the farmer was the primary beneficiary. Between 1961 and 1972 total outlays have grown by 76 percent. A substantial proportion of this increase has been devoted to price-support and income-support activities. Except for the last 2 years, the appropriations for the nonfarm sector have remained somewhat constant over the 10-year period while those for the farm sector have doubled. The other thing to notice is that salaries and expenses for these programs have increased rather substantially. Hence, while the number of farms has declined considerably in the past 10 years, the appropriations for price supports, supply management, and related programs have increased, indicating an increasing emphasis upon income support for agriculture.

Since these programs represent substantial investments in agriculture, the question naturally arises as to their impact. The question can be answered on two levels. On the first and simpler level, the answer requires determining what would have been the level of prices and incomes in agriculture without the price-support programs. A number of studies were conducted during the late 1950s and early 1960s to examine this question. Each of the studies estimated that net farm income would have been reduced 25 to 40 percent under its actual levels without the programs.[11] In addition, the studies indicated that year-to-year variation in prices of specific agricultural commodities was reduced by the price-support program.[12] This finding is important because reduced price uncertainty improves the efficiency of resource allocation.

Another aspect of the benefits question is who within agriculture receives the benefits of the programs? Are they equally distributed among all producers according to their need for income support, or do particular groups such as the largest or smallest farmers receive most of the benefits? Table 11.3 casts some light on this question: the farms producing certain commodities are classified by acreage, from small up to very large, and the benefits received by each segment of this hierarchy are computed. For instance, if the 10 largest cotton-producing farms in the United States received 80 percent of all the benefits of the cotton program, this would be of interest since these 10 are obviously a very small fraction of the total number of cotton farms in the United States. Hence, to read Table 11.3, one must keep in mind that we are comparing the proportion of program benefits going to different segments of farmers.

Consider the 1964 cotton program. Columns 3 and 4 reveal that the lower 60 percent of cotton farmers received only 15.1 percent of the program benefits, while the largest 40 percent of the cotton farmers received 84.9 percent of the benefits. For the same program, the lower 20 percent of the farmers growing cotton received only 1.8 percent of the program benefits, while the top 20 percent of the farmers received almost 70 percent of the program benefits. The reader can investigate the distributional attributes of other programs.

The point of the table is that farm programs are tied primarily to factors of production—land and capital. The larger farms have the greater endowment of these factors and hence receive a larger share of program benefits. Those without many factors, and hence those that might require price and income protection the most, receive very few

11. For the specifics of these proposals, see George E. Brandow, *Interrelations among Demands for Farm Products and Implications for Control of Market Supply*, Pa. Agr. Exp. Sta. Bull. 680, University Park, 1961; Legislative Reference Service, Library of Congress, *Farm Programs and Dynamic Forces in Agriculture*, U.S. Senate Committee on Agriculture and Forestry, 89th Cong., 2nd sess. (Washington, D.C.: USGPO, 1965); Geoffrey Shepherd et al., *Production, Prices, and Income Estimates and Projections for the Feed-Livestock Economy*, Iowa Agr. Exp. Sta., Special Rept. 27. Ames, Aug. 1960; Luther G. Tweeten, Earl O. Heady, and Leo V. Mayer, *Farm Program Alternatives, Farm Incomes, and Public Costs under Alternative Commodity Programs for Feed Grains and Wheat*, CAED Rept. 18, Iowa State Univ., Ames, 1963; and USDA, *Projections of Production and Prices of Farm Products for 1960–65 according to Specified Assumptions*, Senate Document 77, 86th Cong., 2nd sess., 1960.

12. The following is a typical study along these lines: Dale E. Hathaway, *How Price Supports Affected the Dry Bean Industry in Michigan*, Special Bull. 399, Mich. Agr. Exp. Sta., East Lansing, Sept. 1955.

TABLE 11.3. Distribution of farm income and various program benefits: Proportion of income or benefits received by various percentiles of farmer beneficiaries

Item	Percent of Benefits Received by the					
	Lower 20% of farmers	Lower 40% of farmers	Lower 60% of farmers	Top 40% of farmers	Top 20% of farmers	Top 5% of farmers
	(1)	(2)	(3)	(4)	(5)	(6)
Farmer and Farm Manager Total Money Income, 1963[a]	3.2	11.7	26.4	73.6	50.5	20.8
Rice, 1963[b]	1.0	5.5	15.1	84.9	65.3	34.6
Wheat, 1964:						
Price supports	3.4	8.3	20.7	79.3	62.3	30.5
Diversion payments	6.9	14.2	26.4	73.6	57.3	27.9
Total benefits[c]	3.3	8.1	20.4	79.6	62.4	30.5
Feed Grains, 1964:						
Price supports	0.5	3.2	15.3	84.7	57.3	24.4
Diversion payments	4.4	16.1	31.8	68.2	46.8	20.7
Total benefits[c]	1.0	4.9	17.3	82.7	56.1	23.9

Source: James Bonnen, The Distribution of Benefits from Selected U.S. Farm Programs, Rural Poverty in the United States, 1968, pp. 461-505.

a. David H. Boyne, Changes in the income distribution in agriculture, J. Farm Econ. 47 (5, Dec. 1965): 1221-22.

b. For price-support benefits.

c. Includes price-support payments and, in wheat, certificate payments as well.

d. For price-support benefits plus government payments.

TABLE 11.3. Continued

Item	Percent of Benefits Received by the					
	Lower 20% of farmers	Lower 40% of farmers	Lower 60% of farmers	Top 40% of farmers	Top 20% of farmers	Top 5% of farmers
	(1)	(2)	(3)	(4)	(5)	(6)
Cotton, 1964[b]	1.8	6.6	15.1	84.9	69.2	41.2
Peanuts, 1964[b]	3.8	10.9	23.7	76.3	57.2	28.5
Tobacco, 1965[b]	3.9	13.2	26.5	73.5	52.8	24.9
Sugarcane, 1965[d]	1.0	2.9	6.3	93.7	83.1	63.2
Sugarbeets, 1965[d]	5.0	14.3	27.0	73.0	50.5	24.4

of the program benefits. It is for this reason that recent legislation has limited payments to farmers to a maximum of $20,000.

The above answers are somewhat superficial in that they ignore the longer-run impacts upon other sectors of the economy, as well as the secondary effects within agriculture. Certainly consumers and marketing firms have also been affected and this has changed their marketing, production, and consumption pattern. Within the farm sector itself, prices may have been higher because of the price supports but the higher prices in turn affect production practices and patterns. The second and more complex response to the above question requires a longer development. We will devote the final section of this chapter to a more detailed examination of some aspects of current government programs in agriculture.

Before proceeding to this, however, another question has undoubtedly been troubling the reader. Specifically, we know from the tools of economic analysis that low returns should cause resources to shift out of agriculture. If this is true, one might logically ask the question as to why the continual downward pressure on farm prices and incomes has not induced farmers to cut back on their production until the the supply of their products is more in line with demand.

NATURE OF AGGREGATE DEMAND AND SUPPLY

The legislation described in the previous section implies an imbalance between the forces of demand and supply. The imbalance is the culmination of many interacting forces, some of which are peculiar to the agricultural firm on the one hand, and others which relate more to the demand for the output. This section will inquire into some of these peculiarities. The industry supply curve is a summation of the marginal cost curves of firms within that industry, hence one must understand the firm's cost function in order to comprehend behavior in the industry. This section will also lay the foundation for a detailed economic analysis of certain aspects of current farm programs and their impact upon the efficiency of resource allocation.

FARM FIRM SUPPLY CURVE

The short-run aggregate supply curve of agriculture is extremely inelastic, meaning that output is relatively unresponsive to changing prices. The primary reason is that the short-run supply curve of the individual farm firm is extremely inelastic. The short run is defined as a production period. This means that the marginal cost curve of the typical farm firm is very steep. From Chapter 7 we know this implies that the farmer's short-run cost situation is such that changes in output price have little impact on output decisions. The major reasons for the highly inelastic marginal cost curve are discussed below.

PRODUCTION: A BIOLOGICAL PROCESS

The statement that production is a biological process means that the natural growth processes involved in agriculture introduce a time lag into the decision process. Once a production decision is made, the farmer can do little to change the output forthcoming in a later period. For example, suppose a farmer has budgeted his farm operation for the year ahead and decided to plant 100 acres of corn, a decision based on his expected prices and costs. Once the 100 acres of corn are planted, the farmer can do very little either to increase or to reduce the total product from that 100 acres. Adding or deleting a cultivation or an application of fertilizer may, at best, change the yield by a few percentage points. Another example is a farmer with a 50-cow dairy herd. Given that he has the 50 cows producing milk, large changes in the price of milk will have little effect on the total output. Given a substantial increase in price, he may employ additional labor to milk the cows more carefully and for, perhaps, 30 seconds longer; or he may decide to give the cows an extra portion of feed. However, the marginal output he obtains in return for the marginal cost he incurs is very small. In other words, the fact that agricultural production is a biological process which, when initiated, can only be changed within certain very narrow limits, means that the short-run marginal cost curve of the individual farm firm for a particular product will be very steep.

The biological nature of production in the agricultural firm also means that progressively larger portions of the total cost of production become sunk or fixed costs as the output decision matures. Once the costs have been incurred, they are transferred from the variable to the fixed cost category. We know that in the short run fixed costs do not influence the optimum level of output. Hence the closer to harvest the less impact a change in output price will have on forthcoming output. Consider, for example, our farmer with 100 acres of corn who has budgeted out his costs as shown in Table 11.4.

Assume that at 100 acres his marginal revenue is equal to his calculated costs of $120 per acre and, consequently, he plants 100 acres of corn. In the spring before he plants his corn, the marginal cost curves will include all his production costs from planting to harvesting as detailed in Table 11.4. However, after the corn has been planted, the $10 of planting costs will no longer be included in his calculations of marginal cost. These are now sunk. Consequently, the farmer's decisions are based upon the added costs necessary to obtain the marginal revenue from that point in time. As long as the farmer calculates the

TABLE 11.4.   Hypothetical per acre costs of corn production by activity and type of cost for a typical farmer, Burbank, U.S.A.

Activity	Approximate Date	Type of Variable Cost			Total
		Supplies	Labor	Equipment	
Planting	May 1	$ 1	$ 4	$ 5	$ 10
Cultivating	May 20		5	5	10
Fertilizing	June 1	19	6	5	30
Cultivating and sidedressing	July 1	25	8	7	40
Harvesting	October 15		12	8	20
Drying			4	6	10
Total		$45	$39	$36	$120

Note: Assumes a yield of 100 bushels per acre.

added costs of carrying the 100 acres through to harvest to be less than the price of the corn, he will not abandon the 100 acres. For example, if after fertilizing, expected marginal revenue falls below $70 per acre, the farmer would find it more profitable to abandon the corn than to harvest it. At harvest time, as long as the returns from corn are expected to be greater than $30, the farmer will harvest the corn, since any return above $30 per acre can be used to offset some of the previously incurred costs of cultivating, fertilizing, etc.

In summary, the fact that agricultural production is biological means that the decision to produce and the output resulting from that decision are separated by a period of time. The period of time ranges from a few weeks in the case of commodities such as broilers or eggs to several years in the case of milk or beef. During this period, the uncommitted costs that are reflected in the marginal cost curve decline as production proceeds. Furthermore, the influence of changes in the level of uncommitted inputs on the level of outputs is negligible. The net result is a steep marginal cost curve for the individual farm firm reflecting substantial difficulty in short-run output response to price changes.

The sharp rise in feed grain and livestock prices in response to a feed grain shortage is a recent example of this phenomenon. A shortage of feed grains developed early in 1973 because of poor weather during the 1972 harvest. This was accentuated by substantial purchases by several foreign countries, which drove up feed prices to livestock producers and led to high meat prices in the spring and summer of 1973. Farmers responded by planting more feed grains but the new harvest did not affect feed prices until late 1973. Consumers were able to see the impact upon meat prices during the summer of 1974 when the livestock producers' response to the high meat prices was reflected in the marketplace.

INPUTS RELATIVELY FIXED

The fact that inputs are relatively fixed means that resources, once committed to agricultural production, tend to remain rather than to move to other uses. They are "sticky" because few alternatives exist either within or outside the industry. The returns that fixed inputs of land and family labor would earn in the next best use are considerably less than their earnings in agriculture. The opportunity cost of these resources is very low if not actually zero. For example, the alternative economic use of wheatland in Kansas is probably nonexistent with current technologies; consequently, a Kansas wheat farmer prefers any positive economic return on his land to a zero return.

As a second example, consider a 55-year-old farmer. His alternative sources of earning a living are also very limited. Studies indicate that farmers change occupations much less frequently than city people change their occupations. Given his lack of expertise outside agriculture, he has very little hope of earning a reasonable income in other occupations. The only jobs open to him would be in some of the menial, unskilled tasks. A young rural youth usually has alternatives. Once he enters farming, however, his alternative opportunities gradually dwindle. By the time he is middle aged he is locked into agriculture because of age, lack of skills, and location. It requires a move from the country to the city in contrast to the same individual in the city where a change in occupation means a move from one place of employment to another. The urban individual's decision does not require him to uproot his family and break all ties with his community. On the other hand, where agricultural inputs do have alternatives, they adjust quite rapidly, as evidenced by the speed with which land and labor move out of agriculture and into the urban industrial uses around the periphery of all large population centers. However, with the exception of land and labor near large cities, nonagricultural uses for agricultural inputs are very limited.

One might logically ask the question, How about alternative uses within agriculture? Granting the assumption that nonagricultural uses of agricultural inputs are fairly restricted, why can't the farmer shift from product A to product B as he sees his returns declining in commodity A? The reason is that inputs are becoming increasingly specialized and hence extremely limited in substitutability. One can certainly feed a field of corn to beef cattle rather than to hogs, or use a dairy barn for feeder steers rather than for dairy cows, but it is not feasible to use a dairy barn for a broiler-egg enterprise. Furthermore, the rapid advances in technology frequently require more and more specialized capital equipment. Consequently, the corn picker cannot be used for harvesting soybeans, a soybean combine cannot be used for sorghum, dairy equipment cannot be used for hogs, etc.

The alternatives available to a given farm firm are continually declining. As the amount of investment in specialized equipment continues to climb, the ability of the individual farm firm to move from one type of farm enterprise to another diminishes. Tables 11.5 and 6.4 illustrate the growth in specialization. From Table 11.5 one can observe a rapid decline in the number of farms reporting a specific product and a rather large increase in product per farm. For example, in 1949, 1.6 million farms reported harvesting apples. On the average they harvested 4,047 pounds per farm. Fifteen years later, in 1964, the number of farms reporting apples dropped over 90 percent to 112,000 farms, but the pounds harvested per farm increased twelvefold to over 51,600 pounds. All other products in the table show the same sharp drop in number reporting and increases in average product per farm. Table 6.4 portrays the concomitant growth in capital requirements accompanying the growth in firm specialization. Although the data are not on exactly the same products as in Table 11.5, nor for the same time span, there is sufficient overlap to demonstrate the relationship. In most types of farms, it is clear that capital investment has more than doubled over the 10-year period 1957–59 to 1968.

In summary, increasing specialization of resources has reduced their flexibility and hence decreased the individual farm firm's ability to respond to changes in product prices in the intermediate run. Once the decision to become a dairy farmer or a corn, hog, or beef farmer has been made, the decision as to the amounts of capital, labor, and land associated with the most economic-sized unit has also simultaneously been made. Table 6.4 also illustrates a second facet of the resource-fixity problem in agriculture. The $100,000 to $300,000 of capital required to undertake a modern farm operation represent a substantial proportion of the average total cost of producing a commodity. To the entrepreneur these are fixed costs and do not directly influence short-run production decisions. The high fixed costs mean that changes in product prices may have little impact on profit-maximizing output levels because the major portion of the costs included in the average total cost curve for a particular enterprise is the fixed costs of land, family labor, and capital.

The important point is that fixed costs represent a substantial proportion of a firm's total costs. Furthermore, the entrepreneur is continually reevaluating the opportunity costs of these assets in light of how he views the economic climate around him. In an earlier chapter, the fixed-asset theory was developed to illustrate how the portion of the marginal cost curve below average total cost increases as the salvage value of an asset declines. Thus the portion of the MC curve above AVC

TABLE 11.5. Number of farms reporting selected agricultural products and average per farm, United States, 1949, 1959, and 1964.

Product	Unit of Output	1949-50[a]		1959		1964	
		Number of farms[b]	Average per farm	Number of farms[b]	Average per farm	Number of farms[b]	Average per farm
Apples	Pounds harvested	1,557	4,047	185	31,359	112	51,644
Peaches	Pounds harvested	1,102	2,415	144	22,852	81	26,643
Oranges	Pounds harvested	31	121,234	24	206,067	19	223,246
Cattle and Calves	Number sold	2,983	12	2,304	22	1,991	32
Hogs and Pigs	Number sold	2,099	31	1,273	64	803	104
Milk	Pounds sold	1,097	62,546	770	126,725	545	197,179
Eggs	Dozens sold	2,422	996	1,067	3,119	526	8,133
Corn	Bushels harvested	3,202	868	1,990	1,858	1,383	2,431
Wheat	Bushels harvested	1,148	877	931	1,134	740	1,646
Soybeans	Bushels harvested	370	575	500	1,032	560	1,195
Cotton	Bales harvested	1,111	19	509	27	324	45

Source: U.S. Dept. of Commerce, Bureau of Census, Reports on Census of Agriculture 1949, 1959, 1964.

a. 1950 for fruits; 1949 for all other commodities.

b. Thousands of farms.

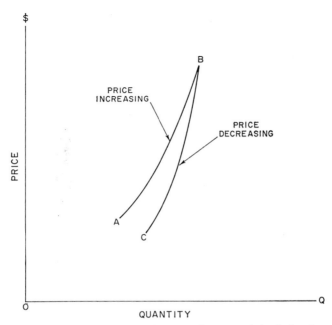

FIG. 11.8. A supply-response curve for an industry with high fixed costs.

is constantly changing. When farm prices rise, the farmer acquires more specialized assets and output increases in response to price increases. When prices fall, the entrepreneur devalues his fixed assets and output is not reduced. Thus we observe that large declines in price do not affect output in the short run, even when the price is demonstrably below ATC of production. This implies that the industry's response to price increases will be larger than to price decreases as illustrated in Figure 11.8. Evidence for this view of agricultural supply response is reinforced by the next major characteristic of agriculture.

FARMING AS A WAY OF LIFE

The farmer generally views farming not only as an economic activity (production) but also as a way of life (consumption). He tends to confuse his role as a manager, as a laborer, and as a capitalist with individual and personal values and goals. As a consequence, the individual agricultural entrepreneur includes in his decisions factors other than profit maximization.

The individual entrepreneur (farmer) in agriculture not only provides most of the labor and management for his firm but also a substantial portion of its capital and land resources. In the farm firm these resources are generally the residual claimant on income. For example, suppose that the farmer in Table 11.4 had anticipated total gross returns of $160 per acre when he made his decision to plant 100 acres of corn. In his calculations he estimated an 8 percent return on his capital and $2.50 per hour for his labor. However, by harvest time the price of corn has dropped to the point that he has a margin of $10 per acre after paying all of his variable costs. Out of this he must pay himself for his own capital and labor. On recalculating his returns, he finds the actual returns on his investment to be 2 percent and his labor to be priced at $0.85 per hour. Ordinarily, economic theory would indicate that since his actual capital returns were substantially less than the 6 percent he could have earned by selling his farm and putting the money in a savings account, the resources should move out of agriculture. However, since the farmer attaches an intrinsic value to farming as a way of life, he accepts the lower returns in order to stay on the farm. If the capital were owned by someone other than the farmer, or he were being paid for his labor by someone else, he would leave the farm to seek higher returns elsewhere.

Economic decisions are diluted by social values, judgments, and personal goals which place a high value upon owning one's own farm. The farmer seems to be peculiar in this respect. Agriculture is perhaps one of the last segments of our economy in which ownership and management still reside in the same individual or group. In few other segments of our private enterprise system can one find as many individually owned and operated firms. Considering that the capital requirements are very substantial, amounting to more than $200,000 in many instances, it is remarkable to observe farmers substantially reducing their standard of living in order to accumulate the needed capital to own their own farms. In other sectors, the entrepreneur does not hesitate to tap other sources of capital via incorporation and stock sales, partnerships, etc. The farmer's preference for sole ownership and his willingness to accept a low return on his labor and capital to preserve this independence means that a substantial block of resources does not readily respond to price changes.

The above three factors all contribute to the inelasticity of the marginal cost curve of an individual farm firm. Summing over all farm firms, therefore, leads one to an aggregate supply curve for food and fiber which is also very inelastic. Generally, the elasticity of the aggregate supply curve for agriculture is estimated to fall between 0.0 and 0.3 within any production period. This means that a 1 percent change in price will result in only 0.3 percent change in output. In a longer period of time, which takes into account the biological nature of the adjustment process, the supply elasticity is estimated at 0.4—still highly inelastic. The supply elasticity for individual commodities tends to be slightly higher than for groups of commodities, but on the whole these supply elasticities are also in the inelastic range.

The above discussion leads to what appears to be a logical dilemma. On the one hand, the aggregate supply curves for agricultural commodities are highly inelastic, yet we saw that agriculture has responded to the post–World War II price-support programs with ever-increasing quantities of output. The dilemma is that on the one hand it appears that farmers do not respond to price changes, yet the available data indicate that over time there have been substantial responses. The next subsection describes the farmer's response over time and resolves the apparent dilemma in terms of the theoretical concepts that have been developed earlier.

AGGREGATE SUPPLY CURVE

Farm numbers have been declining steadily since before World War II. Based on the economic theory of supply, one would expect that the declining numbers of farms would be reflected in an aggregate supply curve shifting to the left at a fairly steady rate. In reality, this is not the case. Increases in gross farm income representing increases in output have more than compensated for the decline in numbers. This is illustrated in Figure 11.9.

Agricultural output has increased fivefold since 1870. In 1870 one agricultural worker fed himself and 5 other people; today he feeds himself and 47 other people. This is the key to both our strength and our concern. In spite of weather, wars, declining farm population, or efforts to limit its growth, agricultural output has grown at an annual rate of about 2 percent. Although 2 percent per year does not seem very high, it means that output doubles in 35 years. In considerable part this has been achieved through the tremendous technological change that has taken place on the farm and because of the increasing specialization of the typical farm firm. Many tasks that were formerly performed by the producer are now performed elsewhere. The net result is a tremendous gain in productivity. As we saw in Chapters 5, 6, and 7, productivity gains in a firm are reflected in a shifting supply function.

Figure 11.9 depicts a steady downward trend in the number of farms in the United States since the mid-1930s. In 1935 there were approximately 6.8 million farms in the United States and the number had decreased to 3.0 million farms in 1968. While farm numbers have been declining, total aggregate farm output as represented by gross farm income (gross income less production expenses) has been increasing steadily. Over the entire period represented by the chart, the growth in aggregate gross farm output is substantial. For instance, gross farm income was $7.6 billion in 1910, while—with the exception of the drastic drop during the Depression years and the short-run declines from the peak levels attained during World War II and the Korean War—gross farm income has grown steadily to $56.5 billion in 1970. Particularly impressive is the growth since 1940. Notice also that the growth

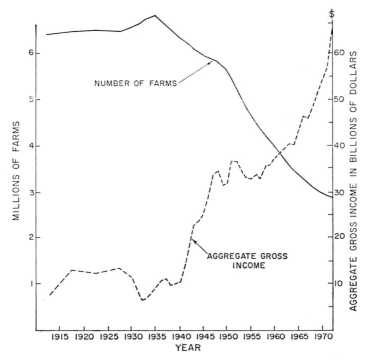

FIG. 11.9. Total farm numbers and aggregate gross agricultural income, United States, 1910–1972. (From USDA, **Farm Income Situation July 1973** and earlier years, Washington, D.C.: USGPO, July 1973 and earlier years, Tables 1H and 3H.)

has not been at a steady pace. It has proceeded in fits and starts with little income growth in the second and third decades of the century, rapid growth during the first two-thirds of the 1940s, a much slower pace in the late 1940s and early 1950s, and a much more rapid pace thereafter.

Figure 11.10 compares gross and net farm incomes, and reveals that an increasing proportion of the value of the farmers' output is left in other sectors of the economy. The figure indicates that while overall growth in agricultural production has been approximately 2 percent per year, net farm income has not changed as rapidly. Up until the end of World War II, net farm income followed the same path as gross farm income. Since that time it has leveled off at approximately $14 to $16 billion per year. The growing difference between gross and net incomes is being absorbed by production expenses, reflecting the technological advances taking place in the industry and the shift of many of the production activities off the farm.

Table 11.6 illustrates in greater detail the changes that have

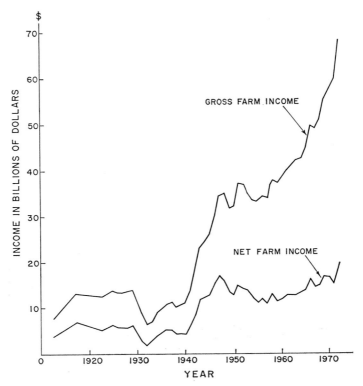

FIG. 11.10. Gross and net aggregate farm income, United States, 1910–1972. (From USDA, **Farm Income Situation**, Washington, D.C.: USGPO, July 1973, Table 1H.)

taken place since the beginning of World War II. Gross farm income has increased approximately 150 percent between the 1941–1945 and the 1966–1970 periods. Gross farm income includes the gross receipts from commercial market sales plus government payments to farmers for programs such as the soil bank and the agricultural conservation and wool programs, plus the value of farm produce consumed directly by the farmer and his family and of housing provided by the farm dwelling.

After deducting farm-operating expenses from gross farm income and adjusting for inventory changes (to account for products produced in the year but not sold), the remainder is farm operators' total net income. Columns 3 and 4 of Table 11.6 indicate that total net farm operator income has not grown very rapidly since the end of World War II. Much of this stability is because production expenses have more than tripled over the same period, growing from $10.8 billion in 1941–1945 to $36.8 billion in 1966–1970. Production expenses include all farm-operating expenses incurred in the production of agricultural com-

TABLE 11.6. A comparison of aggregate gross and net farm income for U.S. agriculture, selected periods 1941–1970

| Period | Average Annual Value of | | | |
	Gross farm income[a]	Production expenses[a]	Net farm income[a]	Total farm income[b]
	(1)	(2)	(3)	(4)
		(billion dollars)		
1941-45	$21.2	$10.8	$10.4	$10.4
1946-50	32.7	17.6	15.1	14.9
1951-55	36.1	22.0	14.0	13.6
1956-60	36.5	24.7	11.8	12.0
1961-65	42.2	29.2	13.0	13.3
1966-70	52.6	36.8	15.8	15.9

Source: USDA, ERS, Farm Income Situation, July 1973, Table 6, 1H, 2H.

a. Including government payments.

b. Net farm income adjusted for inventory changes.

modities. Both variable costs and fixed costs, such as taxes, depreciation, and interest on the farm mortgage debt, are included in operating expenses.

The rapid increase in production expenses is a good indicator of the basic changes that are taking place in agricultural production techniques. With less labor, the same amount of land, and large increases in purchased inputs, the farmer has been able to outpace the increase in the demand for his product. Irrespective of how output or production is measured, the conclusion remains the same; output per man-hour or per unit of land (Figure 11.11) has grown substantially.

The increase in output per unit of input reflects the new technologies, and technological advance is not a simple concept. Sometimes a simple practice or device can lead to a larger output. More frequently one new machine, method, or variety leads the way for the adoption of a whole bundle of new tools, practices, or procedures. It is this total combination which has generally led to the large increases in agricultural output. Greater use of hybrid seed corn, improved varieties of other crops, as well as new and better pesticides and insecticides, have added much to crop yields. More important, however, is the fact that the new varieties made possible the utilization of much higher levels of fertilization, plant populations per acre, and mechanical harvesting equipment. Low-cost fertilizer in relation to the prices of other agricul-

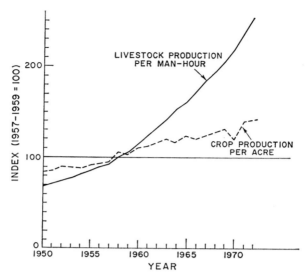

FIG. 11.11. Growth in farm production per unit of input for crops and livestock, United States, 1950–1970. (From USDA, ERS, **Changes in Farm Production and Efficiency,** Stat. Bull 233, Washington, D.C.: USGPO, 1971, pp. 8, 27.)

tural commodities has generated much of the increase depicted in Figure 11.11. Greater use of fertilizer is one of the main reasons for the upward trend in crop production per acre. Fertilizer use in agriculture is now nearly six times greater than in the early 1940s. The improvement in livestock and poultry breeds and in management systems accounts for a large proportion of the increase in livestock productivity. Developing strains of livestock that can more effectively utilize feeds, plus heavier feeding of better balanced rations, have increased livestock production per breeding unit. These factors, when combined with the very spectacular growth in farm mechanization, explain most of the growth in farm output.

As regards mechanization, the number of tractors on farms more than doubled between 1945 and 1965; farm trucks have also increased in about the same proportion. Originally the substitution of purchased inputs for labor was the result of the increasing cost of labor. In the process, farmers became conditioned to seek out new technologies for competitive reasons. The substitution began during World War II when the price of labor was high relative to the price of capital and land. For any given production surface, the higher price for labor meant that profit-maximizing farmers substituted capital for labor until the ratio of the value of the marginal product (VMP) of labor to capital was equal to the ratio of the prices of the two factors. This is illustrated in part a of Figure 11.12 where I_0 is an isoquant for a particular production

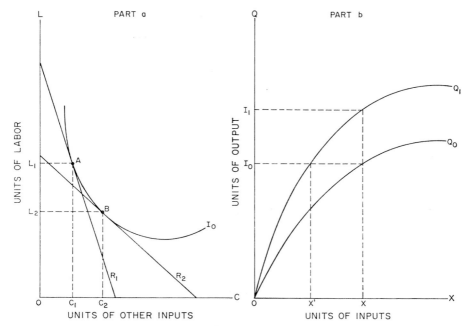

FIG. 11.12. The effects of changes in input prices on input utilization.

surface and R_1 the pre–World War II price-ratio line. The profit-maximizing farmer would be using L_1 units of labor and C_1 units of other inputs. However, during World War II the shortage of manpower drove the price of labor up and the price line shifted to R_2. Given the new relative prices, point B on the old isoquant became the cost-minimizing combination of labor and other inputs to maintain former production levels. The net result is that the farmer uses less labor and more capital to produce I_0 units of output.

Eventually, the substitution of other inputs for labor conditioned farmers to seek out new methods of production for their output-increasing or cost-reducing advantages during periods of low agricultural prices. This is also illustrated in Figure 11.12 (part b). The substitution of capital for labor embodies technological change. The farmer, in purchasing the labor-saving devices, not only substitutes capital for labor but substitutes a new technology for an old one. This in turn shifts the production function upward as illustrated in part b of Figure 11.12. The net result is an increase in output from I_0 to I_1 with the same resources (X), or the same output (I_0) with fewer total resources than previously (X').

World War II and the Korean War also had other less direct impacts upon the supply of agricultural labor. They facilitated the out-migration of the younger residents from rural areas. The draft uprooted young males, transferred them to other areas and, in the process, frequently provided them with training in other occupations. This weakened the linkage with their old communities, making it easier for them to move into nonagricultural occupations. This also helped to keep labor prices high after the war ended.

During the 1950s and into the 1960s, the process of technological advance continued because competitive pressures and low prices forced farmers to continually search for new cost-reducing technologies. The new technologies shift the aggregate supply of agricultural products continually and irreversibly to the right. This shifting aggregate supply is the crux of the agricultural problem.

DYNAMIC NATURE OF AGGREGATE SUPPLY

In the previous section we saw that the farmer originally adopted new technologies in response to a change in the relative prices of inputs. These new technologies have almost invariably resulted in reducing per-unit costs of production but have also led to larger-size firms. Agriculture is an industry in which there are in general substantial economies of scale. Consider Figure 11.13.

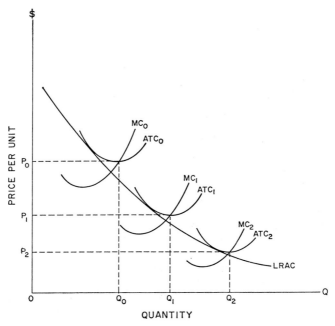

FIG. 11.13.   Long-run average cost curve and short-run average total cost curves of a typical farm firm.

Prior to great advances in technology, we might envision the output of a typical farm as Q_0, with per-unit costs of production of P_0. As technology is introduced, it has permitted the typical farm to expand production along its long-run average cost curve *(LRAC)*. While each new technology has the potential of reducing the per-unit production cost, the competitive nature of the industry mandates adoption, but adoption results in greater output. As the short-run average total cost curves shift out along the *LRAC* curve, marginal cost does likewise. This means that the aggregate supply curve also shifts to the right. If prices in any year are extremely good, such as in 1973, there is often a significant increase in the acquisition of capital equipment and, allowing time for lags, a subsequent rightward shift in the aggregate supply curve for the various commodities as depicted in Figure 11.14.

Now consider Figure 11.15. Here the supply curves for the four time periods depicted in Figure 11.14 are shown with a series of aggregate demand curves for the same commodity. Notice that the rightward shift in aggregate supply is not matched by an equal rightward shift in aggregate demand, with the resultant implication of a falling price.

Because of the inelasticity of marginal cost, short-run price declines do not bring about much decrease in output. The resources which are committed when prices are favorable do not move out of agri-

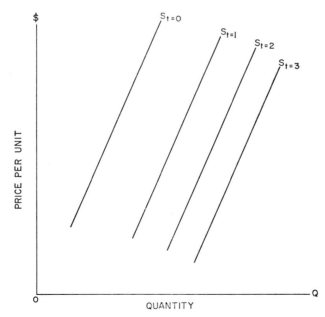

FIG. 11.14. Aggregate supply curves for a specific commodity at four points in time.

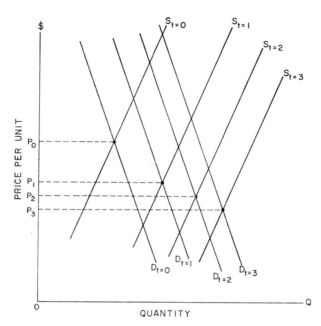

FIG. 11.15. Aggregate supply and demand over time for agricultural commodities.

culture. The farmers caught in this cost-price squeeze are also forced to adopt the innovation to maintain their incomes or be forced out of agriculture. When aggregate demand, which is increasing at a rate consistent with increases in population and incomes, has shifted to the right far enough to remove some of the downward price pressure, the cycle begins again and the aggregate supply curve again shifts rightward, initiating the cycle all over. This is the concept of the agricultural treadmill developed by W. W. Cochrane.[13] It grows out of the view that both the aggregate demand for and supply of agricultural commodities are extremely inelastic. Before turning to the details of the treadmill concept, a few comments on the nature of the demand for agricultural commodities are required.

If the aggergate demand for food were elastic, the agricultural problem would perhaps not exist, or at least it would take on different attributes. If this were the case, as the supplies of food and fiber produced by farmers increased, the prices received by farmers might decline slightly, but total revenues would increase—both in the aggregate and to the individual farmer. But the aggregate demand for food is extremely inelastic. Numerous empirical studies at various times and for various

13. Willard W. Cochrane, *Farm Prices: Myth and Reality* (Minneapolis: Univ. Minn. Press, 1958).

levels of demand (that is retail, farm, domestic, export) all indicate inelastic demands for both individual and aggregate agricultural products. The relatively low price elasticity of demand means that small increases in aggregate supply lead to large price decreases and also decreases in total revenue. The price elasticity for food is generally considered to be on the order of -0.20 to -0.25. This extreme inelasticity stems from two facts:

1. Food is a necessity; consequently, price changes do not affect the quantity consumed.
2. Consumers spend a relatively small portion of their income for food and are thus relatively insensitive to changes in its price.[14]

In the above circumstances, with no change in demand, a 5 percent increase in the aggregate supply for food will require approximately a 20 percent reduction in price in order for the total product to clear the market.

All would still be well if the aggregate demand for food products were shifting to the right at a pace rapid enough to offset increases in aggregate supply. Unfortunately for the United States farmer, this is not the case. Changes in aggregate demand are due primarily to changes in population, per capita disposable income, and export demand. Since the capacity of the human stomach is limited, the United States consumer uses increases in income to substitute better foods for ordinary fare (such as steaks for hamburger). Because, in general, the quantity of food consumed remains unchanged, the income elasticity of demand for food at the farm level is extremely low.[15] Growing per capita incomes cause the aggregate demand for food to shift to the right at a very slow pace. For example, if the income elasticity of demand for food is 0.20, this means that a 5 percent increase in income of a typical American consumer will shift his demand for food to the right by only 1 percent.

The prime shifter of the aggregate demand curve for agricultural products is population growth. In the United States, population is expanding at approximately 1 percent per year, shifting the demand curve to the right at that rate. If it were not for population growth, the United States would soon reach the point where the demand curve for food at the farm level would not shift at all.

14. There is some recent evidence to the contrary. The high food prices during the summer of 1973 have raised more than a little concern on the part of consumers. This may be a short-run reaction that will not be reflected in a change in their expenditure patterns. Alternatively, the higher food prices will increase the proportion of a consumer's income spent on food. At the higher percentage, the consumer may be more sensitive to price changes.

15. It is important to remember that this is the income elasticity at the farm level. The income elasticity for the marketing services attached to farm products is much higher. Hence, the retail income elasticity of demand for food is much higher. See Chapter 8 for a discussion of the effect of marketing charges on elasticities.

TABLE 11.7. Example of the impact of changes in the retail value of farm foods on the farm value
under a constant marketing margin

| | Period | | Percent Change |
	First	Second	
	(billion dollars)		
Retail Value	$30	$27	-10%
Marketing Charges	17	17	0
Farm Value	$13	$10	-23%

When the effects of income change and population growth are added together, it is estimated that aggregate demand is expanding at the rate of 1.7 percent per year. In contrast, aggregate supply is shifting to the right at the rate of 2.6 percent per year. The net effect is illustrated in Figure 11.15.

From previous chapters, the reader is already familiar with the concept of a derived demand. The linkages that operate between the farm and the retail level amplify small changes in retail prices into much larger changes at the farm level. Consequently, the small swings in retail prices and incomes result in large swings in farm prices and incomes. Table 11.7 illustrates the problem.

Suppose that in the first period consumers spent $30 billion for agricultural commodities. Suppose further that a new technology results in a small shift of the aggregate supply curve. With an inelastic demand curve, prices fall and consumers now spend $27 billion for food in period two. This is a reduction, at the retail level, of 10 percent. Assuming that marketing costs in these two periods of time do not change, farm revenues would decrease from $13 billion to $10 billion in the second period—a decrease of 23 percent; a 10 percent reduction in gross income at the retail level reduces income at the farm level by 23 percent. Conversely, increases at the retail level are also amplified at the farm level. This introduces further irregularities into the shifting aggregate supply function. During periods of high prices, innovating farmers have the profits and thus the capital to adopt more efficient production methods. In periods of low prices they face substantially reduced incomes.

In summary, the performance goal society has set for agriculture is an adequate supply of food and fiber at reasonable prices. It has designed and implemented policies and programs that modify structure, conduct, and performance so as to achieve it. The competitive market structure that results has encouraged farmers to meet the growth in demand for food and fiber resulting from increases in population and consumer buying power. The situation is summarized in Table 11.8. Total farm output increased about 12 percent each of the three decades

TABLE 11.8. Changes in farm employment, cropland used in crops, farm output and total population, and per capita income, United States, selected years 1870–1970

Year	Farm Employment Number (million)	Farm Employment Percent change[a]	Percent Change[a] in Cropland	Percent Change[a] in Farm output	Total Population Number (million)	Total Population Percent change[a]	Income Per capita dollars	Income Percent change[a]
1870	8.0				39.9			
1880	10.1	26	52	55	50.3	26	NA	
1890	11.7	16	30	19	63.1	25	NA	
1900	12.8	10	29	30	76.1	21	189	
1910	13.6	6	4	4	92.4	21	292	54
1920	13.4	-1	11	12	106.5	15	672	130
1930	12.5	-7	4	13	123.1	16	605	-10
1940	11.0	-12	-4	11	132.1	7	573	-5
1950	9.9	-10	3	25	151.7	15	1364	138
1960	7.1	-28	-7	21	179.3	12	1937	42
1970	4.2	-41	-5	16	203.7	14	3366	74

Source: 1870–1960, W. W. Cochrane, The City Man's Guide to the Farm Problem (Minneapolis: Univ. Minn. Press, 1965), p. 75; 1970 and earlier years, USDA, Handbook of Agriculture Charts.

a. Percentage change from previous decade.

NA = Not available.

following 1910; 25 percent in the 1950s, 21 percent in the 1960s, and 16 percent in the 1970s. The growth in the 1950s and 1960s was attenuated by specific government programs designed to slow down the rate of growth in agricultural output. Nevertheless, in each decade since 1930, output expansion has been greater than demand growth as powered by the increase in population, per capita income, and foreign demand. This has taken place while farm employment, farm numbers, and cropland have been declining. In return, current price-support programs provide partial compensation to farmers for the economic losses they experience under a national policy of excess capacity. Obviously, not all policies are internally consistent. On the one hand, public policy is aimed at achieving an efficient allocation of resources by promoting structure and conduct which approaches the competitive norm. As an industry, agriculture is probably as competitive as any in the United States. The individual farmer, realizing that he cannot affect market price, continually strives to increase output even though he knows that collectively his actions will create excess output, low prices, and low incomes. On the other hand, the price-support programs which compensate farmers for losses they sustain in such a market environment also operate through the marketplace. The price signals these programs generate have distorted resource allocations. In the process they have also treated agriculture as a homogeneous sector of our economy when it is really heterogeneous. Thus the programs which were viewed as benefiting all farmers have benefited some farmers much more than others.

COMMERCIAL FARM PROBLEM: EXCESS RESOURCES

As was indicated in Chapter 3, there are at least two views of American agriculture. One view is that of the large, very efficient commercial farm which epitomizes the very best of the free-enterprise entrepreneurship we think of as existing in this country. The other view is that of the very small, undercapitalized farm, struggling to stay in operation. Before discussing the farm problem, it would seem well to restate some of the findings presented in Chapter 3.

A study of the data in Table 11.9 indicates that a small portion of the approximately 2.9 million farms in the United States produce substantially all the food and fiber moving through the marketing system. Each of some 1,054,000 farmers annually sells more than $10,000 worth of products. These farmers represent only 37 percent of all farmers, yet sell over 90 percent of all the food and fiber marketed in the United States. As we shall see, it is these farmers who have the production and income problems that we commonly include in the term *the farm problem*. These are the farmers who have pushed total farm output ahead

TABLE 11.9.   Number, average net farm income per farm family, percentage distribution of sales and farms by value of sales
class, United States, 1972

Farms with Sales of	Number of Farms		Percent of Sales	Average Net Income per Farm Family[a]
	Total	Percent of total		
	(thousand)			
$20,000 and over	701	24.4	81.2	$20,138
$10,000-$19,999	353	12.3	9.2	6,736
$5,000-$9,999	359	12.5	4.8	3,533
$2,500-$4,999	420	14.6	2.7	1,929
Less than $2,500	1,037	36.2	2.1	1,061
All Farms	2,870	100.0	100.0	

Source: USDA, ERS, Farm Income Situation, July 1973, Tables 1D,
3D.

a.   Includes direct government payments but excludes nonfarm income.

at a faster pace than demand requirements for food and fiber. This
group of farms we shall term *commercial farms.*

On the other extreme are the low-production farms; those
whose operators sell less than $5,000 of output annually. Some 1.5 mil-
lion farms, representing more than 50 percent of the total, fall in this
category. In total they market about 5 percent of all the food and fiber.
In 1972 the average farm income of this group was approximately $1,300
per farm. Many of the farms in this class are part-time residential or
retirement farms, and many do not depend upon agriculture as their
sole source of income. However, a sizable number of these farms has
only farm-derived income and the policy problem for this group presents
a different dilemma than for the commercial farms.

The economic class of farms $5,000 to $9,999 contains the remaining farmers. This class of farms is comprised primarily of full-time
farmers who are mainly dependent upon agriculture for their livelihood.
Almost 360,000 farms fall in this class. This group of farms is actually
not large enough to be considered truly commercial farms; they are on
the border line. These farms have been described as being "in transition."
Some farms in this group will be successful and move into the top two
categories of Table 11.9. Others will be unable to compete and will fall
into the smaller economic class. While all farmers in this group depend
upon the sale of agricultural products for a major portion of their income, most of them had insufficient resources in 1972 to earn a reason-

able living for themselves and their families; off-farm employment frequently provided supplemental income.

Table 11.10 illustrates the nature of the income differential between these farm sizes. In 1972 the average net income of farmers selling more than $20,000 annually was $28,886 of which $5,132 or 18 percent was from nonfarm sources. The importance of nonfarm income in total income increases consistently and substantially as the size of average farm sales declines. For farms with less than $5,000 of sales per year, nonfarm income comprises 84 percent of total income. Furthermore, the total income of the smaller farms is quite low considering the labor and capital resources these farms employ. Notice also that this group of farms obtains a very small income supplement from government farm programs (3 percent of total income). In contrast, farms selling $10,000 or more per year obtained 13 to 14 percent of their income in direct government payments. This illustrates a point made earlier that government programs are essentially market oriented and the operators of small farms sell very little in the marketplace.

In summary, there are two distinct groups of farmers. One group, comprising approximately one-third of all farms, is highly productive, and the farms have high levels of sales and incomes. The other group, comprising approximately 50 percent of all farms, contains the very small farms with low incomes. There is also a transition group of farmers between these two groups. The characteristics of the two groups are completely different, as are their problems and possible solutions. In the following we concentrate on the commercial farms, defined as those with $10,000 or more of annual sales; it is this group that receives over 60 percent of all direct government payments and indirect benefits of government income support programs.

TABLE 11.10. Comparison of farm family income by value of sales and type of income, United States, 1972

| Sales Class | Average Income per Farm Family | | | | Percent of Total | |
	Farm	Government payments	Nonfarm	Total	Government payments	Nonfarm
$20,000 and over	$20,138	$3,616	$5,132	$28,886	13	18
$10,000-$19,999	6,736	1,694	3,892	12,322	14	32
$5,000-$9,999	3,533	978	5,568	10,079	8	55
Less than $5,000	1,311	327	8,528	10,166	3	84

Source: USDA, ERS, Farm Income Situation, July 1973, Tables 3D-6D.

EXCESS CAPACITY

Estimation of our capacity to overproduce varies from 1 to 14 percent of current levels. In a 1966 study, Daly and Egbert state that "farm output can more than keep pace with population growth and other factors expanding the domestic demand for farm products in the next 10 to 15 years. It can also keep pace with an export expansion during the next 10 years . . . and still leave around 10 percent of the cropland resource idle."[16] Tyner and Tweeten, using several different measures of excess capacity, reach the same conclusion. They estimate excess capacity in the 1955 to 1962 period to range from zero to 13.5 percent, depending upon the assumptions made.[17] As for the future, Heady predicts that by 1975 United States agriculture will have an excess capacity of nearly 73 million acres, implying that we can produce the domestic and foreign food and fiber needs with 73 million less acres.[18] As an indicator of the magnitude of excess resources in agriculture, note that if all the farms with less than $10,000 in annual sales (approximately two-thirds of all farms) ceased production immediately total output would decrease by about 11 percent—less than the estimates of excess capacity.

Other sectors of the United States economy also face the problems associated with the rapidly expanding technological base without also encountering the problems of relatively low per capita income. One explanation is that in those highly capitalized industries there is also a higher degree of market concentration, and hence an ability to control supply. In less concentrated industries (more like farming), there is not the history of federal programs to impede the exit of redundant resources. Hence, while farm programs have aided farmers, they also have dampened the tendency for resource mobility in the face of falling prices.

In summary, one might say that the problems of commercial agriculture arise because of at least four interrelated circumstances:

1. The market organization and structure within which farmers sell their products.
2. The inelasticity of the aggregate demand for food.
3. The high value that American society places on scientific research and technological development.
4. The immobility of resources committed to agricultural production in shifting to alternative enterprises.

16. R. F. Daly and A. C. Egbert, A look ahead for food and agriculture, *Agr. Econ. Research,* Jan. 1966, pp. 1–9.
17. Fred Tyner and Luther Tweeten, Excess capacity in U.S. agriculture, *Agr. Econ. Research,* Jan. 1964, pp. 23–31.
18. E. O. Heady, Potential Shifts in Commercial Agriculture Relative to Technological Change: Policies for Long-Run Solution to Surplus Problems, *Our Stake in Commercial Agriculture, Rural Poverty and World Trade,* CAED Rept. 22, Iowa State Univ., Ames, Jan. 1965, pp. 17–30.

These, in turn, create conditions which can be summarized as follows:

1. A generous publicly supported research and development program which effectively turns out new and improved technological practices year in and year out.
2. The widespread adoption of these innovations by farmers, resulting in sustained increases in aggregate output of farm products.
3. These expanding supplies continually press downward on agricultural prices. This downward pressure in farm prices does not put a brake on agricultural supply because resources employed in farming, once committed, move very slowly in response to changes in price level.

The presence of excess capacity need not necessarily be viewed as a serious problem. Our reserve productive capacity could be very useful in periods of national emergencies. The problem is that excess resources mean low resource returns. Low returns create an intolerable income gap between the agricultural and nonagricultural sectors and mean an inefficient allocation of resources. Hence the real problem is excess resources that are immobile. Recent events have changed somewhat the extent of excess capacity in U.S. agriculture. More is said about this on p. 433.

Many proposals have been advanced to solve the farm problem. Most are aimed at offsetting low returns by raising farm incomes rather than facilitating the transference of resources out of agriculture. More direct policies aimed at the resource immobility problem have at times been suggested. Examples are programs to slow the rate of technological advance in agriculture by placing a special tax or limit on inputs such as fertilizer. These programs have received little support because of the intolerable inefficiencies they would create. Other proposals include government subsidized programs to retrain rural labor, particularly the farm youth, to equip them for nonagricultural employment. Another suggestion has involved government grants to assist farmers in moving from the farm to alternative nonfarm places of employment. Those which have been or are now in operation were described in the first section of this chapter. Essentially they are all variations on three approaches: (1) expand the aggregate demand for farm products, (2) adjust farm production through input controls, or (3) establish income support programs at levels above those established by the intersection of aggregate demand and supply. Each of these proposals will be examined in more detail in the following section.

COMMERCIAL AGRICULTURAL POLICY

In any discussion of government programs for a sector of the economy, the question of guidelines and principles for government policy becomes important. An economic sector is not isolated and policy for it must be consistent with the general goals of the society. Agricultural programs and policies must be consistent with the national goals of free economic growth. This means that they must include a rate of growth in the output of agricultural commodities that at least meets or exceeds the rate of population growth. The nation also seeks to provide economic opportunities for all so that each individual can realize his full potential. Policy also seeks full use of all resources and tries to direct them to their best uses. Another national goal for agriculture is flexibility in production and marketing so that adaptation to changing consumer demands and international markets is facilitated. The nation should encourage the adoption of new technology but should also stand ready to assist when the introduction of this new technology causes economic changes and hardships for certain groups.

In 1966 President Johnson appointed the National Advisory Commission on Food and Fiber to investigate all aspects of United States farm policy. The commission issued a report in 1967 that was intended as a guide for future decisions and policies in agriculture. The report of the advisory commission asks the following questions of agricultural policy:

1. Do the American people get the kinds and quantities of food and fiber they wish at reasonable prices?
2. Is the industry efficient or does agriculture take too many resources away from other types of production?
3. Are the people who are supplying the food and fiber reasonably well off or does the industry contain substantial numbers of people who fall below the income standard necessary for a decent living and an opportunity for human development?

In essence, the commission argued that future agricultural policy should be tied less to land. This is because land is becoming less of a limiting factor in production. Also, it was the position of the commission that progressive policy would provide more help for the groups that bear the costs of agricultural progress—namely the low-income sectors of agriculture no longer able to compete effectively, and the manpower which has been displaced from farming. The role of export demand should assume a more prominant position. Finally, it was argued that the concept of parity is inconsistent with the structure of modern agriculture and should be replaced with a better basis for comparing farm and nonfarm incomes.[19] The reader can judge how closely current programs approach these objectives.

Within these goals we can then describe the many proposals and programs that are currently in existence. Many of these proposals were sketched in the first section of this chapter. The purpose of that

19. National Advisory Commission of Food and Fiber, *Food and Fiber for the Future* (Washington, D.C.: USGPO, 1967), p. 14.

section was to give the reader a sense of the historical evolution of agricultural policy. This section concentrates on the economic implications of current programs. Essentially they can be classified into one of three approaches:

1. To expand the demand of farm products both domestically and in foreign markets.
2. To adjust the growth in farm production to the increases in demand through programs to control production inputs.
3. To control excess production by neutralizing the price-depressing effects in the marketplace.

Each of these three approaches contributes toward the solution of the overall farm problem. However, the relative significance of each has varied over the years. Furthermore, each of the proposals will be found to create undesirable consequences which tend to confound the attainment of meaningful policy.

EXPANDING THE DEMAND FOR AGRICULTURAL COMMODITIES

In Chapter 8 we showed that the demand for a commodity shifts to the right or left depending upon changes in income, population, tastes, and preferences, or the prices of substitutes and complements. Governmental programs offer little potential in expanding demand through population increases or by changing the prices of products which are substitutes or complements. The government is also extremely limited in its ability to increase the demand for farm commodities through increasing per capita income. Even though governmental actions might increase per capita income, the low income elasticity of demand for farm products does not permit much of this increase to be reflected in aggregate demand. Generally such actions are considered as efforts to achieve general economic goals rather than to increase the demand for farm products.

DIRECT DISTRIBUTION

Government-sponsored distribution of food to the needy began in 1933 with the primary intent being to reduce surpluses. The Agricultural Act of 1935 provided funds to be used to purchase surplus agricultural commodities for direct distribution to needy people, to institutions, and to schools. The commodities distributed have varied depending upon what happens to be in surplus at a particular time. Over the years practically all major agricultural commodities have been involved in direct distribution programs; and the number of individuals receiving food has also varied considerably from one year to another (as shown in Table 11.11). Since the original goal of these programs was the disposal of surpluses, the programs often did not provide the type of commodities that would lead to an adequate diet on the part of the recipients. In recent years, the objective of the program has changed, providing a variety of foods that will improve nutritional values of needy families' diets.

The second government program to directly distribute food is the school lunch program, originally part of the same 1935 enabling legislation that provided for direct distribution of commodities to the needy. The main problem of the original program was that it is difficult to build school lunch programs around surplus commodities. In 1946 the National School Lunch Act was passed to provide a more permanent basis for the program. Since then, the program has grown steadily until in 1971 about 24.5 million school children received lunches each day under the program. About one in ten of these lunches was served free or at a greatly reduced price to needy children. In 1966 a school breakfast program was instituted for children of needy families. Unfortunately, approximately 1.5 million children in public schools still do not have access to school lunch programs. In many schools this is because of a lack of kitchen and dining facilities. In 1966 assistance was also provided for the purchase of kitchen equipment.

A third special distribution program is the school milk program which was instituted in the Agricultural Act of 1954 and continued with the Agricultural Act of 1961. Under this program, schools and institutions purchase fluid milk from local marketing firms and, in turn, the federal government pays part of the cost of the milk. It is estimated that approximately 2 percent of all fluid milk consumed by the nonfarm population is under this program. It has also been estimated that the program provides milk to at least three out of every four school children.

Another direct distribution program is the food stamp program introduced for a 3-year trial period in certain areas of the United States early in 1961. It was developed in response to the argument that direct distribution programs handled food outside the regular market channels. Under this program, needy families can increase their food purchasing power by receiving stamps that can be used to purchase food through regular commercial channels. The family buys stamps for an amount approximately equal to what they would normally spend for food, but the value of the stamps is ordinarily substantially higher than this amount. For example, if the family would normally spend $15 per week for food, they would pay $15 to a distribution center which would, in turn, give the family stamps worth perhaps $40 or $50 per week. These are then taken to participating grocery stores and redeemed for food. In some areas the food stamp program has replaced the direct distribution program as the vehicle for increasing the consumption of food by needy families.

Table 11.11 illustrates the growth in the size of the domestic food programs described above. Notice that the food stamp program

TABLE 11.11. Federal food programs, United States, selected fiscal years 1950–1965 and 1969–1971

Program		1950	1955	1960	1965	1969	1970	1971
Commodity Distribution								
Institutions and welfare cases								
Persons participating	(1,000)	1,125	4,624	5,753	7,148	5,032	6,876	6,797
Quantity	(mil lb)	225	297	654	1,313	1,200	1,320	1,466
Cost[a]	(mil dol)	24	97	75	257	250	312	346
School lunch programs								
Children participating	(1,000)	10,129	10,213	15,635	20,390	24,056	24,175	26,000
Quantity	(mil lb)	467	298	523	973	1,042	1,073	1,209
Cost[a]	(mil dol)	55	83	132	175	272	266	279
Indemnity plan[b] (school lunch program)								
Children participating	(1,000)	7,840	10,972	12,839	17,024	22,079	23,127	24,574
Cost[c]	(mil dol)	65	69	94	130	204	300	535

Source: U.S. Dept. of Commerce, Bureau of Census, Statistical Abstract of the United States, 1972, p. 85.

a. Represents cost to the federal government of the commodity as delivered to the state distributing agency.

b. Comprises elementary and secondary schools; government reimburses schools for local purchases of food.

c. Refers to subsidy payments by the federal government; excludes administrative costs.

d. Initiated in Sept. 1954 to increase the consumption of fluid milk in schools and child care institutions.

X = Not applicable.

TABLE 11.11. Continued

Program		1950	1955	1960	1965	1969	1970	1971
Special milk program[d]								
Quantity reimbursed	(mil 1/2 pt)	X	450	2,385	2,967	2,944	2,902	2,507
Federal cost	(mil dol)	X	17	80	97	101	101	91
Food-stamp program								
Persons participating	(1,000)	X	X	X	425	3,222	6,457	10,567
Federal cost	(mil dol)	X	X	X	33	229	550	1,522

415

TABLE 11.12. Comparison of important characteristics of domestic demand expansion programs in the United States, 1930 to the present

	Direct Distribution	School Lunch	Food Stamp	Special Milk	Plentiful Foods
Dates of Operation	1930 to present	1933 to present	1939-43 1961 to present	1940 1954 to present	World War II to present
Major Activity	Distribution of surplus foods	Contribution of foods and financial assistance	Food price subsidy	Subsidy paid on milk sales to school children	Merchandising and informational program
Program Clientele	Needy families, school lunches, charitable institutions	Elementary and secondary school children	Needy families	Elementary and secondary school children	All consumers
Advantages	Is selective in that surplus products are involved	Achieves nutrition objectives while at the same time increasing food consumption	Increases food consumption and nutrition level	Increases milk consumption and nutrition level	Enhances level of knowledge about surplus food products
Weaknesses	May not include food needed to improve diets; does not use normal market channels	Failure of some to participate and is limited to school children	Costly to the government and difficult to administer	Limited to the single food product	Is strictly educational and many do not receive and use the information

Source: J. P. Doll, V. J. Rhodes, and J. G. West, Economics of Agricultural Production, Markets, and Policy (Homewood, Ill.: Richard D. Irwin, 1968), p. 454.

and the school lunch program have grown the most rapidly. The food stamp program grew from 425,000 participants in 1965 to over 10 million participants in 1971. Part of this growth can be attributed to a change in the philosophy of the program from one of disposing of surplus commodities to one of providing adequate diets for families. Similar growth is illustrated for the school lunch program.

Table 11.12 summarizes the types of programs utilized in the United States since 1930 to expand the domestic demand for agricultural products. A short comparative statement on each program's main advantages and disadvantages is also shown.

Economic impacts of direct distribution programs are dependent upon how successfully the program can remove a portion of the commodity from normal market channels and redistribute it to groups within the system without creating negative effects upon the total demand for the product. If successful, the short-run impacts of the program will be to increase the prices paid by nonsubsidized consumers and thereby increase incomes to farmers. Figure 11.16 illustrates the probable impact. Assume the total quantity produced in the given production period is Q_1. In part a of Figure 11.16, assume the government decides to purchase the quantity $Q_1 - Q_2$ leaving Q_2 to be distributed through normal market channels. The normal market price will then be P_2 The more inelastic the demand curve, the greater will be the increase in price and incomes by farmers as a result of the program. For example, if the price elasticity of demand were —0.20 and the government purchased 5 percent of the total supply, farm price would increase 25 percent. It is easy to show in this case that the increase in total receipts of farmers is con-

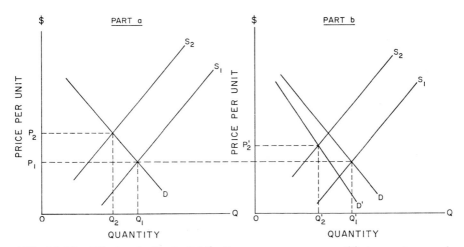

FIG. 11.16. Effects of direct distribution programs on equilibrium prices and quantities.

siderably greater than the expenditures of the government for buying 5 percent of the output. In part a the quantity removed $(Q_1 - Q_2)$ and distributed outside normal market channels had no effect on the market demand curve DD.

In the case where the distribution of food to recipients reduces their normal market demand for the product, the results are much smaller. For example, if distributing free milk to school children causes parents to purchase less milk, the impact on prices will be less. This is illustrated in part b of Figure 11.16. The quantity purchased by the government again shifts the supply curve to S_2, but because of the interaction effects with demand, the actual quantity reduction is greater $(Q'_1 - Q'_2$ versus $Q_1 - Q_2)$, and the price increase is less (P'_2 versus P_2).

In either case, as long as the aggregate demand curve for the commodity is inelastic, the consumer will end up spending more for the commodity than without a direct distribution program. Its impact upon resource utilization is dependent upon the type of commodity involved. In general, the production of livestock commodities requires many more agricultural resources than does the production of an equivalent amount of calories in the form of crops. Consequently, if there are excess resources in agriculture, a direct distribution program which utilizes the high resource-using products such as milk, cheese, butter, and eggs will reduce the extent of redundant resources much more than a direct distribution program involving wheat, rice, and fruits.

The economic effects of the food stamp program depend upon whether or not the basic objective of the program is to support agricultural prices or to provide for improvement in diets. If the primary purpose is to reduce surpluses growing out of supported prices, the program will increase the consumption of a commodity with no change in its price. This is shown in Figure 11.17. Assume that the total demand for a commodity (D_t) can be divided into the demand for those families which could obtain stamps (D_s), and the demand of nonstamp families (D_n). Assume that in the short run (one production period) the amount harvested by farmers is Q_h. If the government wishes to support the price at P_s, it must purchase $Q_h - Q_t$ and store it. Under the food stamp program, the demand for the commodity by families receiving stamps would shift to D'_s, resulting in aggregate demand shifting to D'_t. Under this set of conditions, $Q'_t - Q_t$ would move through ordinary market channels (via food stamps) rather than into government surplus storage. The difference $Q_h - Q'_t$ in Figure 11.17 represents the amount the government would have to place in storage. It is substantially less than without stamps.

Figure 11.18 illustrates the case where no surpluses exist. As before, an increase in the disposable income of needy families through the distribution of food stamps will shift their demand right from D_s to D'_s. There will also be a similar shift in the total demand to D'_t. Assum-

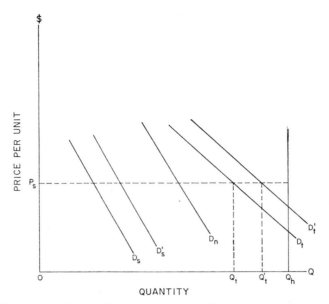

FIG. 11.17. Impact of a food stamp program with price supports.

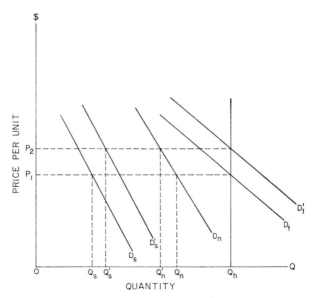

FIG. 11.18. Impact of a food stamp program without price supports.

ing no surpluses and no price-support program, the expanded demand for food will raise food prices since supply is perfectly inelastic at Q_h. Hence, P_2 is now the relevant price and the quantity of food consumed by nonparticipants in the food stamp program will decline from Q_n to Q'_n while that of stamp recipients will increase from Q_s to Q'_s. Under these assumptions, the total quantity of commodity consumed remains constant, with a larger proportion of the total consumed by the low-income needy families who received stamps. Also notice that if there had been a surplus, food stamp recipients would have been able to obtain more than Q'_s, and at prices below P_2. Also, nonstamp consumers would not have experienced a reduction $(Q_n - Q'_n)$.

In either of the above two cases, the food stamp program will increase the consumption of food of those families receiving stamps. There is, however, no guarantee that the diet is adequate or balanced since there is little control over how the stamps are used. Studies of the food stamp program from 1961 to 1964 indicated that recipients did purchase more meat and dairy products, poultry, and fresh fruits and vegetables.[20]

EXPORT DEMAND EXPANSION

The final type of government programs to expand the demand for agricultural products are those which undertake to expand the total worldwide demand for agricultural products. As in the case of the food stamp program (see Figure 11.17), total aggregate demand (D_t) can be defined as total worldwide demand, which is separated into two sub-aggregates: domestic demand (D_n) and foreign demand (D_s). Any successful efforts to shift foreign demand D_s to D'_s will also be reflected in rightward movement of D_t to D'_t and hence a reduction in the cost of carrying the surplus.

These programs are generally conceived to accomplish one of two objectives. First, the efforts may be motivated by mounting CCC stocks growing out of price-support programs. In this case, the objective is to move the surpluses into foreign consumption to reduce the burden of storage costs. Second, the program may be motivated by the desire to minimize the price-depressing effects on domestic markets. Through specific price concessions or subsidies which increase the competitive position of United States agricultural commodities, domestic merchants are encouraged to increase their purchases for resale abroad.

Currently three types of export-demand expansion activities are carried out by the United States government through the CCC: (1) commercial exports with government assistance, (2) concessional sales, and (3) grants and donations. The first activity, commercial exports with

20. USDA, The food stamp program in an initial evaluation of the pilot's projects, *AMS*, No. 472 (Washington, D.C.: USGPO, 1962), p. 31.

government assistance, was originally authorized by the CCC Charter Act of 1933. Under this authorization, the United States government either provides export subsidies per unit of commodity sold by private firms selling abroad or it sells the commodities to the firms from CCC stocks at worldwide price levels. Since world prices are generally lower than domestic support prices, the CCC is in effect taking a loss on the sale of these commodities. Figure 11.19 illustrates the proportion of total United States agricultural exports moving under government assistance. Figures show that in 1972 the United States exported farm commodities amounted to $8.2 billion of which commercial exports made up $6.9 billion. Of the total commercial exports, $1.7 billion moved with some government assistance, such as reduced prices or shipping subsidies. Altogether, $2.8 billion (or 34 percent of total agricultural exports) worth of agricultural commodities moved into world markets with some kind of government assistance in 1971.

The other two types of export demand expansion activities are included in the $1 billion of exports moving abroad directly under government programs. These programs implement the Agricultural Trade Development and Assistance Act of 1954 (PL 480) and the Mutual Security Act of 1953. Under these two laws farm products are sold abroad for foreign currencies which can be used for a number of purposes. Additionally, PL 480 permits the United States to barter or donate surplus commodities to other countries. Title I of PL 480 (Sales for

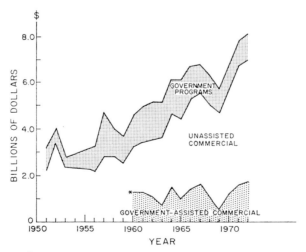

FIG. 11.19. United States agricultural exports under commercial and government-assisted programs, 1951—1972. (From USDA, ERS, **Foreign Agricultural Trade of the United States,** Washington, D.C.: USGPO, various years.)

Foreign Currencies) is the most important provision in the law. It provides for the foreign currency generated under this provision to be loaned back to the foreign government. Smaller amounts are used to support the local operations of our embassies in the respective countries. Title II permits grants of food for disaster relief, and Title III provides for donations of surplus United States food for distribution to nonprofit relief agencies, and the bartering of food for strategically needed materials. Title IV of PL 480 authorizes long-term loans to importing countries to finance the purchase of United States farm products. Title IV was discontinued in 1966. Over the years, more than one-half of all exports under this program were made under the provisions of Title I. As stated earlier, PL 480 started as a surplus disposal operation. However, with the disappearance of large surplus stocks during the mid-1960s, the emphasis of the program changed to one of meeting the special needs of the recipients in foreign countries.

In general, the economic impact of the foreign demand expansion programs is the same as that described earlier for the food stamp program. These programs increase the consumption of farm commodities either by an income effect through a grant (Figure 11.18) or by a price effect which reduces the cost to certain individuals (Figure 11.17). In summary, the demand expansion programs can provide slightly higher incomes for agriculture, but only at a substantial cost to society.[21] These policies are also in accord with our earlier set of goals; they distribute the income according to the individual farmer's contribution to output and avoid interferences with the operation of his business. Furthermore, they do provide incomes that are higher than would be realized without such programs. However, none of these demand expansion policies deals directly with the resource allocation problem in agriculture. Hence, none of them operating alone or in combination provides a complete and satisfactory solution.

CONTROLLING SUPPLY

As described in the first part of this chapter, public programs to affect the supply of agricultural commodities have been substantially more important than those to affect demand. The supply control programs have been both direct and indirect in nature. In terms of long-run impact, we have seen how the indirect programs—which include research and educational efforts by governmental agencies—have dominated the direct supply programs. These indirect programs include research and education by the USDA, research by the state agricultural experiment stations, and support for the establishment of the state and local extension services. Other public programs, such as free rural mail

21. T. W. Schultz, Value of U.S. farm surpluses in underdeveloped countries, *J. Farm Econ.* 42, Dec. 1960.

delivery and public assistance in the establishment of rural electrification and road systems, have also contributed to the tremendous growth in supply. But there are also direct programs to restrict supply.

PRODUCT STORAGE

In the original 1933 act, Congress believed that excess production and hence low prices were the result of better-than-average weather conditions. Thus the original price-support programs conceived of prices for each commodity at a level that would permit crops grown in normal weather years to move into normal consumption. The excess production over consumption in above-normal years would be purchased by the CCC, put into storage, and released back into the market in below-normal years. The idea was to convert the irregular variations in production resulting from the vagaries in weather into a more even flow of commodities.

This concept, called the "ever-normal granary," is illustrated in part a of Figure 11.20. Curve D is the demand for food, S_n the normal supply of the commodity, and P_n the price that would prevail under the demand and supply conditions illustrated. In periods of extremely good weather, the supply curve would shift rightward, and if the government wished to maintain prices of P_n, it must purchase $Q_g - Q_n$ (and store it). In years of adverse weather (part b), the supply curve S_p would be to the left of normal supply (S_n). Given the demand curve, consumers would be willing to pay P_p per unit for the quantity Q_p. In this case, the government would sell some of the surplus from the previous period ($Q_g - Q_n$).

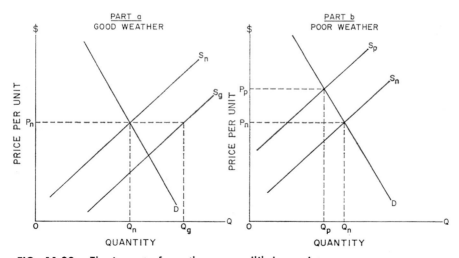

FIG. 11.20. The impact of weather on equilibrium prices.

Here, by selling $Q_n - Q_p$ of the stored surplus, it would be possible to maintain the price at P_n.

For reasons discussed earlier, the program was unsuccessful in stabilizing farmers' incomes and within a few years the objective changed from one of stabilizing prices to one of moving them upward to improve farmers' incomes. In theory, the price-support-through-storage programs can successfully support farm income if the program is large enough. However, such a program does not get to the basic cause of the problem; it in no way solves the problem of high production. Several ways to accomplish that are (1) acreage allotments, (2) general land retirement, and (3) technological limitations. Two other means that are less directly aimed at reducing farm inputs are (1) marketing quotas and (2) farmer bargaining.

ACREAGE ALLOTMENT

From economic theory we know that production requires the inputs of land, labor, and capital. Presently, land is the only input which has been controlled through agricultural programs, and the types of programs employed have varied considerably.

Acreage allotments are an input control device used in combination with price supports. Producers are denied price supports on their output if they plant more than a specified acreage of various crops. The farmer's acreage allotment is usually some fraction of his past acreage. To establish the allotment, the government first estimates the total quantity that will clear the market at an assumed support level. Then estimates are made of average yield per acre, and the total acreage required to produce that amount is determined. Each farmer is then permitted to plant the given percentage of his historical base. If he plants more than his allotted acreage, he receives no price supports on any of his production. While the program was originally mandatory, it is now voluntary.

Controlling agricultural output by limiting the land input has been unsuccessful for three reasons:

1. The actual free-market price tends to stay close to the support price and therefore the penalty for noncompliance has generally been small.
2. Since land is only one input, there is a great deal of substitution of other inputs for land. The effects of the substitution of other inputs were described earlier. The current feed grain program, in effect since 1961, has diverted approximately one-fourth of all feed grain acreage, but the production trend continues upward.
3. The acreage allotments have had no effect on total farm output. They tend to shift the surplus from one crop to another. No effort is made in these programs to obtain cross-compliance.

GENERAL LAND RETIREMENT

The shortcomings of acreage allotments led to an attempt at general land retirement programs as a method of controlling farm output. The objective was to control the amount of total land on which farmers could raise crops or livestock. The national acreage allotment needed for all crops for all uses would be estimated, and this acreage allotment would be allocated to individual farmers. They would then be paid to keep the remainder of their cropland idle and in soil-conserving uses. The soil bank program in the late 1950s operated in this manner. Participation was voluntary and farmers were permitted to retire either parts of their farms or their whole farms for periods of up to 10 years. Under this program, the retirement of land also reduced the use of other inputs such as machinery, fertilizer, seeds, and gasoline; where whole farms were retired, farmers either retired or took nonfarm jobs.[22] Because the retirement of land did reduce other inputs, rural merchants selling to farmers found their volume of business greatly reduced, particularly in those areas where the whole-farm retirements were most extensive. This led to political pressures and the eventual demise of the program.

The voluntary land retirement program has several other faults:

1. If the program is successful in maintaining farm prices and income, there is an ever-increasing incentive by individual farmers not to participate. This happened in 1961 when farmers were paid to idle 25 million acres but cropland acres were reduced by only 19 million acres because nonparticipating farmers increased their acreage planted.
2. The land retirement program also distorts resource utilization in the economy away from the optimum; it reduces the value of the marginal product of labor and capital and increases the value of the marginal product of land. By making land scarce, it raises land prices and its VMP, thereby making it more profitable to use more labor and capital per unit of land. As a consequence, there will be too many of these resources in agriculture and too few elsewhere; total output in the whole economy will be lower than it would be in the absence of a land retirement program.
3. It distorts the benefits of the program in favor of the landowner. If land retirement is successful, the higher incomes will be bid into the price of the land. Thus the owners of farmland find their assets appreciating through no effort on their part.
4. Because marginal land is the first to be retired, the total impact on

22. For more information on the impact on this program, see R. C. Buse and R. N. Brown, *The Conservation Reserve in Wisconsin, 1956–59*, Agr. Exp. Sta. Research Bull. 227, Madison, Wis., June 1961.

output is less than if the more productive land were retired. Thus the reduction in output per dollar of program expenditure is small.
5. Finally, the owner of the small farm, with primarily marginal land, is put at a distinct disadvantage vis-à-vis the owner of the large farm, since the latter can retire parts of his farm (the marginal land) and get paid for doing so, yet continue to produce larger yields on his better land on which he receives support payments.

The feed grain programs of the 1960s were also land retirement programs in which farmers were paid to reduce the acreages they planted to feed grains below the average they planted in 1959–1960. There is also a section in the 1965 act (the cropland adjustment program) which permits farmers to withdraw crop acres for a period of 5 to 10 years. It also contains provisions for land acquisition for public recreational and conservational uses such as for parks, wildlife refuges, and open spaces. The voluntary aspects of this program make it progressively more expensive to keep sufficient acres idle to achieve the levels of prices and incomes sought. While there have been several attempts for mandatory supply management, farm opposition to mandatory participation has always managed to defeat this proposal in Congress. The 1970 and 1973 programs provide even greater flexibility for the individual farmer.

TECHNOLOGY LIMITATION
The knowledge that research on new productive techniques—and educational programs to encourage their adoption—is a powerful supply shifter has resulted in suggesting that this input be restricted.[23] The suggestion is that the subsidy for public research and extension be either reduced considerably or stopped completely. A policy which reduces public expenditures for research and education in new techniques for agriculture is short-sighted because the real costs to the economy are estimated to be very high.[24] It is relatively easy to demonstrate that by slowing down technological progress too many resources would become fixed in agriculture and total national output would be lower than otherwise. Cutting back on research would have two other problems: (1) private industry would soon fill much of the gap and retain most of the benefits through patents and royalties, benefits which are now passed on to the consumer in the form of lower prices; and (2) it would hurt the United States position in world markets for farm products in the long run (since other countries would continue to search for new technologies).

23. For this point of view, see W. W. Cochrane, Some reflections upon supply control, *J. Farm Econ.* 41 (Nov. 1959): 713.
24. See Earl O. Heady, Public purpose in agricultural research and education, *J. Farm Econ.* 43 (Aug. 1961): 566–81.

gain to some groups of farmers and thus an income transfer from the least efficient to the more efficient farmer. Excess resources in agriculture might still be a problem since the large-farm operators with more capital could still outbid small-farm operators for marketing certificates and the pressure on the small-farm operators would continue. Thus the program might result in falling land prices because the marketing certificates become the scarce resource. The program would have the advantage of putting the smallest drain on federal funds for any given amount of production control.

FARMER BARGAINING

Increased bargaining power for agricultural producers is another possible means of gaining higher farm prices and incomes. Government programs to control agricultural supply substitute the discipline of the government for individual discipline. Bargaining is a set of government programs which would help farmers do for themselves collectively what they cannot do individually.

Bargaining is an attempt by an individual or a group to enhance its position relative to those with which they trade; it is the notion of countervailing power. Bargaining power refers to the ability of the group to gain the advantages in terms of prices or other terms of trade. Obviously, there are various approaches to bargaining. While in some cases individual producers may bargain for higher prices or better terms, effective bargaining is generally associated with an organized group—either voluntary or involuntary organizations of producers that wish to influence price. They can approach a collective-bargaining agreement in one of two ways. The first, called the *market gain approach,* attempts to offer advantages to the buyer such as reducing his operating costs, providing him with a dependable supply, or one of more uniform quality in exchange for the higher price. The second approach is called the *market price approach.* Here economic pressure is applied to the buyers of the product if they fail to negotiate. The producer's organization threatens the buyer with withholding supplies of the commodity or by diverting it to other uses in an effort to get a higher price.

In the bargaining process there are essentially three sources of gain for producers: (1) profit margins of processors; (2) higher prices to consumers; or (3) increased marketing efficiency through reduced handling and processing costs. Bargaining gains from profit margins are generally limited. It is estimated that farm prices could be increased by no more than 10 percent if all profits in the food marketing system were returned to farmers. There are some possibilities for gain to farmers if higher prices are passed on to the consumer. However, higher prices tend to reduce consumers' purchases. The extent of the reduction depends upon the prices of the substitutes available. Furthermore, higher prices may actually encourage the introduction of synthetic substitutes such as soybean "bacon," margarine, and nylon. Bargaining gains through more efficient marketing systems offer the best long-run potential by offering the middleman and the final consumer a product uniform in quality and quantity.

Three principal methods can be used by farm groups in bargaining. The first is through marketing orders and agreements. Specific farm legislation was passed in the early 1930s to permit farmers and processors to organize and remain exempt from antitrust action. This subject will be discussed in greater detail in the next chapter. The second approach is through voluntary bargaining associations, while the third is through compulsory bargaining associations. The major difference between these latter two is the legal authority to enforce producers to participate in the provisions of bargaining.

Voluntary bargaining associations have generally been cooperatives organized to obtain a better price for members. Purchasing cooperatives create purchasing power by pooling input needs so that items can be purchased at larger volumes and lower costs. Machinery and fertilizers are the commonest inputs covered. Marketing cooperatives attempt to increase the returns of individual members by enabling them to bargain more effectively in the selling process. These cooperatives are generally set up along commodity lines such as milk, sugar, eggs, fruits, and vegetables. Service cooperatives attempt to increase the individual's return by providing services at reduced rates or by improving existing services.

An example of a voluntary bargaining association is the National Farmers Organization (NFO). It attempts to improve prices by the threat of withholding supplies from market. For perishable agricultural commodities, this procedure is generally difficult; if an industrial worker strikes, he loses only the value of his labor. If the manufacturer refuses to accept the terms of a union, he usually loses the return on his capital. In contrast, if a farmer withholds products from the market, he tends to lose both as a laborer and as an owner of capital. As a result, its success has been limited.

Because of difficulties with producers dropping out of withholding actions, compulsory bargaining holds much more chance of success. Under a compulsory association, enabling legislation is needed to permit farmers to police the procedure. It requires producers' committees which would negotiate price and other terms of trade for all farmers. If, through some procedure such as a referendum, a majority of the producers approved the price or terms of trade, all would be required to abide by whatever production controls or marketing quotas were established. The agreement might also establish methods for disposing of any surplus production.

In summary, successful bargaining through farmer bargaining

associations must meet a number of requirements. First, supply must be effectively controlled; members of the bargaining association must represent a substantial volume of the total supply. Second, production must be restricted. A program must be established and enforced to restrict the supplies to market needs. Third, the agreement must include all similar products. Bargaining must be carried out for similar products simultaneously to prevent producers from overproducing in unregulated products that are substitutes. For example, when bargaining for beef, attention must also be given to lamb, pork, broilers, and other foods consumers would usually substitute for beef. Fourth, substantial control over inputs is required, since successful price bargaining will stimulate the inflow of inputs from other products. Fifth, control over import markets must be established.

Finally, there must be a willingness to accept a loss of individual decision making, as well as some cash costs. Farmer members must be willing to bear the cost of eliminating, diverting, or allocating some of their farm products to other uses to prevent them from depressing the market price. This could include such things as eliminating part of the product through destruction or diverting it to nonfood uses. But the greatest cost may well be in terms of the individual freedom which then must be sacrificed. It only follows that gains which come from extra-market activities such as bargaining and supply control would entail some costs from going outside the free market. If one is unwilling to accept the results of the market, he should not expect to retain all the benefits of that market—such as the right to produce as he wishes. If farmers are to be serious about controlling supply, the myth that they can be successful while retaining their traditional independence must be exposed for what it is—a dream.

SUMMARY: THE CHOICES

Many of the conditions which gave rise to the farm problem were conscious acts of public policy and the public has acted to correct the cost imposed upon particular groups. The problem can be stated as follows:

1. American society places a very high value on technology. Thus it provides for a generous publicly supported research and development program which continually produces new methods and procedures.
2. The market organization and structure within which farmers operate force them to constantly seek out and adopt these new technologies. The best interest of the individual entrepreneur is not the best interest of the industry.

3. The widespread adoption of innovation by farmers creates sustained increases in aggregate farm output.
4. These expanding supplies continually press downward on agricultural prices. This downward pressure in farm prices does not put a brake on agricultural supply because resources employed in farming, once committed, move very slowly in response to changes in price level.

Farmers expect adequate incomes with minimum restrictions on the freedom to produce and market. Consumers expect abundant food and fiber at reasonable cost and low taxes. The ensuing legislation can be inconsistent and fall far short of its intended objective. Support programs are designed to reimburse the producer for the losses he suffers from a public policy of rapid technological advance in a highly competitive market structure. Most of these policies do not directly attack the basic problem. It is industry's rigidities which impede the flow of excess resources to higher-return alternatives, not low agricultural prices.

Parity is presented as a quantitative expression of economic justice in the distribution of income. Parity prices cannot be justified as a measure of income equity between farmers or nonfarmers or between different types of producers. In actual fact, it is tied to price per unit of output rather than to income per farmer. Hence those farmers producing the largest number of units receive the largest benefits. Thus benefits are distributed directly in proportion to the farmers' scale of operation rather than on the basis of need.

Price-support programs have also had a serious effect upon the allocation of resources. They have seriously retarded shifts in production among products, among regions, and between the farm and nonfarm sector. Resources are allocated in accordance with political power rather than market-price signals. Price-cost relationships and production patterns of the past are fixed in a rigid mold. The guiding influence of alterations in consumers' tastes and preferences and in production technologies is ignored or subverted. Market interference through price supports has perpetuated small inefficient farms, frozen the location of production among regions, and diminished the farmer's share of both domestic and foreign markets.

The philosophy of public programs has ranged from rigid mandatory programs to the more recent voluntary participation by farmers. The cost of the programs has been high and there is constant pressure to reduce treasury outlays without completely exposing farmers to the harsh treatment of the marketplace. Programs in terms of public outlays from most to least efficient are (1) mandatory supply controls such as marketing quotas, (2) long-term land retirement such as the Conservation Reserve, (3) short-term land withdrawal such as the feed grain program, (4) set-aside direct payments, and (5) price supports via storage.

Several studies have estimated the cost effectiveness of different types of government programs. Under the long-term land retirement programs such as the Soil Bank Conservation Reserve, it was estimated that each dollar of government expenditure removed $3 of production.[26] Under a shorter-term diversion program such as the 1951 feed grain program, each dollar of government outlay reduced corn production between $0.86 and $1.14.[27] Direct payments without producer controls increased farm income $1 for each $1 expended. Commodity storage programs removed $1 of commodity for each $1 of commodity from the market for each dollar spent but added storage charges doubled government costs in about 4 to 5 years. Another study shows that the multiple-price plan and export subsidies such as for wheat are highly cost effective.[28]

Whether direct or indirect, voluntary or mandatory, the total outlay required to raise farm income a given amount is the same (see Figure 11.3). The difference is in the distribution of costs and benefits. From earlier discussions, most of the benefits go to owners of large farms since they produce the major portion of all output. On the cost side, the choice is not so clear. Mandatory controls, whether through government or through the self-help bargaining approach, raise incomes by restricting supply and are a regressive tax on consumers. They increase the food expenditures more for the low-income segment of the population which spends a larger share of its income on food. Voluntary programs are more progressive in that they compensate the producer directly from the treasury, but government outlay is greater. Treasury funds are obtained from the progressive income tax. The problem with the second approach is that a larger portion of total cost is direct and hence highly visible.

At the end of 1974 the domestic food situation had reversed from large stocks and excess production to a minimum level of stocks and reduced production. Large grain purchases by the USSR and bad weather at home reduced wheat and feed grain stocks to their lowest levels in decades. Additionally, poor weather held wheat production to about 1973 levels; reduced feed-grain production 18 percent below the 1973 crop; and reduced soybean production.

Undoubtedly the U.S. agricultural plant is capable of meeting our domestic needs and some fraction of foreign demand. However, to do so involves a trade-off between farmers' incomes and foreign exchange earnings, and domestic food prices. On the one hand, agricultural commodities could be used to earn foreign exchange with which to purchase needed imports—primarily energy. At the same time this likely would increase farmers' incomes. As world demand for food continues to increase, the economic gains from exporting food will increase. And, unless our energy import requirements slacken, exporting agricultural commodities may be necessary to avoid serious balance of payments problems.

On the other hand, such a policy may result in higher domestic food prices. It is too early to determine all the policy options and implications but many of the economic issues are clear.

SUGGESTED READINGS

BASIC

Breimyer, Harold F. The three economies of agriculture. *J. Farm Econ.* 44(Aug. 1962): 679–99.

>Author argues that agriculture is not homogeneous and hence policies must differ. Economic and technological forces shaping agriculture have produced three distinct and separate sectors: a crop production sector, a livestock sector, and a marketing and processing sector.

———. *Bargaining in Agriculture: Potentials and Pitfalls in Collective Action.* North Central Reg. Publ. 30. Columbia: Univ. Missouri, 1971.

>An analysis of the purposes, sources of power, organizational structure,

26. Raymond P. Christensen and Ronald O. Aines, *Economic Effects of Acreage Control Programs in the 1950's,* Econ. Rept. 18 (Washington, D.C.: USDA, 1962).

27. K. L. Robinson, Cost and effectiveness of recent government retirement programs in the United States, *J. Farm Econ.* 48 (1966): 22–30.

28. Luther G. Tweeten, *Commodity Programs for Wheat,* Agr. Exp. Sta., Tech. Bull. T-118, Stillwater, Okla., 1965.

>costs, sources of gain, and possible courses of action for farmer bargaining.

Brewster, John M. The machine process in agriculture and industry. *J. Farm Econ.* 32(Feb. 1959): 69–81. Reprinted in Karl A. Fox and D. Gale Johnson, *Readings in the Economics of Agriculture.* Homewood, Ill.: Richard D. Irwin, 1969.

>Contrasts the impact of technology on agricultural and industrial firms. Author argues that machine methods have changed the ideology of industry while in agriculture the small, highly competitive, capitalistic unit has persisted. He stresses that many of these differences grow out of the biological nature of agricultural production.

Christensen, Raymond P.; Hendrix, William E.; and Stevens, Robert D. *How the United States Improved Its Agriculture.* USDA/ERS Foreign No. 76, Washington, D.C., Mar. 1964.

>Describes the contribution of inputs and of technology to the increases in agricultural output between 1960 and the early decades of the twentieth century.

Clawson, Marion. *Policy Directions for U.S. Agriculture.* Baltimore: Johns Hopkins Press, 1968.

>A comprehensive analysis of American agriculture and the major issues and alternatives confronting public policy currently and possible directions to the year 2000. Agriculture is defined in its broadest sense to include (in addition to commercial agriculture) policy for rural communities, rural institutions, natural resources, and rural people.

Cochrane, Willard W. *The World Food Problem: A Guardedly Optimistic View.* New York: Thomas Y. Crowell, 1969.

>Describes the nature of the world food problem through an analysis of the basic forces influencing food consumption and their interactions. Presents an analysis of the kinds of policies required to permanently solve the world food problem.

————. *The City Man's Guide to the Farm Problem.* Minneapolis: Univ. Minn. Press, 1965.

Develops the farm problem in terms of the facts, the economics, and the politics surrounding the policy choices. Based upon the author's experiences in Washington as a farm policy advisor to the Kennedy administration.

Griliches, Zvi. Research costs and social returns: Hybrid corn and related innovations. *J. Polit. Econ.* 66(Oct. 1958): 419–31.

An example of the research literature calculating the rates of return on investment in research. The author estimates the rate of return on the public investment in research in hybrid corn and sorghum to be over 700 percent.

U.S. Department of Agriculture. *Farm Commodity and Related Programs.* ASCS Agr. Handbook 345, Washington, D.C.

A compilation, description, and summary of farm commodity, price support, stabilization, and related programs administered by the USDA.

ADVANCED

Benedict, Murray R. *Farm Policies of the United States 1790–1950: A Study of Their Origins and Development.* New York: Twentieth Century Fund, 1953.

A detailed history of the long and complex development of farm programs, policies, and public attitudes.

Cochrane, Willard W. *Farm Prices: Myth and Reality.* Minneapolis: Univ. Minn. Press, 1958.

One of the most influential analyses of farm problems of the time combines the highly competitive market structure for agricultural products with the role of technological advance in agriculture into the concept of the agricultural treadmill.

————. Some observations of an ex-economic advisor: Or what I learned in Washington. *J. Farm Econ.* 47(May 1965): 447–61. The articles by Hardin, Hathaway, and Cochrane are reprinted in Karl A. Fox and D. Gale Johnson. *Readings in the Economics of Agriculture.* Homewood, Ill.: Richard D. Irwin, 1969. (See annotation under Hathaway.)

Fishel, Walter L., ed. *Resource Allocation in Agricultural Research.* Minneapolis: Univ. Minn. Press, 1971.

A collection of papers presented at a symposium on resource allocation for research. Research is viewed as an economic activity requiring scarce resource and producing an output. Covers the problems, issues, and procedures involved in allocating research funds within an economic framework.

Hardin, Charles M. The Bureau of Agricultural Economics under fire. *J. Farm Econ.* 28(Aug. 1946): 35–68.

(See annotation under Hathaway.)

Hathaway, Dale E. Agricultural policy and farmer's freedom: A suggested framework. *J. Farm Econ.* 35 (Nov. 1953): 496–510.

The three articles by Cochrane, Hardin, and Hathaway survey the problems encountered in developing and implementing a national policy for agriculture. The first by Hardin, a political scientist, and the second by Hathaway, an economist, describe the conflicts in rural and urban goals and values. The third provides some insights into the difficulties encountered in attempting to develop a farm policy that is politically acceptable to rural and urban voters.

National Advisory Commission on Food and Fiber. *Food and Fiber for the Future.* Washington, D.C.: USGPO, 1967.

Report of a commission appointed by President Johnson to examine all aspects of U.S. farm policy. The report, based on a series of hearings across the country and a set of 22 special reports and studies by consultants and experts, covers all aspects of agricultural policy. Its recommendations were to be used for establishing national policy.

President's Science Advisory Committee. *The World Food Problem*, vols. 1, 2. Washington, D.C.: The White House, 1967.

Examines the question, Why is the race between food and population being lost? Volume 1 is a concise summary of the world food problem and a set of recommendations for policy. Volume 2 is a set of 14 reports providing the detailed analysis supporting the recommendations and conclusions of volume 1.

Ruttan, Vernon W. The contribution of technological progress to farm output: 1950–75. *Rev. Econ. Stat.* 38 (Feb. 1956) pp. 61–69.

A statement of the role of farm technology and of the interactions between technology and other agricultural inputs.

———. Technology and the environment. *Am. J. Agr. Econ.* 53 (Dec. 1971): 707–17.

An analysis of the significance of the application of new technology to economic growth and development. The author argues that, in view of recent costs such as environmental degradation and the costs of psychological adjustments, rapid technological progress may not be cost-free nor a boon to mankind.

Ruttan, Vernon W.; Waldo, Arley D.; and Houck, James P. *Agricultural Policy in an Affluent Society*. New York: W. W. Norton, 1969.

A set of readings of the most recent writings of prominent economists on the issues of public policy in agriculture.

Schultze, Charles L. *The Distribution of Farm Subsidies: Who Gets the Benefits*. Washington, D.C.: Brookings Institution, 1971.

Analyzes the distribution of benefits by size of farm and income group. Estimates the influence of subsidies on net returns and on the value of farmland.

Tweeten, Luther. *Foundations of Farm Policy*. Lincoln: Univ. Nebr. Press, 1970.

A historical and analytical discussion of agricultural policy. Includes an in-depth discussion of policies relating to rural poverty, foreign trade, and aid.

DISCUSSION QUESTIONS AND PROBLEMS

1. Why does it make economic sense to have society pay for research out of public funds?
2. Does the subsidization of factors of production by public funds always result in a distortion in the best allocation of resources? Explain.
3. Explain how an elastic aggregate demand for farm products would eliminate most of agriculture's problems.
4. How might commodity donations or sales under Public Law 480 affect the derived demand for food in the recipient country?
5. Explain how "dumping" of wheat by the United States affects the international price for wheat.
6. What impact might a welfare program which assured all United States families of a guaranteed minimum monthly income have on the aggregate demand for food? For particular commodities?
7. What impact will the properties of total production controlled by a bargaining association have on their ability to raise the price of their product?

CHAPTER 12: THE AGRIBUSINESS SECTOR

Modern agriculture encompasses a much broader array of economic activities than traditionally held concepts of farmers producing raw food and fiber. In addition to the farmer, agriculture includes the input suppliers who provide him with fertilizer, chemicals, gas and oil, machinery, equipment, and the other supplies he needs; and the marketing firms that process, haul, and store the products. Each sector is equally important to the production of food and fiber, and together they comprise what is frequently termed the *agribusiness* sector of our economy. Table 12.1 shows the relative magnitude of the three components of the agribusiness sector. The input and marketing sectors receive a much larger share of the consumer's expenditures than does the farm sector. In 1967 the consumer spent $126 billion for food and fiber of which the input suppliers received one-fourth and the marketing firms two-thirds, leaving approximately 10 percent for the farm sector. The table clearly illustrates the importance of sectors beyond the farm gate in the production of food and fiber.

Recall from Chapters 5 and 10 that if the market is competitive the price a consumer pays for a product will be just sufficient to pay each factor its *VMP* (the value of its contribution to the final product). Thus a declining share for any sector of the economy means that the contributions of that sector's inputs to the overall production process is declining. This is clearly illustrated in the table; the farm share falls from 22.5 to 9.8 percent of the retail value of total output. Consumer's purchases of agricultural commodities increased from $73 billion in 1947 to $126 billion in 1967—a 73 percent gain over the 20 years. During this same time, the farmer's share of this expenditure has declined 25 percent (from $16.4 billion to $12.3 billion). In other words, in 1947, for each dollar spent by the consumers for food and fiber, $0.225 went back to the farmer to pay him for the resources he used in producing the product. The remaining $0.775 went to either the farm input sector or the marketing sector. By 1967 the farmer's share had declined to $0.10 per consumer dollar.

In summary, the table illustrates three points. First, the magnitude of the task performed by the agribusiness sector is broad. Second, the three subsectors—the agricultural supply, agricultural production,

TABLE 12.1. Comparison of agribusiness volume by sectors, United States, 1947 and 1967

	Year		Percent of Total		Percent Change
	1947	1967	1947	1967	1947 to 1967
	(billion dollars)				
Farm Sector Input Purchases	$12.9	$ 30.7	17.6	24.3	+138%
Farm Sector Value Added	16.4	12.3	22.5	9.8	-25
Food and Fiber Processor Purchases from Farm Sector	$29.3	$ 43.0	40.1	34.1	+47%
Marketing Sector Value Added	43.6	83.0	59.9	65.9	+90
Consumer Purchases of Food and Fiber	$72.9	$126.0	100.0	100.0	+73%

Source: Adapted from materials in Henry B. Arthur and Ray A. Goldberg, The United States Food and Fiber Economy in a Changing World Environment, volume 4 of technical papers published by the National Advisory Commission on Food and Fiber, 1967, pp. 19, 31.

and the agricultural marketing sectors—are all highly interdependent. Third, the farmer, seeing his relative importance in consumers' expenditures declining, feels he is being exploited by the other two sectors.

The problem is quite clear to farmers. They see the share going to the other two sectors of the agribusiness complex growing while their share is declining. They suspect that, because of their market structure, input suppliers and marketers are price makers. Farmers on the other hand always see themselves as price takers. Thus they blame the elements of noncompetitive behavior in the two sectors for absorbing a part of the consumer's dollar that somehow is rightfully theirs. In the next two sections we will demonstrate that the declining shares going to the resources owned by farmers is normal in a market characterized by rapid technological change and low price and income elasticities for farm commodities. The final section is directed to a discussion of the many governmental activities designed to improve the performance of the markets the agricultural producer faces.

INPUT MARKETS

In previous chapters we have illustrated the changing trend toward more dependence upon purchased inputs by agricultural producers. Whereas early agricultural producers utilized inputs that were primarily produced on the farm, today the vast majority come from beyond the farm gate. In Table 12.1 it was seen that total input costs increased 138 percent in the 20 years from 1947 to 1967, while the aggregate value of consumer purchases of food and fiber increased only 73 percent. Table 12.2 illustrates in more detail the extensive shifts in the source of farm inputs to outside the farm gate. The volume of non-purchased inputs declined by 30 percent from 1947 to 1972. In contrast, during the same period of time, purchased inputs increased 60 percent. The two principal components of nonpurchased inputs are farm labor and real estate. A major share of both of these inputs is provided by the farm owner and his family. In contrast to purchased inputs, which are paid first, family labor and land do not represent out-of-pocket costs to the producer. Hence, they are residual claimants to his net income. As total income fluctuates, returns to these producer-owned resources also fluctuate.

The trend in increasing off-farm input cost per dollar of agricultural output has been accompanied by—and has fostered—a number of structural changes in the input-supply industries. These changes, plus the declining share going to the producer, are what has led to the charge of monopolistic exploitation. We shall explore the possibility of a monopolistic structure first since it is easily answered. We shall then return to the discussion of why the shift in types of inputs.

MARKET STRUCTURE

While the evidence is scattered and often incomplete, researchers who have recently examined the more important farm supply industries (feed, fertilizer, farm machinery, and petroleum and chemicals) find little evidence to support the conclusion that the farmer is being exploited by inordinately high prices. After a careful evaluation tion of a USDA study[1] supplemented by other sources, Tweeten recently concluded:

> The performance of industries that supply purchased inputs to farmers . . . has been generally high and is improving. A large number of firms and the many cooperative organizations have provided workable competition, and there has been little evidence of exploitation of farmers by input suppliers in recent years. The farm machinery industry of necessity is highly concentrated but its record of innovation is impressive. The profit rate shows little evidence of monopoly power.[2]

Tweeten goes on to state that the supply curve for firms producing farm inputs is highly elastic. This means that large changes in

1. USDA, ERS, *Structure of Six Farm Input Industries,* ERS-357 (Washington, D.C.: USGPO, Jan. 1968).
2. Luther Tweeten, *Foundations of Farm Policy* (Lincoln: Univ. Nebr. Press, 1970), pp. 297–98.

TABLE 12.2. Index numbers of total farm inputs in relation to purchased and nonpurchased farm inputs, United States, 1947—1972

| Year | Total Input | | |
	All	Nonpurchased[a]	Purchased[b]
		1967 = 100	
1947	93	137	64
1948	94	137	66
1949	97	138	69
1950	96	136	68
1951	99	139	71
1952	99	137	73
1953	98	135	73
1954	98	134	73
1955	98	132	74
1956	96	126	75
1957	94	121	75
1958	94	117	77
1959	95	116	81
1960	94	110	83
1961	94	108	83
1962	94	107	86
1963	95	104	89
1964	96	104	91
1965	97	103	92
1966	98	101	96
1967	100	100	100
1968	101	100	103
1969	102	99	104
1970	101	97	104
1971	102	97	105
1972[c]	102	96	107

Source: USDA, ERS, Supplement V to Changes in Farm Production and Efficiency, 1971.

a. Includes operator and unpaid family labor, operator-owned real estate, and other capital inputs.

b. Includes all inputs other than nonpurchased inputs.

c. Preliminary.

the demand by farm firms do not change industry price significantly; the input supply firms change their output level rather than their prices. He further argues that costs to these firms, principally wages, will continue to rise and to be passed on to farmers rather than to be absorbed by the input industries. He attributes this mainly to labor unions and continued inflationary pressures within the economy.

More recent studies provide some further evidence of how the input industries have changed their structure to accommodate the changing nature of agricultural production. These changes can be interpreted as attempts to change structure to control prices when in fact they are actually responses to the treadmill upon which the agricultural producer finds himself.[3] For example, many input industries have located their manufacturing facilities closer to new sources or users in an effort to reduce transportation costs. They have also integrated manufacturing and distribution activities in their local outlets to achieve economies of scale. In further efforts to compete, each input is increasingly being sold as part of a total product-service package. This serves both to differentiate each supplier's product and to better meet the specific needs of the farmer. For example, fertilizer dealers not only sell fertilizer but they will mix fertilizer to a farmer's specific needs, as well as apply it to his fields. As another example, a vender of chemicals, pesticides, or herbicides, after examining the farmer's fields to determine the exact materials to apply, may deliver them directly to the individual hired to apply them. Additionally, they will extend dealer credit, a practice whereby payment for the service is delayed until following harvest. Farmer-owned supply cooperatives are an important competitive element in this industry. It has been estimated that farmers' supply cooperatives account for over 20 percent of the manufacturing feed market and nearly 30 percent of the fertilizer market. They serve as an alternative supply source preventing input suppliers from increasing prices much above the competitive level. Cooperatives are not important in the farm machinery market, however. Thus the overall evidence indicates that the structure, conduct, and performance of the input-supplying sector is satisfactory.

The explanation for the falling farm share lies in the shift of costs, formerly attributable to the farmer and the resources he owns, to individuals and resources beyond the farm gate. The explanation for this shift is to be found in two types of changes, both of which are an integral part of technological change and at the same time a result of it. The first is the change in relative input costs and the second is the increasing degree of specialization within agriculture. In either case the result has been that many of the production activities formerly performed on the farm are now being located beyond the farm gate.

3. For a more detailed description of structural changes in farm input industries, see Dale C. Dahl, Structure of input supply industries and technique of analysis, *Am. J. Agr. Econ.* 51 (Dec. 1969): 1046–54; Arlo T. Minden, Changing structure of farm input industry: Organization scale, ownership, *Am. J. Agr. Econ.* 52 (Dec. 1970): 678–85.

SPECIALIZATION IN PRODUCTION

The technological revolution has greatly accentuated specialization as a method of reducing per-unit costs. In the process it has made the farmer more dependent upon inputs and service suppliers from off the farm; and it has also increased the degree of flexibility he has in organizing his business.

The farmer not only buys vast quantities of nonfarm inputs but he also employs a myriad of custom services such as fertilizing, spraying, harvesting, and crop dusting by others. Almost any production or harvesting operation can be custom hired from individuals specializing in that service. Modern equipment is much more complex, specialized, and costly than in the past. By being more specialized, it is used only a few days each year on any one farm. It makes economic sense to avoid tying up capital in ownership of such equipment and hence other entrepreneurs buy this equipment and go from farm to farm and from state to state performing this custom work.

As another example of this phenomenon, the machinery that farmers purchase is far different from that purchased in earlier periods. As indicated in an earlier chapter, much of the modern machinery is labor-saving, which means that it performs the task of several men. In earlier times when family labor (usually unpaid) was utilized, this was not a production expense. Today, it is included in purchased inputs and the return is to the capital input rather than to labor. As another example, the farmer may borrow working capital for production expenses rather than tie up his own limited funds. The agricultural production process takes about 6 months for corn and hogs, 2 to 3 years for beef, and 5 to 10 years for tree crops. The farmer may not want to have his capital tied up in production expenses for that long a period. In this case the local bank, production credit association, or input supplier may extend credit, which will be repaid after the product is sold. In some cases they also contract with some other entrepreneur in the agribusiness complex to furnish needed supplies. For example, a broiler producer may be contracted by a feed manufacturer or a poultry processor to deliver birds, say at $0.04 per pound live weight. The contractor furnishes all the supplies, including feed and chicks. Hybrid seed growers, cattle-feeding operations, and vegetable producers are other examples.

In each example the farmer earns his livelihood from his ability as a manager, plus a return for his labor (if any). In some cases he may also receive a sum for rent of the land contributed to the production process. In any case the farmer's total return is a function of that proportion of management, land, labor, and capital that he contributes to production. The important point is that the return to each input factor no longer flows to the same individual—nor even to a farmer.

The new technologies have separated the farming process into many distinct operations, each of which is becoming increasingly specialized. The modern farmer is choosing which of these operations he will perform and what he will leave to others. Thus the farmer has increased flexibility in that he can choose whether he wants to earn his livelihood from the rent of his land, earnings on his labor, interest on the capital he owns, or profits from the management of the resources owned by other individuals. A reduction in the range of the services he performs is accompanied by a reduction in the total consumers' expenditures that can be attributed to him. A substantial proportion of the 25 percent reduction in consumers' expenditures staying on the farm (Table 12.1) can be explained in this manner.

INPUT PRICES
Price trends in agricultural inputs are also responsible for part of the changing pattern of agricultural production inputs. This arises out of the relative changes in prices rather than their absolute

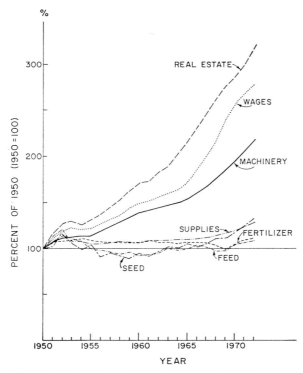

FIG. 12.1.   Indices of prices paid for various farm inputs, United States, 1950–1970. (From USDA, Statistical Reporting Service, **Agricultural Prices: Annual Prices 1972,** Washington, D.C.: USGPO, 1972, p. 10, converted to 1950 = 100; USDA, ERS, **Agricultural Outlook Charts 1972,** Agr. Handbook 397, Washington, D.C.: USGPO, 1972, p. 11.)

levels. Price trends for farm inputs have varied; some show an upward trend while others do not. In Figure 12.1 we have depicted the index of prices paid for selected farm inputs from 1950 to 1972. Generally the nonfarm inputs increased less than the farm-controlled resources of land and labor. Machinery is the only exception.

The average per-acre value of farmland increased 186 percent between 1950 and 1970. This is the largest increase in any input price and the possible reasons for such a large increase are many. Economic theory suggests that the increase is due to a fixed supply of land being confronted with an expanding demand. This could arise out of a number of different circumstances. First, farmers or would-be farmers, anticipating favorable net farm incomes, may attempt to buy land. Second, given the inelastic demand for farm products, farmers know that federal farm programs will raise their incomes. Such expectations will be capitalized into land values as farmers bid up land prices. Third, new technologies usually require larger, more efficient, and more costly machinery and equipment. The farmer finds that this new equipment has excess capacity and he knows that he can reduce its per-unit operating cost by increasing the size of his farm. Competition for land to expand farm size will bid up its price. Fourth, there has been a shift in the method by which land is purchased. Before 1940 most land purchases were for cash or by conventional mortgage. Since 1946 the use of land contracts has increased steadily. Under a land contract the buyer can acquire land for a smaller down payment. In return he pays a higher total price and does not immediately acquire title to the land. The lower down payment permits the buyer to spread his capital over a larger acreage, thereby achieving a larger-sized farm with the same amount of outlay. The results of a USDA study indicate that land prices averaged 10 percent higher when sold under land contract.[4] A fifth factor is population pressure. As expanding population increases the demand for farmland for nonfarm uses such as housing developments, roads, airports, and recreational areas, it also indirectly affects land prices through the increased demand for farm products required by a growing population. Finally, speculation by individuals interested in capital gains is also often cited as an explanation for the increases in land prices. Near large urban centers this is probably an important factor. In agriculture as a whole, speculation is of minor importance in explaining rising land prices.

A recent study by Tweeten and Nelson[5] led them to conclude that

1. One-third of the rise in land prices between 1950 and 1963 was from consolidation pressure to achieve economies of size.

4. USDA, *Farm Real Estate Market Developments* (Washington, D.C.: USGPO, 1964), pp. 19–22.
   5. Luther G. Tweeten and Ted R. Nelson, *Sources and Repercussions of*

2. One-third was from the capitalization of commodity program benefits into the value of land.
3. One-sixth was from the influence of speculators.
4. About one-tenth was from the demand for land for nonfarm users.
5. One-twentieth was from the use of land contracts.

They also state that the increased demand for food due to population growth was mostly offset by increases in farm productivity so that the net effect of population was very small.

    The substantial increases in wage rates illustrated in Figure 12.1 can be explained in terms of higher minimum farm wages, a short supply of skilled farm labor, and the higher wage rates prevailing in nonfarm industries. Although farm workers have fewer laws governing their wage rates than most types of workers, there are regulations setting minimum wage levels for agricultural labor. For example, the Fair Labor Standards Act required certain farm-labor employers to pay at least $1.30 per hour in 1970.

    The most important force in raising farm wage rates is probably the higher wage of industrial workers. Between 1950 and 1970 the average hourly wage rate of farm laborers increased from $0.56 per hour to $1.42, while that of industrial workers increased from $1.44 to $3.36 (Table 12.3). The low levels of unemployment that existed during this period, plus the higher wages, gave the farm laborer attractive nonfarm employment opportunities. This puts a continual upward pressure on the wages of farm labor.

    The increase in the price of farm machinery over the years is a reflection of the larger and more complex machines being purchased. As an example, tractor purchases by farmers are continually shifting toward those with higher horsepower. The size of tractors generally reflects the size of the implements to be used with them. In 1964 the proportion of wheel tractors of 100 HP and over sold to farmers was 2 percent of total tractor sales. By 1970, 18 percent of all wheel tractors sold to farmers were 100 HP or larger. Over the same period of time there was a decline in the sales of all tractors, reflecting a substantial decrease in the demand for smaller tractors. This trend clearly indicates a move by farmers to bigger equipment, which is more costly to own and to operate. It also results in a decreased need for the farmer's labor.

    The changing price ratios between inputs favor the substitution of nonfarm inputs for labor. Table 12.4 clearly illustrates this substitution.[6] The amount of farm real estate has changed little since the first part of this century. In the past 50 years, the total volume of farm labor has declined by 73 percent, while total inputs increased 14 percent

---

Changing U.S. Farm Real Estate Values, Agr. Exp. Sta. Tech. Bull. T-120, Stillwater, Okla., 1966.

    6. Figure 3.5 in Chapter 3 illustrates the year-to-year changes in these indices for the period 1950–1972.

TABLE 12.3. Comparison of average hourly wage
rates of farm and industrial workers,
United States, 1950–1970

| Year | Average Hourly Wage Rates | |
	Farm workers	Industrial workers
	(dollars)	
1950	0.56	1.44
1955	0.68	1.86
1960	0.82	2.26
1965	0.95	2.61
1966	1.03	2.71
1967	1.12	2.83
1968	1.21	3.01
1969	1.33	3.19
1970	1.42	3.36

Source: USDA, ERS, Farm Cost Situation,
1970, 1971, p. 9, p. 22, respectively.

and total agricultural output increased by 100 percent. This has been accomplished by the substantial increase in volumes of fertilizer, lime, mechanical power and machinery, and other capital inputs such as feed and seeds purchased off the farm.

Even if price ratios had not changed, the rising productivity of these inputs continually encourages their use. This is illustrated in Table 12.5. The first column in the table is the index of prices paid by farmers for production inputs. It excludes farm wages and the cost of land. This index, which measures the changes in the cost of inputs the farmer purchases, increased 43 percent between 1950 and 1970. In contrast, the index of farm output increased 51 percent over the same period (column 2 of the table). The ratio of these two components is a reflection of the gross output per unit of production cost (the final column of Table 12.5). When productivity changes in the inputs are taken into account, the change in the cost of purchased inputs per unit of output has increased only slightly over the past 20 years, with no increase apparent in the decade of the 1960s and the early 1970s.

In summary, the squeeze on the cost side as illustrated by Table 12.1 is not an indicator of poor performance in the input sector. Rather it is a combination of several phenomena. First there is an accounting problem. When most of the inputs came from the farm, accounting

TABLE 12.4. Index numbers of total farm inputs and inputs in major subgroups, United States, selected years 1920–1970

Year	Total Inputs	Farm Labor	Farm Real Estate	Mechanical Power and Machinery	Fertilizer and Liming Materials	Feed, Seed, and Livestock Purchased	Miscellaneous
				1957-59 = 100			
1920	93	226	92	32	16	23	67
1930	97	216	91	40	21	26	76
1940	97	192	92	42	28	45	73
1950	101	142	97	86	68	72	85
1960	101	92	100	100	110	109	106
1970	106	61	101	113	226	141	133

Source: USDA, Changes in Farm Production and Efficiency, Stat. Bull. 233, 1964; USDA, Supplements for Changes in Farm Production and Efficiency, 1964 and later years.

TABLE 12.5. Comparison of prices paid for production items and total farm output and output per unit of cost, United States, 1950–1972

Year	Prices Paid for Production Inputs[a]	Farm Output[b]	Output per Unit of Cost
1950	94	100	1.06
1951	104	103	0.99
1952	104	107	1.03
1953	97	108	1.11
1954	97	108	1.11
1955	96	112	1.17
1956	95	113	1.19
1957	98	110	1.12
1958	100	119	1.19
1959	102	120	1.18
1960	101	123	1.22
1961	101	124	1.23
1962	103	126	1.22
1963	104	130	1.25
1964	103	129	1.25
1965	105	133	1.27
1966	108	131	1.21
1967	109	137	1.26
1968	111	140	1.26
1969	116	141	1.22
1970	120	140	1.17
1971	126	152	1.21
1972	134	151	1.13

The "Index of" spans Prices Paid for Production Inputs and Farm Output columns.

Source: USDA, ERS, 1972 Handbook of Agricultural Charts, Agr. Handbook 439, 1972; USDA, Agricultural Prices: 1972 Annual Summary, 1972, p. 11.

a. 1957-59 = 100.

b. 1950 = 100.

practices resulted in a distortion of the contribution of several inputs. Fertilizer from animals was not counted as a productive input and hence no return was attributed to it. Likewise, forage crops were not counted as fuel for motive power and hence this aspect was ignored. Finally, much family labor was unpaid, and it too was ignored in the accounting picture. They were all residual claimants on the producer's income. Over time many inputs have shifted into the purchased input category. The apparent rising costs reflect the growing dependence of producers upon nonfarm firms for their inputs, growing specialization within agriculture, the changing relative factor costs, and the increased productivity of the modern inputs. Poor industry performance is very likely not a factor.

PRODUCT MARKETS

In earlier times farmers took their products to the nearest small town or village and sold them directly to the consumer. The conditions of sale, including the price, quantity, and quality of the product, were subject to individual bargaining in a face-to-face confrontation. At that stage in history, periodic market days with stalls for particular commodities (or peddler carts) were the only form of specialization in marketing. Generally, all facets of the marketing process were performed by the farmer.

As the industrial revolution proceeded, man began to congregate in urban areas. With the growth of towns and cities, the food supply system changed. The farms immediately surrounding each population cluster could not produce sufficient food and fiber to supply the needs of their city neighbors. Furthermore, as the farmer began to specialize in producing commodities, he became less inclined to spend time to transport and distribute the product to the nearby centers. Thus the growth of urban centers required improved transportation facilities to bring the necessary supplies from more distant points. This created the need for country assembly points in each producing area to collect farm products in large enough lots for transportation. It was at this time that processing began to shift from the farm to the factory.

In the cities, terminal market facilities were established to receive, process, package, and redistribute the produce arriving from the country assembly points. Around these facilities another entire group of specialties evolved. It included jobbing, wholesaling, brokerage negotiating, warehousing, transporting, and grading. Since the terminal markets in large cities were the principal price-making centers of agricultural commodities, the need for the establishment and supervision of such marketing services as grades, standards, fair weights, and market news and information arose to protect both buyers and sellers.

At the retail level, changes were also taking place. Up until the 1930s grocery stores, meat markets, bakeries, and other food specialty shops developed in great numbers. The small percentage of the population with automobiles motivated—and in fact necessitated—the establishment of the neighborhood grocery store. After World War II, the self-service concept, facilitated by the invention of open refrigerator display cases and the increasing use of the automobile, generated further changes in the marketing of agricultural commodities. As supermarkets grew in importance, their volume increased until they no longer required all the services of the central market system. Their procurement methods changed because volumes were sufficient to justify these services within their own organizations and give them a cost savings. As a consequence, farm products increasingly bypassed the established country assembly markets and urban terminal wholesale markets. Fruits, vegetables, eggs, and poultry began to flow directly from the farmer or country assembly points to the retailer. Over this period, grain and livestock also increasingly bypassed the large terminal markets as it became more economical to shift processing centers near the producers or near other important inputs.

These large retail outlets were dependent upon supplies of products that were uniform in quality, condition, and appearance. Such supplies were difficult to obtain from the central markets and hence retailers began to place buyers, grading stations, and assembly facilities in appropriate places around the country. They also began to generate their own supplies by specifically contracting with farmers to produce commodities to their own specifications.

Now the marketing system has moved almost full circle: (1) from one characterized by direct dealings of consumers with producers, (2) to one of indirect marketings in which there were many middlemen interposed between producers and ultimate consumers, and (3) back to more direct farmer-retailer transactions. However, there are three substantial differences between the first and the last stage. In the earlier period many producers were selling to many retailers or directly to consumers. Today fewer and larger farmers face fewer and larger retailers. Second, many of the functions performed by the farmer in earlier stages are now in the hands of specialists beyond the farm gate. Third, the consumer today buys not only a food commodity but a very specifically processed commodity. Higher per capita incomes have given rise to a demand for more variety in our foods. This means more manufactured food products, more stages in preparation, and more food eaten away from home. Now, instead of fresh potatoes, the consumer often buys instant potatoes that are mashed, scalloped, or French-fried. Or, rather than purchase ingredients for pies and cakes, instant varieties are purchased. The list is unending and the variety within any given product has also expanded substantially. For example, ice cream is offered in a wide variety of sizes, shapes, flavors, and types. The same is true of items as simple as cottage cheese; it is now available in large and small curd, low calorie, creamed and uncreamed, and with or without chives.

Besides the food retailer, the restaurant trade has exerted its influence on the supply system; the franchise "hamburger heavens," steak houses, and fried chicken chains find it advantageous to buy their meat and other foods according to their own specifications. In this way, it is possible to exercise greater quality control.

In summary, on the product marketing side of the agribusiness sector, we see an increasing number of activities between the farmer and the final consumer. Marketing now encompasses a complex set of activities, institutions, and systems all designed to move the product from the farm to the shopping cart. The system brings together the production from over 2.8 million farmers and redistributes it to over 200 million consumers. Such a large operation is costly and some feel it is inefficiently performed. This is the central issue on the other side of the cost-price squeeze.

Several organizational devices could be used to investigate this issue, and many books have been written on each of them. In the following we briefly sketch some of the various traditional approaches to provide perspective and background, then we turn to an economic analysis of the efficiency of the overall marketing system. Since we could not hope to cover all aspects of marketing, the discussion is written to illuminate the broad issues in the hope that this will serve as a convenient starting point for understanding particular problems, issues, or policies in individual product markets. Rather than approaching the issue of marketing efficiency from the static point of view by describing costs, margins, and profits at particular points in time, we sketch the trends to give the reader a better grasp of the dynamics of the product markets for agricultural commodities. While the date will change from year to year, it is much less likely that the trends, reflecting the underlying structure, will change.

MARKETING DEFINED

Marketing can be viewed as adding consumer utility to the raw material produced on the farm. The job of the marketing system is to change the location, form, appearance, and time of sale of the raw product to that which the consumer desires. *Marketing* is thus defined as the performance of all acitvities involved in the transference of products from the point of the initial producer until it is in the hands of the ultimate consumer. Under this definition, what is included in *marketing* expands or contracts to reflect changes in the nature of the assembly, processing, and distribution system for a particular commodity. It also changes in response to consumer desires.

At least three major ways in which one can describe the marketing system for agricultural commodities are (1) the commodity approach, (2) the functional approach, and (3) the institutional approach. All are different ways of breaking down a complex system into manageable parts so they can be more easily understood.

COMMODITY APPROACH

This approach to marketing concentrates on the specific commodities (such as corn or butter) and follows them through the various stages between farmer and consumer. It describes each marketing function as it is performed. This approach actually combines the following two in describing or analyzing the marketing of a specific commodity.

FUNCTIONAL APPROACH

The functional approach classifies and describes marketing activities according to the services they perform. A marketing function is defined as a major specialized activity performed in the process of transferring the product from farm gate to the consumer. Different lists of functions are used by different lists of authors. The following is a common list:

1. Exchange functions
   a. Buying
   b. Selling
2. Physical functions
   a. Transportation
   b. Processing
   c. Storage
3. Facilitating functions
   a. Standardization
   b. Financing
   c. Risk bearing
   d. Market information

The exchange functions involve the transfer of the title of goods. This is the activity we studied as price formation in Chapters 9 and 10. The physical functions involve the movement, handling, and physical transference of the commodity. The storage function makes goods available at the desired time, the transportation function at the proper place, and the processing function in the proper form. These are frequently referred to as providing time, place, and form utility. The facilitating functions make the exchange and physical functions operate as smoothly as possible. They do not directly involve either title exchange or physical manipulation of the product. Without them, however, an efficient marketing system would be impossible, and marketing costs would be much higher. Standardization establishes a system for measuring and describing the qualities of a commodity. Price quotations have meaning only if the units in which they are quoted are widely understood. Furthermore, it simplifies buying and selling since it makes the transaction possible through simple description rather than inspection. Someone always owns the product as it moves through the system; the financing function helps the persons owning the product in the marketing system bear this cost. Risk bearing permits the marketer to transfer the possibilities of financial loss from either physical or price damage to others who are willing to accept them. The physical risks can arise out of losses due to physical damage from wind, fire, water, accidents, etc. Insurance companies stand ready to accept the burden of such losses. Price risks arise because of the possible change in the price of the commodity during the time in which one of the physical functions is being performed. There is often a desire on the part of the marketer to avoid such price risks, and commodity futures markets are a device whereby price risks can be transferred from the marketer to someone willing to accept such risks. We will have more to say about this system later in this chapter. Finally, we know that optimum resource allocation requires perfect knowledge of market conditions by both buyer and seller. The market information function provides better knowledge by collecting and disseminating pertinent information about the market. As we will show in a later section, adequate storage, timely transportation, and the appropriate form of the product depend heavily upon this facilitating function.

INSTITUTIONAL APPROACH

The institutional approach studies the agencies and businesses that perform the marketing functions and places primary emphasis on the people involved in marketing activities. The approach attempts to answer the "who" in marketing in contrast to the functional approach that focuses on the "what." The institutional approach may be classified as follows:

1. Merchant middlemen
   a. Retailers
   b. Wholesalers
2. Agent middlemen
   a. Brokers
   b. Commission men
   c. Speculators
   d. Facilitators
   e. Processors

While merchant middlemen take title to the product they handle, and both wholesalers and retailers buy products for resale, the agent middlemen act only as representatives (agents) for others involved in the marketing chain; they do not take title to the goods. Their principal function is to provide information or special services for which they receive their fee. Brokers and commission men are individuals who bring buyers and sellers together to exchange goods. The speculator is the one who makes his income from seeking out and accepting the price risks mentioned earlier. The facilitators are the individuals or organizations that provide physical facilities for marketing activities, arrange financing and transportation, police the market, provide market news, and establish grades and standards. For this they usually collect a fee. The processors' function is self-explanatory.

At one time it may have been desirable to present a detailed description or analysis of markets using one or more of the fundamental approaches outlined above. This text will not follow the procedure for several reasons. First, markets and institutions are constantly changing. Today's wholesaler is not the same as 10 years ago, and yesterday's jobber may no longer exist. Second, goods are continually changing channels of distribution in response to new needs. Third, no one channel or institution is used exclusively by any single product. Thus a description of specific processes, channels, functions, or services is quickly obsolete.

Instead, we concentrate on a general description of some of the issues in the marketing system for agricultural products and the role government has played in resolving some of them. One popular issue in marketing, and one discussed earlier, concerns the price side of the so-called cost-price squeeze, that is, how is price established at the farm level and is this price equitable? To analyze this issue, we will examine some typical marketing margins and the magnitude of the overall marketing bill.

MARKETING BILL

The marketing bill is considered a measure of the total cost of moving a farm product from the point of initial sale by the producer to the final sale to the consumer. Its magnitude is indicative of the total cost of performing all the marketing functions and services discussed above. It is computed as the difference between the total food consumption expenditures by all individuals in the United States and the value of food items at the farm level. In 1970 consumers spent $106 billion on all food items, over 7 percent more than in the previous year, and 75 percent more than in 1960. These figures include expenditures for food in retail stores, restaurants, and other away-from-home eating establishments, as well as expenditures in schools, hospitals, and other

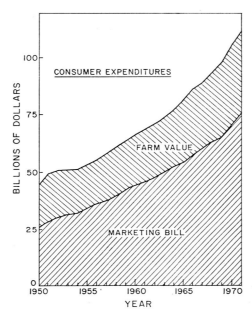

FIG. 12.2. Consumer expenditures for food, the marketing bill, and farm value, United States, 1950—1970. (From USDA, ERS, **Marketing and Transportation Situation,** Washington, D.C.: USGPO, Aug. 1972, Table 7.)

institutions. The trend in the marketing bill between 1950 and 1971 is depicted in Figure 12.2.

Notice that over this period the total marketing bill showed a significant increase while the farm value increased very little; of the $67 billion increase in expenditures over the 20-year period, the marketing bill accounted for 73 percent ($49 billion) of the increase and the farm value for the remaining 27 percent ($18 billion).

The same phenomena exist for most of the individual commodities. In Table 12.6, the change in total United States civilian expenditures for food between 1960 and 1970 is disaggregated into the major food groups to illustrate several important points. The data indicate that between 1960 and 1970 the total retail bill increased by $39 billion and the marketing bill by $26.5 billion. The table illustrates two important points. First, the increases are not equally distributed among all commodities. The commodities with the highest income elasticities show the largest increase in retail expenditures (meat products, fruits and vegetables, and dairy products). Second, the largest increases in marketing costs, as a percent of the retail increase, are for those commodities that require the largest amounts of processing (bakery products and grain products). For example, in 1970, 86 percent of the retail bill

TABLE 12.6. Distribution of the 1960–1970 change in the retail and marketing bill by major commodity groups, United States

Commodity	1970 Marketing of Retail[a]	Change 1960-70 in Retail bill	Change 1960-70 in Marketing bill	Marketing Change as Percent of Retail Change
		(billion dollars)		
Meat Products	55%	$12.8	$ 7.0	55
Fruits and Vegetables	77	7.1	5.6	79
Dairy Products	59	4.2	2.2	52
Poultry and Eggs	55	3.4	2.4	71
Bakery Products	86	3.1	2.7	87
Grain Products	82	0.7	0.7	100
Miscellaneous Products	79	7.6	5.9	78
Total Change	68%	$38.9	$26.5	68

Source: Basic data in USDA, ERS, Marketing and Transportation Situation, Aug. 1972, Table 8.

a. Marketing bill as a percent of total retail bill in 1970.

for bakery products was marketing charges, 82 percent for grain products, and 77 percent for fruits and vegetables. Thus the products with the highest marketing costs show the largest proportionate increase in their respective marketing bill. We will see that these increases are the result of increased costs and services, not inefficiencies in the marketing system.

Increases in the marketing bill can be attributed to three factors: (1) greater volumes of products moving through the marketing system, (2) higher prices for marketing inputs which are not offset by gains in input productivity, and (3) more marketing services per unit of product. The USDA estimates that about 40 percent of the $26.5 billion increase is due to the increased volume of products marketed. The remaining 60 percent was attributed to increases in input costs and more marketing services.[7]

A breakdown of the increased marketing costs indicates a substantial difference among components (Table 12.7). Labor costs constituted nearly one-half the marketing bill in both 1960 and 1970 and also showed a large increase over the period. The 71 percent increase in labor costs over the period accounted for 50 percent of the total in-

7. Jeannette Findley and Leland Southard, The Bill for Marketing Farm Food Products, *Marketing and Transportation Situation* (Washington, D.C.: USGPO, Aug. 1971), p. 16.

TABLE 12.7. Increase in the cost components of the marketing bill between 1960 and 1970

Cost Component	Year		Increase from 1960 to 1970		Percent of Total Increase
	1960	1970	Dollars	Percent	
	(billion dollars)				(percent)
Labor	$18.7	$32.0	$13.3	71	50
Transportation	4.1	5.2	1.1	27	4
Advertising	1.3	2.1	0.8	62	3
Supplies	5.4	8.5	3.1	57	12
Other	8.2	9.1	0.9	10	3
Rent, Interest, and Taxes	2.6	6.0	3.4	130	13
Depreciation and Repairs	2.2	3.7	1.5	68	6
Profits (before taxes)	2.1	4.5	2.4	114	9
Total	$44.6	$71.1	$26.5		100

Source: USDA, ERS, Marketing and Transportation Situation, Aug. 1972, p. 19.

crease in the marketing bill. About $4.9 billion, or another 19 percent of the increase, resulted from increases in the fixed costs of rent, interest, taxes, depreciation, and repairs. Cost of supplies is the other component responsible for a major portion of the $26.5 billion increase.

Profits (before tax) obtained from marketing food products increased $2.4 billion (114 percent) over the 10 years and accounted for 9 percent of the total increase over the decade. While profits were a relatively small proportion of the marketing bill, in 1970 they exceeded the expenditures for components such as depreciation, repairs, and advertising. Although marketing costs have indeed risen, profits are not large enough in relation to sales to be a major contribution to a widening price spread. Furthermore, irrespective of how they are measured, they have remained relatively stable (or even declined) since the end of World War II (Table 12.8). Also, in comparison to other sectors of the economy, they are not unusual. The fact that profits are small relative to sales means that even if profits were eliminated completely marketing costs would be reduced only slightly.

In 1966 the National Commission on Food Marketing concluded that the food marketing system was quite efficient. Its profits were in line with other nonfood industries with which they must compete for resources. They also performed the functions required of them

TABLE 12.8.   Net profits after taxes of leading food companies, United States, selected years 1935–1971

Years	Net Profit as a Percent of Stockholders Equity		Net Profit as a Percent of Sales	
	Food processors	Retail food chains	Food processors	Retail food chains
1935-39	7.2	8.4	3.0	1.5
1947-49	11.7	16.6	2.3	1.4
1957-59	10.1	13.6	2.9	1.2
1960	10.3	12.5	2.4	1.2
1965	11.3	10.2	2.7	1.1
1967	11.1	10.3	2.4	1.1
1969	11.0	10.4	2.4	1.1
1971	11.1	...	2.4	0.9

Source: USDA, ERS, Marketing and Transportation Situation, Nov. 1966 and following years.

quite efficiently.[8] However, the commission did find some evidence of concentration in certain segments beyond that considered necessary to capture all the economies of scale. As a result, they recommended: ". . . that the Federal Trade Commission should be charged with making a continuing review of market structure and competition in the food industry and report annually thereon to Congress."[9]

Since excess profits of food marketing and processing firms cannot logically be used as a cause of the growing farm-retail spread, the major reason must lie elsewhere. Aside from growing volumes and increasing costs not offset by increasing input efficiency, the major reason lies in the growing demand by the consumer for more services included in the food item. In addition to precooked foods, part of this trend is reflected in an increase in away-from-home dining. This trend is depicted in Table 12.9 and reveals that not only has there been a signficant increase in expenditures for away-from-home eating but the marketing bill is a larger percentage of food items thus consumed than of home-prepared meals.

As consumers' incomes continue to grow, the demand for this type of built-in service will likely continue to increase at a much faster pace than the demand for the raw product. Given substantial costs in-

8. National Commission on Food Marketing, *Food from Farmer to Consumer* (Washington, D.C.: USGPO, June 1966), p. 100.
9. Ibid., p. 107.

TABLE 12.9. Consumer expenditures and the marketing bill for U.S. farm foods for foods consumed at home and away from home, 1963–1971

| Year | Consumer Expenditures | | | Percent Away from home of Total | Percent Marketing Bill of | |
	Total	At home[a]	Away from home		At home	Away from home
1963	74.0	56.0	18.0	24	64	78
1964	77.5	58.5	19.0	25	65	78
1965	81.1	60.2	20.9	26	64	76
1966	86.9	64.0	22.9	26	62	76
1967	89.2	64.2	25.0	28	64	78
1968	93.9	67.4	26.5	28	63	78
1969	98.8	70.4	28.4	29	61	79
1970	105.9	74.6	31.3	30	62	79
1971	111.1	77.4	33.7	30	63	78

Source: USDA, ERS, Marketing and Transportation Situation, Aug. 1972, Table 12.

Note: Estimates are preliminary and subject to revision.

a. "At home" is food consumed from the home food supply primarily purchased from retail food stores.

volved in food preparation (primarily labor), the total marketing costs of the built-in services will continue to grow. The proportion remaining for the producer will continue to decline, not because he receives less absolutely, but because the resources he contributes to the final product have been proportionately reduced.

In summary, there are no large profits in the marketing system. The marketing margin widens because many of the services formerly performed by the housewife or on the farm have been transferred to the middleman. The specialization within agriculture has encouraged this process on the input side and is expected to continue. On the output side, the consumer continues to demand that purchases are more ready to eat and wear than in the past. As incomes increase, this trend will likely continue. The extra costs of processing, handling, and packaging the goods in smaller units all widen the marketing margin. The one area of concern singled out for attention—growing concentration of market power—will be discussed later in the chapter where we treat government activities that are aimed at improving market performance. Before turning to that, however, we will develop a conceptual model which depicts marketing services, the marketing bill, the food bill at the farm level, and the total retail food bill. This development will aid in understanding the impact of marketing margins on the demand and supply of food items at both the retail level and the farm level.

MODEL OF THE MARKETING BILL

The preceding discussion was in terms of total expenditures for food at the retail level and at the farm level, and it concentrated upon trends in the shares of the total food bill going to the farmer and to the middleman. In this section, we will present an analytical model of the above concepts. First, consider a given commodity (Q) which requires that certain services be performed prior to its final consumption. These might include transporting from farm to processor, processing, packaging, transporting from processor to wholesaler, handling, transporting from wholesaler to retailer, and handling by the retailer. Assume the aggregate cost per unit of the commodity is P_s, representing the price (cost) of services rendered to the commodity between farm and final consumer. Given these two conditions, we can hypothesize a functional relationship between the number of units of the commodity sold and the cost of services performed on that commodity. This relation is depicted in Figure 12.3.

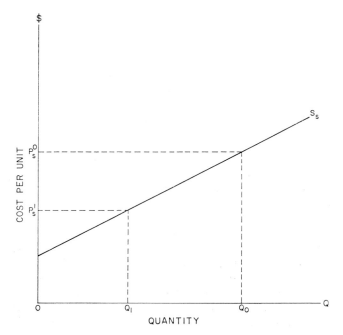

FIG. 12.3. The per-unit cost of marketing services.

The function labeled S_s in Figure 12.3 can be referred to as the supply curve of services since it depicts the per-unit cost of transforming the raw commodity into a marketable product. Before proceeding further, it might be well to point out that the supply of services curve (S_s) need not be linear, nor must it necessarily slope upward. Its shape is determined by the particular nature of the sequence of services provided to Q as it moves from farm to consumer. If the services become cheaper as a larger quantity of Q is processed and handled per unit of time, we might expect S_s to slope downward. If, on the other hand, per-unit economies are insufficient to offset a larger quantity of Q processed per unit of time, its shape would resemble that depicted in Figure 12.3.

Now consider the commodity (Q). It was seen in earlier chapters that it is the demand by consumers which determines what and how much will be produced in a given period of time.[10] For the present discussion, assume a given demand relationship for commodity Q. Demand is defined as the willingness and ability to purchase different quantities of Q at alternative prices per unit of time at the retail level (D_r). It is retail demand that is relevant since a housewife generally buys her food at a retail store rather than from the farmer. Second, we can depict the supply of the raw product that comprises the food item as S_f; that is, we say that there is a retail demand for food and a farm supply. These two concepts correspond to the analysis developed in Chapters 7 and 8. These two curves $(D_r$ and $S_f)$ are drawn in Figure 12.4, along with the supply curve of services function from Figure 12.3.

Since the S_s curve represents the sum of costs for transforming the raw product into a commodity ready for final consumption, it represents the marketing margin. By knowing the marketing margin, and the retail demand and farm supply, we can derive supply at the retail level and demand at the farm level. First consider the demand at the farm level. At each quantity (Q), subtract from the retail demand curve the marketing margin appropriate for that quantity; that is, at Q_0, the magnitude m_0 is subtracted from retail demand (D_r) to determine a point on the demand curve for food at the farm level (point A on D_f). Likewise at Q_1 subtract m_1 from the retail demand curve D_r to obtain point B. Finally, by repeating this process at Q_2, point C can be obtained. By joining these points, we have a demand curve for food at the farm level. The rationale for subtracting the marketing margin for the retail demand curve is that it takes this level of expenditure to convert the raw product into a form desired by the consumer.

We now need a suppply curve at the retail level and the process involves adding to farm supply at each quantity an amount equal to the marketing margin. Thus for Q_0 we would add m_0 to S_f and obtain point

10. Of course we should not overlook the very real impact that advertising has over our perception of what we think we need to consume. It would be naive to suggest that all demands expressed in the marketplace are the result of consumers' wishes alone. See J. K. Galbraith, *The New Industrial State* (Boston: Houghton Mifflin, 1967), especially Chapter 18.

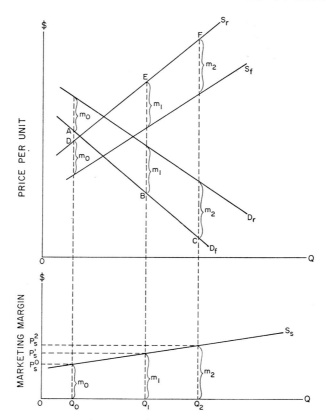

FIG. 12.4. Retail and derived farm demand and supply curves, and the marketing margin.

D on S_r. At Q_1 we would add m_1 and obtain point E, while at Q_2 we would obtain point F. The rationale here is that the farm supply curve merely reflects the quantity of raw product that would be produced by the farmer at alternative prices. To transform that into a desired commodity at the retail level requires the additional expenditure of the marketing margin.

The above model can now be used to analyze the marketing bill for a particular commodity (Q) as well as to discuss the impact of changes in the per-unit cost of services (the marketing margin) applied between the farm and the retail outlet. To facilitate the discussion, the relevant parts of Figure 12.4 have been reproduced in Figure 12.5.

First, notice that the equilibrium quantity is given by the intersection of the retail demand curve and the retail supply curve. This quantity also exactly coincides with the quantity given by the intersec-

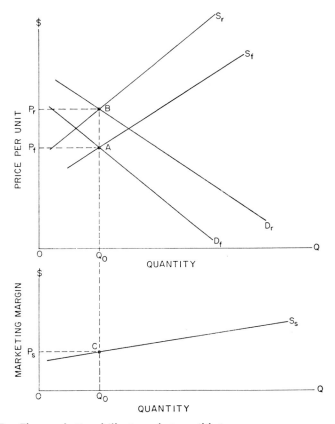

FIG. 12.5. The marketing bill at market equilibrium.

tion of the farm level demand and supply curves. Thus there is perfect correlation in quantities. Second, notice that the marketing bill for commodity Q can be reckoned as the area OP_sCQ_0 in the lower diagram. This follows from the fact that the per-unit marketing margin is P_s, and Q_0 units are currently being serviced. Third, the price at the farm level (P_f) is determined by the intersection of the supply and demand curves at the farm level, and the price at the retail level (P_r) is at the intersection of the retail level supply and demand curves. Finally, observe that P_r exceeds P_f by an amount equal to the cost per unit of servicing the commodity as it moves from farm to consumer, P_s. Furthermore, the marketing bill in the lower portion of Figure 12.5 (OP_sCQ_0) corresponds exactly to the marketing bill in the upper portion of the figure, P_fP_rBA. In other words, the total amount of money spent by consumers on Q in the present period of time is given by OP_rBQ_0. Of this amount, OP_fAQ_0

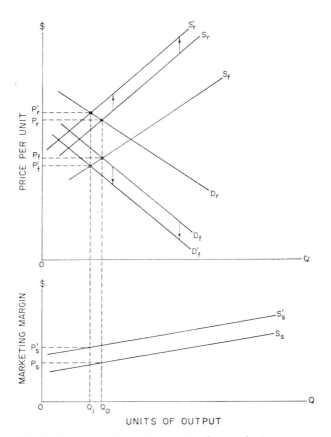

FIG. 12.6. Market impacts of an increase in the marketing margin.

represents farm level receipts for the commodity. The difference, $P_f P_r B A$, represents consumer expenditures which go to all phases of marketing between farm and consumer.

To analyze the impact in the market of an increase in the cost of marketing services, consider Figure 12.6. Assume marketing changes increase as reflected by an upward shift in S_s, with a corresponding upward shift in the supply curve at the retail level, and a similar downward shift in the demand curve at the farm level. Notice that an increase in the marketing margin has no impact upon the demand at the retail level, nor on supply at the farm level; its impact is reflected in shifts in the two derived curves. The net effect of this increase in the marketing margin is to raise the price at the retail level from P_r to P'_r, to lower the price at the farm level from P_f to P'_f, to reduce the quantity of Q

which moves through the market from Q_0 to Q_1, and to increase the total marketing bill.

Notice that the magnitude of the price change is a function not only of how much the marketing margin is changed but of the elasticity of demand at the retail level and the elasticity of supply at the farm level. If retail demand is relatively inelastic, a given increase in the marketing margin will result in a smaller price drop at the farm level and a greater price increase at the retail level than if demand is relatively elastic. Conversely, if supply at the farm level is relatively elastic, a given increase in the marketing margin will result in a smaller price drop at the farm level and a larger price increase at the retail level than if supply is relatively inelastic at the farm level. Thus the changes one observes in farm and retail prices depend heavily on relative elasticities.

In Table 12.10 we have listed some price elasticities at both the farm and the retail level. Additionally, income elasticities of demand at the retail level are also included. Finally, the column labeled "farm price flexibility" depicts the percentage change in price corresponding to a 1 percent change in quantity; this is the reciprocal of the price elasticity. Notice that the demand for the respective items is relatively inelastic with respect to price at the retail level, and even more inelastic at the farm level. The retail level elasticities contain the effect of the demand for marketing services on the farm product. Because the marketing services have higher price and income elasticities than the raw product, the elasticities at the farm level are lower than at retail.

The income elasticities in the last column of Table 12.10 contain the key to explaining the falling farm share of retail expenditures. The average income elasticity of demand for food at retail is estimated to be 0.26. Accurate estimates at the farm level are hard to obtain because of the difficulty of observing farm level demand (D_f). However, one estimate places the income elasticity for food at the farm level at approximately 0.15.[11] This means that a 1 percent increase in consumer incomes will raise the farm level demand for farm products by 0.15 percent and retail demand by 0.26 percent. Thus, as per capita incomes increase, most of the increased income devoted to food is spent on food services rather than for the raw product. This widens the marketing margin and reduces the farm share. As an example, assume an increase in income shifts the demand for marketing services from S_s to S'_s in Figure 12.6. At the new equilibrium, it is clear that the farm share has declined.

Finally, the price flexibilities in Table 12.10 can be used to further expand the earlier discussion on the instability of farm level prices. A price elasticity of -0.2 yields a price flexibility of -5.0, and

11. Luther G. Tweeten, The demand for U.S. farm output, *Food Research Inst. Studies* 7 (1967): 343–69.

TABLE 12.10. Price and income elasticities of domestic demand for selected agricultural commodities at the retail and farm level,
United States

Commodity	Price Elasticity Retail	Farm	Farm Price Flexibility	Retail Income Elasticity
Beef	-0.95	-0.64	-1.6	0.47
Pork	-0.75	-0.45	-2.2	0.32
Lamb	-2.35	-1.78	-0.6	0.65
Chicken	-1.16	-0.74	-1.3	0.37
Butter	-0.85	-0.66	-1.5	0.33
Eggs	-0.30	-0.23	-4.3	0.16
Fluid Milk and Cream	-0.29	-0.14	-7.1	0.16
Cheese	-0.70	-0.38	-2.6	0.45
Fruit	-0.60	-0.20	-5.0	0.40
Vegetables	-0.30	-0.10	-10.0	0.15
Cereals	-0.15	-0.03	-40.0	0.00
Potatoes	-0.20	-0.08	-12.5	0.08
Dry Beans, Peas, Peanuts	-0.25	-0.08	-12.5	0.12
All Foods	-0.34	-0.23	-4.3	0.26
Nonfoods	-1.02	...	...	1.22

Source: G. E. Brandow, Interrelations among Demands for Farm
Products and Implication for Control of Market Supply, Pa. Agr. Exp.
Sta. Bull. 680, Aug. 1961, Tables 1, 10, pp. 17, 50.

an elasticity of —0.5 yields a flexibility of —2.0. The price elasticities
at the farm level are all quite low and hence the price flexibilities are
large. This means that a 1 percent change in the quantity supplied has
a much larger impact on the farm price than on the retail price. Thus
the earlier concern over the instability of farm prices with respect to
retail prices is seen to be a function of the structure of the system; that
is, relative elasticities, which in turn are functions of the size of the
marketing margin, are to blame rather than any monopolistic practices
in the marketplace.

By way of summary, empirical evidence does not support the
hypothesis that excess profits are being earned by those businesses between the farmer and the consumer. The explanation for a declining
share of the consumer's food dollar going to the farmer can be attributed

to higher input costs in the entire economy and to the fact that households now buy a combination of service and commodity rather than just a commodity. It therefore follows that, since the farmer is contributing a smaller share of the final commodity, his share would fall. The food industry does have marketing costs that are quite stable in spite of variations in the volume of products marketed, with the result of large annual variations in farm prices. The solution does not lie in attempts to induce further competition in an already highly competitive industry but rather in programs to improve market performance by other means.

PROGRAMS TO IMPROVE MARKET PERFORMANCE

In Chapter 10 we discussed market structure, performance, and conduct. In this chapter we will briefly describe several programs whose principal objective is to improve the level of performance in the agribusiness sector. To improve performance, society can take a number of approaches. One approach is to improve the structural characteristics of markets. Such steps would include antitrust legislation, eliminating unfair trade practice, or procedures to improve the market position of the disadvantaged group in a price-making process. The first two are negative in that they prohibit certain actions, while the latter type is facilitative in that it sanctions activities of groups such as cooperatives by exempting them from the antitrust statutes. This category also includes the legislation permitting marketing agreements and orders. These two programs will be described in the first subsection below.

A second approach involves regulating the methods by which firms compete and includes such steps as prohibiting specific anticompetitive acts such as price fixing, market sharing, certain mergers, and product-tying agreements.[12] The facilitative policies in this approach include funding agricultural research and dissemination of results through the cooperative extension service. It also includes government efforts to equalize access to information by regularly reporting news and information relative to the market, establishing and maintaining product grades and standards, and establishing and regulating futures markets. These will be discussed under the general heading of market conduct.

The third approach to improve market performance is through direct regulation of performance. On the one hand, these policies include direct regulation of rates, structures, and profits of groups such as public utilities. On the other hand, they include direct government pro-

---

12. These are where the purchase of a certain commodity (say Kodak film) implies an obligation to purchase another commodity (send the film back to Kodak for processing).

grams such as price supports, subsidies, and demand expansion, as well as income maintenance and other welfare programs. The latter will be discussed in later chapters.

PROGRAMS TO IMPROVE STRUCTURE

This section will deal with two types of institutions to improve the structure of agricultural markets. The first is agricultural cooperatives, while the second is marketing orders and agreements. Both institutions have as their objective the bolstering of bargaining power of farmers, often referred to as fostering countervailing power.[13] Government can be said to have two roles in developing countervailing power: (1) permitting it to develop, and (2) where necessary, promoting its development. Cooperatives are an example of the first type, while marketing orders and agreements are of the latter type.

COOPERATIVES

Cooperatives are a type of business organization whereby a group of small units (buyers or sellers) can compete effectively in a world composed of fewer, more powerful units. *Cooperative* has been defined as "a business, voluntarily owned and controlled by its member-patrons and operated for them on a nonprofit or cost basis."[14] Many agricultural cooperatives in the United States provide marketing, purchasing, or service functions for their members. A few are nationally known, such as Land O'Lakes Creamery and California Fruit Growers, but most are small locally owned organizations.[15] Cooperative organizations also include mutual fire insurance companies, rural electric and telephone organizations, health maintenance organizations (HMOs), and credit associations providing financial assistance to farmers. Also, several thousand cooperative livestock improvement associations provide artificial insemination and other herd improvement services.[16]

Originally, the cooperative was defined by the Supreme Court as a combination in restraint of trade, and hence an institution that violated the Sherman and Clayton acts. It took specific legislation to exempt

13. J. K. Galbraith, *American Capitalism: The Concept of Countervailing Power* (Boston: Houghton Mifflin, 1956), p. 111.
14. Marvin A. Schaars, Farmer Cooperative—What They Are and What They Are Not, *News for Farmer Cooperatives* (Washington, D.C.: USGPO, Mar. 1963).
15. For a short historical account of agricultural cooperation in the United States, see H. E. Erdman, Trends in cooperative expansion 1906–1950, *J. Farm Econ.* 32 (Nov. 1950): 1019–30.
16. For greater detail on the types of cooperatives in agriculture and their relative importance by commodity groups, see USDA, Farmer Cooperative Service, *Statistics of Farmer Cooperatives 1968–1969*, FCS Research Rept. 16 (Washington, D.C.: USGPO, Dec. 1970).

cooperatives from antitrust statutes.[17] While for many years the major growth of cooperatives was in agriculture, more recent years have seen this type of business organization evolve into areas such as medical care and housing. To qualify as a cooperative, a business organization must include certain operational characteristics.

First, the ownership and control of the enterprise must be in the hands of its patrons. In other types of organizations, the business is operated to produce a return on the owner's capital investment. Since the users and the owners of a cooperative are the same people, operating a cooperative calls for different behavior than that for the typical business; the cooperative is managed for its member-patrons, not for its members as investors. This means that its primary objective is to buy, sell, or provide services for its member-patrons at minimum cost. This is in direct contrast to the noncooperative which attempts to maximize the differences between cost and returns.

Second, the cooperative allows each of its members one vote. This one-man-one-vote rather than one-share-one-vote insures that the user's point of view is dominant over that of the investor. More recently, several states have permitted limited voting on the basis of dollar volume of patronage which weighs management decisions in favor of the views of the more important member-patrons.

Third, the business must be operated as closely as possible to a cost basis. This recognizes explicitly the notion that cooperatives are nonprofit organizations, and it requires that they refund any returns above operating costs to their patrons on an equitable basis. Usually, any surplus distributed among patrons is on the basis of their past volume of business with the cooperative (patronage refunds). In contrast, the surplus in a noncooperative business organization is distributed as dividends on the basis of ownership (capital stock).

Fourth, the return on owner-invested capital is limited. Cooperative capital requirements are generally the same as for other organizations but its owners are treated differently. In cooperatives, the patrons are also the owners, but their interest in the organization is usually based more on the benefits it provides them as patrons or users rather than as owners. In principle, the return on capital investment is limited to 5 to 8 percent, a figure which reflects its opportunity cost. In practice, cooperatives generally have difficulty raising sufficient working capital. To remedy this, they frequently deduct a certain amount each month from patrons' checks and issue a stock certificate or other evidence of indebtedness to the member. These are returned after a certain period of time from a revolving fund. This procedure keeps the ownership in the hands of its current patrons rather than requiring outside capital.

17. See the discussion of the Capper-Volstead Act in Chapter 11.

A recent development in cooperative organization is the cooperative bargaining association. These associations are cooperatives organized primarily to act as middlemen in negotiating the price of products for their members. Unlike the typical cooperative described above, these associations do not engage in functions such as processing. Currently, there are several hundred such bargaining cooperative associations throughout the United States. These organizations are generally established along commodity lines such as for milk, eggs, and fruits and vegetables for processing. The National Farmers Organization (NFO) is, in effect, a bargaining association.

The primary difference between the cooperative bargaining association and the marketing order and agreement approach to be described below is a lack of police powers in enforcing the provisions of the bargained agreement. A cooperative bargaining association must persuade its producers to voluntarily participate in its program and carry out the agreement that has been negotiated. In this regard, the National Commission on Food Marketing recommended that boards be established which have the power to regulate production or marketing and power to negotiate prices or other terms of trade for agricultural commodities. The purpose of the recommended boards would be to strengthen the bargaining position of farmers in a market composed of large buyers.[18]

In summary, cooperatives are business organizations developed to improve the economic well-being of their members. If they are to be successful, they must achieve one of the following two objectives: (1) reduce the price or increase the quality of the product or service they provide to their members, or (2) increase the net returns to their patrons from the sale of patron products. Their objective therefore is to garner a larger share of any profits that exist in the system for its own members.

MARKETING ORDERS AND AGREEMENTS

Marketing orders and agreements are other means whereby farmers can improve their bargaining power. The Agricultural Marketing Agreements Act (1937) is the legislation permitting farmers or processors to organize and control the marketing of a specific commodity and remain exempt from antitrust statutes. The central purpose of the agreements is to bring about orderly marketing and thereby improve producer prices and incomes. Currently, there are approximately 45 marketing orders in effect for fruits and vegetables, and 59 federal milk marketing orders in operation. In all cases, the requirements for the order or agreement grow out of the imbalance of supply and demand conditions leading to unstable farm prices. The purpose of the agreement or order is to control price directly by negotiation or indirectly

18. The National Commission on Food Marketing, *Food from Farmer to Consumer* (Washington, D.C.: USGPO, June 1966), p. 111.

through the supply placed on the market. In addition to controlling the total volume, it is also possible to set the proportion of total production going into various regions of the country (or uses, such as for processing, or fresh consumption). In some cases, it is also possible to regulate the quantity of a product marketed. In the case of milk, minimum prices to be paid to producers are negotiated.

A *marketing agreement* is a voluntary contract between the United States secretary of agriculture and handlers of the commodity; it is binding upon those who sign it but not upon nonsignatories. A *marketing order* is an order issued by the United States secretary of agriculture for a commodity and makes the terms of the agreement binding upon all handlers or processors of the commodity whether or not they sign it. At present, no marketing agreements are in effect that do not also have a marketing order forcing all to abide by its provisions.

Much of the success of marketing orders and agreements rests upon the fact that there are demand curves with different elasticities in different regions of the country, or for different uses (fresh versus processed), or for different times of the year. If the market can be separated and the quantity offered in each controlled, different prices can be charged which will maximize total net returns over all markets. The technique is essentially that of price discrimination described in an earlier chapter.

In summary, the market order legislation provides producers with a mechanism to force all producers and processors to abide by a set of rules that have been established. In the short run, it has brought about orderly marketing conditions in formerly chaotic markets. Generally, the price of the specific commodity controlled by the order is higher than it would have been in the absence of an order. However, studies indicate that prices do not appear to have been unreasonably high. The inference is that agreements and orders have contributed in a meaningful way to lessening price instability, and hence have established stable incomes for those growing particular farm products. Over the longer run, however, success has not been as great. The orders do not contain effective methods for handling chronic overproduction; they do not permit production controls. Consequently, the problem of regulating and disposing of overproduction becomes progressively more burdensome over the years. This is particularly true for fluid milk markets.

PROGRAMS TO IMPROVE CONDUCT

MARKET NEWS AND INFORMATION

Earlier we described the complicated set of institutions and the many decisions made by thousands of individuals in the agribusiness complex. To make the best decision, each marketer, farmer, input supplier, facilitator, or consumer should have knowledge about the supply and demand conditions of the market. Furthermore, the theory of efficient resource allocation through competition assumes perfect knowledge. If one party has more information than another, he has an advantage and subsequently a potential to exploit the other. In addition to information concerning current market conditions, long-run decisions must also be made with respect to future consumption and production patterns. Here again, information on future market potential and the decisions of others are required if efficient long-run production decisions are to result.

Private concerns in the agribusiness complex spend large sums of money to collect information for their own use. They may maintain a large staff within their own organization or they may support trade organizations such as the American Meat Institute, the American Dairy Association, and the National Grocery Manufacturers of America. In addition, special publications such as the *Progressive Grocer* and *Feedstuffs* collect and disseminate information of particular interest to their readers. Also, a growing list of private research agencies gather, for a fee, specialized information for a particular client. With the exception of general-circulation trade publications, much of this information is available only to those who pay for it. Larger companies that can afford these types of services are thus able to improve their bargaining position through superior information. Small units, particularly farmers, cannot afford these services. Consequently, the federal government has undertaken a program to improve market conduct by providing market information—at no cost—to all parties.[19]

Three principal governmental agencies collect and disseminate statistical information: the Department of Labor, through its Bureau of Labor Statistics; the Department of Commerce, responsible for all censuses; and the Department of Agriculture.

Most of the information on domestic agriculture is centered in two major subdivisions of the USDA: (1) the Economic Research Service (ERS) and (2) the Statistical Reporting Service (SRS). These two services publish both periodic and nonperiodic reports. The periodic reports can be classified into two categories: (1) information relating to factors affecting future prices and the long-term trends in important market variables—generally referred to as outlook information; and (2) information bearing on current market supplies and price situations—generally described as market news. A third category publishes reports on general parameters of the state of the agricultural system. These include estimates of farm numbers, size, production, income, farm real estate, production expenses, and the like. These are published annually as summaries of agricultural statistics. The list of specific reports of commodi-

---

19. Notice that the justification for governmental participation in this activity is parallel to that used in justifying public support of research in agriculture.

ties covered by the periodic reports would cover several pages. To give some appreciation for the extent and type of coverage provided, however, a short description of the market news and information and outlook publications follows.

The outlook information includes approximately 20 different "situation reports" issued from one to six times per year, depending upon the particular commodity. They are designed to provide farmers with information that will help them to make monthly and annual production decisions. They are also useful to others in the agribusiness complex attempting to develop long-range investment and production plans. The reports include

The Livestock and Meat Situation	The Demand and Price Situation
The Feed Situation	The Farm Income Situation
The Fats and Oil Situation	The Marketing and Transportation
The Poultry and Egg Situation	Situation
The Dairy Situation	The National Food Situation
The Cotton Situation	The Tobacco Situation
The Fruit Situation	The Farm Real Estate and Market
The Vegetable Situation	Developments
The Wheat Situation	The Agricultural Finance Outlook
The Wool Situation	The Farm Cost Situation
	The World Agricultural Situation

In addition to these outlook and situation reports, the Statistical Reporting Service provides a large number of reports on estimates of crop and livestock production, inventory, and stocks. It includes monthly reports of field crops planted during the growing season; quarterly reports of grain stocks, number of sows and farrows, and number of cattle and calves; estimates of livestock and poultry numbers; and many other miscellaneous reports.

Many state organizations also publish outlook reports tailored to the needs of their particular areas and farmers. In addition, many agricultural colleges and experiment stations frequently issue public reports and hold informational meetings analyzing and interpreting the data in terms of the interests and conditions of local farmers.

The market news service provides farmers with the information they need to be better decision makers. These reports concentrate on the current situation covering day-to-day and week-to-week market conditions. They report on the movement, quality, and quantity of market supplies; price trends; and bids and offers on livestock, meats, wool, fruits and vegetables, dairy and poultry products, grains, hogs, seeds, feedstuffs, cotton, tobacco, rice, honey, peanuts, and a number of less important commodities.

Assembling the information that goes into these reports is a complex task. Market reporters are stationed at over 140 locations throughout the United States. These reporters gather information daily through personal interview, by telephone, and by mailed questionnaires. In making their reports, they interview buyers and sellers at central markets during trading hours, and they inspect commodities and records of transactions, loadings and unloadings of commodities, and stocks in warehouses and in storage. Information is disseminated by radio, the press, telephone, television, mailings, and bulletin boards. A recent study of the utilization of agricultural market news by farmers indicates that 96 percent of the farmers surveyed list the radio as a source of their market news. Sixty-six percent said it was their most frequent source of market news.[20] Recently, however, television has been increasing in importance as a source of farm market news.

In summary, the government publishes three types of information: (1) *what has been* (the annual summaries); (2) *what is* (market news); and (3) *what likely will be* (outlook). In general, the cost of agricultural production and of marketing services would be substantially higher and competition less if market news and outlook information were not widely and freely available. The information system discourages unfair price practices, reduces marketing risks, and facilitates more rapid marketing adjustments to changing conditions. If the system provides accurate and reliable information, it reduces margins and costs. Depending upon the relative elasticities of demand at retail and farm levels, these savings will be shared by farmers and consumers. However, if market information is to be meaningful, it must completely and accurately describe the product. Grades and standards are designed to fulfill this purpose. They are a natural outgrowth of the use of market news and information and without which such information loses its meaning.

GRADES AND STANDARDS

Grading is the sorting of products into lots, each of which is homogeneous in its characteristics. The characteristics upon which the products are sorted are termed grade specifications. Specifications might include factors such as size, weight, color, shape, taste, odor, length, diameter, strength, texture, contents of various elements such as moisture and foreign material, physical damage such as bruising or by insects, age, degree of ripeness, and tenderness. For example, wheat is graded according to its moisture content, number of damaged or broken kernels, amount of foreign matter, its weight per bushel, and its protein content. The specifications for different grades of wheat cover eight printed pages. The grades for beef are based upon the proportion of fat and lean meat

20. Joe M. Bohlen and George M. Beal, *Dissemination of Farm Market News and Its Importance in Decision-Making*, Iowa Exp. Sta. Res. Bull. 553, Ames, Iowa, July 1967.

in the carcass (reflecting factors of tenderness and flavor) and percent of salable meat in the carcass as an indicator of quality. In summary, the purpose of grading is to establish a common language understood and used by all buyers and sellers as a basis for judging their product.

Standardization is a process of establishing one set of grade specifications among all buyers and sellers. The standards involve defining the weights and measures and indications of quality used in establishing grades. If standards were not established, the grade specifications of two buyers or sellers need not be alike. The top grade of one producer might overlap the middle grade of another producer; or one shipper might choose certain characteristics in establishing the grades for his product and another a different combination of grade specifications. This avoids the chaos in the marketplace that would result if one shipper quoted number one soybeans on the basis of a 50-pound bushel, 10 percent moisture, and 5 percent foreign matter, and another on the basis of a 55-pound bushel, 15 percent moisture, and 1 percent foreign matter. As another example, there is little standardization of containers at the retail level. Although federal law requires that the weights and the contents be plainly marked on the container, packages are often specifically designed to appear larger or fuller than they actually are.

To avoid such problems, a grading system requires that standards be established, recognized, and constantly followed by all traders. For example, suppose grain producers had adopted the bushel as a weight measure or moisture as a quality characteristic. Then someone must define what is a bushel and how moisture will be measured. To meet the need for standard grade specifications, Congress passed laws giving the USDA the power to set up grades and standards for agricultural products sold in interstate commerce. In addition, many states also have laws delegating to state departments of agriculture the authority to establish and supervise grade standards for products sold within the state. Very often, federal standards are used as models by the states in developing theirs. In some states, where this is not the case, higher marketing costs result, since it is necessary to regrade products if they move through interstate commerce. It is estimated that the USDA now either grades or supervises the grading of more than 50 percent of all butter, cheese, skim milk, and beef; over 66 percent of the poultry; 75 percent of the frozen fruits and vegetables; 20 percent of the shell eggs; 25 percent of the canned fruits; and almost all the cotton, tobacco, and grains that are sold off the farm.

From our earlier theoretical discussions, we know that the free market system results in the tendency toward coincidence of supply and demand and the eventual price is one at which the market will clear. The use of grades and standards greatly facilitates this process of price discovery by establishing a basis for which one entrepreneur's product can be related directly to another. The result is a reduction in marketing costs and margins in six ways. First, buyers do not have uniform tastes or purchasing power, and they use products for many different purposes. Grading makes it possible for each buyer to obtain the quality he wants. For some, this reduces waste and gives them a product of higher quality than if they bought it ungraded. For others, the advantage is in being able to buy the lower grades at a reduced price rather than having to buy an average grade and discard the undesirable portion. Through grading, the two qualities are sorted out and sold separately at appropriate prices.

Second, grades make possible the sale of goods by sample or by description. This facilitates sale by mail, telephone, and telegraph, and it reduces the necessity of shipments on consignment. The buyer knows the quality of the products even though he has never seen them; he can buy them with confidence. As we shall see in the next section, this feature of grading also makes it possible to enter into transactions for future delivery.

Third, grading facilitates the settlement of claims. It is much easier for a buyer, seller, or transportation agency to determine the market value of a damaged or lost product that has been graded and inspected than in cases where the quality represented is just a matter of the opinion of one of the parties in the controversy.

Fourth, grading enables a pooling or intermingling of products, and thereby aids the concentration processes of marketing. For example, in cooperative marketing, pooling is an important feature of the operations. The products of many growers are included in various shipments and they lose their identity in the marketing process. Grading permits each grower's produce that is pooled to be paid for according to its actual value. Without a grading system, the identity of a farmer's wheat would have to be maintained throughout the marketing channel if he is to receive a fair price for his product.

Fifth, grading facilitates financing products through the marketing channels. Warehouse receipts indicating the grade of the product can be used as collateral for loans from credit institutions. In addition, sorting of the high quality products that are suitable for storage also reduces spoilage and marketing costs.

Finally, grading may help maintain effective competition. Small sellers can more easily sell to large buyers. If little standardization exists, the large buyer needing uniform supplies finds it to his advantage to limit as much as possible the sources of his supplies. With widespread grades and standards, however, he can satisfactorily obtain his need from many sources knowing that the quality is uniform, whether he buys it from the East Coast, the West Coast, or a southern farmer.

In summary, the advantages of grading are (1) it enables buyers to obtain the particular qualities of a product that they desire; (2) it makes possible more effective distribution by sellers and increases total returns; (3) it improves equity to individual producers, sellers, and buyers; (4) payment for the product on the basis of grade encourages the production and marketing of a better quality product; (5) it facilitates selling and decreases costs by making possible a sale of commodities without personal inspection; (6) it minimizes spoilage costs by separating the poor-quality products from high-quality products that can be stored; (7) it facilitates the settlement of claims; (8) it makes possible the pooling of products; and (9) it provides a common language for buyers, sellers, and market reporters, thus facilitating the exchange of marketing information.

RISKS AND FUTURES MARKETS

In the production and marketing of agricultural commodities, someone must always own the commodity. Ownership exposes the individual to two types of risks: (1) product deterioration or destruction and (2) changes in value arising out of price changes. Those engaged in production and marketing can take certain precautions to minimize these risks. They can buy an insurance policy to hedge against product destruction due to fire, windstorm, hail, or water; or the individual can hedge against product deterioration by buying the latest technical equipment, knowledge, and management techniques available to reduce spoilage and waste. Yet when he agrees to deliver a finished product for a certain price and then finds his raw material costs have soared, wiping out all his profits, he can buy no profit protection insurance. For example, a vegetable canner processes his products during a few weeks of the year, during which time he fills his warehouse with a product he has paid for. During the remaining months of the year, he sells from inventory and thus runs the risk that product price changes in his inventory will wipe out his profits. As a second example, consider a soybean processor. Since most farmers sell their soybeans immediately after harvest, the processor would ordinarily be able to buy relatively small quantities later in the season. If the processor wishes to keep his plant operating, he has to accumulate sufficient inventory to last until the next harvest. If, for example, he can process one million bushels per year at $2 per bushel, he would have $2 million tied up in inventory. Suppose that his plant is valued at $750,000 and ordinarily he would expect a profit of 10 percent on his assets (or $75,000). If soybean prices decline by 10 percent or $0.20 per bushel, he would suffer a loss of $200,000 or almost three times his expected profits.

The need to assume a price risk creates a source of inefficiency in the marketing system. We saw earlier that specialization leads to economies and low costs. Price risk interferes with this specialization. It prohibits the processor of a product, who also owns it, from specializing in processing and obtaining his profits from that particular service.

Therefore, he must include in the cost calculations a margin for price risks. Since he is not a specialist in this activity, it is inefficient for him and, therefore, more costly than when the function can be passed on to someone who desires to specialize in this activity. In the United States there is a method by which the processor can hedge against price changes by using futures markets.[21]

The *futures market* is a market in which commodities are bought and sold for future delivery. The actual article which is bought and sold is not a specific amount of a commodity but a contract for delivery of a specific quantity of a commodity at some specific future month and at an agreed-upon price. For example, when one sells a "May wheat futures," he sells a contract to deliver to the buyer sometime during May a certain quantity and quality of wheat at a certain price. The person buying the May contract agrees to accept delivery of the specific quality and quantity of wheat paying the agreed-upon price. It is a method of contracting for forward delivery. Futures contracts can be bought and sold only at particular locations—called exchanges or boards of trade— throughout the United States. In 1966 there were approximately 15 exchanges or boards licensed to conduct futures markets. They were located in Chicago (2), Duluth, Kansas City, Memphis, Milwaukee, Minneapolis, New Orleans, New York (4), Portland, San Francisco, Seattle, and St. Louis. Chicago is the most important futures grain market, and New York is the largest center for many other commodities.

In Table 12.11 are listed most of the commodities which are traded in futures markets. While the list of commodities continually changes as some are added and others dropped, there are approximately 30 commodities in which futures are traded. Trading in futures contracts can be for one of two purposes: hedging against price risk, commonly called "hedging," or speculation. The object of futures trading generally is not to deliver or accept delivery of commodities. Therefore, only a small portion of all futures contracts is ever settled by actual delivery. Instead, they are settled by an offsetting contract. To settle a contract in which an amount of a commodity was bought, the buyer merely sells an equal amount of the same contract. To settle a contract in which a commodity was sold, the seller merely buys an equal amount on the exchange. This two-way transaction completely clears the books for that individual on that trade. Generally, the speculator will be buying and selling only in the futures market, while the hedger will be buying and selling in both cash and futures markets.

As one might expect, a close relationship exists between cash

21. Firms or individuals use the futures markets for purposes other than to reduce or shift their price risks. For an excellent description of how firms which produce, handle, process, or market agricultural commodities use the futures market for other objectives, see Henry B. Arthur, *Commodity Futures as a Business Management Tool* (Boston: Graduate School of Bus. Admin., Harvard Univ., 1971).

TABLE 12.11. Commodities traded in futures markets in the United States, 1972

Apples	Lumber
Barley	Oats
Beef	Onions
Broilers	Orange Juice
Butter	Pork Bellies
Cattle, live	Potatoes
Cocoa	Rapeseed
Coffee	Rye
Copper	Sorghum
Corn	Soybean Oil
Cotton	Soybean Oil Meal
Cottonseed Oil	Soybeans
Eggs, fresh	Sugar
Fishmeal	Sunflower Seed Oil
Flaxseed	Wheat
Hogs, live	Wool

and futures prices for a commodity. Both are affected by the same fundamental market forces of supply and demand. The major difference between cash and futures quotations is the time factor. The cash price reflects the current demand and supply situation, while the futures price reflects the conditions expected to exist at the time the contract matures (the delivery month). Since each futures contract calls for delivery of the actual product, at maturity the futures and cash prices should be equal. At any time before the maturity date, the futures price should be above the cash price by the cost of storing the commodity until the delivery date. If the futures price were above the cash price by more than the storage cost, traders, observing the chance for a profit, would buy and sell until the two prices were in the proper relationship to each other. For example, suppose the cost of storing grain was $0.025 per bushel per month. On the first of February, the May wheat futures was quoted at $2.00 per bushel and the cash price was $1.90 per bushel. Since the cost of storage was only $0.075, an opportunity existed for a profit of $0.025 per bushel by purchasing wheat on February 1 and storing until May 1. Hence a grain dealer would sell a May future—contract to

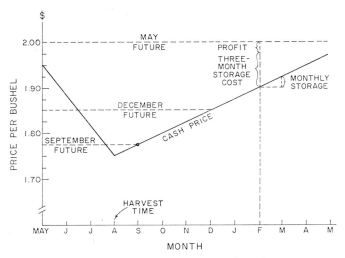

FIG. 12.7   Relationship of cash and futures prices for wheat.

deliver on May 1 a certain quantity of wheat at $2.00 per bushel—and on the same date he would buy an equivalent quantity of wheat on the cash market, store it for 3 months at $0.075 per bushel and then deliver it to fulfill his futures contract at a profit of $0.025 per bushel. Such a hypothetical situation is depicted in Figure 12.7.

While the example in Figure 12.7 is unrealistic in that futures prices are not constant, an important point of the example is that cash and futures prices tend to move up and down together and the cash price approaches the futures price as the contract becomes due. This is the basis upon which hedging operations exist. The other important point is that the futures price is the price that those in the market *expect* will exist in the month the contract expires. In the above example, they expected the price for wheat to be $2.00 per bushel on May first. Since the actual additions to the February cash price for storage would raise the May cash price to only $1.975, traders must expect some change in demand and supply conditions to raise the cash price $0.025 more.

One other important aspect should be noted. Since futures contracts represent transactions that will become due in the future, not the present, they can be bought and sold whether or not the individual actually has the commodity in his possession, or even wants it. This makes futures trading possible for speculators, since they will buy futures if they think the price will rise, hoping to resell them later for a profit. Similarly, they will sell futures if they think the price will fall, hoping to buy themselves out at a lower price. For hedgers, the basis of futures is the same. The difference for them is that they actually have a product to sell or one they wish to buy. If they have it and fear the price will fall before they can sell it, they will sell futures to make a profit (to offset their lower price for the actual commodity). If they need a commodity and are afraid the price will rise before they can buy it, they will buy futures to offset the higher cost of what will have to be paid for the actual commodity. This is what the actual hedging operation is all about. It involves an equal but opposite position in futures and cash. The hedger hopes to offset what happens in the cash market by what happens in futures. A loss in one will mean a gain in the other.

As another example, suppose an egg producer estimates his monthly production at 18,000 dozen eggs and he needs $0.35 per dozen when he sells them in order to make a reasonable profit. To hedge, he sells the 18,000 dozen eggs in the futures market. Since this is a simplified example, assume that the egg futures contract he sells is worth $0.35 per dozen, the same as the cash market price. As a bookkeeping entry, the egg producer's situation would look like this:

CASH MARKET	FUTURES MARKET
Owns 18,000 doz	Sells 18,000 doz
at $0.35	at $0.35

As time passes, assume supply conditions change and both the cash and the futures prices drop $0.02 per dozen. The egg producer sells his eggs for $0.33 per dozen and at the same time he liquidates his futures at $0.33 per dozen. In this example, his bookkeeping situation would now look like this:

TIME	CASH MARKET	FUTURES MARKET
Period 1	Owns 18,000 doz	Sells 18,000 doz
	at $0.35	at $0.35
Period 2	Sells 18,000 doz	Buys 18,000 doz
	at $0.33	at $0.33
	RESULT: $0.02 loss	RESULT: $0.02 gain

The egg producer got his $0.02 per dozen back from futures. If egg prices had risen $0.02 per dozen instead of going down, the egg producer would have had to liquidate his hedge by buying eggs at $0.37 per dozen. This would have cost him $0.02 per dozen in futures; but his cash eggs would have given him an extra $0.02 per dozen so he still would have ended up even. In our simplified example, he is protected either way. This type of hedge is called a selling hedge or short hedge, and it is a tool for any individual owning a commodity vulnerable to a drop in price. It can be used by farmers, grain elevators, warehousemen, merchants, and most processors and manufacturers who own the commodity.

Another hedge—the buying hedge (the purchase of futures)—is used to protect a merchant against the possibility of an increase in the price of a commodity he must buy in the future. For example, suppose a soybean oil exporter receives an order for 900 tons of crude soybean oil to be shipped several months hence. The price at which he agrees to export the oil is related to the prevailing price on the day on which he makes his deal. But since the actual shipment will be made, say, 4 months later, the exporter cannot be certain what price he will have to pay at shipping time.

He has several alternatives. He could buy the oil immediately and store it until time to be exported. But then he would have to pay storage, insurance, and interest costs for 4 months. This would tie up a great deal of capital and raise costs. He could also choose to speculate by not buying the oil immediately, but hoping that the price would drop in the next 4 months at which time he could buy it more cheaply. However, if the price rose during that time, the exporter would suffer a financial loss. For example, if the price rose just $0.01 a pound on his 900 tons, he would lose $18,000.

As a third method, the businessman could prefer to take a reasonable handling profit by hedging through the futures market rather than by speculating on a favorable price change. Assume the sale of the soybean oil for export was based on a cash oil price of $0.08 a pound. To that price, the exporter added the cost of preparing the oil for export, plus a profit. Then the price at which the soybeans are actually sold to the overseas buyers includes a profit margin that can be almost completely protected by the futures buying hedge.

To achieve this hedge, the exporter would buy the equivalent of 900 tons in the soybean oil futures market at the same time he signs the contract to export oil at some future date. Then if the cash price of oil goes up, the price of futures can be expected to rise as well. When the exporter finally buys the oil in the cash market at a higher price, at the same time he would liquidate his oil futures position. The profit from his futures would offset the higher costs for cash soybean oil and he would ordinarily come out even. In this case, here is how the bookkeeping would look:

MONTH	CASH MARKET	FUTURES MARKET
July	Sells 900 tons at	Buys 900 tons Dec.
November	$0.08 per pound	future at $0.0815
	Buys 900 tons at	Sells 900 tons Dec.
	$0.09 per pound	future at $0.0905
	LOSS: $0.01 per pound	GAIN: $0.0090 per pound

By using futures, the exporter hedged himself against most of his loss. The hedging operation also illustrates another very important point. A successful hedge not only protects the hedger against a price loss but also prevents him from sharing any price gain. Hedging is the process of shifting the risk of prices which change in either direction. In the above case, the hedge is not perfect; that is, the cash and futures prices do not move up and down together by exactly the same amounts. In this case the hedger stands to gain or lose a certain amount. Nevertheless, it is much less than the gain or loss he would have experienced without the hedge. It should be apparent that the amount of the price risk actually shifted depends upon how perfectly the cash and futures markets moved up and down together.

Speculators are the keystone of the futures markets because they are willing to accept the risks of price changes that hedgers wish to avoid. A speculator believes that his expertise will yield him a profit. This is the cost the market system pays for permitting risk transference. Speculators are the risk underwriters comparable to the insurance underwriters; without them, there would be no futures trading. In fact, some economists argue that to be effective for hedging a futures market requires much speculation.

Obviously, the potential for market traders to corner the market by buying up large quantities of the commodity, or of contracts, is great. This would allow them to manipulate prices in their favor. In earlier times, traders were able to obtain virtual monopoly positions in certain commodities. The Commodity Exchange Authority was established to supervise the operations of the futures and cash markets. The authority observes the operations of these markets, when necessary investigates certain practices and prosecutes violators, and generally encourages the exchange organizations themselves to police their operations.

When the hedging system operates effectively, it reduces costs. If speculators are willing to assume risks at lower costs than marketing agencies handling or processing the commodities, marketing margins to users of those commodities and to society as a whole are reduced. One can view speculators as specialists in risk-taking providing low-cost price risk insurance.

Futures markets also reduce costs in other indirect ways. Businessmen can usually reduce their interest charge because banks will finance a higher percent of a commodity loan that is hedged. Bankers recognize less probability of price loss on such commodities. It also encourages more rapid adjustments to changes in demand and supply forces. Changes in futures conditions reflected in futures prices are quickly adjusted for in the cash prices. Thus the futures market is another type of institution that improves market conduct.

SUMMARY

In conclusion, a smooth and efficiently operating marketing system does not achieve and maintain this state autonomously. It constantly needs adjusting both from within and through governmental action. The above-mentioned activities are highly beneficial to market operations. Cooperatives, marketing orders and agreements, market news and information, grades and standards, and the futures market all help adjust the market's operation more closely to the ideal of a competitive market, and to a more efficient allocation of resources that this implies.

SUGGESTED READINGS

BASIC

Clawson, Marion. *Policy Directions for U.S. Agriculture.* Baltimore: Johns Hopkins Press, 1968, Ch. 16–21.

Describes the possible form and features of agriculture in the year 2000 by exploring where the present forces, trends, and goals could ultimately lead.

Kohls, Richard L.; and Downey, David W. *Marketing of Agricultural Products.* New York: Macmillan, 1972.

Describes the food marketing system in the United States and the problems involved in obtaining adequate performance from the marketing sector. Devotes a chapter to the institutional and functional problems in each of the major commodity areas.

Shepherd, G. S.; and Futrell, Gene A. *Marketing Farm Products.* Ames: Iowa State Univ. Press, 1969.

A basic text in the marketing of agricultural products.

U.S. Department of Agriculture. *Agricultural Markets in Change.* ERS Agr. Rept. 95. Washington, D.C.: USGPO, 1966.

Reports on past and prospective changes in markets and marketing functions for agricultural commodities. Describes innovations, marketing developments, transportation, and particular aspects of the markets for various commodity groups. Contains an excellent bibliography at the end of each section for those interested in pursuing particular subjects further.

ADVANCED

Arthur, Henry B. *Commodity Futures as a Business Management Tool.* Boston: Graduate School of Business Administration, Harvard Univ., 1971.

Describes the use of futures markets by agribusiness firms to achieve entrepreneurial objectives other than the elimination or reduction of price risks.

Committee on Economic Statistics. Our obsolete agricultural data systems: New directions and opportunities. *Am. J. Agr. Econ.* 54(Dec. 1972): 867–80.

Discusses the design of a statistical data system that can continually adjust to the changing structure it is trying to measure. Argues that the major problem with the current statistical information system is an agribusiness structure that is changing more rapidly than the statistical system constructed to quantify it.

Greig, W. Smith. *The Economics of Food Processing.* Westport, Conn.: Avi, 1971.

Provides a general overview of some of the more important economic and business problems facing the food processing industry and speculates as to the future of the industry.

Helmberger, Peter G.; and Hoos, Sidney. Economic theory of bargaining in agriculture. *J. Farm Econ.* 45 (Dec. 1963): 1272–80.

Outlines the theoretical aspect of bargaining, bargaining approaches, and economic implications of cooperative bargaining.

Hieronymus, Thomas A. *Economics of Futures Trading for Commercial and Personal Profit.* New York: Commodity Research Bureau, 1971.

Describes and analyzes futures trading and its organizations, mechanics, uses, and impact upon the cash market price and market performance.

Moore, John R.; and Walsh, Richard G., eds. *Market Structure of the Agricultural Industries.* Ames: Iowa State Univ. Press, 1966.

Contains 14 chapters, each devoted to a particular food marketing or input supply industry. Each chapter describes and analyzes the recent history and present problems of that industry, the important characteristics of market structure and conduct, and the most important performance results.

National Commission on Food Marketing. *Food from Farmer to Consumer.* Washington, D.C.: USGPO, 1966.

A report of a special presidential commission appointed to study and appraise changes taking place in the food industry. Summarizes the results of a series of public hearings and ten special studies appraising the strengths and weaknesses of the food marketing system.

U.S. Department of Agriculture. *Market Structure of the Food Industries.* Marketing Res. Rept. 971. Washington, D.C.: USGPO, 1972.

Assesses the significant structural changes in U.S. food processing, retailing, wholesaling, away-from-home eating, transportation, and particular commodity groups such as livestock and meat and fruits and vegetables.

Working, Holbrook. New concepts concerning futures markets. *Am. Econ. Rev.* 52 (June 1962): 431–59.

Author traces the emergence of a set of six new concepts in the theory of futures markets arising out of observing the actual market operations. A good example of the interaction of theory and research in advancing economic understanding.

DISCUSSION QUESTIONS AND PROBLEMS

1. How is a futures contract different from most other contracts?
2. Outline how a hedge by a beef producer could assure him of a predetermined level of profit in his feeding operation.
3. Why are grades and market news an integral part of an efficient futures market operation?
4. Describe how the trades of a speculator in a futures market differ from the trades of a hedger.
5. Why do you think futures markets are more prevalent in agricultural commodities than in other types of commodities?
6. If you had the responsibility for establishing grade standards for beef, what groups of individuals would you rely on for developing these standards? Why?
7. In view of the fact that milk producers usually have a supply surplus, what advantages would accrue to producers by restricting supplies by a marketing agreement and order?
8. Would you expect a significant difference in the farmer's share of the consumer food dollar in the sales of farm products to low-income groups as compared to high-income groups? Why?

9. If there was a significant reduction in meat distribution costs and competition forced marketers to pass their savings on, who would benefit—consumers from lower prices or farmers from higher prices? Explain.
10. How would you explain the fact that cash prices in different central markets for the same product tend to move up and down together even though the markets are separated by substantial distances?
11. Under what conditions would cooperatives not improve the competitive structure of the market?
12. Analyze the impact of a reduction in marketing margins upon both farm and retail prices. Which will change the most? What assumptions are necessary to analyze the impact?

CHAPTER 13: HUMAN RESOURCES: THE RURAL POOR

In earlier chapters we have discussed the farm problem and have drawn the distinction among three types of operations within the farming sector. The first of these was referred to as the "commercial" subsector and includes those farms with sales in excess of $10,000 annually. This group accounts for only 36 percent of total farms but for over 90 percent of total farm sales. The average annual net income on these farms in 1972 was approximately $17,000. The second subsector, referred to as "transitional," contains those farming enterprises with gross sales per year between $5,000 and $10,000. This class accounts for approximately 12 percent of the farms and 5 percent of the total farm sales. Here, net farm incomes per year averaged approximately $3,500 in 1972. On the average, operators of these farms earned slightly more than this amount from off-farm jobs, bringing their total income to approximately $10,079. The third subsector, referred to as "marginal," contains the farms with sales of less than $5,000 per year. This class contains almost 51 percent of the total number of farms, yet accounts for only 4.8 percent of total farm sales. The average income from agricultural pursuits in 1972 for these farms was approximately $1,300, with an average of almost $8,528 being earned from off-farm jobs to augment this farm income.

Hence, while in Chapter 11 we talked of the classical farm problem and characterized it as overproduction in the face of a rather static demand situation, it should be obvious that there are at least three farm problems. The remaining two are of a different nature than the classical problem. Essentially, the farm problem for the transitional group of farms is one of acquiring sufficient capital to utilize new, more efficient machinery on larger acreages than currently being farmed. These are the farms that are still attempting to remain competitive through the adoption of better management, better equipment, or acquisition of more productive land.

The third group of farms presents a markedly different picture of the farm problem. Here, with over 80 percent of annual income derived from off-farm sources (on the average), the problem is not one of greatly adding to the nation's surplus of agricultural output, nor is it one of acquiring more capital. While there may be the usual concerns

with productive efficiency, the real problem is one of continued existence
in the face of unfavorable net returns.

The three classes of farms present different problems regarding
the human resources associated with each. The commercial farms are
replacing labor with capital equipment as rapidly as possible, and when
labor is needed, it is most likely seasonal in nature, perhaps even migratory. As these farms expand in size and output, more and more human
resources are displaced from agricultural activity. The transitional class
contains farms that are often viable only for single families. Hence, as
the children grow old enough to play an effective role in the operation,
the income is often inadequate to support them. Here too, labor is
redundant and finds little choice but to move to the urban centers.
Finally, the third class of farms contains the truly marginal operations.
Here, not only is there little opportunity for children to remain in farming but the poverty conditions under which they were reared often
result in poorer educational skills as well as poorer physical health.
Their migration to urban places is often an unsuccessful venture, and
one that can also be rather frustrating. Many of the urban problems of
the past decade are said to be traceable to the massive influx of poorly
educated rural migrants.[1]

Hence, the human resource problems in rural America, as well
as in urban centers, have roots in the three subsectors of farming discussed above. In this chapter, we will first discuss the theoretical aspects
of the generalized labor market to aid in the understanding of changes
which have been occurring in the demand for, and supply of, human
resources in farming. Following this, we will turn to a discussion of
poverty in general, and rural poverty in particular. Finally, we will discuss programs for the future with primary emphasis on human resources.
Recall from earlier chapters the statement that much of the progress, as
well as many of the problems, in agriculture is the result of public sector
programs. In the final section of this chapter we will see how the solutions to many of these problems will also be the domain of the public
sector.

GENERALIZED LABOR MARKET

In analyzing the labor market, the logical place to start is with
the worker's choice between work and leisure. This analysis will
follow closely the methods developed in earlier chapters when
dealing with indifference curves and budget constraints. Specifically, in
Figure 13.1 we have depicted an indifference curve I and a budget constraint. This budget constraint is slightly different from those encountered previously and will require some explanation. Notice that along

1. See, for instance, Niles M. Hansen, *Rural Poverty and the Urban Crisis*
(Bloomington: Ind. Univ. Press, 1970).

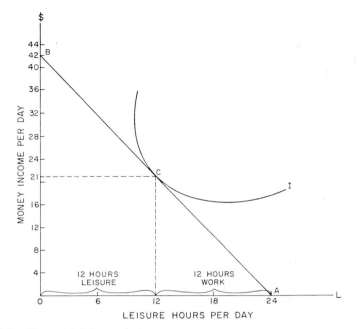

FIG. 13.1. The work-leisure choice.

the vertical axis we have plotted money income, and along the horizontal axis we have plotted the number of leisure hours in a day. Hence the budget constraint in this analysis presents the maximum number of hours available in a day for either work or leisure. Should the individual decide to work zero hours (have 24 hours of leisure), he would be depicted at point A in the diagram and, quite reasonably, would have zero money income.[2] Alternatively, if he could manage to work 24 hours a day at $1.75 per hour, his money income would be at point B ($42). More realistically, we can expect workers to be somewhere between points A and B; the precise point will be, as we have seen from earlier analyses, at the point of tangency between the budget constraint and his indifference curves. In Figure 13.1 this occurs at point C.

At C, the rate at which the individual is willing to exchange work for leisure (given by the slope of indifference curve I) is exactly equal to the relative values of the two endeavors. In this example, he would work 12 hours and earn $21.00 for an hourly rate of $1.75, with 12 hours of leisure per day. Thus the budget constraint represents a wage rate of $1.75 per hour.

2. Note that we are talking about income earned from the "sale" of labor services; it is entirely possible that a person with 24 hours of leisure per day would still have income from, say, rentals, stocks, a benevolent relative, or savings from work in earlier time periods.

Just as consumers react to price differences in their demand for commodities, sellers of labor react to wage differences in the sense that they will be willing to supply different quantities of their services at alternative wage rates. This relationship would be termed the supply curve of labor and is derived through the intermediate step of a price-offer curve. To derive the price-offer curve, we refer to Figure 13.2. In the figure, w_3 represents a wage-rate of \$1.75 per hour as in Figure 13.1, while w_2 and w_1 represent lower wage rates. The indifference curves I_1, I_2, and I_3 represent higher levels of utility. It can be seen from the figure that as the wage rate falls, the tangency point between the indifference curve and the budget line moves to the right. This means that as wage rates fall, workers are willing to supply less labor (have more leisure)—an intuitively obvious conclusion. For instance, the line w_2 represents a wage rate of \$1.00 per hour and we see that instead of working 12 hours as before, the individual now chooses to work only 8 hours (24 — 16). This results in daily earnings of \$8.00. When the wage rate falls to \$0.50 per hour, the individual chooses to work only 4 hours per day (24 — 20), for daily earnings of \$2.00. The line joining points C, D, and E in Figure 13.2 is called the price-offer curve and it traces out the combinations of wage rates and hours worked for the individual depicted by the figure.

By plotting the points along this price-offer curve in "hours-

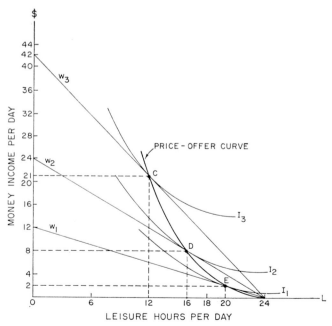

FIG. 13.2 The price-offer curve for an individual.

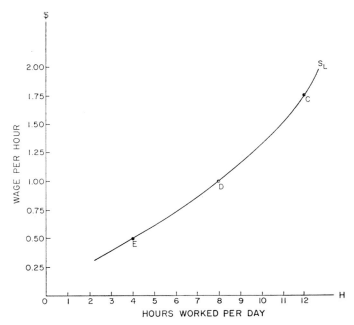

FIG. 13.3. A hypothetical labor supply curve for an individual.

and-wage space," we can construct a labor supply curve for the individual. This is illustrated in Figure 13.3. Notice that it has the slope we would expect of a supply curve—the seller is willing to place more services on the market in a given time period (here 24 hours) as the financial return for those services increases.

Having dealt with the supply of labor of the individual worker, we can now sum over a number of workers in the same market to arrive at aggregate supply, much as we did earlier for the supply of a specific commodity. By a labor market we mean here the group of workers possessing a rather homogeneous bundle of skills, training, etc. Hence, if the individual depicted in Figure 13.3 were a lathe operator, the aggregate supply of lathe operators would be found by summing all individual supply curves of lathe operators.

To develop a market analysis, the demand for labor must also be derived. It was seen in Chapter 5 that the demand for a variable input is derived from the physical aspects of production and the price of the final product under consideration. More specifically, it was shown that when there is one variable input, the *VMP* curve can be thought of as the demand curve for the input (since it traces out the maximum price an entrepreneur would be willing and able to pay for alternative quantities of the input). When the two concepts are combined, it is possible to con-

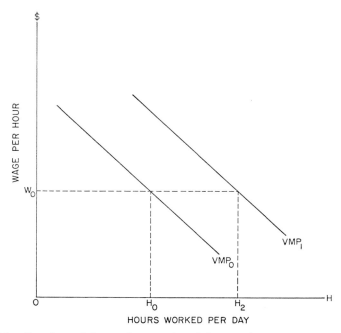

FIG. 13.4. Supply and demand curves in a labor market.

struct a diagram such as in Figure 13.4. The information here can be viewed in the same light as earlier supply-demand relationships, and the notion of market equilibrium can be discussed; that is, the quantity of labor depicted along the abscissa is assumed to be of homogeneous quality, just as for a good or a service. The ordinate measures wage rates, and according to the information in Figure 13.4, the equilibrium wage in this labor market would be w_0. To better understand the essential aspects of the labor market in general, and the labor market in rural areas in particular, we will now turn to a discussion of those exogenous influences and policies that have an impact upon (1) the supply of labor in a market and (2) the demand for labor in a market. We will then integrate the two sides of the market and employ comparative-static analysis to discuss different market adjustments to shifts in the supply of, and demand for, labor.

SUPPLY SIDE

At least four factors can influence the aggregate supply curve in a given labor market: (1) changing preferences regarding work and leisure, (2) alternative employment opportunities, (3) educational attainment and vocational programs, and (4) the size of the labor force.

CHANGING PREFERENCES REGARDING WORK AND LEISURE

It should be apparent that one of the most significant ways in which the supply curve of labor can be shifted is when personal preferences regarding work (income) and leisure are altered. This example is particularly germane in today's attitudes among many of the young. Specifically, as recently as 1965, the aim of most high school and college youth was to obtain a well-paying job and start the ascent to economic security, if not to considerable wealth. The counter culture of many of today's youth rejects this behavior as overly competitive and seems content to merely earn enough to "get by."

This is another way of saying that certain individuals have experienced a change in their preference functions regarding the work-leisure choice and now view work as a more passive endeavor which will permit them to earn a certain level of income—often low, by previous standards—so that they can "enjoy life." This shift in preferences would manifest itself in a leftward shift of the supply curve in many labor markets. If the demand for labor in these markets remained constant, wage rates might be expected to rise; those still in the labor market would benefit as those in need of labor bid for the scarce labor resources in a given market.

ALTERNATIVE EMPLOYMENT OPPORTUNITIES

The second way in which the aggregate supply of labor in a given market may be influenced is through changes in the employment opportunities elsewhere. Of special relevance for rural issues are the employment opportunities in urban areas; rural youths are attracted to the city because of the opportunities for work there and this has an impact on the supply curve of labor in farming.

In a study for the National Advisory Commission on Rural Poverty, Schuh found that the short-run elasticity of labor supply (both hired and unpaid family labor) with respect to nonfarm income was large (a larger negative number than -1). This means that a given increase in nonfarm income relative to farm wage rates will result in a greater than proportionate decline in the quantity of labor supplied to agriculture. Put somewhat differently, this implies that members of the farm labor force are more responsive to changes in nonfarm income than in changes in the returns to agricultural labor.[3] Recall that a supply curve or a demand curve is defined with other things held constant. In this case, one of those other constants—nonfarm earning opportunities—is altered and the elasticity of the labor response is measured; it is a cross elasticity. Schuh concluded that if the supply curves for hired

3. G. Edward Schuh, Interrelations between the Farm Labor Force and Changes in the Total Economy, *Rural Poverty in the United States,* National Advisory Commission on Rural Poverty, Washington, D.C., 1968, p. 176.

labor, unpaid family labor, and operator labor continue to shift to the left as a result of nonfarm earning opportunities, there could be a significant positive impact on labor incomes of those remaining in farming. This would occur because the demand for farm laborers is relatively more inelastic.[4]

In a related vein, Sjaastad correlated migration series for certain time periods with the level (percent) of unemployment in the economy as a whole. His findings seem to indicate that, in the past, migration rates from farming have been dampened by high rates of unemployment in the economy as a whole. This is in contrast to high migration rates from farming causing general unemployment in the economy.[5] Hence, when income earning potential off the farm is stifled, the impact on the supply of labor in farming is positive. When these barriers are reduced, the supply curve of labor in farming shifts to the left.

EDUCATION

The impact of education can have differential effects upon the supply curve of labor in farming—certain kinds of education shifting the curve to the right, and certain other kinds shifting it to the left.

The former kind of influence—increasing the supply—can be observed in programs such as vocational agriculture training, 4-H clubs, and the Future Farmers of America (FFA). Here the intent is to develop those attitudes and skills that would tend to promote the entry of young people into agriculture. In contrast, activities shifting labor supply to the left are probably of more significance. As rural youths receive better education, their opportunities to enter college or the urban labor market are considerably enhanced; that is, their mobility is increased and the opportunity cost of remaining in rural areas rises. Put differently, the costs in terms of income foregone by remaining in rural areas rise as one achieves more education; as this differential grows, there is a greater incentive to move to urban areas. Gisser found that increasing the level of schooling in rural areas by about 10 percent would precipitate a 6 to 7 percent increase in farm out-migration (and a rise in the farm wage rate of approximately 5 percent).[6]

CIVILIAN LABOR FORCE

Schuh found that in the short run labor supply in farming was inelastic with respect to changes in the civilian labor force; that is, *ceteris paribus*, a given increase in the size of the civilian labor force re-

4. Ibid., p. 176.
5. Larry Sjaastad, Occupational Structure and Migration Patterns, *Labor Mobility and Population in Agriculture* (Ames: Iowa State Univ. Press, 1961), pp. 8–27.
6. Micha Gisser, Schooling and the farm problem, *Econometrica* 33 (1965): 582–92.

sults in a less than proportionate increase in the quantity of labor sup-plied to farming.[7]

These then are four of the factors that can influence the quan-tity of labor supplied to the production phases of agriculture. Before general conclusions can be drawn, however, it is necessary to investigate the other side of the market—the demand side.

DEMAND SIDE

On the demand side, at least four factors can influence the quantity of labor being sought in farming: (1) physical produc-tion factors, (2) the price of the final product, (3) the price of other inputs used in conjunction with labor, and (4) wage rates being paid in farming. The influence of the latter factor is more long run in nature but is still important.

PHYSICAL PRODUCTION ASPECTS

As will be recalled from Chapter 5, the basis of a demand curve for one variable input being combined with several fixed inputs is the marginal physical product function. The position and slope of this function are critical factors in the position and elasticity of demand for a variable input such as labor. The way to view this effect is to divide technology used in an industry into three categories: (1) labor neutral, (2) labor using, and (3) labor saving. Since the first is trivial in the present context, we will discuss the latter two.

Labor-using technology is that technology which, when adopted, increases the demand for labor; that is, the demand curve for labor is shifted to the right with the adoption of the technology. Inasmuch as most new technology falls into the labor-saving category, examples here are not common. One example is in the area of livestock husbandry. It seems that certain measures can be used to increase the probability of twinning in cattle. However, twinning increases the possibility of com-plications at parturition and the need for someone to assist in the birth process. Hence, the demand curve for labor would shift to the right. This would be an example of labor-using technology.

Labor-saving technology is the commonest variety in most sec-tors of the economy including farming. New harvesting machinery for most crops not only replaced labor when first introduced but continues to evolve in such a manner as to reduce the need for labor. The new hay-cutting equipment introduced 10 to 15 years ago drastically reduced the need for hand labor but still required that labor be employed to operate equipment to bale the hay, gather it from the field, and stack it. Now, with new machinery, this process is handled by one or two ma-

7. Schuh, Farm Labor Force and the Total Economy, p. 179.

chines and can be done with but one individual. These influences cause the aggregate demand curve for farm labor to shift to the left.

PRICE OF THE FINAL PRODUCT

The other component of the derived demand for a variable input such as labor is the price of the product being produced. Recall that when one input is variable, the VMP function is the demand curve for that input, and the VMP function is the product of the marginal physical product function and the price of the commodity. Hence the exact position of the demand curve for labor in a sector is a function of the product price. Schuh found that the short-run elasticity of the quantity of labor demanded in farming with respect to real farm prices was less than one. This means that if real farm prices fall by, say, 10 percent, the demand for farm labor will fall by something less than 10 percent. Conversely, should real farm prices rise by 10 percent, the demand for farm labor will rise by something less than 10 percent.[8]

PRICE OF OTHER INPUTS

We saw in Chapter 5 that the ideal combination of two variable inputs is a function of their relative price; every time their relative price changes, a new combination is required if the entrepreneur wishes to produce a given output level at least cost or maximize output for a given outlay for variable factors. As the following discussion illustrates, this complicates the derivation of a demand curve for one variable input. In Figure 13.5, the curve labeled VMP_0 depicts the demand for labor when all other factors and prices are held constant. The price of labor is shown to be w_0 and the entrepreneur is currently utilizing H_0 units of labor. It is also assumed that this is the appropriate level of labor use in relation to other variable inputs such as water, fertilizer, and machinery.

To analyze the impact on the derived demand for labor from a change in relative input prices, consider Figure 13.6. Here, several isoquants are depicted in input space, with labor plotted along the abscissa and fertilizer plotted along the ordinate. The isocost line labeled TC_0 indicates the ideal combination of fertilizer and labor as F_0 and H_0, respectively. The H_0 here corresponds to the H_0 in Figure 13.5, and w_0 is similarly analogous.

From the discussion in Chapter 5, we know that when the price of fertilizer rises, its use will be decreased. In Figure 13.6 this price rise would be manifest in an alteration in the slope of the isocost line to TC_1. This latter curve depicts a price of labor at w_0 (unchanged), and a price of fertilizer at P_{F_1} (higher than P_{F_0}). In addition to the sizable reduction

8. Ibid., p. 176.

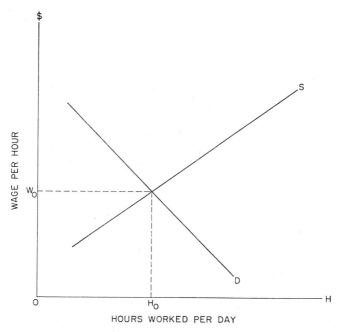

FIG. 13.5. Hypothetical demand curves for labor under alternative prices for other inputs.

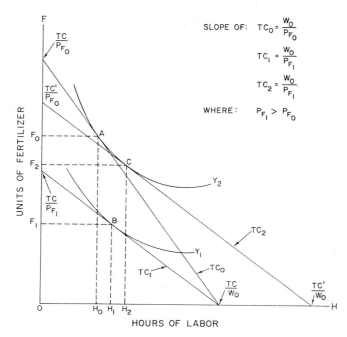

FIG. 13.6. The least-cost combination of labor and fertilizer.

in the use of fertilizer (from F_0 to F_1), there has been a small increase in the hours of labor employed. But, notice that for the same level of cost outlay (TC), output Y_2 is no longer attainable. Output is reduced to Y_1 as a result of the significant reduction in fertilizer. To achieve the same output level as before the rise in the price of fertilizer—that is, to get back to original isoquant (Y_2)—it is necessary to increase total outlays for variable inputs. The new total cost curve (TC_2) would have the same slope (reflect the same relative price between fertilizer and labor) as TC_1 and be tangent to Y_2. This occurs at point C. Here the new combination of fertilizer and labor is F_2 and H_2, respectively.

Note that while the use of labor has increased from H_0 to H_2, its price has remained unchanged. Hence, what must have happened is that the derived demand for labor has shifted out to VMP_1 in Figure 13.5; that is, a change in the price of another variable input has shifted the demand curve for labor. This result is rather intuitive since one can reason that as electricity becomes more expensive, the demand for natural gas will be enhanced, or that as the price of meat increases, the demand for potatoes will be enhanced. It all points to the familiar substitutability among several inputs to achieve a certain output.

However, not all production relationships are epitomized by substitutability and it is conceivable that complementary relationships exist wherein a rise in the price of one input (say a tractor that requires one driver) will bring about a reduction in the demand for another input (the driver). This would be reflected in a reduction in the demand for labor from VMP_1 to VMP_0 in Figure 13.5.

FARM WAGES

The final factor that influences the demand for farm labor is the wage paid to laborers in farming. As indicated earlier, in the long run, the wage rate is reflected back in the demand for labor: in the short run it is now obvious that an increase in the price of one input leads the entrepreneur to utilize less of that particular input; that is, there is a movement up the VMP curve for that input until its use is brought in line with its value at the margin. But, if this process continues, it may soon reach the point where the entrepreneur would rather use other means to accomplish the same task. Consider the earlier example of labor use in haying. As the price of seasonal help rises, the farmer may initially cut back on its use, partially substituting other inputs. If wages continue to rise and he continues to cut back on labor, he eventually reaches the point where he completely alters his production methods. As in our earlier example, he finally purchases a single machine that permits him to do without any seasonal labor. Hence, a long-run view of the demand curve for farm labor would show a shift to the left.

In Figure 13.7 we have depicted the trend in selected farm

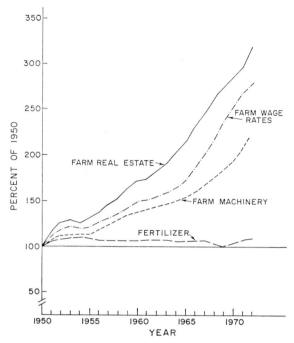

FIG. 13.7. Trends in the index of prices of selected farm inputs. (From USDA, **1972 Handbook of Agricultural Charts,** Agr. Handbook 439, Washington, D.C.: USGPO, 1972, p. 11.)

input prices (as a percent of 1950 prices) since 1950. Notice that both farm real estate prices and farm wage rates have increased the fastest, while the price of fertilizer has actually fallen.

In Figure 13.8 we have depicted the quantities used of selected inputs since 1950 as a percent of their usage in 1950. A comparison of the two figures indicates that those inputs that experienced the greatest percentage price increase (land and labor) also experienced the greatest percentage decrease in utilization. Hence, though the impact may not work itself out in the short run, the long-run demand for a factor is influenced by its price.

DEMAND AND SUPPLY

The previous discussion has highlighted four factors on the supply side and four factors on the demand side that result in shifts in the labor supply and labor demand curves. In this section we will employ the comparative statics of Chapter 9 to analyze several hypothetical situations in the labor market.

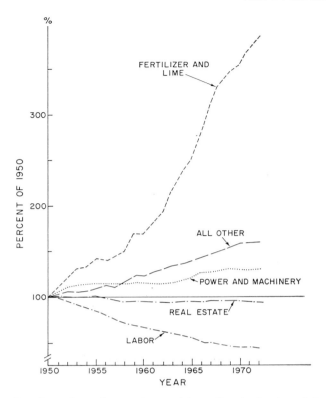

FIG. 13.8. Trends in the indexes of quantities utilized of selected farm inputs. (From USDA, ERS, **Changes in Farm Production and Efficiency,** Stat. Bull. 233, Washington, D.C.: USGPO, 1973; USDA, ERS, **Supplement V to Changes in Farm Production and Efficiency,** Washington, D.C.: USGPO, 1973, p. 29.)

First consider shifts in the labor supply curve brought about by enhanced employment opportunities in urban areas. From earlier discussions, we know that this would cause the supply curve of labor in farming to shift to the left as in Figure 13.9. As this shift occurs, the new equilibrium in the labor market would be established at H_1 and w_1 (point B). Notice that if the same amount of labor services were to be used as initially (H_0), a wage of w'_0 would be required (point D). Further notice that at this higher wage producers would be willing to hire only H'_0 (point C). If a new equilibrium were to be established at the old wage (w_0), it would require a leftward shift in the demand for labor to D_1 (point E). Here, the former wage would obtain, but the quantity of labor employed (in this case hours worked per day) would be only H^*.

The factors which might precipitate the shift from D to D_1 were

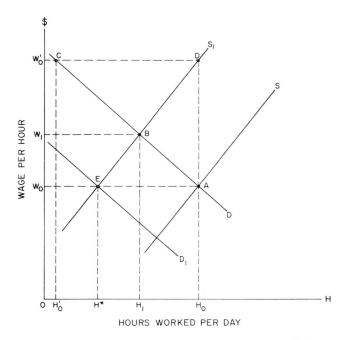

FIG. 13.9. Comparative statics in the labor market: shifts in labor supply.

discussed above and include a fall in product price, a change in the price of other inputs, and the long-run response to a rise in the price (wage) of labor. Notice that the latter two factors—a change in the price of other inputs, and a change in the wage rate—are actually subsumed under the heading of a change in relative prices of inputs.

Next consider the adjustment in the labor market brought about by a shift in the demand for labor. Assume that the consumer demand for a product increases, driving up the price of that product. We know that the demand curve for labor by an industry is the product of its *MPP* function for labor and the price of the product; when the price of the final product rises, the demand curve for labor to produce that product will rise, *ceteris paribus.* In Figure 13.10 this is illustrated by a shift in the demand curve for labor from D to D_1. Under these more favorable market conditions, producers would be willing to hire H_1 of labor inputs and pay a wage of w_1. At point C the former wage (w_0) would obtain, but this would entail more labor services employed in the industry (H'_0). Hence, it would necessitate a rightward shift in the supply curve to S_1 to enable producers to satisfy their demand for more workers at the previous wage.

Should producers wish to employ the same number of man-

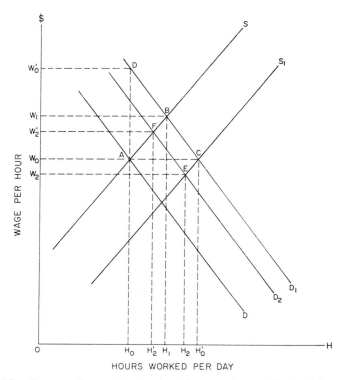

FIG. 13.10. Comparative statics in the labor market: shifts in labor demand.

hours of labor as before the change in demand for their product, they
would be justified in paying a wage of w'_0 since this level reflects the contribution of a man-hour to the value of the final product under the new
demand conditions. From earlier analysis, however, we know that the
tendency would be to expand the use of labor and so to increase production.

Finally, should the producers in the industry view this fortuitous situation as durable, the tendency might be to invest in more capital
equipment. If, as is usually the case, this new technology is labor saving,
we could expect the demand curve for labor to shift back to the left;
assume the shift is to D_2.[9] Here, with the labor supply curve (S_1), wages
would fall to w_2. Under the original supply curve (S), wages would be
w'_2. Under either labor supply assumption, wages are lower (w'_2 versus

9. Again we remind the reader that the degree of shift in all supply and
demand curves in this sort of analysis is purely arbitrary—the sole rationale is for
expository clarity. It will be helpful in understanding economic logic to experiment
with shifts of different magnitudes, tracing out the economic consequences of each
configuration.

w_1 for S; w_2 versus w_0 for S_1), and the quantity of labor hired is less (H'_2 versus H_1 for S; H_2 versus H'_0 for S_1) after the introduction of the labor-saving capital equipment.

Two issues are yet to be explored. First, recall from the discussion of Chapter 11 that one aspect of United States farm policy has been a program of price supports for certain commodities. To depict the impact of this policy on hired labor in farming, consider Figure 13.11.

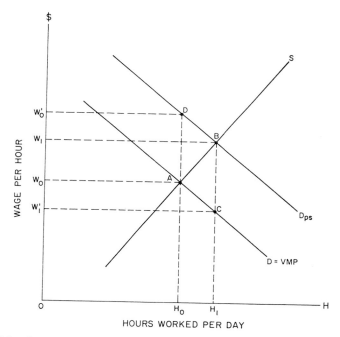

FIG. 13.11. Impact of government price support programs on the market for farm labor.

Here the demand curve D depicts the derived demand for labor without any government price-support programs. The curve D_{PS} is the derived demand curve for farm labor with government price-support programs. Assume that the producers of the product whose labor situation is depicted by Figure 13.11 do indeed employ H_1 man-hours per day at a wage of w_1. Now, if D represents the demand for farm labor under product prices which would prevail in the unfettered market, we can conclude that the demand curve D depicts the true social value of labor in producing that product at the margin. Put differently, the curve D represents the maximum amount any entrepreneur could pay for an hour's labor in the production of the product under consideration; for H_0 hours of labor, the industry could pay no more than w_0. However, with the government supporting the price of this commodity at an artificially high level, the amount that producers could pay for H_0 hours of work is w'_0 (point D). Alternatively, if H_1 hours of labor are employed at an equilibrium wage of w_1 (point B), we can assert that the true value of the contribution of labor is only w'_1 (point C). Government price supports give an incorrect signal as to the true social value of the commodity (D_{PS})— and consequently to the amount of labor to employ.

Several conclusions are possible. If farmers in fact perceive D to be their demand curve for labor, they would employ H_0 man-hours and pay a wage of w_0. However, D_{PS} depicts labor's actual contribution, and a wage of only w_0 implies exploitation of labor ($w'_0 - w_0$). Or, if farmers in fact perceive D_{PS} to be their demand curve for labor, they would employ H_1 man-hours and pay a wage of w_1. Here, however, labor, while receiving the value of its contribution at the margin, is overpaid with respect to its correct value at the margin (w'_1). In this latter instance, a government program to aid the income of farmers results in a distortion in the labor market which affects the allocation of labor between farm and nonfarm occupations.

Finally, consider the issue of minimum wages. In Figure 13.12

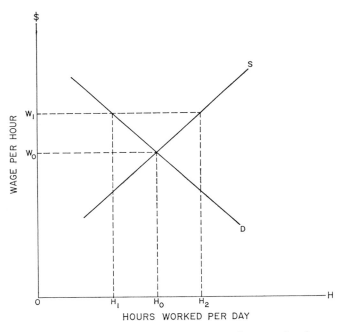

FIG. 13.12. The effect of a minimum wage on employment levels.

we have depicted a labor market in equilibrium at a wage rate of w_0 and the number of man-hours employed at H_0. Now, assume that a minimum wage of w_1 is established. At this higher wage, the derived demand for labor indicates that entrepreneurs would be interestetd in hiring only H_1 units of labor. But, notice that at this wage, workers would be willing to be employed at a level of H_2. The magnitude $H_2 - H_0$ represents the increment that would be willing to work at a wage of w_1 in contrast to w_0, while $H_0 - H_1$ represents the increment that is unemployed at the higher wage rate. Hence, unemployment would be the magnitude $H_2 - H_1$.

SUMMARY

In this section we have presented the general theory of labor markets. Indifference curves depicting the trade-off between work and leisure were combined with a budget constraint to derive the supply curve of labor. Concepts from production economics were employed to derive the demand curve for labor. The two sides of the labor market were integrated to permit the analysis of certain factors which cause shifts in these curves. The effect of government price-support programs for certain farm commodities was explored, as was the impact of minimum wage legislation.

We now turn to a more specific discussion of the labor market in rural areas.

THE POOR AND THE RURAL POOR

While our focus in this chapter is on the rural poor, it is insufficient to ignore the general phenomenon of poverty in the United States.

THE POOR

. . . I see tens of millions of . . . citizens . . . who at this very moment are denied the greater part of what the very lowest standards of today call the necessities of life.

I see millions of families trying to live on incomes so meager that the pall of family disaster hangs over them day by day.

I see millions whose daily lives in city and on farm continue under conditions labeled indecent by so-called polite society half a century ago.

I see millions denied education, recreation, and the opportunity to better their lot and the lot of their children.

I see millions lacking the means to buy the products of farm and factory and by their poverty denying work and productiveness to many other millions.

I see one-third of a nation ill-housed, ill-clad, ill-nourished.[10]

This famous quote came not from the Reverend Martin Luther King, nor from John or Robert Kennedy, nor from Senator George Mc-Govern. It came instead from President Franklin D. Roosevelt nearly 40 years ago. The topic of his concern was particularly relevant in the post-Depression years, but waned as an issue with the advent of World War II and the postwar prosperity. It was not until the Kennedy-Johnson years (1960–1968) and the civil-rights activism that poverty again became a pertinent topic for public discussion and government action. It is our intent in this section to ascertain the relevancy of Roosevelt's diagnosis for contemporary America. What indeed is the extent of poverty today? To facilitate the discussion, we will first describe two aspects of the poor —how many there are, and who they are. Then we will discuss several reasons why they are poor.

WHO IS POOR?

To determine how many (and who) are poor, it is necessary to establish a standard. Such a demarcation point will be the subject of much debate, yet it cannot be avoided. The President's Commission on Income Maintenance Programs has employed a standard developed by the Social Security Administration. The index is based on the USDA's measure of the cost of a temporary low-budget, nutritious diet for households of certain sizes. Then, to arrive at the necessary expenses of a low-income family, this food budget is multiplied by three to reflect the fact that food typically represents one-third of the total expenses of a low-income family.[11] The index is thus said to represent the minimum income needed to purchase a subsistence level of goods and services. Table 13.1 depicts the poverty index for families of various sizes in 1968.

Using this definition, the Office of Economic Opportunity estimated that in 1966 there were 30 million poor in the United States. Hence, if one is satisfied with the above definition of "poor," we have made some progress since President Roosevelt's speech. Indeed, between

10. From Franklin D. Roosevelt, *Second Inaugural Address,* Jan. 20, 1937.
11. The President's Commission on Income Maintenance Programs, Poverty in America: Dimensions and Prospects, *Poverty Policy,* ed. Theodore R. Marmor (Chicago: Aldine-Atherton, 1971), pp. 3–27.

TABLE 13.1.   Poverty thresholds for different family size by place of residence, 1968

Family Size	Poverty Index	
	Nonfarm	Farm
1	$1,748	$1,487
2	2,262	1,904
3	2,774	2,352
4	3,553	3,034
5	4,188	3,577
6	4,706	4,021
7 or more	5,789	4,916

Source: The President's Commission on Income Maintenance Programs, Poverty in America: Dimensions and Prospects, Poverty Policy, ed. Theodore R. Marmor (Chicago: Aldine-Atherton, 1971), p. 5, Table 1-2.

1947 and 1967, median family income grew by 76 percent (corrected for inflation). Also, using these figures of poverty, some conclude that we reduced the extent of poverty from 22 percent of the population in 1959 to 13 percent of the population in 1968.[12]

Using the above criteria to establish the poverty line, the Office of Economic Opportunity has summarized the poor and nonpoor by different characteristics. Notice in Table 13.2 that while the aged (over 65) constitute only 9 percent of the total population, they constitute 18 percent of the poor; they are overrepresented by a factor of two. Also notice that while nonwhites make up approximately 25 percent of the total population, they make up over 31 percent of the poor—again a situation of overrepresentation. While farm residents compose 5 percent of the total population, they compose over 8 percent of the poor population—a case of overrepresentation. Finally, rural residents make up 30 percent of the total population but almost 40 percent of the poor.

While the above data classify people according to an index based on budgetary needs, there are other ways in which to view poverty; that is, one way is an *absolute* indicator, the other is a *relative* indicator. Consider Table 13.3. Here we see that, according to an absolute criterion (column 2), the percentage of families below a poverty line has dropped drastically since 1947. However, in relative terms, the picture is less heartening. Specifically, the median income is defined as that level where exactly one-half the population receives more, and one-half re-

12. Ibid., p. 3.

TABLE 13.2. Selected characteristics of the poor and nonpoor, 1966

Characteristic	Number Poor	Number Nonpoor	Percent Distribution Poor	Percent Distribution Nonpoor
	(million)			
Age				
Total	30.0	163.9	100.0	100.0
Under 18 years	13.0	57.4	43.5	35.0
18-21	1.6	10.4	5.3	6.4
22-54	7.4	68.7	24.7	41.9
55-64	2.5	14.7	8.5	9.0
65 and over	5.4	12.6	18.0	7.7
Race				
Total	30.0	163.9	100.0	100.0
White	20.4	150.2	68.3	91.6
Nonwhite	9.5	13.7	31.7	8.4
Family status				
Total	30.0	163.9	100.0	100.0
Unrelated individuals	5.1	7.6	17.1	4.6
Family members	24.9	156.3	82.9	95.4
Head	6.1	42.8	20.3	26.1
Spouse	4.1	38.5	13.5	23.5
Other adult	2.1	17.7	7.2	10.8
Child under 18	12.6	57.3	42.0	35.0
Type of residence				
Total	30.0	163.9	100.0	100.0
Farm	2.5	8.5	8.2	5.2
Nonfarm	27.5	155.4	91.8	94.8
Rural	11.2	46.7	37.3	28.5
Urban	18.8	117.2	62.7	71.5

Source: Office of Economic Opportunity, unpublished tabulations from the Current Population Survey and draft report, "Dimensions of Poverty, 1964-1966." Reproduced in the President's Commission on Income Maintenance Programs, Poverty in America: Dimensions and Prospects, Poverty Policy, ed. Theodore R. Marmor (Chicago: Aldine-Atherton, 1971), p. 4, Table 1-1.

TABLE 13.3. Percentage of U.S. families poor by changing and fixed standards, 1947–1965 (1965 dollars)

| | Percentage of Families | |
Year	Income less than one-half the median	Income less than $3,000
	(1)	(2)
1947	18.9	30.0
1948	19.1	31.2
1949	20.2	32.3
1950	20.0	29.9
1951	18.9	27.8
1952	18.9	26.3
1953	19.8	24.6
1954	20.9	26.2
1955	20.0	23.6
1956	19.6	21.5
1957	19.7	21.7
1958	19.8	21.8
1959	20.0	20.6
1960	20.3	20.3
1961	20.3	20.1
1962	19.8	18.9
1963	19.9	18.0
1964	19.9	17.1
1965	20.0	16.5

Source: Victor R. Fuchs, Comment on Measuring the Low Income Population, Six Papers on the Size Distribution of Wealth and Income, ed. Lee Soltow, Natl. Bureau of Econ. Res., 1969, p. 200.

TABLE 13.4. Median income and the poverty line for non-farm families of four, 1959 and 1968

Income Measure	1959	1968	Percent Increase
Median Income	$6,355[a]	$9,948	57
Poverty Line	2,973	3,553	20
Poverty Line as Percent of Median Income	47%	36%	

Source: U.S. Dept. of Commerce, Bureau of Census, Current Population Reports, Series P-60, No. 35; Series P-23, No. 28; and Series P-60 released on Dec. 1, 1969. Reproduced in the President's Commission on Income Maintenance Programs, Poverty in America: Dimensions and Prospects, Poverty Policy, ed. Theodore R. Marmor (Chicago: Aldine-Atherton, 1971), p. 26, Table 1-8.

a. Median income for 1959 is for urban families.

ceives less. Notice in Table 13.3 that in 1947 almost 19 percent of United States families had incomes less than one-half this median income. In contrast, 1965 shows that 20 percent of United States families suffered this fate. Hence, while absolute indicators reveal an optimistic picture, the proportion of United States families receiving less than one-half the United States median income has actually increased slightly.

The comparison of median income and the poverty line is useful in discussing the increasing gap between the living standards of the affluent and those of the poor. Table 13.4 reveals that, while the median income has risen by 57 percent between 1959 and 1968, the poverty line increased by only 20 percent. Whereas the poverty line used to be 47 percent of median income, it is now only 36 percent of median income.

Yet another way to view the relative income of different groups in the United States is with the aid of a distributional breakdown as presented in Table 13.5. Notice that in 1970, 20 percent of United States families at the lowest end of the income scale obtained only 5.5 percent of total family income, while 20 percent of United States families at the highest end of the income scale had over 40 percent of total family income. Hence, however one measures relative income, there is a substantial group of United States families that can be called poor.

WHY ARE THEY POOR?

While some still maintain that people are poor because they are lazy, facts do not bear this out. First of all, of the 30 million poor in 1966, 5.4 million were beyond retirement age and hence could not work even if they wanted to (Table 13.2). But what of the remaining

TABLE 13.5. Percent of aggregate income received by each fifth and top 5 percent of families and unrelated individuals, 1950–1970

Item and Income Rank	1950	1955	1960	1965	1967	1968	1969	1970
Families[a]	100.0	100.0	100.0	100.0	100.0	100.0	100.0	100.0
Lowest fifth	4.5	4.8	4.9	5.3	5.4	5.7	5.6	5.5
Second fifth	12.0	12.2	12.0	12.1	12.2	12.4	12.3	12.0
Middle fifth	17.4	17.7	17.6	17.7	17.5	17.7	17.6	17.4
Fourth fifth	23.5	23.7	23.6	23.7	23.7	23.7	23.5	23.5
Highest fifth	42.6	41.6	42.0	41.3	41.2	40.6	41.0	41.6
Top 5 percent	17.0	16.8	16.8	15.8	15.3	14.0	14.7	14.4
Unrelated Individuals[a]	100.0	100.0	100.0	100.0	100.0	100.0	100.0	100.0
Lowest fifth	2.3	2.5	2.6	2.6	3.0	3.2	3.2	3.3
Second fifth	7.0	7.3	7.1	7.6	7.5	7.8	7.8	7.9
Middle fifth	13.8	13.4	13.6	13.5	13.3	13.8	13.8	13.8
Fourth fifth	26.5	25.0	25.7	25.1	24.4	24.4	24.3	24.5
Highest fifth	50.4	51.9	50.9	51.2	51.8	50.8	51.0	50.5
Top 5 percent	19.3	21.7	20.0	20.2	22.0	20.4	21.1	20.5

Source: U.S. Dept. of Commerce, Bureau of Census, Statistical Abstract of the United States: 1972, 1972, p. 324, Table 528.

a. Beginning with 1969, the data are based on revised methodology; for a description, see Current Population Reports, series P-60, No. 59.

24.5 million? Of those, nearly half (13 million) were under 18 years of age; for them most would agree that work should not yet be considered a way of life. This leaves 11.5 million persons between the ages of 18 and 64 that in 1966 were officially classified as poor. Why?

After considerable study, the President's Commission on Income Maintenance Programs concluded that our economic and social structure virtually guarantees poverty for millions. Excluding the aged, there are several reasons for this startling result. Consider the following:

1. Six percent of the nonaged persons that were poor in 1966 lived in families headed by aged (over 65) poor persons.
2. The heads of almost 2 million poor families (42 percent of the total) worked full time for more than 40 weeks per year.

3. Of the 4.5 million nonaged heads of poor families, 73 percent (3.3 million) worked for some period during 1966.
4. Of those 3.3 million, nearly 60 percent worked full time.
5. The balance worked either less than 40 weeks a year or less than 35 hours a week.
6. Of the 1.2 million poor nonaged family heads who did not work in 1966 (see items 3 and 4 above):
   a. Nearly 50 percent were women with responsibilities for young children.
   b. Another 33 percent were unable to work because of illness or disability.
   c. Of the remaining 230,000, 40 percent were in school and unable to work.
   d. Fifteen percent were unable to find work.[13]

We are left with approximately 100,000 nonaged poor who in 1966 did not work for reasons other than those listed above. Less than 3 percent of the nonaged heads of poor families might have willingly decided not to work; they might have also possessed certain disabilities not recognized in official statistics (primarily mental). Hence, while there are no doubt some lazy poor, it is an unfair generalization to argue, as some who were more lucky in life often do, that people are poor because they choose to be poor.

Hence, the "why" of poverty turns out to be much more complex than most imagine. The primary reason is a national rate of unemployment that has recently varied between 3.5 and 5.5 percent that hits the undereducated disproportionately hard. Second, in 1966, 3.1 million men working full time (two-thirds of them family heads) earned less than $1.60 per hour. A full-time job (2,000 hours per year) would thus result in a gross income of only $3,200. Locational aspects are also important as will be seen later in the chapter. While approximately two-thirds of the poor lived in urban areas (1966), the risk of being poor has been seen to be greater (Table 13.2) for those who live in rural areas where job opportunities are fewer. And finally, there is racial discrimination; nonwhites were earlier seen to be overrepresented among the poor.

In summary, why people are poor is impossible to answer with such clichés as laziness or personal choice.

THE RURAL POOR

We have already seen how the probabilities of being poor are greater for rural residents than for urban residents. It is our

13. See the President's Commission on Income Maintenance Programs, *Poverty amid Plenty: The American Paradox* (Washington, D.C.: USGPO, Nov. 1969).

TABLE 13.6. Persons in poverty, by rural and urban residence, March 1965

Residence	All Persons		Poor Persons[a]		
	Number	Percent distribution	Number	Percent distribution	Percent poor
	(million)		(million)		
U.S.	189.9	100.0	33.7	100.0	17.7
Total rural	55.3	29.1	13.8	40.9	25.0
Farm	13.3	7.0	3.9	11.6	29.3
Nonfarm	42.0	22.1	9.9	29.4	23.6
Total urban	134.6	70.9	19.9	59.1	14.8
Small cities	27.1	14.3	6.4	19.0	23.6
Metropolitan areas	107.5	56.6	13.5	40.1	12.6
Central cities	58.6	30.8	10.2	30.3	17.4
Suburbs	48.9	25.8	3.3	9.8	6.7

Source: President's National Advisory Commission on Rural Poverty, The People Left Behind, Sept. 1967, p. 3, Table 1.

Note: Because of different periods, different sources, and rounding, numbers here are slightly different from those in Table 13.2.

a. Income data for 1964. Based on Social Security Administration poverty lines (preliminary estimates).

intent in this section to discuss in greater detail those changes in the rural labor market which may help explain that situation. Table 13.6 presents a more detailed breakdown of the poor by urban and rural areas as of March 1965. Of interest here are those factors on the demand and supply side of the rural labor market that have brought about this marked change.

In essence, four factors—two on the demand side and two on the supply side—summarize the major changes in the rural labor market over the past 25 to 30 years. On the supply side, better education of rural youth, coupled with improved earning opportunities in nonfarm occupations, has brought about a considerable leftward shift in the supply curve of labor in farming. Concomitantly, the increased utilization of labor-saving technology, and an alteration in the relative prices of labor and other inputs (fertilizer and machinery), have tended to cause a leftward shift in the demand for labor in agriculture. Figure 13.13 illustrates the change in employment by industry groups for rural and urban resi-

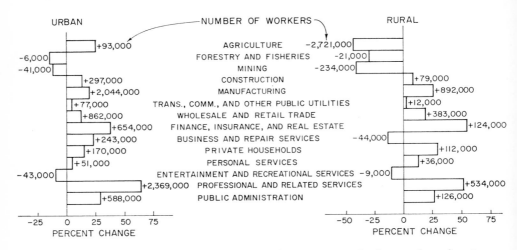

FIG. 13.13. Change in employment by industry groups of urban and rural residents, 1950–1960. (From President's National Advisory Commission on Rural Poverty, **Rural Poverty in the United States,** Washington, D.C.: USGPO, May 1968, p. 8, Figure 3.)

dents during the period 1950 to 1960. The trends evidenced there would seem indicative of probable future changes.

Shortly after the turn of the century, farm people made up a significant proportion of the total rural population. Between 1920 and 1940, the urban population increased by almost 40 percent, while the rural population increased by only 11 percent. Within the rural population, the nonfarm rate of growth was nearly as high as the urban, while the number of farm people declined very little (due to the Depression). However, in the following decade, the urban growth rate more than doubled its previous level, while the rural population experienced no growth. In spite of this lack of growth, certain changes were going on. Specifically, the farm population declined by nearly 25 percent; by 1950 the farm population was down to 23 million. By 1965 it was estimated that there were only 12.4 million farm residents. Figure 13.14 summarizes the average annual net migration out of agriculture for 5-year periods between 1920 and 1966.

The changes discussed above have not been equally distributed in all regions of the United States. For example, the Northeast has been considered predominantly urban since about 1900. Likewise, the North Central and Western regions have been considered predominantly urban since around 1920. Following the large decline in its farm population between 1950 and 1960 (40 percent decline), the South finally became predominantly urban at the end of the 1950s.

By way of summarizing this section, we will present some of

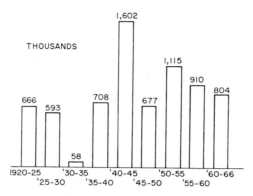

FIG. 13.14.   Average annual net out-migration from the farm population, 1920–1966; net change through migration and reclassification of residence from farm to nonfarm. (From President's National Advisory Commission on Rural Poverty, **Rural Poverty in the United States**, Washington, D.C.: USGPO, May 1968, p. 4, Figure 1.)

the recommendations of the President's National Advisory Commission on Rural Poverty.[14] These, when viewed along with the programs to be discussed in the following section, will provide the reader with a basic understanding of the current problems of human resources and with some suggestions for improving the lot of the less fortunate.

GUARANTEED EMPLOYMENT
        The commission strongly recommended that the spirit of the Employment Act of 1946 should be fulfilled. To quote from the act:

> The Congress hereby declares that it is the continuing policy and responsibility of the Federal Government to use all practicable means consistent with its needs and obligations and other essential considerations of national policy, with assistance and cooperation of industry, agriculture, labor and State and local governments, to coordinate and utilize all its plans, functions, and resources for the purpose of creating and maintaining, in a manner calculated to foster and promote free competitive enterprise and the general welfare, conditions under which there will be afforded useful employment opportunities, including self-employment, for those able, willing, and seeking to work and to promote maximum employment, production, and purchasing power.

        Given the rates of unemployment in rural areas, this attempt by the government to provide work for all those willing and able to

14. The President's National Advisory Commission on Rural Poverty, *The People Left Behind* (Washington, D.C.: USGPO, Sept. 1967).

work would be a significant social program. The programs during the Depression such as WPA (Works Projects Administration), PWA (Public Works Administration), and CCC (Civilian Conservation Corps) were all intended to put people to work in the public sector. The above programs concentrated on the construction of sewage and water systems for many towns, as well as on the development of certain conservation programs such as stream-bank protection, campgrounds, and forest trails. At the present time, Operation Green Thumb utilizes elderly rural residents to perform similar tasks in rural areas. An expansion of this program, or a revival of the public works projects of the Depression years, would go a long way toward fulfilling the spirit of the Employment Act of 1946.

MANPOWER

The commission recommended that the Employment Service be separated from the Unemployment Compensation system. This would permit the Employment Service to concentrate on developing an ability to serve the employer and the person seeking work. An elaborate computerized system should be developed so that those with skills could be matched effectively with those seeking skills. The scattered programs of manpower development, training, and retraining could then be organized as a single comprehensive operation. Additionally, a relocation program with training and assistance was recommended for the disadvantaged worker.

EDUCATION

The commission recommended that every 3-year-old child should be afforded the opportunity of participating in a comprehensive preschool program. We saw in Chapter 3 the extent of the disparity between rural and urban schools. Thus this type of program, coupled with a program whereby schools, regardless of their location, would have access to specialists, could mean that youngsters entered school with the best possible preparation. Further, it was recommended that an educational extension service be created linking all schools in the nation with national and regional educational laboratories and universities. Federal funds would be provided to upgrade teachers' salaries in rural areas and hence to induce the better teachers to work in these areas. It was suggested that rural schools might have to pay higher salaries than their urban counterpart to overcome the higher transportation costs associated with commuting.

HEALTH AND FAMILY PLANNING

The commission urged that professional and paraprofessional rural health manpower be expanded, and that community health centers be established. The role of planned parenthood is stressed with the recommendation that family planning centers be established. Much interesting research is going on at the present time dealing with the ideal type and extent of delivery systems for health services. Rural areas create a phenomenon referred to as the "social cost of space." This is simply another way of saying that population densities are so low as to make the provision of many public services very expensive. With modern technology, space is becoming less of an obstacle to many programs and hence we might hypothesize that the social cost of space is a decreasing function of technological advancement. Exciting studies to lend some rigor to these notions are being conducted in many states.

PUBLIC ASSISTANCE PROGRAMS

One troublesome aspect of current public assistance programs is that qualifications for access to programs vary across cities, counties, and states. What this means is that two people equally poor, or equally incapacitated, receive differential assistance depending upon the location of their place of residence. In addition to the moral inequities this creates, it also places a burden upon those localities that have more lenient requirements or higher benefits. The president's commission on rural poverty recommended that city and state residency requirements for public assistance programs be abolished. Also, it urged that the federal government provide funds to the states sufficient to cover payments required to meet nationally established minimum needs standards. There is progress here and these programs will be discussed in more detail in in the following section.

HOUSING

The commission recommended that the present program of rent supplements be expanded to facilitate the rental of housing by the rural poor. Countywide housing authorities were recommended to administer the programs of public housing in rural areas. Housing programs will be discussed further in the following section.

AREA DEVELOPMENT

The commission recommended establishing multicounty districts which cut across rural-urban lines so that the planning and coordination of area development could be accomplished in a comprehensive fashion. The commission also urged that federal grants, loans, and subsidies to industries be created so that both the goods and services produced by the private sector and those produced by the public sector are readily available to rural residents. This topic is the special subject of the following chapter.

With this partial listing of the recommendations of the President's National Advisory Commission on Rural Poverty, we now turn to a general discussion of those programs with special relevance for the betterment of human resources, which are either in existence or on the horizon. Some of them will deal specifically with human problems in rural areas. The majority are programs conceived with the intent of altering the lot of the nation's disadvantaged, regardless of their place of residence.

PROGRAMS FOR THE FUTURE

Earlier we stated that in the future the public sector would play a more significant role in the area of human resources. If there was any doubt about that statement, the above recommendations should partially dispell it. The exact nature of this role will be different, depending upon the area of concern. Also, because many of these programs are still in the formative stages, it is difficult to be specific. Nonetheless, enough information is available so that a few generalizations are possible. To conclude this chapter, we now turn to a brief discussion of several human-resource–oriented programs most likely to be instituted or expanded in the near future. These programs will be grouped under the headings of (1) welfare and family assistance, (2) manpower programs, (3) social security, (4) medical care, and (5) housing.[15]

WELFARE AND FAMILY ASSISTANCE

Perhaps because of our belief in the propriety of the free market as an allocative mechanism, the present system of welfare and public assistance is, in some experts' views, a national scandal. Taxpayers, administrators, politicians, and recipients are said to be unsatisfied. Many of the difficulties can be attributed to the fact that the system was never conceived as a unified package addressed to the problems of low-income persons. Instead, it is the result of an ad hoc patchwork approach. The initial efforts at public assistance appeared in the 1930s when major concern was directed toward job creation and social insurance. The main targets were those people who could not work and those who were not yet covered by social insurance.

By historical precedent, public assistance has been a state responsibility; the federal government would match, using a rather complex formula, the amount spent by the states. As a consequence, public assistance benefits vary widely among states.

The current public assistance program is not a general pro-

15. Much of the following material, excluding the theoretical discussions, is based upon Charles L. Schultze et al., *Setting National Priorities: The 1972 Budget* (Washington, D.C.: Brookings Institution, 1971).

gram, but it is intended to assist certain categories of people such as the aged, the blind, the disabled, and families with dependent children. The program of aid to families with dependent children (AFDC) was designed for those families with no husband, although in 1962 it became possible to assist families with unemployed fathers. However, because of state control only 23 states had initiated such expanded aid by 1970. Additionally, families of employed men are not eligible for assistance, even though they may be poorer than the families covered by the program. In addition to excluding the working poor from aid, the program encourages a husband to leave his family, even if he has a low-paying job, so that they will qualify for public assistance benefits.

When public assistance programs were first initiated, the expectation was that they would be short-lived. Such has not been the case. Public assistance expenditures, especially AFDC payments, have expanded continuously. Between 1966 and 1970, total money payments for AFDC programs (federal, state, and local) rose from $1.8 billion to $4.8 billion, or almost 27 percent per year. Rising unemployment and factors such as increasing numbers of broken families, more liberal eligibility standards, increased awareness of the program, and increased migration from the South to the North have been the primary causes of this expansion.

In 1968 President Johnson appointed the Commission on Income Maintenance Programs. This interest was continued by President Nixon, and in the fall of 1969 Nixon outlined the rudiments of a Family Assistance Plan (FAP). The Family Assistance Plan was never enacted and while the exact nature of any federal income program is still to be determined, five major attributes of FAP are worth noting. First, there would be uniform eligibility standards. These would replace the current maze of requirements that vary according to place of residence. One proposal would have this be a family income of less than $3,920 (for a family of four) and assets of less than $1,500 (excluding the value of the family's home, household goods, personal effects, and property essential to the earning of an income).

Second, there would be a uniform schedule of minimum benefits, regardless of place of residence. The federal floor would be $500 per person annually for the first two people in a family, and $300 per person annually for additional family members. Also, the family would be allowed to earn $720 annually with no reduction in benefits. A family of four would receive a minimum of $1,600 and would continue to receive some benefits until total family income, including earnings and benefits, reached $3,720. By way of contrast, a family of seven would have a cutoff at $5,720. Figure 13.15 illustrates the benefits for a family of four. Up to an earned income of $720 annually, the family would re-

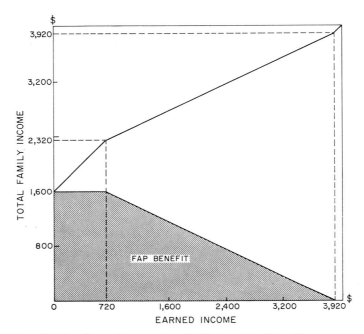

FIG. 13.15. The family assistance plan (FAP) for a family of four.

ceive all its FAP benefits. Beyond that level of earned income, FAP benefits begin to decline (shaded area).

Third, the Family Assistance Plan would provide for the inclusion of the working poor. For the first time, a family with a fully employed, able-bodied male head would be eligible to participate if his total family income fell below the poverty line for that size family.

Fourth, there would be an accompanying work incentive. Specifically, all of the first $720 earned could be retained. Thereafter, each additional dollar of earned income would decrease benefits.

And, finally, the Family Assistance Plan would provide job training and child care. For those employable participants lacking full-time jobs, FAP would provide for the development of an employability plan, incentive training allowance, training programs, and child-care services.

It is estimated that the Family Assistance Plan would reach 4 million families and add approximately $3.8 billion to the federal cost of current programs, but would result in savings at the state level of approximately $0.4 billion, for a net cost addition to the nation of $3.4 billion. The impact is summarized in Table 13.7.

TABLE 13.7. Comparison of estimated full-year cost of the family assistance plan and the current welfare system, by level of government and program, fiscal year 1972

Level of Government and Program	Total Cost under Family Assistance Plan[a]	Cost of Current Welfare System	Net Cost of Family Assistance Plan
	(billion dollars)		
Federal Government	16.1	12.3	3.8
Payments to families with children	5.0	3.7	1.3
State fiscal relief[b]	0.6	...	0.6
Adult categories	2.5	2.1	0.4
Day care and training	0.9	0.3	0.6
Administration	0.7	0.4	0.3
Medicaid[c]	4.0	3.8	0.2
Food stamps[d]	2.4	2.0	0.4
State and Local Governments	4.1	4.5	-0.4
Payments to families	2.8	3.1	-0.3
Adult categories	1.3	1.4	-0.1
Total	20.2	16.8	3.4

Source: Department of Health, Education and Welfare (for the House Committee on Ways and Means, 92nd Cong., 1st Sess.), Welfare Reform: Costs and Caseloads, Feb. 1971), Tables II-1, II-3, II-4.

a. Assuming 100 percent participation of persons eligible for the plan.

b. State fiscal relief results from a proposed 90 percent freeze on state expenditures, which would produce state savings, increasing with increased case load over time, but would result in a net flow of funds from states to the federal government if FAP benefits are raised high enough to eliminate most of the state supplemental payments.

c. FAP would result in some increase in Medicaid coverage, but this would not occur if Medicaid is replaced by the proposed federal health insurance plan.

d. If approved, a simplified proposal for the cost of food stamps to be automatically deducted from welfare checks, with the stamps then sent directly to the client, will result in increased cost.

In spite of the rather liberal coverage of assistance to many segments of the population, individuals living alone or in families without children would not be eligible for benefits unless they are blind, aged, or disabled. To include these would expand the number of beneficiaries by about 4.5 million persons and would cost an estimated additional $1 billion annually.

Families currently in poverty receive a variety of income-in-kind benefits such as food stamps, commodity distribution, public housing, Medicaid, Medicare, and others. It is impossible to go into the interrelationships among all these programs, but Table 13.7 indicates the estimated impact of FAP on several of these. Notice that federal outlays for food stamps and Medicaid will increase $0.6 billion annually, while state and local government payments will fall $0.4 billion.

The expense of FAP to the federal treasury has been estimated at approximately $3.8 billion. Some estimates run as high as $5 billion. This is a substantial difference in cost and there is much debate over proposals to redistribute income to this extent. However, to provide some perspective, some comparative figures are appropriate. The gross national product in calendar year 1970 was $977 billion. In the 1970 fiscal year, the federal government had budgetary outlays of approximately $197 billion. Of this amount, $88 billion (45 percent) went to national defense, space programs, and foreign affairs. Hence, even the liberal estimate of $5 billion for FAP represents less than 6 percent of what we currently spend on the above programs, or approximately 2.5 percent of total federal outlays in 1970 (or one-half of 1 percent of GNP).

The student should be clear on the implications of a family assistance program for the demand side of the market. To relate the discussion on a family assistance plan to our earlier economic concepts, recall that the budget constraint reflects the consumer's *ability* to purchase certain goods and services, while the indifference curves reflect the consumer's *willingness* to purchase certain goods and services. Benefits of the type discussed under the heading of FAP would result in an outward shift in the consumer's budget constraint, thereby permitting tangency at a higher indifference curve (attain greater utility). Knowing the price and income elasticities, the student should be able to predict the effect of FAP benefits on the demand for normal goods, inferior goods, necessities, and luxuries.

MANPOWER PROGRAMS

As indicated earlier, the 1930s saw an increase in the creation of jobs by the public sector with the expectation of doing something for people as well as for the nation. The Works Projects Administration (WPA) emphasized the creation of jobs rather than the usefulness of the project. WPA primarily took the unemployed and put them to work doing whatever they were capable of doing—building post offices or writing local histories. By way of contrast, the Public Works Administration (PWA) concentrated primarily on useful projects such as schools and kindred structures. Whereas WPA produced more jobs, it is generally recognized that PWA resulted in a greater product for the nation.

With World War II, unemployment ceased to be a problem and the programs were abandoned. It was not until the mid-sixties, with President Johnson's war on poverty, that job creation again became a popular topic of discussion. At this time, there were essentially two schools of thought on unemployment. The first notion, and one referred to as the aggregate demand view, was that unemployment was the result of an inadequate level of aggregate demand in the economy. It was argued that an increase in aggregate demand would push the level of unemployment down to approximately 3.5 or 4 percent. Admittedly there would have to be some training programs to relieve labor shortages in specific skill categories, but a major job-creation program was not needed. In the other "camp," one found the structuralists who argued that the current unemployment problems resulted from a disparity between an increasing demand for certain skill categories and an over-supply of unskilled laborers. For them, the solution was to be found only in altering the mismatch between the demand and the supply for labor skills. This could be accomplished through job training.

Over the years we have learned several things about unemployment—knowledge which now argues for public action of a new sort. Specifically, it is now obvious that even full employment will not solve the job problems of the poor. There is a trade-off between unemployment rates and the price level. Pushing unemployment down to 3.5 percent creates inflationary pressure in some manpower categories long before unemployment in other categories is eliminated. This is illustrated in Table 13.8 where it can be seen that unemployment rates of blacks and other minority groups, and of all races between 16 and 19 years of age, are uniformly greater than unemployment rates for whites. While there is not a necessary correlation between race and skill possession, past educational neglect of most minority groups is reflected here.

There is also a definitional problem here that merits elaboration. First, rates of unemployment are computed as the percentage of the work force that is out of work but actively seeking work. This is misleading since many of the poor and the low skilled or unskilled soon become discouraged and cease "actively seeking work." Hence, unemployment rates *underestimate* those out of work who would like to have a job. Another problem is semantic and concerns what is meant by full employment. When the Employment Act of 1946 was passed, full employment was considered as an unemployment rate of approximately 3.5 percent. However, recent difficulties in achieving this have prompted

TABLE 13.8. Unemployment rates for persons 16 years and over and for teenagers, and percent of adult men not in labor force, in metropolitan areas, by color, 1970

| | Unemployment Rate | | | | Percent not in Labor Force | | | |
| | Persons 16 years and over | | Teenagers 16 to 19 years | | Men 25 to 44 years | | Men 45 to 64 years | |
Place of Residence	White	Negro and other races	White	Negro and other races	White	Negro and other races	White	Negro and other races
Central Cities	4.9	8.3	14.3	31.8	4.2	6.6	10.3	15.2
Suburbs	4.5	7.4	14.0	26.6	2.2	5.8	8.5	14.2
Poverty Areas[a]	6.3	9.5	16.3	35.8	6.3	9.4	17.3	18.6

Source: U.S. Dept. of Labor, Manpower Report of the President, 1971, p. 87, Table 2.

Note: Data for central cities and suburbs apply to all standard metropolitan statistical areas; those for poverty areas, only to SMSAs with 250,000 population or more.

a. Poverty areas were derived by ranking all census tracts in SMSAs of 250,000 or more population on the basis of 1960 data on five poverty-linked characteristics. The tracts in the lowest quartile form the poverty areas. About 85 percent of the residents of these poverty areas live in their SMSAs central cities; the other 15 percent are in the suburbs.

TABLE 13.9. Differential rates of unemployment when average unemployment is 3.5 percent, 1969

Age	Male		Female	
	White	Black	White	Black
16 - 17 years	11.1	18.0	12.9	22.8
18 - 19 years	7.0	19.0	9.1	23.3
20 - 24 years	3.8	8.6	4.8	13.0
25 years and over	1.6	2.7	2.7	5.5

Source: Robert E. Hall, Why is the unemployment rate so high at full employment? Brookings Papers on Economic Activity 3(1970): 391.

administrations to redefine full employment to mean anything up to and including unemployment rates of about 4.5 percent. Hence, full employment still leaves many unemployed—particularly the unskilled, the minorities, and the young.

Another lesson is that, in periods of general unemployment, manpower programs supported by the private sector are scaled down since industry is, in general, laying workers off. Those programs in the public sector lead to cynicism and discouragement since there are few, if any, jobs once the participant successfully completes the program.

Third, if the economy is at full employment, it is extremely difficult to design comprehensive job-training programs because those out of work are a heterogeneous mixture of the young, the old, the rural poor, and the urban slum dweller. In addition to the previous table, Table 13.9 illustrates unemployment rates by race, age, and sex, as of April 1969, when the overall unemployment rate was only 3.5 percent. Note the differential rates of unemployment among the different categories.

Although the following focuses on rural labor problems, this does not imply that the problems of rural labor markets are any more significant than those of urban markets. In its 1971 *Manpower Report of the President,* the Department of Labor argued for the following kinds of programs for rural areas.[16]

First, it is necessary to improve the functioning of the rural labor market by creating the full range of employment services offered the unemployed in urban areas. More timely and comprehensive labor market information is required to better inform those seeking work. Particular attention should be devoted to aiding migrant and seasonal laborers in making the transition to nonfarm jobs. The report stressed

16. U.S. Department of Labor, *Manpower Report of the President* (Washington, D.C.: USGPO, 1971).

the relocation of workers and the development of manpower programs. It argued that the traditional exclusion of farm workers from most of the protective social and labor legislation must cease. There is also an urgent need to extend the federal-state unemployment insurance system to farm workers. The report recommends, too, that the right to collective bargaining be granted to farm workers. The gains of grape and lettuce workers in California represent steps in this direction.

The above analysis can be related to the earlier theory of labor markets by visualizing two markets: one for skilled workers, and one for unskilled workers. Each has a demand and supply curve, and each has an equilibrium wage. In the unskilled market, the equilibrium wage lies below that in the skilled market. Manpower programs would attempt to shift the supply curve of labor in the unskilled market to the left by training people so that they become skilled, thereby shifting the supply curve of labor in the skilled market to the right. In essence, the programs attempt to redefine workers from unskilled to skilled (think of it as firms leaving one market and entering another). Under such a reallocation, the wage rate in the unskilled market would rise and the wage rate in the skilled market would fall. It is this conceptual framework that prompts unions to adopt strict entrance requirements. While classic examples are usually confined to labor unions, the American Medical Association and the American Bar Association face similar situations in the skilled market and hence also influence wages by controlling entry.

The future of manpower programs is uncertain at this time—mainly in regard to their specific nature rather than to their evenutal existence. If unemployment remains high, manpower programs will be implemented soon. If, on the other hand, fiscal policy brings about a reduction in unemployment, their implementation will be delayed. However, given the existence of a permanent pool of unemployed, it is highly likely that a new form of manpower program will eventually emerge.

SOCIAL SECURITY

Depending upon one's values and beliefs, the social security program can be viewed as either the greatest step toward socialism this country has yet taken or as the most enlightened social program we have enacted. To proponents of the free market economy, social security is anathema since it allocates income outside the market system. To those inclined to view the market economy as a means to some higher end, the social security system guarantees a means of support to those too old to be productive or those harshly treated by the market system. In contrast to a private insurance program, the premiums paid into the social security program over the productive life of a citizen need bear no resemblance to the total benefits received after retirement. In general, the typical retiree receives benefits in excess of the total amount paid in. Additionally, the social security benefits are income redistributive because higher percentages are paid to low-wage earners than to high-wage earners, while the tax itself is regressive.

The system operates on the principle that the current working generation supports earlier generations of workers. Those currently employed pay into a trust fund which is invested in government securities. The interest earned from these investments, plus current receipts from social security taxes on income, are used to pay benefits to the retired. In the past few years, social security benefits have been raised a number of times. Inflation is primarily responsible for reducing the purchasing power of individuals living on fixed incomes. Without these increases in benefits, those living on fixed incomes would have assumed the disproportionate share of the costs of our inflation. The largest single category of individuals in this group are the retirees living mainly on social security. Frequent increases in their benefits are the only way that such groups can be maintained on a parity in terms of purchasing power with other groups in our economy.

While the payroll tax was 2 percent on the first $3,000 of income when the program was first initiated, the tax as of January 1974 was 11.7 percent of the first $13,200 of income. As it now stands, the wage earner pays one-half of this tax, and the employer pays the other. The social security tax is a regressive tax. It is assessed as a constant percentage of total gross income for incomes up to $13,200 (currently 5.85 percent for the individual's contribution). It makes no allowances for differences in net incomes of different families. As a consequence it requires a larger percentage of net incomes for lower income families than for the higher income families. For example, for a family of 4 earning $13,000, its social security tax represents 9.4 percent of its taxable income. The same family with a gross income of $9,000 paid 11.3 percent of its taxable income in social security taxes and at the $6,000 level, 16.7 percent. There are now several proposals to reduce the extent of regressiveness of social security taxes; these include refunding the payroll taxes paid by the poor, introducing personal exemptions into the tax, or crediting part of the payroll tax against the income tax. Regardless of these changes, many argue that the program is an inefficient way to provide minimum incomes to the retiree or widow where prior wages were not high enough to permit an adequate retirement income.

The major proposals under consideration at this time include (1) an increase in widow's benefits, (2) liberalizing the retirement test, (3) increasing the minimum monthly benefit, and (4) providing for automatic cost-of-living increases in the future (in contrast to the current frequent battles in Congress).

As of 1974, a wife or a dependent husband of a retired worker received a benefit equal to 50 percent of the retiree's benefit. A couple therefore received 150 percent of the basic benefit. Also, when a worker died, his widow received a benefit equal to 100 percent of his benefit if she was over 65. Under the present law, for each dollar of earnings above $2,400, social security benefits are reduced by $0.50. Under a new proposal, there would be an increase in the amount a recipient can earn and still be entitled to full benefits. Additionally, there is a Senate proposal to raise the minimum benefits to $100 for a single person and $150 for a couple. The current minimums are $84 for a single person and $126 for a couple.

The social security trust fund was expected to generate a surplus of $8.9 billion in 1972. It was this surplus that was used to earn dividends to further augment the fund. Whatever happens to the social security program in general, it is obvious that significant changes will be necessary when the current large number of people from the post–World War II baby boom reach retirement age.

MEDICAL CARE

One of the important debates of the 1970s will be the exact nature of a medical care program. While some might be perplexed over why medical care is a problem, anyone who has checked the facts would not be puzzled. In spite of rather high levels of expenditure for health care, and in spite of all the publicity given to certain aspects of our medical system (excellent technology, organ transplants, etc.), the United States has a poor health record when compared to other industrialized nations. Additionally, the access to health care is a significant problem; health care is considered by many to be a basic right of every individual, yet unbearable financial barriers prevent many of those most in need of health attention from receiving it. The problem is aggravated by the fact that medical costs have risen much faster in recent years than the rate of increase in general prices.

Between 1960 and 1969, the consumer price level increased at a rate of 2.5 percent per year, while the index of medical prices rose by 5.2 percent per year. Additionally, since 1965, daily service charges in hospitals have risen an average of 14 percent per year. It is not uncommon to pay $200 per day to receive good hospital care. To believe that the poor or the aged can afford this level of expenditure is unwarranted. Table 13.10 indicates the distribution of family personal health expenditures. In 1963 average expenditures for medical care were $370, with 8 percent of United States families spending in excess of $1,000. This 8 percent accounted for more than one-third (36 percent) of family medical expenses. By 1969 average family medical expenses had risen to $785.

TABLE 13.10. Distribution of family personal health expenditures, 1963

Total Expenditure for Health per Family	Percentage of Families	Percentage of Total Health Expenditure by All Families
(dollars)		
0 - 99	29.5	3
100 - 299	31.5	16
300 - 999	30.9	45
1,000 and over	8.1	36
Total	100.0	100

Source: Ronald Andersen and Odin W. Anderson, A Decade of Health Services (Chicago: Univ. Chicago Press, 1967), pp. 57-58.

In fiscal year 1970, total outlays for medical care of both private and public sources approached $62 billion—roughly 7 percent of our gross national product, and a larger share of GNP than in other major nations. If present trends continue, it is estimated that by 1975 we will spend, on hospital care alone, twice what was spent in 1960 for all medical services. In spite of this, fourteen industrial nations have lower infant mortality rates than the United States, and eighteen have a longer life expectancy for 20-year-old males.

In spite of our substantial expenditures as a nation, those living in rural areas, and the poor, regardless of their place of residence, get much poorer health care than the general population. For example, in 1967 the infant mortality rate in several low-income Mississippi counties was approximately 45 per 1,000 live births. In contrast, the rate for the whole United States was 22.4 per 1,000 live births, and in certain very wealthy areas—such as Montgomery County, Maryland—the rate was 17 per 1,000 live births.

In recognition that something must be done to improve the quality, accessibility, and cost of medical care, many proposals have been made to establish some form of national health care for all. Early in 1971 President Nixon introduced a National Health Insurance Partnership. This plan would require employers to provide a minimum standard health insurance policy for employees and their dependents. No federal subsidy would be involved. The cost was to be shared by employers and employees. This program would cover approximately 150 million persons but would exclude over one-fourth of the population. Governmental employees would be excluded since they already are covered by rather comprehensive programs. Also, part-time workers, seasonal workers, domestic help, the self-employed, and obviously the unemployed would be excluded. To cover these, a variety of other programs would be designed to supplement current Medicare and Medicaid programs.

A number of other plans are also being considered by Congress, the most widely known is the Health Security Act sponsored by Senator Edward M. Kennedy and Representative Martha Griffiths. Unlike the Nixon proposal, this legislation would establish a national health care program where the federal government administers health insurance for everyone. Either proposal requires a vast administrative structure. The Nixon plan would utilize present private insurance companies— a point of criticism to some. Under the Kennedy-Griffiths proposal, a much larger share of national health expenditures would appear in the federal budget, estimated to be as much as $70 billion in the first year of operation. Under the Nixon plan, only certain supplemental expenses would appear in the federal budget since employees and employers share most of the costs directly. Under this proposal, federal outlays would be expected to approach $16 billion in the first year.

What is important here is not whether Americans receive better health care as measured by the amount appearing in the federal budget but the changes that can be made in the delivery systems of our present medical knowledge to improve citizen well-being. This is particularly important to the residents of rural areas where great distances to doctors and hospitals currently compound the often exhorbitant costs associated with adequate medical care.

The point is that any medical delivery system must be income redistributive. Medical care is costly and the low-income family does not have the resources to acquire it. Hence, any program whose objective is adequate medical care for all individuals must tax those who can afford it to provide it to those who cannot.

HOUSING

Concern over housing at the national level is directed at three objectives: (1) the need to construct housing to meet the expected increase in the number of families growing out of the baby boom of the mid-1940s, (2) the desire to improve the quality of existing housing, and (3) the need to provide adequate housing for the poor and near-poor families who now spend an inordinate proportion of their income on shelter. To meet these objectives, the federal government has been active in housing programs under the Housing and Urban Development Act of 1968. The act set as a national goal for the subsequent decade the construction of 25 million new housing units, and the public subsidization of 6 million new and refurbished units for poor and near-poor families. To achieve these goals, the federal government is prepared to spend between $5 and $6 billion during the next decade to subsidize housing directly. In addition, it stands ready through monetary and fiscal policy to influence housing starts through the interest rate as well as through the availability of loanable funds in the nation's banks and lending institutions.

As indicated above, the act was designed to create 25 million new units by 1978. The estimate of 25 million units was based on a number of demographic and economic factors that are expected to affect the demand for housing, including the level of household formation (e.g., the number of new families being created), the price of housing relative to the general price level, changes in after-tax income of households, and general monetary conditions. As shown in Table 13.11, the estimate of

TABLE 13.11. Comparison of national housing goals with projections based on high and low rates of household formation and varying economic conditions, 10-year totals by type of housing unit, fiscal years 1969–1978

Type of Projection	Single Unit Starts	Multi-unit Starts	Total Housing Starts	New Mobile Homes	Total New Housing Units
			(million)		
National Housing Goals	10.8	10.2	21.0	4.0	25.0
Alternative Projections					
High rate of household formation					
Favorable economic conditions	10.7	7.7	18.4	5.0	23.4
Slower economic growth	10.0	7.8	17.8	5.0	22.8
Unfavorable construction prices	9.8	7.9	17.8	5.2	23.0
Tight monetary policy	10.1	6.8	16.9	5.0	21.9
Low rate of household formation					
Favorable economic conditions	10.2	6.5	16.7	4.9	21.6
Slower economic growth	9.5	6.6	16.1	4.9	21.0

Source: Charles L. Schultze, E. R. Fried, Alice M. Rivlin, and Nancy H. Teeters, Setting National Priorities: The 1972 Budget (Washington, D.C.: Brookings Institution, 1971), p. 287, Table 14-7.

25 million units is substantially above those assumed under the most favorable economic conditions. In fact, they are much higher than those observed over the past two decades. The effect on estimated housing units required under less optimistic assumptions are also shown in Table 13.11. For example, if relative construction costs increase as they have in the past, 23 million new units will be created with multifamily units and mobile homes being a larger share of total housing units. The purpose of this discussion is to illustrate the point that our national goals are substantially above the level of housing that the market is estimated to provide. Furthermore, government activity in monetary and fiscal policy has a substantial impact on the number of new units created. Estimates range from a low of 21 million to a high of 23.4 million units. The Housing and Urban Development Act was designed to close this gap.

In Table 13.12 we present estimates of federally assisted housing starts for fiscal years 1971, 1972, and 1975. The bulk of housing starts

TABLE 13.12. Federally assisted housing starts, by program, for fiscal year 1968 and estimates for fiscal years 1971, 1972, and 1975

Subsidized Program	1968 Actual	1971 1970	1971 1971 (estimates)	1972 1970	1972 1971	1975[a] 1970 (estimate)
		(thousand)				
For Poor Families						
Low-rent public housing	51	94	100	94	95	121
Rent supplements	12	13	20	32	32	30
For Moderate-Income Families						
Home ownership	44[b]	141	162	128	163	144
Rental housing	15[c]	73	124	151	188	144
Total, excluding rural housing	122	321	406	405	478	439
Rural housing[d]	35	101	...	147	...	147

Source: Charles L. Schultze, E. R. Fried, Alice M. Rivlin, and Nancy H. Teeters, Setting National Priorities: The 1972 Budget (Washington, D.C.: Brookings Institution, 1971), p. 279, Table 14-1.

a. 1971 estimates for 1975 are not available.

b. Loans for low-income and moderate-income housing.

c. Housing for the elderly and rehabilitation loans and grants.

d. Farmers Home Administration housing program. Not reestimated in 1971.

in 1972 was expected to be for moderate-income rather than for low-income families. The rationale is that, as the near-poor move into these new units, their old housing will become available for the poor. The major programs provide that (1) the federal government will pay the difference between 20 percent of the family's income and the mortgage payments on approved housing, (2) the federal government will pay the difference between 25 percent of the family's income and fair market rents in special housing projects, and (3) the Farmers Home Administration makes loans at subsidized rates of interest to moderate-income families in rural areas. For the first two programs, federal outlays were expected to increase from the 1970 level of $23 million to $450 million in fiscal 1972.

In addition to the 25 million new units described above, plans have been made to build 5 million new units and to rehabilitate 1 million existing units under a subsidy that will bring their price or rental rate within the reach of low-income and moderate-income families. This program is predicated upon the premise that the current housing of the poor and the near-poor is substandard. Some of the attributes of families occupying substandard housing are shown in Table 13.13. Substandard is defined as dilapidated or as nondilapidated but lacking facilities such as hot and cold running water and separate kitchen and toilet facilities for each household in the dwelling. Of the 6.5 million substandard units in 1966, 1.5 million were occupied by nonelderly single persons (6.5 — 5.0), primarily those residing in rooming houses or similar units. Of the remaining 5 million, more than one-half were in rural areas, 2.7 million units. More than 50 percent of the rural poor, and almost 30 percent of rural households with moderate incomes, lived in substandard housing in 1966. Additionally, only a small percentage of poor urban households, and an even smaller proportion of the moderate-income urban households, lived in substandard units. Hence, substandard housing is a particularly severe problem in rural areas.

One difference between rural residents and their urban counterparts is found in the share of income that must be allocated to housing. In urban areas the overwhelming proportion of low-income renting families must pay more than 25 percent of their income for rent and household utilities, while for rural areas, where the bulk of the substandard housing is to be found, a small proportion of poor households utilize more than 25 percent of their income for housing. Put somewhat grossly, the rural poor get their substandard housing at a bargain, while the urban poor pay substantially more for the same "privilege." This is evident in Table 13.14.

In summary, the data in Tables 13.13 and 13.14 indicate that there is proportionately more substandard housing in the rural than in the urban areas. The cost of such housing is also lower in the rural areas, reflecting the lower population pressures. In other words, there is a relatively larger supply of housing units in the countryside because of

TABLE 13.13. Number of substandard housing units, by location and income class of occupant households, 1966

Location	Total	Occupancy[a] Poor households	Moderate income households
	(million)		
Distribution of Substandard Units			
All locations	6.5	3.5	1.5
Central cities	1.6	0.8	0.5
Other urban areas	1.9	1.0	0.6
Rural areas	3.0	1.7	0.5
Distribution of Substandard Units, excluding Those Occupied by Single-Person Households under Age 65			
All locations	5.0	2.8	1.1
Central cities	0.9	0.5	0.3
Other urban areas	1.4	0.8	0.4
Rural areas	2.7	1.5	0.4
	(%)		
Percentage of Households Occupying Substandard Units, excluding Single-Person Households under Age 65			
All locations	9.5	27.9	7.0
Central cities	5.5	14.8	4.6
Other urban areas	5.5	20.9	4.9
Rural areas	24.3	52.3	28.3

Source: Charles L. Schultze, E. R. Fried, Alice M. Rivlin, and Nancy H. Teeters, Setting National Priorities: The 1972 Budget (Washington, D.C.: Brookings Institution, 1971), p. 291, Table 14-9.

a. For purposes of this tabulation the following annual income criteria were used to define "poor" and "moderate income" households: poor-elderly, less than $2,000; nonelderly single-person households, less than $2,000; nonelderly multiperson households in rural areas, less than $3,000, and in urban areas less than $4,000. Moderate income-elderly, $2,000 to $4,000; nonelderly multiperson households in rural areas, $3,000 to $4,000, and urban areas, $4,000 to $8,000.

TABLE 13.14. Percentage of households paying more than 25 percent of their income for rent and household utilities, by income class and location, 1967

Annual Income	Central City		Other Urban Areas		Rural Areas	
	Elderly	Non-elderly	Elderly	Non-elderly	Elderly	Non-elderly
Less than $2,000	85	84	72	81	29	22
$2,000 - $3,000	74	75	69	50	26	13
$3,000 - $4,000	55	48	40	38	a	13
$4,000 - $6,000	25	18	37	19	a	10
All incomes	59	22	54	18	24	9

Source: Charles L. Schultze, E. R. Fried, Alice M. Rivlin, and Nancy H. Teeters, Setting National Priorities: The 1972 Budget (Washington, D.C.: Brookings Institution, 1971), p. 292, Table 14-10.

Note: Based on data for renter households, nonelderly data include only multiperson households.

a. Less than 1 percent.

the migration of much of our population to the cities. The data do not take into account the quality of substandard rural housing, but it is likely to be older than in the cities where houses are generally of more recent vintage. This may also partially explain the apparent cost differential. The lower-cost housing may have attracted low-income elderly households to the countryside where they now find themselves trapped by a lower level of all the services they require and which are much more difficult to provide because of the distances involved.

Whatever the exact form of future national housing policy, it is obvious that incentives for new construction and rent subsidies will be an integral part of that policy. Currently there is a move to separate programs for housing subsidies from those used to stimulate construction of new units. Then, national monetary and fiscal policy could be used to stimulate new housing starts as needed. Low-income households could be granted subsidies in the form of income supplements to live in existing housing rather than in new housing. Estimates indicate a housing allowance that would provide an income supplement of this type would provide adequate housing at a cost 50 to 60 percent less than the current subsidy program, primarily because it would emphasize the use of existing housing, as other families upgrade to new housing.

Housing programs of this type also have disadvantages. First, it must be recognized that present zoning regulations, and racial biases, might obstruct families from occupying much of the existing housing as it is vacated. An additional drawback is that the policy would tend to concentrate the poor and the near-poor in certain sections of cities—a practice that has had undesirable effects in the past. Sociologists point out that a certain degree of mixing is desirable. Extensive reliance on housing allowances would probably not accomplish this.

Finally, let us examine the economic implications of housing programs. Two programs—a rent subsidy and an income supplement—were discussed above. Each holds different behavioral implications for the recipient. Consider first the rent subsidy. In part a of Figure 13.16, housing quality is plotted along the abscissa, and all other goods along the ordinate. It is labeled "money," whose price is unity. Thus money income is fixed at OC. The line TI represents the total income of the individual to be allocated between housing and all other goods. The vertical intercept shows how much could be spent on other goods if nothing were spent on housing, while the abscissa intercept shows how much would be allocated to housing (in this case to buy a certain quality of housing) if nothing were spent on other goods.

The initial position is at point A where housing quality H_0 is purchased, requiring an outlay of CB, and leaving OB to be spent on other goods. Assume that a rent subsidy is instituted which reduces the real cost of housing to the individual from P_H to P'_H. The new income constraint becomes TI', permitting the individual to reach indifference curve I_1. In this case a significant increase in housing quality is possible $(H_1 - H_0)$ for only a very slight increase in total money spent on housing $(CE$ versus $CB)$. Hence, a rent subsidy permits an individual to acquire much better housing for a fraction of what it would cost otherwise—an intuitive conclusion. There is more to the issue.

If the individual had no desire to obtain better housing, we

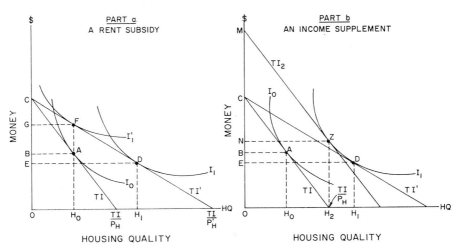

FIG. 13.16.   The impact of a rent subsidy and an income supplement for housing on housing demand.

would expect H_0 to prevail, and this would imply the individual possessed an indifference curve of I'_1 not I_1. Notice now that the individual need spend only CG on housing, leaving OG for the purchase of other goods. Hence, a rent subsidy, while it may lead to better housing, need not. It depends upon the preferences of the recipient. If no increase in housing quality is purchased, the subsidy will be reflected in an improved standard of living through the increased purchase of other goods (GB). Note that a subsidy for housing could shift the demand curve for housing to the right (if recipients indeed desire better housing) and hence the initial price without the subsidy (P_H) may be increased.

Consider the income supplement in part b of Figure 13.16. Here, rather than a housing subsidy, the program consists of an income supplement that permits the individual to reallocate income between housing and other goods. Specifically, the initial position is again point A where H_0 of housing quality is purchased (requiring CB), with OB to be spent on the other goods.

Assume that we wish to provide the individual with the same level of utility as represented by I_1 under a rent subsidy (part a). A parallel shift of TI out to TI_2 would be required and would lead to point Z rather than point D. Here, at the same level of utility (I_1), an income supplement of MC results in lower quality housing than with the rent subsidy (H_2 versus H_1), but higher than without the supplement (H_2 versus H_0). Also, more is spent on housing (MN versus CE), and more is left to spend on other goods (ON versus OE).

The conclusion that follows from the above is that a "tied" grant, such as a rent subsidy, results in greater expenditures on the subsidized item than does a straight cash grant (income). In part b, the difference between points Z and D represents the price effect, while the difference between points A and Z represents the income effect. The difference between points A and D is the total effect; that is, if an individual is given sufficient income to reach I_1, the difference between points A and Z is due to the higher income. Any movement along I_1 is because of price differentials.[17] This means that if the desire is to upgrade housing quality, a housing subsidy will be more effective than an income supplement.

SUMMARY

In this chapter we presented the theory of labor market equilibrium by first deriving supply curves for labor and then integrating the supply and the demand side to examine the adjust-

17. Remember that the conclusions are a function of our assumptions regarding the indifference curves (the preferences) of the individual in Figure 13.16. Nevertheless, if housing is a normal good, we would expect its consumption to increase as income rises.

ments that will take place. It was seen that farm programs result in a misallocation of labor between farm and nonfarm industries and that minimum-wage policies may lead to unemployment.

With respect to the problem of poverty, there has been a decline in the absolute poverty of United States families in the past 30 years but virtually no change in relative poverty. In 1966 there were an estimated 30 million poor persons in the United States. In 1959 the poverty line was 47 percent of the median United States income. By 1968 it had fallen to 36 percent of median income. Since 1947 there has been little change in the distribution of the total income in the United States; in 1947 the top 20 percent of the families in terms of income received 43 percent of total United States income, while in 1966 they received 41 percent of total income. In contrast, in 1947 the lowest 20 percent of the families received only 5.1 percent of United States income, while in 1966 that 20 percent received 5.4 percent of the income.

The popular notion that people are poor by choice (laziness) was exposed as a popular myth. Of the 30 million poor, approximately 100,000 were unemployed, apparently by choice. The balance were aged (over 65), in school, mothers of young children, sick, injured, or unable to find work.

Finally, a discussion of the economic implications of five human resource programs was presented. These programs are (1) welfare and family assistance, (2) manpower programs, (3) social security, (4) medical care, and (5) housing.

The objective of the discussion was to illustrate the methods by which society, through its government, modifies the economic results of the marketplace. For a number of reasons the remuneration of the marketplace to resources controlled by particular individuals is less than what our society considers desirable. The above programs are all examples of governmental attempts to compensate the poor, the disadvantaged, the unemployed, the aged, etc., for these discrepancies.

SUGGESTED READINGS

BASIC

Batchelder, Alan B. *The Economics of Poverty*. New York: John Wiley, 1971.
    An introductory treatment of poverty, this book covers some of the economic issues.
Ginsburg, Helen. *Poverty, Economics, and Society*. Boston: Little, Brown, 1972.
    A collection of articles by economists, politicians, and activists on the problems of poverty. This book provides a good perspective on poverty. Contains an excellent bibliography.
Harrington, Michael. *The Other America*. Baltimore: Pelican Books, Penguin Books, 1969.
    Perhaps the single most important book in pointing out the nature and extent of proverty in America.

Marmor, Theodore R., ed. *Poverty Policy.* Chicago: Aldine-Atherton, 1971.
    An excellent series of articles by experts in the field of poverty.
President's National Advisory Commission on Rural Poverty. *Rural Poverty in
    the United States.* Washington, D.C.: USGPO, 1968.
    A compilation of studies that form the basis for the commission's recom-
    mendations.
————. *The People Left Behind.* Washington, D.C.: USGPO, Sept. 1967.
    A condensed volume of the commission's recommendations.
Schultze, Charles L.; et al. *Setting National Priorities: The 1972 Budget.*
    Washington, D.C.: Brookings Institution, 1971.
    An excellent synopsis of economic issues and the budgetary process.
Theobald, Robert. *Free Men and Free Markets.* New York: Doubleday, 1965.
    A popularized argument for the guaranteed income, this book is very
    provocative—and also very interesting.
U.S. Department of Labor. *Manpower Report of the President.* Washington,
    D.C.: USGPO, 1971.
    A government document containing the Nixon administration's posi-
    tion on labor policy.
Will, Robert E.; and Vatter, Harold G., eds. *Poverty in Affluence.* New York:
    Harcourt, Brace & World, 1965.
    An anthology like Ginsburg's, this book is excellent for a perspective
    on poverty.
                            ADVANCED
Bawden, D. Lee. Welfare analysis of poverty programs. *Am. J. Agr. Econ.* 54
    (Dec. 1972): 809–14.
    An advanced discussion of the benefits of poverty programs.
————. Implications of a negative income tax for rural people. *Am. J. Agr.
    Econ.* 53 (Dec. 1971): 754–60.
    Discusses the negative income tax concept with special reference to
    the rural poor.
Browning, Edgar K. Alternative programs for income redistribution: The NIT
    and the NWT. *Am. Econ. Rev.* 63 (Mar. 1973): 38–49.
    The author evaluates the economic implications of a negative income
    tax (NIT) as compared to a wage subsidy in the form of a negative
    wage tax (NWT) as methods of income redistribution. He concludes
    that the NWT will produce a lower welfare cost.

DISCUSSION QUESTIONS AND PROBLEMS

1. Justify our assertion that there are three farm problems rather than only
   one.
2. Explain under what conditions one might expect a supply curve of labor
   to resemble the curve in Figure 13.Q.1.
3. Contrast the underlying foundation for a supply curve of labor with one
   for a commodity.
4. Why do cash income figures give an incomplete picture of poverty
   thresholds?
5. Justify public intervention in human resources to someone of unfaltering
   faith in the virtues of the free market economy.
6. Discuss the undesirable consequences of the above intervention.
7. Discuss the "social cost of space."

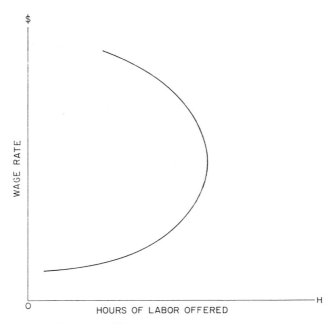

FIG. 13.Q.1. Supply curve of labor.

8. Contrast the work incentive aspects of the FAP with existing public assistance programs.
9. What are the weaknesses in current unemployment rate estimates?
10. What indices would you suggest for evaluating the adequacy of health care in the United States?
11. Discuss the likely success of traditional monetary and fiscal policy for stimulating the demand for low-income housing.
12. What would be the implications on the medical "industry" from a subsidy for medical services? From a cash income grant that need not be spent on medical care?

CHAPTER 14: THE RURAL COMMUNITY

Title V, Section 501, of the Rural Development Act of 1972 states: The purpose of this title is to encourage and foster a balanced national development that provides opportunities for increased numbers of Americans to work and enjoy a high quality of life dispersed throughout our Nation by providing the essential knowledge necessary for successful programs of rural development.[1]

In recent times, we have observed an interesting phenomenon in American geographic living preferences. Beginning in the early 1940s, there was a relentless movement of people from rural areas to the cities. Following the Korean War, the movement was from city to suburb. Now there is a mini-exodus back to rural areas. The role of the rural community has changed; first it was an exporter of raw materials and labor for the factory (and for the table), now it is a refuge for the harried city dweller. The Rural Development Act is the latest in a long series of national efforts concerned with the viability of the rural community and with balanced economic and population growth in a geographic sense.

We will discuss first the role—both past and present—of the rural community and, second, the important changes in the economic organization of society and how these changes affect the rural community. Finally, we examine the future of the rural community through several theories of regional growth and the federal programs aimed at altering the viability of rural communities.

ROLE OF THE RURAL COMMUNITY

The rural community arose from the need for goods and services as the frontier pushed westward. Early studies have shown that the network of rural communities in the Midwest was such that no farm was generally more than 25 miles from a town; most families could get to town and back in the same day. The location of county seats also meant that most legal business of the farmer could be transacted within a day's journey of his farm.

Some sociologists describe the broader role of the community as a combination of social units and systems that perform the major soci-

1. Public Law 92-419, 86 Stat. 671.

ological functions to which people require daily access. These functions have been grouped into (1) production-distribution-consumption, (2) socialization, (3) social control, (4) social participation, and (5) mutual support. The first category contains the bulk of the communities' private market transactions; the second consists of the process whereby prevailing knowledge, social values, and behavior patterns are transmitted to individual residents (for example, schools); the third includes the legal and other institutional guidelines; the fourth, the various groups and organizations which people join for one reason or another (for example, churches); and the last, those functions essential to the communities' operation such as the local press, radio, and the chamber of commerce, as well as voluntary health care organizations.[2]

This is a system of interacting parts with an equilibrium that permits it to adapt to external and internal changes so as to minimize the disruptive impact of changes on the organizational structure. This concept of a community implies an effective demarcation from surrounding communities; otherwise the notion of a community is meaningless.

Sociologists argue that strong communities have locally oriented actions across a gamut of human interests, that these are coordinated through various associations, and that they are integrated through a common ideology. The "instruments of integration" are said to be the political and economic systems, the local press, the various citizens' councils, and the churches, schools, and other kindred organizations. These lead to the enhancement of various integrative aspects: (1) cultural, (2) normative, (3) communicative, and (4) functional. The first implies consistency or harmony among cultural standards; the second implies agreement between cultural standards and the behavior of individuals; the third involves a ready exchange of communications; while the fourth implies the mutual support of various units to each other. To this group we should add the notion of economic integration—the extent to which economic entities rely upon each other for supplies, as well as customers. As will be seen in the next section, this is a particularly relevant consideration.

Hence, one might think of a community as a multidimensional web of interactions, both sociologic and economic, which give it the ability to provide the essential daily needs of its citizens. This web of interactions involves two distinct types of interrelationships: vertical and horizontal. A community's vertical pattern is the structural and functional relation of its various social and economic units and subsystems to extracommunity systems. Its horizontal pattern is the structural and functional relation of the various social and economic units and subsystems to each other. Examples of the former would be the tie between local activities and their respective main offices outside the community.

2. Roland L. Warren, *The Community in America* (Chicago: Rand McNally, 1963).

The horizontal ties are essentially the integrative aspects mentioned above. This manner of viewing communities and the systems they encompass is useful in understanding the nature of the changes observed in rural America.

CHANGES AFFECTING RURAL COMMUNITIES

According to some sociologists, great changes are taking place in communities all over America, and the implications of these changes for rural communities are very important for our present discussion. Warren argues that there is an increasing orientation of local units in a community to the extracommunity systems to which they are linked and a corresponding decline in community cohesion and autonomy. In other words, the horizontal ties of the community are deteriorating relative to the vertical ties. With this change, the locus of decision making is shifting elsewhere; the former ties among different subsystems have deteriorated and the control by local people over the establishments, their goals, their policies, and their operation is weakened. Although the initial incentive for change usually comes from the economic sphere, the more significant impacts are probably felt in the sociologic sphere; that is, it is economic reasons primarily that strengthened the vertical ties but the sociologic aspects are more far-reaching. To fully appreciate this point, we digress momentarily.

As we have seen, as the frontier pushed westward the rural community grew out of a need for locality-relevant functions. These communities were founded upon and were meant to serve those economic activities directly related to a natural resource base. Over time, at least four fundamental economic changes have occurred—each with implications for the rural community as it has evolved: (1) a change in the demand for the local raw material or in the product produced from the local raw resource, (2) a shift in the comparative advantage of various areas, even with demand for local goods remaining constant, (3) exhaustion of the resource base upon which the community was founded, and (4) structural changes in the industries exploiting these natural resources.

DECLINING DEMAND

An example of this kind of economic change is the development of substitute raw materials that results in a drop in the exports of the local area. For example, with the advent of natural gas and atomic power plants, coal-mining areas have declined economically. A region can be conceptualized in terms similar to those for the firm, hence a decline in the demand for a region's product brings about economic

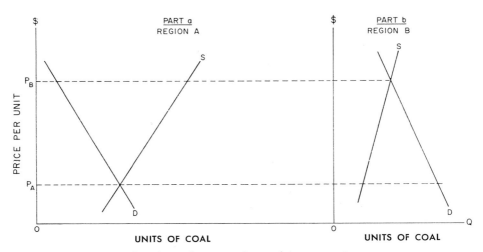

FIG. 14.1. Demand and supply curves for coal in two regions.

changes of similar impact. This can be illustrated with the use of the
following diagrams.

In Figure 14.1 are depicted the demand and supply curves for
two regions; let region A represent Appalachia and region B represent
the rest of the United States. The horizontal axis in each part of the
figure represents the units of coal, demanded and supplied, with region
A showing an ample supply (S) of coal but a rather restricted demand,
while region B shows a more substantial demand for coal and a more restricted supply. Accordingly, the price of coal in A would be P_A, while
the price of coal in B would be P_B. Note that between prices P_A and P_B
there will be a surplus of coal in region A and a deficit in region B. Because of the significant disparity in coal prices between the two regions,
producers of coal (coal-mining companies) in region A would like to
export as much coal as possible. In this case, consumers of coal in region
B would benefit by lower prices while the prices in region A would increase. To examine the economic impacts of trade in these two regions,
we introduce the notion of excess demand and supply curves. The problem is to find the equilibrium price at which the excess supply in region
A is just equal to the excess demand in region B.

Excess demand and supply curves depict precisely that—the extent of excess demand and supply between two regions. *Excess demand*
in a region is defined as the schedule of the differences between the quantity consumers will demand and the quantity firms will be willing to
supply at each price; that is, for region B,

$$E_D{}^B = Q_D - Q_S \tag{14.1}$$

where

$E_D{}^B$ = excess demand in region B
Q_D = quantity demanded if the price is P
Q_S = quantity supplied at price P

Excess supply in a region is defined as the schedule of the difference between the quantity that will be supplied and the quantity that will be demanded at each price; that is,

$$E_S{}^A = Q_S - Q_D \qquad (14.2)$$

where

$E_S{}^A$ = excess supply in region A
Q_D and Q_S are as defined above

The astute reader may wonder why both quantities are required. In practice, for any particular region, both E_D and E_S are not used. If the region is one of predominately excess supply (such as region A) excess supply is calculated. Conversely, in region B the excess demand curve is calculated. Given the excess demand and supply curves between two regions, their intersection indicates the equilibrium price, the quantity demanded and supplied in each region, and the quantity that will be traded. Consider Figure 14.2. At a price of P_B, the market for coal in region B is in equilibrium, but at prices below P_B, there is a demand for

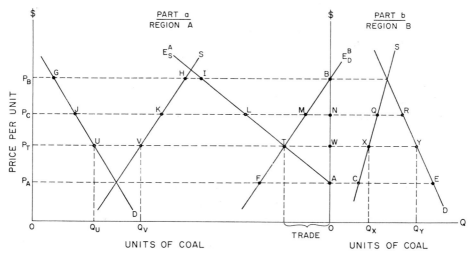

FIG. 14.2. Excess demand and supply curves and interregional trade in coal.

coal in excess of the region's ability to produce coal. The amount of excess demand at each price level can be determined from the figure. For example, at the low price of P_A, there is an excess demand of CE. If we were to plot this magnitude of excess demand (CE) at a price of P_A, we could locate point F which is CE units of coal to the left of point A in Figure 14.2; that is, $FA = CE =$ the extent of excess demand for coal in region B at the low price of P_A. Since at a price of P_B there is no excess demand in region B, we can plot point B on the vertical axis separating the two regions. Point M on $E_D{}^B$ is the quantity QR for price P_C. We can similarly obtain point T. Hence, the curve $E_D{}^B$ traces out the locus of points depicting the extent of excess demand at different prices for coal in region B. Note that for prices above P_B there is a negative excess demand—excess supply.

For region A we will calculate excess supply $E_S{}^A$. At a price of P_A, the market for coal is in equilibrium, with no excess supply (point A). This is one point on region A's excess supply curve. At prices above P_A, producers are willing to produce quantities significantly greater than those which consumers would purchase. Indeed, at a price of P_B, there is an excess supply in region A of GH units of coal. By plotting this magnitude to the left of the vertical axis (at the price P_B), we have a second point on the excess supply curve for region A (point I). Notice the distance $IB = GH$. Similarly, point L on $E_S{}^A$ is found by plotting the distance JK at price P_C ($JK = LN$).

As in normal equilibrium analysis, the intersection of the (excess) supply curve and the (excess) demand curve (point T) is an equilibrium point. At this intersection, the magnitude of excess demand in region B (XY) is exactly equal to the magnitude of excess supply in region A (UV); that is, $XY = UV$. Also notice that $XY = UV = TW$. This amount of coal could be exported from region A (an area of excess supply) to region B (an area of excess demand) at the equilibrium price of P_T. Region A would produce Q_V but consume only Q_U, and would export the difference (TW). Region B would produce Q_X, import TW, and consume Q_Y. Note that transportation costs are assumed to be zero, and hence the extent of trade is greater than would prevail if our analysis included transportation costs. Still, the analysis is useful for our purposes below.

As an illustration, assume the foregoing is a statement of the conditions in a coal-producing region, such as A (say, Appalachia), and the rest of the nation, represented by region B, and let us examine the implications for coal exports. Figure 14.3 depicts most of what was presented in Figure 14.2, with several important exceptions. First, assume that nuclear generators and natural gas developments in the rest of the nation bring about a decline in the demand for coal required to power electricity-generating facilities. Further assume that the demand for coal

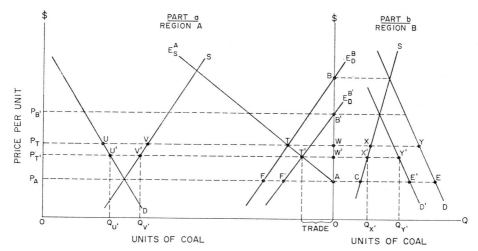

FIG. 14.3. Interregional trade under declining demand for coal in region B.

in Appalachia remains constant. Finally assume that the supply side of the coal market remains unchanged. Under these assumptions there would be a new demand curve for coal in the rest of the nation (D' in region B) and a new excess demand curve ($E_D^{B'}$) for the same region. Note that the excess supply curve for region A is unchanged.

The derivation of the new excess demand curve $E_D^{B'}$ is the same as for the original excess demand curve. In Figure 14.3 there is no excess demand at a price of $P_{B'}$ and this would be plotted as point B' on the center vertical axis. At the price of P_A there is now an excess demand of CE', and when plotted, this yields point F'. The excess demand curve is obtained by joining points F' and B'. In summary, the impact of a decline in the demand for coal from D to D' in importing region B is a decline in the excess demand for coal facing the exporting region.

Assuming zero transportation costs, a price of $P_{T'}$ could be charged in both regions and result in exporting the quantity $Q_{V'} - Q_{U'}$ from region A to region B. Note that the quantity to be exported ($T'W'$) is less than that quantity previously exported (TW). Thus the decline in demand results in region A being able to export less and receiving a lower price for its product ($P_{T'}$ versus P_T).

The analytics can be extended to cover any commodities that are traded between regions or nations. In all cases, a decline in the demand for the particular product in which a region happens to specialize will bring about a decrease in the well-being of the local economy as the external price falls. More will be said on this later.

SHIFT IN COMPARATIVE ADVANTAGE

We know that certain areas have a comparative advantage in the production of specific commodities and that this is reflected in the aggregate supply curves of the commodity or commodities for each area. In fact, the concepts of excess demand and supply developed above can be utilized to describe the effect of changes in the comparative advantage of a given region. Before doing this, however, it is worthwhile to briefly review the nature of the economic changes which result in shifts in a region's comparative advantage. The most obvious factor that would likely alter the comparative advantage of a certain region would be the development of improved transportation facilities; that is, the location of an interstate highway or a major airport can bestow significant cost reductions on producers fortunate enough to be located near the new facilities. Producers not so fortunately situated are at a comparative disadvantage regarding transportation costs. Another example of an economic change that could alter regional comparative advantage would be the establishment of a large university in an area. In this case, the existence of an abundant supply of student labor plus graduate student wives means that local producers have access to reliable sources of labor usually willing to work at relatively low wages. In both cases, factors external to the firm or industry have created favorable cost conditions for producers in one area vis-à-vis those in other areas and hence have altered an area's comparative advantage.

Consider Figure 14.4. Assume that a process is invented which permits coal producers to extract the coal more cheaply from most coal deposits, but not from the Appalachian coal deposits. This would result

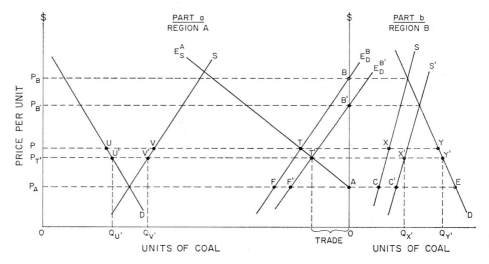

FIG. 14.4. Interregional trade with shifts in comparative advantage.

in a shift in the supply curve for region B producers from S to S' and a corresponding rightward shift in the excess demand curve from $E_D{}^B$ to $E_D{}^{B'}$. Note that the extent of excess demand in region B is reduced, with the result that there would be a reduction in exports from region A (imports to region B). The equilibrium price would decrease from P_T to $P_{T'}$. This would have a detrimental effect on the demand for labor and other productive factors in region A, as well as have a depressing impact on the level of general business activity in the region.

EXHAUSTION OF THE RESOURCE BASE

The third kind of adjustment with implications for rural communities is related to the gradual exhaustion of the resource base which forms the foundation of the region's economy. The coal fields of Appalachia are a classic example, as is the case of the cutover area of northern Minnesota, Wisconsin, and Michigan. In both instances, the primary basis of the local economy has declined in quality or quantity, with the result that the export base of the region has deteriorated. Consider Figure 14.5. Here, as the resource base (coal) of region A is depleted, and as costs of extraction rise, the supply curve for coal in the region shifts from S to S'. This results in a shift in the excess supply curve from $E_S{}^A$ to $E_S{}^{A'}$. Assuming no change in excess demand, the intersection of $E_S{}^{A'}$ and $E_D{}^B$ at T' indicates the equilibrium price has risen to $P_{T'}$. Thus the increasing scarcity of coal in region A results in a higher price, reduced exports from the region ($U'V'$ versus UV), and correspondingly reduced imports of coal by region B ($X'Y'$ versus XY). As exports

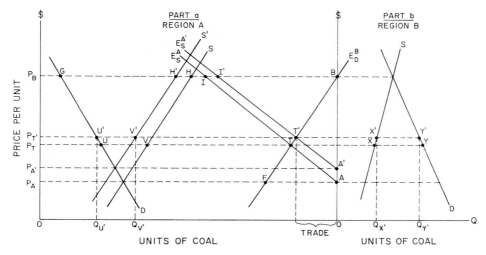

FIG. 14.5. Interregional trade with resource exhaustion in region A.

from region A decline, the main source of employment may shrink. While the price per unit is higher, production costs have also risen as a result of the increased resource scarcity, and the demand for labor will fall as firms seek new least-cost resource combinations.

STRUCTURAL CHANGES

The final type of change with implications for rural areas which we wish to examine concerns structural changes within an industry or within several industries. While the previous examples were also relevant for agricultural pursuits, the structural changes within agriculture are a major source of concern for those wishing to preserve the rural communities.

Specifically, as local resource-based industries such as mining, lumbering, and agriculture have undergone internal reorganization and expanded to exploit economies of large scale, the nature of their linkages to both the output markets as well as to the input markets has changed. In the case of agriculture, these changes were described in detail in earlier chapters. On the input side, as farms and ranches become larger, the nature of their input purchases takes on a different form. Whereas most input purchases formerly were made at the local level—from the local business community—the greater scale of present operations plus improved transportation means that many purchases will be concentrated in cities often some distance from the enterprise. In other words, the local community no longer serves as a source of input supply for many agricultural producers.

On the output side, one observes the same structural change. The move toward contract selling to large processors and the volume of output of many agricultural firms mean that the local mill, processor, or assembler is bypassed in favor of a larger processor, mill, or assembler at some distance from the production site. Again, improved transportation has enhanced this trend.

In summary, structural changes within industries such as agriculture, coupled with significant improvements in transportation, have combined to displace many of the economic functions of the local rural community. Indeed, it is said that much of the push for the preservation of the family farm—and the legislation in some states to prohibit large corporate farms—originates with the rural merchants who view this as the final blow to the viability of the rural community. As was seen earlier, rural merchants played a significant role in the controversy over whole-farm land retirement programs. The concern over corporate farms is rather similar. As the rural merchant sees it, part of his product is a close personal contact with the farmer or rancher and a customer loyalty that accompanies it. When large and often absentee-owned operations become prevalent, the merchant is fearful that his personal contacts will decline considerably, and so will his business.

IMPLICATIONS

The above four types of economic changes are important not only because of the direct impacts which they precipitate in a rural area but also because of the indirect ramifications—sociologic as well as economic. We will discuss the economic ramifications first, and then turn to a brief treatment of some of the other noneconomic impacts on a rural area.

The first type of economic change was that of a declining demand for the particular raw materials in which the region specializes. This could come about either as a result of the development of substitute materials or products or the shifting of tastes and preferences for certain commodities of which the raw material is a component. We earlier described the role of natural gas and nuclear generators in altering the demand for coal.

When the demand for exports from an area begins to decline, the first effect would be a drop in the price of the raw material (see Figure 14.3). With a lower product price, the derived demand for variable inputs—particularly labor—will decrease. The exporting businesses now buy less labor from households and purchase fewer other inputs from the local businesses as well. Hence the households of those no longer employed by exporting industries have less personal income to spend, and those who own or work in the businesses that sell to the exporting industries or their employees also face a falling demand for their products. These businesses are frequently referred to as secondary and tertiary industries, in contrast to the exporting industries which are called primary industries.

The secondary and tertiary firms, in turn, hire fewer persons. Not only are some household heads faced with unemployment but the youth of the area are also affected; that is, there are few if any part-time jobs, and little prospect for permanent employment. This fact, coupled with attractive employment possibilities in most urban centers, tends to encourage out-migration of the young. This further compounds the decline in retail trade. If this situation persists, some businesses will eventually be forced to close. Once this happens, the range of choice for rural residents is reduced, further encouraging the trend to shop in the larger urban places. This in turn further aggravates the downward progression in the economic viability of the rural community.

The second type of economic change was a shift in the comparative advantage of one region relative to other regions producing the same commodity. We used as examples the advent of a technological process that could only be used in certain areas and the building of a major highway or airport in a particular region. There is another governmental activity which has had a significant impact on the relative production capabilities of certain regions in the United States. Specifically, the federal government, through the Bureau of Reclamation, makes sizable investments in irrigation facilities in the 17 contiguous western states. As of 1970, the bureau had constructed 217 reservoirs, 132 diversion dams, 111 major pumping plants, 6,935 miles of canals, and 763 miles of pipeline. The total cost from the inception of the reclamation program (1902 to 1970) is estimated at over $6 billion. For the crop year 1964, it is estimated that over 8.5 million acres were receiving water under some aspect of the reclamation program.[3] This has meant substantial increase in the economic activities of rural communities in those states.

While this has meant a significant increase in economic activity in many areas of the arid West, there are some negative aspects. The irrigation of many acres of dryland in the West meant that cotton production, which was formerly confined to the Cotton Belt of the Southeast, was able to expand into parts of Texas, New Mexico, Arizona, and California. But the demand for cotton has not increased, and because of synthetics, it has even decreased slightly. The subsidization of irrigation facilities gave producers in the Southwest a competitive advantage over those in the Southeast and some rather painful adjustments were required in the cotton-producing areas of the Mississippi Delta.[4]

When comparative advantages are significantly altered, prices of the product from the higher-cost area must fall to maintain the existing share of the national market. If it is assumed that little positive profit was being earned prior to the shift, prices cannot fall very much before producers begin to look for alternative means to remain competitive. The most obvious is to move the facility to the low-cost area. However, this is not a universal solution since some types of economic activity are not that mobile. Moreover, when plants do move out of a rural area, the sequence of events is predictable. With few exceptions, it is similar to the progression spelled out above: fewer jobs, out-migration, declining retail trade, stores closing, less local shopping, more stores closing, and so on.

Alternatively, the firms could remain but take drastic steps to counter the cost advantage enjoyed by producers elsewhere. This might take the form of significant investments in new capital equipment to become more efficient. If this is the case, the new least-cost combination of resources many reduce the demand for labor. This would set into motion the familiar sequence detailed earlier. Furthermore, with capital

3. U.S. Bureau of Reclamation, *Summary Report of the Commissioner*. Statistical Appendix Parts I, II, and III (Washington, D.C.: USGPO, June 1970).

4. For an interesting analysis of this, see George S. Tolley, Reclamation's influence on the rest of agriculture, *Land Econ.* 35 (May 1959): 176–80.

equipment it is likely to be more specialized. Hence, a larger share of the inputs required by the plant(s) would be purchased in major urban places since rural communities would be unable to supply these more specialized inputs. Repair needs would also be met by specialized craftsmen from the urban center. In summary, the outcome for the rural community is much the same as in the earlier situation, even though the principal cause is different.

The third type of adjustment—resource exhaustion—can be discussed in the same terms as the previous two examples. Here production costs rise as the process of extraction becomes more difficult. The three choices open to local producers are to cut back on output levels, to close down, or to maintain former output levels by changes in production (extraction) processes. Closing down is the trivial case, although the indirect ramifications for the residents of the area are far from trivial. Short of closure, certain adjustments might be made. If output is cut back, exports must necessarily fall. If demand has not shifted, this means local producers are able to get a higher price for their product (see Figure 14.5). However, as in the earlier types of economic change, the sequence of events leads to undesirable consequences for the community. If producers attempt to maintain exports at previous levels, there would likely be extensive investment in new technology, just as in the case of a shifting comparative advantage. Here again, the sequence of events would resemble that spelled out above.

Finally, consequences of the fourth economic change—structural changes in the local industries—have been covered in the first three types of change. As the typical lumber, mining, or agricultural firm becomes larger, the nature of its input purchases will change, and the extent to which its output is processed locally will also change; both carry implications for the rural community that are similar to those already articulated.

The above discussion has been limited to the economic ramifications to a rural community of changes in the characteristics of economic production in an area. While important, it should not be inferred that these are the only kinds of adjustments taking place. Some would argue that the sociological adjustments are of more significance. We will briefly discuss these latter ramifications.

Earlier we mentioned the concept of horizontal and vertical ties, the former referring to the relationship that exists among different units and systems within the rural community and the latter referring to these relationships with units and systems outside the community. It was also stated that the major way in which adjustments are occurring in rural communities is that these horizonal ties are becoming weaker vis-à-vis the vertical ties. The sociologist Roland Warren would classify these changes into seven categories.[5]

5. Warren, *The Community in America.*

First is the division of labor. Warren contends that increasing specialization of labor has not only increased the fragmentation of tasks performed within firms but has greatly fragmented economic structure. The former mercantile or general hardware store has been replaced by at least 4 to 5 different stores, all specializing in a few product lines. This has tended to fragment human functions into many fine categories; now units are held together less by values and behavior patterns than they are by the artificial interdependence necessitated by the highly differentiated nature of their respective tasks within a complex whole. In other words, people who live and work in the same small community are increasingly having less and less in common with one another.

The second aspect of the "great change" is the more pronounced differentiation of interests and associations. The neighborhood, once the focal point of individual interaction, has been largely replaced by what Warren calls "categorical groups." Examples of such groups are bowling leagues, bridge groups, garden clubs, and so on. In many rural communities, where firms may be small enough to preclude the formation of such affiliations, the result could be individuals being cut off from human interaction. While the neighborhood is perhaps more significant in small rural areas than in urban places, Warren does not appear optimistic that the trend toward categorical groups will be reversed.

The third aspect of change is to be found in the increasing relationship with the larger society; that is, national politics have become more interesting than local politics and the allegiance of persons is displaced to the larger sphere. Another example is athletics where major league teams have tended to displace local high schools in the eyes of many sports fans. Improved communication facilities vis-à-vis television have promoted this substitution.

The fourth aspect of change is the increased bureaucratization and impersonalization of daily life. As jobs have become more specialized, each individual has less stake—and hence less pride—in a particular commodity or service. Additionally, the increasing dependence on economic units outside the local community implies that many decisions are made elsewhere. For example, the drugstore is indeed local; but the fact that it is a franchise of a national firm means that many pricing and product decisions are beyond the scope of the local manager.

Warren would list as the fifth aspect of community change the transfer of many duties from the voluntary sphere to the private or public spheres. Previously, when the family and neighborhood roles were well defined and active in the community, the needy usually had someone to assist them. This is no longer the case, and there is an accompanying rise of both private and public institutions to deal with these problems. As the rural community becomes more depersonalized—as the horizontal ties are further weakened—this trend is expected to continue.

The sixth aspect of community change is the trend toward suburbanization. While this is not as pronounced in small rural communities, it is a definite factor in many medium-sized communities. Currently, the individual seeks to move out and away from the core of the community. The emphasis is on the acquisition of a private domain. The quest for privacy and elbow room is a further blow to the role of the neighborhood as a socializing device.

The final aspect of the great change discussed by Warren is changing values. Conventional wisdom has it that the true strength of America lies in the rural countryside; that as long as people are reared in rural settings we will be assured a pool of hard-working, righteous, compassionate, and patriotic citizens. In addition to being far too quixotic, this Jeffersonian view is probably incorrect as well. As Hathaway points out, the bitter struggle over civil rights for blacks—with its roots in the rural South—suggests that rural people have no monopoly on justice and compassion. Additionally, the treatment accorded migrant workers by some farmers tends to corroborate this doubt. Local control of schools is one of the more inflammatory issues in America, yet the poor quality of many rural schools has produced a large number of rural to urban migrants that are unable to integrate into an industrialized society. Finally, the enthusiasm with which many rural areas support conservative candidates implies most rural residents are against the types of social legislation required to combat high unemployment and the concentration of economic and political power.[6]

Given the above, rural areas no longer hold the appeal that they once did, and many of the younger generation cannot move to the urban places soon enough. This means that our traditional view of the good life is in the process of changing, and with it, the hope for many rural communities.

These then are a sociologist's view of the great change taking place in communities of all sizes in rural and urban America. Let us review these vis-à-vis the notion of horizontal and vertical ties. As Warren points out, at the local level it is possible to locate a structured interaction which displays characteristics which can be described as a social system. The behavior of local units at the community level consists of a dynamic interplay of vertical and horizontal forces. Fluctuations between the two constitute an equilibrating influence on the behavior of the community. While the vertical pattern is typified by deliberate and rational planning and a bureaucratic structure, the horizontal pattern is characterized by sentiment, informality, impulsiveness, and a diffuse and ad hoc structuring that is essentially nonbureaucratic in nature. The vertical ties are intraorganizational, the horizontal are interorganizational. The bureaucratization of social organizations has had a greater

6. Dale E. Hathaway, The Implications of Changing Political Power on Agriculture, *Agricultural Policy in Affluent Society*, ed. V. W. Ruttan, A. D. Waldo, and J. P. Houck (New York: Norton, 1969), pp. 63–68.

impact on vertical organization of local units than it has had on the nature of the horizontal. To combat this effect, entities such as chambers of commerce and local planning boards are utilized to strengthen the horizontal ties.

Yet most of the crucial factors—economic as well as sociologic— are beyond the control of the community. For example, on the economic side one can mention the four economic changes discussed above, plus others such as changes in federal and state tax structure, changes in various federal and state policies governing the use of the natural resource base, changes in the stock market and national wage settlements, and changes in the bank discount rates. On the sociologic side, as the communications media, primarily television, bring the rest of the world into every living room, they simultaneously replace the sociologic link to the local community. As the community becomes smaller, the sociologic ties become more important, yet are ever more difficult to maintain.

The sequence of events which we observe might be described as the emergence of domestic colonialism. A colony is ordinarily the possession of a large industrialized nation and performs certain functions for that large nation. One function such a colony performs is supplying that nation with raw materials (for example, coffee beans, balsa wood, certain minerals, rubber, and so on). These are transported to the industrial country, processed, and used domestically or sold to other nations. The colony does little besides supply the raw material. The capital that is invested in the colonial country is usually from the industrial power; and the control, as well as the profits, remains in that large nation. Without too much imagination, one can view the changes that have been occurring in rural America as similar to the problems of domestic colonies.

The bulk of the important economic and social decisions affecting the community are made elsewhere. The community and the rural area around it exist to provide some raw materials to the colonial powers (the metropolitan area) and to serve as a limited market for the manufactured goods from these latter areas. The political and economic power of these colonies has atrophied and their only hope seems to be in the proliferation of regional planning commissions, citizens' councils, and imaginative chambers of commerce to provide the local input and control for rural development.

FUTURE OF THE RURAL COMMUNITY

The future of the rural community cannot be examined in isolation from the hierarchy of communities in America. The linkages articulated in the previous section highlight the extent to which all communities are interdependent, regardless of their size.

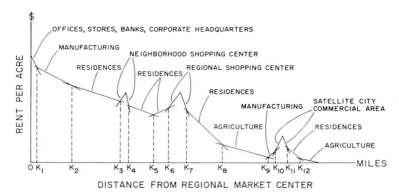

FIG. 14.6. Spatial aspects of economic activity from an urban center. (From Hugh O. Nourse, **Regional Economics: A Study in the Economic Structure, Stability, and Growth of Regions,** New York: McGraw-Hill, 1968, p. 120, Figure 5–17.)

To underscore this interdependence, we can utilize a modified version of Figure 4.3 to demonstrate the relationship between a regional market center, a regional shopping center, and a satellite city. In Figure 14.6 we plot rent per acre as a function of distance from the regional market center and the location of economic activities and communities. In Chapter 4 we talked of the location of production around marketing points, and derived net receipts functions for several kinds of agricultural production. That discussion can now be generalized to include all types of land use. In Figure 14.6 we have presented a diagram similar to Figure 4.3. Here, however, we are dealing with a range of land-use activity from manufacturing, residences, and neighborhood shopping centers to regional shopping centers, agriculture, and satellite cities. This should illustrate the extent to which the rural community is linked to the major urban place, primarily as a satellite in the hierarchy. It also clearly illustrates the nature of and the reason for the strength of the vertical linkages described earlier.

RURAL DEVELOPMENT

The very nature of this linkage is what concerns those who view with alarm the demise of the rural community. Rural development is the general term which is used to describe all those efforts aimed at altering the present and anticipated level of economic activity in rural communities. There is no universally accepted definition of what constitutes development. There are, however, some indices which can be used to indicate the difference between a community that is likely to prosper and one that will continue to become less significant in the hierarchy. Some of these indices are per capita income of the residents, per capita tax burden, unemployment rates, seasonal fluctuations in unemployment, bank deposits, business loans outstanding, private investment, the degree to which personal income is concentrated in the hands of a few persons, the proportion of high school students going on to college, participation of the citizenship in local politics and elections, the quality of available housing, infant mortality rates, proportion of the population with a high school education, and perhaps certain mental health indices.

It should be emphasized that the above list is not intended to reveal any cause-and-effect relationship; high bank deposits, high per capita income, or large proportions of students going on to college do not cause the development of rural communities. Nevertheless, there seems to be a high correlation between many of these indices and the degree of development of the community. The astute reader will recognize this as a definition of development based on what we observe, with little notion of how to manipulate these factors to bring about development. In the language of Chapter 2, the development of a rational policy for bringing about a greater degree of economic activity in a rural area (development) is dependent upon the identification of certain causal factors. One sets as an objective the attainment of certain levels for specified target variables—say increasing per capita income by $500, increasing per capita manufacturing income by $200, upgrading the available housing by ten dwellings per year, and increasing the proportion of high school graduates that finish college by 3 percent per year over a 10-year period. However, the identification of those steps necessary to assure the attainment of the objectives—that is, the identification of the initial cause of development—is rather more difficult.

For example, it is safe to conclude that the establishment of a manufacturing plant will facilitate the attainment of one or more objectives, but what will this do for the others? What sort of product will be manufactured? What guarantee is there that skilled labor is available to work in the plant? What burden will the plant place on available water and sewer facilities? Will this improve the rate at which local youth graduate from college? We cannot even assume that per capita incomes will be increased very much if the plant is capital intensive, or if laborers commute to work from another area. Hence, to talk of rural community development is to embark upon a discussion which can only be couched in very general terms.

ALTERNATIVE APPROACHES

As should be obvious, we have been describing development as if it were a simple process of attracting factories, or building a new school, or hiring better teachers, or paving some streets. This is what is called the task-oriented approach. The emphasis is on the specific tangible output of a group effort. However, some view the real essence of community development as the process which it goes through in the quest of change. It is a process of social actions and interactions by which the residents organize themselves, define common and individual problems and wishes, make individual and group plans to meet these wishes, perform the necessary work to implement these plans, and then assess the results. Hence, the act of following through from problem identification to evaluation of the solution to that problem may be as important to the tangible results of that action as cleaner water, more retail trade, a better hospital, or more jobs.

In terms we have used before, rural development can be viewed as strengthening horizontal ties at the expense of the vertical ties. Rural development as viewed from the sociologist's perspective is in sharp contrast to rural development as viewed by the economist. The economist would tend to favor the task-oriented approach where emphasis is on improving the level of exports from the area or improving the efficiency with which certain factors of production are utilized (make labor more productive, thereby increasing labor incomes), while the sociologist would tend to concentrate on the process whereby change is realized in a community and be less concerned with the tangible results of that process.

In the foregoing, we have attempted to summarize as briefly as possible the notion of rural communities as part of a hierarchy of communities in America, and to discuss the concept of rural development. There is no universal definition of rural development and hence we wish to reemphasize that our discussion was necessarily in general terms. Development is defined by pointing to a few quantitative indications the level of which can be said to correspond to the level of development of a community. We now turn to a discussion of a few of the existing programs, largely sponsored by the public sector, aimed at achieving development. This does not imply that all the programs to be described here will result in something which might be called development. Nevertheless, the fact that they are federal programs aimed at altering conditions in rural areas indicates that they merit discussion. Additionally, it exposes the student to various approaches to development and the problems inherent in them.

To set the stage for the discussion of present programs designed to alleviate the income problems of rural residents, we briefly discuss some past programs. The primary objective of these efforts was to improve incomes by altering economic activity in rural areas.

DEVELOPMENT PROGRAMS

One such government activity was the Farmers Home Administration, established in 1946, and another was the Rural Electrification Administration. The first provided financing to farmers and rural communities for economic activities that were ineligible for loans from conventional private lending sources. It either made direct loans or insured the loans from conventional sources. FHA replaced the Farm Security Administration, an agency established in 1935 to grant supervised rehabilitation loans to destitute rural families. The agency was also authorized to make loans to public and nonprofit organizations in rural towns (population less than 5,500) to develop domestic water supplies and waste disposal systems. In 1967 their lending authority was expanded when they were authorized to make up to $200,000 available (for up to 50 years) to private nonprofit corporations and cooperatives to build housing for low-income senior citizens. It was also authorized to loan money for purposes that would stimulate the economy to public agencies and nonprofit organizations in rural areas. Such things as the purchase of land for flood control, soil erosion protection, or recreational facilities, loans for the construction of access roads, recreational sites, and the purchase and improvement of grazing areas were all eligible for loans.

The Rural Electrification Administration was established at a time when only 11 percent of the farms in the United States were said to have electricity. It was started in 1935 and is often described as doing more for rural development than any other government endeavor. By 1968, largely through the efforts of REA, the percentage of farms with electric power had risen to 98 percent.

In the 1950 census, 1.5 million farm families or 28 percent of the total had net cash incomes of less than $1,000. Over 50 percent of all farm families had a net cash family income of less than $2,000. Generally, these families lived on small farms located in areas bypassed by modern technologies and by the urban-industrial development of most of the rest of the country. One solution to the problems of these low-income farm families was legislation called the Rural Development Program (RDP). The Rural Development Program was recommended by President Eisenhower in 1954 and was formally initiated in 1956. The general approach was to be educational and developmental; research and extension efforts were to be refocused on the problems of low-income rural areas. By 1960 there were estimated to be over 200 counties involved in the program and at least 18,000 new full-time jobs were created in that year alone as a result of industrial development in rural areas. Yet there were disappointing results as well. The program did little if any good for the hard-core unemployed in rural areas.[7] Another problem was the inability of these families to take good advantage of new technical knowledge. Making capital readily available to some farmers with marginal operations and no hope of ever achieving an economic sized unit may be more of an injustice than to expedite the operations' demise.

7. Willard Cochrane, *City Man's Guide to the Farm Problem* (Minneapolis: Univ. Minn. Press, 1965).

Under the Kennedy Administration, the Rural Development Program was renamed Rural Areas Development (RAD). The focus did not change much; the central aim was still to concentrate the programs of existing agencies to alleviating rural poverty. In 1961 the Area Redevelopment Act created the Area Redevelopment Administration in the Department of Commerce.[8] The objectives of the agency were to (1) provide loans for job-creating commercial and industrial enterprises, (2) provide grants and loans for public facilities, (3) provide technical assistance, and (4) implement manpower retraining programs. In 1965 the latter function was transferred to other manpower programs and the balance of programs in the Area Redevelopment Administration was transferred to the Economic Development Administration (EDA). There was also a shift in program focus. More emphasis was to be placed on regional development plans. The Economic Development Administration was created by the Public Works and Economic Development Act of 1965. The act designated four types of areas that were eligible for assistance from the Economic Development Administration: (1) a redevelopment area, (2) Title I areas, (3) economic development districts, and (4) economic development regions. Each type of area qualified for one or more types of loans or grants from EDA.

A redevelopment area was defined as an Indian reservation, a county, a labor area, or a municipality having at least 250,000 residents. It qualifies for EDA assistance on the basis of criteria which indicate "chronic economic distress." The primary indicator is an index of unemployment. An unemployment rate of 6 percent over a several-year period was an indication of "distress." Additionally, an area was classified as a redevelopment area if it had lost at least 25 percent of its population between 1950 and 1960, providing median family incomes were less than $2,830 in 1960. Finally, if a state did not have an area that qualified on the basis of high unemployment, low family income, or population loss, the area in the state that most closely met those criteria could be designated as a redevelopment area.[9]

The second type—the Title I area—is one with substantial unemployment. It is eligible for public works and development facility grants assistance. These will be explained below.

The third type of area is the multicounty economic development district. It was created for the express purpose of encouraging several counties to join together (often up to 12) to facilitate the achievement of development objectives impossible on an individual

8. In 1962 and 1963 Congress appropriated $850 million for the Accelerated Public Works Program for the improvement of public facilities in rural areas. Cochrane estimates that 220,000 man-years of employment were provided during the first two and one-half years of the program. See Cochrane, *City Man's Guide*, p. 205.

9. This is an example of Congress trying to equalize the extent to which all can benefit from a federal appropriation. By this last clause, each congressman can hold an elaborate press conference to announce the establishment of a redevelopment area in his state. None is left out!

county basis. Not every rural community can hope to prosper by its own efforts; the only hope of many rural communities is to join with others in the immediate region in hopes of improving the level of regional economic activity, with the ultimate hope that the indirect effects will trickle down to the local community. It was required that each economic development district must contain an economic development center—a city with sufficient population, natural resources, public facilities, industry, and commercial services to insure that any investment can be self-sustaining. Thus the definition implies an assumption of the trickle-down theory. The trickle-down theory states that the development of the central place will stimulate ancillary development in the satellite towns of the region.[10]

The final type of geographic area eligible for EDA assistance is the economic development region. This is a multistate area where long-range planning with federal and state cooperation can be accomplished through a regional commission. In 1966, five regional commissions were established: (1) the Ozarks region, (2) the Upper Great Lakes region, (3) the Coastal Plains region (parts of the Carolinas and Georgia), (4) the New England region, and (5) the Four Corners region (where Arizona, New Mexico, Colorado, and Utah meet). These are patterned after the Appalachian Regional Commission and are joint federal-state organizations composed of one member from each state and a federal member who is appointed by the president and confirmed by the Senate. Each regional commission is charged with analyzing the problems of its area's economy and developing an overall strategy for promoting the long-run growth of the region.[11]

To conclude, each type of area is eligible to receive economic and technical assistance under one of the following EDA programs. First, EDA is authorized to make grants of up to 50 percent of the cost of qualified projects for public works, public services, or development facilities. Second, it can make supplementary grants that may be used to reduce the local reimbursement obligation for other federal programs. Third, EDA is authorized to make loans for up to 100 percent of the costs of public works and development projects in redevelopment areas. Fourth, it is to encourage business and industry to build or expand in redevelopment areas by providing incentives such as long-run low-cost loans. Fifth, while not permitted to make loans for working capital, EDA may guarantee such loans from private lenders to high-risk borrowers. Finally, EDA can conduct a program of research on the causes and effects

10. Actually, it would be better to refer to this as "trickle out" rather than "trickle down." Economists talk of trickle down as the extent to which increased economic activity in one area extends down to other persons within that direct location. On the other hand, trickle out refers to a spatial distribution of the effects of increased economic activity in a specific location.

11. Niles M. Hansen, *Rural Poverty and the Urban Crisis* (Bloomington: Ind. Univ. Press, 1970).

of chronic unemployment.[12] As a major part of its technical assistance program, it also provides studies of economic and business problems which afflict depressed areas. This can include assistance for planning and programming economic development projects, for managerial assistance, and even for demonstration projects.

Recently the Rural Development Act of 1972 was passed. It continues the philosophy of federal loans and grants to encourage the location of future economic growth so as to assist the rural communities. The general purpose of this act was quoted at the start of this chapter. Specifically, the act calls for providing "the best available scientific, technical, economic, organizational, environmental, and management information" to all possible units of local, state, and regional organizations concerned with public services and investments in rural areas. Additionally, the act calls for research in all fields that have as their purpose the development of knowledge useful to those engaged in promoting activities contributing to rural development. Finally, there is a call for expanded research on innovative approaches to small-farm management and technology.[13] The appropriations for the act are small and hence little is expected in the short run.

FINANCING

To this point our emphasis has been on the role of the federal government. In addition there are 50 state governments, 3,000 county governments, 25,000 municipalities and townships, and more than 40,000 school and sewage districts. Each of these units can become involved in community development and each must have revenues to finance its public activities. Not all units of government have equal access to revenue, nor equivalent views of how public funds should be allocated. State and local governments rely primarily upon property, sales, and excise taxes for their financing. These tend to rise more slowly than per capita income or to place an increasing burden upon the individual if incomes are falling. Thus we see, on the one hand, increasing pressure for more governmental services and developmental efforts at the local level, and on the other, growing inability of the local units to finance those projects they deem worthwhile.

Past federal programs of grants and loans to local units have provided funds but at a cost of red tape and rigidities which make it difficult to adapt the programs to local conditions. In contrast, locally developed and financed programs have created many inequities. Public assistance is the most widely known example. Federal revenue sharing is an attempt to increase the revenue base of local units of government,

12. Ibid., p. 143.
13. Public Law 92-419, 86 Stat. 671.

provide uniformity among programs, and simultaneously provide an increased level of local autonomy. Revenue sharing can be defined as the sharing of funds collected by one unit of government with other units of government. In the case of federal revenue sharing, the federal government collects revenue and in turn shares it with states, counties, and local jurisdictions throughout the nation. Two questions immediately arise: Why share revenue at all? Why do it in this manner? We consider each in turn, starting with the latter question.

The income tax collection system of the federal government is the most efficient method of collecting revenue (for public purposes). Hence, it is more efficient to collect federal income taxes and return some proportion to the locality from whence it came than to collect it at the local level.

Three arguments are usually advanced in favor of revenue sharing: (1) the existence of a fiscal crisis at the state and local levels, (2) the transfer of power to state and local levels, and (3) the need to redistribute wealth from the affluent to the less affluent by shifting part of the burden of government from the generally regressive state and local sales taxes to the more progressive federal income tax, and by redistributing resources from richer states to those states less well off.

As stated earlier, the need for revenue sharing has been accentuated by the changing magnitude and nature of spending by the public sector over the past several decades. As recently as 1929, expenditures by all levels of government accounted for only 10 percent of the gross national product (2.4 percent by the federal government and 7.5 percent by state and local governments). By 1970, however, total government expenditures were up to 32 percent of the gross national product, with 18.6 percent being federal and 13.4 percent being state and local government spending. The source of public funds has also changed substantially. Initially, federal revenues from the sale of lands and other sources were adequate to cover federal expenses. By early in this century, however, taxes on personal income became the main source of revenue for the federal treasury; they now provide about 85 percent of federal revenues. In contrast, state and local governments rely rather heavily on the property and sales taxes, both of which are regressive and grow more slowly than the income tax. Through a program of general revenue sharing, the extent of reliance by state and local governments upon these latter two kinds of taxes would be reduced. Perhaps more importantly, the local levels of government would receive a larger share of responsibility in allocating federal funds to meet local problems.

Additionally, the recent recessions, coupled with inflationary pressures, have created serious fiscal conditions in many state and local governments. As the economy slows down, the demand for certain services from the public sector expands; examples are welfare requirements and unemployment payments as people become unemployed. Figures indicate that during 1970 the number of welfare recipients increased by 23 percent over the previous year.[14] Also, since the beginning of 1966, evidence indicates that the prices paid by state and local governments for goods and services have increased by 32 percent, more than one-third faster than the general level of consumer prices.[15] Unions and the new militancy among teachers and other public employees have pushed up wages faster than in other sectors of the economy. Table 14.1 indicates the extent to which costs of state and local governments have risen since 1955. In contrast to the rising expenditures of state and local governments, their revenues have risen much more slowly.

The second major issue in revenue sharing is mostly political: returning power to the people. The argument is that local decision makers are more cognizant of local problems and hence are in a better position to evaluate where federal money should be allocated. It is indeed true that in recent times the proliferation of federal programs has greatly confounded the problems of rural areas seeking help. In fact, some planning commissions in rural areas often hire a person whose sole function is keeping track of federal programs and potential funding sources.

There are also some compelling arguments against more local control. Because of the spillovers that exist, there are persuasive arguments for control at a level considerably larger in scope than many rural areas. Education is the most obvious example. The local school board is an old and revered American institution. There are probably few areas of more concern than that of local control over education. Yet, the fact that the vast majority of rural youths migrate to urban areas means that some other region bears the social costs of decisions made elsewhere. If rural schools continue to concentrate upon vocational agriculture curricula—and exclude the humanities, social sciences, and other areas of study—the youths that migrate to urban areas are ill prepared to function effectively in the more complex urban environment. Another factor is the quality of elected officials at the local level in contrast to those at the national level. Students of American politics generally agree that grass-roots politicians are noted for their lack of administrative ability.

The third area of discussion is that of income redistribution. As indicated earlier, revenue sharing would shift the tax burden from low-income to high-income groups, and from low-income to high-income states. Revenue that is collected would be allocated on the basis of area characteristics such as population, urban congestion, or public assistance recipients. It would reduce the disparity with which states and localities can respond to social needs by offsetting a portion of the difference in their financial resources.

14. Charles L. Schultze et al., *Setting National Priorities: The 1972 Budget* (Washington, D.C.: Brookings Institution, 1971), p. 137.
15. Ibid.

TABLE 14.1. Comparison of state and local expenditures, by function, fiscal years 1955 and 1969

Function	Amount (billion dollars) 1955	1969	1955-69 Percentage increase	1955-69 Percentage of total increase	Percentage of 1955-69 Increase in Expenditure Attributable to Increase in Workload	Price	Scope and quality
All Functions	39.0	134.1	244.1	100.0	...	...	...
General Expenditure	33.7	116.7	246.1	87.2	26.2	43.8	30.0
Local schools	10.1	33.8	233.2	24.8	31.7	52.4	15.9
Higher education and other education, except local schools	1.8	13.5	657.6	12.3	25.1	35.5	39.4
Public welfare	3.2	12.1	282.2	9.4	...	29.7	70.3
Highways	6.5	15.4	138.9	9.4	50.8	42.3	6.9
Hospitals and health	2.5	8.5	237.5	6.3	18.8	43.8	37.4
Basic urban services[a]	4.3	14.9	243.7	11.1	22.8	50.6	26.6
Administration and other[b]	5.3	18.5	247.4	13.9	18.5	38.0	43.6
Utility Deficit	0.4	1.4	234.5	1.0	...	...	...
Debt Retirement and Additions to Liquid Assets[c,d]	3.9	12.0	206.1	8.5	...	...	...
Contributions to Retirement Systems	0.9	4.0	339.8	3.2	...	...	...

Source: Charles L. Schultze, E. R. Fried, Alice M. Rivlin, and Nancy H. Teeters, Setting National Priorities: The 1972 Budget (Washington, D.C.: Brookings Institution, 1971), p. 139, Table 6-1.

a. Includes fire protection, police protection, correction, sewerage, other sanitation, parks and recreation, housing and urban renewal, and transportation and terminals.

b. Includes administration and general control, general public buildings, interest on general debt, employment services, and miscellaneous functions.

c. Excludes assets of social insurance funds.

d. Estimated.

There are two classes of federal revenue sharing: (1) general revenue sharing and (2) special revenue sharing. General revenue sharing means the earmarking of a portion of federal revenues for distribution to the individual states on the basis of a formula. These funds will automatically transfer to the states without annual appropriation by Congress. The states, in turn, would be required to share their funds with their local governments on the basis of guidelines spelled out by the legislation.

The act creating federal revenue sharing became law on October 20, 1972, and checks covering amounts retroactive to January 1, 1972, were mailed out shortly thereafter. For the calendar year 1972, $5.3 billion were distributed back to local jurisdictions. The act expires December 31, 1976. An additional $25 billion are to be disbursed in slightly increasing annual installments before that time.[16]

At present no one knows what will be the impact of general revenue sharing on local jurisdictions. The funds are allocated one-third to state governments and two-thirds directly to local jurisdictions. They can be spent for high priority items such as ordinary and necessary maintenance and operating expenses for public safety, environmental protection, public transportation, health, recreation, social services, and normal capital expenditures. This still leaves local towns and villages considerable discretion in buying items such as new fire engines and police cars, while spending very little on human resource needs. Although $5 billion appears to be a substantial sum, it still represents a small proportion of total state and local expenditures.

The $5 billion distributed under federal sharing in 1973 represented less than 4 percent of total state and local expenditures in 1970. To expect this amount to significantly alter the fiscal position of state and local governments is expecting far too much.[17]

In contrast to the general revenue sharing, special revenue sharing involves a substantial restructuring of current programs. Under current proposals, 130 existing aid programs would be consolidated into 6 major grants. Under this scheme, recipient governments would not be required to provide matching funds or to maintain their current level of expenditure to obtain the grant; each of the 6 grants would be distributed among the states and localities on the basis of a formula established in the legislation, and the recipients would be free to spend the money as they saw fit. The 6 categories designated for special revenue sharing are (1) urban community development, (2) rural community development, (3) education, (4) manpower training, (5) transportation, and (6) law enforcement.

The rationale for special revenue sharing is largely an efficiency

16. Public Law 92-512, 86 Stat. 919. The correct title for the act is the State and Local Fiscal Assistance Act of 1972.
17. Schultze et al., *Setting National Priorities*, p. 146.

argument. Presently the federal government provides aid to state and local governments through more than 500 categorical grant programs. The confusion and conflicts in this system are well known. Specifically, the system of grants would be designed to channel federal funds into those programs that will serve a particular national goal. Currently this legislation has not been passed by Congress.

SUMMARY

This chapter stresses the economic and sociologic role of the rural community and analyzes those factors which, over time, have combined to exert detrimental impacts upon the economic viability of such communities. The four dominant economic factors are (1) a decline in demand for locally produced products, (2) a shift in the comparative advantage among producing regions, (3) exhaustion of the resource base upon which the local economy is based, and (4) structural changes within the major exporting industry.

In spite of the tremendous growth in the productive capacity of our food and fiber system, rural areas and communities have been unable to single-handedly generate the enterprises and jobs to employ the labor it has released. Conditions cannot be turned around simply by the development of commercial agriculture. A prosperous agriculture can contribute to the economic well-being of rural areas but it does not solve the total income-employment problem in either the well-to-do or the poorer regions. A number of public programs including the Rural Development Act and the State and Local Fiscal Assistance Act were described in detail. Their success is still to be established and much remains to be done.

The free market economy results in the allocation of factors of production to those endeavors in which each factor can contribute the most to the value of the final product. If there is too much labor being applied to the production of "widgets" relative to the capital being used, labor could receive higher returns (contribute more to the value of the product) by transferring to the production of "gidgets." The same principle applies to spatial aspects of production. Factors of production (labor, capital, entrepreneurial skill) are allocated to certain regions of the nation because they contribute the most to the income of the nation in that region. Because of this, certain regions of the country lag behind others in terms of the level of economic activity. Because labor is the least mobile of the productive factors, people tend to remain in these lagging regions. This is the domain of public policy. When the differential grows sufficiently large, public action is requested to alleviate the undesirable consequences of differential rates of mobility between labor and other productive factors (primarily capital). The problem is to design a set of signals which will modify economic behavior from that which would prevail if the market were allowed to continue operating in an unrestricted fashion.

But what form should this policy take? Do we attempt to take jobs to the people or encourage people to move to the jobs? In the absence of a conscious population policy,[18] much of the discussion of rural development still centers on taking the jobs to the people—that is, the industrialization of the countryside. As indicated by Hansen, the 1968 Manpower Report of the President, while admitting that some out-migration from rural areas will continue to be inevitable, proposes that the basic need is for programs designed to help discover "their economic potential and to promote their output and employment growth."[19] These measures would take the form of improving transportation and other infrastructure, and improving the education and training opportunities for rural residents. Additionally, it might be necessary to institute investment grants, loans, special tax advantages, and other preferential incentives.

Yet there is pessimism that such efforts will be successful. Whatever advantages rural areas may have in terms of a stable labor force that is often willing to work for less than union wages, land that is abundant and relatively cheap, and an environment that is both healthful and refreshing, there are some disadvantages as well. The cheap land and low taxes are likely to be matched by a low-quality array of public services. The absence of ancillary economic activities means that many inputs must be acquired at rather long distances from the business. Furthermore, the abundant labor is often of low quality. This fact also generally means that educational and cultural facilities are lacking—a drawback to plants that want to attract good management and technical personnel.

A second factor which tends to dampen plans for the industrialization of the countryside is that the fastest growing sector of the economy is the tertiary sector—for example, services such as insurance, real estate, medical care, legal services, etc. The largest market for these kinds of economic services is in the populated urban centers. Thus the potential for attracting industries from the most rapidly growing sector of the economy is extremely limited. Those industries that do move to rural areas are often in search of cheap labor (they have been known to threaten to leave if a union organizer is even seen on the premises) and are often those from sectors experiencing relative stagnation or decline.

The solution must be sought in two different ways. The word *sought* is used purposely since the appropriate solution is still unknown.

18. The *Report of the President's Commission on Rural Poverty* has been criticized for its failure to address this important issue. See Hansen, *Rural Poverty*, pp. 222–38.
    19. Ibid., p. 222.

First is the need for improved delivery systems of social and economic services by public agencies. These would include improved education, health services, employment services, credit availability, planning, and other technical assistance. Much of this approach was discussed in the previous chapter. Revenue sharing can assist the local community in developing the appropriate delivery system. The federal government, with revenue sharing as the incentive, can motivate local units to develop programs which are consistent, standard, and uniform in their treatment.

The second route requires stimulating new firms and businesses to create new jobs and incomes in the countryside. This cannot be limited to either rural or local regions. Programs to reduce poverty and unemployment in urban areas and across large regions trickle out to other regions and to rural areas. Perhaps what is needed is a national program to search for the solution and deal with the problem.

DISCUSSION QUESTIONS AND PROBLEMS

1. What are the three main roles that a community plays?
2. Criticize the notion of horizontal and vertical ties in a community.
3. Explain "domestic colonialism."
4. Trace through the impact (as in Figure 14.2) from an increase in the demand for an exported product from a rural region. What will be the impact on equilibrium price?
5. Introduce transportation costs into the analysis of Figure 14.2. What would be the impact on quantity of coal exported from region A and on the equilibrium price?
6. Discuss the potential conflict between the "environmental movement" and rural development efforts.
7. Evaluate the following: Since the government alters the comparative advantage of areas by building highways, it should equalize the positive effects by subsidizing activities located some distance from such highways.
8. Define the "trickle-out" theory and comment on its plausibility in the urban-rural hierarchy.
9. Discuss the advantages and disadvantages of more local control over the spending of federal monies.
10. Develop a definition of rural development and formulate an economic model (see Chapter 2) for testing your definition. Be specific as to your assumptions, your hypotheses, and necessary data.

SUGGESTED READINGS

BASIC

Cameron, Gordon C. *Regional Economic Development: The Federal Role.* Washington, D.C.: Resources for the Future, 1970.

An interesting book for the general reader; nontechnical but thorough.

Goetz, Charles J. *What is Revenue Sharing?* Washington, D.C.: Urban Institute, 1972.
> An excellent primer on revenue sharing, what it might become, what it might accomplish, and what it will not accomplish.

Hansen, Niles M. *Rural Poverty and the Urban Crisis.* Bloomington: Ind. Univ. Press, 1970.
> A description of regional development problems and programs. It contains a discussion of minority problems, rural industrialization, and urban growth policies.

Nourse, Hugh O. *Regional Economics: A Study in the Economic Structure, Stability, and Growth of Regions.* New York: McGraw-Hill, 1968.
> A very basic book on regional economics.

Perloff, Harvey S.; et al. *Regions, Resources, and Economic Growth.* Lincoln: Univ. Nebr. Press, 1967.
> A good historical description of regional growth in the United States. An excellent reference source.

Richardson, Harry W. *Regional Economics: Location Theory, Urban Structure, and Regional Change.* New York: Praeger, 1969.
> Extensive coverage of regional economics for beginning or intermediate students.

Sundquist, James L. *Making Federalism Work: A Study of Program Coordination at the Community Level.* Washington, D.C.: Brookings Institution, 1969.
> An interesting book covering community action, model cities, and rural development.

ADVANCED

Bressler, Raymond G., Jr.; and King, Richard A. *Markets, Prices, and Interregional Trade.* New York: John Wiley, 1970.
> An outstanding book on interregional trade.

Iowa State University Center for Agricultural and Economic Development. *Benefits and Burdens of Rural Development: Some Public Policy Viewpoints.* Ames: Iowa State Univ. Press, 1970.
> A collection of papers from a symposium on the economic and sociologic aspects of rural development.

Isard, Walter, ed. *Methods of Regional Analysis: An Introduction to Regional Science.* Cambridge, Mass.: M.I.T. Press. 1960.
> One of the classic texts in regional analysis.

McKee, David L.; Dean, Robert D.; and Leahy, William H., eds. *Regional Economics: Theory and Practice.* New York: Free Press, Macmillan, 1970.
> An anthology of many articles on regional economics.

Needleman, L., ed. *Regional Analysis.* Baltimore: Penguin Books, 1968.
> An excellent anthology of articles on various topics central to regional economics.

CHAPTER 15: NATURAL RESOURCE ECONOMICS

It is impossible to cover in one chapter all the pertinent issues of natural resource use and, hence, we set more modest goals here. One area of recent interest is that of the concept of the earth as a spaceship and the problems inherent in its economic growth.[1] This line of inquiry is much too complex to treat adequately in the space available. The Suggested Readings at the end of the chapter offer a choice of interesting and provocative books on the issues involved in the debate.

As an overview, we start with a discussion of natural resource issues at the national level and explore the various ways in which public policy has evolved to deal with these specific problems. In the second major part of the chapter we discuss in some detail four economic issues in the area of natural resource use: (1) conservation, (2) natural resources as free factors of production, (3) the general problem of pollution, and (4) the valuation of natural resources in formulating public policy. In the final section we focus on problems and programs of future significance.

OVERVIEW

When the nation was young, our overriding concern was to establish a viable and self-sufficient economy capable of supporting the local population with minimal dependence upon other nations, such as the industrial giant of that period, Great Britain. With this as a motivating force, and given the apparent boundlessness of the nation's natural resources, the predominant ethic in our early stages of development was to conquer nature as an adversary.

1. The notion of the earth as a spaceship is a result of the realization that we live in a closed system; that is, when something is thrown away or used up, it is still with us. It may be in some other location or in a different form, but it is still with us. Put differently, if we foul our life-support system—our land, our air, and our water—there is little chance of survival. See Kenneth E. Boulding, The Economics of the Coming Spaceship Earth, *The Environmental Handbook,* ed. Garrett DeBell (New York: Ballantine Books, 1970), pp. 96–101.

Whereas the Indian moved in response to the availability of resources for food and for clothing, the new settlers, with their culture of landed property, established homesteads to extract a living from the soil.

At that time in our nation's history, there was little concern for conserving natural resources, and there was certainly no concern for creating national parks so that future generations might see wild animals and forests. To a population living among wild animals and forests, the thought was incredulous. But we have changed since that time, and now over one-third of our total land area is controlled and managed by the federal government. Indeed, few examples better illustrate the changing nature of our policy toward natural resources than the history of land policy. Figure 15.1 depicts the major eras in federal land ownership and management since approximately 1800, and up through the year 2000.

Figure 15.1 indicates that there have been at least five distinct modes of behavior on the part of the federal government regarding land. Initially, as a condition for statehood, the federal government obtained title to large blocks of land from the territories. Next is an era of disposal when, in an effort to encourage settlement of the large uninhabited regions of the country, land was offered to homesteaders, miners, and railroads. Following that era, we entered one of reservation where large tracts of land were set aside. By 1893 some 13 million acres had been designated as forest reserves, but there were no funds to carry on even the most superficial degree of administration. Other tracts of land were added to the reserves during the administration of Theodore Roosevelt but still with little, if any, funds for management. With the most desirable (productive) lands in private hands, with some of the most scenic lands in national parks, and with the balance of the forested lands in forest reserves, there was still a large block of unreserved and unappropriated public domain left in federal ownership. In the early

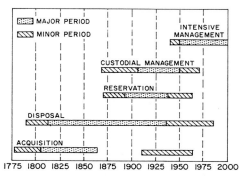

FIG. 15.1. Major eras in federal land ownership and management in the United States, 1800—2000. (From Marion Clawson and Burnell Held, **The Federal Lands,** Lincoln: Univ. Nebr. Press, 1957, p. 17, Figure 1.)

1930s this land became the responsibility of the Grazing Service (later Bureau of Land Management). The next era, custodial management, is characterized by rudimentary management efforts to control grazing and timber trespass, and to promote "wise" use of the forests and rangelands. Although it is impossible to set an exact date for the beginning of intensive federal resource management, the period following World War II is generally recognized as the turning point in federal land management—from a custodial attitude to one of aggressive and scientific management.[2]

Today we have the Forest Service, the Bureau of Land Management, the National Park Service, the Bureau of Indian Affairs, the Tennessee Valley Authority, the Council on Environmental Quality, the Environmental Protection Agency, Federal Power Commission, the Office of Minerals and Solid Fuels, the Office of Oil and Gas, the Bureau of Reclamation, the Army Corps of Engineers, the Office of Water Resources Research, the United States Fish and Wildlife Service, the Bureau of Sport Fisheries and Wildlife, the Bureau of Mines, the Geological Survey, the Bureau of Outdoor Recreation, the Soil Conservation Service, and the Natural Resource Economics Division of the Economic Research Service (USDA) all concerned with some aspect of natural resource use, management, or development. As should be clear from the above listing, natural resource policy not only involves action within a public agency but also involves interagency action. Certain economic concepts and principles apply, irrespective of the agency or agencies involved in resource management. Rather than describe policies or goals of specific government groups, we will approach natural resource policies from the viewpoint of the economic concepts involved in their management.

ECONOMIC ISSUES

We have selected four important areas of interest in natural resource use and management for detailed discussion: (1) conservation, (2) natural resources as free factors of production, (3) the general problem of pollution, and (4) the valuation of natural resources in public policy decisions. As indicated, we will not be able to treat each of the four issues in complete detail, but our hope is to show how economic analysis is useful in understanding some of the pressing natural resource problems. However, before turning to that

2. For an excellent treatment of land management practice (and history), see Marion Clawson and Burnell Held, *The Federal Lands: Their Use and Management* (Lincoln: Univ. Nebr. Press, 1957).

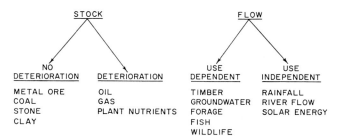

FIG. 15.2. A classification scheme for natural resources.

treatment, it is necessary to make a distinction between natural resources that are characterized as "stock resources," and those characterized as "flow resources." Figure 15.2 depicts these two classes of natural resources, along with a further subdivision within each.

RESOURCE TYPES

The distinction between stock and flow resources is that the former (stock resources) are nonrenewable within a meaningful time horizon. Metal ores and coal are indeed being formed, but that rate of transformation is economically and technically irrelevant. Flow resources, on the other hand, are renewable. Within this two-part classification there is a further distinction: stock resources are classified as either (1) not significantly affected by natural deterioration (metal ores, coal, stones, clays) or (2) significantly affected (refined metals subject to oxidation, oil and gas seepages, leaching of plant nutrients, evaporation of surface water). Flow resources can be categorized into (1) use-independent (flow not significantly affected by human action) and (2) use-dependent (flow significantly affected by human action). Use-dependent resources are characterized by the presence of a critical zone in their utilization. A *critical zone* is defined as a more or less defined range of utilization rates above which a decrease in flow cannot be reversed economically under presently foreseeable conditions. Frequently, such irreversibility is not only economic but also technologic.[3]

3. As an example, a flow resource such as a fish population may be depleted to the point where it is economically impossible to harvest, but it still survives in limited numbers. In this case, it has been fished beyond the point of economic irreversibility because it will never become more abundant, but not technologic irreversibility. If the population were completely destroyed (made extinct) we would term this the point of technologic irreversibility. Note that technology has a profound impact on the level of economic irreversibility, but not on the level of technologic irreversibility. For a discussion of this, see S. V. Ciriacy-Wantrup, *Resource Conservation: Economics and Policies* (Berkeley: Univ. Calif. Press, 1963), p. 39.

STOCK RESOURCES

As seen in Figure 15.2, stock resources are typified by metal ores, coal, stone, oil, gas, and some plant nutrients. The characteristic which distinguishes these resources from the flow resources is that their rate of renewal is so slow as to be imperceptible. Coal is the obvious example; the processes which produce coal are still going on, but the rate of formation is so small as to be irrelevant from an economic viewpoint.

The difference between those stock resources susceptible to deterioration and those not affected hinges on the existence of physical loss while still in the natural state. Whereas coal, the ores, and stone are not subject to disappearance prior to mining, oil and gas can leak into more inaccessible areas in the earth's structure, or, in the case of gas, escape unnoticed into the atmosphere.

The economic problem in the utilization of stock resources is to devise a system of incentives which will encourage the extraction of these resources at a rate which is consistent with the demands for them, to monitor this extraction so that the resource is not completely exhausted before alternative sources of supply can be found, to encourage the exploration of these alternative supplies, and finally to encourage the development of substitute materials for the day when all available supplies are exhausted.

Hence, wise use of stock resources is a very complex issue. Wise use does not mean nonuse, for there is little sense in preserving the coal reserves of the United States if a perfectly suitable substitute can be developed in the laboratory—particularly if it can be produced synthetically for less than the expected costs of mining coal. Put differently, coal has no intrinsic value; its value is only as an input into a process which creates energy. *Wise use* means a rate of extraction of a stock resource such that the present value of all future net returns from the sale of that resource is as large as possible. Although this sounds simple it is a very complicated problem. To determine net revenue, one must know future costs of coal extraction, future costs of manufacturing synthetics, relative efficiencies of coal and its substitute in the production of energy, and several other factors. Once the future net revenues have been estimated, their present value must be calculated. Obviously a dollar obtained next year is not as valuable as a dollar now. One could loan it out and have something more than one dollar next year. The formula for calculating the present value of future income streams is delayed until later in this chapter. The point is that the difficulty of calculating future net revenues results in policies to control the extraction of stock resources that are very conservative. In other words, instead of trying to maximize the present value of all future receipts, the operational policy is to mine that quantity of coal which leaves a considerable margin of error to allow time for new discoveries and the development of substitutes.

FLOW RESOURCES

In contrast to the stock resources, flow resources are replenishable. Those that are renewed at a rate independent of their rate of utilization are called *use-independent* resources. Examples are rainfall, a river, and solar energy. Because they are use independent, rainfall and solar energy are not usually considered as resources on which economic issues exist. This is not the case. But, before discussing that, river flow merits some discussion.

The extraction of water from a flowing stream is governed by a very elaborate system of legal constraints rather than economic considerations. Most are intended to insure that all those along the course of the river with prior claims take precedence in their rights to its flow. It is impossible to go into detail here as volumes have been written on the matter. What is relevant is that the market has very little if any role in the allocation of most water taken from rivers and streams. In the West, the doctrine of "prior appropriation" operates—meaning essentially first come, first served. Once use patterns are established along a water course, it is impossible, without legal revision, to alter that allocation. This is part of the reason for the water shortage in the arid Southwest. Agriculture, being one of the first economic pursuits carried on in the West, has appropriated the vast bulk of the available water.[4] To acquire water needed for industry and domestic purposes, the Southwest has had to look elsewhere, primarily the Pacific Northwest, for surplus water.

In the case of rainfall and solar energy, we see many interesting issues evolving from induced precipitation, otherwise known as cloud seeding or weather modification. Western agriculturalists view this as the solution to their ever-present problem of inadequate moisture. Various experiments if successful may significantly alter the rainfall in certain regions of the West. However, those familiar with the hydrologic cycles argue that more rainfall in one area is at the expense of rainfall in another area. While certain farmers in the West need more rainfall during certain parts of the year, other farmers—producing other crops—depend upon the dry weather to mature their crops. Thus conflicts will inevitably arise. Hence, the question of weather modification includes a number of legal and economic issues, most of which are still unknown and certainly unresolved.

Let us turn to the more conventional flow resources—those characterized by the presence of a critical zone in their rate of utilization (use-dependent). These natural resources are heavily dependent upon the rate at which they are harvested; their future existence is a

---

4. It is estimated that approximately 90 percent of the consumptive use of water in Arizona is for agriculture. Consumptive use is defined as a use which results in a loss of the water to other users. Evapotranspiration is an example—although the water returns in the form of precipitation, it may be in another place, and in another time.

direct function of present use. Figure 15.2 lists the common examples in this category as timber, forage, fish, wildlife, and groundwater. While the first four are obvious, there may be some question as to why groundwater is a use-dependent flow resource. The answer lies in the fact that underground aquifers are subject to certain changes if excessive groundwater is extracted. Along coastal areas, a withdrawal of groundwater may lead to the intrusion of salt water which will ruin the water supply. Away from the coastal areas, excessive withdrawal from aquifers can compact the porous material, making it impervious, thereby reducing its ability to be replenished.

To develop the concept of a critical zone, we will use a fish population and develop the dynamics of a fishery. Although brief and oversimplified, it should facilitate the understanding of the economic problems of harvesting a use-dependent flow resource. A common expression for the biological production (biomass) of a fishery in a natural (unharvested) state can be stated in gross terms as

$$\text{Biomass} = f \text{ (recruitment, growth, natural mortality)}$$

As long as fishing does not occur, these three primary influences will govern the size of the population; its biomass. All three variables on the right-hand side of the equation, in turn, are a function of the biomass and its relationship to its environment. For example, recruitment is low at very low population levels because the number of spawners is small. At very large population levels (in relation to environment), recruitment may also be low because the fish are not healthy, and there is severe competition for food. At some intermediate population level, the ability of the spawners to recruit progeny into the standing population is a maximum. A similar condition prevails for individual growth. At low population levels, the growth rate of the individual fish is a maximum, decreasing as a function of the size of the standing population. The third factor, natural mortality, is low for very low population levels but increases as a function of the standing population. The system is one of simultaneous relationships. The three influences combine to provide the idealized relationship between the number of spawners in one time period and the mature progeny surviving in the following time period, as shown in Figure 15.3.

The 45° line $[g(P)]$ is called the *replacement line* and indicates the level of mature progeny which would just maintain the parent stock at its present levels. At a population of P_1, the production of mature progeny over and above that needed for replacement is a maximum. At a parent population of P_2, the production of mature progeny is a maximum in an absolute sense. At P_3, the production of mature progeny is just adequate to replace the natural attrition of the parent stock.

From Figure 15.3, it is possible to define equilibrium catch as

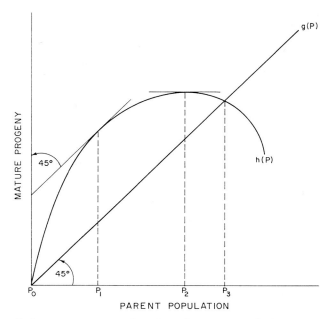

FIG. 15.3. Mature progeny as a function of parent population.

that level of fish mortality which will leave the population at its present level. It is the difference between the number of mature progeny produced and the line $g(P)$. At P_3 there is no positive net recruitment, and the equilibrium catch would be zero. Suppose the population is at P_3 and fishing is introduced into the system. This additional source of predation reduces the parent population but permits the remainder to increase its production of young. As fishing is increased further and the population further reduced, the ability to produce young (and the capacity of the young to grow) increases until at P_1 the production of a surplus over that needed for replacement is a maximum. If, in any one year, the catch is less than the equilibrium catch, the population will move in the direction of P_3. If more than equilibrium catch is taken, the population will be further reduced. If exactly the excess over that needed for replacement is taken each season, it is possible to hold the fish population at P_1. At this level, the sustainable yield will be maximized and the population will be held in a state of artificial equilibrium, artificial in that it is man-caused and man-controlled.

It follows from the definition of equilibrium catch that by taking the difference between the $g(P)$ and $h(P)$ functions in Figure 15.3, it is possible to derive equilibrium catch, $f(P)$, as a function of parent population. This relationship is shown in Figure 15.4. At P_0, equilibrium catch is zero, the same as at P_3. For intermediate values of P, the yield increases, reaches a maximum at P_1, then declines to zero. Note that it is possible to obtain the same equilibrium catch from two different population sizes. For example, population sizes P_a and P_b both provide an equilibrium yield of Y_e.

The aggregate catch of fish depends both upon the size of the fish population and total fishing effort; either can be fixed while the other varies. For example, a given level of effort applied to a large population will yield a larger catch than the same effort applied to a smaller population. Figure 15.5 illustrates some possible aggregate production functions for a fishery. Each represents a different size of fish population.

Assume that Y_e is the equilibrium catch of fish from Figure 15.4. For a small population, P_a, the amount of effort (E^*) required to harvest the equilibrium catch, Y_e, is greater than that required (E') to harvest the same equilibrium catch from a larger population, P_b. Population sizes exist between P_a and P_b, however, where equilibrium catch is greater than Y_e (see Figures 15.3 and 15.4). The maximum equilibrium catch, Y_{me}, is obtained with a parent population of P_1 utilizing E_1 units of effort. However, with biomass of P_1, the fishing industry could maximize

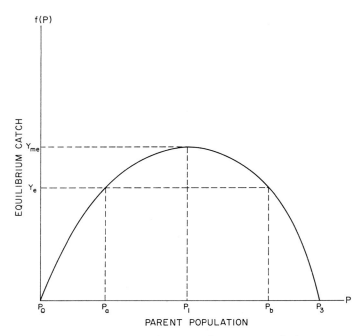

FIG. 15.4. Equilibrium catch as a function of parent population.

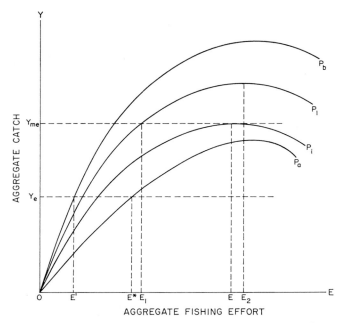

FIG. 15.5.   Aggregate catch as a function of aggregate fishing effort.

total catch by expending E_2 units of effort. If the cost of effort was zero, this would also maximize their profits. If costs were such that the industry maximized profits by applying a level of effort between E_1 and E_2, the biomass would decline toward P_i and P_a. Thus a conflict can exist between the optimum level of fishing from the fishing industries' viewpoint and the optimum harvest to maintain the parent population.

The relationship among fishing effort, profit-maximizing yield, and equilibrium yield is crucial. Furthermore, fishing effort as dictated by profit-maximizing yield directly affects the size of the fish population which, in turn, affects the equilibrium yield.

The relationship between fishing effort and profit-maximizing yield is a crucial one in the fishery and the above should make this point obvious; there is a different production function for each population level. The concept of a critical zone is that, if the equilibrium catch of the fishery is exceeded over several successive seasons, the ability of the population to replenish itself may be permanently impaired. When it becomes impossible to reverse the flow economically, the critical zone has been surpassed.

The economic problem in harvesting a flow resource is to find and maintain that level of harvesting activity (fishing effort) which maximizes the net returns to society. Again, while simple in concept, this is a most difficult operational goal. The conflicts between optima on the firm production function and the natural resource production function, the interdependence of different fish species, the uncertainty of future demands for fish, and the imperfect knowledge of the exact biological relationships are but a few of the reasons why this goal is difficult to obtain.

In summary, it can be stated as a general proposition that the utilization of stock resources is particularly sensitive to the economic factors such as the state of technology employed in extraction, while for flow resources, economic, technological, and legal factors are important. As extraction equipment becomes more sophisticated, the potential for depleting the available stock resources is enhanced with no possibility for replacement. On the other hand, as technology becomes more advanced, the probability of discovering good substitutes also improves. For stock resources, the firm generally recognizes the importance of its decisions on the level of stocks available in future periods. For flow resources, technology is also important since improved methods of spotting fish (sonar) mean that the probability of capturing more fish is enhanced. In this case the likelihood of conflict between the firm's actions and the level of future resource flows is greater. Hence legal controls are necessary. The establishment of quotas and the shortening of fishing seasons in response to this new technology are ways to prevent the critical zone from being encountered.

With this foundation in the nature of stock and flow resources, we turn to the four substantive issues of natural resource use and management.

CONSERVATION

Conservation is often defined in terms of use rates at some constant level, say, sustained yield. This notion is useless for stock resources and has little meaning for flow resources. Specifically, in the previous illustration of a fishery, a sustained yield would preclude the possibility of speeding up or slowing down the growth rate of a natural resource—an act which may be economically rational. For example, if the demand for a particular species of fish (perhaps flounder) decreases as incomes rise, it makes little economic sense to continue the harvest at a sustained-yield level.[5]

Ciriacy-Wantrup argues that a proper definition of conservation is possible only when related to the time distribution of use rates. Specifically, *conservation* is defined as changes in the intertemporal distribution of physical rates of use in the direction of the future. Conversely,

5. In the concepts of demand theory (Chapter 8) we would say that the income elasticity of demand for flounder is zero or negative.

depletion would be a change in the intertemporal distribution of physical rates of use in the direction of the present. Conservation always implies comparison of two or more time distributions of use. The *optimum state of conservation* is that distribution of use rates over time which results in the greatest possible present value for expected net revenues.

One of the major issues in conservation is the time horizon. The optimum state of conservation was just defined in terms of the present value of expected future net revenues. The crucial element is the time preference of those making the decisions, the planning horizon. There is a disparity between the planning horizon for individuals and the planning horizon for societies and their governments. Generally individuals have a shorter time horizon than governments. Each individual knows that his presence on earth can be measured in rather finite terms and generally is less than 100 years. On the other hand, societies exist for centuries and, assuming nuclear holocaust is averted, the population of any country expects to continue into the indefinite future.

To bring this back to the issue of conservation, recall that conservation is defined as the manipulation of use rates over time such that the present value of a future stream of net benefits is as large as possible. Thus the problem of the conservation of a natural resource is intimately related to the length of that future stream. Is it to be calculated using the next 5 years? the next 10 years? 50 years? or 200 years? Some individuals would opt for the shortest time horizon and others for the longest.

The importance of time preference is perhaps best illustrated by describing how the present value of a future stream of income is calculated. Assume that you were offered, with no strings attached, $100 today. Alternatively, you could have $102 exactly one year from now. If you are like the vast majority of people, you would prefer the $100 today. This choice is a reflection of your time preference. Further assume that you were 65 years old. Now, the possibility of $100 today is even more attractive than $102 one year from now. It might even be that you would prefer $100 today to $500 one year from now. Every individual has a particular time preference, and the rate at which you are willing to forego present consumption in favor of future consumption is termed your *private rate of time preference*. Put differently, the rate at which one is willing to discount future income possibilities is an indication of his time preference. If he is willing to discount future earning possibilities by a significant amount ($100 today preferred to $500 one year from now), it means that he has a high rate of time preference. Conversely, if he prefers $101 one year from now to $100 today, he has a low rate of time preference.

To compare different streams of income over future periods of time, it is necessary to reduce the streams to a comparable base called their present value—their worth to you today. Consider the following example: you are offered \$100 today and \$100 exactly one year apart for the next five years. To calculate the present value of this bequest, it is necessary to calculate the sum of Equation 15.1.

$$PV = \$100 + \frac{\$100}{(1+i)^1} + \frac{\$100}{(1+i)^2} + \frac{\$100}{(1+i)^3} \qquad (15.1)$$
$$+ \frac{\$100}{(1+i)^4} + \frac{\$100}{(1+i)^5}$$

where PV stands for present value and i reflects the discount rate consistent with your private rate of time preference. If you are 65 years old and do not figure to live much longer, the stream of annual quantities would have a present value of a lesser magnitude than if you were young and could be reasonably sure of being around to collect it. To illustrate this, we will assume that the 65-year-old person has a high rate of time preference and let $i = 0.06$ (as in a 6 percent rate of interest). On the other hand, the young person will likely have a lower rate of time preference and here we will let $i = 0.03$. The present value for the first individual will be

$$PV_{65} = \$100 + \frac{\$100}{(1.06)} + \frac{\$100}{(1.12)} + \frac{\$100}{(1.19)} \qquad (15.2)$$
$$+ \frac{\$100}{(1.26)} + \frac{\$100}{(1.34)}$$

$$PV_{65} = \$100 + \$94.34 + \$89.00 + \$83.96 \qquad (15.3)$$
$$+ \$79.21 + \$74.73$$

$$PV_{65} = \$521.24 \qquad (15.4)$$

For the 20-year-old person, the present value of the same stream of income is

$$PV_{20} = \$100 + \frac{\$100}{(1.03)^1} + \frac{\$100}{(1.03)^2} + \frac{\$100}{(1.03)^3} \qquad (15.5)$$
$$+ \frac{\$100}{(1.03)^4} + \frac{\$100}{(1.03)^5}$$

$$PV_{20} = \$100 + \frac{\$100}{(1.03)} + \frac{\$100}{(1.06)} + \frac{\$100}{(1.09)} \qquad (15.6)$$
$$+ \frac{\$100}{(1.12)} + \frac{\$100}{(1.15)}$$

$$PV_{20} = \$100 + \$97.09 + \$94.26 + \$91.51 \\ + \$88.85 + \$86.26 \tag{15.7}$$

$$PV_{20} = \$557.97 \tag{15.8}$$

First, note that the younger person views this income stream as yielding $36.73 more in present value than does the older person. Second, note that the same amount of money ($100) in the fifth year is worth $86.26 to the young person and only $74.73 to the older man. This clearly illustrates the role of subjective time preference in viewing a future stream of income. Third, a high rate of time preference is another way of saying that one prefers income now rather than in the future. Alternatively, a high rate of time preference means that it requires a high rate of interest to entice an individual to trade consumption today for future consumption. For instance, the older individual in our example would be indifferent between $100 now and $115 in the fifth year. In contrast, the younger person would be willing to trade $100 now for $106 in the fifth year.

To tie the above into our earlier discussion on conservation, recall that the optimum state of conservation is that schedule of use rates over time which maximizes the present value of expected future income streams. To understand the problem which arises between private decisions on resource use (say, a forest plot) and the public (society) desires regarding the use rate, it is only necessary to recognize that individuals making decisions over use rates will have different time preference rates than will the society as a whole. It is this disparity in time preferences between private owners of natural resources and the public at large (represented by their government) which is the heart of much of the conservation movement. To illustrate, refer to Equations 15.1 through 15.8. The annual income received in $100 increments can be viewed as the net income from harvesting an acre of forested land. The rate of use is the same in both examples but the present values are quite different. The present value for the older person can be increased by shifting some of the use closer to the present—to harvest more timber in the earlier time periods. Consider Figure 15.6. Here are plotted two curves tracing out the present value of $100 received at different intervals in the future. At a high interest rate (time preference), the present value declines much more rapidly. After 50 years the present value—at a discount rate of 6 percent—is only $5.43, whereas the present value at a discount rate of 3 percent is $22.81.

Hence, for the person with a high rate of time preference (a high discount rate), the ideal strategy is to move use rates of a natural resource toward the present. To illustrate with our example, assume that the 65-year-old person decides to harvest his forest in a fashion that will increase the present value of his net earnings. Further assume that he cannot simply harvest the entire amount in one year because some of

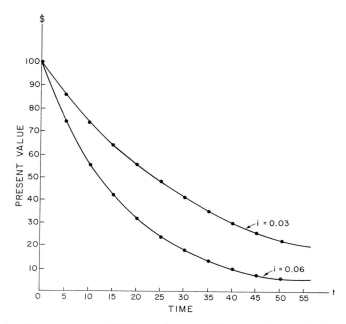

FIG. 15.6. Present value of $100 received at different points in the future under alternative discount rates.

the trees are needed to protect the stand. In this case, he might choose to harvest trees such that his annual net income was $125 during the first four harvests, and $50 for the two remaining harvests. He would still be selling a net value of $600 worth of timber, but the time distribution of that harvest is now moved toward the present. His present value is now

$$
PV_{65} = \$125 + \frac{\$125}{(1.06)^1} + \frac{\$125}{(1.06)^2} + \frac{\$125}{(1.06)^3} \qquad (15.9)
$$
$$
+ \frac{\$50}{(1.06)^4} + \frac{\$50}{(1.06)^5}
$$

$$
PV_{65} = \$125 + \$117.92 + \$111.25 + \$104.95 \qquad (15.10)
$$
$$
+ \$39.60 + \$37.36
$$

$$
PV_{65} = \$536.08 \qquad (15.11)
$$

The alternative harvesting strategy has increased the present value of his expected earnings by $14.84. Note also that the new present value is still $21.89 less than the present value of the person with a longer planning horizon (a lower rate of time preference).

The above illustrates the significance of rates of use in different periods of time, and the impact that different rates of time preference have on the decision governing the "when of use." In summary, conservation is concerned with the time distribution of use rates; an increase in those use rates toward the present implies *depletion,* the opposite movement implies *conservation.*

In concluding this section, some of the factors that influence an individual's time preference are described. They are the income level of the resource owner, the degree of uncertainty facing that owner, price levels and expectations for the resource, the nature and security of property rights, the individual's access to credit, taxation policy, the degree of competition in the market in which the individual operates, and general economic stability.

The first factor is the income level of the resource owner. The natural resource can be viewed as a capital stock under control of the private entrepreneur, in much the same way an individual treats a savings account—as money in the bank. If the owner is financially insecure, he will want to harvest some of the resource to generate income. On the other hand, if income in the current period is adequate, there is a greater tendency to save the resource—much as one would save money—until it is needed.

The second factor is that of uncertainty. If the resource owner does not know what to expect in the way of income and prices in the future, the wise decision may be to avoid risk by harvesting the resource now. This also holds if there is some chance of possible damage to the resource from exogenous forces, say, an insect or disease infestation. Additionally, if the resource owner has an insecure claim on the resource—if his property rights are tenuous or in jeopardy—there is a greater tendency to harvest soon. As for credit, if the individual has access to sources of financing to help him through the economically difficult periods, he is less likely to harvest the resource in a way that might be depletive. Tax policy of the government can have a significant impact upon an individual's attitude toward the timing of harvest. For example, the time of property assessment might encourage a resource owner to harvest prematurely. Individuals operating in a monopolistic market tend to restrict output and to charge a higher price.[6] Hence, it might be that a monopolist would be more protective of a natural resource than would someone operating in a perfectly competitive market. Finally, the general economic conditions of the nation will play a significant role in influencing the rate of use of natural resources. If the government is viewed as being secure, there is less need to rush harvesting; the contrary is true if there is fear that next year, or the following year, the current government—or current economic conditions—might change.

6. Review parts of Chapter 10 if this statement is not clear.

The above listing and discussion of economic forces are factors which collectively constitute the time preference of the individual. Nations intent on preserving their natural resource base could view the factors as a set of policy variables. For instance, if there were a desire to adjust the rate of resource use away from the present (toward the future), reasonable national policy would include (but not necessarily be confined to) a taxation policy that rewards future rather than present use, a flexible credit policy, guaranteed future prices to dispel the fear that resource prices might fall over time, secure property rights, a set of national economic policies that assure stability, and a resource protection plan that assists the entrepreneur in preventing disease. If there is doubt as to the efficacy of these measures, it is always possible to institute licenses, harvest quotas, or other means to insure that private decisions with respect to the rate of utilization of natural resources are in accord with broader social objectives.

NATURAL RESOURCES: ZERO-PRICE INPUTS

In earlier times, when population was not as concentrated, most economic activities could be carried out with little concern for their impact on other economic enterprises. There were few if any instances where the production of one commodity by a firm would interfere with the production of the same or a different commodity by another firm. Economic thought at that time was dominated by the primacy of the unfettered market and the wisdom of Adam Smith's "invisible hand." It theorized that each individual entrepreneur in seeking to maximize his private gain would behave in such a way that, in the aggregate, social gain was also as great as possible. In such an economic system, factors of production would be optimally allocated; and no one could be made better off without at the same time making at least one person worse off. The term *laissez faire* is used to identify this situation.

In the 1930s economists began to recognize that this idealized world was not in fact the world in which they lived. The British economist A. C. Pigou argued that there are circumstances in which the private decisions of a profit-seeking entrepreneur would not result in the greatest possible social product. He referred to this disparity as a divergence between private value and social value or as a difference between private costs and social costs.[7] He probably did not suspect that he had identified the essence of the environmental crisis as we know it today.

Private cost measures the value of the best alternative use of a resource as evaluated by the firm undertaking the production. Frequently private cost is measured by the market price the firm pays for the

7. See A. C. Pigou, *The Economics of Welfare* (London: Macmillan, 1962).

factor. *Social cost* measures the value of the best alternative use of a resource as evaluated by the society. In some cases the best measure of the social cost may be the market price; in others the social cost may deviate substantially from the market price. The problem is to identify the social costs and to integrate them into the resource allocation process.

This disparity between the actions of the private decision maker and his ideal actions from a social point of view can be attributed to a divergence in time preferences, to the absence of property rights in certain factors of production, and to the lumpy nature of production.[8] It is the property rights in resources that most concern us here. We will argue that market failure leads to divergence between private costs and social costs and, hence, to a disparity between optimum private decisions and optimum society-wide decisions.

Market failure exists when there are no markets for scarce and valuable goods and services or when a market exists but functions improperly. In earlier chapters we studied how the ideal factor allocation results from the movement of factors from one use to another in response to price signals. An improperly operating market is one that misallocates resources. Property rights are important because it is this institution plus a market which leads to the allocation of scarce and valuable goods and services to production. Owners of land, labor, and capital are rewarded for the use of their factors through the market mechanism. If there is no price or an incorrect price signal either because of market failure or because there is no owner of the factor to limit or allocate its use, there will be a divergence between the private and social optimum level of output.

In summary, when scarce and valuable resources are used in production or consumption process—and no price is paid for those resources—a nonoptimal allocation of resources exists; and the value of the social product is less than it might otherwise be. In what follows we describe this particular form of market failure.

We have repeatedly used the terms *scarce* and *valuable* when discussing the essence of market failure. It was seen in Chapter 2 that without scarcity there is no allocation problem. While scarcity is necessary for an economic problem, it is not sufficient; there must be more. Value in use must also be present. Wagon wheels are now relatively scarce, but with the exception of a few collectors, they do not appear to have much value. On the other hand, sunlight is extremely valuable as an input in agricultural production, yet it is not particularly scarce (except perhaps in several polluted cities). So our concern here is when signals do not exist, or they exist in the wrong magnitude, for resources that are both scarce and valuable.

8. By "lumpy" we mean that certain items, if they are to be produced at all, must be produced in fixed quantities. A dam must block the river and hence there are lower limits to the scale on which a dam may be built.

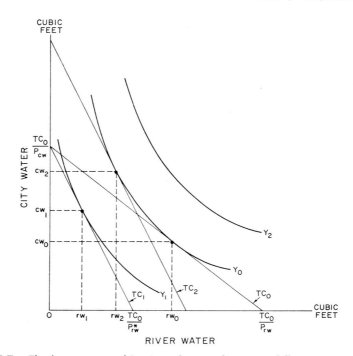

FIG. 15.7. The least-cost combination of water from two different sources.

Furthermore, the input must be valuable in exchange in contrast to having use value. It is property rights which give rise to the exchange value of a productive factor. In our development of production theory, sunlight was never treated as an input, although it is definitely a productive factor. It was not included because it is not a scarce factor of production that can command a price. It commands no price because there is no value in exchange, although there may be considerable value in use. Because there are no property rights to sunlight, its allocation is not subject to the normal forces of the market.

Consider the water in a river flowing by a pulp mill. The mill utilizes this water in conjunction with other inputs to produce pulp for the manufacture of paper. This situation can be illustrated by the two-space isoquant map. In Figure 15.7 we have depicted two inputs: water purchased from the city (cw) and water pumped from the nearby river (rw).* The other inputs used in the manufacture of pulp—such as labor, chemicals, wood chips, and machinery—are assumed held constant. We are concerned only with the mix of water from the two sources. The price

* *Note:* The isoquants imply that city water and river water are not perfect substitutes in the production process. Assume, for the moment, river water contains some sediment and city water is heavily chlorinated. With these assumptions, the isoquants in Fig. 15.7 are justified.

of city water is given by P_{cw}, while the price of river water is given by P_{rw}. It can be seen that a total outlay for water of TC_0 would result in Y_0 units of pulp, with the relative prices of city and river water indicating that the mill utilize cw_0 units of the former and rw_0 units of the latter.

The price paid by the mill for water from the city is P_{cw} and reflects the actual cash outlay for each unit (cubic foot) of water. In contrast, P_{rw} is different. Because the mill is allowed to pump water from the river without paying anything for it, its only cost is the expense of pumping the water into the mill. So, $P_{rw} =$ (pumping costs $+$ actual water charge) or $P_{rw} = (PC + WC) = PC$ because in this example, $WC = 0$. As discussed earlier, the fact that the mill pays nothing for the actual water cannot be judged as undesirable per se unless it can be shown that water has some use downstream—unless it is scarce and valuable. If there is no use for the water once it passes the pulp mill, a zero price is proper. This then is the opportunity cost of the water.

The opportunity cost of a unit of water is the value of that unit in producing another good or service. Perhaps the only activity going on downstream from the mill is swimming and recreation. While it is difficult to impute values to water for these purposes, a value still exists.[9] Or, perhaps the water being removed by the mill could be used to process camera film. If that were the case, the amount that the film processor would be willing to pay for a unit of river water would be its opportunity cost. If the pulp mill cannot afford to pay the opportunity cost of the water, the allocation of productive factors (and hence the output mix of society) would be enhanced if the water were utilized in film processing rather than in the manufacture of pulp.

Since the pulp mill views the opportunity cost of the river water as zero, it will overutilize this factor of production. Social efficiency would be served by establishing an institutional arrangement which charges the pulp mill at least as much as the film processor would be willing to pay. In this manner, the mill would be encouraged to utilize water more efficiently than at present. Assume that the pulp mill were to be charged for its river water based on the opportunity cost of water downstream (to the film processor); hence, WC is no longer zero. This will alter the slope of the isocost line, say, to TC_1. This new isocost line has the slope given by the new relative prices:

$$- P^*_{rw}/P_{cw} \tag{15.12}$$

where

$$P^*_{rw} > P_{rw}$$

9. The determination of value for recreation sites will be the subject of a subsequent section.

given that

$$P_{rw} = PC$$
$$P^*_{rw} = PC + WC$$

Assuming that the new isocost line (TC_1) is tangent to the isoquant (Y_1), the payment of a fee for river water has altered the relative magnitudes of water used by the pulp mill to cw_1 and rw_1 and has reduced the output of pulp as well. The difference in use of river water by the pulp mill $(rw_0 - rw_1)$ is available to the film processor to increase his output. Notice that if the pulp mill wishes to increase production to reach former levels (Y_0), it is necessary to increase total production costs for the purchase of water (TC_2). The new input levels will be cw_2 and rw_2, respectively.

The above demonstrates the physical linkage of productive activities utilizing a scarce and valuable natural resource. In economics, this is termed *technological interdependence*. The fact that the two industries are linked technologically is necessary for there to be market failure as defined here, but it is not sufficient. Two activities must be linked physically, and there must also be an absence of prices for the resources they both use in production. When both conditions are met, we say there is a *technological externality*. Under an optimal pricing scheme, both the pulp mill and the film processor will be paying the opportunity cost of the water they use in their production processes. If this is the case, the externality is said to have been *internalized*. Notice that market failure ceases to exist after this internalization, even though the industries or firms are still linked in a technological sense.

POLLUTION

The natural environment—whether air or water—can be thought of as a cleansing agent insofar as it is a receptacle for certain by-products from production. For example, when a ton of sugarbeets is processed, a significant quantity of other inputs is required, and there is a large quantity of residuals that must be disposed of. Furthermore, there are alternative production techniques available and some are less polluting than others. For instance, a high-residual process with no recirculation converts a long ton (2,200 pounds) of sugarbeets into 285 pounds of sugar, but requires 45,150 pounds of water, 120 pounds of limestone, 260 pounds of coal, and 2,545 pounds of air. It also produces almost 22,000 pounds of flume waste (water, soil, and suspended and dissolved organics), 5,000 pounds of pulp waters, 540 pounds of lime slurry cake, and over 16,000 pounds of condensed water, plus 90 pounds of molasses and 500 pounds of wet pulp. In contrast, the low-residual process with extensive recycling converts the same quantity of sugarbeets

(2,200 pounds) into 285 pounds of sugar (the same), but requires only 3,370 pounds of water, 120 pounds of limestone (the same), 350 pounds of coal (more), and 3,425 pounds of air (more). The low-residual process produces only 150 pounds of lime cake (much less) and 800 pounds of clarifier sediment in contrast to the much larger quantities with the high-residual process.[10]

The natural environment is capable of absorbing certain quantities of these residuals, providing the level of concentration is not too great. It is this last point that gives rise to the environmental crises. As our population has increased and become more concentrated, and as per capita consumption of goods and services has increased, the assimilative capacity of the natural environment has been approached or exceeded. This accounts for the sudden awareness of pollution by people as they notice smog-bound cities and sludgelike rivers.

The relationship between an economic activity and the ability of the environment to absorb residuals is at the heart of pollution policy. It can be represented by a functional relationship depicting offsite damage as a function of output of a firm. Assume that the pulp mill, located upstream from a film processor, pays the proper rate for the river water it utilizes but, as an outgrowth of its pulp manufacture, it dumps its waste by-products into the river. Again, if there were no activity downstream making use of the water, this act would not result in market failure.[11] Assume for this example that the film processor downstream is faced with using river water that is contaminated by the wastes from the pulp mill. If we assume that the dumping of wastes is directly (and linearly) related to the production of pulp, a function depicting this would resemble part a of Figure 15.8.

The next step in the analysis is to determine the effect of this dumping on downstream users. For this purpose we construct a damage function. A *damage function* relates the quantity of waste being discharged by the upstream firm to the costs that are incurred downstream as a result of that dumping. Assume that for every unit of waste dumped in the river by the pulp mill, the film processor must spend $1 to clean the water before he uses it in processing film. This information permits one to construct a damage function as illustrated in part b of Figure 15.8. The diagram shows the economic costs incurred by the film processor as a direct function of the level of pulp production (and, indirectly, the dumping by the mill). These costs are often referred to as "offsite costs," "downstream costs," or "spillover costs."

The damage function is used to construct a total cost curve for

10. For more on this subject, see Allen V. Kneese, R. U. Ayers, and Ralph C. D'Arge, *Economics and the Environment* (Washington, D.C.: Resources for the Future, 1970).

11. This fact is troubling to ardent environmentalists who insist on pure water at any price. We do not wish to imply that some rivers should not be "pure," but what constitutes purity is an empirical question. Additionally, an absolutely "pure" river is economic nonsense.

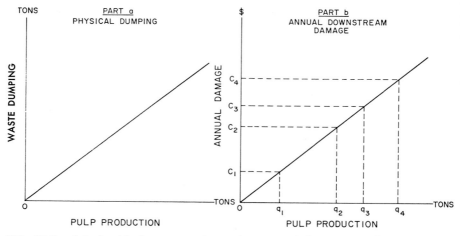

FIG. 15.8. Relationship between pulp production and downstream damage.

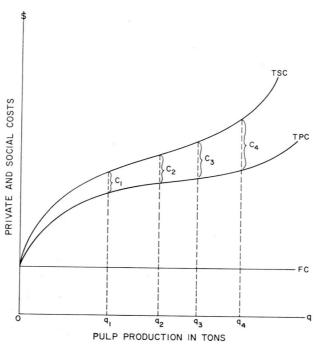

FIG. 15.9. Total private costs and total social costs of pulp production.

the pulp mill which reflects this damage. This cost curve is called the "total social cost curve" in contrast to the "total private cost curve" derived in Chapter 6. Its derivation is as follows. Assume that TPC in Figure 15.9 reflects the total private cost of producing pulp as determined by the mill's production function. At each level of output per unit of time, an amount equal to the downstream damage is added to the total private cost function (Figure 15.8). At an output of q_1, the amount C_1 is added. At q_2, C_2 is added, and so on at all levels of pulp production. The end result of this process is a total social cost curve which reflects all the costs of producing pulp, both internal (private) and external (offsite). If the pulp producer were made to pay all the costs of his production (private plus social), he would use TSC instead of TPC as his relevant total cost curve in determining his optimum level of output. The optimum output level will be different using total costs TPC than if he uses total costs TSC. Before discussing possible ways to make him aware of the offsite costs of his activity, we will examine this difference in more detail.

From Chapters 5 and 6 we know that the marginal cost curve is derived from the total cost curve, and that the profit-maximizing entrepreneur produces the output level where marginal cost equals price. The marginal cost and average total cost for the two total cost curves in

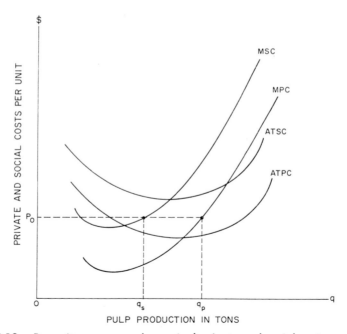

FIG. 15.10. Per-unit average and marginal private and social cost curves.

Figure 15.9 are presented in Figure 15.10. They are labeled *MPC* and
ATPC, and *MSC* and *ATSC*. At a price for pulp of P_0, the ideal output level for the mill is less (q_s) when social costs are considered than
when only private costs are used (q_p). Thus failure of the individual
entrepreneur to include offsite costs in his profit-maximizing calculus results in a larger than socially optimum level of output. Assuming that
the cost curves in Figure 15.10 are typical of all firms in the industry,
we can describe the impact of pollution on the mix of goods and services produced by an economy. Consider Figure 15.11.

     Part a of Figure 15.11 resembles Figure 15.10. In part b the
industry is assumed to be made up of the individual firms producing pulp.
The supply curve S_p represents the case when all firms in the pulp industry are concerned with only private costs, while the curve S_s is the
industry supply curve if they are made to pay the offsite costs they impose downstream. If the offsite costs are included in their decision calculus, the typical firm would have a marginal cost curve such as *MSC*.
In this case the industry supply curve representing social costs would be
S_s (the summation of all *MSC* curves). Given this, Q_s would be the
proper industry output (not Q_p) and the prevailing price would be P_s.
The typical firm would be producing an output level q_s rather than q_p.

     In summary, the fact that pulp mills can ignore the offsite costs
of their production (the spillovers) means that too much pulp is being
produced (Q_p rather than Q_s), and also that the price of pulp is too low

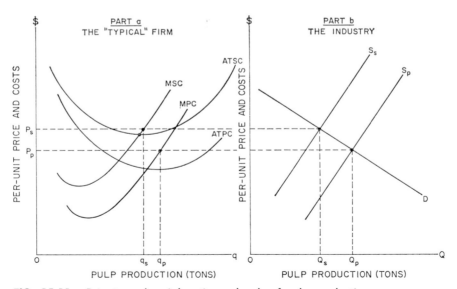

FIG. 15.11. Private and social optimum levels of pulp production.

(P_p rather than P_s). The consumers of pulp are not paying the full social cost for the product they purchase. With the price artificially low, they are led to purchase more of the commodity than they would otherwise buy if its price reflected all the costs of its manufacture.

To analyze the impacts of pulp production upon film processors, let us assume that the downstream uses of water are limited to film processing. This merely facilitates the example. Hence, the offsite costs of the pulp industry are those incurred by the film processing industry to clean up river water prior to its use. At this point the analytics become more complicated because the level of waste dumping affects the film processor's costs (technological interdependence). Recall that waste dumping by the pulp industry is assumed to be a linear function of pulp production and that this dumping causes damage downstream which must be added to the private costs of producing pulp. However, for the film processing firm, each level of pulp production (and hence waste dumping) implies a different set of cost curves.

In Figure 15.12 we have depicted several total cost curves for a typical film processor. FC represents fixed costs, and TC represents variable costs (not shown) plus fixed costs for alternative levels of film processing. The pulp mill upstream makes it necessary that the film

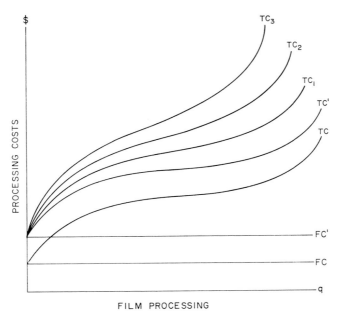

FIG. 15.12. Technological interdependence, the impact of pulp production on production costs of a downstream film processor.

processing firm acquire water purification equipment in addition to the equipment necessary to process film. The curves FC' and TC' reflect fixed and total costs, respectively, for this latter equipment.

The added costs of using this purification equipment will depend upon the production of pulp and the level of upstream dumping by the pulp mill. If little pulp is being produced, pollution will be low and the purification equipment is utilized at a low level. If, on the other hand, the production of pulp is substantial, the film processor must purify the river water to a greater extent. The curves labeled TC_1, TC_2, and TC_3 represent the total production costs of the film processor as a function of the output of pulp as well as of his own output level. TC' represents the total costs of processing film with no waste dumping by the upstream pulp mill (but including the fixed cost for the purification equipment), while TC_3 represents total costs of processing film when water pollution is very high. The two intermediate curves represent levels of waste dumping between these two extremes. *Technological interdependence* is the term that describes this linkage between the output of pulp and the production costs for film processing.

To relate the above to the equilibrium indicating output and price, examine Figure 15.13. The left side of the diagram represents the typical firm in the film processing industry, while the right side represents the entire industry. The average and marginal curves for the typical firm are derived from the total cost curves in Figure 15.12. Only TC_2 and TC_1 were used to simplify the diagram. In the static case and assuming that pulp production is at a level which causes the downstream film processor to operate along TC_2, the curves ATC_2 and MC_2 in Figure

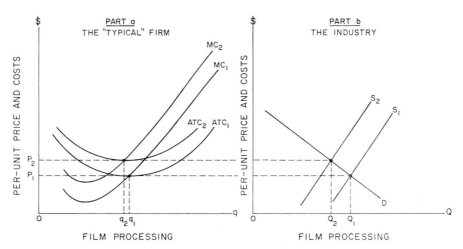

FIG. 15.13. Film processing costs and output as a function of upstream pollution.

15.13, indicate that the typical firm is making zero profit (but covering all opportunity costs). In this case, S_2 in part b of Figure 15.13 would represent the industry supply curve as long as upstream pulp mills continue to produce a constant quantity of pulp. When pulp production is varied, and hence water pollution also, the marginal and average curves of the typical downstream film processor shift up or down, and the industry supply curve shifts similarly. For example, if the pulp mills reduce production somewhat, the marginal and average cost curves of the typical film processor would shift downward to MC_1 and ATC_1, respectively, and the industry supply curve would shift to S_1. This new supply curve reflects the fact that total production costs of film processing have fallen to TC_1 (Figure 15.12). Note that the typical film processor would now produce a larger quantity (q_1 rather than q_2) since his production costs have fallen. The net result is that consumers of film processing obtain a larger quantity of film processed at a lower price (P_1 rather than P_2).

In summary, the ability of the pulp mill to ignore spillover costs (offsite costs of production) reduces its production cost below the social cost. This leads to a greater-than-optimal level of pulp production. On the other hand, if film processors bear the full brunt of offsite costs, we saw that their production costs are directly affected by the decisions of firms in another industry, the upstream pulp mill. This means that the costs of film processing are artificially high, and that there is a less-than-optimal level of film processing; society gets a nonoptimal mix of outputs because one scarce and valuable productive factor (river water) is not bargained for in the marketplace. An institutional system should be created whereby the upstream pulp mills could bargain with the downstream film processors. This would create a market for river water which would allocate it to that use where the value of the social product would be maximized.

The obvious question is, What is the proper level of waste dumping by the pulp mill? This can be analyzed with the aid of Figure 15.14. The curve AB is the downstream damage for every unit of waste not discharged; that is, at point A, there is not any waste that is not discharged (all is discharged), and damages are OA. At point B, OB units of waste are not discharged (none are discharged) and damages are zero. Curve DC relates the marginal cost of cleaning up the waste at its source (pulp mill) rather than dumping it in the river. The point at which these two curves intersect (Z) represents the ideal level of waste not to discharge (W^*).

The problem is how to achieve W^*. If a sanitary authority were created, it could levy charges equal to the damages associated with each unit of waste discharged. The classical economic solution to the problem is to tax the pulp mill an amount equal to the difference between MPC and MSC to make the operator aware of these offsite costs. When

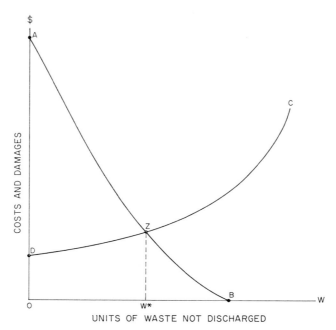

FIG. 15.14. Optimal level of polluting.

the pulp mill entrepreneuer recognizes these costs and reduces output accordingly, the production costs of the film processor are also reduced. The film processing industry supply curve shifts rightward and the market price of film processing falls. At the same time, the higher costs of producing pulp (now including the tax) shift the industry supply curve for pulp leftward, resulting in a lesser output level, and a higher pulp price. The result is the socially optimum output mix.

As always, conceptual solutions are much easier than operational ones. To ascertain the "ideal" tax to encourage the "optimal" mix of pulp and film processing (that is, to find point Z in Figure 15.14), it is necessary for all the production functions to be known in both industries. As if this were not enough, it is also imperative to know the exact relationship between the dumping of waste by the pulp industry and damage inflicted downstream. This is difficult enough when there is only one downstream use. It is impossible in the more realistic situation of many downstream uses. To further complicate the matter, it is also unrealistic to assume that only one upstream activity exists. In fact, there are many kinds of consumptive and productive activities utilizing a waterway, all of which may impinge on its quality, and all but one of which are, by definition, upstream.

Many pollution problems involve bodies of water where the distinction between upstream and downstream is not at all clear (a lake). As another example we have the matter of air pollution in a city. The point is that the design of *optimal* economic incentives and sanctions to correct the behavior of firms in the marketplace is at best a hopeless task. This is why legal sanctions are very frequently utilized. However, courts of law are not intended to insure the efficient solution to economic allocation problems and do not consider the marginality of economic decisions. Given this, economists argue that national income is likely to be impaired by legal sanctions. In the meantime, biologists, engineers, and economists struggle to collect the information necessary to construct the taxes which will encourage optimum economic behavior on the part of the private sector. The legal sanction then is the end result of political action brought to bear on a specific problem. It is likely that we will see an increasing reliance on the system of legal sanctions to correct problems of "market failure." We will return to this issue in the final section of this chapter.

Our final area concerns the valuation of natural resources. This problem arises, for example, when there is a public debate over the future use of a forested area which is particularly scenic. In this instance, the conflict is over its preservation for hiking and camping versus its harvesting for timber. In the following section we explore ways in which the value of this site as a wilderness might be derived for comparison with its market value as a timber-producing area.

NATURAL RESOURCE VALUATION

The statement "you cannot put a value on the sight of a beautiful sunset or on a beautiful coastline" is frequently used to avoid the pricing of natural resources and amenities. Before developing the economic issues here, we comment on the validity and propriety of economic evaluations of natural amenities such as a sunset, a coastline, a wilderness, or a timber tract. Of course, one can put a value on these amenities. The crucial question is, Is it the correct value? Unfortunately, there is no way to determine correctness, but valid procedures do exist. Furthermore, if one is to make decisions with respect to the use of scarce and valuable resources, it is appropriate to utilize the best economic data available rather than proceeding without whatever illumination the values provide.

Consider the question raised earlier over whether a particular forested area should be harvested or left for camping and hiking. It is fairly easy to determine the value of the site for timber. To value it as a recreational site is most difficult, since there is not likely to be a price attached to its use. On the assumption that the site is currently being used for recreation, there is a solution. Recall that the definition of conservation requires maximizing the present value of all future uses; in our example, this means maximizing the present value of the future use of recreation or timber production to see which will result in the greatest net present value for society.

It is fairly straightforward to estimate the net present value of a site for the production of timber, and the discounting would be reckoned as in Equations 15.1 through 15.11. We would estimate the annualized value of the sustained yield of timber from the site, or any other form of temporal distribution of harvest, and calculate the net present value of the total income stream. For the recreational use, it may be sufficient for our decision to know the lower bound (or the minimum estimate) of its value as a recreational site. For example, if we know that the site has a net present value for timber production of, say, $5 million, we have sufficient information to make a policy decision if a crude estimate of its net present value in recreation is $5.3 million. Since the lowest estimate of its recreational value is in excess of its fairly precise estimate for timber, we can be confident that it is best left as a recreational site. In this instance we need not estimate its total value as a recreational site. We know that our ability to precisely ascertain the full value of the site as a recreational resource is imperfect, but the lower bound on its net present value is sufficient for our decision making.

If our lower bound estimate of net present value as a recreational resource is less than the timber value, say, $3 million, we do not have sufficient information to conclude that harvesting the timber has a higher net present value. In this case we would attempt to improve our estimate of its *full* economic value for recreation. There are other bases for reaching decisions than just its economic value. For example, suppose we calculate that on a present value basis, the most this particular site is worth as a recreational resource is $4.5 million. There are a number of valid and compelling reasons which would lead us to keep it as a recreational site even though its value as a timber resource is higher. One reason might be that it is a very unique recreational resource, or one particularly close to a metropolitan area. Another might be that technology is capable of developing alternatives to wood products, but incapable of producing a recreational site. Still another might be that we wish to preserve the options of future generations to use it as a recreational site or as a timber-harvesting site. If it were severely harvested, future generations would not have that choice. Alternatively, if it were harvested on a sustained-yield basis, it would be possible to use it as a timber site in the present and still have the option of making it a single-use recreational site in the future. Finally, we could use the site for both timber and recreation. In this case, limited harvesting might yield a net present value of $3.5 million, and compatible

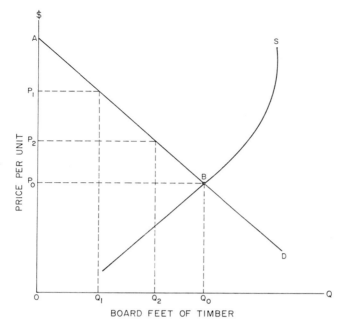

FIG. 15.15. The demand curve for timber on a specific site.

recreational use a value of $3 million. The joint net present value exceeds either of the two individual values.[12]

Having discussed the need for values in making rational economic decisions with respect to a natural resource, we return to the problems involved in determining its value. For timber valuation, consider Figure 15.15. The curve D represents the derived demand curve for timber on the site under consideration. It would be derived from various producers' willingness to purchase the timber on that site. Note that the supply curve has a positive slope and, at a particular level of supply, becomes infinitely elastic. This arises out of the fact that as timber prices rise, the owner or manager would be willing to sell increasing quantities. However, at some point, the resource is exhausted (or the maximum allowable cut is reached) and no more can be supplied regardless of the price offered.

Given the demand data in Figure 15.15, one possible method of valuing the timber would be to compute the total revenue for each possible quantity demanded from the site. If Q_0 units of timber could be sold at a price of P_0, its value is $\$P_0Q_0$, or, OP_0BQ_0. However, this is

12. The student should review the product-product concepts in Chapter 5 if the reason is not clear.

not a full measure of the timber's value. Note that for a quantity of Q_1, the timber has a price of P_1 per unit and at Q_2 a value of P_2. Thus if we could sell Q_1 units at P_1, Q_2-Q_1 at P_2, and Q_0-Q_2 at P_0, total revenue would be greater than if one sold all Q_0 units at a price P_0. Hence, to estimate the full value of the timber, we could calculate the entire area under the demand curve for timber to the left of Q_0. By this method, the value is $OABQ_0$ instead of only OP_0BQ_0. The additional area (P_0AB) is referred to as *consumers' surplus* and reflects the difference, at any quantity, between what consumers (in this case the firms that want to purchase the timber) would be willing to pay (as depicted by the height of the demand curve) and what they have to pay (P_0). Consumers' surplus is derived from the notion that the consumers obtain a surplus value. The total area $OABQ_0$ is termed *total willingness to pay* and reflects the aggregate value of the timber on the site. With this concept one could determine future demand conditions and calculate a net present value of the total willingness to pay for timber on the site. It is this value that should be used to compare with its value as a recreational site.

Inasmuch as there is no market for recreation, except in certain instances, our task of valuing it for recreation is more complex. One line of methodology which has shown considerable durability is to determine what individuals at various distances from a recreational site must pay to travel to the site. In a questionnaire, a hypothetical entrance fee is presented to them and efforts made to ascertain the recreationists' responses to this fee. In this way, it is possible to conjecture as to their valuation of the direct experience of visiting the site—as distinct from the cost of getting to and from the site. The methodology is too complex to detail here, but the method has been used to develop estimates of the recreational value of estuaries that are not allowed to become polluted, of the recreational value of a polluted lake that might be cleaned up (here the cleanup costs are compared with the value of a clean lake), and of the value of a hydroelectric dam on a wild river.

Other methods of resource valuation also exist. They are complex and beyond the scope of this text. Suffice it to say that much still remains to be done. This does not mean that all choice issues should be resolved on the basis of economic value alone. Nevertheless, if the economic aspects are ignored, the resulting decisions may turn out to have unfortunate long-run consequences. If economics can at least help one to avoid the obvious mistakes, then it has made a valuable contribution to public natural resource policy.

NATURAL RESOURCE POLICY

Most of the decisions in the area of natural resources are made by public bodies rather than by private entrepreneurs. This is not to say that some decisions are not made in the private sector, but in most instances, explicit federal policy establishes guidelines or quotas. The need for such public action is, by now, little cause for question, but the exact form of that action is of great interest. We shall consider three areas as examples of the types of public policies existing in current natural resource programs: (1) pollution, (2) water resource management, and (3) general land use policy.

POLLUTION

In a previous section, economic incentives in the form of effluent taxes were mentioned as the most efficient solution to the pollution problem. We also stated that the *correct* tax requires considerable knowledge of all production functions, all damage functions, and the location of pollution sources. With over 40,000 sources of industrial and municipal pollution in the United States, such a task is impossible. Hence, explicit regulations were instituted.

The most significant form of pollution regulation, and the most controversial, is the October 1972 Amendments to the Federal Water Pollution Control Act. Title I of the act's amendments contains a declaration of federal policy:

> Sec. 101. (a) The objective of this Act is to restore and maintain the chemical, physical, and biological integrity of the Nation's waters. In order to achieve this objective it is hereby declared that, consistent with the provisions of this Act—
> (1) it is the national goal that the discharge of pollutants into the navigable waters be eliminated by 1985;
> (2) it is the national goal that wherever attainable, an interim goal of water quality which provides for the protection and propagation of fish, shellfish, and wildlife and provides for recreation in and on the water be achieved by July 1, 1983;
> (3) it is the national policy that the discharge of toxic pollutants in toxic amounts be prohibited;
> (4) it is the national policy that Federal financial assistance be provided to construct publicly owned waste treatment works;
> (5) it is the national policy that areawide waste treatment management planning processes be developed and implemented to assure adequate control of sources of pollutants in each State; and
> (6) it is the national policy that a major research and demonstration effort be made to develop technology necessary to eliminate the discharge of pollutants into the navigable waters, waters of the contiguous zone, and the oceans [Public Law 92-500, 86 Stat. 816].

The act suggests that by 1985 there be no pollutants discharged into the nation's waters. To achieve the complete elimination of all pollutants by 1985 would be a very costly process. Current policies generally call for *secondary treatment* of all effluent, a process which results in the removal of 85 to 90 percent of the significant pollutants. A recent estimate is that attaining this level of treatment by 1980 will require annual expenditures of $23 billion to $28 billion. It is estimated that the level of treatment required by the 1972 amendments would require annual expenditures of $60 billion to $70 billion.[13] This significant increase in cost for removing the last 10 to 14 percent of pollutants should come as no surprise, given the principle of diminishing marginal returns (and its corollary, increasing marginal cost). This approach is not necessarily the most efficient way to achieve complete elimination of all pollutants. It relies solely on treatment of the wastes rather than on the possibilities of changing production processes to generate less waste.

Many are concerned that it is financially absurd to comply with the "no discharge" mandate, and furthermore that it is unnecessary. It is unnecessary because water courses have an assimilative capacity. This means that they can absorb certain quantities of most pollutants without becoming polluted. This seeming contradiction arises from the fact that *pollutants* are defined as any substance discharged into a water course that is not in (virtually) pure water. In contrast, *pollution* is defined as a degradation in the "natural chemical, physical, biological, and radiological integrity of water."[14] Hence, water courses can assimilate some pollutants without causing pollution, and it is unnecessary and uneconomic to insist on zero discharge of pollutants.

In addition to the federal goal of no discharge, the amendments call for federal financing assistance (up to 75 percent) for publicly owned waste treatment works, areawide planning for implementation of waste treatment management, and the increased participation of the public in the development, revision, and enforcement of regulations, standards, and programs. These particular portions of the legislation are much less controversial than the "no discharge" aspects and will likely cause little concern.

For several reasons, improvements in air quality are often more difficult to attain than improvements in water quality. One reason is that there is not a clear distinction between upstream and downstream. A second problem is that much of the blame for air pollution lies with the automobile, a nonstationary source. While it may be politically possible to impose restrictions on 40,000 industrial polluters, to attempt the same on over 100 million trucks, buses, and automobiles is clearly a significant problem.

There are a number of clean air acts regulating air pollution, and standards have been established for the 274 airsheds in the nation.

---

13. Charles L. Schultze et al., *Setting National Priorities: The 1973 Budget* (Washington, D.C.: Brookings Institution, 1972), pp. 367–93.
14. Public Law 92-500, 86 Stat. 887.

Each state has the responsibility for developing plans for attaining emission levels in its own airsheds so that the national air quality standards can be met.

For automobiles, the Environmental Protection Agency (EPA) has the responsibility for setting deadlines for the removal of certain percentages of hydrocarbons and carbon monoxide. Initially, the hope was that standards could be met by the internal combustion engine. The process is costly and reduces gas mileage significantly. In the summer of 1973, automobile manufacturers were successful in postponing the deadline for compliance with certain standards. As indicated by the gasoline shortages in the winter of 1973–74, this also has implications for natural resource policy since it results in an increased demand for petroleum. Hence, instead of attempting to add a waste-treatment plant to each internal combustion engine, there is growing interest in cleaner forms of locomotion. Rotary engines, turbines, and electric motors are three possibilities currently being given serious consideration.

WATER RESOURCE MANAGEMENT

In the 6-year period 1967 to 1972, the federal government spent over $14 million on "water resources and power." Much of this was for water development projects such as irrigation, navigation channel improvement, flood-control structures, and hydroelectric facilities. June 1973 may very well mark the beginning of the end of an era that dates back to the Flood Control Act of 1936. In June 1973 the National Water Commission released its report to the president and to Congress, culminating 5 years of study, analysis, and public hearings.[15] The more than 230 recommendations of the commission—if all adopted—would bring about a significant departure from traditional federal-state-local relations in the use, management, and development of the nation's water resources. The commission was created in September 1968 at a time when interest in (and opposition to) large-scale interbasin water transfers was at a peak. The arid Southwest wanted the "surplus" water that was "wasting to the sea" from the Columbia River. The act that created the commission also imposed a moratorium on federal studies of such transfers until such time as the nation possessed a comprehensive plan for managing its water resources.

The commission went on record as being opposed to the "no discharge" policy established by the 1972 amendments to the Federal Water Pollution Control Act and in favor of a return to the water quali-

15. The report is National Water Commission, *Water Policies for the Future* (Washington, D.C.: USGPO, 1973). The condensed summary is National Water Commission, *New Directions in U.S. Water Policy* (Washington, D.C.: USGPO, 1973).

ty standards of the Water Quality Act of 1965. Additionally, it favored improving the transferability of water rights, increased repayment obligation by those who benefit from federal water resource projects, and an end to large-scale water developments in one region of the country that have significant impacts on the economy of other regions. In this latter regard, the analysis in Chapter 14 is a good example of the possible effects on price and exports from a producing region when the supply of that same commodity is increased elsewhere through a water development project that permits irrigated agriculture.

The traditional pattern in water resource developments has been for a small local group of citizens who expererience a water-related problem, such as flooding, to approach one of the federal water development agencies for assistance. The main agencies are the Army Corps of Engineers, the Bureau of Reclamation, and the Soil Conservation Service. Through their planning activities, the agency would formulate a development project to solve the water-related problem. The principal assistance these agencies provide is the financing for the projects. Under this procedure, the general public through taxes assumes the cost and the local group receives the benefits. If the recommendations of the commission are adopted, this would be significantly changed. The principal beneficiaries of each development would assume the major share of the financial obligation. Additionally, state and local government agencies would become more active participants in the planning and evaluation process, rather than the current procedure of relying entirely upon the federal agencies.

GENERAL LAND USE POLICY

In closing this chapter on natural resources, two major items warrant discussion: the recommendation of a national land commission, and proposed legislation that could have far-reaching effects on national land use policy.

The Public Land Law Review Commission was created in September 1964 and released its final report in June 1970. Its principal charge was to review all the laws pertaining to public land management, as well as the policies and practices of the public land management agencies,[16] and make recommendations. The recommendations were much less numerous than those of the National Water Commission. However if adopted, they would still result in a significant alteration in the use and management of the public lands.

The most controversial recommendations pertain to several aspects of public land use by commercial operators. For instance, the commission urged that "dominant" uses of each tract be identified and

16. These are, primarily, the Bureau of Land Management, the U.S. Forest Service, and the Bureau of Sport Fisheries and Wildlife.

given priority rights. This does not mean that multiple uses of certain tracts of land were prohibited, but it was thus interpreted by conservationists who saw this recommendation as a gift to the mining, grazing, and timber interests. In another controversial recommendation, the commission urged that users should pay for the full use value of the lands, except where there is no "consumptive" use of the resource. Since grazing and timber production can be on a sustained yield basis, there is no consumptive use. This was viewed as another concession to the commercial interests, particularly ranchers who were paying considerably less than the market value for their grazing privileges. A third controversial recommendation was that current users—and this applies almost exclusively to grazing activities—be granted more secure tenure over their current access to the public lands; to wit, if the federal government must terminate the lease, compensation should be paid. Since grazing on the public lands is not a right but a privilege, this recommendation created considerable opposition among those who oppose grazing as a legitimate use of the public lands. Finally the commission recommended the sale of those public lands "required" for particular uses such as mining, grazing, and other commercial or residential purposes. Conservationists viewed this as a most undesirable position.

In the 3 years since the release of the commission's report, few of its recommendations have been formally enacted, although many of its suggestions have been adopted by the land management agencies. More significant, however, may be proposed legislation to establish national land use policy guidelines. At this writing this legislation is still in the early stages of development. It calls for the states to take a more active role in planning and regulating land use so that future development is environmentally sound and in the public interest. There is also a special provision to protect critical areas of national concern.

The fate of the proposal is still unknown, but its formulation is a clear indication that we have progressed far from the days when the landowner was presumed to be master of his own landed estate. We now recognize that technological interdependencies exist, not only in the areas of water and air pollution but in the area of land use as well. The presence of unsightly urban sprawl, the proliferation of junkyards, and the seemingly endless array of small signs and large billboards are constant reminders of these spillovers.

SUMMARY

In this chapter we have presented some issues in natural resource use and management and have illustrated the applicability of the theoretical concepts developed in Part II. The concept of conservation was seen to involve a redistribution of use rates toward the future, while depletion was seen to involve a redistribution of such use rates toward the present. The concept of time preference was introduced, and its impact upon present values was explained. The factors which influence an individual's rate of time preference were discussed and were seen to comprise a reasonable set of possible variables for the design of a nondepletive natural resource policy.

We introduced the concept of technological interdependence and viewed that phenomenon from two different perspectives. The first perspective was that of an upstream firm utilizing a scarce and valuable natural resource as if it were not scarce and valuable. The downstream use of water gives it an opportunity cost which requires consideration in the decision calculus of the upstream firm. When this value is recognized, the upstream firm will use less of the resource, thereby freeing more of it for the downstream firm. This readjustment in input usage will also result in a readjustment in the output of the two activities. Another area where there is an incorrect output mix was demonstrated using pollution as an example. Here, the upstream firm uses a scarce and valuable natural resource to dispose of production wastes, thereby imposing offsite costs (external diseconomies) on a downstream firm. When this market failure is corrected through a pricing scheme for the natural resource, the upstream firm produces a lesser quantity of its output, and the downstream firm produces more of its output. The prices of the respective products also change, reflecting the new equilibrium quantities.

The problem of valuing natural resources was seen to be serious, though not an impossible task. The public choice process is aided by comparative values of different goods and services, and the fact that certain goods and services are not produced in a factory, or in a shop, in no way precludes the validity or propriety of estimates of their economic worth. This is not to say that all decisions should be made on this basis, but such information can be an important form of data for the decision process. The concept of aggregate willingness to pay was introduced, and seen to be the area under a demand curve for a good or service, but to the left of the quantity which is consumed. If empirical estimates can be made for natural amenities that do not ordinarily have a market value, natural resource policy will be enhanced significantly.

Finally, we presented a discussion of general policy issues in the natural resource area and cited the recommendations of several commissions charged with suggesting statutory and operational revisions. Additionally, recent and proposed legislation of significance for natural resources was discussed.

As this final chapter was being written, some important events occurred. As a result of Arab-Israeli hostilities in the early fall of 1973— and because of support for Israel by some nations—many consuming nations were faced with an oil embargo by most of the oil-producing countries in the Middle East. Traditionally, the majority of petroleum imports to the United States have come from Canada and Venezuela, with lesser amounts from North Africa, Indonesia, Nigeria, and the Middle East. By October 1973 (just prior to the embargo), oil arriving at United States ports from the Arab nations reached approximately 2 million barrels per day[17] (both crude and refined products)—approximately one-third of our total daily imports.[18]

With this supply virtually eliminated, United States citizens encountered a phenomenon that had not been experienced in this country since World War II—shortages of certain items, such as gasoline and heating oil, that we had begun to take for granted. By early spring of 1974 the worst of the gasoline shortage appeared to have passed. But, the basic economic issues remain to be resolved.

These can be viewed as economic problems on the consumption (demand) side and on the production (supply) side. As for the former, energy consumption in total has more than doubled in the United States since 1950, in spite of a population growth of approximately one-third. In most years, our consumption of energy has increased at a rate almost twice the rate of population growth. While our own use of energy has been rising at slightly more than 4 percent annually, world energy use has been increasing at approximately 6 percent per year. Still, with 6 percent of the world's population, we in the United States consume about 33 percent of the world's energy.[19] Most experts agree that mankind's voracious appetite for energy must be curtailed if we are to avert serious ecological problems.

On the supply side, the United States has, in recent years, become extremely reliant on imported petroleum and petroleum products. As the effects of the Middle East embargo became apparent, President Nixon announced the intention to achieve energy self-sufficiency for the United States by 1980. Called "Project Independence," the stated goal would be to preclude the necessity of the United States ever again being at the mercy of oil-producing nations. This does not necessarily mean that we will never import petroleum or petroleum products, but it does mean that our economy will never again be quite so dependent upon foreign oil as we had become early in the 1970s. Indeed, the oil embargo was a blessing in disguise in that it forced us to reassess our national energy policy while only partially dependent on foreign oil. Some experts believe that if the embargo had not come until 1975–1976, we would have suffered greater impacts than those that have arisen from the 1973–1974 experience.

A national energy policy is just now in the formative stages,

17. One barrel contains 42 gallons.
18. Ford Foundation, *Exploring Energy Choices: A Preliminary Report,* Energy Policy Project of the Ford Foundation, 1974, Table 2, p. 6.
19. Joel Darmstadter, Appendix to "Energy Consumption: Trends and Patterns" in *Energy, Economic Growth, and the Environment,* ed. Sam Schurr (Baltimore: Johns Hopkins Press, 1972).

but its economic implications are already clear. First of all, the period of cheap energy is probably gone forever. As new sources of energy are discovered and utilized, there is very little likelihood that petroleum products will ever again be as cheap as they were prior to the fall of 1973. Crude oil that formerly sold for $3 per barrel will probably bring $7 to $8; with the deregulation of natural gas, its price will also rise; with rehabilitation of strip-mined areas, the price of coal will also likely rise.

More expensive energy will cause many changes in our daily lives. The size and horsepower of automobiles will become a crucial variable in new and used car sales; the leisurely drive will be questioned; homes will be cooler in the winter and warmer in the summer; offices and homes will be less well lit; mass transit in urban areas will become more attractive vis-à-vis the traditional one-person-per-car pattern now so prevalent.

In the area of food production and distribution, there will also be some change. The move toward an even more mechanized agriculture will be tempered by higher energy prices; not only will fuel be more expensive, but the energy component in equipment manufacturing will become more expensive. Convenience foods, which are energy intensive compared to other foods, will become more expensive.

Other issues of relevance to natural resources pertain to the potential impacts from renewed efforts to become more self-sufficient in energy. What are the potential hazards of increased oil production from the Outer Continental Shelf? What are the possible resource implications of increased strip-mining? Will development of geothermal energy be environmentally acceptable? What are the economic and environmental issues surrounding increased oil production from the North Slope, and its movement (by ship, pipeline, or both) to markets in the United States? There are economic aspects to all of these questions and they indicate the role that economics must play in the formulation of rational public policy in the natural resource area.

DISCUSSION QUESTIONS AND PROBLEMS

1. Compare the role of technological advances in the exploitation of stock resources with that of the exploitation of flow resources.
2. What is "wise use"?
3. Criticize the following statement: Since future generations will be wealthier than the present generation, it makes little sense to transform use rates in favor of the future.
4. Discuss the likely disparity in rates of time preference between a rich man and a poor man of the same age. Between a wage earner and a salaried individual of the same age.
5. What are examples of scarce items of little value?
6. What are examples of valuable items that are not particularly scarce?

7. Discuss the role of property rights in a market economy.
8. Why would a tax equal to the difference between MSC and MPC elicit socially desirable behavior from a profit-seeking entrepreneur?
9. Suppose a firm were offered a "bribe" equal to the difference between MSC and MPC to not pollute. What would be the result of such an offer? Why?
10. What are the drawbacks to economic sanctions in air pollution control?
11. What are the drawbacks to legal sanctions in air pollution control?
12. Criticize the following statement: If one-half of this nation's forests burn, the price will double and their total value will remain unchanged.
13. Analyze recreation and timber production in the context of the product-product theory of Chapter 5. How would one decide the merits of joint use as distinct from single use for a forested site? How would one arrive at relative prices?

SUGGESTED READINGS

B A S I C

Barkley, Paul W.; and Seckler, David W. *Economic Growth and Environmental Decay: The Solution Becomes the Problem.* New York: Harcourt Brace Jovanovich, 1972.
> An introductory text that treats the possible conflicts between economic growth and environmental problems.

Cicchetti, Charles J. *Alaskan Oil: Alternative Routes and Markets.* Baltimore: Johns Hopkins Press, 1972.
> An analysis of the controversy over the trans-Alaskan pipeline versus the Canadian route.

Ciriacy-Wantrup, S. V. *Resource Conservation: Economics and Policies,* rev. ed. Berkeley: Univ. Calif. Press, 1963.
> The earliest and best-known book on natural resource economics. Complete and incisive as well as insightful.

Clawson, Marion; and Knetsch, Jack L. *Economics of Outdoor Recreation.* Baltimore: Johns Hopkins Press, 1966.
> Probably the first definitive work on the economics of recreation, it contains chapters on recreation demand, valuation, economic impacts of recreation, and major policy issues.

Crocker, Thomas D.; and Rogers, A. J. III. *Environmental Economics.* Hinsdale, Ill.: Dryden Press, 1971.
> An introductory book developing the essence of market failure, pollution, and market solutions.

Freeman, A. Myrick; Haveman, Robert H.; and Kneese, Allen V. *The Economics of Environmental Policy.* New York: John Wiley, 1973.
> A well-written book of interest to the beginning student.

Goldstein, Jon H. *Competition for Wetlands in the Midwest.* Washington, D.C.: Resources for the Future, 1971.
> A well-written and interesting book on the issue of preserving wetlands as wildlife habitat versus draining them for agricultural production.

Haveman, Robert H. *The Economic Performance of Public Investments: An Expost Evaluation of Water Resources Investments.* Baltimore: Johns Hopkins Press, 1972.

A good treatment of the actual economic performance of large public water resource investments.

Howe, Charles W.; and Easter, K. William. *Interbasin Transfers of Water: Economic Issues and Impacts.* Baltimore: Johns Hopkins Press, 1971.

A very good treatment of the economic issues involved in transferring water between two basins. Highly recommended.

Kneese, Allen V.; and Bower, Blair T. *Managing Water Quality: Economics, Technology, Institutions.* Baltimore: Johns Hopkins Press, 1968.

A good basic book on the different aspects of controlling water pollution.

Landsberg, Hans H.; Fischman, Leonard L.; and Fisher, Joseph L. *Resources in America's Future: Patterns of Requirements and Availabilities, 1960–2000.* Baltimore: Johns Hopkins Press, 1963.

An excellent (though dated) look at natural resource availability.

Meadows, Donella H.; et al. *The Limits to Growth: A Report for the Club of Rome's Project on the Predicament of Mankind.* New York: Universe Books, 1972.

The center of an emotional controversy over economic growth and natural resource availability. Much of the debate concerns the assumptions that permit certain conclusions regarding the catastrophic demise of population when resources are exhausted. Highly recommended though the assumptions must be viewed critically.

National Water Commission. *Water Policies for the Future.* Washington, D.C.: USGPO, 1973.

This complete final report of the commission contains much valuable information in addition to the specific recommendations.

——. *New Directions in U.S. Water Policy: Summary, Conclusions, and Recommendations.* Washington, D.C.: USGPO, 1973.

A much briefer account than the full report. This is a valuable book.

Public Land Law Review Commission. *One-Third of the Nation's Land: A Report to the President and to the Congress.* Washington, D.C.: USGPO, 1970.

An interesting document with some valuable information in addition to the recommendations.

ADVANCED

Gaffney, Mason, ed. *Extractive Resources and Taxation.* Madison: Univ. Wis. Press, 1967.

An excellent anthology of articles on natural resources and taxation.

Herfindahl, Orris C.; and Kneese, Allen V., *Economic Theory of Natural Resources.* Columbus, Ohio: Merrill, 1974.

A recent book covering time and natural resource use, as well as investment decisions, and environmental quality.

Kneese, Allen V.; and Bower, Blair T., eds. *Environmental Quality Analysis.* Baltimore: Johns Hopkins Press, 1972.

An excellent anthology of articles on the environment and economic growth, quality management, and political and legal institutions.

Mäler, Karl-Göran, *Environmental Economics: A Theoretical Inquiry.* Baltimore: Johns Hopkins Press, 1974.

A highly mathematical treatment of several traditional natural resource issues.

Mishan, E. J. *Cost-Benefit Analysis: An Introduction.* New York: Praeger, 1971.

A good analysis of the techniques often employed to evaluate public policy in natural resource development.

INDEX